Pray for

Very Rev. Jeremiah Rustel SSF
and Community

THE THEOLOGY OF
THE MYSTICAL BODY

THE THEOLOGY OF
THE MYSTICAL BODY

By

EMILE MERSCH, S.J.

Translated by

CYRIL VOLLERT, S.J., S.T.D.

Professor of Theology
St. Mary's College, St. Marys, Kansas
The School of Divinity of St. Louis University

B. HERDER BOOK CO.
15 & 17 SOUTH BROADWAY, ST. LOUIS 2, MO.
AND
33 QUEEN SQUARE, LONDON, W. C.

IMPRIMI POTEST

Daniel H. Conway, S.J.

Provincial

Missouri Province

St. Louis, Mo., May 31, 1950

NIHIL OBSTAT

Frederic C. Eckhoff

Censor Librorum

IMPRIMATUR

✠ Joseph E. Ritter

Archiepiscopus

Sancti Ludovici, die 24 Julii, 1951

Copyright 1951

B. HERDER BOOK CO.

Third Printing, 1955

2303
m t

Library of Congress Catalog Card Number: 51-7383

Vail-Ballou Press, Inc., Binghamton and New York

AUTHOR'S PREFACE

This book is the sequel of a previous work, which is a sort of preface to the present volume.

The work I am referring to is *Le Corps mystique du Christ: Etudes de théologie historique.*[1] The book showed how Sacred Scripture and the Fathers explain the nature of the mystical body in treating of dogma generally: the mystical body is the whole Christ, God and man, head and body.

A doctrinal, speculative study had still to be made, a study that would endeavor to investigate how and in what measure all dogmas discourse of the whole Christ. This could be regarded as a sort of hypothesis that had to be verified, with the purpose of ascertaining whether dogma is always and everywhere Christ. Such a speculative and doctrinal study of theology is the object of the present work.

"We would see Jesus" (John 12:21). We are setting out in search of the truth which Christ has brought. Our aim is to see Christ who is the truth, to see Him in it and it in Him. For the truth is like a great panorama that shows forth what He is, depicting Him in His divinity, in all mankind, and in Himself, and nothing but Him. Is He not light and life?

My earlier work closed with some lines which I may be permitted to set down here: "If then we were to show what it is that makes Christian truth the light of all Christian souls, we should have to point out how that truth speaks to men, always and everywhere, of the union with God that they all receive in Christ. We should have to make a kind of synthesis of Catholic teaching, embracing two points of view: that of Christ and that of the Christian. Such a task is, of course, too vast to be given here, even in outline

[1] Translated by John R. Kelly, S.J., under the title, *The Whole Christ* (Milwaukee: Bruce, 1938).

iii

form; but with God's help we hope to undertake it later on." [2] God has granted the realization of this hope. May He continue to aid us, so that the realization may not fall too far short of what it should have been.

Although each of the two books is a self-contained unit, they are related by ties of closest union. The documents that reveal what Scripture and the Fathers have said of the whole Christ when treating of the various dogmas, also show what these same sources teach about the various dogmas when discoursing of the whole Christ. Therefore the reader will understand that, since we have quoted Scripture and the Fathers so abundantly in the earlier work, we need not quote them so frequently and at the same length in the present study. We shall limit ourselves to quoting sources at points of special interest, and thus we can dispense with copious footnotes. But we should like to remark that this meager display of critical apparatus by no means implies negligence in the consultation of sources. The investigation has been made, but its results are recorded in *The Whole Christ*, which thus, in a way, serves as a storehouse of annotations for the present book.

Indeed, the earlier work was written with the later one in view. A word of explanation will here be pertinent. The book which was first conceived, and which through all subsequent preoccupations ever retained the first place in my thoughts, actually appeared as the second of the two. Years and years have been spent on its composition. But shortly after I started it I perceived that it had to include a preliminary chapter that would explain, according to Scripture and tradition, in what the whole Christ consists. How could I otherwise express exactly what I had in mind in my ambition to recapitulate all Christian teaching in the doctrine of the whole Christ? Such a chapter, therefore, I set out to write. But the farther I advanced, the more clearly I saw that the territory to be explored stretched out in every direction. A single chapter, or even several chapters, would never be enough to record the results of such immense researches. A whole volume was needed. I also saw, before I had gone very far, that a man's life would be too short to bring such an undertaking to anything like completion. And yet I was unwilling to renounce the main enterprise for which this research was only a preparation. Hence I

[2] *The Whole Christ*, p. 581.

became reconciled, not only to leaving the investigations un-
finished, but even to breaking them off while they were as yet
far from giving up all they promised. Rightly or wrongly, I believed I had discovered the main theme. I thought that the chief
landmarks pointing to the doctrine and the history of its progressive
disclosure were sufficiently ascertained, and that the moment had
come for publishing my findings. Thus appeared the studies on
historical theology in *The Whole Christ*. They form a self-contained
unit. But beyond that, they take their place in the vaster project
which is realized in the present volume.

The latter also requires a few words of explanation. First of all,
I must avow that it is likewise incomplete. To study all dogmas
and all points of doctrine, and to show how they all lead eventually
to the truth of the whole Christ, would be an endless task. Hence
I have confined myself to the chief teachings. But all the rest converge toward these supreme summits. In showing how the doctrines treated lead to Christ, we show at the same time how
everything else tends toward Him.

These dogmas have been studied one after another, in the best
order I could devise. And this procedure is not free from defect:
it is an analysis, and what is needed is a synthesis; the truths are
studied successively, and each is called upon to contribute toward
an explanation of the others. But it is impossible to say everything
at once. By force of necessity I had, at times, to introduce elements
of solution that ought not to have been brought in until later, or
to draw attention to aspects of truth having an importance that
would not be clear except in the sequel.

The synthesis, which could not have been enunciated in a word,
can hardly be taken in by the reader at a single glance. Inevitably,
when he comes to the last page of the book, he will have lost sight
of points made at the beginning; yet such truths will not receive
their full illumination till the end.

The remedy would be a willingness to reread the whole book
after going through it once, or at least to reread rapidly the earlier
chapters and the outlines of the rest in the Table of Contents. But
the author cannot well count on this additional labor. Let me express one desire: that the reader will refrain from pronouncing
definite judgment on the pages that follow until he has perused
them all.

The task I have undertaken is delicate in the extreme. The theological formulation of many Christian truths has not yet been definitely fixed. Who, for example, would venture to assert that accord has been reached among Christian teachers on the nature of the divine missions or the appropriations, on the essence of the redemption, of grace, or of the Sacrifice of the Mass? Yet these are truths of capital importance. And as long as theological science has not definitely agreed on the essences of things, it will evidently have great difficulty in determining how these essences are related to one another.

Moreover, the scientific formulation of such truths, even when most perfect, is deficient. We are in the realm of supernatural truths, which natural concepts cannot adequately represent. Hence every effort bearing on their rational elaboration must be highly prudent and cautious in order to preserve fidelity to the light that has been given us.

Accordingly—although so obvious a remark scarcely needs to be made—the author submits every word of this book to the judgment of him who has been charged with the upholding of Christian truth and who pronounces his decisions in the Church. This is not a matter of resignation; it is a matter of desire and of joy. When a man is in quest of truth, what better fortune can befall him than to find it where it is disclosed? These lines are also submitted to the judgment of the reader; and let Christ judge in the persons of His servants.

He who is on the watch for inexactitudes and defects in this book, will be sure to find them in abundance. However, since what is looked for is often found, we prefer to beg the reader to join us, if he will be so good, in searching for the truth. We beg him to complete, by drawing on knowledge gained from other sources, whatever is deficient in this exposition, and to use passages that are more fully developed as a commentary on those which unfold too rapidly. And we also request him to apprise us of corrections to be made and of further elucidations to be added.

When truth such as this is in question, to seek is to pray, and to seek together is to be heard. In studying dogma thus, perhaps the reader may come to love it with more enlightenment and to cling to it with more spirited tenacity. Perhaps he may discover in himself a greater appreciation of it even in its lesser parts, for in all of them he will find Him who is the delight of his life, Christ:

Tantum esse sub fragmento
Quantum toto tegitur.

"By their fruits you shall know them" (Matt. 7:20). This will be a sign by which the reader may judge. This is the principal sign which has emboldened us to publish this work, to the praise of the Lord who in His gracious kindness gives us such a magnificent message, so full of light and goodness and love and power, so full of truth because, throughout its length and breadth, it is full of Christ.

INTRODUCTION [1]

▲▲

The French original of this book, *La théologie du corps mystique*, was published in 1944. A second edition, from which the present translation was made, appeared two years later. The work is the author's masterpiece, the culmination of all his studies, and the climax toward which the theological investigations of his entire scholarly life were directed. He began planning the book as early as 1917 when, as a student in the last year of his course in theology, he presented a long paper on "The Mystical Body of Christ" in two meetings of a seminar. His ambition was to group all the great Christian dogmas around this central idea; and during the quarter century that followed he devoted every hour he could spare from his many apostolic and teaching assignments to the carrying out of this project.

After several years of preliminary study, he perceived that the theological synthesis he envisaged had to be preceded by more thorough researches into the scriptural and patristic sources of knowledge about the mystical body than any scholar had undertaken before him. These researches, conducted with patience and perseverance, lasted from 1920 to 1929. In June of the latter year he requested some of his associates to read his manuscript; on their advice, especially that of the renowned patristic scholar, J. de Ghellinck, S.J., he refrained from publishing at that time, so that the work might be perfected by further historical study and thus gain in value. The two volumes of the monumental *Le corps mystique du Christ. Etudes de théologie historique*, at length appeared in 1933; an English translation from the second edition, by John R. Kelly, S.J., was published in 1938 under the title, *The Whole Christ*.

As soon as he was satisfied that his historical researches were approaching their term, Father Mersch lovingly went back to his

---

[1] By the translator.

original project, the theological synthesis of the doctrine of the mystical body, which was the true goal aimed at in all his labors. He had never lost sight of his main undertaking, and from time to time had sketched out various aspects of it. About 1929 he began the serious composition of the first draft, which he finished in 1935. During these years of study, meditation, and writing his knowledge matured; no sooner had he completed the preliminary redaction than he set himself to the task of rewriting the whole work from beginning to end. This labor occupied most of his time until 1939. He continued to work on the book for another full year; at the beginning of May, 1940, he confided to some of his friends that the third and definitive draft of his work was about ready for the press. He was engaged in touching up the last chapter or two when the German armies invaded Belgium.

Louvain, where Father Mersch had been stationed since 1936, was one of the main objectives of the German assault. As the invading hordes approached, he was charged by his superiors with the responsibility of leading a group of aged and infirm Jesuit priests to some haven of safety. The band proceeded to Tournai which, however, soon had to be abandoned because of the repeated air bombardments that were demolishing the city. Father Mersch found refuge for most of his companions in various villages, and with the two feeblest priests secured transportation in a crowded automobile that was setting out for France. In the terrible confusion of those days he became separated from his aged friends, who still had with them the baggage of the little party; the luggage consisted of a small brief case, containing over half of the manuscript of the new book, and two larger valises, in which the remaining chapters were distributed among clothing and other traveling necessities.

Father Mersch made his way to the town of Lens in northern France and was given lodging at the local priest's home. The next day, which was the feast of Corpus Christi, May 23, 1940, he celebrated the last Mass of his life. All that day the town was under furious air attack. In the early afternoon two soldiers reported that many wounded people were lying along the Douai highway. Father Mersch hurried to their assistance, and several hours later was found dead beside the road, apparently a victim of one of the bombing raids.

The two aged priests who had become separated from Father Mersch were taken to Saint-Pol. One of them was admitted to the local hospital, where he died a few days later. The other died shortly after arriving in the town. With him had been left the brief case containing the larger portion of the precious manuscript, as well as the two valises. When the corpse was removed for burial, forty-eight hours later, only the brief case could be found. The other bags had been stolen, along with the ten chapters of the manuscript placed in them. In spite of many efforts made to trace them, they have never been recovered.

An editorial board, composed of the author's former friends and associates, worked loyally to prepare the manuscript for publication. Eleven of the twenty-one chapters had received final revision and were ready for the printer. The two earlier drafts of the book were discovered intact in Brussels and Louvain. The second redaction, written during the years 1935 to 1939, represents in most respects the author's definitive ideas; it exists in a form that is almost suitable for publication, and indeed several of the chapters had been published as articles in theological journals. The editors drew upon this second draft to supply the chapters lacking in the final redaction. The problem of filling in several missing pages was met by having recourse to the first redaction, composed between 1929 and 1935. As eventually published, the book exhibits some lack of balance in a few of the later chapters. But J. Levie, S.J., head of the editorial board, assures us that nothing essential has been lost. The work is substantially the synthesis of theology planned so many years before by Father Mersch.

The editors of the French edition have carefully noted the condition of the manuscript used in each chapter of the published book. Such references have been omittted in this translation. Chapters 2, 11, 13 to 17, 19, and 20 are taken from the author's second draft, with occasional lacunae filled in from the first redaction. The rest of the chapters, representing the larger part of the final redaction, had been approved for publication by the author himself.

On June 29, 1943, Pius XII issued his great encyclical, *Mystici corporis Christi*, on the mystical body of Christ. Father Mersch never had the happiness of reading the splendid dogmatic treatise. The document would have brought keen joy to the theologian who had consecrated his life to a study of the same doctrine. His many publications, particularly the present book, constitute a sort of anticipated commentary on the encyclical. At the same time, the encyclical would have enabled Father Mersch to achieve greater precision in several phases of his exposition.

The encyclical has been eagerly welcomed in theological circles because of the clarity and decisiveness of its doctrine. In the course of the centuries controversies had arisen about some aspects of the mystical body; confusion reigned especially as to the relation between the mystical body and the Catholic Church. Pope Pius XII teaches unequivocally that the two are identical. A second debate dealt with the question of the soul of the mystical body. This point, too, has received clarification: we are taught authoritatively that the soul of the mystical body is the Holy Ghost.

Mersch's doctrine, developed prior to the appearance of the encyclical, is not as firm in these details as it would have been had he been able to study the document. But nothing in his book is opposed to the Holy Father's teaching. Although he does not identify the Church with the mystical body as emphatically as the Pope does, he repeatedly states that the Church is indeed the mystical body of Christ. This is true especially in chapter 16, in which he discusses the nature of the Church; his "purpose is to study the Church regarded as the body of Christ and its continuation here on earth." He holds that authors who "declare that the mystical body in the strict sense of the word is exclusively the Church militant" are "quite orthodox." He says that Christ "has members in a body that is the Church" and that "the visible Church is the continuation of Christ's humanity." He points out that "Christ acts in the Church, for the Church is His body," and that the sacraments are the "acts of the Church, the body of Christ." Sin is a dreadful disorder, because "every sin in a baptized person is an offense against his baptism, a violation of his character as a member of Christ, and hence an attack on the whole body which is the Church." "The Church is a body, and the faithful are its members." The Eucharist perfects our "union with the visible and invisible mystical body that is the Church."

Occasionally his language is less exact, as when he says that "the mystical body represents the assemblage of those who live or ought to live in Christ." His study of tradition leads him to the conclusion that "in the ordinary language of the Church, 'mystical body' connotes the entire multitude of those who live the life of Christ, with a life that admits of degrees, whereas the word 'Church' represents the society of the baptized faithful as organized under their lawful pastors." Hence a person can "live the life of Christ without being actually attached to the visible society that is His Church; an example is a pagan who would have received grace and charity without being aware of the Church, or a fervent catechumen."

Such statements, if clarified in the light of other, complementary passages, are reconcilable with the teaching of the encyclical. The Belgian theologian is but following the lead of St. Thomas who, in a famous article of the *Summa*, IIIa, q. 8, a. 3, distinguishes between actual and potential membership in the mystical body. Mersch is careful to point out that "as the head is truly head only of the members proceeding from it, so the members are truly members only in union with the head whence they proceed." All others, not actually united to the head by baptism, profession of the true faith, and communion with the Catholic Church, are merely potential members. This understanding of Mersch's doctrine seems to be required by the qualifying phrases he often introduces, as when he writes that Christ is continued in the Church "which, in the divine vocation, contains all men." "Every man is a member of Christ, at least in God's invitation." "Christ is the head of a mystical body which, in the divine vocation, takes in all mankind." "Christ is present, at least according to the divine vocation and in a rudimentary way, in every man."

These views find their justification in the encyclical. The Holy Father affirms that Christ is the head of the whole human family (cf. the official English translation, *America* edition, no. 37). Then, after recalling that, properly speaking, only those are members of the Church who have been baptized, profess the true faith, and are not cut off from union with the body by schism, heresy, or excommunication (*ibid.*, no. 29), the Pope declares that persons outside the fold may be related to the mystical body by unconscious desire and resolution (*ibid.*, no. 121), that is, according to the Latin text, *inscio quodam desiderio ac voto ad mysticum Redemptoris corpus ordinentur*. Baptized non-Catholics preserve a bond with the Church; although the absence of the other two conditions prevents them from being true members of the mystical body, they are not strangers to the Church, which beckons to them and awaits their return. The infidel is in a worse state, for no baptism connects him with the Church; yet such a one remains a potential member of the Church, as St. Thomas says in the *Summa*, IIIa, q. 8, a. 3 ad 1, and can become an actual member if he heeds the invitation Christ sends him.

Before the publication of the encyclical, various proposals were made about the soul of the mystical body. The most common opinion was that the Holy Ghost should be regarded as corresponding to this factor in the analogy. At the end of the encyclical *Mirae caritatis* of Leo XIII, the Eucharist is considered as the quasi-soul of the Church. Others thought that the Logos might be so regarded; yet others held that sanctifying grace exercised this function. On the other hand, St. Thomas, in the *Summa*, IIIa, q. 8, a. 1 ad 3, refers to the Holy Ghost as the heart of the Church. Pius XII repeats the doctrine taught by Leo XIII in the encyclical *Divinum illud*, that the Holy Ghost is the soul of the mystical body (cf. *America* edition, no. 69). Yet the Pope goes on to say: "If that vital principle by which the whole community of Christians is sustained by its Founder be considered now not in itself, but in its created effects, it consists in those heavenly gifts [that is, especially sanctifying grace and charity], which our Redeemer together with His Spirit bestows on the Church and which He and His Spirit, from whom come supernatural light and holiness, make operative in the Church." It is according to this aspect that Mersch speaks of the soul of the mystical body.

Father Mersch did not live long enough to receive enlightenment from the clear directives of the encyclical. He briefly discusses the theories current among theologians, and favors the view that the soul of the mystical body is sanctifying grace. However, he qualifies his preference by insisting that his "way of representing the doctrine does not imply a denial that the Holy Spirit is the soul of the Church." He then proceeds to describe the activity of the Holy Spirit in the Church in words that harmonize with the teaching of the Supreme Pontiff (see no. 68 of the English translation of the encyclical).

Although the encyclical of 1943 eliminates several of the views which Mersch, in common with all theologians, could discuss in 1940 as freely debatable alternatives, the brilliance of the theologi-

cal synthesis he presents in this book does not on that account suffer
impairment.

Cyril Vollert, S.J.

St. Mary's College
St. Marys, Kansas

Contents

Book Four

THE BLESSED TRINITY

Book Five

IN CHRIST

BOOK ONE

Theological and Philosophical Introduction

CHAPTER I

THE UNDERSTANDING AND SUPERNATURAL TRUTHS

> "By God's gift, reason attains
> some understanding of mysteries."
> Vatican Council

I. Text of the Vatican Council and Its Propositions

THE Constitution, *De fide catholica*, defined at the Vatican Council, contains some lines we wish to set at the head of this book. They express its spirit and its scope so exactly that our theological introduction will be no more than a commentary on them. "When reason, enlightened by faith, seeks earnestly, piously, and calmly, by God's gift it attains some understanding of mysteries, and indeed a most fruitful understanding: partly from analogy with truths it knows naturally, partly from the relations of the mysteries with one another and with man's last end." [1]

In the original form in which the definition was proposed to the Fathers, this passage was much shorter, consisting of only a few words: "Although, with faith casting its beams ahead, some understanding of them may be reached. . . ." [2]

We are not informed, either in the official report of the proceedings [3] or in the remarks contributed by some of the Fathers,[4] why a more positive and expanded text was adopted. The remarks made in the discussion touch only on questions of style,[5] with a single excep-

---

[1] Vatican Council, *Constitutio de fide catholica*, 4 (Denz., 1796).
[2] Mansi, *Amplissima collectio conciliorum*, L, 62; see the extremely brief *Annotationes, ibid.*, 84.
[3] "Verbale LII," Mansi, XLIX, 724.
[4] Mansi, LI, 252, 363.
[5] *Ibid.*

3

tion, which was proposed in the seventh general Congregation, but which has disappeared without leaving a trace.[6] We may well believe that the author withdrew it of his own accord. This indicates a unanimous agreement in the Council,[7] arrived at without debate.

We wish to call attention to three affirmations or theses in the passage. According to the Council, an understanding of the mysteries themselves is possible. This understanding is undoubtedly imperfect, but is real and fruitful. The Council further states that this understanding has to be sought for by the intellect, with the aid of grace of course, yet by an effort which is no less rational on that account. Lastly, the Council indicates three ways of conducting the inquiry. One of these is that which is adopted in this book. It consists in studying and meditating the bond of union existing among the mysteries: *e mysteriorum ipsorum inter se nexu.*

II. A Certain Understanding of the Faith

First of all, then, some understanding of the mysteries may be gained: *aliqua mysteriorum intelligentia.*[8] Assuredly this is an imperfect understanding, but it enables us to acquire some little comprehension of the mysteries: comprehension in the French or English sense of the word, although not in the sense of the Latin *comprehendere* as defined by the Scholastics, that is, a complete grasp, once for all.

Nevertheless it is an understanding that bears on the mystery itself. Its object is not merely the philosophical terms or the expressions of common usage that enter into the doctrinal definitions; no grace would be needed for this; a good dictionary would be enough, even for a pagan. Its object is not the images employed to represent the dogma, or the theological theories advanced to show the intelligibility of the enunciations of the faith or the absence of contradic-

[6] Msgr. P. M. Ferré, bishop of Casale, would have preferred a text that would restrict this understanding to the possibility of demonstrating the existence of mysteries but would exclude the possibility of penetrating deeply into them; *ibid.*, L, 203, 294. The proposal does not appear in the "Emendationes," *ibid.*, LI, 34.

[7] The Constitution, *De fide catholica*, won a unanimous vote; cf. Mansi LI, 436. The few reservations made by eight of the Fathers on the eve of the session do not concern either the doctrines enunciated or the point we are occupied with.

[8] Cf. Pius IX, ep. *Gravissimas inter*, Denz., 1670.

tion in them. Its object is not only the historical arguments which establish the fact that these mysteries have really been taught by Christ. All this is external to the truths believed, and the external is not at all in question. As the text itself says plainly and as the context makes clear, the question concerns a genuine supernatural knowledge of truths surpassing reason; it has to do with mysteries, and even with what is mysterious in the mysteries.

So much and no more is necessary for the Christian populace. All the rest, at bottom, is an affair of specialists; but this is the bread that all must eat: "Not in bread alone doth man live but in every word that proceedeth from the mouth of God" (Matt. 4:4).

In spite of the sublimity of its object, this understanding is real. God Himself who gives it by His grace could never rest content with granting some faint reflection, some indecisive glimmer, some semblance of light. The Council affirms that the understanding is most fruitful; could an uncertain gleam, a superficial phosphorescence produce rich fruits?

Far from suppressing faith, this understanding, as has been indicated, tends to make faith more perfect and firm and hence more credible. It does not dispel the mystery; though it gains some insight into the mystery, it leaves the character of mystery intact.

Thus the understanding of mysteries is *sui generis*, just as faith and dogma are *sui generis*. Faith, we may say, is a union with God: a union of the intellect. Dogma is likewise an expression of union with God. The understanding proper to dogma and faith is an understanding through union and in union, an understanding that comes to the intellect from the union granted to it, in Christ, with the first intelligible and the first truth.[9] God is light as well as love, and Christ who is the way and the life is also truth.

Sacred Scripture itself proclaims the intellectual splendor of the Christian message. Indeed, one of the main ideas of the Fourth Gospel, made known in the prologue and resumed in the course of the development, is that Christ is the light, the true light,[10] the light that has come down from heaven to enlighten the world and to shine into the eyes of all men.[11]

[9] Cf. what is said later about the "being of union," the causality of union, and so on.

[10] John 1:4, 9; cf. 3:19; 8:12; 9:5; 12:45. On this entire matter, see *The Whole Christ*, pp. 134, 142, 174-77.

[11] John 1:5, 9.

By believing in Christ we dwell in the light. We receive the light into ourselves and at the same time we ourselves are received into it.[12] Scripture suggests the comparison that, just as Christ is in the light, we also are in the light.[13] This is the decisive light, the light of God,[14] the light brought down by the Son of God,[15] the light He brings to the whole world and to the whole human race.[16] The true light has been shining ever since the Word was made flesh and lived in the flesh,[17] and we open our souls to drink in that light of life [18] by devoting ourselves to our brethren and by believing in the Gospel.[19]

St. Paul speaks in the same way. In his very first letters, those written to the Thessalonians, he presents his preaching as a light. But at this period the light seems, in his mind, to indicate the moral order rather than the intellectual order; it is the luster of moral purity shining forth in the midst of pagan dissoluteness rather than a clear illumination flooding the souls of his converts.[20] In any case, either light is impossible without the other.

In the great epistles the Apostle's thought ranges farther, and he speaks of the intellectual splendor proper to the gospel, of the magnificent, divine glory reflected in Christian revelation. He writes to the Corinthians that the Jews are blind; a veil covers their eyes and keeps God's work hidden from them. But the Christians, he continues, face the light without obstruction:

But we all, beholding the glory of the Lord with open face, are transformed into the same image from glory to glory, as by the Spirit of the Lord. Therefore, seeing we have this ministration, according as we have obtained mercy, we faint not. But we renounce the hidden things of dishonesty, not walking in craftiness nor adulterating the word of God; but by manifestation of the truth commending ourselves to every man's conscience, in the sight of God. And if our gospel be also hid, it is hid to them that are lost, in whom the god of this world

[12] John 11:9 f.; 12:35 f.
[13] Cf. I John 1:7.
[14] Cf. I John 1:5 ff.
[15] John 1:4–9.
[16] John 9:5; 1:9.
[17] Cf. I John 2:8.
[18] John 8:12.
[19] John 3:19 ff.; I John 2:8 ff.
[20] Cf. I Thess. 5:4; II Thess. 2:16.

hath blinded the minds of unbelievers, that the light of the gospel of the glory of Christ, who is the image of God, should not shine unto them. For we preach not ourselves but Jesus Christ our Lord; and ourselves your servants through Jesus. For God, who commanded the light to shine out of darkness, hath shined in our hearts, to give the light of the knowledge of the glory of God, in the face of Christ Jesus.[21]

Thus Christianity is the glory of God shining forth, it is light in the midst of darkness, it is day.[22] The more the Apostle meditates on this splendor, the more he is elated at the thought of being its bearer.

In the letters dating from his captivity in Rome, which come after the great epistles, he writes of the matter with poetic exaltation.[23] What he has to teach is doubtless a mystery.[24] But it is a mystery for the very reason that it shines with a brilliance that is too dazzling. If we but have the courage, or rather the happiness, of adhering to it by faith, its glory will flow into us. This is what he desires for the Colossians: "That their hearts may be comforted, being instructed in charity and unto all riches of fullness of understanding,[25] unto the knowledge of the mystery of God the Father and of Christ Jesus, in whom are hid all the treasures of wisdom and knowledge." [26]

"All riches of fullness of understanding, unto the knowledge of the mystery." Paul certainly does not hesitate to insist. This mystery, which is so abundant in its fullness and so rich in its brightness, is evidently in his eyes more than a simple formula designed to mortify man's mind. In itself it is astounding intelligibility, for it contains Him who possesses in Himself all the treasures of wisdom and knowledge.

We should not imagine that the joy thrilling in his words comes merely from the magnificent graces he has received; it is also caused, or indeed is mainly caused, by the overwhelming realization that

[21] Cf. II Cor. 3:18—4:6.
[22] Cf. I Cor. 1:24, 30; 2:6-16.
[23] Eph. 3:3 f., 14 ff.; Col. 1:23, 25.
[24] On mystery conceived as enlightenment, see *The Whole Christ*, pp. 89-100.
[25] To the Corinthians, Paul had already written: "I give thanks to my God always for you, for the grace of God that is given you in Christ Jesus, that in all things you are made rich in Him, in all utterance and in all knowledge" (I Cor. 1:4 f.).
[26] Col. 2:2 f.; see Eph. 3:18 ff.

God Himself gives these graces. Joy, understanding, enlightenment, gratitude, the union of all in Christ, must all have a place in a frame of mind that is at once most simple and conscious of its overflowing riches. Such is the Christian attitude. "Let the peace of Christ rejoice in your hearts, wherein also you are called in one body; and be ye thankful. Let the word of Christ dwell in you abundantly, in all wisdom: teaching and admonishing one another in psalms, hymns, and spiritual canticles, singing in grace in your hearts to God." [27]

A hymn singing in the souls of men and a peace rejoicing in their hearts clearly have nothing in common with a resigned submission or a stifling of a desire to understand. Obscurities will assuredly persist, and unaided natural reason cannot grasp God's mysterious gift.[28] But this is because reason is too shortsighted and because the brightness is beyond its range.

Respect for man's mind and for the splendor of the divine message has remained in the Church. We may recall the magnificent terms with which the liturgy extols the light uncovered in Christian preaching, and the maternal solicitude with which it begs for the faithful the grace to understand.

O Lord our God, Father Almighty, Thou unfailing Light who art the source of all light, bless this light that has been sanctified and blessed by Thee who enlightenest the whole world. Grant that we may take fire from that light and may be illuminated by the flame of Thy brightness. And as Thou didst give light to Moses in his coming out of Egypt, so make it shine on our hearts and minds that we may deserve to reach eternal life and light. Through Christ our Lord.[29]

Almighty God, we beseech Thee to grant to us, who are bathed in the new light of Thy incarnate Word, that the faith shining in our minds may be reflected in all our actions.[30]

Almighty God, we beg Thee that the splendor of Thy brightness may shine upon us; and by the radiance of the Holy Spirit, may the light of Thy light impart strength to the hearts of those who have been born anew through Thy grace.[31]

[27] Col. 3:15 f.; see Eph. 5:19.
[28] Cf. I Cor. 1:18 ff.; 2:4; Rom. 1:17 ff.; Col. 2:8.
[29] Prayer at the blessing of fire on Holy Saturday.
[30] Second Mass on Christmas, oration.
[31] Vigil of Pentecost, oration.

According to the Son's promise, the Holy Spirit is so to enlighten the minds of the faithful and bring them to the fullness of truth,[32] that with purified hearts they may attain to an understanding of what they venerate with solemn worship.[33] For its catechumens, the Church begs God to open the ears of their hearts and to give them an increase of faith and understanding.[34]

What the Church thus expresses in its prayers it reproduces in its life. We have shown elsewhere how the writers and doctors of the Church contemplated revealed truth with love and joy in order to comprehend it as clearly as possible and to impart an understanding of it to others.[35] The strictest orthodoxy never repressed or imprisoned their minds; on the contrary, it was the inspiration of their labors.

St. Augustine is perhaps the outstanding example of this endeavor. He may be said to be an intellectualist to the extent that he is a believer; he holds that we believe in order to understand. "Unless you believe you will not understand," he says in explaining Isaias.[36] "Believe that you may understand," he repeats whenever the occasion warrants.[37] Faith purifies the mind and understanding fills it,[38] even here below.

If God has spoken to us, He has done so because He wishes us to understand. "Since He has deigned to speak to us, He Himself opens up our minds. He would not wish to say anything unless He wished it to be understood. Having deigned to speak, He has undoubtedly aroused the interest of His hearers; do you think He would desert the man whose interest He has awakened for the express purpose of getting him to listen?"[39]

Hence our effort to understand is but obedience to God's designs. "I have said this to stir up in your faith a love of understanding, to

[32] Mass for Wednesday after Pentecost, first oration.
[33] Feast of Epiphany, postcommunion.
[34] Good Friday, prayers for catechumens.
[35] The Whole Christ, pp. 134, 229, 249, 263 f., 385, 419, 465, 538.
[36] Isa. 7:9.
[37] See, for example, In Ioannis evangelium, XXIX, 6; XLV, 4; LXIX, 2 (PL, XXXV, 1630, 1722, 1817). St. Cyril of Alexandria is fond of referring to the same text: In Ioan., VI, 54, lib. IV, cap. 2 (PG, LXXIII, 576).
[38] In Ioan., XXXVI, 7 (PL, XXXV, 1667). "If any of you is able to grasp more than I explain, let him not be satisfied with this little rivulet, but let him hurry to the overflowing fountain; for the source of life is in Him in whose light we shall see light" (Sermo 362; PL, XXXIX, 1614).
[39] In Ioan., XXI, 4 (PL, XXXV, 1566).

which true reason leads and for which faith prepares the soul." [40]
"Love of understanding"—that is well said. A little later in the same
letter the saint urges: "Love understanding very much." [41] Love
understanding, be eager to grasp, *intellectum valde ama*. The turn
of the phrase is typically Augustine, but what it expresses is pure
Christianity.

And ought it not to be so? Faith is surely an intellectual virtue,
elicited by the speculative intellect. *Credere est cum assensu cogitare*,
to believe is to think with assent, according to the Augustinian definition which has remained classical. "To believe is nothing else than to
think with assent. Not all who think believe, since many think so as
not to believe. But everyone who believes thinks, and thinks by
believing and believes by thinking. . . . If faith is not charged with
thought it is nothing." [42]

An act of thinking can dispense with everything but what is
thinkable, and an intellectual virtue can renounce everything except
what is intelligible. The intelligibility may be highly specialized in
nature, and we shall see that it is necessarily so: it admits and implies
elements of obscurity and dogmatism; but it has to be real. Otherwise
faith, as an intellectual process, would have no meaning. If there
were question merely of a volitional process, of a firm intention to
repeat, whenever occasion required, a formula guarded in the
memory,[43] the case would be different. Faith would then lie outside
the understanding and could well dispense with intelligibility.

If we were to rest satisfied with grasping the preambles of faith,
the motives of credibility, and the philosophical sense of the words
used in the dogmatic formulas, the problem would be simple: all this
is the work of natural reason. But then the intelligible would be com-

---

[40] *Epist. ad Consensium* (PL, XXXIII, 454).

[41] *Ibid.*, 458.

[42] *De praedestinatione sanctorum*, 5 (PL, XLIV, 963).

[43] This is the notion some would favor. See, for example, the passage in
Jansenius, *Augustinus*, II, prooem., cap. 4, col. 7 (Louvain, 1640): "As the
intellect is the faculty for learning philosophy, so memory is the faculty for
possessing theology. The former, by penetrating into principles as understood, makes the philosopher; the latter, by registering what has been handed
down, makes the Christian theologian. . . . No one should hold it ridiculous
or strange that wisdom is born of Christian memory, unless he is unaware
that the eternal Wisdom which is the Father's Word . . . has come forth
from the Father's prolific memory." A comparison between this theology and
the psychology of the passages from St. Augustine quoted in the preceding
pages is not without interest.

pletely outside of what is formally believed, and the act of faith, as such, would find nothing intelligible to deal with; it would not be an act of thought, and hence would not be an act of faith.

A virtue is a power, a perfection. Faith is a virtue of the intellect; what power, what perfection, can it have except to understand? If a supernatural virtue is in question, as it certainly is, it ought to convey understanding with a supernatural perfection.[44] By faith, says St. Thomas, God communicates His own knowledge to souls [45] through an infused light, analogous to the light of the agent intellect which makes first principles manifest.[46] Could such light be nothing but obscurity? By faith, says St. Paul, Christ who is the splendor of the Father dwells in our hearts; [47] and shall we remain out in the night? How then could St. John characterize Christianity as a manifestation of brightness? "This is the declaration which we have heard from Him and declare unto you: that God is light, and in Him there is no darkness." [48]

Christianity has brought us a higher and moral way of willing. How could it fail at the same time to bring us a new and higher way of thinking, and how could it have brought the latter if its message were not intelligible and thinkable in all that is most central and essential to it? How could a gospel incapable of appealing to the mind have revolutionized men's habits of thought? How could it have remade the world, which is guided by ideas, if it had not been a magnificent idea? And is an idea nothing but a formula repeated without comprehension?

Faith is the beginning of vision, even though it differs specifically from vision and does not remain the same knowledge, *eadem numero*,

[44] Such elevation of the cognitive faculty is supposed in the following passage from St. Thomas. He says that one way of knowing divine things is according to our human manner, and this is natural; another way is according to the manner of the divine things themselves, and this is supernatural. The latter is expressed thus: "The second way of knowing is according to the nature of divine things as they are grasped in themselves. This is a kind of knowledge which we cannot possess perfectly in our earthly life; but even in this life we have a certain sharing in such knowledge and an assimilation to divine knowledge, in the sense that, through the faith which is infused into our souls, we adhere to the First Truth itself on account of itself" (*In Boethium de Trinitate*, q.2, a.2).

[45] *In Boethium de Trinitate, prooemium.*
[46] *In III Sent.*, d.23, q.2, a.1 ad4.
[47] Eph. 3:17.
[48] See I John 1:5; cf. 2:8.

when it passes from earth to heaven. St. Thomas declares that faith is "a certain foretaste of that knowledge which will beatify us in the next life, a foretaste of vision." [49] Or, as Suarez says, it is "a unique kind of sharing in the divine light and the supernatural order, and a certain inception of beatific light." [50] Face-to-face vision, the sudden, blissful bursting forth of eternal splendors, will be for the faithful not an absolute beginning, but the flowering of a seed. And although it is a glory coming forth from God, it will be the final revelation of a possession, even of a knowledge, already existing under a specifically different form in the soul. How, then, can we entertain the notion that faith is a negation of sight?

An objector may contend that understanding will come later, on the day of eternity. Meanwhile the act of faith implies understanding only as something yet to come, something whose possession is undoubtedly assured for those who persevere, but nevertheless something transcendent that arises, not from the act which perseveres, but from the justice which rewards the men who persevere.

But in that case, we should have to reply, you may not say that faith is an inception, for an inception has to contain the initial stages of what it introduces. If vision is in faith only in the sense that God promises it for later giving, then, to tell the truth, it is not present in faith either as in a seed or in any other way; it exists only in the infinite goodness from which it will later come forth. The act of faith would be a mere extrinsic disposition, juridically requisite, no doubt, but pertaining to a wholly different order of things.

Here we should like to interject a remark, not with the intention of making odious comparisons, but for the purpose of bringing out the precise bearing of various opinions: the complete isolation that would hold faith back from understanding suggests the complete isolation interposed by Protestants between the substance of the soul and the justification it receives. According to them, God sanctifies us by covering us with a holiness that remains foreign to us, and not by making us internally holy. This perfecting which stays outside, this amelioration which does not ameliorate but only puts our enduring wretchedness in contact with distant affluence, corresponds rather well, in the line of being, to that which purports, in the line

---

[49] *De veritate*, q. 14, a. 2; *In III Sent.*, *loc. cit.* Cf. *Compendium of Theology*, chap. 2, and *Summa*, IIa IIae, q. 5, a. 1.
[50] *De fide*, disp. III, sect. 13, no. 4.

of knowledge, to be an illumination that does not illuminate but gives only a hope of future brightness, and an intellectual aid that does not engender understanding but only reconciles us to do without understanding. Both views betray a misconception resembling a false notion of the Incarnation: one opinion will not allow that the incarnate Son is truly sanctity within us, the other will not allow that the Word made flesh is truly light within us.

The admitting of human reason into divine truth, as is done in theology, is not an unnatural commingling or a sacrilegious intrusion, any more than the entrance of a believer into a church or the union of a human nature with the Word is an intolerable profanation. Luther regarded theology as a monstrous hybrid, a sort of centaur: human reasonings coupled with divine truth. St. Thomas spoke quite differently. Human reasoning is the act, the cooperation of an intellect divinized by living faith. Hence "they who employ philosophical demonstration in sacred science by bringing reason to the service of faith, do not mix water with wine but change water into wine." [51]

III. The Quest of Understanding

If to believe is to think, to think with assent, then the duty to believe is a duty to think. A duty to think! Many Christians, alas, never give a thought to such a duty.

1. **The error of anti-intellectualism.** Kantianism and Positivism, which have surreptitiously contaminated even authors who believed they were fighting against these tendencies and actually did combat them at many points, have discredited thought. They have engendered the conviction that thought, like a careful housemaid, can, in a true sense, rearrange and put in order what the senses have discovered, but that any endeavor to advance independently and gain self-mastery is a rash undertaking. Its efforts, always somewhat clumsy and ponderous, are represented as ridiculous and even tragic; and wise men busy themselves with bringing back to solid earth the poor ox that would like to soar aloft. There are manuals of philosophy, excellent in other respects, that make verification by the senses the ultimate criterion and judge of thought.

This timidity is taken for prudence, this unconscious nominalism

[51] *In Boethium de Trinitate*, q. 2, a. 3 ad 5.

passes for the critical spirit. For a time the subservience of the angel to the beast was regarded as submission to reality and loyal service of being. But all the while the mind was ill, and its illness was its shamefaced distrust of itself.

If men were afraid to let the intellect range unaccompanied through a domain that is, after all, its own, how much greater were their misgivings to see it mount up, as though on wings, into what is in itself a transcendental zone, an indescribable region full of mystery and, as was vaguely suspected, of danger. Its explorations there seemed like the terrible game of a child playing with explosives; and some Christians, especially among the fervent, felt a chill creeping along their spine. What might not happen if anyone set to thinking about his faith?

Among certain of the faithful, this attitude results from a lack of intellectual curiosity. Among others it springs from the unconscious annoyance of a mind that has reached adulthood but has remained in an infantile stage as regards religious formation. With others it is diffidence in the presence of their own intellects, which they know are more inclined to object and hesitate than to construct. With yet others, it is a reverential dread: they remember Oza and fear to touch the ark.[52] With others, finally, it is perhaps an unavowed mistrust in the presence of Christian truth, as though a serious investigation might reveal weaknesses.

These varying attitudes may be assigned a number of different names: abandonment to God, simplicity of faith, a wise prudence, modesty, reverence. But this is sure: we cannot find in all this any trace of a great love for the intellect or of an ardent passion for the faith. They are a proof of debility, like the many precautions of the aged. Intrepid faith, genuine faith, does not shrink back from a current of air; it fears nothing, neither prisons nor persecutions; above all, it is not afraid of light.

In everything that regards the will, Christians profess spiritedly that their Christianity is their noblest and strongest inspiration and that it bids them: "Will! Will with all your might, with your whole soul, and even more; will as a man ought to will when he wills with God." Apparently, however, with less appreciation of the intellect than of the will, they do not venture to suppose that the Word may have imparted new energies to their thinking and that dogma tells

[52] See II Kings, 6:6 f.

them: "Think! Think with all your power, with all your love, with all your loyalty; think as a man ought to think when he is thinking with God."

But when God entrusted His truth to their intellects, in answer to their need for understanding, did He not impose on them an obligation to seek it out? In uniting Himself to them in the incarnate Word, did He not wish to give them a new knowledge, and hence to awaken in them a new understanding, that would be worthy of Him who helps them to achieve it and also worthy of the children of light?

When God comes to dwell in the intellect as truth, does He intend the intellect to be saved without its cooperation? When He lodges His truth in the mind, is not the withholding of a desire to know it equivalent to casting it out from the soul? Is not lack of interest in comprehending that truth a sin of omission, is it not contempt and blasphemy, analogous, in the order of knowledge, to indifference regarding good and neutrality regarding duty in the order of volition? A faith that renounces understanding renounces life. "Everybody who believes thinks, and thinks by believing and believes by thinking. . . . If faith is not charged with thought, it is nothing." [53] A desire to gain some understanding of the faith is a desire to believe.

2. **How this understanding is to be sought.** The same quality that makes this understanding so useful, *fructuosissima*, and even so essential, likewise indicates the way it is to be sought. This way is described by the text of the Constitution *De fide catholica* in a few words. We are told that reason ought to seek understanding in the light of faith, *fide illustrata*, and as a gift of God, *Deo dante*. But reason must do the seeking, and is to reach the goal by its own labor: *ratio . . . cum quaerit . . . assequitur*. This labor has to be earnest, pious, and modest: *cum sedulo, pie, et sobrie quaerit*.

This is exactly what we have been saying. The understanding in question consists in intensifying within the mind the act of faith so far as it is an act of thinking. It consists in thinking with a thought that is as sincere and profound as we can make it, and in an assent, an adherence, and a surrender to the God of truth as complete and spontaneous as possible. The act intends to plunge into the very light of faith: *fide illustrata*. It must rely on the eternal truth, with which it wishes to satisfy the intellect, in an atmosphere of peace,

[53] St. Augustine, *De praedestinatione sanctorum*, 5 (PL, XLIV, 963).

certitude, and firmness. The satisfaction is of a special kind proper to this special act of thinking, which is the act of thinking *cum assensu*, with adherence and union with God. To some extent the satisfaction can be expressed in terms that describe the natural satisfactions of the spirit; but in itself it pertains to an order that is unique and transcendent.

The understanding is present in faith itself as its final perfection and its most complete assimilation by man. We do not step outside faith and then stand opposite it to see whether it is reasonable; we plunge into faith in order that reason may, by believing, perceive that belief is reasonable and good. The act of faith will be all the easier for this inspection, because it will be more prompt; and hence it will be more meritorious.[54]

We hardly need to point out that such endeavor cannot be successful without grace: *Deo dante*. The same grace of God that made faith possible must endow faith with the perfection enabling it to gain full ascendancy over reason. The serenity, power, and contentment in the light experienced in adhering with all one's intelligence, and hence in an intelligent manner, to the gospel message, cannot be attained "without the illumination and inspiration of the Holy Spirit, who imparts to all men sweetness in assenting to and believing in the truth." [55]

As the Word became incarnate by taking on our ways and being made the heir of mankind's past, His light will reach us through the medium of our intellectual acts. It will proceed from us, but without ceasing on that account to come to us from God, in the same way as living water which we draw from its source and which springs up from the earth is the water that comes down from the clouds.

The procedure in the order of knowledge resembles that which we observe in the order of volition. The human will can elicit supernatural acts, for example, of theological virtues; but a divine aid must have incited, sustained, and fecundated it. God begins and God finishes; but to begin and finish thus, God requires and arouses a free cooperation. When the work has been accomplished, it is assuredly His work, and in a certain sense it is His alone; yet it is also and quite

[54] St. Thomas, *Summa*, IIa IIae, q. 2, a. 10.
[55] Vatican Council, Constitution *De fide catholica*, 3 (Denz., 1791), quoting the Council of Orange, can. 7 (Denz., 180).

literally our work. God makes our knowledge fruitful in the same way and divinizes it by grace. Aided by this grace, the mind seeks, reasons, and reflects; and God grants that its efforts are crowned by a better understanding of the revealed doctrine. This understanding is a divine gift; but it is also, in strict truth, the fruit of human endeavor. The Council puts the matter very well: "Reason seeks and, by God's gift, achieves understanding."

Therefore reason must set to work; reason itself, along with grace, must elicit the act of understanding. And the Council specifies: reason must labor with earnestness, piety, and modesty: *sedulo, pie, sobrie.*

Sedulo: reason does not possess excessive resources for so sublime a task. Only by perfecting itself to the highest possible degree does it become capable, in its own measure, of receiving divine enlightenment.

Pie: this is even more important. So saintly a work can be performed only in a saintly way. Not that prayer is to replace the exacting efforts of reasoning; but the reasoning has to be carried on in a prayerful manner. There is question here of an ascent toward God, since it is an ascent toward divine truth and is made in union with this truth. Adaptation to the object of investigation is one of the prime conditions of scientific work. When a sacred object is investigated, therefore, the research must be conducted in a reverential spirit if it is to be scientific. The method of reasoning must be different in history, mathematics, and medicine; it must also be different in theology. But if it has to vary with the science, adaptation to the object of the science must be the same in every case. If, in an apologetic study, a dogma is formulated in cold and impersonal phrases, almost as a rationalist might express it, the explanation, at least in part, is this: the author is addressing adversaries, and is constrained to use a language they understand. But, in a work in which a dogma is studied in itself for the benefit of those who wish to reproduce it in their lives, if we were to treat it as we would treat indifferent or profane things, we would depreciate ourselves and them and it, and from the very outset would place ourselves in a false position.

Sobrie: we are in God's house. We must go up to the sanctuary serenely, modestly, humbly. The advance is not slower on that account. On the contrary, such reserve, like the piety from which it flows, is an adaptation to the object; therefore it is objectivity and preparation for the special light belonging to these matters. It is progress toward clear sight.

"O Lord, one God, O Triune God, whatever I have written in these books about what is Thine, let those who are Thine receive; if I have written anything that is mine, may Thou and Thine overlook." This prayer, which brings to a close one of the masterpieces of Catholic theology,[56] expresses a deep conviction every theologian ought to make his own: the conviction of being gravely inadequate to the task, without even knowing to what extent.

Evidently we are unequal to the undertaking. Anyone who would begin such a work with confidence in his ability would show that he is unaware of what is at stake. Christian teachers, following Scripture, repeat the words: "He that is a searcher of majesty shall be overwhelmed by glory" (Prov. 25:27). The wisdom of the world and the prudence of the wise are too small to measure the divine gift.[57] Pius IX bids us to expose the arrogance lurking in the proposal to sift the mysteries the merciful God has revealed to us and in the attempt to grasp and sound them with the limited and feeble mind of man. He points out that nothing is more stupid and senseless than the rash venture to penetrate and explain mysteries with the sole resources of human reason.[58]

Such words are not rare; this is not the only occasion on which the Church has forewarned its sons against the peril of presumption. We do well to recall them as we set out on our researches: not to discourage the enterprise, but to make a good beginning.

We have only to read these words with a little attention to see that what they condemn is not the simple effort to understand, but the effort made in a spirit of pride, vain self-sufficiency, and rationalistic assertiveness. This alone is what the Church rejects. Far from rebuking the desire to understand, the Church encourages it; all that it requires is that the light be sought where it is to be found. One of the documents that is most severe in repressing intellectual pride encourages such desire with exceptional emphasis: "Through its inherent power faith comprehends what is believed by the understanding it freely bestows, and intrepidly penetrates to depths which natural reason cannot reach." [59]

[56] St. Augustine, *De Trinitate*, XV, 28 (*PL*, XLII, 1098).
[57] Cf. I Cor. 1:18 ff.; Rom. 1:20; Eph. 5:6; Col. 2:8.
[58] Allocution, *Singulari quadam*, December 9, 1854 (Denz., 1642, 1645).
[59] Gregory IX, Epist. *Ab Aegyptiis* (Denz., 442).

Even in the natural order, a certain humility and dependence, consisting in submission to the exigencies of the object, are a condition of investigation. This, to be sure, is but a temporary tactic: nature rules only by conforming; an investigator allows himself to be guided by his facts only for the purpose of gaining control over them by discovering the bonds that hold them together. In theology such aspirations to dominate would be puerile. The student bows before dogmas and the object they express in order to receive and to continue to receive light from them, the light that is always brighter than the light of the intellect.

Submission to doctrinal formulas, submission to the intimations of grace and the directives of the teaching authority of the Church, submission also to reason and its light—these three submissions required of the theologian are, when clearly grasped, but one. For the same Christ resides in dogmatic pronouncements, in the official teaching authority, and in the life of grace. On the other hand, this triple and single submission to the one Christ is nothing else than scientific integrity and exclusive concern for truth, for the Truth is Christ. In freely obeying their pastors, Christians are not less determined than others to see nothing but the truth. On the contrary, they are doubly resolute to see nothing but the truth, for they, the privileged ones, are able to see it in two ways, since it gives them, along with itself, a double contact: it displays itself from without and it guides them from within.

Therefore the humility in question in no way restricts liberty but increases it, in the sense that it increases efficacy of action. On principle, no one is as free as the theologian who searches into the theology.

Perfection, of course, is not to be found in this world, and successes achieved are the more infrequent in proportion as the goal aimed at is more sublime and richer in varied aspects. In view of human shortcomings, it can happen and does happen that theologians do not always keep their hearts sufficiently detached from human fear and personal interest to see Christ living on in the teaching authority of the Church. In view of these same shortcomings it can happen and does happen—except at those solemn moments when the teaching Church speaks with the full assistance of Jesus Christ and His infallibility—that those who hold authority are not sufficiently distrustful of their own lights and individual preferences to be impartial bearers and witnesses of the pure light. The result may be that they obscure its intense clarity with their own murky limitations.

All this is inevitable in a society which, like the Church, is essentially composed of men. However, God makes use of these very imperfections to promote the good of His Church, and this is the good of the heads as well as that of members and theologians. As regards the latter—for these pages deal largely with theology—it is through the very defects of theologians and those in authority that God forms them to humility, prudence, obedience, confidence in Himself, and an unyielding and enduring love of truth. To ring the changes on the well-known saying, "What is not worth working for is not worth loving," he who has not had the experience of suffering for truth, does not know what loving it means. Perhaps many scandals of the weak, many awkward stumblings and errors among theologians themselves, have been avoided thanks to the restrictions issued by the teaching authority, even though they seemed harsh and possibly were so. But if a modest degree of heroism is required in such circumstances, that heroism does not lessen either enthusiasm or intellectual honesty. In any case, whatever may be the good procured by God through man's shortcomings, the defects are incidental and do not keep the humility and submission imposed on the theologian from being principles of high-mindedness, liberty, and adaptation to reality and light.

Thus, if we may be permitted to repeat, when Christians and theologians think about their faith, they have absolutely nothing else to do than think. No constraint is imposed, no arbitrary precautions are laid down; nothing but desire for truth prevails. Docility to grace and obedience to the Church are not orders coming from without but are the very requirements of the pure act of thought when it is brought to bear on dogmas. Mention of these matters is superfluous for those who are capable of understanding the situation; they need only to be urged to contemplate their faith, and will perceive immediately that, to comprehend it, they must look for it where it is to be found, in union with Christ who guides by His grace and directs by His Church toward the same truth.

3. **Role of theology in the quest for understanding.** The role of theology regarded in its proper sense consists in performing this labor in a scientific, technical, methodical fashion, with a procedure

that is strictly controlled and closely reasoned, just as is done in other sciences in other fields.

Accordingly we may define theology as the science of the faith, the human discipline that studies divine truth in a human way. Its aim is to present this truth in the most intelligible manner so that the human mind may contemplate it, and as far as possible, to make the object of faith an object of science. As means it employs the procedures and methods familiar to human reason in the systematic study of its objects.

What theology does is approximately the same as what Christian thought has always and everywhere done. Hence we may say that, considering the matter in its first beginnings, the great theologian is the entire Church, the Christian people. It is such in the measure in which it believes and thinks in union with Him who is the Truth, and not through some prodigious feat of universal suffrage. We should not imagine that the first on the scene was a teacher of exegesis or of Scholasticism; all men are capable of living their faith intelligently, for all are obliged to profess their faith with their whole intelligence. On the other hand, we should not imagine that every man can express clearly, not to say scientifically, his manner of comprehending his religion; but everyone in the Church and in Christ possesses, within the living mystery of his conscience, the only good way of comprehending it by living it. For this is an understanding—and a theology —that is lived, that informs the whole of life, and is not detached from life. It may not be scientific theology, but it is the living germ of theology.

Scientific theology expresses systematically what this ordinary theology contains implicitly and indistinctly. It is a science of the specialist, as all sciences are; indeed, it embraces almost as many sciences as it has different parts. But even so, it has but to define, codify, and unify what is formed in the soul of every Christian.

Thus it is a public service performed, not for the gratification of exposing personal views, but for the purpose of helping one's brethren to contemplate joyously the message of the Father for the benefit of God's people. Theologians such as St. Bonaventure, St. Thomas Aquinas, and Suarez are assuredly gigantic figures; but above all they are the organs of a great body, the voice in which all mankind hails the dawning day.

In this sense theology is something Catholic and sacred. It is liturgy. It is not a genteel occupation reserved for those who close the door on life. It is an essential, vital function in the dispensing of truth; and Christianity lives on truth.

This fact lays social and ecclesiastical duties on theology: the duty of being extremely careful not to bruise the faith of the simple by one's way of speaking and criticizing, and even more the duty of not scandalizing forthright and sincere souls by far-fetched explanations and inaccurate apologetics; the duty also of devoting special study to vital questions and of seeking answers to current problems.

As a public function, its work is the work of the Church. Theologians are not called on to give decisions in matters of faith, any more than the teaching Church is called on to construct a theology: the business of the Church is to teach. But because it has to teach, it has to know and direct the explanations given of its teaching and the science fashioned from that teaching. Otherwise such teaching will not be basically its own.

Theologians also have to listen to the Church, and that on two scores: as believers and as theologians. Their entire competence, their very authority—for they have such—come to them from their connection with the official teaching authority. Hence the Church guides theologians. But we must add that the Church directs them with respect, because of the sacred truth to which they devote themselves and which is the Church's own truth. The Church has always held their profession in honor, and its very severities are a mark of esteem. Even on the most solemn occasions, and especially then, popes and bishops are careful to consult theologians, and they would sin against prudence and truth if they neglected to consult them. That the body may live fully, each of its organs has to perform a definite part in its functioning.

As a work of the Church and a function of the mystical body, the theologian's work is, we may say, Christ's work, because the Church is the continuation of Christ. Through this work the Word continues to be made flesh, to be made man; the Word utters Himself in concepts and systems, in a way of knowing and understanding that is human.

In thus prolonging the Incarnation theology is holy with the holiness characteristic of Christianity. That statement is not too strong. It makes plain the element of blasphemy—or rather, fortunately, of ignorance—present in a certain contempt that is sometimes expressed for what is well called "sacred theology."

Some critics have asserted that theology is a Tower of Babel, a mass of disparate notions: history, textual criticism, philosophy, sociology, psychology; all this arranged in a certain order, no doubt, but giving forth an impression of a shallow universal science. But, we have to reply, what can the theologian do about this, if Christ has ties with everything: *omnia et in omnibus Christus*, and if, to proclaim so tremendous a gospel, human words are ever inadequate?

The greatness of Christ makes the greatness of theology, in matters which inattentive minds may mistake for incoherences. But this very greatness gives theology the right to refrain from assuming its definitive form at the first trial. As the mystical completeness of the Incarnation, which is the constructing of the mystical body and which theology describes, never comes to an end here below, theology likewise is never finished on earth.

Have profane sciences reached their goal? On what date did physics and chemistry, or meteorology and medicine, attain their full perfection? Yet these are easy sciences whose objects are open to the hand's touch. Should we be astonished if difficult sciences, whose objects lie on a higher plane, have not yet reached mature form? Philosophy in our day, we may well believe, is still in the groping stage, and theology much more so. And we are right to regard them thus: if man has but begun the sciences of matter, how could he have finished the science of the spirit and the science of God? Ought not theologians to exult with joy and enthusiasm at the realization that they are cooperating in an enterprise so magnificent that it will never be completed, for the reason that human thought-processes are too complicated and too sluggish to express the whole simplicity of the splendor that has to be described?

This does not imply that nothing has been accomplished. The *Summae* our fathers have constructed are marvelous cathedrals. But their merit is precisely their conviction that the truth is more beautiful than all that has been said about it, and their brave undertaking to set to work with the help of God.

As their example is a lesson, their discoveries remain a definite acquisition. Even in natural sciences, the new theories which progress brings to light do not, as a rule, suppress the earlier theories they replace; they preserve what is essential and improve it. Of course in those fields of investigation in which growth takes place mainly by the accretion of new elements, we can readily perceive that a new conception may entail the negation of older ideas.

With much greater reason, in the sciences of the spirit advance toward the future is respectful of the past. For in these sciences progress is made internally, by better understanding, and hence not by suppression, of what was known previously. In these sciences all the essential data are furnished at the outset; likewise at the outset the mind can supply the whole answer in its general outlines. In philosophy, for example, from the moment a man sets himself to reflect, he finds himself in the presence of thought, of being, of cause, of finality, of all the great realities on which he is to discourse. Nothing prevents him from perceiving rather early the chief and most evident of the truths he has to discuss. The difficulty, which is real and extremely grave, was and still is to understand correctly what was presented for consideration in the initial stages.

Theology likewise found itself, from the beginning, in possession of all the essential factors of the solution. Revelation was closed with the death of the last apostles, and moreover God has never ceased to assist the Church in its task. The definitive formulas of dogmas could be phrased very early, and speculative syntheses and theological systems could be outlined. But the seed did not die the day it was planted. As there is a development of dogma, so also, and much more, there is a development of theology, which likewise takes place within its own genus, that is, in the same dogma, the same sense, the same doctrine.

God's supernatural work is always accomplished progressively, in slow and imperceptible growth. The work of God which is the acclimatization of divine truth in human minds ought, as far as we can judge, to advance in the same way. The road to be traveled is long, and mankind's pace to which God adapts His activity is not very swift. Tremendous stretches of time will be required. During the centuries or milleniums to come, we may well believe, theology will be much more magnificent than we perceive it to be at present; but it will resemble the theology of today and the theology of the past more than we can imagine.

Hence we should not be astonished if new shoots spring from the sturdy ancient trunk and if these pages, while constructing theology in the traditional mode, do not express the truths in exactly the same way as they have always been expressed.

There is a *profana vocum novitas*, a novelty in the usage of words, that ought to be avoided like the plague. This is a way of speaking that is scornful of tradition. But there is also a rigid formalism that is no less dangerous, for it is false to the very life of the faith, transforming into a repetition of formulas what was the glowing unity of an expanding life, benumbing the ardor of contemplation that belongs to the essence of the faith, and scorning the tradition of progress that flourishes in the Church.

In His omnipotence God could have given us a theology fully formed at the beginning, just as He could have created for Christ a soul and body fully matured, so that they would not be the culmination of a long human preparation. But then Christ would not have been a man from among men. In the same way, as regards theology, knowledge of the supernatural would not have been a human knowledge in the complete sense. God, in coming to us, would have turned us out of doors and would not have entered into us.

God in His goodness had no intention of acting thus. As He graciously invites us to cooperate in His work, He graciously invites us to devote our intellectual industry to the expression of His message. The response to His summons is theology, the consecration of the human intellect, in its scientific capacity, to divine truth.

Thus theology calls forth not only the respect but the love of Christians. Love, I say, for in itself it is love. To see nothing but abstractions and subtleties in its massive folio volumes, a man must be incapable of penetrating to the soul of things. To smile at it as though it were a presumptuous effort to express the divine, one must be ignorant of what man is and what God is. God, who can make the tongues of infants eloquent and raise up children to Abraham from the stones of the wayside, will also know how to impart to His friends the power of meditating on His truth.

"Loving Savior," wrote Henry Suso, "the very frogs praise Thee in the ponds, and, not knowing how to sing, they croak. O my sweet Jesus, I know and I recognize what I am; I recognize perfectly that I ought rather to weep for my sins than seek to praise Thee. But, O infinite Good, do not despise my desire, even though I am nothing but a wretched worm of the earth. . . . Lord, the cherubim and seraphim and the whole company of heavenly spirits praise Thee with all their might; but what can they do more than the slightest of creatures, in the presence of Thy Majesty, which is above all praise?" [60]

So let us praise the Lord in our own way, poor men that we are; and, since we cannot sing like the angels, let us, with our ponderous minds, fashion our theology as men—in the man Jesus Christ.

[60] H. Suso, *The Book of Eternal Wisdom*, chap. 24.

CHAPTER II

THEOLOGY AS SCIENCE AND AS SEARCH
FOR UNITY

> "Everything is intelligible so far as it
> is one. He who does not understand
> one, does not understand anything, as
> the Philosopher says."
>
> St. Thomas, *De veritate*, q. 21, a. 3

I. THE SEARCH FOR UNITY IN EVERY SCIENCE

IF theology is truly a science and a quest of understanding, we
shall be well advised, in undertaking to treat of it, to ask ourselves
how the human mind sets about constructing a science and achieving
understanding in the spheres that are its own domain. The answer
is simple. Always and everywhere, when the mind desires to comprehend—and what else does it desire?—it unifies.

The Scholastics defined science as knowledge through causes. In
our day, mainly because of the positive sciences which did not exist
in the Middle Ages, science is defined rather as knowledge through
laws. Whatever may be our judgment about these two different
conceptions, we see at once that they coincide at one point: the
relations determined by causality, like those measured by laws, are
bonds among phenomena; in both these viewpoints, science is regarded as knowledge through connections, through unification.

This characteristic of science is brought out by another consideration that comes to our notice from the moment we may call
the birth of science in every individual. This feature is well known
to adults who are harassed and embarrassed by the perpetual "why"
of children. The little mind is scarcely open to knowledge when it
is off in pursuit of synthesis and unification; the terms, technical

though they may be, are exact. The young mind tries to associate new ideas with those already possessed, and the questions outwardly asked but reveal the inner need. The intellect, from the time it is aware of its contact with external reality, is conscious of its essential aspiration, the inclination toward unity.

Recognition of this bent was the first achievement, the stroke of genius, and the human reaction of the founders of European science, the physiocrats of Hellas. Out of the endless variety of phenomena striking the senses, they sought a single basic reality of which all the rest would be but the manifestation and the product. They suggested that everything is made of water, or of air, or of fire; everything is number and proportion; everything is the same; everything is the mind and its work. These reconstructions and syntheses may appear childish to us; but the adult always begins by being a child, and the first step is the indispensable condition of all the steps that follow. Their aphorisms represent the first conscious and whole-hearted attempt, at least in the Greco-Roman world, to achieve the grouping and unification which science is still aiming at today. The proper and unique task of science has been the same from the outset: the reduction of the different and the many to unity.

But this activity did not have to await science for its discovery. From the first gropings of the first man, as we may conjecture from our observation of infants, it has asserted itself, implicitly and indistinctly perhaps, but resolutely. In coming to birth, science did not have to invent it, but only to disengage it.

Indeed, we would be inaccurate if we were to affirm that science was born on some fairly recent day, after long centuries during which it did not exist. In the form in which we now view it, it has grown and matured; but it existed much earlier. It has lived from the time that man lived; but it was mixed up with man's life, without having won as yet a place apart and without having arranged its features into an orderly symmetry.

It still lives on in this way among those who are not reckoned as "scholars." It exists under the form of everyday knowledge, under the form of ideas grouped in small units. Thus associated in the mind of every man, ideas, whatever their nature, tend to organize and unify themselves. Resemblances come to the fore and mutual dependencies become manifest by their relation to some common cause; in a word, connections are apprehended, to show that, from the first beginnings, the act of thinking is an act of uniting.

Scientific knowledge tightens these bonds and reduces their number; it does not innovate but carries on a task already begun. Its movement has become more conscious and more rapid. Are we forced to conclude that it is more resolute and victorious? After all, the initial advance was made into uncharted territory, through tangled underbrush, in a direction not yet ascertained. Are the pioneers less deserving than those who make their way over an explored countryside? In any event, in ancient times as today, in uncultured knowledge as in science narrowly so called, the endeavor is the same: reason lays hold of its data with the purpose of putting the universe in order in the heads of men, and at the same time tries to subject its order to their activity. Immersed in multiplicity, reason seeks unity.

The scientist may not explicitly advert to this tendency. He will tell you that he is studying electrical discharges in a condition of reduced pressure, he will talk about the effects of a virus on the intestines of a guinea pig; he is not even thinking of a search for unity. Perhaps he may not be thinking of it; but his work thinks of it for him; and if it is not one of the matters falling under his observation, the reason is not that it is absent from his work, but rather that it is the soul, the stimulus, and the basis of his work. What else is observation of connections, or inquiry into relations, or the desire to express in equations, than the pursuit of unity? Of course unity is not pursued in its pure and isolated state, with the object of discovering what it is in itself; that is the office of philosophy. But it is pursued as realized in things, as being the very cohesion of facts and the framework within which phenomena are arranged. Wholly intent on the task of synthesizing, the mind has no time to reflect on this task; what is known overshadows the investigator's realization of his knowledge, and the unities he is intent on describing cause him to lose sight of the fact that he is conducting a search for unity.

The sciences, especially those that have advanced farthest and are the best formulated, furnish striking examples of this fact. Let us consider the science of physics. The object it investigates is, at first sight, extremely varied and even changeable. This object embraces movements, sounds, colors, lenses, phenomena of electrical power, conduction, polarity, hydrostatics, in brief, an uninterrupted succession of diverse things. A superficial observer would say that all this is sheer multiplicity; what connection is there between motion and color, between expansion and heat? But let a physicist come on the scene, let a college of physicists take over, let them observe and perform their calculations. They will require centuries; no matter. When they finish, or rather, since they will never finish, when they have labored for a time, the whole aspect of the undertaking will have changed. They will take these disconnected facts, hem them in, and fit them together in a thousand ways; gradually a vast network of steel wires will cover the whole, transforming this seeming incoherence into a rigid unity. These wires are laws; each of them is an inflexible relation requiring a fact to be fixed, measured, set off, and determined by others. These latter, in turn, are accounted for by yet others, or by the first ones; and these others by others, and so without end, until the same has been done, on some distant day, with everything that has individual existence in the physical universe.

Thus science advances through the mobility of phenomena, like the frost that takes possession of a body of water, changing fluidity into rigidity by forming a single block out of disparate elements. Each fact henceforth emerges as a simple consequence of others, almost in the way a solution results once a mathematical operation has been set in motion. One might say that there are no longer any isolated facts, nor even any absolutely new and autonomous facts; there is only an immense and all-embracing interdependence, in which everything is completely governed by the rest and nothing governs itself. This conception of the world which physics sets out to elaborate may appear inadmissible and strained, and so it is; but no one can deny that it is a pursuit of unity.

However, physics does not stop there; it advances farther, and always in the direction of unity. These laws which reduce the universe to a single whole are diverse and numerous; it strives to group them together. It does so by endeavoring to unite them under general formulas, of which isolated laws would be particular cases. It then goes on and tries to combine these more general laws into yet more general laws. In this way are formed the great theories and systems of physics, of which the system of universal gravitation is a good example, and which are, if we may say so, laws of laws, laws to the second or third power, statements embracing a multitude of laws in their unity. As the laws unify the phenomena, the theories and systems unify the laws, and thus the drive toward unity never slows down.

This same tendency is observed in the way physics, like all the positive sciences, formulates its laws: mathematical language is employed. The introduction of such language supposes unification, and that for two reasons. It supposes unification, in the first place, because it implies that we can represent phenomena by figures; this is impossible unless we are able to decide what equality and addition are in each category among the phenomena, or, in other words, that we can determine on a measure in this category, a recurring type that is always the same in all the individuals of this category. But such a type is evidently a unity of the class of universal ideas, a unity which, being found identical in many, reduces the many to one in itself. And what is that if not unification?

The other unification which the introduction of mathematical language supposes is that required for calculation. For figures and the assigning of various quantities in mathematics are merely the creation of a vocabulary; its true language consists in ascertaining the relations of these figures and quantities, so as to discover the equalities, equivalences, and identities among them. But such relations cannot be ascertained unless the existence of similar relations among the phenomena has been established. Consequently the introduction of mathematical language supposes the unification which the laws constitute.

This is not the place to discuss the researches, artifices, and postulates necessary for such an introduction of figures and calculus. What we are intent on emphasizing is the quest of unity revealed in the translation of experimental data into mathematical language.

Mathematics is eminently the science of unity—a unity, clearly, of a material order. It is generally defined as the science of quantity, since quantities are the objects it treats of. But we may just as aptly define it as the science of unity in quantity, for its whole endeavor is to reduce to unity an object that in itself is pure multiplicity.

For the object of mathematics is pure extension, pure divisibility, extraposition with reference to itself: that is, pure multiplicity. Therefore its first procedure has to consist in constructing, in the midst of this multiplicity, the very entities it proposes to treat of. It performs this task by deciding on classifications. In this way it obtains the numbers and figures, or the quantities it is going to study.

This is its initial act, by which it acquires its object, quantities; and this act, as is evident, is already a synthesis, a unification. The second procedure of mathematics, that which constitutes its proper function, consists in determining a priori the relationships among all these magnitudes; theoretically it aims at determining all these relationships, or at least all those which appear to have a special interest. We are able to know whether these relationships are rigorous, close, thoroughgoing, inflexible: out of the inconsistency, the discontinuity, and the multiplicity which are the starting point of the science, they construct an inexorable unity, unyielding as a block of steel. We may say that mathematics is the science of absolute concatenation, of compact and unbreakable bonds that are linked to one another and that require, necessitate, and grapple one another: an impregnable and dominating citadel, which the mind has constructed from the absolute and intrinsic discreteness which is quantity.

This is no doubt a dream castle, a necessity emptied, by its own exactions, of concrete reality, a form of unity that imprisons something alien and not a unity that is self-contained. But it is a significant dream, a dream vividly expressing the nature of the mind, at least in its function of knowing quantities, extension, and matter. This may be said to be its play and its occupation, in which, by sheer activity, without being heedful in the first instance of external things, but only in obedience to its interior structure and caprice, it exhibits to itself the spectacle of itself and of its free unfolding. This play consists exclusively in making unity out of nothing, that is, in transforming into pure unity, into a sytem of intolerant and total enchainment, what in itself is absolute discontinuity and non-identity with itself, or non-unity.

And all this is as nothing: the mind pushes much farther ahead, revealing much more clearly what it is. It proposes to force the supple movement of experience into this adamant unity, as though the fluid and variable universe could not really exist for it unless that universe were changed into this rigid unity.

To this work physics has consecrated itself, and the same goes for the other natural sciences. It discourses of phenomena, of things, of events; but it speaks of them in figures. When it has accomplished its task, colors, sounds, and motions have become magnitudes, functions, equations, derivations, a whole amorphous and abstract world which mathematical unity absorbs, not without difficulty but, on principle, without definitive resistance. Nothing is left but formulas; and science organizes these formulas into more and more general formulas, and the latter into others yet more general. The ideal animating the whole endeavor is, evidently, the ambition to find a single formula of which all the rest would be particular instances. It is an inaccessible ideal, to be sure; even a contradictory ideal, as could be demonstrated; yet an undeniable ideal, for the entire undertaking converges to it; above all, a significant ideal. To construct science and to achieve understanding, the human mind seeks unity.

Philosophers of a nominalist or positivist persuasion have tried to locate the motive for this quest of unity in a desire for facility. The mind strives to group and synthesize facts merely to grasp them more easily and, in grasping them with a single effort, to lighten the work of the memory, to enjoy the satisfaction of making calculations about them, and to make them serve practical purposes more conveniently. Moreover, they sometimes add, the mind experiences a special pleasure, a sort of esthetic delight, in contemplating the rigid molds in which it succeeds in unifying reality.

All these fine results are assuredly produced by the effort toward unification. But we may ask whether the mouse is the explanation of the mountain, and whether a journey so protracted, so tiring, so unremitting is adequately accounted for by a number of effects that are after all incidental. Furthermore, whence comes this particular pleasure the mind experiences in contemplating unity, if there is no contact between the unity and it? What is the power which the unification can impart for foreseeing and utilizing things, if there is no connection between it and those things? We have to search much deeper, we have to go into the very nature of things, into the nature of the mind and of reality, to find the explanation of all this.

What do we mean by comprehension if not the grasping, with a single act of the mind, of the object to be comprehended, and how can we grasp it with a single act unless we unify it? The greater the object, the more difficult the synthesis and the more imperative our need of combining and comparing in order to effect it; but such synthesis is always indispensable. Either we shall not comprehend at all, or else everything that is to be comprehended will be inserted, and hence unified, into the one act which understands.

However, we are aware that we need not belabor this point here; the soul is one, and consciousness of self is one.[1] Comprehension, for the soul and for consciousness, is assimilation of the object and the finding of it in oneself in recognizing oneself in it. But how can that which is one assimilate that which is multiple and recognize itself in the latter without unifying it?

What, after all, is knowledge of an object if not—and we beg pardon for mentioning so evident a truth—the power to say and think: "I know this object." [2] But that cannot be said and thought unless two things are thought of at the same time and in the same act: oneself and the object. To know, therefore, is to be aware of an object in the act by which one is aware of oneself, it is to be conscious of the object, it is to make of the object, as known, an element of consciousness itself. From that moment, the object as known has to be living and has to be one with the life and the unity of consciousness. As we need scarcely point out, the unity of consciousness is a most perfect unity, since consciousness is the complete coinciding of a being with itself, the possession of the whole of oneself in oneself. Accordingly the known, to be known, understood, and comprehended, must also have a most perfect unity in us.

In speaking of this matter, we may well advert to the scholastic axiom: "Whatever is known exists in the mind in a way that is conformable with the nature of the mind." Since the person who knows is one, and especially since he is one precisely as knowing, the object known, as known, must likewise be one. No knowledge is gained without achieving a certain identity, and "the person actually knowing and the object actually known are one and the same." If the knower is so completely one, how can the known be other than one? Hence St. Thomas declares that the intellect has only one way of comprehending, and that is by unifying: "The intellect can understand many things as one, but not as many." [3] In fact, "to understand many things as one is, in a sense, to understand one thing." [4]

---

[1] Consciousness will be discussed later.

[2] To every man his due: the formula is from Kant; it is even the magnificent discovery of Kant. However, Kant integrates it in a general conception of knowledge that suppresses the mind from the very outset, and ignores the very essence of consciousness, as we shall have occasion to point out soon. Here, as will be seen more and more clearly in the course of these pages, no question of agnosticism can arise.

[3] *Summa*, Ia, q. 85, a. 4.

[4] *Ibid.*, q. 58, a. 2 ad 1.

Our reasoning, up to this point, has considered only the act of knowing. We must now go farther and penetrate to that which is the foundation of knowledge, namely, being. If unity is necessary for knowledge, the reason is that it is necessary for being.

For, according to the scholastic principle, *ens et unum convertuntur:* being and unity are functions of each other. A cognate principle asserts: *ens et verum convertuntur, unumquodque est intelligibile in quantum est actu:* intelligibility and truth on the one hand, and being on the other hand, are functions of each other. In joining these principles together, therefore, we have to say: *unum et verum convertuntur,* unity and intelligibility are functions of each other; the intellect cannot comprehend anything except one as one, because it cannot understand anything except being as being. Being, in the measure in which it exists, is intelligible of itself, for it cannot have any explanation or need of explanation outside of being; such explanation and its need would be in the realm of nothing. In the same way, since being and one go together, one, to the extent that it is one, is intelligible of itself; any explanation drawn from outside would be in the realm of the incoherent and unthinkable, according to Aristotle's profound remark: "He who does not understand one, does not understand anything." One, as far as it is one and for the very reason that it is one, necessarily satisfies the mind; for being is essentially a self-possession, a perfection of meaning and a fullness in need of nothing for their completion.

When scrutinized to its depths, the inclination toward unity, like the inclination toward being, is seen to be a constitutive element of the mind and of all reality. It is not at all a passing caprice; indeed, when it has become conscious in the faculty of consciousness, it is recognized as the impulse of everything that exists toward Him who is the supreme source of all existence. For God is pure One just as He is pure Act. As pure Act, He is the first cause without which nothing would exist; as One, He is the first principle without which nothing would hold together, nothing would be one, nothing would be at all. To tend toward that principle of all inner cohesion is as necessary as to be united to one's own being and to be oneself; and to tend toward Him is to tend toward unity.

"Hear, O Israel, the Lord our God is one Lord." [5] This great precept of the Old Law, this preamble of the first of the Christian com-

    [5] Deut. 6:4.

mandments,[6] is also at the basis of true epistemology. The mind must gravitate toward unity with all its weight; it must love unity in its own special way as befits a mind, for it must aspire after God with its whole strength.[7]

The long study the intellect engages in to organize its knowledge and to synthesize phenomena is doubly revealing. First, it bears witness to what the intellect, in all its activity, is in itself and in its nature. Secondly, it bears witness to the great need the intellect has of Him who is both the Necessary Being and Unity.

In itself, therefore, such study is religious. They who undertake it in a profane attitude of mind lack the right spirit and expose themselves to the danger of doing it badly. They who do it well, they who, if only implicitly, feel the need of unity which is its soul, perceive in themselves at least the beginnings of a desire which is a prayer and which moves toward God of its own impetus. Such study is religious, not by reason of some accidental accretion or some practice of devotion or cult required of the investigator; it is religious because of its nature, because of its appetite for unity. This religious aspect does not directly bestow any moral rectitude on the will, for in itself it resides in the intellect. Yet it has a relation to morality, for the intellect is not separated from the will. In any case, and so far as the subject treated in these pages is concerned, we have ascertained an important point: the instituting of a search for unity in religious science properly so called and in theology involves nothing sacrilegious and should cause no astonishment.

II. The Search for Unity in This Work

> "The more perfect a science is, the more unified it is."
>
> Summa, IIIa, q. 11, a. 6, 1

1. **The search for unity in theology in general.** Since theology is a science, and since every science seeks unity, theology must likewise seek unity. We shall do well to consider for a moment the attitude impressed on the will by religion; at bottom, that attitude is an aspiration toward unity.

Even natural religion and morality are summed up in this aspira-

[6] Mark 12:29.
[7] Mark 12:29 f.; Deut. 6:5.

tion. For what is the search for God or the purpose to do one's duty or the maintaining of peace, confidence, and justice, if not the endeavor to be in harmony, "to be one" with oneself, with nature, and with God—to live consistently, as the Stoics would have said?

Supernatural religion also requires unity, and does so much more emphatically. Its great precept, its single precept, is charity; and what is charity but a unity of wills? We need but recall the counsels of ascetic perfection. The solicitude to see nothing but God and His fatherly providence in all that happens, purity of intention, sincerity with oneself, the desire to think, act, and live for Christ and in Christ —what else is all this than an ardent, concentrated, and exclusive aspiration of the soul that wishes to unite itself completely to Him who is complete Unity? What is mortification, recollection, detachment, what are the renunciations imposed on self by the religious vows, but an effort to escape multiplicity, the encumbrance of wealth, the complexity of affections, and the incoherence of desires, so as to mount up with more unified soul toward Him who is Unity?

The whole of Christianity is unity. And it has to be if the intellect is to point out what, in Christianity, is its essence. Christianity is the taking up of the universe of mankind into the unity of God through the unity of Christ. The science that explains Christianity, theology, must give expression to this tendency toward unity. It will be more truly itself, it will be more truly a science and the science of Christianity, in proportion as it resolves itself systematically, energetically, and exclusively into unity.

In order to contemplate this unique and eternal truth, theology evidently need not lose sight of particular truths, since knowledge of the primary truth is arrived at through these particular truths. The task of theology will be precisely to study these fragmentary truths, in order to show that they engender a knowledge of the one source from which they all flow, and to disclose that which constitutes the unity of them all.

"My God and my all": this exclusive preoccupation with God is immediately seen to be essential to religion in the sphere of volition. Why, when understanding is in question, is the intellect less clear-sighted? "Do Thou alone speak to me." [8] Absorption in the infinite is the mark of adoration and love; how could it be other than the characteristic of that science which is the science of adoration and

[8] *The Following of Christ*, I, 3, 2.

love? "What have I in heaven, and besides Thee what do I desire upon earth?" (Ps. 72:25.) The voice of Moses does not touch me, nor that of the prophets, nor that of the councils, unless I hear Thee underneath their words. "As the hart panteth after the fountains of water" (Ps. 41:2)—is not the whole of life, especially that of the spirit, a search for Him who is necessary because He is the One?

Unfortunately the multiple confuses us and diverts us from unity. It lays hold of us so strongly that it keeps us from perceiving that unity accounts for the very solidity of its multiplicity. Some even go so far as to say: "What is the good of seeking unity in dogmas?" May God forgive us; they might as well say: "What is the good of bothering about God and the faith?"

In all our cognitive activities, Christianity counsels us to turn our eyes toward unity: on that side the sun rises. Christianity reminds us that even when we contemplate the material universe the search for a remote reflection of infinite unity in things is religious and true. "From one Word are all things, and all speak this one." [9] True wisdom is the unity to which "all things are one, which reduces all things to one, and sees all things in one." [10] How much more is this counsel in place when we contemplate Christianity itself! "O Truth, my God, make me one with Thee in eternal love." [11]

Although the quest of unity is essential to theology, it will be conducted in different ways according as theology itself unfolds in different ways. To fix more precisely the method of undertaking the search in this book, a review of other methods employed in other departments of theology will be instructive.

In historical theology, for example, unity is achieved in two ways: the two procedures proper to history. Each point of the theologico-historical exposition is first unified, in the endeavor to recapture its proper individuality. Then the general bearing of these points is unified as well as can be done, in the effort to see how they may be connected in a single, coherent historical exposition. Thus scholars will try to express clearly what was the doctrinal teaching of a Father, of a school, of an epoch; how, at this period, particular details explain one another and how they are related to the circumstances of the times. They will then inquire how the various partial doctrines

[9] *Ibid.*
[10] *Ibid.*
[11] *Ibid.*

are extensions of one another, how they all express the same Christian teaching, and how, although stressing now one point, now another, they all end up by expressing it fully.

In scholastic theology, likewise, two methods of unification are employed, and they are the methods that befit Scholasticism. In the first place, unity is aimed at in the search for the clearest, most precise, most sharply defined formula for each dogma: the formula that best brings out the characteristics and unity of this dogma. This initial unification prepares the way for the second unification; for, in tracing the shape of its outlines, it traces the projections and indentations by which each formula is fitted to the others and takes its place among them, so as to constitute with them all a single general formula. This second unification, the unification of synthesis, is very pronounced in scholastic theology. We have but to recall the theological *Summas*, their systematic designs, their exhaustive divisions, and their announced objective of being complete and self-contained. We will thus be convinced that what the Scholastics had in mind was the construction of a coherent system in which all supernatural wisdom would be comprised, marshaled, and organized; this is truly the achieving of unification.

Among the procedures employed to realize this goal, two merit special mention, because they have been used more often and with greater success, and because they have won a more authentic approval. The first, pre-eminently the scholastic method, consists in applying the classifications furnished by philosophy, particularly by scholastic philosophy, to the unification of dogma. And indeed, within the limits attainable by natural reason, what can we find that is better adapted to such an end, and that is more worthy and suitable? Among all fields of knowledge, is not philosophy the most exalted? Is it not precisely philosophy that deals with many of the objects revelation speaks of, such as God, man, destiny, and duty? What programs of unity could better be transferred from the domain of reason to that of faith than those of philosophy?

A second procedure employed, one that enjoys a certain favor in our own era, is the synthesizing of dogma in function of human finality. This procedure is not adequately distinct from the first one; how can we speak of finality without speaking of philosophy? But it has its own clearly marked characteristics. It lends itself, better than the preceding method, to psychological and moral developments, and more easily admits of appeals to interior experience and even to sentiment. On the other hand, the consideration of finality leads naturally to discourse about God who is the last end and about means for attaining God; with this as a starting point, the way is open for expressing the whole of Christianity.

Synthesis in function of finality, synthesis in function of other sciences and especially of philosophy, synthesis also made on the model of historical syntheses: all these are unifications. Now historical theology and scholastic theology are the two main branches of theology. In sacred science, therefore, unification may be said to be a traditional procedure, and it is also accredited by usage which is, as we have seen, justified by reason and by the example of natural disciplines.

However, we must add, the syntheses in question are, in themselves, extrinsic to revealed truth as revealed. They unify revelation on the level of history or on that of the natural sciences, of moral science, and of philosophy. They do not formally unify revelation on its own level.

Assuredly, divine truth has become a fact through the Incarnation, and under God's guaranty it has been embodied in formulas and judgments derived from natural science and natural speculation. On this basis it not only can but must be synthesized in the way befitting facts or doctrines, in the way of history or philosophy. Such unification particularly befits certain traditional and necessary enterprises of theology that are undertaken on these grounds, for example, apologetic expositions, works of controversy, and the discussions of the schools. But we should note that these undertakings, because of some aspect treated in them, remain external to divine truth itself, and consider in divine truth some point which the adversaries can grasp as well as the theologian can, or which so lightly touches its essence either in itself or in the manner in which it is conceived that it can be made the subject of dialectical bouts. We may have to combat the enemy, we may have to run after straying brethren, or we may engage in domestic disputations for exercise; but in all such cases we remain outside the sanctuary.

The fact that the unity disclosed by these methods is an extraneous unity need cause no surprise. It is a natural, not a supernatural unity; a human, not a divine or Christian unity. Since nature is suited to grace, unity of this kind will clearly be suited to dogma. But the harmony will be such as is found between two distinct things; it will not be the unity of the thing itself, the unity which is one with that thing.

Being extrinsic to revelation, this sort of unity can furnish no more than an extrinsic understanding of revelation. In other words, it enables us to understand the judgments and concepts in which a revealed truth is formulated, the virtues it requires, the efforts it calls forth, and the events in which it is expressed. But in itself it does not disclose the inner mystery of that truth.

2. **Method of searching for unity in this book.** The unity just mentioned, and it alone, is what we are seeking in this book. The only unity to occupy our attention is the unity intrinsic to revelation. What we hope to accomplish, with God's help, in this investigation is the attainment of a certain understanding of what is intrinsic in revealed truth.

Consequently ours is a limited task. The whole of theology has been thoroughly studied by others who are intellectual giants; we are not so naive as to attempt to do their work over. But at least we desire to perform this limited task in a technical and reasoned way, by penetrating to the ultimate principle of theology and by endeavoring to acquire an accurate grasp of its spirit.

Such an undertaking is no novelty in God's Church; if it were, it would be suspect. It is an ancient and traditional enterprise and is therefore, on this head, fully authorized.

We wish to make this clear, for the preceding pages, which had to insist on some very real distinctions, may have raised suspicions of ruptures with the past and consequently of presumptuous innovations. The Scholastics, to speak of them first, for it is to them that we owe reparation, have had frequent recourse to the method we are going to follow, even if they did not employ it as their major procedure. Hence, as we are happy to point out, in raising it to the status of a system, we may still count ourselves among their followers. Repeatedly in their works, and often in passages that are well known as well as in the introductions or conclusions of their expositions, they bring to light hidden connections by which dogmas are drawn to one another and joined together. Frequently also, even in their most metaphysical argumentations and their most controversial discussions, they are fond of showing that one truth of faith irresistibly evokes another, and that within the interior of truth all things hold together in unity.

Well ahead of the Scholastics, and to a greater extent than they, the Fathers of the Church proceeded in the same way. In the eyes of St. Irenaeus, for example, dogma is so unified that it constitutes a sort of body [12] of which the various parts are so many members. When one member of a body is injured, all the members protest; "all the members suffer with it" (I Cor. 12:26). The same is true in Christian teaching: when heresy has attacked one dogma, the others are marshaled to repel it. This is the way the Fathers refuted the Macedonians; they showed that the Holy Spirit must be God because He vivifies us by grace. They refuted the Adoptionists by pointing out that Christ had to be the true Son of God, since He endows us with adoptive sonship in Himself. They refuted Arianism, Gnosticism, and Pelagianism by appealing continually to the unity which Christian teaching possesses and which establishes solidarity among all its parts.

We can go back still farther. What we find in tradition we find also in the Scriptures. St. Paul, for example, long before the Fathers, loved to set off the various dogmas by one another. Thus he shows how undeniable Christ's resurrection is by linking it up with our resurrection; [13] he explains the power of baptism by recalling the effects of Christ's death; [14] he brings out the excellence of grace and the gospel by exalting the greatness of Jesus Christ and His sufficiency for our salvation. [15]

Beyond St. Paul, beyond Sacred Scripture, we come to Jesus Christ. Since we are merely noting our Lord's descent to our level, we are not rash in remarking that in presenting His message He shows that it is one. We have observed this elsewhere, when studying the Gospel according to St. John [16] in connection with the most sublime and essential truths of our faith, such as the solidarity existing between Christ and Christians, and the new and single life which all the faithful receive. Our Lord loves to propose these different dogmas in series so closely linked that He does not even indicate

[12] *Adversus haereses*, I, ix, 4 (*PG*, VII, 548); see also *The Whole Christ*, pp. 231 f.

[13] Cf. I Cor. 15:12–18.

[14] Gal. 3:27; Rom. 6:3; Col. 2:12.

[15] Gal. 2:16–21. Cf. *The Whole Christ*, pp. 414 f., 453, 480 ff.

[16] *The Whole Christ*, pp. 166–74. Cf. John 3:3 ff.; 5:17–24, 26; 6:57.

when He has left off speaking of one topic to impart instruction on another. He discourses on them all together, passing from one to another without break or transition, as though He were not treating of a different subject. The discourse after the Last Supper is typical in this respect: Christ follows no strict plan, He introduces no air-tight divisions, and yet He discusses a multitude of different truths. They are all uttered, and with emphasis; but they are uttered within one another, because each of them is, at bottom, present in all of them. Let no one say that it is the Evangelist who has blended these truths and reduced them to living unity. The inspired author, the inspired witness, has but given testimony [17] of what Jesus taught; and the Master, with sure touch, knew no less well than His disciple how to bring out the unity of His teaching.

When we reflect on our Lord's procedure, which is also that of the inspired writers, should we not conclude that God, in the very act of confiding His revelation to us, instructs us to reason on it, and hence that at the same time He implants in the heart of mankind both the seed of faith and the seed of theology?

Thus theology keeps recurring; theology, the sacred science, and doubly sacred: by reason of the object occupying it and the aids required for it, and also by reason of the initial impulse setting it in motion.

As soon as our search for intrinsic understanding and unity discloses what is essential to theology, we perceive that its beginnings coincide, so to speak, with the beginnings of Christian life on this earth. Peter, John, Paul, and the others who belonged to its first period, were theologians at the same time as they were apostles and inspired writers. At the same time, we repeat; for it is as apostles that they bear witness, not to the faith alone, but also to the unity and intelligibility of the faith; and it is as inspired writers that they set forth, not only the revealed truths, but also the manner in which these truths are implied in one another and are intelligible in being unified, that is, in being what at bottom they actually are. Although the following statement may seem somewhat bold, we are going to propose it because it seems to us exact: they were apostles, not only of the faith, but also of a theology that is nothing but a flowering of the faith, since it is nothing but a manifestation of the unity of this faith, an intrinsic theology without which the faith is not whole; they

[17] John 19:35; 21:24.

were inspired to teach a theology which, in them, was inspired like everything else contained in Scripture.

May we go even farther? And why not, if God's love is not straitened? The very first theologian was not an apostle but—God be praised for His measureless goodness!—our Lord Himself. Everywhere throughout the supernatural order, in the order of virtue, in the order of preaching, in the order of testimony rendered, in the order of martyrdom, it is He who has blazed the path. He has also led the way in the order of human reflecting on divine truth, "that in all things He may hold the primacy" (Col. 1:18), that theologians might have no other model than Him, the Child in the midst of the doctors, the Master in the midst of the apostles.

As a theologian He was of course free from the defects which ordinary theologians are inevitably subject to at times. But He was a theologian, because He thrilled with joy in His human intellect when He saw how His divine message grew luminous for His little ones and because He always drew attention to the unity of His revelation. He was a theologian in the harmonious teaching He proposed in so splendidly coherent and intelligible a fashion, and in the supreme skill with which He led men into the light. This is evidently a highly special and exalted sense of the term "theologian," but one that is closely connected with current usage.

Thus, as we see once again, theology, and particularly theology as here described, that is, theology conceived as a quest of unity, is deeply Christian. It is intimately associated with Him who is absolutely first in Christianity, Christ.

The idea of synthesizing theology, which is familiar to the whole of Christian tradition, is authentically approved by the official teaching authority of the Church. On this subject we possess a document of capital importance. The preceding pages are but a commentary of it, and we have saved it for the last because of this very importance. It will be the definitive word pronounced in this chapter; there is no court of higher appeal. It is a passage from the dogmatic constitution, *De fide catholica*, promulgated at the Vatican Council. We have already quoted several lines from it on a former occasion, and also gave some indication of its historical background.[18] We now present the entire passage:

[18] Cf. chap. 1.

When reason, enlightened by faith, seeks earnestly, piously, and modestly, it attains, by God's gift, some understanding of mysteries, and indeed a most fruitful understanding: partly from an analogy with truths it knows naturally, partly from the relations of the mysteries themselves with one another and with man's last end; but reason never becomes capable of understanding mysteries as it does those objects that constitute its proper object. For by their very nature divine mysteries so transcend the created intellect that even when communicated through revelation and received by faith, they remain covered with the veil of faith and enshrouded in a certain obscurity, so long as we are wayfarers during this mortal life, "absent from the Lord: for we walk by faith and not by sight" (II Cor. 5:6 f.).

But although faith is above reason, no real dissension can ever arise between faith and reason, since the same God who reveals mysteries and infuses faith has also endowed the human mind with the light of reason, and God cannot deny Himself and truth can never contradict truth.[19]

The first lines of this text concern the object of the present chapter. The Council asserts that a certain understanding of mysteries can be acquired; it then indicates several methods of arriving at such understanding. We have already had occasion to consider and ponder the assertion; we now wish to touch on the declaration of methods that follows. The Fathers point out that reason has at its disposal several ways of arriving at this understanding: *tum ex eorum quae naturaliter cognoscit analogia, tum e mysteriorum ipsorum nexu inter se et cum fine hominis ultimo*. That is, reason is able to gain some degree of understanding of the mysteries, basing its study on the analogy existing between these mysteries and natural truths, or on their relations with one another, or on the connection they have with man's last end.

The first and the last of these means are, as we stated previously, among those currently employed by theology. The first, in its most developed form, is represented by the study and synthesis of dogma in the framework of metaphysical organization; the last is represented by the study of human destiny and of man's most basic needs. These are the two procedures we have examined with particular care. The remaining method, occupying the second place in the

[19] Mansi, *Amplissima collectio conciliorum*, LI, 433.

decree, *e mysteriorum ipsorum nexu inter se,* is that which we desire to employ throughout the rest of this work.

Our aim is to acquire some degree of understanding of the mysteries by pondering on their mutual interconnections and by reflecting on the way they are implied in one another to the point of forming a single whole, a single unity composed of all of them. This procedure is in no sense a profane method arbitrarily introduced into sacred science, but is, as we explained above, a means of apprehending that is natural to the human mind. Moreover, as we now perceive, it is a mode of procedure that is authentically ecclesiastical.

Conclusion. Existence of unity in dogma. A last word will bring this chapter to a close. We must seek unity in dogma. But someone may inquire whether such unity exists.

The answer to this question is at hand. God sends us off on our quest through His Church, by the example of His saints, and by the very structure of our minds; could the search be nothing but a chimera? God has given us dogma for our contemplation, and He has made our minds in such a way that they can apprehend nothing but unity; could dogma, then, fail to possess unity? Especially He has made the search for unity in science a sort of prayer, adapted to the capacity of science, and a sort of act of love. Could He, who glories in always heeding our prayer, have prepared in advance a refusal to this petition? What kind of mockery of man would that be? And how could God steal away at the very moment of His coming to give Himself to men without reserve?

CHAPTER III

UNITY IN THEOLOGY: THE WHOLE CHRIST

> "In Him was life, and the life
> was the light."
>
> John 1:4

I. The Question of Unity

THE question occupying us at present is to find out what is the unity of dogma, what is the center around which the whole is organized, what element in it is the first intelligible with respect to its unification.

This question was not asked by scholastic theologians, at least not as one of the primary questions. They asked another question, however, which is closely allied to ours and is most important: the question of the formal and ultimate object of theology, or of its *subiectum*, as they termed it.

To tell the truth, the word *subiectum* was not understood by all of them in the same sense.[1] In general we may say that it signifies the noblest object to which theology reduces all that it studies, the aspect it investigates, the supreme element which, to its mind, imparts value to all the rest, the formality it considers, the unique point of view on which it takes its stand in order to know and judge the whole.

This *subiectum*, according to the teaching we may regard as unanimous, is God; the term "theology," *quasi sermo de Deo*, indicates this sufficiently.[2] St. Thomas takes a definite stand on this matter in the first pages of the *Summa:*

[1] See, for example, Capreolus, *Defensiones theologiae divi Thomae*, prol., q. 4, a. 1, nos. 5 f.; Vasquez, *Commentarii ac disputationes in primam partem S.T.*, q. 1, disp. 10; Tanner, *Theologia scolastica*, disp. I, q. 3.

[2] Cf. St. Thomas, *In I Sent.*, prol., q. 1, a. 5, 1 et *sed contra; Summa*, Ia, q. 1, a. 7. See also the texts from St. Albert the Great, *In I Sent.*, d. 2, a. 2, and *Summa theol.*, I, tract. 1, q. 3.

Whether God is the subject matter of this science.

I answer that God is the subject matter of this science. Subject matter is related to a science as an object is related to a potency or a habit. Properly speaking, the object of a potency or habit is held to be that which is the reason why all things are referred to the potency or habit in question. Thus man and stone are referred to sight inasmuch as they are colored; hence anything that is colored is the object of sight. But in sacred doctrine all things are treated under the aspect of God, either because they are God Himself or because they are directed to God as to their source and end.[3] Consequently God is the subject matter of this science. This is also clear from the principles of this science: these are articles of faith, which is about God. The subject matter of the principles and of an entire science is the same, for the whole science is virtually contained in its principles.[4]

Earlier, in the *Commentary on the Sentences*, the saint had attacked the same problem, and his solution had also been clearly the same. "If we wish to specify the subject matter embracing all this, we may say that the divine Being as knowable through revelation is the subject of this science." [5]

In these selections from St. Thomas, not all the details, apparently, are equally certain. He himself introduces modifications: *quodammodo ordinantur*,[6] *ordinata aliqualiter;* [7] and the context suggests several restrictive precisions.[8] Moreover, as some of the later Scholastics observed,[9] the two passages exhibit slight variations. In the *Commentary on the Sentences*, the saint assigns as the subject matter *ens divinum cognoscible per revelationem;* in the *Summa* he corrects, or rather perfects his statement, and gives simply God, *Deus*, as the subject matter.[10]

[3] On these last words, see the passage from St. Albert the Great, quoted in note 67 *infra*.

[4] *Summa*, Ia, q. 1, a. 7.

[5] *In I Sent.*, Prol., q. 1, a. 4; cf. ad 1.

[6] *Ibid.*, ad 2.

[7] *Summa*, Ia, q. 1, a. 7 ad 2.

[8] *Ibid.*, a. 1, 3, 6.

[9] See, for example, J. P. Nazarius, *Commentarii et controversiae in primam partem S.T.*, q. 1, a. 7.

[10] The explanation of the difference is perhaps to be found in the preceding article of the *Summa*: "Sacred doctrine most properly treats of God viewed as the highest cause, for it treats of Him not only with reference to what is knowable about Him through creatures (in the way that philosophers knew Him, as is said in Rom. 1:19: 'That which is known of God is manifest in

In any case, a certain variety of opinions is noticeable among the theologians of the school on this point. Some say that the subject matter of theology is God as revealing, or divine truth as capable of being revealed.[11] Others hold that it is God so far as He can be known through Sacred Scripture; [12] others, that it is God as the infinite Being; [13] yet others, that it is God as Savior and Rewarder.[14] Others, finally, maintain that the subject matter of theology is God as God: *Deus ut Deus est, Deus sub ratione deitatis*.[15] As we see, the divergencies bear only on the manner in which God is the *subiectum*; but that He actually is the *subiectum*, is affirmed in common by the whole school. This is equivalent to saying that a denial of this position would be rash.

For that matter, what could be more certain, once the question is clearly understood? The problem is to assign the ultimate subject matter, the formal object of theology. On the other hand, theology studies the truths of faith. But the truths of faith are what they are because they speak of God or of what leads to God, and of God's work in communicating Himself; that is, if we may repeat, because they speak of God. To study them in their proper character, consequently, theology must study them so far as they speak of God. Even theodicy, which is plain natural theology, has God for its proper object. Can we conceive that supernatural theology, which is theology strictly so called, should not have that object? Moreover, God is the ultimate goal which all the sciences, each in its own way, envisage; accordingly the noblest of all sciences must do so more explicitly.

But this question is not the only one that can be asked; and so, without in any way ignoring the decisive answer given by the Scholastics, but rather making it our own, we go on to consider other questions. The Scholastics asked what is the supreme and formal object of theology; we may ask what is its material and interior ob-

---

them'), but also with reference to what is known about Him to Himself alone and is communicated to others through revelation." *Summa*, Ia, q.1, a.6; cf. *ibid.*, a.1, 3.

[11] Capreolus, Palauco, Gonet, Toletus, Vulpes.

[12] Thus Bacon.

[13] Scotus; cf. Albert the Great and Dionysius the Carthusian.

[14] Giles of Rome.

[15] This is the definitive view of St. Thomas, and is shared by the majority of Thomists, as well as by Henry of Ghent and Vasquez.

ject. They inquired into the unity toward which it tends as a whole; we may inquire into the unity within which it is organized as a whole. They asked about the ultimate end which makes theology wholly a science of God; we may ask about the means by which this science of God, without in any way being less the science of God, is also a human science.

The same question keeps recurring under these various forms: the inquiry into the object of sacred science as it is in itself, into the nature of its unity; the investigation of the tie that binds the whole together and makes it a single object of science, a single intelligible thing; the examination of the unity of the mysteries among themselves, *mysteriorum inter se nexus:* not the unity that unites them in relation to a transcendental term, but the unity that is interior to all of them.

That is our question. What, in Christian teaching, is the point, the aspect, the mystery which is present in the whole and in which the whole is present? What is the thing which makes that doctrine one by enclosing it in itself? What, within the very heart of Christian teaching, is the first intelligible with respect to which the entire doctrine is one and intelligible?

The absolutely first intelligible, present in Christian truth as nowhere else, is God Himself, God as God. But the intelligibility of this intelligible is beyond the range of men. "No man hath seen God at any time," unless God communicates and gives Himself, as He has communicated and given Himself in Christ alone, "the only-begotten Son who is in the bosom of the Father," in Christ who for those belonging to Him is life and truth, "full of grace and truth." [16] This is so because Christ, who has access to the interior of every soul, places within the reach of every soul the divine intelligibility that is in Himself.

This Christ is the whole Christ, God and man, head and body. Reflection on the question is all that is needed to let the question itself suggest the answer: if God is the ultimate object of theology, we may say that the whole Christ, God as far as He has made Himself completely ours, is its material, integral, and immediate object.

This assertion evidently requires formal demonstration. Before undertaking such demonstration, however, we feel called upon to explain briefly what we mean by the whole Christ.

[16] John 1:14, 18.

II. THE IDEA OF THE WHOLE CHRIST

The whole Christ is Christ considered with all that is inseparable from Him in the reality of things: with the entire Trinity in which He is one God, and with the whole of mankind of which He forms one body, His own. This is the *totus et integer Christus* mentioned in the documents of our faith; Christ who possesses the fullness of divinity and who is the fullness of humanity; this Christ who is all in all, in whom all men form but one, and who is one of the Trinity, *unus de Trinitate.*

This Christ is exactly the same as the historical Christ, the same as Jesus, Son of the Blessed Virgin, now present in the Eucharist; there is but one Christ. But, as He Himself said during His mortal life, He is a vine and we are branches in the vine. He dwells in us and we dwell in Him so truly and intensely that, living in Him as He lives of the Father, we are one in Him as He is one with the Father.

The expression "mystical Christ" primarily indicates Christ so far as He contains in Himself the fullness of humanity; the expression "whole Christ" is more extensive and indicates Christ as containing in Himself not only this fullness of humanity but also the fullness of divinity in the fullness of His unity. But the term "mystical Christ" often has this fuller sense. The mystical body [17] represents the assemblage of those who live or ought to live in Christ, and sometimes includes the humanity of Christ who floods them with this life, and even includes, in this humanity, the divinity in which the latter exists and in virtue of which it can flood men with life.

This notion of the mystical Christ and of the mystical body can be wrongly understood, and it can fail to be understood altogether. This would be the case if we had in mind some sort of organism resembling the human body in which Christians would be fibers or cells, or if we imagined an immense and formless entity in which everything would be confused and indistinct.

The best definition we can give of it, in our opinion, is that which exhibits it as a unity, for life is a unity. But the unity has to be supernatural: the supernatural unity of all creation, and more particularly, since men are in question, the unity of mankind in the God-man.

[17] This book in its original French form appeared prior to the publication of the Encyclical *Mystici Corporis* of Pius XII. On the term "mystical body" as used by Father Mersch and in the Encyclical, see Introduction.—Tr.

This definition is suggested by the most vivid and solemn scriptural passages that refer to the mystical body, especially the climactic prayer of Jesus Christ, repeated over and over again during His last hours: "that they may be one" (John, chap. 17). The very texts that employ the image of a body strongly emphasize, and even place first, the idea of unity.[18] Moreover this notion is metaphysical and psychological as well as scriptural and theological; it enables us easily to join together the lights that philosophy may shed.

The word "mystical" in the expression "mystical body" means imperceptible to sense, mysterious, supernatural.[19] The unity it implies surpasses in excellence and reality all the unities known to experience and all the natural concepts we may turn to for aid in expressing it. The vagueness and imprecision always accompanying our knowledge of it come from its transcendence and "supra-rationality," not from any inconsistency or "infra-rationality" in it.

The pages to follow will explain how a notion of this unity may be arrived at. Here we need say no more than that the main resources at our disposal for this purpose are the various indications which Scripture and tradition furnish, and which we tried to collect in our earlier work. In that book, as the reader may verify for himself, we described the full Christian teaching about the union of the Christian with Christ. There we also listed the numerous suggestions bearing on this same union that are comprised in Christian living, the reception of the Eucharist, the practice of charity, the liturgy, and also in the life of the Church and of the saints. Further aids are ideas on the natural unity existing among men, as gathered from the sciences, psychology, sociology, and philosophy; all these constitute a point of departure and a guide for arriving at a notion of supernatural unity.

We would still be orthodox, no doubt, if we were to think of this unity in Christ as a simple moral unity: a union of resemblance, dependence, gratitude, imitation, love, reception; in a word, a unity like those familiar to us on earth, except that it would be far more excellent and hence more perfect and complete. But such a concep-

[18] Cf. I Cor. 6:17; 10:17; 12:12 ff., 20; Rom. 12:4 f.; Eph. 2:14-22; 4:3-6; Col. 3:10-15.

[19] On the original sense, see H. de Lubac, "*Corpus mysticum.* Etude sur l'origine et les premiers sens de l'expression," *Recherches de science religieuse,* XXIX (1939), 257, 429.

tion, we believe, would not go far enough to do justice to all that is brought to light on this subject by Scripture, tradition, Christian teaching, and Christian living. In any case, it falls short of the conception that is the theme of this book.

Throughout the present work the union between Christ and the faithful is regarded as real, and even "super-real"; for it is a supernatural union, a union pertaining to the ontological order, or to the physical order if that is preferred. The book will be intelligible only if a union of this kind is envisaged. If anyone should find such a union inconceivable, a perusal of these pages will prove disconcerting. All we can ask of him, unless he prefers to close the volume immediately, is that he may grant such a union provisionally, by way of hypothesis. Perhaps, in gradually perceiving the implications and fullness of sense it brings to light in Christian teaching, he will consent to judge it by its fruits.

III. Unity of the Whole Christ

The unity of revealed truths and the first intelligible in theology must be sought in the truth of the whole Christ. This may be gathered from what we have already said on the subject. The whole Christ, we pointed out, is God: He is the Word, the Son of the Father, the Spirator of the Spirit; He is the Redeemer, the head of the body which is the Church, the living fount that floods Christians with grace, the power that is operative in the sacraments. Moreover, He is one. The whole Christian religion is drawn together in His unity, and all dogmas but express the totality of what He is.

A dogma that would speak only of God or of the divine persons would not contain the truths that concern our justification, and hence would not unify them in Him. Although this justification comes entirely from God, it is not God, and all truths about God would be exactly the same even if no justification and no creation had taken place. In that case we would not exist and of course would not know any truths about God; but would they be affected in any way by that?

A dogma that would speak exclusively of the work of God, taken in itself alone, prescinding from Christ and from the whole Christ by whom it is performed, would not contain truths that are about God, and no reason is apparent why it would contain any other truths that also deal with the work of God. For this particular work of God is neither God Himself nor the other works; in knowing it, we should not thereby know God or these other works.

The central truth, the truth that discloses to us the unity and intelligibility of the whole, must be a truth that announces both God and all the works of God, a truth that expresses the union between God Himself and mankind, and indeed all mankind.

This truth is precisely the truth of the whole Christ, of Christ God and man, head and body, and one. Accordingly the truth of the whole Christ must be the bond of unity in the science of supernatural truths.

Is it not true that, throughout Christianity, unity is established by Christ? The human race had been split into fragments and divided against itself by falling into sin. It is Christ who died that God's children may be gathered together again in unity.[20] It is He, the one mediator between God and men,[21] who restores union between heaven and earth in His lacerated body,[22] who gives us access to the Father in the unity of the Spirit,[23] who makes us all one among ourselves by making us one with God.[24] Does not the conclusion naturally follow that in dogma also, that is, in the divine truth which He brings to our earth and which proclaims this unity, He should be the bond of unity, precisely for the reason that He is the unity of all else, by being the whole Christ? According to the doctrine given to us, He is all in all; should He be less so in this doctrine itself?

He, and He alone, regarded in this totality, imparts to Christianity its whole essence, uniqueness, and completeness as a religion, as the union of man with God. Since *ens et unum convertuntur*, does not logic demand that He should also impart to it its unity? Is not the whole of Christianity God's gift, and is not the whole of God's gift summed up in Christ?[25]

The place thus occupied by Christ in Christian teaching, whereby He is everything and everywhere in that teaching, is brought out by Sacred Scripture. When we examine the New Testament, the first realization that strikes us is that its chief and most sacred books,

[20] John 11:52.
[21] Cf. I Tim. 2:5.
[22] Cf. II Cor. 5:17 ff.; Col. 1:18–21; Eph. 2:12–21.
[23] Eph. 2:18.
[24] John 17:21 ff.; I Cor. 15:22–29; Gal. 3:26 ff.; Col. 3:1–11.
[25] Rom. 8:32.

those containing the earliest lessons of Christian life and thought, are the books that narrate the life of Jesus, the Gospels. These books have formed the great bulk of Christian teaching throughout the centuries; they invest Christian preaching with its characteristic features. At the same time they are the reflection of Jesus and nothing but the reflection of Jesus. What does this imply if not that this teaching holds together completely in Christ?

He Himself preaches His doctrine, not as a system or as a series of propositions, but as the expression of Himself, as His own manner of thinking, reacting, and judging. It is He Himself who appears clearly in all His deeds and reactions; He who enables us to see, in the depths of Himself, what He is, what God is, and what man ought to be; He who, by living His noble life, makes us understand what it is to be a child of God and a divinized man.

The Synoptic Gospels show us this from the outside; the Gospel of St. John exhibits the same to us from the inside. Frequently in the Fourth Gospel the recitation of what Jesus has done is continued in the recollection and meditation of the truth He has announced, without any sign of separation or even distinction: the message becomes one with the Master.

As has often been remarked, Jesus frequently speaks of Himself in that Gospel. But He also appears at the center of all the realities He talks about: He is in the Father, He is in Christians, He animates them and gives all to them. Hence we may say that He, in His firmly self-enclosed unity, appears as the center around which all the realities spoken of by Him and by Christian truth are united with one another, and from which they pass to His followers. Always Christ, and He alone; but everything is found in Him, all light and all revelation: the whole of Christian dogma is one in Him and proceeds from His unity. In seeing and touching Him, His disciples had contact with the word of life in all its fullness. "That which we have heard, which we have seen with our eyes, which we have looked upon, and our hands have handled, of the word of life: for the life was manifested; and we have seen and do bear witness and declare unto you the life eternal which was with the Father, and hath appeared to us." [26]

This method of teaching Christianity which was employed by Christ remained that of the apostles. Their title of apostle, *apostolus*

[26] Cf. I John 1:1 f.

Iesu Christi,[27] informs us, not that they profess a metaphysic, but that they are the representatives and heralds of a person.[28] They have been sent to give testimony of Christ's life, of His risen life, of His life that raises to life those that believe in Him.[29] They speak of nothing else. As we are told in the Acts of the Apostles, their teaching is confined to an explanation of matters concerning the Lord Jesus [30] and, as the same book declares, the whole of the good news they announce is Jesus Christ: *Evangelizavit illi Iesum*.[31] The formula is not a convenient abbreviation but an authentic summary.

The apostles themselves were not Christians in any other sense. Their formation was the product, not of courses taken in a school, but of contact with the Master. They had seen Him,[32] they had eaten and drunk with Him,[33] they had been His companions from the first days of His preaching to His ascension.[34] What better opportunities could be desired for them? That is why, whenever an occasion presented itself, they spoke to every well-disposed soul of nothing but Him, of His attitude toward God and His attitude toward men. What more could anyone ask? [35] In making Him known, they announced all truth.

This conception of Christian teaching is especially clear in St. Paul, the apostle whose ministry is best known.[36] What launched him on his apostolate and gave him a gospel to preach was the revelation he had received that Christ is everything in the Church.[37] Accordingly the doctrine he proclaims in founding the Churches is that Christ is all, and all in all.[38] He sums up his entire gospel in this teaching, just as Christ sums up everything in Himself.[39] His

[27] Titus 1:1; Gal. 1:1; Rom. 1:1-4; II Cor. 8:23; Eph. 2:20.

[28] John 15:26 f.; 19:35; Mark 8:38.

[29] Acts 1:8, 21 f.; 2:32; 3:15; 10:39, 41; 26:16; I Cor. 9:1; Gal. 1:1.

[30] Acts 28:31.

[31] Acts 8:35; 5:42; 11:20; cf. 10:36 ff.; Gal. 1:16; Eph. 3:8. We may compare with this the announcement made by the angel to the shepherds: "I bring you good tidings of great joy that shall be to all the people, for this day is born to you a Savior, who is Christ the Lord" (Luke 2:10 f.).

[32] Acts 4:20; 26:16; I Cor. 9:1; I John 1:1 ff.

[33] Acts 10:41.

[34] John 15:27; Acts 1:22.

[35] See the discourses reported in Acts 2:22 f.; 8:34 ff.; 10:37-42.

[36] Cf. *The Whole Christ*, pp. 80-150.

[37] Acts. 9:3 ff.; 22:4; 26:13 ff.; Phil. 3:12.

[38] Col. 3:11; Gal. 3:28.

[39] Eph. 1:10. On what follows, we refer the reader to *The Whole Christ*, pp. 104-8.

gospel, Paulinism, has been variously said to sum up everything in man, or in God, or in Christ. The truth is that St. Paul sums up everything in the whole Christ, in Christ living in men and causing them to live in God, in Christ who dwells in God and causes men to dwell in God. This is the mystery into which Christ initiated His eminent apostle: the immense plan of goodness by which God wishes to unite all men, including pagans and sinners, in His well-beloved Son; all Christianity holds together in this plan, and it holds the whole together in Christ. Of course Paul declares many truths and precepts; his epistles are full of such, sometimes to the point of being overloaded with them. But the multiplicity is only apparent; in reality, all this but indicates the way we have to think and act in order to think and act in Christ. Thus, in whatever St. Paul teaches, he teaches Christ alone, the whole Christ, and we can take in its most literal sense his assertion: "I judged not myself to know anything among you but Jesus Christ, and Him crucified." [40]

What Scripture thus proclaims, tradition repeats: the recapitulation of the whole of Christian teaching is Christ.[41] But to demon-

[40] Cf. I Cor. 2:2. On the connection between this formula and the whole Christ, see the context, from 1:17 to 2:11, especially 1:23, 30; 2:7 f. Cf. Gal. 6:14 f.

[41] John 17:3. The saying of St. Ignatius of Antioch is well known: "Why do we not all become wise, by making our own the knowledge of God, that is, Jesus Christ?" *Epist. ad Eph.*, XVII, 2. On this subject we may quote some lines from that warm-hearted and congenial author, Clement of Alexandria: "Since the Word Himself has come down to us from heaven, we need no longer, in my opinion, attend schools taught by men in Athens or in the rest of Greece or even in Ionia to search for learning. For if our teacher is He who has filled the world with His holy power, His works, His salvation, His benefits, His laws, His preaching and His teaching, we have the teacher from whom all instruction comes; and the whole world, including Athens and Greece, has already been made the domain of the Word. And you, who gave credence to the poetical fable that Minos of Crete was the bosom friend of Zeus, will not find it hard to believe that we have become the disciples of God and have received true wisdom: that wisdom which the leaders of philosophy only vaguely surmised, but which the disciples of Christ have learned and proclaimed. The whole Christ, if one may use the expression [*totus Christus*, a term that was to become classical for designating the mystical Christ], is not divided: there is neither barbarian nor 'Jew nor Greek; there is neither bond nor free; there is neither male nor female' (Gal. 3:28; cf. 6:15; Eph. 4:25), but a new man, transformed by the Holy Spirit of God. All the other counsels and precepts are less important and deal with particular matters . . . only that command which urges us to piety is general, only that one pertains to the whole course of our existence and always and in all circumstances directs us to our final end, which is eternal life. . . . 'The com-

strate this assertion by appealing to the immense bulk of doctrine left behind by tradition, which still awaits its full formulation, would be too long a task. We shall content ourselves with bringing forward two indications of such proof.

The first is found in the plan that has been followed most often at all epochs for explaining the Christian faith, and that reduces it to two classes of truths: one concerning the Godhead, the other concerning humanity and the work accomplished in it by the Godhead. But is not this class fully and coherently realized in Christ alone? The Fathers declare that there are two great categories of truths: those that speak of God and those that speak of man, or, as they frequently put it, those that speak of heavenly and eternal things, and those that speak of earthly and temporal things. The name "theology" [42] was often assigned to the first part, and the term "economy" was applied to the second part. The first includes dogmas dealing with the divine nature, the Blessed Trinity, and the Trinitarian processions; the second embraces dogmas treating of God's works here below and the "dispensation" or dispensing of divine life among creatures, that is, the dogmas on creation, original sin, redemption, sanctification, the Church, and so on.

This division is suggested even in the Creed; but from the time of the Creed the affirmation of a connection between the two parts is also observed. Jesus Christ, who has charge of the distribution of graces and the restoration of the world, that is, the whole economy, is likewise the unique means by which we acquire knowledge of God's interior life and the Trinitarian processions, that is, theology. As God, He is the object of the latter; as man, He sums up the former in Himself. In His living unity and totality as the God-man, He is the unity and totality of all that is taught in Christian instruction.

---

mandment of the Lord is lightsome, enlightening the eyes' (Ps. 18:9). Receive Christ, receive sight, receive the light. . . . Let us receive the light that we may receive God. Let us receive the light, and become disciples of the Lord. This is what He said to the Father: 'I will declare Thy name to My brethren; in the midst of the church will I praise Thee' (Ps. 21:23). Praise, then, and declare to me Thy Father, God; Thy utterances bring salvation." *Protrepticos,* c.11 (*PG,* VIII, 229).

[42] Among the Greeks, the term at first referred to pagan conceptions about the origin of the gods; it was not restricted to signifying the science of the true God and of Christ until the time of Eusebius. Among the Latins, the use of the term by Christians must have come much later, and the word did not bear the meaning it has today until the time of Abelard.

The same twofold division of Christian faith is still found during the scholastic period [43] and in St. Thomas himself.[44] We have to conclude that it belongs to the traditional background of teaching. Theologians ordinarily propose it, however, not when they study the content of theology, but when they make an inventory of the content of the faith. If we examine their works, either in commentaries on the *Summa*, IIa IIae, q. 1, a. 6 ff., or in commentaries on Book III of the *Sentences*, q. 24, we see that, in explaining different ways of dividing the articles of the Creed, they generally distinguish two groups, articles dealing with the divinity and articles dealing with the Incarnation. Occasionally they may add a third group, as St. Thomas has done.[45] In that event, they place in this third group the articles dealing with the effect produced in men by the Incarnation under the action of the Holy Spirit; in other words, this last group does not contain anything that is not already comprised in the second group.

In any case, the economy of Christian teaching thus envisaged is the economy of the Incarnation. Therefore in saying that this teaching has God and the Trinity for its object on the one hand, and Christ and grace that gives life to men in Christ on the other, the masters of former days said that theology from beginning to end discourses on the whole Christ. Thus they taught implicitly that the object of theology is the whole Christ. Indeed, they did not confine themselves to implicit statements. Some of them taught this doctrine expressly; others, if they did not teach it distinctly, left to all the

[43] The division is given by a number of authors belonging to the school of Abelard, by Roland Bandinelli (Alexander III), by Hugh of St. Victor, and others.

[44] *In I Sent.*, prol.; *In Epist. ad Ephesios*, cap. 3, lect. 5; *In Epist. ad Hebraeos*, cap. 9, lect. 2; *Summa*, Ia, q. 2, prooem.; Ia IIae, q. 106, a. 1 ad 1; IIa IIae, q. 1, a. 8; a. 6, 7; q. 174, a. 6; IIIa, prooem.; *Compendium theologiae*, cap. 2. We quote the latter (from C. Vollert's translation, B. Herder, St. Louis, 1948): "Faith is a certain foretaste of that knowledge which is to make us happy in the life to come. The Apostle says, in Hebrews 11:1, that faith is 'the substance of things to be hoped for,' as though implying that faith is already, in some preliminary way, inaugurating in us the things that are to be hoped for, that is, future beatitude. Our Lord has taught us that this beatific knowledge has to do with two truths, namely, the divinity of the Blessed Trinity and the humanity of Christ. That is why, addressing the Father, He says: 'This is eternal life: that they may know Thee, the only true God, and Jesus Christ, whom Thou hast sent' (John 17:3). All the knowledge imparted by faith turns about these two points, the divinity of the Trinity and the humanity of Christ."

[45] *Expositio primae decretalis*, near the beginning.

undisputed right of doing so. This is the second of the indications which we have mentioned above, and to it we shall now turn our attention.

To appreciate the situation, we must go back to the great epoch of Scholasticism, which established the classical doctrine that God is the subject of theology. Up to that time, the golden age of precise thinking and rigorous definition, the question had not been proposed with the intense clarity that subsequently marked it. But another, closely allied question, which we must consider briefly, strongly attracted attention: the question of the object of Sacred Scripture and its content, or, as was commonly said, its matter.

The answer to this question, formulated by St. Augustine and, we may say, unanimously accepted, was that this object is Christ: Christ as God and man, head and body; in a word, the whole Christ.[46] "All this proclaims Christ, the head that has ascended into heaven and the body that toils on earth to the end of time," St. Augustine wrote on the subject of the sacred Books.[47] This assertion refers explicitly to the Book of Psalms, but applies to the whole of Scripture.[48] As was acknowledged on all sides, the whole of Scripture is like the field mentioned in the Gospel: a single pearl is hidden there, and this pearl is Christ,[49] the whole and complete Christ.

During the epoch in question the Scholastics, especially at the beginning, envisaged theology as a study dealing with the doctrine of Sacred Scripture, with the content of the holy Books: *scientia de divina pagina.*[50] They do not ignore tradition, of course, as could easily be shown were this the place to do so; but their main preoccupation is with Scripture. We shall meet with several examples of this; and St. Thomas himself, in the very passages in which he establishes the subject matter of theology, proceeds to discuss the content of Sacred Scripture, without in any way apprising the reader of that

[46] For an exposition of this point, the reader is referred to *The Whole Christ*, Part III, chaps. 4 and 5.

[47] *Contra Faustum manichaeum*, XXII, 94 (*PL*, XLII, 463).

[48] Cf. St. Thomas, *In psalmos Davidis expositio*, prooemium. "The subject matter of Sacred Scripture is the whole Christ, head and members," we read in the *Glossa ordinaria*.

[49] Cf. St. Irenaeus, *Adversus haereses*, IV, xxvi, 1 (*PL*, VII, 1052); Origen, *In Matt.*, X, 4; XIII (*PG*, XIII, 844; XVII, 296).

[50] Alexander of Hales, for instance, regards the expressions *sacra doctrina* and *sacra scriptura* as synonymous; see his *Summa theologica*, I, q.1. See also the opening words of the first book of Peter Lombard's *Sentences*.

fact.[51] Thus, in keeping with accepted practice, when the Scholastics of those early days came to determine the subject matter of theology, they adapted to theology the traditional doctrine of their time on the subject matter of Sacred Scripture.[52]

If theology has the content of Scripture as its object, and if this content is the whole Christ, we have to conclude that the object of theology is likewise the whole Christ.

When, therefore, at the beginning of the scholastic era, the most ancient current of thought, the Augustinian current as we may call it, which saw in the whole Christ the object of sacred science and of Scripture, met another and more Aristotelian current, which assigned God as the ultimate object of sacred science, it could not fail to sweep the latter along with it, or at least to produce some commotion at the point of confluence.

One of the earliest examples of this meeting occurs in Robert of Melun.[53] In his *Sententiae*,[54] written about 1160, he sets forth the object of his work by declaring, according to the ancient formula, that the object of Scripture and of the science he is going to study [55] —note the connection between Scripture and theology [56]—is the "Incarnation with all the sacraments [57] that precede it, accompany it, and follow it." [58] In other words, this object is the whole Christ,

[51] *Summa*, Ia, q. 1, a.9, 10. See also a.2 ad 2; a.3; a.4 ad 2; a.7 ad 2; a.8 ad 2; *Quodl.* VII, q.6, a.15 et ad 1, 2, 4, 5.

[52] Thus St. Bonaventure, *In I Sent.*, prooem., q.1; Alexander of Hales, *Summa theologica*, I, 1. The *Glossa* of Walafrid Strabo was often appealed to, and even more frequently the *Complexiones in psalmos* of Cassiodorus (cf. *PL*, LXX, 17).

[53] He was born toward the end of the eleventh century and died as bishop of Hereford in 1167.

[54] The *Sententiae* appeared in two editions. One is more developed, and is dated 1155–60; the other, in abbreviated form, was issued 1160–63.

[55] Thus theology, like Scripture, has two parts, and these two parts make up the plan of the *Sententiae*.

[56] As soon as he comes to describe theology he calls it *Sacrae scripturae doctrina*, lib. I, par. 1, cap. 1. Robert of Melun is by no means forgetful of tradition, as the prologue attests.

[57] On the meaning of *sacramentum*, cf. lib. II, par. 1, c.3: "Sacrament at times means the sacred thing itself hidden under certain signs, and at times means the sign that conceals the sacred thing. The latter is the notion Augustine gives of sacrament when he says: 'A sacrament is a visible sign of God's invisible grace.'"

[58] Lib. I, par. 1, c.8. Mention of the "sacraments" that preceded and followed the Incarnation is also found in Hugh of St. Victor, *De sacramentis*, I, prol. 2 (*PL*, CLXXVI, 183).

God, man, and the life of mankind. As Robert explains farther on, the Incarnation contains all Christianity, and all the graces man receives are from it, just as heaven and earth are composed of the matter created by God in the beginning.[59] What does this imply if not that Christ, whom the Incarnation defines, contains in Himself the whole of Christianity and all Christian truth?

About a century later another Robert, who was also an English bishop, Robert Grosseteste (born around 1175, died 1253), bishop of Lincoln, undertook to explain the subject with all the clarity that could be desired. In this case, too, theology and Scripture are considered together: the work in which is found the text we are going to cite, the *Hexameron*, evidently deals with the sacred Books, as its title plainly indicates. The text treats explicitly of theology. For this reason it has attracted much attention ever since the scholastic epoch, and Robert of Lincoln is one of the names repeatedly mentioned as an example of the authors who see in the whole Christ the object of theology.

Until recent times this text has been known only in a summary of it given by Duns Scotus.[60] It was published a few years ago.[61] The passage is rather long and somewhat complicated. In it Robert Grosseteste declares that, according to some authors whom he does not name, the subject matter of theology is the whole Christ, that is, the incarnate Word with His body which is the Church. For his part, Robert prefers another formula which, however, as far as substantials are concerned, has exactly the same sense. Instead of speaking of *Christus totus*, he chooses to speak of the unity of grace that is recapitulated in Christ. This is the unity Christ had in mind in His last words when He prayed to the Father "that they may be one, as We also are one" (John 17:22); this is likewise the unity that expresses so strongly the incorporation of Christians in the Savior and their attachment to God.[62] What impressed Robert Grosseteste most

[59] Lib. II, par. 2, c. 1.

[60] Cf. *In 1 Sent.*, prol., q. 3, a. 5. According to Grosseteste, we are told in this passage, Christ is "the first subject . . . as Christ is one with a triple unity, the first being a union with the Father and the Holy Spirit, the second a union of the Word with the assumed nature, and the third a union of Christ the head with the members."

[61] Gerald B. Phelan, "An Unedited Text of Robert Grosseteste on the Subject-matter of Theology," *Revue néo-scolastique de philosophie*, XXXVI (1934), 172–79. The passage we are interested in is on p. 176.

[62] See *The Whole Christ*, pp. 185 ff.

in this unity is its wealth of diverse aspects, and this equips it admirably to be the sole object of a science so extensive and varied as is theology. He calls attention to the unity that unites the two natures in the one person of Christ, to the unity by which Christ unites Himself to the Church by having the same nature as ours, and to the unity by which the Church, in turn, is united to Him in the sacrament of the Eucharist. These are the three unities constituting the mystical Christ. Furthermore, Grosseteste continues, the unity Jesus speaks of also includes the unity that unites Him to the Father and the unity of grace and divinization that unites us to Him. Yet all these unities are joined together in Christ, and whatever is comprised in Christianity can, in some way, be derived from the unity they have in Him. Therefore this unity, this *unum* or rather this *unus*, can be regarded as the adequate object of theology. To bring out the thought more clearly, we may add: What is this unity, if not the whole Christ, God and man, head and body?

This text from the Bishop of Lincoln is the most emphatic known to us; collections of manuscripts or printed works with which we are not familiar may possibly contain stronger expressions. Grosseteste is an Aristotelian, and even translated some of the Philosopher's works. Hence the thought might occur that the position dear to the Augustinian tradition, that the object of theology is the whole Christ, enters fully into the peripatetic tradition with Robert. But such a conclusion would be unwarranted. The rest of our survey records the gradual effacement of the idea, although the idea itself by no means completely disappeared. The position that should have been accorded the place of honor retires to a remote corner, somewhat like a seed that is buried only to germinate in due time.

We now come to the truly great names among the Scholastics. One of the first in point of time, Alexander of Hales (born in the decade 1170–1180, died 1245), is even slightly anterior to Robert Grosseteste. In the beginning of his *Summa universae theologiae* he inquires into the object of theology. He replies that this object is God, so far as He makes Himself known in the work of man's restoration. In this sense, he continues, it is exact to say that the object of Scripture—here, too, and throughout the whole context, no distinction is made between Scripture and theology—is the whole Christ, head and members.[63] The idea is the same as that of Grosse-

[63] *Summa theol.*, I, lib. I, q. 1, a. 3.

teste, but it is relegated to secondary rank; primarily, the object of theology as assigned by the *Doctor Irrefragabilis* is God; Christ is mentioned only in an accessory manner, to give precision to the primary consideration.

Some years later another Franciscan and a disciple of Alexander of Hales, St. Bonaventure (1221–1274), takes up the same question in his commentary on the *Sentences*.[64] In the introduction he asks what the subject matter of sacred science may be, and replies by distinguishing between a "radical" subject and an "integral" subject, that is, between a subject in which theology finds its first origin and ultimate basis, and a subject in which it is adequately summarized. The radical subject, he says, is God; but the integral subject is Christ: Christ as God and man, head and body. This integral subject so truly comprises the whole matter of theology that the saint derives from it the plan of his work. The first two books of the *Sentences*, he explains, treat of Christ as God and man; the last two treat of Christ as head and members.[65] The Seraphic Doctor expresses a similar thought in his *Breviloquium*. He declares that in theology the subject *a quo omnia* is God; the subject *per quod omnia* is Christ; the subject *ad quod omnia* is the work of our restoration.[66] As we perceive, the saint views the question as Alexander of Hales does: the whole Christ is truly and really the object of theology, but only in a secondary way.

With the beginning of the Thomist school, mention of the mystical body as the subject matter of theology is much in evidence. St. Albert the Great, it is true, makes no reference whatever to it in the first of his important theological works, the *Commentary on the Sentences*. But the question of the subject matter of theology is treated there in very summary fashion; only one point seems to interest the master: that God is this subject matter, as the name of theology clearly indicates.[67] But in the *Summa theologiae*, begun some

---

[64] St. Bonaventure began his *Sentences* about 1248. The *Summa* of Alexander of Hales, begun shortly before 1231, was left incomplete by his death in 1245.

[65] *In I Sent.*, prooem., q. 1.

[66] *Breviloquium*, I, 1.

[67] The work is dated about 1250. The subject of theology, the author says, is, in general, things and signs, as Peter Lombard taught; but specifically it consists of all the points studied in it. Finally, "the special subject is said to be that which is the noblest of all the topics treated in a science, and hence the subject matter of this science is God, from whom it receives its name.

twenty years later, he takes up the point we are investigating. A number of "positions," he says, have been taken on this question. The first, proposed by St. Augustine, is that *res* and *signa* are the subject of theology; the second, held by Hugh of St. Victor, declares that the works of redemption are the subject; a third asserts that the subject is Christ and the Church; a final opinion maintains that God is the subject. We shall quote St. Albert's own words to show how he expresses the last two views, and this will also enable us to see how he associates theology with Sacred Scripture.

In the beginning of the commentary on the Psalms we are told that everything in Sacred Scripture pertains to Christ or the Church. Therefore the head and the body, the Bridegroom and the Bride, Christ and the Church, in a word, the whole Christ completely considered, is the subject matter of sacred theology. Another view is that God is the subject of Sacred Scripture, as is indicated by the very name of theology.[68]

The saint admits all four opinions: to his mind they are all valid, each according to its own point of view.

We answer that, if the subject matter of theology is assigned in accord with the main end of this science and in terms of the truth that has to be known before anything else in it can be treated, God is the subject matter of theology, which also receives its name from Him.

But if subject matter is understood in the second way, as the object of demonstrations and determinations, Christ and the Church are the subject, or the incarnate Word with all the sacraments He administers in the Church. And this is the same as saying that the works of redemption are the subject: for theology shows that these flow from the head and are received in the Church.[69]

Thus our view accords with that of St. Albert, although he attributes a subordinate place to it. God is the chief object of theology; Christ is the object in a secondary sense. God is the ultimate object to which everything in sacred science is referred; Christ is the integral object in which everything is recapitulated. Yet Christ is truly the object in the latter sense, and the saintly doctor is so convinced of this

However, the subject matter is not only God as absolutely considered, but also as He is alpha and omega, the beginning and the end." *In I Sent.*, d. 1, a. 2.

[68] *Summa theol.*, I, tract. 1, q. 3.

[69] *Ibid.*, q. 3, membr. 1.

truth that in developing the topic he refutes objections lodged against this "position."

Albert the Great's favorite disciple, Ulric Engelbert of Strasbourg (died 1277), speaks like his master but in firmer tones. He says that the subject of theology is God as God, as alpha and omega, beginning and end.[70] However, he continues, because of the vast matter treated in this science, Augustine and others defined its subject differently. "Others say that the subject matter of this science is the whole Christ, that is, the head with the members. For in Christ is understood the entire Trinity, the anointing Father, the anointed Son, and the Holy Spirit as ointment. As the head, furthermore, Christ is the principle of all. And as the head of the members of His body which is the Church, He is the first source of all truths that are known by faith alone." [71]

Not a word of disapproval: from the point of view taken by these "others," the point of view of the material object of theology and of the unity of this object, Ulric admits that they are right.

Finally we reach the Angel of the Schools. When he comes to assign the object of theology, St. Thomas ascribes a larger place than is ordinarily thought to the mystical Christ. Unquestionably, his clearly formulated and invariable teaching is that the subject matter of theology is God as God. Yet throughout his works he acknowledges that, in a certain sense, the whole Christ is also the subject. With regard to sacred science, he declares that we may ask, not only what is the ultimate object with which it deals and to which it subordinates whatever else is treated in theology, but also what is the central object, the material object in which all that it studies is summed up. He does not undertake to investigate this latter point, but he finds nothing inappropriate in the contention of those who maintain that the object in question is the whole Christ.

The following passage from the *Summa* comes immediately after the lines we quoted near the beginning of this chapter. After noting that in theology "all things are treated under the aspect of God," the saint continues: "Some authors, attending to what is treated in this science rather than to the aspect under which it is treated, have assigned something else as its subject matter: either things and signs, or the works of redemption, or the whole Christ, that is, head and mem-

[70] These are the very terms employed by Albert; cf. above, note 67.
[71] Ulrich of Strasbourg, *Summa de bono*, I, tract. 2, cap. 2.

bers. All these matters are, indeed, treated in this science, but according as they are referred to God." [72]

The *Commentary on the Sentences* has a few lines that are quite similar: "A subject is related to a science in at least three ways. The first is that everything treated in the science must be comprised in the subject matter. Aware of this condition, some have maintained that things and signs are the subject matter of this science; others have proposed the whole Christ, that is, the head and members, since everything treated in this science is apparently reduced to this subject." [73]

In these passages, the mention of "things and signs" is a bow to the Master of the *Sentences* [74] and to St. Augustine.[75] The reference to "works of redemption" alludes to the *De sacramentis* of Hugh of St. Victor [76] and to Alexander of Hales. The mention of the mystical Christ recalls, as we have said, Robert Grosseteste or, more accurately, the entire ancient tradition which declares that the mystical Christ is the object of Sacred Scripture.

Cajetan remarks, in his commentary on this passage of the *Summa*, that we should advert to the moderation with which St. Thomas refutes these opinions to establish his own thesis with greater firmness. More to the purpose, we should note that he does not refute anything, and that he does not set out to refute anything. He merely distinguishes various points of view. He observes that the authors referred to do not treat the question he is speaking of, but another question; and this other question, as he recognizes without further discussion, is treated in a way that meets with no objection from him.

Accordingly, if we keep these various points of view in mind, we can regard the text from St. Thomas as an approbation. If our avowed purpose is to seek the object in which theology is recapitulated, "attending to what is treated in this science," and in which "everything treated in the science must be comprised," we have the right to declare that St. Thomas readily admits that this object is the whole Christ.

Indeed, the saint goes even farther than this, especially in his com-

---

[72] *Summa*, Ia, q. 1, a. 7.
[73] *In I Sent.*, prol., q. 1, a. 4.
[74] *I Sent.*, d. 1, c. 1.
[75] *De doctrina christiana*, I, 2 (*PL*, XXXIV, 19).
[76] Lib. I, prol., cap. 3 (*PL*, CLXXVI, 183): "The subject matter of the Sacred Scriptures consists in the works of human restoration."

mentaries on Sacred Scripture. "As a man who possessed a book containing all science would seek only to master that book, so we ought no longer to seek anything but Christ." [77] This contention is borne out particularly in the case of the Psalms: "Whereas the individual books of the canonical Scriptures have special subject matters, this book treats of the whole of theology." "Theology," St. Thomas says; hence, in studying Scripture and the Psalter, he is thinking of the object of theology. He continues: "Its subject matter is universal, for it includes everything. And since this pertains to Christ, 'because in Him it hath well pleased the Father that all fullness should dwell' (Col. 1:19), the subject matter of this book is Christ and His members." [78]

Accordingly, as we see, the declaration that Christ is the object of theology does not involve any departure from Thomistic orthodoxy, provided we understand it in such a way as to acknowledge that God as God is the ultimate object to which everything refers and leads.

The secondary place thus accorded to the opinion in question has never, so far as we know, been contested by any of the Scholastics. [79] At times they show at considerable length that the view is legitimate. For example, we need do no more than read what John of St. Thomas has to say on the subject [80] to convince ourselves that the most authentic Thomism leaves abundant room for it, although only, we must recognize, as an open question.

In general, the Scholastics do not delay over the idea, and the only ones to undertake brief and variously conceived justifications of it and cognate ideas are a few Nominalists, such as Gabriel Biel, [81] William Ockham, [82] Peter of Ailly, [83] and, we may add, likewise

[77] *In Epist. ad Col.*, cap. II, lect. 1.

[78] *In psalmos Davidis expositio*, prooemium, near the beginning.

[79] See, for example, Henry of Ghent, *Summa quaestionum ordinariarum*, par. I, a.19, q.1 f.; F. Polanco, *Tractatus theologici de Deo uno*, disp. prooemial., q.2.

[80] John of St. Thomas, *Cursus theologicus*, I, q.1, a.2.

[81] "Christ may be regarded as the main subject by a priority of content, for He has a divine and a human nature." *Collectorium super I Sent.*, prol., q.9.

[82] Ockham admits that Christ may be said *valde improprie* to be the subject of theology, inasmuch as in Him is comprised, in some fashion, all that Ockham indicates as the subject, namely, the divinity, the Trinity (because of Christ's union with the Father and the Spirit), and creatures. *Super quattuor libros Sententiarum*, prol., q.9.

[83] *Quaestiones super libros Sententiarum*, prol.

Durandus.[84] But their aim in speaking about the object of theology is not to show that theology is one, as it is summed up in the unity of Christ, while everything in it leads to union with God. On the contrary, they hold that a search for strict unity in theology, especially the absolute unity pertaining to a single and formal subject, is a fruitless task. According to them, theology is no more than a collection of truths that are similar and that have some relation to Christ; but it is not a truly unified system in which all is ordained to a single end. We mention these authors, not to claim their patronage, but to draw a line marking them off from us. Thanks be to God, no anti-intellectualism will be found in these pages.

Apart from them and several others,[85] the masters of Scholasticism manifest indifference about the problem engaging us.[86] Vasquez declares that a search for an object comprising all that theology treats of is a task not worth the trouble: "As we said, there is no reason why we should bother about the matter." [87] This way of speaking expresses the general attitude as well as his own view.

The comparison made in preceding pages between the object of theology and the object of Scripture is accurate enough, but should not be pressed too far. These two objects are not identical in every respect: we may say that they are materially identical, but not formally identical. In other words, Sacred Scripture and sacred science deal entirely with the whole Christ, that is, with God's donation of Himself to mankind in Christ. But Christ and this self-donation are viewed differently in the two cases. In Scripture, they are viewed from the side of man and of mankind, for Scripture is a message from God to men, and therefore everything in it is addressed

[84] The object of theology is the meritorious act, or also God considered as Savior. *Super Sententias theol. Petri Lombardi commentarii*, prol., q.5.

[85] Among theologians of a later date, we may single out L. Thomassinus, whose formulas, however, are not always clear. See his *Theologica dogmata*, III, tract. I, cc.8–11.

[86] Even the disciples of St. Bonaventure, who was so clear on these points, have little or nothing to say. The most resolute we have found among them display timidity. An example is Boniface de Augustinis, O.M.Conv., *Seraphici Bonaventurae Ecclesiae doctoris super quatuor Sententiarum libros theologia iuris et facti in summam redacta*, tract. I, disp. 1. q.4. He sets forth and defends the saint's idea, but reduces it to a minor role, whereas the Seraphic Doctor had made much of it. M. Hauzeur, O.S.F., *Collatio totius theologiae inter maiores nostros*, I, q.1, no.3, is even more reserved.

[87] *Commentarii et disputationes in primam partem Sancti Thomae*, q.1, disp. 10, cap. 4.

to man. Theology, on the contrary, is an effort made by man to know God in Christ, and therefore everything in it tends toward God. Although we may say that the object of Scripture is the whole Christ, we must be more specific when we come to theology, and say that its object is indeed the whole Christ, but that Christ is its object only because He is God.

If this explanation is kept in mind, the proposition that the object of theology is Christ cannot, as may be gathered from a reading of the preceding pages, be said to constitute a rash and novel way of speaking. It is but a synthesis of two formulas, both of them ancient and traditional, each of them clarifying and completing the other. Of these two formulas, that which affirms that the object of theology is Christ, is the older. As employed in its day, it lacks precision but not truth; it did not distinguish what in Christ is formally the ultimate object of theology, and what is the material object. But that is not surprising, for the question had not yet been distinctly phrased.

The necessary refinements were added by the Scholastics when they came to determine that God as God is the ultimate object, the *subiectum* of theology; and this is the second and more recent of the two formulas. The Scholastics put it forward with vigor, as was right; but this incidentally involved the setting aside of the earlier formula which they had no occasion to defend.

Now that their thesis has become a definitive acquisition, may we not be permitted to resurrect the other one, which theologians of an earlier time expounded with so much love and upheld with so much loyalty? For, in the last analysis, to maintain that the whole Christ is the object of theology, is no departure from the doctrine that the object of theology is God alone, provided that the new and more precise sense won by the labors of the Scholastics is assigned to the older words. Is not Christ literally God? Is He any other than God?

Indeed, to speak thus is to state more emphatically that God is the object of theology. For if reference to Christ is omitted, God is less the object of our knowledge; so far as natural reason goes, God is known as though unknown, *cognoscitur tamquam ignotus*,[88] since He is known only by way of negation, analogy, and transcendence.

[88] St. Thomas, *In Boethium de Trinitate*, q. 1, a. 2 ad 1. "God is honored by silence; I do not mean that we may say nothing about Him or may make no inquiries about Him; but we lack ability to understand Him." *Ibid.*, q. 2, a. 1 ad 6. Cf. St. Augustine, *De doctrina christiana*, 6 (PL, XXXIV, 21).

"No man hath seen God at any time: the only-begotten Son who is in the bosom of the Father, He hath declared Him" (John 1:18). Not only is God better known in Christ but, also in Christ, He who is better known is more clearly God, for He is God as known in what is most interior and transcendent in Him, that is (we beg the reader's forbearance for our efforts at expression), in His most intimate life and nature, since the object of knowledge is God in the mystery of His immanent processions.

Thus, to tell the truth, we may, if we wish, retain the scholastic formula and say quite simply that the object of theology is God as God. But we should take the formula in its fullest sense and understand that God is the object with regard to what is most inaccessible and proper in Him; that He is the object in such a way as to be truly attained and grasped by the human intellect; that He is the object, not only as He is reflected in creation, but as He lives in Himself and for Himself alone; not merely as He is enshrouded in darkness, but as He gives Himself unreservedly to the substance and to the thought of men. Hence the fomula ought to be pushed to its limits so as to express what God really is in Christian theology. So understood, it means that God gives Himself in Christ, and that Christ, the divine life and light enveloping mankind, is the whole Christ: God who gives Himself to men in the God-man.[89]

Nothing more is needed to make the expression prevail. Once its rich meaning is allowed to sink into the mind, the very definition of the ultimate object of theology, while remaining the definition of that object, is seen to become in addition the definition of the integral and material object of this same theology.

Conversely, when we say that the integral and material object of theology is the whole Christ, *Christus totus*, do we not at the same time assert that the supreme and ultimate object is God as God? Indeed, do we not thus express the truth more clearly and systematically, as the explanations that have been given indicate? The solution lies in understanding the expression in all the precision conferred on it by the distinctions which the Scholastics, relying on dogma, have so successfully introduced.

All that is in Christ subsists in His divinity. This is His sole per-

[89] V. L. Gotti, in his *Theologia scolastico-dogmatica*, I, tract. 1, q.2, dub. 1, attempts to show that Christ is not the object of theology by proposing the amazing argument that theology would have existed even if the Word had not become incarnate.

sonality, this is the ultimate subject in which His humanity exists, this is the deepest source of His life that animates the entire race of regenerated man. Hence the divinity is also the ultimate in the whole Christ, God and man, head and body. Therefore, in asserting that the whole Christ is the complete object of theology, we assert that His divinity is the ultimate object of theology.

The same development occurred in the case of the first formula, through a reverse procedure. As the formula that specifies the ultimate object of theology became the formula that also specifies the material object without ceasing to specify the ultimate object, so now the formula that specifies the material object becomes the formula that specifies the ultimate object, without ceasing to be what it was. This is a sign that we are at the very center of unity. And, to tell the truth, it is in Christ that everything is united.

Moreover, Christ is wholly orientated toward the Father. He is the type, the ideal, and the principle of such orientation for all mankind. God is the goal toward which all His actions are directed in splendidly human fashion, the terminus which His entire psychology has in view, and the end of all His aspirations. As the whole Christ, He shares with His members this mounting up to the Father who sent Him, this undeviating ascent toward God. Everything in the world of reality that flows toward God and empties in God is a tendency in Christ, and has only to issue from Christ to attain its objective: the divine persons are in one another by circumincession. The formula that is valid in the order of realities may be transferred to the order of knowledge. In the latter, too, the only efficacious tendency toward God is the tendency that operates in Christ. In asserting that theology studies the whole Christ, we assert that theology reaches all the way to God in the purest fashion possible to men; in other words, since science is in question, theology is the science that has God as God for its ultimate object.[90]

Christ is not a sort of middle term or intermediary between the infinite God and the lower world; He is the infinite God communi-

[90] "What is the Father's doctrine, if not the Father's Word? Therefore Christ Himself is the Father's doctrine, if He is the Father's Word. But the Word cannot be the Word of no one, but has to be the Word of someone, and the doctrine that He announced is Himself and not just His, because He is the Word of the Father. What is so much yours as you? And what is so little yours as you yourself, if what you are belongs to another?" St. Augustine, *In Ioan.*, XXIX (PL, XXXV, 1629).

cating Himself to the lower world, and also the mediator in whom earth is joined to heaven. We should never imagine Him as a midway stopping point; He is the pure pouring out of God over men, as He is the pure ascent of men toward God. As Christ is the head of every man, so God is the head of Christ.[91] In being Christocentric, therefore, theology is but the more theocentric, and in exactly the way that befits men; so much so that to be truly theocentric it must be Christocentric. Theology has access to so high an object only through Christ.

Indeed, we must further remark that Christ has His ultimate intrinsic unity in the divinity alone, for His ultimate intrinsic unity is that of His person, and this person is exclusively the second of the divine persons. His human nature, assuredly, lacks none of the constituents of our race, and in particular has its inner coherence and immanence, or briefly, its unity, in our race. But this unity which, in other men, is the product of human personality, has in Christ's human nature a foundation incomparably deeper: His unique personality, which is that of the Word.

Accordingly the unity imparted by Christ to Christian teaching must, to be truly Christ's unity, be the unity of the divinity; and when we say that He is the center toward which all dogma converges, we say that God is that center in Him. But we must add that God, by nature, is too high above man to be the unifying principle in any human science. It is only in Christ, who dwells in us at the center of our life as well as of our science, that God becomes the unity of a human discipline.

IV. The Whole Christ as the First Intelligible

The Incarnation is the "abbreviated word" in which all revelation is enclosed. "Of all the works of God, the Incarnation most surpasses reason. Nothing done by God could conceivably be more wonderful than the fact that the true God, the Son of God, has become true man. And because the Incarnation is the most wonderful event in the world, all other wonders are ordained to belief in this greatest of all wonders; for what is greatest in any order, is perceived to be the cause of all the rest." [92] These lines of the holy doctor exhibit Christ

[91] Cf. I Cor. 11:3; 3:23.
[92] St. Thomas, *Contra Gentiles*, IV, c.27.

as the supreme sun from which radiates all the light that is in Christianity. He is the first intelligible and the source of all Christian truth, just as He is all its unity. Since the notion of first intelligible and that of unity are connected, all that has been said of the latter in the preceding pages applies also to the former. Here a few words will be enough.

The first intelligible, which is the whole Christ, has all the primacy of the absolute first intelligible, that is, of God Himself, for Christ is God. Moreover, Christ has this primacy in a way that suits man, in a human way, for He is man; and He has such primacy in His unity, for He is the God-man. Therefore this first intelligible is wholly perfect, as it ought to be in theology, which is the queen of sciences. The assertion that Christ is this first intelligible needs no proof, after what has been said about the quality of His unity in Christian teaching and the role of unity in understanding.

Everything in Christianity comes from Christ; the intelligibility proper to Christianity ought also to come from Christ. All the mysteries have come to mankind through Christ or in view of Christ; the understanding that can be gained of these mysteries ought likewise to come from Him: *ens et verum convertuntur*.

Christ is the first universal principle in Christianity: the first principle of grace, of satisfaction and merit, and of the revelation of mysteries. How could He be other than the first principle of the understanding of the mysteries? Supernatural truths have come to mankind through Him or in view of Him. For this very reason, the understanding of these truths, in the measure in which they may be intrinsically understood, must come from Him.

CHAPTER IV

UNITY: THE HUMAN CONSCIOUSNESS OF CHRIST AND THE CONSCIOUSNESS OF CHRISTIANS

I. The Consciousness of Christ and the Consciousness of Christians as Unity in Theology

> "Let this mind be in you which was also in Christ Jesus."
>
> Phil. 2:5

A. NOTION OF CONSCIOUSNESS

WE can advance yet farther in our search for unity. We have shown that the unity of theology is Christ. We are now going to show that it is Christ's consciousness, His human consciousness.

But some preliminary clarifications are necessary, because Modernists have likewise spoken of dogma as a consciousness, and the notion of consciousness is more complex than it appears at first sight. In this matter particularly the present work rejects the modernist error; but we do not intend to reject the error by running away from it. If arguments are to reach an adversary, they must take up the challenge of his denial, and should not be afraid to employ concepts and terms used by him.

Truth and error are not separated by a no-man's land which is neither the one nor the other and which prudence would urge us to shun. On the contrary, truth and error touch along their whole course. Truth advances up to error all the way, but no farther; to stop short of that limit, if only to remain at a safe distance, would be to fall into error and to stamp as false what is still true. Everywhere, but especially when in dangerous territory, truth must suppress any tendency to excessively anxious precautions that would make systems swerve to keep from skirting a possible abyss. If the systems are true, they will shun the peril by themselves; for truth of itself, without any need of our apprehensions and our stratagems, has the resources to avoid conversion into error.

The effective tactic is to pay no attention to error, except for the purpose of bringing to light and of firmly recovering the ideas and words which error has presumptuously appropriated. *Verum iudex sui et falsi:* truth, just by being truth, is the refutation of error.

Accordingly we must define consciousness. The notion is not as simple as it may appear to be at first sight. Its hasty identification with the deeper reaches of sensation or with coenesthesia or with the contents of empirical consciousness is an over-simplification. Such conceptions open the way to confusion without end.

Consciousness in general is a possession of oneself in oneself, an immanence of all that a person is in all that he is, a perfect identity of being with himself, a manner of being whereby a person exists in himself and for himself, so that not existing for oneself is the same as not existing at all. In a word, it is a way of existing fully.

Thus the notion of consciousness is connected with the notion of being. A being is knowable and knowing in the measure that it is in act. To be conscious, then, is the same as to be. But it is such by being so powerful that in virtue of it a person is himself for himself and possesses his own proper being in himself merely by being. Non-conscious beings are unaware of themselves, and they forever remain strangers shut off from themselves.

This close connection with being shows how consciousness can have the first place in knowledge: it is first inasmuch as knowledge is an apprehending by a knowing subject, a possessing by that subject. For two aspects are distinguishable in knowledge: the act of grasping elicited by the subject, and the object that is grasped. In virtue of the first aspect, knowledge is subjective and interior, a personal thing terminating in the person; in virtue of the second, it is essentially objective, an apprehension of being as being.

The more perfect knowledge is, the more these two aspects tend toward complete identity. But one always supposes the other. Knowledge of being, hence true knowledge, is impossible without self-knowledge. For, as long as there is no knowledge of self, the knower is unaware of himself from every point of view, and therefore is unaware of himself in his very act of knowing. The converse is also true: genuine consciousness, true knowledge of oneself, is impossible without true knowledge of being as being. If anyone does not know his own person as a being, he cannot claim to know it as it is, and therefore cannot claim to know it at all.

Because of its close connection with being and with knowledge, consciousness is analogous, just as being and as knowledge are. Accordingly there will be as many different types of consciousness as there are different types of being.

As there is only one Being that exists fully, there is only one Being that is fully conscious. Since He is Being without limit, He knows, simply by knowing Himself, all other beings in all their being. On this level consciousness implies—but only on this highest level, by identity—the supremely objective and eminent knowledge of everything. Therefore identity of a being with himself by no means prevents him from expressing in himself all the rest precisely as the rest.

Immediately below God are the angels. They exist fully on the plane of their forms, but not on the plane of their act of existence. Hence they are fully conscious of their forms, but not of their act of existence. Therefore something remains unexplained for an angel, namely, his very being.

Man does not exist fully either on the plane of the act of existence or on that of form. The individual has existence only by receiving it from God. Moreover, the human individual is not humanity. Or rather, to express the whole tenor of the paradox in a word, the human individual is not the human universe. He is part of a whole that has given him place in the world and supplies him with his energies, his matter, his experiences, his very life. Without all this he would be nothing; and yet he is not it. The universe is outside of him, the infinite Being is immeasurably above him; nevertheless man, in himself, is what he is only in unceasing dependence on these two that are not he. Cut off from them, he would no longer be himself, he would no longer be anything at all; and he is in himself only by being with them and in virtue of them.[1]

The same paradox recurs in man's consciousness. To be aware of himself, he must at the same time be aware of these others without which he would not be himself. In its very immanence and inwardness, his consciousness is the product both of the transcendent Being from whom it comes and of the external universe whereby it lives.

[1] Cf. St. Thomas, *De anima*, q. un., a. 17 ad 10.

Man is too poor to suffice completely for himself. At every moment his being is composed of forces and elements derived from the universe, and at every moment his existence is absolutely and totally dependent on the pure Act. Hence his being is in their possession before becoming his. The same is true of his consciousness: to be his consciousness and to express him, it must at every moment express other beings through whom he is what he is. In fact, since he exists through them, his consciousness must express them before it expresses him: either the empirical light of the act focuses on them before focusing on him, as is the case with his knowledge of the universe, or the absolute value of the affirmation directly envisages the Other before falling back on him, as is the case with his knowledge of God.[2]

B. THE HUMAN CONSCIOUSNESS OF CHRIST

The term "consciousness" must be clearly understood. Consciousness can signify the person who expresses himself, and also this same person as expressed by himself. It can mean the expression thus formulated, and can also mean the faculty, or rather the aspect of the faculty or even the act, by which this expression is formulated.

According as we understand the word in one or other of these senses, we may say that one or several consciousnesses, one or several egos, are found in Christ. Since Christ is but one person, there is in Him only one consciousness, one ego, one subject that is the point of departure of all His acts and is the ultimate terminus of attribution. Consequently there is only one who is conscious in Christ. But since this one who is conscious has two natures and two intellects, He has also two powers of saying "I," and in this sense He has a twofold consciousness. Each of these powers forms in Him a notion, or the equivalent of a notion, representing the "I," and thus Christ has two ways of expressing "I" or two expressions of consciousness.

The consciousness of Christ to be considered here is that belonging to Him as the first principle in the supernatural order, as the principle of unity in Christian teaching, as mediator; that is, the consciousness He has as man: His human consciousness. Since His human nature is complete, it has to possess this power of complete reflection or consciousness, without which man would not be an intellectual being.

---

[2] St. Thomas, *In I Sent.*, d. 3, q. 4, a. 5, has several lines that suggest the same thought without directly expressing it.

C. ITS PLACE IN THEOLOGY

In Christ, this consciousness had to possess unique characteristics, for He was man in a unique way. As was mentioned in the preceding chapter, He united and recapitulated the whole of Christian teaching in His humanity. To express Him, therefore, and to be a true consciousness in Him, His consciousness had to express this entire doctrine. Is not the man Jesus Christ primarily characterized by the fact that His humanity is that of the Son, that He is God who became incarnate and was crucified for us, that He is what Christian teaching says He is, that He is the mediator between God and man? Does not His human consciousness first of all have to express this to Him, and is not His human consciousness the doctrine taught by Christianity?

To express Christ, the consciousness of Christ had to express the whole of Christianity which is summed up in Him, is complete in Him, and reaches its zenith in Him. It expressed Christianity in a most simple and adequate manner, because Christ's humanity was already in possession of its ultimate end, and was the humanity of the God-man. Accordingly this consciousness was the perfect unity of Christian teaching. Christ's humanity, by its very nature, is that unity in the order of being; it is also the unity in the order of knowledge.

We said above that consciousness is the first intelligible in every man and with reference to him. In the whole of mankind, therefore, the consciousness of this Man who is the unity and center of all mankind is the first intelligible with reference to men.

We shall have occasion to speak frequently of Christ's consciousness, and we shall point out that it is most human, since it is the consciousness of a man, and at the same time most divine and quite impossible without grace, since it expresses God. Hence we need not delay over that truth here. But before going on, we should pause before this tabernacle, where God Himself speaks to man in a Man. Ever since Eden, the marvel of revealed religion is that God deals with man in a way that is completely fitting and completely human. Thus in the fullness of time, when God chose to speak to all mankind, He did not ensconce Himself on some remote, inaccessible Sinai. On the contrary, He draws near, He enters, He descends to us, we may almost say He loses Himself among us, so closely does He unite Himself to those He teaches. From the midst of men He singles out a Man to be the center and the recapitulation of the race, and in the inmost part of this Man, in the intellect which is the very center of man, in the consciousness which is the center of the intellect, He deposits His truth. There He places it, not to be an alien accretion like a seed or a foreign body, but to be a necessary constituent and an essential activity of that unique consciousness, and to proclaim itself in the very act in which this unique God-man asserts Himself even as man.

God did not become man by half-measures. Gently, delicately, He follows our course with us. The eternal light flashes forth; or rather, since nothing equals it in softness and tenderness, it dawns in the intellect, which is the manifestation of man in man.

D. THE CONSCIOUSNESS OF CHRISTIANS
AS THE FULL EXPRESSION OF CHRISTIAN TEACHING

If Christians are members of Christ, they must, in the degree proper to members, be what He is as head. The primacy Christ possesses in the order of unity, intelligibility, and the grasp of knowledge that develops within consciousness, He transfers to His members; for He communicates Himself to them in such a way that they, living His life, become sharers of His primacy.

This statement evidently lacks meaning unless we admit the doctrine of the mystical body in a realistic sense, unless we admit that the Christian, as a Christian, is intrinsically and ontologically a member of Christ and that he is such in the innermost essence of His Christian being. The present book is based on this supposition.

Christians, then, as Christians, are Christ's members. As such, they are definable only in terms of Christ; and Christ, as we have said, is definable only in terms of the totality of Christian teaching. Therefore Christians, too, are definable only through this totality. To know themselves, they need this totality; and on the other hand, since they are spiritual beings, they must know themselves and be conscious. Hence we must conclude that Christian teaching expresses the consciousness they have of themselves as Christians.

What is this consciousness? It is clearly something wholly unique, *sui generis*, and must possess the unique characteristics which theology recognizes in supernatural knowledge. What does this imply? The Christian, formally as a Christian, is a member of Christ, that is, of the Word, who is the Son of the Father and the co-principle of the Holy Spirit. The Christian lives as a member of that sacramental reality which is the Church. He lives in an immense redemption. He is made and animated by all that is expressed in the doctrine of Christianity. To express himself to himself, he must express this whole doctrine.

The necessity of this consciousness in the Christian is made clear by the following considerations.

1. Christ's supernatural knowledge, which we have been regarding as consciousness, must be similarly regarded as possessed by Christians. The two form a single reality in the order of grace, just as Christ and Christians form a single supernatural organism: *operari sequitur esse.*

2. Supernatural elevation has its roots in the inmost depths of men. Hence the elevation of knowledge must likewise be rooted in man's innermost depths. What is this but consciousness? In the order of being, a person is a member of Christ by a grace affecting the very substance of the soul. In the order of knowledge, therefore, a person will also be a member of Christ by a grace affecting this same substance of the soul that expresses itself in knowledge. Again, what is this interior expression if not consciousness?

3. All life is immanence. Supernatural life is endowed with a supernatural perfection. Hence it must imply an immanence that is likewise endowed with supernatural perfection. Consciousness expresses this immanence in the highest degree. If God becomes the very being of our being and the soul of our soul, He must also be, as it were, the consciousness of our consciousness. Consciousness is the very cry of the soul, the act of a being that clasps itself. How can its knowledge become truly interior to us in our human way, unless it penetrates our consciousness and unless the latter expresses it in expressing ourselves?

4. Every being in the spiritual order is conscious. But supernatural being is spiritual being. Therefore it must be conscious being.

E. SPECIAL CHARACTER OF CHRISTIAN CONSCIOUSNESS

The consciousness of Christians must be of a special kind. The Modernists, as we remarked above, also affirmed that supernatural knowledge is at bottom a consciousness. But by consciousness they meant an interior impression, a sort of sensible consciousness, rather than an intellectual consciousness. Following Kant, they held that the intellect is imprisoned in the world of phenomena: it can know nothing of the Absolute, of God. But, they added, as Kant had done before them in speaking of the postulates of the will, in the sphere of sentiment the intellect has a confused but persistent impression that such realities must exist. It does not know them, but it does yearn for them: it is harassed by a thirst for the ideal, a nostalgia for the infinite and the divine, a need of aspiring. Being essentially rational, man necessarily expresses this indefinable attitude of his soul in rational utterances which are its symbol and which account for religious formulas. Thus, according to them, are born those beautiful and inimitable pronouncements, those Christian and Catholic formulas that are called dogmas.

We need not here pass judgment on this conception in its entirety; anyone can perceive the agnosticism, that is, the suicide, to which it entices the intellect and religion. It is clearly poles apart from our own conception. The following points will suffice to indicate succinctly the essential differences.

A person is conscious in his own personal way; a member of Christ, as such, is conscious in the way befitting a member of Christ. A man is a member of Christ by being attached to Christ; his consciousness will be in him as continually received, just as his quality as a member is continually received. But this reception, as we indicated above, must be both interior and exterior; it must be a reception of interior light and a reception of formulas. The two are complementary: the formulas lead us into the light, and the light imparts meaning to the formulas. Accordingly the interiority here in question is not that which man, as man, has in him, but is that which, as a member of Christ, he has in the transcendent God.

With regard to its characteristics, this consciousness must be both free and restricted. It must be free, because attachment to Christ is not brought about against one's will; it must be restricted, because, once the attachment is effected, consciousness does no more than affirm the attachment.

Further, this consciousness will be clear and mysterious: clear, because it manifests to a member what he is; mysterious, because a member is what he is by attachment to Him who in Himself is mystery and transcendence.

It will be both unchangeable and capable of being lost, assured and uncertain, gratuitously infused as a grace and absolutely indispensable in the hypothesis of supernatural elevation.

It will also be essentially personal because the life of the spirit is such, and essentially dependent, social, and ecclesiastical, because this life is imparted by incorporation into Christ and hence by incorporation into the immense unity of those who live the life of Christ.

Lastly, this consciousness will be essentially divine and essentially human. It will be essentially divine because it exists only in union with God and to express that union. It will be essentially human because it exists in man and exists to express to man what is henceforth best in him. Accordingly it is theocentric, anthropocentric, and Christocentric. It is all this together, and each aspect has its place; for in His own unity Christ effects in man the unity of all that is human with the whole of divinity.

Because of Christ and our incorporation in Him, the doctrine of Christianity, as a message about God, a theological message, is not at all a collection of formulas imposed on our memory in a system that is coherent though cold. It is, we may say, ourselves: the life of us who know, springing up in us from the living God.

To be our own, this supernatural knowledge must come to us from God. In giving it to us, God deals with us as a mother would deal with her child. The child is as yet too young to express its confused thoughts to itself and to others. The child tries to speak, falters, and bursts into tears. Then the mother catches it up in her arms, gazes into its eyes, and speaks to it, slowly, using the child's own language. Between mother and child there is so great a resemblance, so close a tie, so much love, that she divines what it is trying to say but cannot; nothing is so perfectly the language of this child as the language issuing from the heart of the mother. This is what God lovingly does for His children on earth. Through His bounty, they have treasures in their souls which they will never be able to express, but which they ought to express since they are spiritual beings. Then God, using human words, the only words His little ones understand, describes to them the marvelous beings they have become. What He tells them is what their very nature as members strives to tell them, so much is it their own, but does not succeed, so amazing is the beauty. God awakens the consciousness they have as members by illuminating it with the only light that is suitable; and that is the light of the sun.

But God's loving care goes much farther than a mother's. The mother tells the child what the child is half able to express, and what it will soon be completely able to say. But God tells us, and gives us power to express, what we, left to ourselves, could never in any way say or be. And though His generosity is unlimited, it is perfectly adapted to the one who is to express his thoughts. It is even more than this. God knows much better than a mother what He has and what He makes over to His children, and with far greater love He is able to find the words that awaken understanding. His voice is perfectly the voice of our divinized nature, for our divinized nature is His.

F. THE CONSCIOUSNESS OF CHRISTIANS
AS THE UNITY OF DOGMA AND THE FIRST INTELLIGIBLE

In this conception, the Christian's consciousness may be said to be the unity and the first intelligible of Christian truth. It is such because Christ is such.

Christians truly possess all that is needed to understand mysteries in the measure in which they are understandable here below: *aliqua, Deo dante, mysteriorum intelligentia e mysteriorum ipsorum nexu inter se*. This is because Christians, by the grace of God, are products of mystery, as Christ is; they are products of mystery in their faculty of comprehension, in their act of understanding, and in their consciousness which, like all that they are, is from Christ and in Christ. The nexus between mysteries that is accomplished in Christ is also accomplished in them as far as they are His members and as far as He unites Himself to them in the substance of their souls where their being is joined to Him and in those intimacies whose voice is their consciousness.

Thus the unity of the whole Christ, which pervades all Christian teaching, also pervades the entire Christian organism that accepts it on faith. This unity is the reason why each dogma in its own way expresses the whole doctrine, for in its own way it expresses Christ. The same unity is the reason why every Christian and his consciousness, in constituting the whole Christ in the manner proper to members, likewise constitute the unity of doctrine and its totality in the manner proper to members. Thus the objective unity of supernatural knowledge corresponds to its subjective unity.

II. Reduction to This Unity

> "Thou art the Master teaching most
> secretly in the school of the heart."
> St. Augustine, *Confessions*, IX, 9

A. REDUCTION TO CHRIST AND HIS CONSCIOUSNESS: OUTWARD EXPRESSION

The task of theology is to reduce everything to the first intelligible, which is Christ and His consciousness. "To reduce" means, etymologically, to lead or bring back. Accordingly our purpose is to bring everything back to Christ as to a more perfect unity.

The physicist reduces everything to a first intelligible in his science, that is, to equations. Our endeavor in this work is similar. We propose to show how all knowledge of supernatural truths is reduced to the knowledge Christ has of Himself, both in Himself and in His members, and to the knowledge His members have of themselves as members. We wish to make clear how all Christian truths are connected with the truth of the whole Christ.

The rational expression of such a study will resemble the technical expression of other sciences; it will involve reflection, comparison, reasoning, and the like. Yet it will have its own characteristics, the first and most essential of them being an undeviating orientation toward Christ.

The physicist, while pursuing his investigations, is obsessed with his formulas. Similarly the theologian, as theologian, ought to be wholly wrapped up in Christ. In all his ponderings he should see only Christ: *omnia et in omnibus Christus*. Since Christ is a mystery, we shall be tracing all other mysteries back to a mystery when we trace them back to Him in our effort to comprehend them. Therefore our understanding of them will be mysterious, and will remain obscure and a source of humiliation for us even in the satisfaction and light it confers. We can gain no more than *aliqua mysteriorum intelligentia*.

B. REDUCTION TO CHRIST AND HIS CONSCIOUSNESS: INTERIOR REALIZATION

This conceptual reduction to Christ, outwardly expressed in scientific formulations, is the expression of a living reduction of

Christian thought that lives by the living consciousness of Christ. For knowledge is life: *cognoscere cognoscentibus est esse*. Supernatural knowledge is life at its fullest; it is eternal life: "This is eternal life, that they may know" (John 17:3).

To reduce our knowledge to Christ and His consciousness, to share by union in the understanding, certitude, and clarity possessed by Him, we must lead our minds back to Christ, we must think in terms of surrender, adherence, and insertion into Him: "To believe is nothing else than to think with assent." [3] Faith, as participation in Christ, has its source of life and light in that participation, through Christ.

Therefore to believe with a faith that is thought and adherence, with the full consent of the heart joined to the clear thinking of the mind, is the primary condition for reduction to Christ. Such is the faith by which we forget ourselves and consecrate ourselves to God and to our fellow men in charity. It is a faith animated by a considerate love, in union with the Lord, a faith that rejoices to think in the Lord. When we have that faith, we judge as He would have judged, we evaluate as He would have evaluated, we say what He would have said. Above all, we resay what He actually said, and what He says still in Scripture and the Church, like Mary, who "kept all these words, pondering them in her heart" (Luke 2:19).

Thus we reduce ourselves and our thoughts to the thoughts and consciousness of Christ. Or rather, it is He who draws us to Himself. He is the one who makes us one; He is the life that upholds those who live by that life: "The peace of God, which surpasseth all understanding, keep your hearts and minds in Christ Jesus" (Phil. 4:7). The activity needed to achieve such reduction is cooperation with Christ's work, and indeed is its effect, so long as it is good; all the vigor of the vine-branch comes from the trunk. "The members of Christ must understand, and Christ must understand in His memmers, and Christ's members must understand in Christ; for head and members are one Christ." [4]

The initiative comes from Christ. And we must leave the initiative and the priority to the first intelligible and its spontaneity, since this is consciousness, and consciousness is by nature free. How could activity that is exercised from without be successful in dealing with

[3] St. Augustine, *De praedestinatione sanctorum*, 5 (PL, XLIV, 963).
[4] St. Augustine, *In ps. LIV* (PL, XXXVI, 629).

something that is purely interior? Christ's consciousness, the first principle in supernatural intelligibility, must be the first principle in the act of understanding. Free with a liberty that is one with the first cause and that is absolute liberty, it must freely intervene in our comprehension of the supernatural, by initiating and giving the very act of understanding.[5]

Theological science, like every human science, is essentially incomplete. Everything in it tends to a clarity that nothing in it can furnish. Other sciences may come to a halt when they have said their last word. Theology has to end in silence. "Speak, Lord, for Thy servant heareth" (I Kings 3:10). Its final step is to lead us to the Master, who remains always the unique Master, the only one who speaks within at the same time that He instructs from without.

C. REDUCTION TO THE CHRISTIAN AND TO HIS CONSCIOUSNESS AS MEMBER

Christ speaks to His members through the nature they have as members. The explanation of Himself in His own consciousness comes to them through their consciousness, so far as this is a consciousness belonging to them as members. Accordingly reception of this full, interior explanation is not beyond their powers of interiorly receiving a whole.

To set forth all that is implied in such reduction to the consciousness of Christ, we must speak of a reduction to the consciousness of Christ's members. To bring a truth to the consciousness of a Christian is the same as to concentrate and reflect on this truth as far as it expresses Christian life and is clarified by that life, and actually to be, as intensely as possible, what it requires of Christians. This amounts to saying: to be a child of God, a member of Christ, a brother to all men, so that the conformity between such an attitude and the basic life of the soul may serve as a personal verification of the doctrine, which is in this way unified.

But as Christians are members of Christ by attachment to Christ and to God, the witness thus borne by their Christian nature comes to them through their attachment to Christ and to God. Hence this testimony can confer on the act of the man receiving it a firm-

[5] The Council of Orange, can. 5, teaches that not only every increase of faith, but its beginning and the very desire to believe, are gifts of grace. Cf. Denz., 178.

ness surpassing human firmness. The possibility of being unified and established in this consciousness as members comes from the inner unity of that consciousness, a unity resulting from attachment to, and participation in, the consciousness and unity of Christ.

Everything in that consciousness is unity, everything is the same: the act of thinking, the truths adhered to, the aspect of these truths that induces adherence, the motive for which adherence is given, and the promulgation of the truths leading to adherence. At first sight, and looked at from without, all these factors appear to differ; but when they are attentively and thoroughly examined, they are seen to come together in Christ and in His members.

The act of thinking is an act of adhering, of believing. But this act, as such, is an act of a cognitive faculty and of a nature that exist in adherence and attachment; it is the actuation, in the order of knowledge, of what this manner of existing is in the order of being. Therefore it is the expression, under the form of knowledge, of that which, in the reality of things, is the gift of God to men in Christ.

The truths to which this act adheres are the same; for they are dogmas, and dogmas express Christ and the donation of God to all men in Christ. The aspect of these truths that induces adherence is likewise the same. For this aspect is the fact that the truths are communicated and revealed by God Himself in Christ. This revelation is the same donation of God to men in Christ.

The motive for which adherence is given is the authority of God who reveals. But this very authority of God, which of itself guarantees only the acts of God Himself, establishes an intellectual attitude in the mind of man because it is communicated; and it is communicated through God's donation of Himself in Jesus Christ.

Lastly, the promulgation of these truths through the Church, as considered in its mysterious totality, is still this same donation of God, this revelation of God by God. For in the Church, which is the continuation of Christ, it directly reaches all souls.

Thus the intellectual attitude actuating the consciousness of Christ's members is in itself perfectly one, just as the activity that expresses the life of the spirit ought to be one. And this attitude merely expresses in the cognitive order what the Christian character is, for what makes men Christians is the same donation of God. In this attitude, which is complete unity, the Christian can achieve perfect unity and can find the inner consistency, the peace and intellectual satisfaction, the *determinatio ad unum*, which is certitude.

All this may be anthropocentrism, but it is also Christocentrism and therefore in the last analysis theocentrism.

This reduction to the member's consciousness is not entirely an individual operation. When the Christian undertakes it and attempts to enter into himself and his consciousness as a believer, to find in his faith the immovable rock, he communes with himself in God and Christ; or rather, God, in Christ, brings him to commune with himself; for in Christ the whole mystical body of Christ enters into such communion, whenever the act of knowledge is exercised. Does not any living being instinctively and characteristically gather itself together and tense itself when it is going to spring forth? Such is the action of Christ in His body, such is the action of that organism of living light which is the body of Christ when the act of knowledge is exercised; for knowledge is life, and the light of knowledge is also life.

Accordingly this reduction to Christ is also a reduction to God; God alone is the ultimate goal. Thus we see once more that God alone is the formal object and the *subiectum* of theology. But God is wholly in Christ.

At the same time this reduction has its starting point and runs its whole course in every man: Christ is the way, Christ in us. All the members of Christ have a right to a part in it and a capacity to understand His doctrine through it. Not all have a mind sufficiently subtle and trained to engage in scientific theology; but all have what is required to engage in the living theology that is here in question. They have the capacity in the same way as they have their being and their power to understand; for they are created, by a second creation, in Jesus Christ. Like all theologians, they will have such power of understanding only by believing. They will have it in their reason, evidently, but their reason will have it because, in the act of believing, reason will perceive that belief is good for reason, the reason of a member of Christ.

D. MORALITY AND THEOLOGY

There is a moral conscience, a power to judge between good and evil that is properly Christian, just as, according to the preceding pages, there is a speculative, cognitive consciousness that is properly

Christian. There is a Christian moral conscience because there is a Christian morality, a moral science that is specifically and intrinsically Christian.

Christian morality is by no means a profane ethics of Aristotelian or Stoic character, augmented by arguments drawn from dogma and by various refinements subserving the commandments of the Church. Christianity is too perfectly one and consistent with itself to be constructed of second-hand materials. As it has its own knowledge which is highly unified and specialized, namely, theology, so it has its own code which is similarly unified and specialized, namely, its moral science.

As the knowledge possessed by Christianity stems from its own first principles, so its moral science stems from its own great notions of morality. Its notion of end differs from that which is found in the simple science of natural morality. God is of course its last end, but is envisaged under a different light, as a given truth and not as inaccessible; He is exhibited in His own inner life, as He is in Himself, and not merely in external reflections and infinitely deficient images. It is in Christ that God, as He exists in His own inner life, becomes accessible. Hence Christian moral science finds its last end in Christ. Since Christ possesses the fullness of divinity and the fullness of humanity in complete personal unity, He possesses all that is necessary for man's complete perfection. When we say that Christ is the end, we do not deny that God is the end; all that we say is that God is the end in a supernaturally perfect way.

This notion of end dominates all other notions. In the first place, it dominates the notion of the supreme state toward which man ought to tend, that of the moral ideal, of the *finis quo*. In Christian morality this is the divinized life, the quality of adoptive sonship in the one Son by participation in Trinitarian life, the perfection of a son who ought to be perfect as his heavenly Father is perfect; or, what comes to the same, the incorporation of the whole man into Christ. On earth, while man is yet in process of formation, this incorporation is effected by grace; it will be brought to perfection in the state of glory. But in both states it is the same life, lived in the same Christ.

The notion of the actions leading to this end, this ideal, is also new. Since the question concerns divinization and union with God in Himself, these actions must be performed by God along with man; or, since the union of God and man is complete in Christ, they must be continuations of Christ's activity: continuations realized as the continuation of Christ is realized, embracing what is invisible and what is visible, an influx of new love from within and an influx of grace from without through the sacraments. Christian morality is essentially sacramental, as it is essentially personal.

Further, the notion of liberty, of the power to realize such an end, is new. Union with God is in question; power to rise so high must be a power joined to God, a liberty elevated above its native condition. This is a liberty that is divinized and reinforced by grace; a liberty belonging to man not merely as man, but as a member of Christ. Such a liberty is designed to bring about, within the deepest recesses of each member of Christ, a union between God and man that calls Christ to mind. Christian morality is essentially theological, and is "charitological" as well as Christological.

According to this norm, the whole moral law must be summed up in Christ and must consist in imitating Him, in acting, feeling, or willing as He would have done and as He actually does within the soul, from the first vigorous stirrings of Christian life.

All our duties toward God consist in being, in God's eyes, what Christ is, that is, what He is in His members. Our duties toward men lead back to Christ. In incorporating us into Himself, He makes us all members of one another, *commembra, concorporales*. Because of Him and in Him, our manner of willing is a willing in communion with all. When a man becomes a Christian he lives, acts, thinks, prays, and suffers not in solitude, nor with Christ alone—for Christ is not alone—but with all mankind. His love ought to reach out to every man and to the limits of the universe, and ought also to reach up to God and infinity, in Christ who is all in all. Consequently this morality is thoroughly human, as it is mysteriously divine. Our duties toward ourselves likewise bring us back to Christ. We must be pure out of respect for a body He has made His own. We must be kind, patient, joyous, and strong because we are members of Him who is the most splendidly human of all the children of men.

Such a morality supposes a conscience that is not confined to the natural plane but is raised to a perfection that enables us to arrive at judgments in the divine order and to have reactions and quasi-instincts befitting Christ and the mystical body of Christ. This moral conscience of the Christian is a human conscience as elevated by the gifts of counsel and fortitude. Through it the Christian moral law becomes a sort of new natural law, a law written in the depths of the soul and the heart, according to the classical text in this matter: "This is the testament which I will make to the house of Israel after those days, saith the Lord: I will give My laws into their mind, and in their heart will I write them." [6] Through this conscience the Christian law is truly instilled before being written, as St. Thomas says with so much insistence: "The New Law is in the first place a law instilled into our hearts, and secondarily it is a written law." [7]

In the natural order man is essentially conscious, and his consciousness has two aspects: a cognitive aspect and a practical aspect. He knows what he is: this is cognitive consciousness or psychological and intellectual consciousness. He also knows what he ought to be; and this is his practical consciousness, his moral consciousness, or, as is usually said, his conscience pure and simple. The two, as we see, are intimately connected, for they are expressions of the same being, and one is a beacon for the other; in willing as he ought, a man knows himself for what he is.

In the supernatural order, the elevation of man's nature implies a corresponding elevation of these two aspects of consciousness. They retain the close union that is essentially theirs. They possess the characteristics of supernatural elevation that have already been considered in connection with cognitive consciousness. They are received from Christ and from the organism in which Christ is continued; they are received in formulas and in the internal directives of grace, without ceasing to be the intimate voice of nature, for this nature itself, in its utmost depths, is a received nature, the nature of a member.

Accordingly moral conscience is in a state of dependence with respect to the Church, for its need of precepts reveals its dogmatic and ascetic character. But Christian morality also has the personal character it ought to possess, the character of a law imposed on liberty from within. Man's nature requires him to direct himself freely, and what God most expects of him in Christianity is the initial and spontaneous movement of the soul. Hence man must have a guide within him that will point out to him how to act truly in his own way by acting as an adopted son of God and a member of Christ.

In judging according to this conscience, in summoning every-

[6] Heb. 8:10, quoting Jer. 31:33.
[7] *Summa*, Ia IIae, q. 106, a. 1; cf. ad 2 and the whole question.

thing before it and reducing all to it, the Christian judges according to Christ. He judges in Christ, and Christ judges in him. Thus Christ is wholly present in the Christian's moral code, especially when it is formulated in the depths of consciousness. Conscience is likewise wholly in Christ. It is one in Him, always expressing Him in all the great notions that constitute it, as we have seen, in the same way as theology is one in Him and expresses Him in all the truths that compose theology. And this is exactly what is required in order that conscience may aid toward an understanding of theology.

Christ Himself is so completely in conscience that we may say that He is it and it is He, in the sense that He gives life to His members in a way that is suitable for those who belong to Him while remaining free. The expression of conscience in formulas and precepts is secondary; the chief factor in it is an influx of love that enters into the soul with its own tendencies, a charity and a life that accompany its divine morals.

Christian conscience is less a system than a person, less a code than a living teacher who is incessantly imparting life. We can never master it to the point of being able to decree its conclusions imperiously; we follow it by endeavoring to be docile toward Him who alone possesses the words of eternal life. To contemplate Christ in the Gospel is more necessary than to reason about principles, to allow ourselves to be formed by Him is more important than to acquire self-mastery.

We have called theology a unique science. Unlike other sciences, it has no need to proclaim the last word, but should lead us to Him who utters it. The same is true of Christian moral: it ends in silence, in an appeal, in love.

E. APOLOGETIC VALUE OF THIS THEOLOGY

Theology thus envisaged has an apologetic function. But this is a special apologetic, an apologetic which is intrinsic to Catholic doctrine and which avails for those who are within the faith; an apologetic which, as the Vatican Council says—for the idea is not unknown to tradition—is directed to the children of the Church, assuring them "that the faith they profess rests on a most solid foundation." [8]

This apologetic is a justification that is connected with Christian

[8] Constitution *De fide catholica*, c.3 (Denz., 1794).

life itself as an object of reflection. It is related to that life as health and its signs are related to bodily life. It imparts assurance and strength. It does more than solve difficulties: it keeps difficulties from agitating the depths of the soul. It is, so to say, like a process of reasoning that returns on itself, and thus retains all its forces in unity. By it, faith justifies itself in the manner of a universe that stands firm because of its very bigness, in virtue of its inner fullness and living solidity.

Undoubtedly this justification can to a certain extent be expressed in formulas. But such expression will not be adequate. To make the most of it we must, in our opinion, take our inspiration from one of the most striking arguments used by apologetics to demonstrate the transcendence of the Church. When everything else is tottering, it has been said, the Church holds together and remains unshaken despite the falterings of its heads and members. We should do better to say that the doctrine of Christianity holds together in the Church and in Christians, and that it enables the Church and Christians to hold together in it. It holds together in spite of all the wavering, the cowardice, the opportunism beclouding the intellects in which it resides. It holds together under the blows delivered by life and history; all such shocks but strengthen it and provide it with the occasion for pronouncing the decisive word at every epoch, in the face of the timidities and erroneous forecasts of its adherents. It holds together, and will continue to hold together all the better the more frankly we view it, the more sincerely and fervently we live, and the more importance we attribute to it.

According to the Vatican Council,[9] the Church itself is its own proof, a testimony which divine grace renders irrefutable. Since the doctrine of Christianity defines the Church and since each Christian is in miniature what the Church is on a large scale, we can say of the Christian what we say of his doctrine. Christians are themselves a proof, a testimony, and this witness receives decisive force from the grace informing it: not only a firmness in the will, but an intellectual certitude, for grace acts on the intellect as it does on the will. Grace does not bring to light anything else than what men see, but it causes us to see, in what appears to be something purely human, the God-man who is living on.

The God-man Himself is the great argument that convinces by the

⁹ *Ibid.*

power of God appearing in man, that wins over the masses and the children, that wins over His very persecutors: witness St. Paul. He is such even today, in His teaching and in the Christian. A few men have succeeded in charging the lines they write with a spark of their own souls and their human truth; and some of their phrases have moved their readers, like a look that penetrates the eye. How much more this Man, who spoke as no other has ever spoken! He has expressed the whole of His personality in His doctrine. Let us but meditate it, particularly in the light which is He Himself in our souls, in the light of the Christian life which He pours into His members. Then the doctrine will appear as deep as consciousness, it will be one as life is one, it will be as ardent as love and as compelling as Christ.

If Christ alone utters the last word in theology, He alone, likewise, utters the last word in the apologetic that is intrinsic to theology. If we assert that He is living, the least we can do is to let Him perform the acts of life.

This apologetic differs greatly from the apologetics of immanentism spoken of by the Modernists. The latter apologetic is immanent to man as man, the former is immanent to the man who lives in Christ, to the whole Christ; that is, it is immanent to Him who is purely transcendent, and hence it is strictly transcendent. The transcendent Christ nowhere so strikingly displays His transcendence as in the inner depths, or, if the word is preferred, the immanence of His action on souls.

Therefore this apologetic avails only for those who are already Christ's members, for Christians who are already fashioned by grace. For those who lack any beginning of a tie with Christ, who are completely passed over in God's design to unite all men in His well-beloved Son, it has no force. But are there any such souls?

CHAPTER V

THE TEACHING OF PHILOSOPHY ON MAN AND HIS UNITY

I. Unity of the Universe in Man

> "Every corporeal creature tends to likeness with man, since thereby it is assimilated to supreme goodness."
>
> St. Thomas, *In II Sent.*, d. 1, q. 2, a. 3 ad 3

AN understanding of the nature of man is necessary for an understanding of the whole Christ and of the mystical body. Too often the notion of man is restricted to that of his body, with an added corrective imposed by spiritual principles; we are told that this figure, with a stature of such and such dimensions, this biped, is capable of certain immaterial activities. This inadequate conception eventually engenders a deficient notion of Christ and the Church.

We wish to show that man is quite different from anything that can be represented by sense, imagination, and even concepts. Man is a certain immensity. In his relations to the universe he is more than a part: he is a center, a totality, a culmination. With respect to the whole of mankind, he is likewise more than a mere part: he is a recapitulation, a totality of a special order. This is what we must now make clear.

A. THE UNITY AND MEANING OF THE UNIVERSE SOUGHT IN MAN

Science supposes and at every turn asserts that the universe is one. Does not science continually revert to the claim that it can express everything in one synoptic table, in a coherent collection of laws, and perhaps in a single law? The great postulates it builds on, such as the postulates of the conservation of energy and of universal invariance, are affirmations of unity. Even the idea that physical laws are but statistical laws is reduced to the view that the multiplicity present in disorder ends up by producing order and unity.

Apart from this unity, another fact striking the observer is that the universe everywhere appears to be joined in a hundred different ways. Every part in the whole is so affected and modified by attractions, influences, and vibrations emanating from every other part that it seems to be the resultant of all the rest, like a sort of soft clay on which the universe has left its impression, or a sort of microcosm within the macrocosm.

The impression thus stamped varies with the degree of perfection of each object. The universe is inscribed on inorganic things in a purely external way, as a garden is reflected in balls of silvered glass strung above it. In living beings endowed with immanence, it is inscribed within the immanence, though imperfectly and materially in the case of lower organisms. We perceive this in the phenomenon of assimilation. Eating is a transfer of an organism's external surroundings to its interior, to the point of identification. All external matter is potentially internal for a living being. A single plant of corn-poppy or wild mignonette could absorb and transform into itself the entire terrestrial globe in some ten years—supposing, of course, that the whole were assimilable and that the plant's seeds were suitably distributed. After this, the whole solar system would be an affair of several years, and all sidereal matter of a few more: twenty at the most.

But this is negligible in comparison with what takes place in the higher animals. On its higher levels life, confronting the universe, shows itself yet more grasping; or rather the universe, in the living beings it contains, is seen more clearly to be in gestation of itself. The power of sensation, for example, is more rapid than the power of assimilation. It annexes the universe, not grain by grain or mouthful by mouthful, but at a single stroke, and by a movement so easy that it can be repeated over and over without being noticed. We may describe sensation as an exploit that consists in appropriating entire regions, oceans, and heavens by merely opening the eyes. For the animal that seems surrounded on all sides, it is a fantastic sortie outside itself and a triumphant return—in the limited capacity the animal has of dwelling within itself—in which it brings back the whole universe as booty.

Yet this is only a hint of what occurs in the act of understanding. Sensation may succeed in grasping the universe, but it cannot grasp itself.

There is in the universe a part of that universe, well comprised within the aggregate, closely connected with the animal kingdom in which it finds place, a true part of the universe in virtue of its body. But by its soul it is able to express the whole universe in the perfectly undivided act by which it folds over on itself; it can express the universe in its own being, in its own reality which, much more truly than irrational beings, is the whole universe in miniature within the great universe—if, indeed, we are bound to add the qualification, "in miniature." [1] This being is man.

In man, therefore, the striving toward unity that is found everywhere in the universe comes to a head. The human act of thinking in which the universe is confronted with itself, though now as understood and unified, is not exclusively a human activity; it is a cosmic function. The unity pervading the mass does not have its principle anywhere else, because it does not properly exist anywhere else. In man alone it succeeds in finding itself and realizing its inherent potentialities. Therefore, if it is internal to man, it is internal to the world; it is the unity of the world.

What is true of knowledge is also true of action; what begins in the universe culminates in man. Determinism reigns throughout the universe; its parts move one another, but nothing in it ultimately moves itself, so that we cannot see whence the movement comes. Undoubtedly science has never proved that this determinism is absolute. Nor has philosophy, in our opinion, ever established it. Philosophy requires that the universe, to exist, must be one in its own way, that is, in the way of an aggregate, through connections and ties, and hence by a unity resembling the unity described by determinism. But it also requires that this unity should be imperfect, as the being of the universe is imperfect, and therefore that the determinism in the universe should be imperfect. In any case, we have to note that this determinism, so far as it exists, is a unity that joins all the parts of the world together by a thousand bonds of steel.

[1] The idea is ancient. Aristotle, *Physics*, VIII, 2 (252 b 26), refers to man as a microcosm. Cf. St. Thomas, *Summa*, Ia, q.91, a.1; q.96, a.1.

But we must be no less careful to note that this unity, such as it is, does not find its explanation or its principle in itself any more than it has its totality from itself. If everything is determined by the rest, nothing is determined by itself; the determinant, being always somewhere else, is everywhere absent, and we ask how anything can be determined in such absence of a determinant.

The unity of determinism is achieved only in the liberty in which it finds the adequate grounds of its existence and its definitive form. In the immense flux of things moved by other things, eddies and whirlpools arise in which the movement strives to turn back on itself and grasp itself. This takes place, to a limited extent, even in inorganic bodies, which have their characteristic reactions; it takes place particularly in living beings, which, in their phenomena of growth and reproduction, and still more in their phenomena of sensation, have the power of self-movement.

But these movements remain external to themselves. They do not release themselves or assign their types to themselves, and they are not their own terminus. The vital cycle does not close down on itself, but issues in a new living being that begins the cycle all over again. Sensation has its culmination, not in itself, but in the reaction it calls forth; the eddy is lost in the current, and the unity that embraces some phenomena does not embrace itself.

Only the free act can do this: the act that is conscious, that is its own beginning and end to the extent it is free, that is complete in being one: *liberum est quod est causa sui.* Thus we come to perceive that without man the universe is truncated and inexplicable: it has no center, no ultimate, no issue. It is nowhere conscious; therefore at no point does it take possession of its own being, and so it does not exist intrinsically. Can we call that the full realization of existence? Nowhere is it free; hence at no point does it assimilate its being by receiving its natural law into itself.

Accordingly, since creation comes to a successful issue in man alone, we may say that man is its end. Man is the intrinsic end of the world, and is the relatively last end for the world. God is the transcendent and absolutely ultimate end, but the world tends to God only in man. "Since a thing is assimilated to the best [i.e., God] by coming to resemble what is better than itself, every corporeal creature tends, as best it may, to a likeness of the intellectual creature, which attains divine goodness in a more perfect way. And therefore the human form, namely, the rational soul, is said to be the ultimate end aimed at by lower nature." [2]

B. MAN'S FULLNESS SOUGHT IN THE UNIVERSE

Man's deep-rooted dependence on the universe emerges clearly from a study of the life of his body and his soul.

To compose a complete history of man's body, we should have to go back to the time when its components were as yet buried in the waters of the original sources and in the minerals of geological strata. We should have to begin with primeval chaos, just as, to compile the sacred history of the God-man, the divine Author began His narrative with the creation of heaven and earth. To give an adequate description of man's body, we have to describe the kingdom of animal organisms. Man lives like them, and indeed cannot live without them. For he is unable to assimilate many of the elements of inorganic nature, which must first be adapted and transformed by other living beings.

Related to the whole universe through his animal life and the inorganic elements of his body, man is also related to that universe through his soul. The human intellect, wholly spiritual though it is, is not without affinity to the material universe. The human soul is the form of the body; and when it exercises the intellect in the act of knowledge, the soul is the form of the body as knowing, that is, it is the form of sensations and imaginations.

The soul, which during the present life does not exist without the body, does not know without the body; and the body, which requires the universe for its existence, is actuated in its organic apprehensions by the vibrations and influences of the universe. In order that the soul may know, even that it may know itself, this whole mechanism has to go into action. The soul's thought is, in a very real sense, the thought of the universe, the thought that emanates from crags and from clouds, from biochemistry and from geology, but that does not take form except in the unique part of the universe which is man. Is it not a scholastic principle that the concept is the joint product of sense and intellect?

Thus man does not deal with the universe as with a stranger, but as with himself, with an aspect of himself. He seeks himself there, and there he finds himself.

[2] St. Thomas, *In II Sent.*, d. 1, q. 2, a. 3; cf. also ad 3.

This is first manifested, as we indicated before, by eating and assimilating, and also by sensations. It is next manifested by man's love of nature. That love of nature is not merely a pastime. Imperious as love always is, it demands a detached soul, a soul ready to forget itself and its cares and its definite ideas, so as to let itself be carried away by the beauty of things. Christian detachment is the best preparation for this. Let a man but approach nature preoccupied with the idea of gain or exploitation, and the charm will never reach him.

We must forget ourselves and allow ourselves to be swayed. And the marvel is, that in thus giving ourselves we find ourselves. Love of nature is not drowsy passiveness or curtailment of personality, it is development and realization. The statement has been made, and is deeply true, that it expands the soul to the proportions of the universe for which it arouses love. This is but an application of the proverb, "Tell me with whom you associate, and I will tell you what you are."

Science discloses the same relationship between man and the universe. Scientific labor consists in translating phenomena into terms which man derives from himself, as though they had no separate existence in themselves. So true is this that we see them readily embodied in a category of thought or an equation as in their proper domain. They exist as though they were potential thought and nourishment of thought, as though they had something human in them and were waiting to be taken up by man. And man, by advancing toward them, advances toward the reconquest of himself.

How explain the impassioned interest which throughout the ages and the centuries, has led men to devote their lives to science, unless we admit that science in its own way answers the engrossing question: What is man? Indeed, are not the world's phenomena the explanation and commentary of the body's phenomena, and is not the body the material aspect of man, and that which the soul informs? [8]

This is why science arouses in the soul all the love it has for itself.

[8] "Since intellectual being is superior to sentient being, just as intellect is superior to sense, and since lower beings imitate higher beings as best they may, just as bodies subject to generation and corruption imitate in some fashion the circulatory motion of heavenly bodies, it follows that sensible beings resemble, in their own way, intellectual beings. Thus from the resemblance of sense to intellect we can mount to some knowledge of intellectual beings." St. Thomas, *Compendium of Theology*, p. 74 (Part I, chap. 80).

To gain knowledge of its own immanence and of its interior nature as a spirit, the soul undoubtedly does well to speculate on being as being and on the existence that must characterize spirit. But the soul must also, although to a lesser degree, perceive the immanence in animal life, for it is essentially related to that immanence.

Lastly, to render full account of his moral attitude, man has need of the universe. For his moral attitude is that of a rational animal, of a being made by God to live in a universe governed by laws, and to live his bodily life in conformity with these laws. The soul is the expression of the body in the spiritual domain. During the period of union with the body, it is designed to exercise its will in accord with the laws of the body. God has placed it in the midst of matter to perceive the moral significance of material phenomena, and thus to assimilate the universe into the spirit.

Therefore man must come to love and will these laws of the world which are also his own laws. He must enact them in some fashion even when they cause him suffering; and this, not with Stoic stiffness but with fraternal tenderness and ontological sympathy. Thus he will discharge one of his noblest functions: that of transforming the entire material order into the life of the spirit and into moral activity, and of making, along with the whole human race, an immense act of love of the good and of God.

Thus the universe provides man with an occasion of exercising his chief moral acts: acts of patience, of serenity, of courage. The illnesses and discomforts of age are his great educators; and his supreme human act, that by which he releases his hold on his own being, the act of dying by accepting death, is likewise owing to the universe and its laws to which he is subject. Accordingly man is cosmic even in his morality. He advances toward the good in his human fashion, in the rhythm of events.

C. THE UNITY OF THE UNIVERSE IN MAN
EXPRESSED IN TERMS OF MATTER AND FORM

We should understand clearly that the human form may be viewed in two different ways: one is purely ideal and impossible of realization, the other is real but less elevated.

In the ideal conception, the human form takes its place in the category of subsistent forms, although as the very last among them. If it were meant to exist without any relation to matter, in the way higher subsistent forms exist, it would be resplendent in its complete humanity. In its unity it would command all the resources needed to explain man fully and to make him live intensely, and would possess everything to which man is intrinsically relative. In its perfect unity, moreover, it would be equivalent, if not superior, to all the perfections actually represented by the multitude of forms in the universe. But the human form does not exist in this way. It has to inform matter, and therefore it is restricted in the way material forms are restricted. Such restriction is assuredly not absolute, for the soul is a spiritual form; yet it is real, just as this form's union with matter is real.

A notable difference is apparent between this realization and the ideal existence referred to; and this difference lies in the form. The superiority of a form existing in the first way is brought out by a consideration of the various material forms in the universe. Although material forms are essentially not the human form, since the latter is realized in real man, they represent the vast riches of human meaning that would constitute the riches of the pure form of man, the additional, complementary perfections, the aspects of animality, life, structure, and material qualities necessary to express adequately what a rational animal is. All of this would be required to enable the rational animal to exist fully, but cannot be verified in the concrete existence of this rational animal, for matter imposes its limitations. Therefore such additional perfections will exist alongside of man and with man, in an immense aggregate constituting the human universe.

This line of reasoning is not intended to suggest the multiplying of individuals within the same form; we are merely considering the multiplication of forms necessary to express, so far as this is possible for material forms, what a spiritual form is, so that what one of them cannot achieve may somehow be compensated by many of them.

We saw earlier how the universe is intrinsically human and man is intrinsically cosmic, and also how the world may be sought in man and man in the world. We now draw the conclusion. If man is all this in the universe and if the universe is all this in man, we begin to perceive what the God-man will be in the entire universe. When God, in the phrase of St. Irenaeus, recapitulated His ancient creation in the God-man, this was, by the very nature of the Incarnation and not by some accessory manifestation of power, the supreme cosmic event. At this point we merely call attention to the fact, to indicate that the anthropological reflections dominating this chapter have a Christological bearing.

II. The Realization of All Mankind in Every Man

> "As the various members of the body are parts of one human person, so all men are parts and in a way members of human nature. Wherefore Porphyrius says that, by sharing in the species, many men are one man."
>
> St. Thomas, *In Rom.*, cap. 5, lect. 3

From the preceding pages we gather that the whole universe is like a pyramid whose sides lead up toward a summit, which is man. The striking feature in this matter is that the pyramid is truncated. It does not end in a sharp point. No single and complete man exists; only men exist. In place of unity, we find plurality occupying the summit.

Nevertheless the lines of a truncated pyramid continue to draw toward the lacking pinnacle and converge above the material mass to trace out the ideal profile. The same is true of the universe. Complete man, humanity as such, may not be found anywhere in matter; yet everything points in that direction. Although humanity itself has no concrete existence, it has a certain existence that is real in its own way. This is the existence we propose to discuss at greater length in the present chapter.

We have already investigated the unity of the universe, and we came to the conclusion that this unity is man. We now go on to inquire into the unity of man himself. And the first thing to note is the great multiplicity in mankind. Mankind is multiple beyond all other species, for each individual is a whole, a truly original whole in virtue of his spiritual soul, which causes men to differ from one another in the manner of wholes, with a difference that in a sense is total. Accordingly mankind is grievously multiple. The fact is incontestable, and we would no more think of denying it than we denied the multiplicity of things or concepts in the preceding chapter.

What we wish to look for, in spite of this, is the unity that may be underlying the multiplicity: a unity which would not destroy this multiplicity, for that is impossible, but would be its product and would bring out its coherence and self-consistency; in a word, a unity that would make it somehow one. Hence we shall continue the task we have begun, and shall consider the relations man has, no longer with the universe, but with other men.

A. EVERY MAN FOR MANKIND AND MANKIND FOR EVERY MAN

The unity of the human species is manifested in the past and in the present. In the past: starting from the endless variety of types and individual characteristics, the farther we go back into mankind's past, the closer we draw to the unity of origin. For mankind has a single common father, and successive generations send forth ever lengthening lines that, without ever breaking, join men together in an evident relationship.

Thus we have heredity of flesh and blood, but also psychological heredity. Each man, as he resembles his ancestors in physical features, also resembles them in spiritual features, with the exception of some traits that may be modified by his liberty; the visage is the mirror of the soul. If, then, provided we go back far enough, these ancestors are the same for all, it follows that at the bottom of their hearts all will have the same basic dispositions, and, in their mental life, the same reactions, except for slight variations. Even these, produced as they are by a liberty that is common to all on the occasion of circumstances which are often identical for all, will not lack resemblances.

Also at the present time men are one. Like material things that are formed and conditioned by one another, men, too, are in large part molded and influenced by one another. In every age and environment there is a sort of median type of humanity, an agglomeration of aspirations, prejudices, and dispositions that are more or less expressed and diffused on all sides and that work their way into a man at every turn, like the air he breathes. Each man, by a shifting interchange of actions put forth and influences transmitted, helps to form this type, but each is also being continually formed by it. In this way the entire race imposes itself on each person and almost supplants him in the depths of his individual characteristics.

A particularly significant indication of this close community is language. In any given culture, language is like an act of century-old thought that has become crystallized and that now, rich with all the spiritual acquisitions permanently attached to its structure, powerfully intervenes in all the intellectual activity of the group. And language does not only appear on the lips but manifests itself in the mind at the very origin of the intellectual act, to accompany and sustain it, and not merely to give it subsequent expression. Thus language is not a burden that weighs down the intellect, but a steed that carries it farther and faster than it could go alone. Accordingly language penetrates to the very center of personal consciousness.

Furthermore, speech is essentially an orientation toward others, a communication with others. It joins a man to other men in the interior of his intellectual life. A man is really not alone even when he gives himself to solitary reflection; others are there, not at his side, but in him. Whether he wishes it to be so or not, he reflects in function of them all, and hence in union with them all. We pointed out above that the human act of thinking is a cosmic activity, because the energies of the whole universe contribute to its separate existence and sustenance, at the same time that they form a necessary part of its content. We must now add that the human act of thinking is a universally human act, for in the individual man the instrument that shapes it and enables it to issue forth has been forged by all mankind.

Thus a man is joined to the whole race in what concerns the past and the present. The same is true as regards the future. Each individual has a far-reaching, multiple, indefinable influence on the men of the future, for each individual by all his words and deeds swells the current that transfers to future generations the immense heritage of the past. God alone can follow the events that may succeed one another before the eddies cast up to the surface what a man may have casually dropped into deep waters. A word uttered today may pass without notable effect; but when it is carried farther by intermediaries who do not reflect on it, it may end up by touching some person at a great distance and cause repercussions like bombs which, after lying buried for years in a field, are one day detonated by some incautious prodder. Mankind of today shapes the human race of tomorrow, and thereby the race of the remote future. And mankind of today, by a jumble of intercrossing influences, is shaped in part by every man, just as every man, except for the play of the will's freedom, is shaped by the whole race. And every man of today, no less than the whole of mankind today, is molded by mankind of the past—always, of course, making due allowance for free will.

Thus the race lives like a single man. And every man, in solidarity with all the rest by the heredity that fashions him, by the relations that mold him, and by the influences that bear on him, possesses all men.

Who, then, can describe all that a man is? Even material organisms are unfathomable mysteries. No one, whatever may be his convictions about the matter, has ever seen an acorn. We have of course seen the outer contours, a small, round-shaped object of no value; but that is not the acorn. The real acorn is a potency and a fertile principle of an oak tree, and through it of other oaks and yet others without end; it is a far-off shimmer of forests stretching to the horizon. It is all this within, in a secret interior that no microscope or microtome can discover, in the absolute inner heart of life.

So also with man. Inside, in what really makes the man, he is immensely, infinitely man. He is the whole of mankind in germ; but all this is within him, where no eye can penetrate. And thus no one has ever seen man.

B. ALL MANKIND IN EVERY MAN: BY IMAGINATION AND MEMORY

Every man, enclosed though he is within himself, is open to the action of others; they invade him without any exertion on their part, and without any possibility of repelling them on his part. The humanity present in each man makes him pregnable for all the others in whom humanity is found. If every man is thus a refuge to which all men have access, he must have some immense capacity within him to receive them. This capacity will be studied in the following pages.

It makes its appearance, first, in the memory and the imagination in a way that is sentient and even animal; for its analogue—and it is no more than an analogue—can be discerned in animals to a striking degree. Like other animals, the rational animal, placed in the midst of the universe and surrounded by his kind, is a sort of mirror capable of reflecting everything. This appears in the work of the imagination which can call forth a representation of the limitless wastes of the universe and people them. This operation is more than a registering of things seen; it is a true construction.

The creative faculty can do more than this, and acts much more frequently, but so gently and naturally that even when our attention is called to its processes we do not notice that it is at work. Indeed, it is continually in operation whenever we exercise our power of sight, not only when we look at outlines but whenever we look at anything. Whatever we may be regarding, the only element at our disposal for seeing the object we are looking at, is a tiny sketch. In the depths of the dark chamber we call the eye, bright rays have painted a miniature hardly a few square centimeters in size, smaller than a walnut shell, a trifle in comparison with the outlines of the thing before us. Nothing more is needed; from this slight image, without difficulty, without even noticing that anything is going on, we have created a limitless scene, perhaps of interminable series of forests and distances that lose themselves in the remote haze.

We may well pause here a moment and endeavor to ascertain and experience this interior immensity. Do not object that these are but dreams: nothing is more real than the power to dream. This power reveals the measure of the person in whom it resides, just as the quality of ordinary musing marks the value of the soul engaging in such a practice. And what a measure it is! The whole of space which is literally without measure is present in this power. And it is truly present, for it is there not as one of the unreal things called forth in a dream, but as the condition of all such calling forth and dreaming, and even of all vision, as we have pointed out. To imagine anything at all, we must imagine it in a place. Therefore space has all the reality of this power.

Space is not, surely, a mere form of sensibility and a wholly subjective entity, as Kant held. Everything in sensation, like everything in its nature, manifests it as something external and empirical. On the other hand it is not, as positivist or materialist ideologies so easily fancy, a completely external reality which the thinking subject does not comprise within himself at all. In that case, how would a person truly grasp and know external objects, and what would become of the senses and knowledge, and in particular what would become of the knowledge of space itself?

What are the properties of the immensity of the imagination? It cannot be formal or partially real or unreal; it must be virtual. The faculty itself cannot become extended; but it can provide indefinite extension for the objects of knowledge and, under the present or past stimulation of the outer world, can engender in itself the sensation of extension. Therefore it is not space, but rather a power bearing on space, a superiority with reference to space. Accordingly it is not in space, but space is in it, not formally, we repeat, but virtually, that is to say, eminently, *eminenter*.

By gaining full possession of himself, or at least by beginning to do so, man is able to comprise within himself everything that is not self-contained. In the presence of extended objects that are purely external to him, man can assert that his own interior is far greater than they, although in a different way. This assertion is made with regard to the universe, but also with regard to mankind. And this is what we have mainly to consider here. When a man exercises his imagination, he may summon up before him all other men and even himself, so far as he is extended, and he is able to comprise them all within himself. Men are extended in their material nature, and matter is the reason why they are multiple and separated from one another. Thus their material multiplicity, without being suppressed, begins to be surpassed; its inaccessibility is in some way undermined at its base, and the unity of form begins to acquire some mastery over the multiplicity of matter.

Through his imagination, therefore, every man becomes an adequate receptacle and, in a sense, a center of reunion for all mankind, just as every man may be regarded as a culminating point and a center of diffusion relative to all the generations of mankind.[4] Although man is an individual, this phase of his interior life is a public thing: here he comes into contact with others, while remaining enclosed within himself. And this is precisely the point: man is not enclosed within himself except by embracing the very same immensity of the universe which all the others comprise within themselves.

As is evident, men are found living together in outward space. To be convinced of this, we need do no more than follow them in their conversations and discussions on the subject of their affairs. But they are also found together in interior space. This is seen to be the case whenever a number of them gather to listen to an account of the same events. As the discourse unfolds, each thinks of the same things, each one imagines the room he is in and, surrounding it, the house and the streets, and the garden with its vistas. In each of them almost the same universe is conjured up, with the same objects occupying the same places. Assuredly, by reason of the imaginations which call all this forth and the psychologies to which the imaginations are joined, the inner visions are distinct to the point of being

[4] Cf. p. 106.

incommunicable. But how can we conceive that the objects evoked remain outside one another? By what distinct immensities would they be separated?

Thus the outer contact, without ceasing to be what it is, becomes an inner contact, and the external, material environment, which already brought about a certain union, accomodates itself to an internal, psychological environment, which further promotes unification.

Indeed, one of the characteristic activities of life is the construction of an internal environment for itself. This characteristic is encountered even on the lower levels of life. What physiological life achieves in a physiological way, psychological life achieves in a psychological way. It takes its environment into itself, becoming in a sense the whole of which it is a part, with the aim of gaining possession of its totality and of becoming an absolute totality. Space, for men, is the medium in which relations are entered into and alliances and associations are formed; everything finds room in it. And life absorbs this space, at the same time drawing into itself the medium of junctions and unions. The communication which had been external, and which by its nature must remain external, becomes internal by reason of the place where it is made and the faculty that effects it.

In this way the unity of mankind begins to be revealed within mankind. But this is only a beginning. For there is something else in man besides memory and imagination; there is intelligence. And intelligence meets with extraordinary success when it undertakes to produce the unity that unifies multiplicity without destroying it.

C. ALL MANKIND IN EVERY MAN: BY INTELLIGENCE

The unity of mankind and of the human universe is chiefly manifested in human intelligence. Because of its spiritual nature, the intellect is the culmination of being in the world of man, and also, in consequence, the point of maximum unity. This is the unity we wish to consider in the present section.

In the order of intellectual beings, man is the least perfect found in God's creation. His intellectual soul forms a single nature with the opposite of intellect, that is, with matter, so that man is rational only in the manner of an animal; he is a rational animal. Nevertheless he has an intellect, and in it he must possess, at least imperfectly, what

is essential to intelligence. But it is essential to intelligence to be
capable of expressing the very being of the objects it knows, and
therefore to have an ontological immensity of an absolute order.
Such an immensity enables the human individual, in his own way, to
be the unity of mankind far more perfectly than immensity in the
spatial order can make him.

Demonstration of the truth that intelligence is essentially a faculty
that has to do with being, need not detain us long. The truth is
evident, and the preceding pages have thrown light on it. Here we
may content ourselves with repeating that we have to attribute to
the intellect all or nothing: either it knows being as being, as least
imperfectly, or it does not know anything of value.

The fact is that things are received into the human intellect, although, of course, in the special way that befits the human intellect.
Knowledge, as it exists in man, is only in the judgment. But judgment
is an affirmation of existence, and indeed is nothing else. Kant's error
consisted precisely in seeing in the judgment nothing but a simple
connection, a simple power of synthesis. In reality, the judgment is
the taking of an absolute position, it is an unconditional affirmation.

The inherent energy of this affirmation carries it far. We need
only to examine it closely to perceive that it equates existence and
affirmability, if we may use the expression. It gives assurance that a
sensible object is affirmable because it is a being, not that a being is
affirmable because it is sensible. It goes on to assert, without saying
so expressly, that a purely contingent being is only contingently
affirmable, and that the absolute being, God, and He alone, is absolutely affirmable.

Operari sequitur esse, activity is determined by a being's nature.
Man's affirmation of being must correspond to the way he possesses
being. Man is a being that is far from simple; his manner of affirming
will be no more simple. He is a being that is doubly composite, for
he is composed of matter and form and of potency and act. His
mode of affirmation will also be doubly composite: it is composed
of an affirmation of form and an affirmation of existence. Man is this
particular being because he is a part of the universe, and a part that
is what it is by reason of a special form that is a human form. His
affirmation of being is likewise what it is because it is an affirmation
of a part of the universe and of a form, the form suitable for this
part; or, to combine the two, we may say that it is what it is by being

the affirmation of a part of the universe, of a thing, through the realization of a form or an idea.

This is exactly what the judgment is. The thing, the part of the universe, is represented by the subject; the form, the idea, is represented by the predicate; and the double affirmation, that is, the affirmation of the idea with reference to the object and of existence with reference to the synthesis of the two, is expressed by the copula.

We may add that the affirmation itself, which is the form and, as it were, the soul of the judgment, has its own act. It does not stop with uniting subject and predicate; it reflects on the union and knows it: *veritas est in iudicio tamquam cognita in cognoscente.* It goes even farther: as epistemology and metaphysics show, it goes so far under its own impulse as to imply, although not to reach, Him who is absolutely affirmable, as the necessary basis for every solid position and every definitive intelligibility. This is precisely the role the human form, which is the soul, plays in man. The soul is not limited to informing the body; it grasps and knows itself; and in this knowledge it possesses in germ a yearning toward Him who is the first being and the last end, God.

In affirmations of existence, therefore, the judgment presents the structure that is proper for man as an intelligent being, and human intellectual knowledge is a knowledge of being as being. Hence we should be completely mistaken if we were to imagine that intelligence is a sort of superior sensibility that would restate in ethereal, abstract terms, almost devoid of content, what the senses report about colors and sounds. This is what happens when we discern in knowledge no more than a collection of intellectual images and representative ideas. To understand what intellectual knowledge really is, we have to admit that the object known in knowledge and the object known in itself are identical and not merely similar. Otherwise knowledge is impossible.

The act of knowing establishes a relationship of identity between the world as known and the world as it exists in reality. Judgment is an act that is in tendency toward a goal. It never acquires full possession of the universe by its thought, which is its essence. Or, to put it in another way, this act, by which the universe becomes conscious of itself in that part of it which is man, never attains its objective; neither the universe nor man ever reaches the complete perfection that is possible. Consequently the judgment is an advance and a tendency toward a conquest of matter by spirit rather than a definite annexation. In this sense it is in tendency; the identity it affirms is doubtless realized, but only in the striving toward more adequate realization. From this point of view it is an *identitas intentionalis*, a "certain kind" of identity: an identity between two things which, being in process of production, are in process of becoming identical, and which, tending toward themselves, are still tending toward their unity.

Complete man, cosmic and fully human man, is fashioned gradually. The same is true of his knowledge and of the identity between the object known and the idea formed of it, which is the essential element in knowledge. Therefore the identity is likewise fashioned and tends toward itself; it is an *identitas intentionalis*.

We ought to add that the cognitive operation which is the judgment involves, as man himself does, an implicit tendency toward transcendent and infinite being, and that in the infinite Being alone the being of all things is contained supereminently and in supereminent unity. This may further serve to explain the *identitas intentionalis* that must exist between the object known and knowledge.[5]

Operari sequitur esse. As the faculty of knowing being, the intellect is a faculty of knowing every being, but especially the human being, since it is a human faculty. This is the marvel and the mystery: the intellect is a universal capacity with reference to everything and the totality of everything. With full competence and in actual potency with reference to the human universe, and remotely but with intrinsic possibility with reference to all being, it is by its very nature capable of containing in itself and of comprehending absolutely everything that exists. For what are all things but beings? Such interior possession of what belongs to others is possible for man, not only as regards material things, but as regards other men. Does man not devote most of his thoughts to men, and can he know them otherwise than as beings?

It follows from this that all men are virtually present in every man. Indeed, they are actually present, although in implicit fashion; for knowledge, being universal, necessarily implies a reference to the universality of men. They are present in an imperfect way, assuredly, just as the soul has its act in an imperfect way. But the perpetual

[5] On judgment and its dynamism, see J. Maréchal, S.J., *Le point de départ de la métaphysique*, especially Vol. V.

marvel and the paradox is this: they are present truly and in their very being. Each man receives what is most intimate in others into what is most intimate in himself, and in the consciousness of each the whole of humanity is affirmed.

Herein appears man's greatness. The spectacle of the immensities of his imagination and his memory aroused wonder; what astonishment must be caused by the sight of the limitless and overwhelming vastnesses present in his mind? Aware of man's small place in the domain of knowledge, and taking into account the fact that his mind can grasp or discard at its pleasure, we realize that man has no adequate notion, no well-defined, sharply pointed concept, for expressing himself to himself, or for expressing other men in their spiritual nature, or for expressing the angels of God. Things that are no more than parts of a whole, that is, material things, may be sufficiently represented by ideas that are but parts of knowledge. But things that are wholes are not known except by a knowledge that is whole and that engages the whole knower. Such is man so far as he is spiritual: no idea expresses him; it is rather he, the source of all his ideas, who is for himself the expression of himself. He is a self, and his way of appearing to himself is to act as a self, to utter and think a self. This is an absolute knowledge which is not dependent on any external sign, and which is presented as obvious in itself, or at least, when man is in question, as obvious to him who thinks and knows.

Attention must be drawn to these absolute, interior characteristics: in order to express himself, each man affirms an absolute unity deeply within himself whenever he affirms being. In the case of external manifestations and concepts, this unity is gauged by the limited unities of the objects known and the concepts attributed to them. But in the interior of life it shows itself to be unlimited and immensely human, and it confers on each man an ontological capacity for the whole of humanity. This complete humanity, however, is still on the way toward self-discovery, for man, and hence humanity in him, is still being formed here below, and is still in process of being born.

The identity between the object known and the knowledge which the knowing subject has of it is in tendency toward itself: it seeks itself. It is like a being that is coming to birth; the unity of the universe and of humanity begins in man and in the cognitive act that expresses man, the judgment. As though it were a real being, it begins to be a living form, but one in the travail of its birth. And in fact it has something in common with birth. This is what we shall investigate in the next section.

D. ALL MANKIND IN EVERY MAN: THE HUMAN FORM AND ITS ACT

We begin with a principle that may seem banal; but it has enormous consequences. All men have the same form in the abstract. In itself, this form is transcendent with regard to its concrete realizations. Therefore the latter must be endlessly multiplied in order to convey as well as possible, although always inadequately, the fullness of humanity that is in the form. The conclusion necessarily flowing from this is that the multiplicity of men is at bottom a unity, and that all men are one through their form.

Mankind possesses this unity in the way it possesses existence. Since it exists only in individuals that are many and distinct from one another, it can be one only in them. Need we point out that the unity of mankind cannot have separate existence any more than humanity as such can? Yet humanity, although it exists only in individuals, has a real existence, and this existence is found in men. In truth, we have but to give ear to what is affirmed within men to hear the whole of humanity affirming itself within them.

For the substantial form, which among animals is wholly submerged in the matter it informs, retains among men enough of its individuality to grasp and know itself. Every one of them can say: "I am a man." And that implies all the depths of inner, hidden, conscious life. Since it is the individual who speaks and lives among his kind, the same word that defines him and sets him apart, likewise, in what regards essentials, defines all the others.

"I am a man": this is a sort of brief summary of anthropology. It states that there is in each man a formal unity of humanity, that is, a unity in the form and through the form. Such a unity is evidently of a high order, since the form is the principle of all the determinations of a being. It is deep-seated, active, and alive, because the form in a human being puts forth the most profound vital actions, those of knowing and willing. Lastly, as we shall see, it is most real, for, since it resides in the form, it can be real with all the reality of that form.

When we say that the human form subsists only in individuals, we must avoid the idea that this form has no proper subsistence or act of its own. Other forms have no act of their own and are merely principles by which matter is informed; but the human form, which is able to grasp itself even while it is rooted in matter, has an operation of its own, an operation it does not exercise exclusively through matter and in matter, an operation that is wholly simple and spiritual, that of saying "I," and of knowing and willing itself. This operation is possible only if the form producing it has its own existence which, though not separate, is nevertheless proper and distinct; it is possible only if the form has its own act.

These considerations establish the universally human character of the soul. Personality is again shown to be related to universality. For, if the form has its own act and therefore its own spirituality and personality, it must have them in its own way, and hence the form in the individual man must be the complete human form, that is, all men and the whole human universe.

Undoubtedly this form possesses its act imperfectly. The universality pertaining to it exists only in a real individuality, and this universality does not attain its full realization during the present life. But one of the principles of Thomist philosophy is that an act is not limited by itself: *actus in quo genere est irreceptus, in eo est illimitatus.* Therefore, if it is found to be limited, the limitation can come only from outside, from something that is not itself. In man, the form is the soul. The latter is both received in matter and unreceived. It is received in the sense that along with matter it constitutes a single being that is man; it is unreceived in the sense that its activity extends to operations that are plainly immaterial, such as the act of saying "I." Consequently this form must be at once unlimited and limited: unlimited, so far as it is not received in matter; limited, so far as it is received.

If we reflect on all this and on what human nature is, we must come to the conclusion that the human form is the reason why the individual in whom it is found is intrinsically one, interior to himself, and capable of bending back on himself, or in other words, is conscious and personal; and furthermore, that this individual is intrinsically united to all other individuals and possesses them all within himself through that union and through the interior knowledge and love the union makes possible. In accordance with the principle, *operari sequitur esse,* a being that is only itself and is absolutely nothing but itself, cannot know anything else than itself. To be able to know and will others, one must be these others to a certain degree: to the precise degree in which they are truly to be known and willed. This is the only way of accounting for such knowledge, and it comes back to the universality we have been speaking of.

And it is not only other individuals that the form thus contains: as we have pointed out, mankind is not complete unless it embraces the universe. In order that the human form may be free from limitation, it must, in the words of the ancient phrase, be *aliquo modo omnia;* in a sense it must become the whole human universe, and must possess and express that universe as it actually exists.

This is the way the soul appears to itself; and a truth of common sense, which is at the same time one of the great scholastic theses, is that man does not know himself unless he knows the universe of man and humanity. This explains the interest man takes in other men and in material phenomena. They truly concern him; they make up his completeness, not only so far as he is body and hence a part of the universe, but also so far as he is form which has its own act and which, being on that score unlimited, is itself only by including all that belongs to it.

The universality thus found in every man is not at all opposed to the distinction among men. On the contrary, it consecrates that distinction. But it does so by incorporating the distinction into a larger unity. For the universality arises from the fact that the form has its act. But the fact that the form has its act is precisely what makes it conscious and personal, and hence radically distinct from all others.

Therefore human forms are distinct from one another both by the matter they actuate and by the act each of them has in relation to this matter. Two men differ from each other because they are this man and that man, but also because each of them has his own, strictly personal consciousness. Each of the two will lose his matter; and who can say whether the matter of one of them will not some day come to be a part of the matter of the other? But consciousness is definitively the constitutive and incommunicable property of each of them: it is eternally an individual thing.

If we take man's spiritual soul into account, we cannot say simply and purely that he is less than the whole of humanity. In his own way he has all humanity within him. Therefore he cannot from every point of view be subordinated to humanity. He is high enough in the scale of being to have rights and duties that cannot give way before the whole human race taken together.

If this principle is translated into certain formulas, it can appear quite revolutionary. It authorizes all forms of pride and egoism, and we may not see how we can overcome them. Who, then, will be able to establish the reign of order? For order requires the adjustment of individual and collective interests, and neither of the two ought to be sacrificed to the other. The reply is that order need not be established, for it is already established by the very principle that seemed revolutionary and that turns out to be, on the contrary, the basis of morality and of its harmonious unity. When we proclaim that the individual is an end in himself and not a simple means, even in relation to the whole of mankind, we have but to recall that the individual has consciousness and freedom, and that consequently he is the subject of morality. Furthermore, in stressing the sacred character of the person, order emphasizes the sacred character of humanity which is made up of persons. Humanity is sufficiently strong and perfect to have its own act in the individuals in whom it is realized and whom it thereby invests with the character of persons.

To conclude, we may say that absolute human perfection, if by a miracle it were to become possible, so that man would be humanly perfect, would require a man to be deeply and completely himself, capable of expressing himself entirely by being true to his nature. Thus it would require that he should be interior to every man and that every man should be interior to him, by the very plenitude each would possess, and not in virtue of any advantage each would receive from their contact. Hence it would require that a man, in living his own full interior life, should be able to share in all human life, to experience all human suffering, and to think all human thought. It would further require that this human universality should not in any way destroy man's inwardness, but should find complete expression by deeply participating in it without at the same time violating it by undergoing disintegration. Lastly, such perfection would require that this plenitude should not encroach on the minor plenitudes of other men, but that on the contrary it should be full of respect and tenderness for them, so as to welcome them graciously and refrain from anything that might injure what a man ought to possess.

Human nature has no means of realizing this absolute unity and transcendent universality. But we may say that, so far as our reflections on human nature and its activity give us some knowledge of it, there is nothing in it to rule out the possibility of such perfections. How these marvels may be realized and how we may show that they are capable of going together, is another question. But that they represent man's absolute and superhuman perfection, cannot be called in question. The moment we recognize that man has a soul, that is, that the human form really existing in an individual has its own act and hence the act proper to the human form, we have no difficulty in perceiving that, to be man in a perfect way, a man must be what he is immensely and universally, and this merely by being himself.

III. Unity of Mankind in the Future

"It hath not yet appeared what we shall be."
I John 3:2

Man fails to recognize that all humanity is in him, because he is not yet a man but is only becoming one. Adults will perhaps feel astonishment when they are told this. They readily admit that children are not yet men but are on the way to manhood. But the assertion that they themselves, magistrates, industrialists, and property owners are not men, strikes them as whimsical. "What in the world is a man," such a one would say, "if I am not a man?"

Yet nothing is more true. Life on earth is a time of formation for mankind; therefore mankind is not yet formed. It is the time during which humanity must assert itself and win its spiritual plenitude in the conquest of flesh and matter. Man does not yet enjoy the full realization of his spirit. The present time is the time of his ascent toward his end; therefore he has not yet attained his definitive growth.

We wish to show that the greatness toward which mankind is aspiring is humanity, man such as no one has ever imagined him: man as completely man. We shall thus be dealing with a natural eschatology that will put the finishing touch to the anthropological notions discussed in these pages. We call this a natural eschatology, because it envisages man from the point of view of a purely natural finality which does not exist and is only possible, but which will aid toward an understanding of supernatural finality.

A. MAN AS AN END FOR MAN

Of course God alone is man's end. As He is the first cause of everything, so He is the end beyond which there is no end. But God is the last end of each being conformably to the nature of each being, and therefore He is the last end of man conformably to the nature of man. In the natural order He remains strictly inaccessible in Himself, and the possession of Him that creatures can acquire is not distinct from the possession they can have of their own being and its activities.

Our familiarity with the supernatural in the order of grace may be an occasion of error for us and may lead us to suppose that in a natural order God would be possessed in almost the same way. That is impossible. The possession of God as He is in Himself is absolutely beyond the capacities of simple human nature. A being's good is determined by its nature; an excessively great good would leave us indifferent or would crush us. If God were to give Himself to man without preparing him and elevating him supernaturally, He would demolish him. Such a union with divinity is a suitable end for those who have been divinized. For all others, with their merely natural capacities for perfection and happiness, it is too heady a wine. The only possession of God they can bear and rejoice in, is that which is mitigated and adapted to the measure of their being: a possession in humanity and through humanity.

Deus est omnis boni bonum.[6] This is the classical formula for expressing the truth that God is the good of every good. When a being possesses its proper good, it possesses God, because God is the goodness of that good. Evidently, as the ultimate in a being is its relation to God, the ultimate in its action will be this same relation, especially in those actions which have being as being for their object, such as the action of knowing and willing. Among all human actions, therefore, knowledge and love of God are supreme; they have a character of finality, and will have it in a maximum degree when man attains his maximum development, that is, when he arrives at his goal, his end.

But *operari sequitur esse.* Such a character is found in action because it is found in being. The perfection achieved by attainment

---

[6] St. Augustine, *De Trinitate*, VIII, 3 (*PL*, XLII, 949). St. Thomas, *Contra Gent.*, I, 40; *Summa*, Ia, q. 6, a. 4; *De veritate*, q. 21, a. 4.

of the end is ontological before it is operative. In the natural order this perfection, with all its components and the internal logic binding them together, is purely human. God remains completely transcendent in regard to it, and He is as inaccessible for fully developed man as for man in formation.

If, therefore, by end we mean the supreme perfection that can be reached (*finis quo*, not *finis qui*), the summit of being which a man can acquire by his own forces and which is truly his, we have to speak, not of God, but of man; understanding, of course, that man is an end only by participation and by analogy with God. In this sense man, as he is on the way toward realization of himself, is also his own end. He is even his last end, for his supreme realization is his supreme assimilation of being and hence his union with God. He is his end by participation in God and analogy with God. In declaring that he is his own end, man does not deny that God is his end, but explains how God is his end. Man will be a sort of recompense for himself, a recompense coming to him from God, just as his being and all his powers come from God.

This does not imply a system of extrinsic sanctions. The natural law and natural finality pertain to the essence of nature. The question is about being, of a man's being himself, conformed to the law which he is for himself, and of existing completely; for God, the cause of being as being, speaks to His creatures through their very being.

This is why freedom is given to man, that he himself may attain his end by attaining his full development. Freedom is the power a man has to achieve self-realization, to desire it, to make his being his own, so as fully to be through himself what he already is through God: *liberum est quod est causa sui.*[7] A free being is so faithful an image of God's creative power and, in some sense, of the divine aseity —*omne agens agit sibi simile*—that he is capable of freely causing himself to be within himself what he already necessarily is through God. In producing him, God makes him incomplete but gives him power to perfect himself; or rather, man is so complete a product

[7] This definition is often encountered in St. Thomas. But he frequently applies it to liberty as opposed to slavery, to which, following in Aristotle's footsteps, he devotes considerable attention. Then *qui est causa sui* means: who exists for himself. Cf. *De veritate*, q.24, a.1; *Summa*, Ia, q.21, a.1 ad 3; *Contra Gent.*, I, 72. The saint also says that freedom is a dominion over one's act, especially in *Contra Gent.*, I, 88, and *Summa*, Ia IIae, prol.

that he has power to perfect himself. Such a being has his norm in himself, because he ought to perfect himself; he has his sanction in himself, because he himself is the prize at stake in the struggle; he has in him the means of realizing himself, liberty, because his sole task is to realize himself; lastly, and this is in question here, he has his end in himself, because he is, as it were, a goal to attain for himself. But he is an end unconditionally imposed on himself and his intellect, just as he is an obligatory norm, only because he is his own way of going to God and of gaining possession of the absolute good.

B. MANKIND AS AN END FOR MAN

This end is not only personal perfection, but is the perfection of union among all men and the most complete realization of mankind that is possible in the natural order.

Union with others is the condition of one's own perfection. For one's own perfection requires the possession of all human excellences. But the latter cannot coexist in a single individual; one person cannot at the same time have all degrees of virtue or all types of intelligence and will, any more than he can have white hair and black hair at the same time. The endless variety of goods can be possessed only through union, inasmuch as a man becomes one with others who have them; and the perfection will be greater in proportion to the closeness of the union.

The very substance of these other men is human; in leaving them outside himself, a man would renounce all opportunity of possessing the fullness of humanity. To exist fully, he must make the latter his own. He does not do this by taking it from them; by destroying their personality he would destroy the very perfection he desires to possess; no, he accomplishes his objective by becoming one with them.

The precepts of justice, of mutual love, and of sincerity, which enjoin us to treat others as we ourselves would like to be treated and to regard them as other selves, are precepts of union. We may even say that our duties toward ourselves are also directly duties toward others, since they are duties that impose respect for human dignity. And our duties toward God in the natural order are, in part, duties of collective worship and of full acceptance of duties toward others and toward ourselves, because they are imposed by God. Thus they are also duties toward others.

Therefore mankind ought to be recognized as an end for man, and actually is such an end. Human psychology attests this need of union with all, this aspiration toward the whole species, an aspiration which human nature places in every man. An indication of this is furnished by the tendency in every man to perpetuate mankind. This tendency affects what is most personal in man and is one of the main factors in his psychology, one of the great stimulants of his labors and of his moral formation; but it is also something that extends beyond the individual, something that pertains to all mankind. So obvious a truth does not require further emphasis.

A second indication is found in man's social nature, in the inclination man experiences, always and everywhere, to associate with other men and to form one social body with them. In every way, at every moment, an impulse rises in the race toward its own social good, just as in autumn a nostalgia for warm regions rises in migratory birds. This ambition is clearly too vast to be fully realized on earth. Accordingly mankind employs numberless expedients to approach what it cannot achieve by a single effort; this accounts for the partial unions whereby sections of mankind are formed into limited and imperfect groups. All such unions bear witness to the same tendency, the profound instinct that makes man a political animal, and that causes him to seek his own fullness of being in the totality and unity of mankind.

C. DESCRIPTION OF THIS UNITY: ITS NATURE

Let us next endeavor to gain some idea of the natural totality and unity which mankind is able to achieve. This is not an easy task. Even the individual man is not adequately represented in any sensation, phantasm, or concept; still less is all mankind. Yet the difficulty should not deter us from making an attempt. Abandonment of the attempt would be renouncement of self-knowledge and of man's end and full realization.

To understand the nature of this complete humanity, this unity and fullness of mankind, we must study it in the man who has reached his end. Since man reaches his end and arrives at his goal by way of death, we must turn our thoughts to death and what it means for man, if we would gain an idea of what humanity is. This investigation, we repeat, is undertaken on the merely possible supposition of a purely natural order.

At death the soul is separated from the body. But the separation is not absolutely complete, for the soul retains an essential relation to the body; otherwise it would not be a definite soul. This relation is the basis for the possibility of the body's resurrection, that is, for the possibility of a renewed existence for the same body.[8]

For the soul, death is the crisis of a second birth, not of annihilation. Its period of formation has come to a close, and now at length knowledge may be gained of what a soul is in its full realization. Union with the body had immersed the soul in a world of conflicts, rivalries, and divisions. This union, involving an endless multiplicity of parts and a throng of passions and diverging tendencies disruptive of the whole, was a burden on the soul within the man whose form it was. But all this falls away with the departing body, and the soul can at length enter into a more expansive life. It is no longer in the world of bodies and dissolutions, but is now in the world of the spirit, of the infinite, of unity.

The principle of limitation for the soul is matter. *Actus, in quantum est irreceptus, in tantum est illimitatus.* Therefore death, the breaking away from matter, is humanity's flight toward infinity. After its separation from the body, the soul asserts itself completely; it turns to itself and takes possession of itself. Man had sought himself; now at last he "is." [9] Now at last, in touch with his own humanity within himself, through the perfection of his personality, he is also in contact with all mankind. He encloses all men within himself, at least all those who are not excluded from this unity of mankind by their hatred and malice.

May we not say further that he touches and contains within himself the physical universe by possessing its center? If humanity is ontologically the ultimate unity here below, man gains possession of the unity of the world when he gains possession of the unity of humanity. Here on earth, he was only in process of becoming, and he had to win this cosmic greatness by accepting his part in the universe

---

[8] This enables us to understand that, if the soul is to attain all possible perfection, as is the case in the supernatural order, a resurrection of the body and a renewed heaven and earth are required.

[9] Yet we must note that, since man is a composite of soul and body, the separated soul is not a man. It remains a human entity, however, and even, as we are trying to show, a human entity that has acquired its ultimate natural perfection. This is the sense in which, in the present passage and in several others, we call it "man."

and the laws of the universe. These laws, like his own being, were partly external to him and were capable of opposing him. But now, perfected in his being, he is perfected in his cosmic greatness, not in the sense that he has power to act on natural laws from without and to produce exceptions, for then he would no longer be their unity, but in the sense that he is the interior principle of cohesion and union and perfect accord. And this accord is achieved through possession, comprehension, and superiority, not through subordination.

But there is something that is more certain and essential than the future possession of the world, and this is what chiefly interests us: the possession of humanity. In the life to come, man will at length know what it is to be a man, a "whole." Up to that moment, he has known nothing about such matters. He has scarcely caught a glimpse, in himself and in others, of anything beyond insignificant organisms. But from that time on, he will have a revelation of his human immensity and of other human immensities that are interior to themselves and to one another. On earth, as he was but a man in course of development, he had no more than a developing knowledge of man; and this knowledge, through reasoning and reflection, was in pursuit of an ever-receding idea. But then, of a sudden, he will find himself face to face with himself. The veil of matter will drop, and in his full union with himself he will perceive his full union with all.

In that life, therefore, he will reach culmination, achievement, and the ultimate Being, and hence beatitude. This is natural beatitude, consisting essentially in a relation to God and a union with God; for he who fully possesses his being, thereby possesses the bond with God of which he is capable by nature.

D. DESCRIPTION OF THIS UNITY: ITS OPERATIONS

What we have said of being, must be applied to activity. In the pages that follow we shall devote particular attention to knowledge, since a number of good questions suggest themselves on that subject, especially as regards the way it functions and its manner of knowing God.

1. **The way in which knowledge functions.** By separating the soul from the body, death will efface from knowledge all that pertains to sense. There will remain only the spiritual element of notions acquired and the intellectual actuation resulting from the exercise

of thought here below. This leaves little of positive and technical science; but what purpose can any longer be served by such science? The knowledge of self and of being is everything for true knowledge. What difference does it make that the rest disappears? What good is the springboard once the leap has been made?

Previously the act of knowing extended beyond its own confines and sought itself outside itself, by being absorbed in matter. But now it exists in the soul that has found itself and finally learns, by coincidence, what knowledge means and what self-knowledge is.[10]

To compensate for the absence of matter and sensation, the Scholastics had recourse to the hypothesis of an illumination emanating from pure spirits. This supposition would be explicable in the supernatural order; but in the natural order we do not see how these pure forms that are quite self-sufficient could intervene in human activity, since they do not intervene in human existence. Nor do we see how mankind could be passive with regard to the angels.[11] And the appeal made to God's activity in infusing the intelligible species requisite for natural knowledge is an avowal of defeat and an acknowledgment that the soul, in its definitive state, is a useless being that does not possess all it needs to exist and act in its own way. This is to assign to God a function that ought to belong to one of the constituents of nature.

A different explanation is suggested by ideas developed in the present study. Since separate souls are united to one another and support one another in their being, why should they not be united and aid one another in what concerns knowledge? *Unumquodque intelligit in quantum est actu.* During the present life, each man acquires his clearest knowledge through the human instruction imparted by other men; and what he learns through personal experience is also taught him by the human universe, hence by humanity. Quite naturally we conclude that, when man passes on to his definitive state,

---

[10] The separate soul "will know itself directly, by an intuition of its essence, and will not know a posteriori, as it does now." St. Thomas, *De anima*, q.17. See also Cajetan, in his Commentary on the *Summa*, Ia, q.89, a.2, no.1. In this article St. Thomas says that the separate soul will have a perfect knowledge of other separate souls. *seipsam per seipsam intelligit. . . . Et ideo de animabus separatis perfectam cognitionem habet.* But he does not make much of this knowledge (*ibid.*, ad 3; cf. especially *Quodl.* III, q.9, a.21, where he greatly restricts it). He does not consider the social aspect of knowledge.

[11] St. Thomas regards such knowledge as preternatural. Avicenna thought it was natural. See Cajetan, *In Iam.*, q.89, a.1, no.3.

this receptivity will accompany him. As the soul remains its personal self in its union with all other souls, it will have its own personal knowledge through this same union. Understanding always arises from unity; the unity of the future state will be a union of each individual with all other individuals. Understanding will come from this union and will follow the nature of the union; it will be personal in each one, in the distinct but unseparated consciousness of each one.

No language will be required for this. Besides, words would be insufficient, since total knowledge is in question. The totality of man and of all humanity is to be communicated, not the partial notions expressed by words. The soul has in itself all that is needed for this, without any recourse to words: it needs only to be and to act.

However, owing to lack of experience, we have no definite information about the mechanism of such intercourse of consciousness with consciousness.

2. **The manner of knowing God.** The soul will have knowledge of God. Otherwise perfection and beatitude would be impossible. But the soul will have such knowledge in a way that is proportionate to its state.

In the revelation of itself and of humanity, the soul will have clear, evident, immediate, and complete knowledge of one of God's works as such, for it will know itself as a being, and as a being it is a work of God. Therefore it will have a definite, luminous, total knowledge of God so far as He is the cause of man, and so far as knowledge of God is necessary for the perfection of the human intellect. On earth, as we have pointed out, the soul had enjoyed a certain kind of demonstration of God's existence. This was a demonstration that had to be sought out and constructed; it was a vivid and interior demonstration, based on the soul's attitude in presence of itself as a being, and was expressed in long, abstract arguments, conformably to the searching processes of reasoning. But now that the soul has gained full consciousness of itself, it has full consciousness of the demonstration it gives of God and comprehends that demonstration with an evidence that is its very life, finally disengaged from all encumbrances.

This is not the beatific vision; the intellect cannot bear its brilliance. Yet it is a vision: a vision of a work of God. Its essential imperfection does not prevent it from being wholly satisfying and beatifying for human nature, because it corresponds exactly to the essential imperfection of human nature. To represent man's supreme natural knowledge of God as an attenuated form of the beatific vision is to attribute both too much and too little to it: too much, because the natural end is essentially inferior to supernatural destiny; too little, because on its own level it is more complete and yields a greater natural satisfaction. On the other hand, to define it without including God and union with God, is to renounce all clarification of its proper structure.

But if we assign the difference to man himself, we see that everything drops into place. Man can be considered in two different states, each of them subdivided into two different periods: the natural state and the supernatural state, each of them with its period of formation and its period of achievement. Each of these states and periods has its own way of knowing God, and in each of them knowledge can be complete in its own kind, while being different in each case.

E. CONCLUSION

Man alone is truly adjusted to himself. That is why, in the supernatural state, God appears to him in human form: in the God-man and in the God-man's mystical body, which is regenerated humanity.

This mystical body, which is the central theme of all the pages to come, this supernatural unity of mankind effected in the God-man, is the perfecting and the divinization of the unity effected in man. For this reason we had to consider the former before treating of the latter.

Consequently we may say that the truth of the mystical body is pre-eminently a truth which is made for mankind and for which mankind is made. Therefore it is a truth that must be set in prominent relief in Christian teaching. And we may add that it is a truth especially befitting man of today, because man of today seems to be aware, to a greater degree than ever before, of what mankind means for him, and also because the Spirit seems in our day to shed a more vivid light on this truth in the thoughts of the faithful. Accordingly it ought to be investigated with particular attention by the theologians of our time.

BOOK TWO

The Coming of Christ

CHAPTER VI

CREATION

> "When the slime of the earth was being
> fashioned, Christ the future Man was in
> God's thoughts."
> Tertullian, *De resurrectione carnis*, 6

SINCE Christ is at the center of everything, He is not only a beginning but a culmination, as well as a plenitude in Himself. To declare Him fully, Christian teaching has to take account of what He is and of what precedes and continues Him: "the incarnation of the Word of God along with the sacraments preceding and following Him," according to the formula of Robert of Melun.[1] In dealing with such matters, Christianity but speaks of Christ. All things converge on Him and lead back to Him, although not always in the same way.

In Book Two of the present work we shall treat of what went before Him: creation, the Fall, the preparation going on throughout the entire epoch of the Old Testament, and the Blessed Virgin. During these endless ages the long-awaited coming of Christ was gradually being made ready.

He Himself has made known most of these preliminaries. The dogma of original sin, for example, seems to have been unknown during the whole of the Ancient Covenant. From this point of view we could well treat of Him before taking up these matters. On the other hand, they disclose what Christ came on earth to do; from this point of view, they form an introduction to the study of what He is. This is the way we consider them here.

[1] *Sententiae*, I, pars 1, c.8.

I. Creation as a Dogma

The first of the dogmas to presage this long-awaited advent of Christ is the dogma of creation and the creative decree. The coming of Christ was intended from the very beginning, and the dogma that deals with the beginning of everything by that fact deals with the beginning of Christ, so far as He is man.

This dogma is by no means identical with the truth of creation as it may be naturally known. The latter speaks only of contingent things; it tells us that these things do not possess their reason for being in themselves, and that consequently they must have such a reason in a being that is not contingent, finite, and imperfect like themselves. They exist because they are produced by God. Their quality as creatures is a relation and a dependence intrinsic to them: "creation is the dependence of created being on the principle by which it is produced, and hence is a kind of relation." [2] Therefore the relation is real with all the reality and entity of the finite being; it is an essential, constitutive, total relation. Since this relation makes the finite being what it is, it endures as long as the finite being endures. When this being begins, the relation begins by making the being begin. As long as the being continues to exist, so does the relation. And when the being that is endowed with freedom causes itself to be in a more complete sense, the relation also becomes more complete.[3]

But knowledge of this relation does not enable the mind to reach the transcendent Being that is infinite and inaccessible. The mind grasps only the finite. But it grasps the finite as unintelligible and unknowable in itself, and hence as requiring a cause that is not finite. The mind postulates that cause, affirms it, and knows it by knowing its necessity, but does not know it in itself.

This is a paradoxical knowledge, an understanding whose positive content is something finite that is unintelligible and whose sole explanation is something inaccessible that is superintelligible. The mind, inacapable of resting satisfied with the finite, is also incapable of reaching the infinite and so it does not succeed in fixing definitely on anything; all it has is a tendency, an unrequited appeal, an essential dynamism, a tormenting, heady idea resembling altitudes where the

[2] St. Thomas, *Contra Gent.*, II, 18.
[3] Cf. St. Thomas, *De potentia*, q. 3, a. 3 and ad 2; ad 6.

air is too thin for breathing. In ordinary life, as we know, the vagueness condenses: we are dimly aware of a very powerful activity,
and the idea, though remaining indistinct, comes to lose something
of its humiliating character. But it is humiliating, and well for us
that it is: for it thus becomes a continual goad to the mind, and
moreover, it remains capable of being supernaturally perfected.

The dogma of creation supplies such perfection: it exhibits creation, not as it is naturally knowable by man, but as it is known by
God. Since men are divinized and are united to God in Christ, they
must have a divinized knowledge of things through union with the
knowledge God has of them; in other words, men must have knowledge of things in Christ. God knows things by knowing Himself,
in His decision to give them existence; men will likewise know them
in that decision, through their contact with it in Christ. Christ is the
Creator Himself; by being members of Christ, men are members of
the Creator. Therefore they must know creation as it appears to the
Creator; this knowledge they acquire by faith in Christ and through
the revelation of Christ.

The Creator has become creature, the creature who is the Creator,
by hypostatic union in Christ, by mystic union in Christians. This
interchange, which is everything in Christianity, places man at the
beginning and center of everything, because it places God in the
heart of man. And it requires a corresponding interchange in man's
knowledge, which must now grasp being and its organs in a different
way, no longer from the standpoint of effects and through effects,
nor from the standpoint of man, for man is an effect, but from the
standpoint of God and, in the most rigorous sense of the word,
through the cause of being.

Isolated from all context, the formula of the dogma bears a close
resemblance to that of a rational truth. But it requires its context,
and this context invests it with its special meaning. Man does not
express his conclusions in it, but God declares His love in it: creation
is the first token of a total donation. If God gives men their whole
being, He means to give them His whole being, in Jesus Christ.

"I believe in God, the Father Almighty, Creator of heaven and
earth." [4] This first article of the Creed expresses the complete inter-

[4] The first part of this article is the most ancient; it mentions creation only
implicitly, in the word "Almighty." The second part is very explicit, but less
ancient. Cf. Denz., 1, 3, 6, 9, 54, 86.

change. Man no longer says: "I look on the world, and I see that it is frail." He says: "I no longer wish to see anything but God, and I see that He has made everything." Or rather God says: "See, I am your Father, and I have made everything." He does not say this from heaven, which is too high above us; we would not hear. He says it from close by, in Christ and in the Church; He says it from within; through grace present in the soul's substance, we are incorporated into Him in Christ.

Later we shall have occasion to dwell on this new knowledge of being; it is a way of knowing brought about by union with the source of being and the very act that creates it, by union with the inner life of this principle. All that we wish to point out here is that belief in creation takes its place, through Christ, in belief in the Trinity. Our faith is based less on a sense of awestruck inferiority than on a conviction of the fatherly tenderness of God, who surrounds His children with His solicitude and His providence. Jesus Christ Himself has asserted that creation serves as a commentary on His gospel of adoption and as a lesson to Christians on filial confidence in the Father who is in heaven. In Christ, creation is a message not only about itself and its complete dependence on the pure Act, but about God and the fatherly love He had in creating. Contemplation of creation almost becomes a contemplation of the way God's adopted children should act: we come to the point at which we do not think about anything except the Father, thus heeding Christ's words: "Glorify your Father who is in heaven" (Matt. 5:16).

II. Creation as a Revelation of Christ

The genesis of the world was a presage of Christ; it was the commencement of His coming and the remote beginning of man's adoption in Christ. Ought not the whole universe, whose origin He calls forth, to be recapitulated in Christ, so that Christ may be all in all? When the world came into being, did not the advent of the Savior begin? When the original chaos rose up, all the elements that in the fullness of time would go to form the body of the Savior were there, scattered throughout the universal mass. God was even then fashioning a body for Himself. The human race, which He summoned into existence on the sixth day, was in truth His race. In producing it, He began to produce the God-man and that regenerated mankind which would fill out the measure of the God-man.

Humanity, as we have said, is identical with the human universe. Christ is a rightful member of humanity, and all its members possess the whole of it through union. Christ Himself, as the God-man, is the supreme achievement of all creation. Accordingly, when God created, when He caused the universe to be, He was raising up Christ from afar. Thus, when God recounts the history of His incarnate Son, He goes back to this instant which is the very first, beyond the whole of the Old Testament, beyond the original defection. "And Jesus Himself was beginning about the age of thirty years, being (as it was supposed) the son of Joseph, who was of Heli, who was of Mathat, who was of Levi . . . who was of Adam, who was of God." [5]

In many of the most important passages that mention the Incarnation, Scripture views it as a union that is undoubtedly proper to Christ, but also as an event that concerns creation in its entirety, a cosmic event.[6] The Incarnation is described as a second creation which is greater than the first creation.[7] Christ is depicted as the second Adam, of whom the first Adam is only a figure.[8] The Fathers insist on the same truth against the Docetists and the Gnostics; that salvation might be effective, the Word had to assume the matter of which man is made, the ordinary matter of the universe, the ancient creation.[9]

God knew this from all eternity and He knew it when He created; what He made was the humanity of His Son and the mystical fullness of that humanity. In God's eyes, how could Christ's humanity fail to excel all else with the very pre-eminence by which God Himself excels everything? This gives us some understanding of the mysterious but realistic sense in which creation, as relating to the Son, is by

---

[5] Luke 3:23 f., 38.

[6] John 1:1–18; Col. 1:15–21; Eph., chap. 1.

[7] Cf. II Cor. 4:6; 5:17; Gal. 6:15. See also what St. Paul has to say about God's ancient, mysterious design in creating, at length revealed (Eph., chap. 1; Col., chap. 1). Cf. *The Whole Christ*, pp. 133 f.

[8] Rom. 5:14; I Cor. 15:22–49.

[9] See especially St. Irenaeus, *Adversus haereses*, III, xviii, 7; xxi, 10 (*PG*, VII, 938, 955). We may add that a classical exegesis sees the figure of the Incarnation in the account of creation: Adam is Christ, and Eve is the Church.

a special title the work of the Father: "I believe in God, the Father Almighty, Creator of heaven and earth."

III. The Decree of Creation and the Decree of the Incarnation

If we turn our thoughts to creation as a dogma, as divine knowledge communicated to the human mind, we have to trace it back or reduce it to Christ. In this connection we should like to suggest the following considerations.

According to Thomists and many other theologians, the purpose of the Incarnation was redemption from sin. Logically, therefore, the Incarnation comes after sin and hence after creation. But according to others, especially Scotists, the Incarnation was willed in the first instance as the most excellent of all possible works and, if one may say so, as the work most worthy of God. Sin had but the effect of giving it a new incidental aspect, the aspect of redemption.

Each of these two opinions is backed up by such strong arguments that some theologians have attempted to make room for both of them. Suarez, for example, holds that the Incarnation was decreed for two reasons: on account of its inherent excellence and hence as the principle of all of God's other works, and as a remedy for sin and hence in consequence of sin and creation.[10] Similarly Godoy and other Thomists teach that in the order of execution Christ was decreed subsequently to creation and sin, but that in the order of intention He was decreed before all else and that God permitted sin and created the world only in view of Him and His magnificent work of redemption.

In the order of intention Christ was willed, not only as regards the substance of the Incarnation but also as regards the circumstance of proximate possibility and as the actual Redeemer, prior to the natural order and the order of grace and the permission of sin.[11]

[10] *De Incarnatione*, q. 1, disp. 5, sect. 2–5.

[11] P. de Godoy, *Disputationes theologicae in tertiam partem divi Thomae*, q. 1, tract. 1, disp. 8, no. 6; J. B. Gonet, *Clypeus theologiae thomisticae*, pars III, disp. 5, no. 6; J. P. Nazarius, *Commentaria et controversiae in tertiam partem divi Thomae*, controv. XIII, q. 1, a. 3, concl. 2. P. de Cabrera, *In tertiam partem sancti Thomae commentarii et disputationes*, q. 1, a. 2, disp. 1, no. 25. See also Medina, *Expositio in tertiam divi Thomae partem*, q. 1, a. 3.

By His passion and death He merited our existence, for our substance, as we showed in the treatise on predestination, was an effect of our predestination and therefore a reward of the merit of Christ's passion and death.[12]

This is the sort of synthesis we wish to propose. Since creation, the Fall, and redemption are distinct from one another, they certainly have a basis for their distinction in God. Hence we may legitimately speak of successive divine decrees. However, since God is infinite unity, we may also legitimately reflect that these decrees are aspects of a total decree that is one in Him. We may without rashness seek to understand this single decree as it exists in God, since as Christians we are obliged and accustomed to live in God and to know in God.

Sin is, indeed, a complete break; but only on the side of creatures. On the side of God and His unity, sin cannot mar or shatter anything. And it is on the side of God that we are united in Christ, and Christ, who has initiated us into the divine world, shows us what God's work, of which He is the summit, could have been from the beginning. Furthermore, Christ is a redemption and a restoration. And in fact, by conceiving God's total work as a redemption and restoration, we are seemingly enabled, within the limits of human speculation, to account for all the details it presents.

God is love, and love is more active the more it gives itself and the more unworthy its beneficiaries are. We can readily conceive that God, in the mystery of His gratuitous love, would have chosen in preference to any other a universe in which He would be good in fullness, even to excess, toward a creature that had voluntarily become evil. In this way He would be good with all the greatness of His infinity in contrast to the depth of sin. Among all the worlds He could have brought into being, there was one in which man, after being loaded with all sorts of gifts, would break with His Creator and would debase himself to the lowest possible degree, and in which angels also, despite splendid graces, would allow evil to enter among them. This is the universe He created to show forth His love the more strikingly to a world that had merited nothing but wrath. "God

---

[12] P. de Godoy, *op. cit.*, q. 24, disp. 57, no. 4; cf. disp. 56, no. 1, and *In primam partem*, q. 22, disp. 62, no. 1, 4; disp. 63, no. 3. See also John of St. Thomas, *De Incarnatione*, q. 1, disp. 3, a. 3.

judged it better to draw good from evil than not to permit evil to arise." [13]

These are plans of love and mercy that go to extremes, and that embrace men and angels in two different ways, corresponding to their different natures.

As regards the angels, we have little information; but we do not need much. If we recall the supernatural state they were raised to, we can catch a glimpse of an analogous sense in which we may speak of mercy and redemption for them. In the hypothesis of a natural order an angel, because of his total existence, would either sin totally with an unforgivable sin or else would not sin at all. But in the supernatural order each angel, while retaining his complete individuality, is caught up into eternal life. In this life, which is his most precious possession, an angel forms a single whole with his fellows, as we shall show at greater length when we come to man. We can conceive of sin invading this whole through the evil deed of some of its members. We can understand that, because of the supernatural unity binding them all together, this fall would affect even those who did not fall, and that the latter are capable of receiving aid which would preserve them from the taint threatening them because it has entered into the whole. We can even see that they are capable of profiting by a restoration which would repair them by repairing their environment. The nature of this preservation and reparation cannot, of course, be accurately determined, since we lack data on the subject. Yet it suggests some points of resemblance with the redemption of her who is the queen of the angels and who was redeemed in a more sublime way by being preserved from contracting sin. The reparation of the angels thus proposed would be associated with the redemption whereby men are properly redeemed, to constitute two species under a higher genus for which we lack a suitable name, but which would be God's matchless design of goodness, charity, and kindness toward a sinful collectivity.

We may add, by way of hypothesis, that this supernatural life and unity offered to the angels have as their summit and principle Him who, being the God-man, is at once infinite and finite, necessary and contingent. The angels, created for the supernatural state, ought in their very first act to have accepted this state which God had already made their own, and to have been willing to be preserved

[13] St. Augustine, *Enchiridion*, 27 (*PL*, XL, 245).

in existence, unity, and life in a transcendental way by this necessary and contingent God-man. They could conceivably have refused. Although they were perfect, fully actuated, and hence impeccable on the level of form, they were imperfect, deficient, and hence peccable on the level of act; and the supernatural state, being a divinization, is essentially a perfecting on the level of act. Thus the angels could have maintained a closed front against Him, and could have preferred to rest content with themselves rather than receive an elevation that would incorporate them into a whole and would increase their dependence on God; especially as this elevation, while raising them, in a way, to God's level by grace, also lowers them to the level of man and gives them everything in a man, who is Christ.

If this is so, the creation of the angels themselves is recapitulated in Christ the Savior.

As regards men, our knowledge is more complete, and we hope in the following pages to make more and more clear the concept that from the very beginning God has willed for man an immense redemption, pardon, and restoration that has all its meaning in Christ. This is a pardon such as God alone can grant, a splendid, total, overflowing pardon, a pardon so loving and considerate that it exalts those whom it reinstates.

The pardons we grant are always a little distant, like an inadvertence we let fall from on high. They are also deficient, for any change they produce occurs in him who pardons; the one who is pardoned remains exactly as he was before. If a pardon were no more than this, God's action would not be one; actually it accomplishes much more. The changeless God undergoes no change, but the Almighty brings about a change in the sinner, and so the pardon is creative. In response to God's action the sinner effects a change in himself, and to restore himself he employs the very consequences of the evil and the punishment that goes with it. God brings this about, not as from outside or without any desire to touch the soul, but from within, by becoming a man Himself; this He does in the God-man and in the members of the God-man. Thus men accomplish the whole task; the autonomy of their personality and initiative is jealously safeguarded; their beatitude, their stainless moral purity, and their holiness is their work; and they will not enter heaven humiliated. Yet all this is even more the work of Him who has made and remade all, and His creative omnipotence becomes more splendidly and impressively manifest in the precision and magnificence of such a restoration: "O God, who showest forth Thy almighty power most strikingly by sparing and by having mercy," the liturgy sings.[14]

All this is summed up in Him who is forgiveness, life, and union with God fully restored; the entire divine plan is recapitulated in Christ the Redeemer.[15]

The plan, we may say further, is that of an immense resurrection by which man, after having lost life by his sin, enters more excellently into life: "I am come that they may have life, and may have it more abundantly" (John 10:10). The entire universe is a perpetual breaking up leading to a perpetual renovation: astronomical cycles make a full turn and begin all over, vegetation stops growing and starts again, living beings mature and multiply, the vibration of matter results from innumerable comings and goings: everywhere in the universe there is struggle for life and struggle to the death, and from the common hecatomb the rich life of the world rises unceasingly in the splendor of the sun.

Thus the creative plan is a plan of resurrection, a plan in which the resurrection of nature accompanies the resurrection of man. If at the beginning man was for a brief time in a more delightful economy, this economy too has its place in the design of the whole; for in order to rise, man must first have lived another life. And during that period he was withdrawn from the universal struggle and was, so to say, isolated from the world in a Paradise made expressly for the purpose.

If such is the case, the creation of the world was the first beginning of the birth of Christ, the Redeemer, the Risen One. The decision that decreed creation was one of the phases of the single decree that willed the Incarnation. The God-man, the well-beloved and only-begotten Son, was willed, prepared, and predestined in all and

[14] Tenth Sunday after Pentecost, oration.

[15] Cf. St. Ambrose, *In hexaemeron*, VI, 10 (*PL*, XIV, 272): "I thank God our Lord that He has made a work in which He might find rest. He made the heavens, and I do not read that He rested. He made the earth, and I do not read that He rested. He made the sun, the moon, and the stars, but I do not read that He rested in them. But I do read that He made man and then rested, having at length someone whose sins He might forgive. Perhaps even then was foretold the mystery of the Lord's future passion, in which it was revealed that Christ would find repose in man."

through all, and we, together with the entire universe, were chosen and blessed in Him, "that in all things He may hold the primacy" (Col. 1:18).

Thus conceived, the Incarnation remains essentially, as the majority of theologians teach, the remedy for sin. Nothing indicates that the Incarnation would have taken place without sin, for without sin there would not have been so much goodness to show forth nor, consequently, so much glory for the divine love. At the same time, the Incarnation is willed for itself, for a redemptive Incarnation is but an Incarnation pushed to the extreme; the Incarnation is an act in which God gives Himself, and when God gives Himself to sinners, He but gives Himself the more generously. In this case the redemption is essential, but we need not mention it at every turn. In speaking of the Incarnation in its full sense, we implicitly include the redemption.

If God undertakes to give Himself and to love, we may say that it is almost natural and becoming for Him to go to these mysterious excesses. They make Him appear all the greater in His divine initiative, an initiative of love. As the infinite Being, He causes being; similarly, as gratuitous and free love, He calls forth love in creatures endowed with freedom.

IV. ORIGINAL JUSTICE

Thus created as a remote inception of Christ, man was created in a supernatural state, and at the same time was adorned with sanctifying grace and preternatural gifts.

To recall the Christian teaching on this subject, we believe we can do no better than quote from the dogmatic draft of Catholic doctrine prepared for the Vatican Council. The doctrine there outlined was not defined, but it was composed with meticulous care as a short and authentic exposition of Christian faith by theologians chosen for the purpose, and it was revised and corrected several times in accord with instructions issued by the Fathers of the Council, so that it had every chance of being accepted without any major change. A more thoroughly authorized formula could hardly be found. Mansi gives it in four separate stages of its development; [16] we shall quote only the last revision.

[16] *Amplissima collectio conciliorum*, L, 60–119; LIII, 164–77; 230–36; 287–307.

Christian faith acknowledges a great mystery of divine generosity at the very beginning of the human race. Man, made to the image of God, is ordained by his very nature to know, worship, and love God in a way befitting his natural capacity. But the supreme Creator and Lord, whose power is not hemmed in by the properties and laws of created nature, willed in His inexhaustible goodness to elevate the race of men in their first parent to a state in which man would share in the divine Good beyond the limitations imposed by nature. Accordingly, in addition to the endowments by which man was perfected in his own nature, God bestowed on him an admirable gift of holiness and justice, so that he who was a servant by nature but a son by the gift of the Holy Spirit might carry out the divine commands and perform the works of virtue no longer by the powers of nature alone, but by the grace infused into him from above, and thus might merit eternal happiness. For this purpose man's grace kept the flesh in subjection to the spirit and freed his mortal body from the tyranny of death. For man was mortal by the condition of his animal body, but was made immortal by the beneficence of the Creator.[17]

No doubt sanctifying grace in this original period was not quite the same as ours. It had no sin to efface and was not the grace of the Redeemer as such. Yet, if what we have said is correct, it was given solely in view of the God-man who was to come. The excellence of the latter already required and demanded it, so as to be able to increase it, not of course as a continuation without interruption, but as a more wonderful restoration.

To understand grace, therefore, we have to study it in Christ. As Christ received grace in fullness at the first instant of His existence, the first man received grace at his creation. And as Eve received grace through Adam in a special way and as associated with him rather than as dependent on him, the new Eve received it through the new Adam in an unparalleled way and so as to be associated with Him in the work of redemption.[18]

But these comparisons hold good only in a few details. To go to the heart of the matter, we must say that in Adam as in Christ, and because of Christ, grace is a divinization, a Godlike transformation brought about in human nature by union with God. The chief dif-

[17] Mansi, LIII, 288 f.

[18] The Scholastics did not speak of Eve's sanctification. Similarly the way the Mother of Christ and of Christians was sanctified at her conception was defined rather late.

ference to be noted here, as concerns men and prescinding from Jesus Christ, is that this change took place in a nature as yet completely unsullied, whereas now nature is defiled by sin.

This is the source of everything that can be said about original justice, which was above all a divinization. If, as we shall bring out later, a divinization is incomprehensible without a literal and substantial union with God, we have to conclude that in Adam too it was impossible without such a union. This does not mean, evidently, that Adam received the hypostatic union. Nor does it mean that, if Adam had not sinned, a God-man would have been born of his race, that is, a God-man free from suffering and wholly glorious. For, in the hypothesis we are discussing, Adam was chosen as the first sinner and as a man to be restored; the question of what would have happened had he not sinned does not arise. We mean only that Adam was willed as the ancestor of the race from which Christ was to issue, and hence as the ancestor of a divinized race.

Since sanctifying grace in Adam was a divinization, that is, an assimilation to Him who is very being and unity, it caused him, as we shall explain at greater length in the proper place, to be a man in a transcendent fashion that is impossible unless one is assimilated to Being itself; and it caused him to be unified in himself and to be united to his whole being in a way that is impossible unless one is assimilated to unity itself. But in Adam this elevation and unity did not encounter the obstacle of a nature fallen through sin, as is the case with us, and so grace could produce all its effects in an instant. The result was the existence, in the primitive state, of gifts not found in the present state: integrity, knowledge, immortality, impassibility, and let us add, a more perfect possession of human nature.

These gifts did not in any way transport mankind to a region of fairy tales. Humanity thus described was real and concrete, and was not necessarily at variance with the human origins which paleontology and prehistory are able dimly to discern. For that matter, we should be wasting our time if we desired at present to settle points of agreement with a science that is still far from being settled.

Man's glory consists in being the culmination and crown of the whole hierarchy of nature. He was that in his original state even more than now; let us not imagine him cut off from the grand life of the cosmos. His glory further consists in his ability to develop himself and thus to develop the humanity in him; we should not fancy that from the outset he was so endowed by God with every perfection that he did not have to work out his own perfection. He surely had to do so. More closely united to God, he found himself more solidly established in the domain and dynamism of reality. He was not like an adult of the twentieth century, burdened with a long and hard human experience, far off from his origins; he was a man scarcely risen from matter, a child just come forth from his Father's hands. And children, with their clear vision, have such magnificent powers of perception.

Therefore man, at the birth of mankind, must have been more unified than he is by nature; he was supernaturally one. All the tendencies, impulses, and instincts that now hurry him off in various directions were then united in his unity. His soul and will, being more closely united to God, were more capable of unifying his lower powers. The latter, thus sharing in man's unity, also shared in his innocence. Neither in his dreams nor in his desires nor in his body did man have anything to hide from himself, from others, or from God. Such was the gift of integrity. Such a state must have appeared quite natural to man, almost as a thing may now appear natural in the eyes of children.

Further, being at one with himself and the human universe, man was in a better position to know himself and everything else. He was not limited to knowing from without, by observing signs or by testing phenomena through experimentation; rather he knew by a sort of sympathy, of divining instinct, of connaturalness, an ability we no longer possess. He knew not merely the outside of things, but their inner nature; he perceived the human meaning that makes them parts of the human universe, and the image of God that is the very substance of their being. Is this not the essential perfection of all knowledge, far exceeding the knowledge of the engineer and the scientist? Moreover, without having a direct vision of the divine essence, he enjoyed, in the magnificence of nature and the purity of his soul, a near and familiar presence of God in the midst of the verdant garden.

Besides, his soul and body were more closely united; separation of the two would not have occurred, nor was there any place for those half separations, those lacerations of man we call sufferings. How such a situation could have endured for a long time, we do not know; but it was not intended to endure long. In any case, we should not entertain the notion of a Providence bustling about and perpetually intervening to keep man from being bruised by the universe. When prints of polychrome pictures come out wrong and colors overlap, the printer does not have to make as many corrections as there are points of intrusion; he has to make only a single readjustment on his press. In the same way the relations between man and determinism are not external; to be perfectly adapted to each other, they have only to be put right in their own lines.

To these gifts we must add another that is usually passed over in silence, although it follows necessarily from the preceding considerations. If man is inherently social, if his perfection includes the possession of all humanity, the original divinization must have perfected this social aspect and this possession. At the beginning, therefore, since man was supernaturally man, he must have been supernaturally united to the whole species, and must have possessed the entire nature in a supernatural way.

Scholastic tradition indicates this when it speaks of society as it must have existed then,[19] and we may say that Christian doctrine expressly asserts the same when it teaches that grace and the preternatural gifts were conferred on the whole of human nature in the first man and were to have been transmitted from generation to generation along with nature. This can hardly be understood if nature as such did not have some sort of real existence in the first man besides its existence in individuals.[20] We shall speak of this point at greater length when we come to the question of original sin.

Of course the first man was not a sort of universal idea of man, as was imagined by a certain Francis Georgius, whom Suarez refutes.[21] In the beginning, he claimed, God created man in general, *hominem communem et supra ab individuis abstractum*; it was only later that He created a concrete man. We are not dealing here with

[19] Cf. St. Thomas, especially the *Summa*, Ia, q.96, a.4; q.98, a.1 ad 3. The commentaries are interesting: see Suarez, *De opere sex dierum*, V, 7, no. 17.

[20] St. Thomas, *Summa*, Ia, q.100, a.1; *Compendium of Theology*, p. 205, Part I, chap. 187.

[21] *De opere sex dierum*, I, cap. 4, no. 1. Much along the same line of thought is the rabbinic tradition popularized by certain teachers, as reported by Moses Bar Cepha, *De Paradiso*, I, 14 (*PG*, CXI, 497). Adam and Eve were represented as being of so great a size that they could have forded the ocean. All mankind could have found place in such huge individuals, as in a Noah's ark. We mention these ravings to put the reader on guard, if need be, against the imagination, which is deceptive and dangerous in these difficult matters.

any such fanciful unity. Nor are we dealing with a unity pertaining to the experimental order, such as are all those unities we can easily represent, or even with a natural unity, such as are necessarily those unities of which unaided reason can form an idea, even though it be with difficulty. We are dealing with a unity that is essentially supernatural, a unity that is unthinkable except in function of theological premises, such as elevation to the order of grace, the divinization of man in his very being and hence in his unity, and the original state of innocence, which in no way prevented this divinization from producing its effects.

To form some idea of this unity, we have to think of it as it was in Christ and in the unity established in Him; it was a sort of preliminary sketch of what was later to be the mystical body of Christ: not precisely this body itself, but that of which the mystical was to be the restoration.

This original unity had to contain more than men; the human universe entered into it, as we have said, but also the angels had their place in it. For if, on the level of form and in the natural order the angels are so fully complete in themselves that each of them is a whole universe, yet in the order of act they are all, along with man, in a common condition of need with regard to God, and therefore they are in a common potentiality with reference to supernatural elevation through union with pure Act. Union with God equally unifies all finite beings in God; the instant they begin to live eternal life in Him, they all live together in a living unity.

God is one. He is the source of all unity. He has conferred on every being the power to enter into union with all other being and also to be one in itself for its very being is the principle of its unity.

But since the ontological perfection of supernatural unity respects personality and liberty, it cannot exist fully unless it is freely received. That reception was refused, and the refusal is original sin.

CHAPTER VII

ORIGINAL SIN

FOR many thinkers the dogma of original sin is a tremendous difficulty, and for some it is even a scandal. This attitude is perhaps owing to a failure to conceive original sin in the exact way faith proposes it.

If it consisted merely in a physical debility affecting men because of some ancestral crime, it would be readily intelligible. The laws of natural solidarity need not be moral laws, and repeated experience shows that men can be injured by faults they have not committed. But it is a real sin that burdens a conscience without the commission of any fault whatever. The Council of Trent is explicit on this point.

The sin of Adam is one in its origin and, being transmitted to all by propagation, not imitation, is in each man as his own.

If anyone asserts that Adam's transgression injured him alone and not his posterity, and that the holiness and justice he received from God and lost, he lost for himself alone and not for us also; or that he, defiled as he was by the sin of disobedience, has transmitted only death and punishments of the body to the whole human race, but not sin also which is the death of the soul, let him be anathema.[1]

A sin that is proper to each man without any defection on the part of each, has the appearance of being something in the moral order that flatly contradicts the moral order. Assuredly this sin is not like other sins, and therefore some theologians attempt to explain it partly by minimizing it as much as they can. But in that case a full explanation would consist in denying it completely; and suppression is not explanation.

[1] Sess. V, can. 2 and 3 (Denz., 789 f.).

After what we laid down in the preceding chapter, an explanation consistent with the theme of this work is at hand. But before giving our explanation, we may observe that it is suggested by the dogma itself. And the dogma does indeed suggest an explanation. The very way the most authentic teaching proposes the dogma for our belief indicates, and with insistence, the lines along which an explanation must be sought: this truth is an object of understanding in the same way it is an object of belief and a dogma and a mystery; the explanation must be sought in Christ.

I. DOCTRINAL INDICATIONS ON THE THEOLOGY OF ORIGINAL SIN

The great scriptural passage which is almost unique in its mention of original sin is very instructive. This text is found in the fifth chapter of the Epistle to the Romans. As a rule theologians confine their attention to the common fall in Adam, for this is nowhere else proposed so clearly. But what St. Paul is most intent on bringing out is a common restoration in Christ. However, since that restoration is taught in many other powerful texts and indeed throughout the entire epistle, theologians do not delay in pointing to this truth here.

But we have only to read these famous lines to see what has the primacy in St. Paul's thought and preaching.

By one man sin entered into this world, and by sin death; and so death passed upon all men, in whom all have sinned. For until the law sin was in the world, but sin was not imputed, when the law was not. But death reigned from Adam unto Moses, even over them also who have not sinned after the similitude of the transgression of Adam, who is a figure of him who was to come. But not as the offense, so also the gift. For if by the offense of one, many died, much more the grace of God and the gift, by the grace of one man, Jesus Christ, hath abounded unto many. And not as it was by one sin, so also is the gift. For judgment indeed was by one unto condemnation; but grace is of many offenses, unto justification. For if by one man's offense death reigned through one, much more they who receive abundance of grace and of the gift and of justice shall reign in life through one, Jesus Christ. Therefore, as by the offense of one, unto all men to condemnation, so also by the justice of one, unto all men to justification of life. For as by the disobedience of one man, many were made sinners, so also by the obedience of one, many shall be made just. Now the law entered in, that sin might abound. And where sin abounded, grace did more abound. That as sin hath reigned to death, so also grace might reign by justice unto life everlasting, through Jesus Christ our Lord.[2]

The structure of the passage stands forth clearly. The Apostle's reason for speaking of a contracting of evil, of a common sin, is to bring out a fellowship in life, a universal grace. The original fall is but a point of departure; the whole movement of the text is in the direction of grace, of the gift, of insertion into justice. As soon as the comparison with the original iniquity has been made, Paul advances to a second stage: the first Adam appears on the scene only to serve as a figure of the second Adam.[3] What is associated with this second Adam is much more important, universal, glorious, and vital than anything connected with the first Adam: [4] "Where sin abounded, grace did more abound." This grace, this life, this justice, is in question throughout the entire letter, and is the climax of the present passage: "That grace might reign by justice unto life everlasting, through Jesus Christ our Lord."

This verse is significant because, as is shown by a comparison with many other texts scattered throughout the letter,[5] it recalls the general thesis,[6] and because it enables us to see how the whole passage fits in with the great idea St. Paul is perpetually trying to instill: that justice, grace, redemption, and the mystery of life and holiness come to every man by incorporation into Christ. Accordingly the great scriptural announcement of original sin may be said to take its place as an element in the announcement of the mystical body.

The entire passage is continued in another that expresses the same truth, although less clearly. Here, too, the Apostle speaks of a collective sin, but without connecting it explicitly with Adam. He describes a sort of tremendous, hostile force, a universal sin that operates in this world, and he says that we escape its clutches by being caught up into the embrace of Christ and by being buried with Christ in baptism, which makes us die to this sin and live a new life in Jesus Christ.[7] The solidarity in evil we dimly discern in this passage is manifested only in function of a solidarity in good.

[2] Rom. 5:12–21.
[3] Verse 14.
[4] Verses 15–19.
[5] Rom. 3:21–31; 4:25; 6:23; 8:1, 39.
[6] Rom. 1:16 f.
[7] Rom. 6:1–23.

Tradition takes up the same teaching. During the first centuries the dogma of original sin was not formulated separately from the dogma of redemption. Redemption is universal; therefore a universal defection has occurred. All men, including infants, need to be baptized to secure remission of sin; all have to die and be buried with Christ by baptism for the destruction of sin and resurrection to justice, as we are told in the passage from the Epistle to the Romans cited above. Consequently all are in sin, even those who have not committed any personal sins.

St. Irenaeus in particular repeats over and over that Christ's work was a remaking, a recapitulation: Christ repaired the whole of creation that had fallen in Adam.[8] St. Cyril of Alexandria expresses himself in a similar way. He never found a perfect formula for defining original sin, but he shows clearly that solidarity in Christ has its basis in a solidarity in Adam, a solidarity that embraced all nature, so that it could not be restored except in the God-man. The whole of nature, he says, was in Adam to lose life and freedom from corruption, just as it is in Christ to receive anew the Spirit and immortality. The following passage is a little long, but it well shows the relation between original sin and redemption in Christ.

Scripture says that He who is God and was begotten by the Father before all ages is begotten today (Ps. 2:7), in order that in Him the Father may receive us into sonship, for all human nature is in Christ so far as He is man. In the same way the Father, who has the Spirit, is said to give Him to the Son, that in the Son we may receive the Spirit. For this reason, as it is written (Heb. 2:16 f.), the Son took hold of the seed of Abraham, and in all things was made like unto His brethren. Therefore the Only-begotten receives the Holy Spirit, not for Himself, for the Spirit is of Him and in Him and through Him, but that He who was made man and had our whole nature in Himself might refashion all nature and restore it to its former state. We must further consider, if we wish to reason rightly and employ the Scriptures to advantage, that Christ did not receive the Spirit for Himself but rather for us, for all good things come to us through Him. After our forefather Adam lost the grace of the Spirit, being enticed by the devil to turn away from the service of God to disobedience and sin, with the

---

[8] See *The Whole Christ*, pp. 232 ff. and St. Irenaeus, *Adversus haereses*, III, xviii, 1, 7; xxi, 10; V, xvi, 3; xvii, 1 (*PG*, VII, 932, 938, 954 f., 1168 f.).

result that the whole of nature suffered the loss of the divine gift in him, God the Word who is without change became man, in order that, receiving that good as man, He might for the future preserve it safely for our nature. . . . Therefore the Only-begotten became man like us that in Him first the goods might be restored to us and the grace of the Spirit might be rooted in our nature for all time to come. . . . This is why Sacred Scripture calls Christ the second Adam. For in the first Adam the human race proceeded from non-being to being, but soon became corrupt, because it broke the divine law. But in Christ, the second Adam, it rises up again to a second beginning and receives a new life.[9]

The saint does not imagine a sort of presence of all men in Adam; all this takes place through the intermediary of nature. As he says expressly elsewhere,[10] nature received the gifts and nature lost them. In his conception, this nature had, in Adam as in Christ, an existence real enough to include the whole ruin or the whole resurrection of the human race.

This theology receives its clearest expression in St. Augustine.[11] As he is pre-eminently the doctor of original sin, so he is also the one who best describes this sin as a solidarity in evil, which however is secondary and dependent with reference to a solidarity in good. In Adam all men form, as it were, a single mass, a mass of sin and sinners,[12] a mass of wicked men,[13] a mass of perdition,[14] a mass of damnation, a condemned mass,[15] a mass of death and mortality,[16]

[9] In Ioan., V, 2 (PG, LXXIII, 753, 756).

[10] In epist. ad Rom., V, 18 (PG, LXXIV, 789); De recta fide ad Reginas, 2 (PG, LXXVI, 1384); Adversus anthropomorphitas, 9 (PG, LXXVI, 1092).

[11] We could also mention Tertullian, De anima, 40 (PL, II, 719) and a text of St. Ambrose which St. Augustine often refers to, In Lc., IV, 67; VII, 234 (PL, XV, 162, 1762).

[12] The word massa, at first occurring rarely in this sense, appears rather often after letter 186 (PL, XXXIII, 815, 823).

[13] Sermo 301 (PL, XXXVIII, 1383); De diversis quaest. LXXXIII, 71 (PL, XL, 71); De diversis quaest. ad Simplicianum (PL, XL, 121, 124).

[14] Enchiridion, 99, 107 (PL, XL, 278, 282); Epist. 136 (PL, XXXIII, 817); Sermo 26; 71 (PL, XXXVIII, 177, 466); De gratia et peccato originali, II, 29 (PL, XLIV, 402).

[15] Sermo 26, 301 (PL, XXXVIII, 177, 1383); Enchiridion, 27, 99 (PL, XL, 245, 278); Opus imperfectum contra Iulianum, I, 141 (PL, XLV, 1140); Contra adversarium legis et prophetarum, 1 (PL, XLII, 635); Epist. 194 (PL, XXXIII, 876, 879, 881).

[16] Epist. 186 (PL, XXXIII, 823); In ps. 72 (PL, XXXVI, 924).

a mass of ruin,[17] a mass vitiated in its root,[18] a mass depraved and punished and lost,[19] a mass of dispersion and corruption. "Man was created good; he did not make himself good. What he made of himself we know: he fell from the potter's hand and broke." [20] "Brethren, I have already mentioned that Adam was one man and that he was the whole human race. That is what I said, if you remember. As though he had been broken and scattered he is gathered up, and is again made whole in union with others and in spiritual peace." [21]

Christ came to take this mass into His saving unity. It is an unfit and sluggish clod of earth, but a seed dropped down from heaven to make it bloom. "One came to do battle against one, One who gathers against one who scattered, One who gives life against one who spread death." [22] "Such is our faith, such is truth; this is the foundation of Christian faith. One and one: one man through whom ruin, another through whom restoration; through the former comes ruin, through the latter restoration. He who did not remain standing fell, He who did not fall raises up. The former fell because he abandoned Him who remained standing; the latter, still standing, stooped down to him who was lying prostrate." [23] These two unities, these two cities, these two loves, these two masses, these two groups, these two men, as Augustine often puts it, sum up the entire religious history of mankind. "Christian faith is wholly bound up with the causes of these two men." [24] "All die in Adam, because by a man came death; likewise all are brought to life in Christ, because by a man comes the resurrection of the dead. Therefore man and man: as the latter is one, so is the former." [25]

One and one: hence two unities, and two unities that go together. In St. Augustine, we may say in consequence, the dogma of original sin is viewed in the perspective of the dogma of redemption, and exhibits a similar structure. Obviously the two are not placed on the same level; although the saint speaks frequently and forcefully of union in evil, he speaks more frequently and with greater light and

[17] Epist. 186, 189, 190, 194 (PL, XXXIII, 845, 851, 860 f., 876).
[18] Sermo 96 (PL, XXXVIII, 587); Enchiridion, 99 (PL, XL, 278).
[19] Opus imperfectum contra Iulianum, III, 161 (PL, XLV, 1315).
[20] Sermo 26, 2 (PL, XXXVIII, 172).
[21] In Ioan., X (PL, XXXV, 1472).
[22] Sermo 90 (PL, XXXVIII, 563).
[23] Sermo 30 (PL, XXXVIII, 190).
[24] De gratia et de peccato originali, II, 24 (PL, XLIV, 398).
[25] Opus imperfectum contra Iulianum, VI, 31 (PL, XLV, 1585).

love of unity in good. Therefore an explanation of the former must be sought in the latter.

The same connection is observed in St. Thomas. His soteriology, easily the best among the Scholastics, is acknowledged to be a soteriology based on unity.[26] All the faithful are sanctified by Christ because together with Him they form a single living reality, a single person,[27] for the whole of human nature is found in Christ by reason of His divinity.[28] This is not a haphazard formula, escaping the Angelic Doctor's vigilance; it is deliberately intended, and at critical junctures is brought forward as the ultimate argument.

His theology of original sin is firmly anchored to the same principle, which he brought out more clearly than the other Scholastics, and with increasing effectiveness as his genius matured.[29] In Adam all men are as one man; Adam is, in a sense, human nature. This is why all men and the whole of nature could have sinned in him.

The Thomist explanation does not appear in the *Scriptum super libros sententiarum*, the first of the saint's works to take up the problem of original sin.[30] Not until some years later, in the *Summa contra Gentiles*, is it encountered for the first time, already considerably developed, but not yet closely synthesized. In the following passage St. Thomas explains how a transmission of sin from one man to another may be envisaged.

Matters stand differently with an individual than with the nature of a whole species; for, as Porphyry says [*Isagoge*, cap. II, 36], by sharing the same species many men are like one man. Therefore a sin pertaining to a single individual or person is not imputed as a fault to anyone but the sinner, because one person is different from another. But if a sin affects the specific nature itself, it may not unreasonably be transmitted from one man to another, just as specific nature is. . . . Hence a defect of this kind, communicated by our first parent to other men, is culpable in them, according as all men are reckoned one man by sharing in the common

[26] See below, pp. 249 ff., and *The Whole Christ*, pp. 467 ff.

[27] *Summa*, IIIa, q. 19, a. 4; q. 48, a. 1; a. 2 ad 1; a. 3 ad 3; q. 49, a. 1; *In III Sent.*, d. 18, a. 6, sol. 1 ad 2; *De veritate*, q. 29, a. 7 ad 11.

[28] *In III Sent.*, d. 18, a. 6, sol. 2; d. 20, a. 2 ad 4.

[29] Here as elsewhere, chronological data on the works of St. Thomas are taken from P. Mandonnet and J. Destrez, *Bibliographie thomiste* (Le Saulchoir, 1921) and M. Grabmann, *Die Werke des hl. Thomas von Aquin* (Münster, 1931).

[30] *In II Sent.*, dd. 21–24 and 29–33.

nature. And this sin is perceived to be voluntary through the will of our first parent, just as the hand's action is sinful on account of the will of the moving principle, which is reason. Thus in the case of the sin of nature various men may be considered parts of common nature, just as in the case of personal sin there are various parts in one man.[31]

A decade later the saint had recourse to the same comparison in the *De malo*, with developments that were more carefully worked out though still sketchy.[32] It is only in the second part of the *Summa*, which is but slightly later if at all, that we find a fully systematized exposition. It occurs in the first lines of the short treatise devoted to original sin.[33]

According to Catholic faith we must hold that the first sin of the first man is transmitted to his descendants by way of origin. This is why children are taken to be baptized soon after their birth, that they may be cleansed of some infection of sin. The contrary doctrine is typical of the Pelagian heresy, as Augustine shows in many of his books. But in investigating how the sin of our first parent can pass to his posterity by way of origin, various theologians have proceeded along various lines.

After reviewing a number of unsatisfactory theories, the saint proposed his own.

Therefore we must have recourse to some other explanation. I hold that all men descending from Adam may be regarded as one man, inasmuch as they have a common nature received from their first ancestor. Thus in civil matters all men who are members of one community are reckoned as one body, and the whole community as one man. This accords with what Porphyry says, that by sharing in the same species many men are one man. In this sense the many men derived from Adam are like many members of one body. But the action of one of the body's members, the hand for instance, is voluntary not by the will of the hand, but by the will of the soul which first moves the member. Hence a murder committed by the hand would not be imputed to the hand as a sin if the hand were considered in itself apart from the body, but is imputed to it as something that belongs to the man and that is moved by the man's first motive principle. In this way, then, the disorder in the man descended

[31] *Contra Gent.*, IV, 52.
[32] *De malo*, q.4, a.1 ad 18 and 19; a.2; a.6 and ad9.
[33] *Summa*, Ia IIae, q.81–83.

from Adam is voluntary not by his own will, but by the will of his first parent who, by the motion of generation, moves all who take their origin from him, just as the will of the soul moves all the members to action. Accordingly the sin thus transmitted by the first parent to his posterity is called original, as the sin flowing from the soul to the members of the body is called actual. And just as an actual sin committed by a bodily member is not a sin of that member except so far as that member is something belonging to the man himself, which is the reason why the sin is called a human sin, so original sin is not a sin of this particular person except so far as he receives his nature from the first parent, which is the reason why it is called a sin of nature, according to Ephesians 2:3: "We . . . were by nature children of wrath." [34]

"All men descending from Adam may be regarded as one man." This is the explanation at which the saint pauses. In the *Compendium of Theology* [35] and in his commentary on the Epistle to the Romans,[36] he comes back to it and develops one or other detail. But he has nothing essential to add; for him, clearly, the whole explanation is there. And when he reflects on the comparison that so aptly illustrates the problem, he allows himself some optimism in expressing his satisfaction. "This question," he says, in uttering what is perhaps his last word on the subject, "is easily solved." [37]

[34] *Ibid.*, q. 81, a. 1.

[35] Here the saint tries to show yet more clearly how original sin can be a real sin in every man. "But there remains a more pressing question: whether the privation of original justice can have the nature of sin in those who descend from the first parent. . . . This question is easily solved if we but distinguish between person and nature. As there are many members in one person, so there are many persons in one human nature. Thus, by sharing in the same species, many men may be thought of as one man, as Porphyry remarks. In this connection we should note that in the sin of one man different sins are committed by different members. Nor does the notion of sin require that the various sins be voluntary by the wills of the members whereby they are committed, for it is enough that they be voluntary by the will of that which is most excellent in man, that is, his intellectual part. For the hand cannot but strike and the foot cannot help walking, when the will so commands. In this way, then, the privation of original justice is a sin of nature, in the sense that it has its origin in the inordinate will of the first principle in human nature, namely, of the first parent. Thus it is voluntary with respect to nature, that is, by the will of the first principle of nature. And so it is transmitted to all who receive human nature from him, for they are all, as it were, his members." *Compendium of Theology*, p. 211, Part I, chap. 196.

[36] Cap. V, lect. 3.

[37] *Compendium of Theology*, loc. cit.

The solution, as we see, is the same as that given in his soteriology. He says that Christ and those who are saved in Him are, as it were, one person, because God is powerful and is above all human nature; he likewise says that Adam and his descendants are regarded as one man, and that the sin of nature results from the inordinate will of the first principle in nature.

Hence there are two unities, two solidarities that go together. Here as elsewhere the dogma of original sin appears in connection with the dogma of redemption and, in a sense, it is shaped on the same model. But again, here as elsewhere, these two unities are not on the same level. Unity in Christ is presented, along with its proofs, scriptural as well as theological, as a truth inseparable from the whole treatise on the Incarnation. In the questions devoted to the grace of headship, to the power of Christ, to the influence of His life and death on all Christian life, and to the action of baptism and the Eucharist, we may say that the saint constructs the metaphysics of this unity.[38]

Far less study is consecrated to our unity in Adam. The comparison with a living organism is developed at some length, more perhaps than in relation to our unity in Christ. But it is not so fully reasoned out. To give some justification of it, St. Thomas contents himself with quoting a text from Porphyry [39] which, as he knew well, generates more darkness than light; [40] To this he merely adds that Adam, head of the race, virtually contained all his descendants in himself,[41] and recalls that Adam received the supernatural gifts for all men and lost them for all.

Two of these considerations are within the capacities of natural reason, and only one of them is based on theology. None of them, not even the first, which is open to serious difficulties, is closely scrutinized. The saint does not delay over the matter, but hurries to his conclusion by declaring that the first ancestor moves his descendants by generation as the will moves the members of the body by the control it exercises over them, so that the descendants can become

[38] Cf. *The Whole Christ*, pp. 472–76; *Summa*, IIIa, q. 7, 8; q. 13; q. 48 ff.; q. 56, a. 1 ad 3; *In III Sent.*, d. 13, q. 3; *De veritate*, q. 29, a. 3–5.

[39] *Isagoge, De specie* (in H. Busse, *Commentaria in Aristotelem graeca*, IV, 1 [Berlin, 1887]).

[40] The endless quarrel about universals stems from the *Isagoge*.

[41] *Summa*, Ia IIae, q. 81, a. 4, 5.

sinners by the deed of the first ancestor just as the members of the body share in sin through the act of the will.[42] That is all; the paradoxical comparison which condemns the whole universe is stated in a few words that are well chosen, no doubt, but that scarcely bring out its violent character, and the reasoning is so rapid that it has embarrassed the commentators.[43]

To draw attention to such shortcomings,[44] to point out the abyss between the real unity of an individual man and the unity of the collectivity that makes of a society a sort of human being and a moral person, would be futile, for all that is clear enough. What we have to stress is the inequality of conclusiveness achieved by the two theories. Obviously, the one which comes first in Christian thought and imparts the light that has to clarify the other,[45] is the theory of redemption, of the unity of the saved in the Savior.

But we are not sure that St. Thomas expressly searched the one for the light it could shed on the other. The mention of Porphyry which, beginning with the *Summa contra Gentiles*, becomes more and more frequent in connection with our unity in Adam, also occurs in connection with our unity in Christ, but less and less in the later works. It figures in the *Commentary on the Sentences*,[46] but in this passage it has nothing to do with original sin. Later it is dropped. From this point of view, a comparison between the theology of the redemption as developed in the *Summa* and in the *Commentary on the Sentences* is not without interest.

To complete the saint's doctrine an investigation should have been made, we believe, into the supernatural, mystical, real, almost or-

[42] *Ibid.*, a. 1.

[43] "This example of the members has been sharply attacked," writes Medina. He goes on to say that if anyone refuses to admit it, "let him find some that are better and more apt." This is a bit of humor, and seems to imply a concession. *Expositio in primam secundae angelici doctoris divi Thomae Aquinatis*, q. 81, a. 1.

[44] Dominic Soto acknowledges all this, and his discontent contrasts with the satisfaction of St. Thomas, his master. "The comparison is very hard to explain even for a most learned man; I confess my own inability to do so, and I have read nothing on the subject that I would not like to see developed more fully." *De natura et gratia*, I, 8.

[45] St. Thomas clearly perceived the link between the two; see, for example, *Summa*, IIIa, q. 19, a. 4 ad 1 and 3; q. 69; q. 81, a. 3 ad 3; *Ad Rom.*, cap. V, lect. 3; *Contra Gent.*, IV, 5.

[46] *In III Sent.*, d. 18, a. 6, sol. 1.

ganic, and in any case vital unity that can bind all men together in Adam, as that sort of unity does bind them together in Christ. But the commentators, even the best of them, have not pursued that line of thought.[47]

The development of theology has taken a different direction. Explanations similar to those undertaken to give some account of the dogma of redemption, by appealing to juridical considerations, were attempted for the dogma of original sin.[48] Even in this endeavor the dogmas retain their solidarity. The occasion for undertaking this task was furnished by controversies with Protestants, for the latter made generous use of juridical considerations in theology. But their procedure was not the same as that of the Catholics, and it is worth while to note in passing a difference, that is a contrast.

According to the Protestants, as is well known, the justification of Christians is a juridical imputation and a sort of legal fiction: God, in looking on the faithful, consents to see nothing in them but the justice of Christ, which He is pleased to regard as though it were their justice.[49] This is consequently great holiness, but it lacks roots in men; it is an extrinsic and adventitious holiness. In the depths of their souls, Christians remain sinners. Original sin, the innovators continue, has corrupted their whole substance; in all that they are,

[47] Exceptions are rare. We note here only P. Capponi a Porrecta, because of several words he wrote in his annotations to the *Summa*, Ia IIae, q.81, a.1. He speaks of a "deordination that is voluntary, not by the particular will of a given man himself, but rather by the will of the mystic supposit (for, as we have said, Adam is one man with his posterity and consequently one supposit)."

Likewise Medina, after giving a summary of the Thomistic figure of a single individual, says: "But another example, no less apt perhaps, occurs to me"; and he suggests the allegory of a king who ennobles one of his subjects. *Expositio in primam secundae angelici doctoris divi Thomae Aquinatis*, q.81, a.1.

[48] St. Thomas had already done the same. Cf. *Contra Gent.*, IV, 52; *Summa*, Ia IIae, q.81, a.1; *De malo*, q.4, a.1.

[49] "By faith in Christ the justice of Christ becomes our justice, and all that is His and He Himself becomes ours. . . . He who believes in Christ, cleaves to Christ and is one with Christ, having the same justice as He." Luther, *Sermo de duplici iustitia*, 1519, in *Werke* (Weimar, 1884), II, 146. "Therefore we are not said to be formally holy, as a wall is said to be white because of its inherent whiteness. Inherent holiness is not enough. Hence Christ is our whole sanctity." *In epistolam ad Galatas commentarius*, 1535 (*ibid.*, XL, 1, 197). "We wish to remain in the justice that is in the category of relation and not of quality, that God may regard us as pious and righteous; we cannot regard ourselves as such." *Tischreden*, 2933 a (Weimar, 1914), III, 96.

they are sinners and sin itself: "natural things are wholly corrupt in the sight of God." [50] In a word, sin is as real and deep-seated for Christians as justification is extrinsic and superficial.

The opposite is true in Catholic theology. Redemption, the good, is intrinsic, and sin remains relatively superficial. Though the two may be formulated in juridical terminology, that does not mean that sin takes priority over restoration.

The juridical theory of original sin is ancient, as is understandable; theologians are men, and the juridical spirit is natural to many men, if not to all. In any case, the theory enjoyed immense favor during the epoch we are speaking of, and has not disappeared in our day. It comes to this: in bestowing grace on Adam, the physical head and the common ancestor of mankind, God appointed him to be the representative of the entire species and made him the juridical head of the race, equipped to act in the name of the whole human family. The justice and gifts he received, he received for all men, and all received them in him. But if Adam lost them, he would lose them for all, and all would lose them in him.

Whether this involves a pact, a contract, a decree, or a number of decrees, matters little. In virtue of the divine dispositions, human nature received in the first man a sort of legal existence, a juridical personality that enabled it to receive and transmit God's gift and even obligated it to do so. God, for His part, wished human nature to be clothed with this nuptial garment.

But Adam sinned, and the precious raiment was lost for all men. From then on, when men received their nature at birth, they received it simply as such, lacking the grace with which it should have been adorned. Therefore nature in Adam's descendants was not as God wished it to be; it was in a state of disorder and sin: *peccatum naturae*. Nature comes to men without the grace that had been given and that ought to be possessed; consequently nature was deprived of this grace because of a sin committed in the first parent. Original sin was defined as *privatio gratiae, residens in natura et voluntaria voluntate Adae.*

Such, in general outline, is the juridical conception of original sin. Its clarity and coherence are immediately apparent, and we need but read any theological treatise to apprehend all the details it ac-

[50] Luther, *Enarratio psalmi LI*, in *D. Martin Luthers Werke* (Weimar, 1914) XL, 2, p. 324.

counts for in the fall of man. But, as St. Robert Bellarmine noted,[51] we also perceive straightway that it does not eliminate the difficulty. In particular, it is based on an affirmation which recurs frequently in tradition and therefore has to be true, but which nothing in the theory makes conceivable: the affirmation of a sin of nature.

According to the juridical view, God regards nature as sinful because it is no longer such as He wishes it to be and because sin is precisely deviation from God's law. Undoubtedly so; but what is this law of God and to whom is it addressed? Nature in general does not exist. God's will, the foundation of all that is real, is directed to what is real, that is, to individual natures. God could evidently impose on Adam, to whom He had given grace and the means of guarding it, the duty of preserving grace forever. But as for Adam's descendants, who did not exist at that time, how could God impose on them the duty of possessing a thing which, as He foresaw, they had no means of receiving?

Prius est esse quam esse sic. Before God could require nature as such to preserve anything at all, He would first have to give it existence. Whatever commands God may have laid on Adam, nature is not obliged to do anything as long as it does not exist. We have to bear in mind that Adam is only a human individual. Whether he is the first or the last, whether he is the object of a pact or of a decree or of nothing, the fact remains that he is what he is. He is an individual, and can perform only individual acts. In certain cases these acts can assuredly take on a special gravity: they can bring down disastrous consequences on his entire race. But this gravity will affect him alone. His descendants will be miserable because of the ruin inflicted on them; but this does not necessarily involve the consequence that they are defiled and sinful. "How could I have committed sin, if I was not as yet born?" one might ask, were it not for fear of verging on irreverence.

Nevertheless, the retort might be made, is not nature truly deprived of grace? Are we so sure of this? By what right can we say that absence of grace in a man who has not sinned personally is a privation? Grace, as we know well, is supernatural; nothing in nature as such has a claim to it. In treating of original sin we may not overlook what we insist on when we treat of grace or the end of

[51] *Secunda controversia, de amissione gratiae et statu peccati*, V, 16.

man. Some theologians will not even admit that the beatific vision is in a certain sense desired by finite intellects, for fear of compromising the transcendence of the supernatural, although the desire in question could be frustrated without entailing any real privation. How, then, in the present instance, can we say without inconsistency that the absence of grace is a real privation, and a privation that is a sin? Surely it is such in him who had received grace and who could and ought to have preserved it. But what did the others do to deserve that affliction? Can we say that anything is lacking to their nature, if their nature is complete?

The objector may insist that at least with reference to the divine will, the divine plan, something is lacking to Adam's posterity, and the divine will is the norm of good and evil. But is that possible? Is it possible that God should seriously will to find in men something which He does not give them any means of possessing? Is it possible for God to regard them in any way as bound by a commandment which the laws of the universe, His very own laws, prevent them from observing and even from knowing? Would not God display as much justice, more truth, and much more goodness if He did not look for grapes on brambles and figs on bushes? Indeed, God is the norm of good and evil, but only because He is being itself and the principle of all being and of all good. Why then does He have to uphold, and why should He wish to uphold, a plan that does not correspond to anything inherent in real being? Is He not the super-eminent prototype as well as the source of all reality? In the last analysis, who causes human nature to come into existence thus defiled in every generation? Adam is dead; the present question concerns an order of the world that did not create itself. Who then, if not He who created it, is responsible for what it now produces by its own power?

After all, the privation, if there is privation, does not exist except in Him, that is, in the sort of deception He practices in seeing that men are born merely as men. Or, if we insist that the privation exists in men themselves, it exists in them only with reference to Him and because of the way He regards them. The sin is said to consist precisely in this privation; hence the consequence follows—we scarcely dare express the thought—that it exists in Him or because of Him. It is He who, by His way of regarding men, makes them sinners; and He need only change this attitude to enable them to be perfectly in order; nothing would have to be modified in them. In that case, can we go on defining sin as opposition to God and His will? [52]

All these considerations, as is apparent, are designed to focus attention on one defect: the absence of any explanation that might enable us to understand a certain physical, ontological presence of all nature in Adam, a real union of all men in their first origin. Yet this is the essential point in the doctrine of original sin and is, so to speak, the heart of the mystery.

The point thus clearly called to mind by a lacuna in the juridical theory, which in itself is so clear, is brought out by the convergence of all Christian teaching. For the latter asserts that there is a solidarity in evil by asserting that there is a solidarity in the Redeemer. To recall what has been said on this subject, we here transcribe some lines from the draft De doctrina catholica.[53] "Just as in the first Adam, who is the type of Him who was to come, the human race fell in its head, so in the last Adam, that is, in Christ Jesus, the race was reconciled to God in its second head." [54]

This economy of Christian teaching is a signpost. When we thus see the doctrine of original sin resolutely orientated toward redemption and solidarity in the Redeemer, we can perceive exactly how the doctrine stands and how it is intelligible, without wasting time in seeking the precise point where theology ought to insert it. "A thing is intelligible so far as it is in act." We must reduce this teaching to unity in Christ, that is, to the whole Christ, to Christ the Redeemer.

II. Theology of Original Sin
According to Christ's Unity and Redemption

The preceding chapter prepared the way for a theology of this kind. There we showed that man at his origin ought to have been divinized in his unity, because he was divinized in his being. He ought to have possessed the whole of human nature more truly and really than men can possess it through their own powers, and ought to have been more intimately united to all possible men.

Moreover, this unity ought to have been perfectly adapted to nature, since nature had not yet set up any opposition to God through sin. It ought to have been propagated along with super-

[52] The answer to all this is given below.
[53] Already referred to above.
[54] Mansi, Amplissima collectio conciliorum, LIII, 291.

natural life, in the way that nature is propagated; and marriage in that state would have been a sort of equivalent of our present sacraments. Should not the act which actuates humanity to the highest degree in the natural state, to the point of making it a cause of man, have actuated its elevation to the highest degree so as to communicate this elevation? Furthermore the unity ought to have existed originally where nature itself existed originally, that is, at the beginnings of the race. If we are able to imagine a condition of things that was destined never to take place, we can conceive that the sin of any man whatever would have had disastrous consequences; but at the same time we see that the result could never have been so disastrous as it actually was because of the sin committed at these first origins.

Humanity, in the full, supernatural measure of its existence, deprived itself of the gifts that were to have made it more happy and more unified by making it divine. But the offer of the gift was not retracted; the sin had been foreseen even in man's first elevation, and in virtue of this elevation and its definitive character, nature remained destined for the gift. Hence nature is in opposition to the gift and to itself, in absolute interior disorder, in sin.

We should note well that there is sin only in relation to the supernatural order, and because of God's persistent, obstinate goodness. If God withdrew His offer, nature would then recover its equilibrium, or would almost do so. Humanity would be confined to the human sphere; but what other exigency does it have? The reason why humanity is not as it ought to be is to be found in its opposition to the infinite, divine love with which God continues to love it. Let no one complain of divine severity in connection with original sin; nor should anyone speak chiefly of justice: originally there is nothing but unstinted charity. There is no inexplicable divine decree declaring men sinners when they have as yet done nothing; there is nothing but an inconceivable tenderness that continues to pursue men, whatever evil they may have committed. The privation of grace which is their sin is but the negative expression of an interior orientation toward the grace that God is keeping for them, and this orientation itself is but the effect corresponding in them to the eternal offer that refuses to be withdrawn.

In a purely natural order the juridical personification of nature and the coming of a sin to each man through the act of an individual appears to us incomprehensible. If absurdity is to be avoided, original sin has to be so minimized that it ceases to be a sin. But then, what becomes of the dogma of redemption? And in the supernatural order the whole juridical structure merely expresses in the realm of law what is first realized in the depths of being. The will of God is the cause of things and the expression of truth itself. If God decides to love all mankind in the first man and to give it, in this man, His grace and His gifts, so that in him all mankind would receive or lose them, He truly causes mankind to exist in that man, at least sufficiently to make it capable of receiving and losing. This grace and love have precisely the effect of making mankind exist in such a way.

We have no need of recourse to a multiplication of arbitrary decrees. Everything holds together naturally. The supernatural elevation, by supernaturally perfecting man from the social as well as from the individual point of view, establishes a supernatural solidarity in virtue of which a collective sin will destroy the elevation. In the same way the hypostatic union of the Redeemer's humanity with the divinity, which invests the humanity with its redemptive power, perfects it in its social aspect and its union with other men, and enables it to communicate its justice to all.

As is evident, the two unions are not equal in perfection. The union in the Redeemer, who is God, has its ultimate principle and its fullness in itself. The union in the first man, who is but a divinized human being, has not reached its culmination; it is, as has been said, a union that merely began, and that began only to collapse. Hence it is essentially imperfect and incomplete.

An exact determination of its limits and a fixing of its coefficient of depth and intimacy would surely be interesting. But this is impossible. God has not given us much information about it; it is an affair of the past that no longer exists. All we can say is that its reality is gauged by the results it has produced and by the sin it truly engenders in each man.

Therefore this union is real, because this sin is real; it has to be real also because the original elevation to grace is real. But it is imperfect, as the sin is imperfect. For if original sin is the gravest of all sins by the extent of its diffusion, it is the slightest of all from the standpoint of the malice it leaves in the soul: it does not imply any personal deordination toward evil, it is not the object of any true repentance or of purpose of amendment, and it does not of itself make us incapable of natural beatitude nor, consequently, of natural moral perfection.

All these restrictions must be found in the unity in virtue of which original sin comes to each man: this unity does not penetrate to the ultimate basis of our personal being, and so is not the ultimate human unity. We may not be able to describe it in greater detail, but we can say that it is imperfect.

Such as it is, however, this unity, in unifying men, joined the human universe to them, as we have pointed out. Therefore the universe has been drawn down with them in their fall, and the Apostle says that all creation has been subjected to frustration despite its resistance and has been reduced to the servitude of corruption.[55] It also united the angelic world to the world of men, and caused all finite intelligences to form a sort of luminous and living whole in God who made them all alive with the single life of grace.

Indeed, this is the way the sin came; it descended from on high. A cleavage occurred in the angelic world: some of the angels broke with God, and thus broke themselves. The whole was so closely united that the evil tended to invade the whole.[56] That was the temptation of Eden; the unity was shattered by an inevitable concussion, because one of its columns collapsed. The man remained free, no doubt, and did not fall except by his own fault; [57] but he fell with and through the devil. Thus he put himself under the power of him who has empire over death, that is, of Satan; [58] he was an accomplice in the same crime and so was condemned to the same punishment.

Man contracted original sin. Because of this sin he was drawn down through a variety of errors and terrors to that final unending punishment with the rebellious angels, his corrupters and masters. . . . Thus the matter stood; the whole condemned mass of the human race lay prone in evil and, indeed, wallowed in it, and rushed headlong from evil to evil;

[55] Rom. 8:20 f.

[56] "If you are looking for an example of change, you find it in the devil; if you are looking for the contamination of generation, you find it in Adam. Therefore, when the Apostle said, 'By one man sin entered into this world,' he meant the sin propagated by generation. But the sin committed by imitation entered into the world through the devil, not through one man." St. Augustine, *Opus imperfectum contra Iulianum*, II, 49 (*PL*, XLV, 1163).

[57] St. Thomas, *De malo*, q.3, a.3, 5; *Summa*, Ia IIae, q.81, a.1.

[58] Council of Trent, Sess. V (Denz., 788).

and having joined the party of the angels who had sinned, mankind was paying the richly deserved penalties for its wicked insurrection.[59]

Here we behold the order of sin—if one can speak of order in this connection—the power of evil, which continues to rage in man and the world. Sin that is now committed is not merely the isolated act of an individual: freely welcomed and accepted, it is the immense apostasy of all apostates. The world, in the sense frequently occurring in the Gospel, is not only the place where men sin, but is also the domain where the evil one, the "prince of this world," works his havoc.

We delude ourselves if we cherish the idea that we are not tempted by ourselves. The disorder is within, and solicitation from outside would remain ineffective without internal complicity. But we should also err were we to imagine that we are not tempted by another, by him whom Scripture calls the tempter.

Personal sins are a sort of continuation of the original fault. The sinner makes the sin of the race his own, he actuates it in himself, and assimilates it by a sort of ratification. He sins "after the similitude of the transgression of Adam" [60] by deliberately entering into the solidarity of evil.

If we conceive the matter in this way, we understand how original sin can be a privation of grace in each man, owing to Adam's sin, which is truly a privation. For if nature is complete without grace so long as it has never had grace, once it has received grace it is wounded to death when it loses grace, because the gift has actuated splendors of life which were but possible before and which, vanishing with the grace that departs, leaves nature bereft of what had become its supreme necessity, and so it is desolated by the strictest kind of privation. By the gift of original justice, each man has received an actuation of these splendors, to a lesser degree undoubtedly than if he had received grace by a personal title, but nevertheless really, in the measure of his union with Adam. In losing grace, therefore, he loses a life that had been his own, and so this sin is for him the death of his soul.[61]

But if grace remains his own, the reason is that God continues

[59] St. Augustine, *Enchiridion*, 26 f. (*PL*, XL, 245).
[60] Rom. 5:14.
[61] Denz., 789.

to offer it to him; and therefore God intends a restoration and a redemption. Belief in original sin is but an aspect of belief in God's redeeming love.

Accordingly we may say that this sin leaves human nature at once unharmed and wounded, that God could have created man in the condition in which he now comes into the world,[62] that nature is not injured in anything that is natural to it,[63] as contemporary theology teaches with ever-growing conviction, and that, nevertheless, man is less attracted to good and more heavily weighed down by matter than his normal state would have permitted, as writers on spiritual and ascetical subjects often aver. Nothing is lost except the supernatural gift; but this loss is a true privation for nature, as we have said. This leaves in nature an inner emptiness, an upsetting of equilibrium, a defect that is less than in the case of mortal sin, yet real.

To describe all this in detail is impossible; but we see clearly enough that this rupture with unity, charity, and good readily manifests itself in a certain egoism, a certain duplicity of conscience, a certain indifference to good. We wished to do no more than explain the principle of this collapse. But the principle lacks precision, since we cannot fix exactly the measure and the manner of the unity and existence of all nature in Adam; hence we cannot specify the exact consequences.

Moreover no one can venture to clarify this principle by natural reason alone, for we are dealing with a unity that is essentially supernatural. The mystery may not be suppressed or restricted in any way; that is out of the question. All we can do is to perceive exactly where the mystery is situated and to what order of truth it belongs. It consists essentially, not in the transmission of a sin or in a complicated juridical process, but in that which permits and produces this transmission, that is, in the divinization of unity entailed by the divinization of being.

To understand this, we have to understand the order of divinized being; and we can understand the latter because we are included in such an order, and especially because we are included in a unity that is similar but far more perfect: the unity of Christ and His mystical

---

[62] Denz., 1055. We know, according to the system of Baius, what meaning to give to this disputed proposition.
[63] Denz., 817 ff.

body. Thus the mystery is explained by another mystery, with an explanation that is fully adapted to it, and hence fully adapted to man; for this mystery embraces man as he is in himself, and joins him to Christ.

CHAPTER VIII

MARY, MOTHER OF JESUS

> "If anyone will not admit . . . that
> the Blessed Virgin is the Mother of
> God, let him be anathema."
>
> *Anathem. Cyrilli*

THE final step in the long preparation for Christ is His mother.
We cannot say anything more glorious or more beautiful about
her than that, as the mother of Jesus Christ, she is inseparable from
Christ and from all that is Christ.

This is what we wish to write about in the present chapter. *Dignare me laudare te, Virgo sacrata.* The subject is delicate because it
is so stupendous.

In speaking of Our Lady, we ought not to make improbable assertions
about matters that are beyond our knowledge, for example, that when
she was a small child she went up to the Temple to offer herself to God
with extraordinary fervor and a heart on fire with love. For all we know,
she went simply in obedience to her parents. Again, why should we say
that, after the Blessed Virgin heard the prophetic words of the old man
Simeon, she ever afterward had the passion of Jesus before her eyes? . . .
"Thy own soul a sword shall pierce" (Luke 2:35). You see well, my
dear Mother, that this was a prediction of future events.

If a sermon on the Blessed Virgin is to bear fruit, it must describe her
real life, such as the Gospel gives us a glimpse of, and not her fancied life.
And we perceive clearly that her real life at Nazareth and later on must
have been quite ordinary. . . . "He was subject to them" (Luke 2:51).
How simple it all is!

Sometimes the Blessed Virgin is represented as being quite unapproachable. Instead, we ought to show that she was imitable in her practice of
hidden virtues; we ought to point out that she lived a life of faith, just as
we do.

We know well that the Blessed Virgin is queen of heaven and earth; but she is more of a mother than a queen, and we ought not to give out the idea, as I have heard it done more than once, that because of her prerogatives she eclipses the glory of all the saints, just as the sun, rising in brilliance, makes the stars disappear. My God, what a strange thing to say! A mother who makes the glory of her children disappear! For my part, I believe just the opposite; I think that she will greatly increase the splendor of the elect.

We do well to speak of her prerogatives. But we should not stop there. We should make her loved. If, when we hear a sermon on the Blessed Virgin, the preacher tries to do nothing from beginning to end but call forth our admiration, we become bored, and that does not lead to love and imitation. Who knows but what some souls will not experience a certain sense of estrangement from a creature so lofty? [1]

This is what the little St. Theresa said on her deathbed, and her protest shows well what piety can add to theology, *ut legem credendi lex statuat supplicandi.*

The grandeurs of Mary are such that, if we consider them in isolation, they make those of Christ appear less unique and those of Christians less fair; a strange glory for a mother, to cast a shadow over the splendor of her Son and her children! Does this not make her appear to be a sort of intermediary between Christ and Christians, separating Him from them by all the distance intervening between her and them, and between Him and her? To make her out as an exceptional and isolated being introduces confusion into our thoughts and perplexity into the devotion that the Christian religion ought to have toward her. As though the essence of Christianity were not union and unity!

Devotion to the Blessed Virgin goes with devotion to Christ. Indeed, for many centuries the two had no separate existence. The martyrs had long had their special feasts—going as far back as 155 or 156 in the case of St. Polycarp—and Mary did not as yet have one. The first feasts dedicated to her, the Annunciation and the Presentation, date from the fourth century, and are mainly feasts of our Lord. It is only beginning with the fifth century that feasts properly dedicated to Mary, such as the Nativity and the *Dormitio*, begin to ap-

[1] St. Theresa of the Child Jesus, *Novissima verba* (Lisieux, 1926), pp. 154-57.

pear in the East, and such celebrations are not found in the Church of the West until the seventh century.[2]

Nevertheless, as thus included in the cult of Christ, devotion to the Blessed Virgin did not fail to grow and develop, although in restricted fashion. But once it was established, we see it flourishing with extraordinary vigor, like new sprouts which do not appear until after the buds, but which are remarkably strong because they spring up from the roots. As soon as churches begin to be dedicated to her, we find many of them, and they are the greatest ones.[3] And as soon as feasts begin to be consecrated to her, they multiply rapidly, and the faithful cannot have enough of them. Even in our own day the cult of the Blessed Virgin closely parallels that of Christ; we have the same cycle of feasts, the same titles, the same mention in public prayer, the same perpetual presence in Christian piety.

Such, if we may say so, is the Mariology that flourishes in the Church: it is inseparable from Christology. And, in fact, is not the great and the first doctrinal definition of Christology also the great truth of Mariology, the definition concerning the Mother of God? Such is the Mariology we envisage in this work: a Mariology in which Mary's glory consists in being united to Christ and Christianity, in being the Mother of Christ.

I. MARY'S MATERNITY

In speaking of Christ, our first and essential task is to declare what He is. The same is true in speaking about His mother. The essential thing about Christ is that He is God, man, and one; He is perfectly God, perfectly man, perfectly one. The essential thing about the Blessed Virgin is her part in making her Son what He is, her causality in making Him perfectly man. In order that He might be man, a mother of God was needed. Without her, God could indeed have created a human nature for His Son, but it would not have been of our race; God could have created all possible likenesses to us in this human nature, but these common traits would have been deceptions of a sort. Without a mother of God, God would not have recapitu-

[2] We take these data from L. Duchesne, *Les origines du culte chrétien* (Paris, 1920), pp. 285–301.

[3] Thus at Rome, in the fourth century alone, we have St. Mary Major, Santa Maria in Trastevere, Santa Maria Antiqua.

lated in Christ His creation that had fallen, as St. Irenaeus says.[4] Without a mother of God, the Word would have been merely similar to us but would not have been perfectly consubstantial, *homoousios*, in the formula of St. Athanasius,[5] and the triumphant and magnificent verse of Scripture that speaks of the absoluteness of the divine plan would have to be effaced: "Of the seed of Abraham he taketh hold." [6]

Nothing more sublime could be conceived. We have here the supreme principle of Mariology, which is also the supreme principle of Christianity and Christology. The mother of God defines the Incarnation, for the part that concerns men. And the Incarnation defines Christianity. It is in Mary alone that the Incarnation is the assumption of the concrete human race, the taking up of all of us into one of us. Without her, the God-man would not be my brother, He would not have my blood in His veins and my heredity in His background; and real and concrete man would not be fully united to God in Him.

Without Mary, accordingly, Christianity would be altered as a religion. Christianity is the absolute and perfect religion because it is the perfect bond between God and men; and it is such a bond through the God-man who is one with God, one with men, and one in Himself. But without the Blessed Virgin the God-man would not be completely one with men; the bond with God would not encircle men in themselves; they would not be made, in Him, full sharers in the divine nature, in grace, in divinization.

Without her, furthermore, the divine unity that incorporates all men in itself would not be interior to the race of men; it would in some way be superimposed on them, but would not be their own unity. In other words, the mystical body would lack its final perfection, and Christ would not be "whole" in all fullness. This point has to be stressed in the present work: it shows how Mariology is necessarily connected with the theology of the mystical body.

This last glory of the Blessed Virgin is expressed both well and poorly by calling her the "neck" of the mystical body,[7] or, as some

---

[4] *Adversus haereses*, II, xxi, 10; cf. III, xix, 3 (*PG*, VII, 955, 941).

[5] Cf. *Epistola ad Epictetum*, 4, 5, 7 ff. (*PG*, XXVI, 1056 ff.).

[6] Heb. 2:16.

[7] The formula comes down from the Middle Ages, in commentaries on the Canticle of Canticles. Cf. "Thy neck as jewels," Cant. 1:9; see also Cant 4:4; 7:4.

authors of our day explain with considerable zeal, by saying that she is its heart.[8] For our part, we do not care much for either of these formulas. Prudence must be exercised in employing allegories; if we push them too far we come to unpleasant details that cast a shadow of unreality on the doctrine itself. The best thing to do is to adhere to the truth signified, that is, to say that the mystical body is a super-natural unity and that in this unity the Blessed Virgin is the point of junction, the means by which the unity enters into the mass and holds it fast. Thus she is not so much a particular member as the channel through which life flows into the whole body; her role is not partial but total, although secondary. As the mother of God she is in her way what the God-man is in His way: both have a universal func-tion.

Mary has a part in the Church, no doubt, just as she has a part in the mystical body. But she has her part in a special way, in the way of a whole: she joins Jesus Christ to the whole Church by joining Him to mankind. In view of her special position and universal func-tion in passive redemption, of which we shall speak later, it seems that she does not, like the rest of the faithful, enter into the sacramental order, which applies the fruits of the redemption by degrees. Did she not give us Christ, who is the principle of this entire order? And, except for the Eucharist, which is a totality in the sacramental econ-omy, what special fruit could the sacraments have conferred on her?

She is more a type than a daughter of the Church. Her role, like that of the Church, is to give Christ, to be the mother of Christians and the spouse of the Spirit. As the Church is holy, she is holy; as the Church is preserved from all error, so she is preserved from all fault—and the same pope who defined papal infallibility also defined the Immaculate Conception. As the Church is the only house of God, outside which there is no salvation, so she is the gate of heaven, through which all grace comes down to Christians. As the Church is all this exclusively for the benefit of men, so she is all this in order to be completely the mother of Christ and of Christians. Moreover, as heresy has reproached belief in the Church as a belittling of devotion to Christ, it has cast the same reproach at piety toward the Blessed Virgin.

[8] Thus P. E. Mura, C. Feckes, M. J. Scheeben. According to Scheeben, Mary may also be regarded as the head of the mystical body, considering the latter as the assembly of the faithful, therefore not including Christ.

This position of the Blessed Virgin relatively to the human race is unique, like that of Christ and like her own part in the work of Christ. In thus intervening in the union of men among themselves and in their union with God, she intervenes in procuring the very end of mankind, whether the absolutely last end, which is the possession of the absolute Good, or the last end relative to man, which is the possession of the supreme human good.

In the order of human sanctity, consequently, she has a total sanctity, which is of course inferior to her Son's sanctity. It is a sanctity that befits the mother of Him who is holiness itself: she is "full of grace." [9]

Other saints, however great they may be, can be thought of as having never existed; their place would have been taken by others who would have been as good or perhaps better. But Mary could not have been removed without gravely modifying the very physiognomy of Christ and of Christianity; the precise point at which God establishes contact with us would have been suppressed.

The other saints have particular kinds of holiness exclusive of one another. Their sanctity is that of members. The foot is not the hand, and the ear is not the eye; St. Benedict Labre is quite different from St. Francis de Sales, and St. Peter Damien is different from St. Theresa of Lisieux. But Mary, who is holy in her capacity as the mother of Christ, possesses all holiness: the unblemished splendor of the woman clad with the sun is in striking fashion the splendor of the sun itself.

This holiness partakes of all the matchless perfections of Christ. Its excellence, which consists in uniting Christ to all men, makes of it a holiness of union with all; it is a common and everyday holiness, an imitable and approachable holiness, because it is pure holiness.

There is nothing extraordinary in Mary's life, nothing to excite wonder. As Jesus was quite simply a man who did not exalt Himself above His station and did not harden Himself against pain or despise the slight value to be found in us, so she was simply His mother, the woman whose Son is Jesus.

All the facts at the disposal of Christian piety show her living, in faith, hope, and charity, the life that God appointed for her. She does not hesitate to ask herself exactly what the future will bring,

---

[9] We cite the following very instructive passages from St. Thomas: *Summa*, IIIa, q.27, a.5 et ad 1; *Expositio in salutationem angelicam.*

but at the same time she always and in everything sees, loves, and carries out fully the will of God. She needs no scientific reflections or scholastic formulas. She grasps, as a mother can, with an intuition born of love, which is adequate but may remain indistinct, what her Son is and what mission He came to accomplish. She accepts and wishes what He wishes, and with all her heart allows her consent to be fixed and carried out in His. Because of this unique excellence of hers she is the Christian par excellence; and that is exactly what she ought to be.

She is the means which God in Christ employs to be the neighbor, the equal, and the blood relative of all men. How could anything in her be remote or hopelessly raised above us? In the order of the Incarnation, sublimity and God-likeness consist in being near, in being given.

What is true of the divine maternity is true of the privileges that flow from it. At first sight these privileges may seem to set the Blessed Virgin apart from mankind; actually they join her closely to mankind. We have to consider them as they are, that is, in the whole Christ, by reducing them to Christ.

The first privilege to consider is Mary's universal mediation, which merely expresses the divine maternity under another form. We have to speak of the two in the same way. Mary is the mediatress of all graces for all men.

No less truly and properly we may affirm that, by God's will, nothing whatever of the inexhaustible treasury of all grace which the Lord heaped up is imparted to us except through Mary; for "grace and truth came by Jesus Christ" (John 1:17). As no one can draw near to the Father on high except through the Son, so in general no one can draw near to the Son except through His mother.[10]

She it is "of whom was born Jesus" (Matt. 1:16). She is His true mother, and therefore is the worthy and most acceptable mediatress to the Mediator.[11]

But her mediation is essentially derivative; it depends on the mediation of Christ, which it serves to clarify. As God's mother, she shows

[10] Leo XIII, encyclical *Octobri mense* (Denz., 1940 a).

[11] Leo XIII, encyclical *Fidentem* (Denz., 1940 a). In the Mass of Mary, Mediatress of All Graces, she is called "Our mother and mediatress with Thee," and "Thy mother and our mediatress."

precisely how Christ has truly united mankind to God in Himself. For Mary, the mother of God, is also our sister, as St. Athanasius pointed out long ago.[12] She is not a mediatress placed by Christ between Himself and men in order to keep them at a distance. On the contrary, she is the means employed by Him to abolish remoteness and to put the human race in direct contact with God.

Therefore we have only one Mediator, and He needs no other to help Him. But one element in His complete mediation is supplied by His mother. Mary's mediation is, in the first instance, contained in that of Christ and is exercised in Him: the mediation of Jesus is perfect on its human side because of the quality it receives from Mary. This mediation, as found in the Blessed Virgin, who is a person, is exercised in a way befitting a person, through personal acts, prayers, and intercessions. But it is by no means an isolated and detached mediation added to Christ's mediation from without. It expresses and actuates one element in Christ's mediation, the element by which His mediation is fully adapted, donated, and made accessible to men. In a word, it is exclusively a mediation of God's mother, that is, a mediation of the God-man who, because He has a mother, is perfectly man.

Operari sequitur esse. Mary's mediation, which has the purpose of serving as a bond and of conferring the final perfection on the bond between God and men, operates by engendering union. Her function, her natural inclination, and her spontaneous action in the order of grace is to unite, to intercede, to request, to obtain. "Even when she is not invoked, of her own accord she is always at hand to help us." [13]

This is true, not only at the moment of the Incarnation, but forever. As long as Christ exists He is man, in God's designs, because He is Mary's Son. And since He is her Son physically and not merely in a moral sense, her mediation is likewise not merely moral but is physical and ontological; it is a mediation of grace and merit, and not only of prayer and intercession.

On the possibility of meriting for others, some explanation will be given when we come to speak of merit. But if, as we shall see then, this possibility is based on the vital union that makes men members

---

[12] *Epist. ad Epictetum,* 7 (PG, XXVI, 1061).
[13] Leo XIII, encyclical *Magna Dei mater* (*Acta Sanctae Sedis*, XXV [1892–93], 141).

of a single body, and if, on the other hand, Mary is a member of that body with a perfection belonging to her alone, we perceive immediately that her life-giving, supernatural influence must have a unique and plenary character. The communion of saints, which is the basis of that possibility, is fully operative in her alone, because she is the means through which Holiness itself comes into contact with the whole race.

Through this fellowship of prerogatives and will between Mary and Christ, she richly deserved to be made the repairer of the lost world and the dispenser of all the gifts Christ procured for us by His blood and death. . . . Since she excels all in holiness and union with Christ and has been taken into association with Christ in the work of man's salvation, she merits for us *de congruo*, as said in theology, what Christ merited *de condigno*, and is the chief agent in the conferring of graces.[14]

The same is true of the title "Coredemptrix," which is even more open to misunderstanding.

She so grievously suffered and almost died with her suffering and dying Son, she so wholeheartedly renounced her maternal rights over her Son for the salvation of men and immolated her Son, as far as was in her power, to placate God's justice, that she may deservedly be said to have redeemed the human race along with Christ.[15]

Undoubtedly there is only one Redeemer, as there is only one Mediator; no one adds anything at all to His superabundant redemption, as though something might be lacking. Nevertheless He is the Redeemer of men by being united to them; He can transmit His satisfactions and His holiness to men because He is, as it were, one person with them.[16] But He is united to them because He is the Son of the Blessed Virgin. Therefore Mary, who makes it possible for the God-man to belong to a sinful race, also makes it possible for Him to be the Redeemer of that race.

Accordingly, as Christ's mediation is closely bound up with Mary, His redemption is closely bound up with her. The Immaculate

[14] Pius X, encyclical *Ad diem* (Denz., 1978 a).

[15] Benedict XV, apostolic letter *Inter Sodalitia* (Denz., 1978 a; see also the texts of Pius XI and of the Holy Office there quoted, and the text of Pius X cited in the preceding note).

[16] Cf. chaps. 10 and 11.

Virgin, wholly pure as she is, establishes the Word in solidarity with sin by joining Him to mankind,[17] and it is this solidarity that primarily dedicates Him to the redemption and to death. Thus, as Christ takes His origin, on the human side, in her, so also Christ's redemption takes its origin in her.[18]

Such, we believe, is essentially the redemption we can speak of in the case of the Blessed Virgin: it is wholly contained in the one Redeemer. It is the expression of the great principles of soteriology in God's mother and in Mariology, just as all that has been said of her holiness is the expression of the great principle of Christology in God's mother.

Since the Blessed Virgin is a person, however, this essential redemption by union is expressed by her personal attitudes and actions. Theologians endeavor to determine their nature and bearing; they speak of the offering she made of Christ, the renouncement of rights she may have had over Him, her intimate fellowship with His dispositions as Redeemer, and such compassion as befitted her role in the coredemption. But they are careful to stress that all this had no value except through her union with Christ and His redemption; the part of a mother is to unite. God did not wish her to suffer martyrdom; Christ alone was to undergo that, for fear lest anyone might regard her apart. Jesus and His cross alone occupy this height; but "there stood by the cross of Jesus His mother" (John 19:25).

Moreover, as we shall point out in a later chapter devoted to the matter, Christ's redemption, which is superabundant, is given a mystic continuation where He Himself is given a mystic completion, in the members of His mystical body. The Blessed Virgin has a unique and total function in this body, as we have explained. Therefore redemption by this member will have a unique and total function in this continuation of the redemption.

II. Mary and the Preparation of Christ

If Mary is thus inseparable from Christ, she is associated with all that belongs to Christ, with the lengthy preparation that was the beginning of His coming as with the lengthy continuation by which He is prolonged in Christianity. To perceive all that Christ is, we

[17] Cf. Rom. 8:3; II Cor. 5:21.
[18] Cf. the pages that follow, on the Immaculate Conception.

have to bear in mind these two long periods in the history of mankind. We have to do the same if we wish to have an adequate knowledge of what His mother is. To bring the Blessed Virgin before our eyes, the liturgy calls up the remote past and the very origins of eternity. "From the beginning and before the world, was I created." "The Lord possessed me in the beginning of His ways." [19]

As soon as the Incarnation is in question, from the very decree that decided it, she is likewise in question. For God as for us, the God-man is man through His mother; and in willing and predestinating Him as man, God also willed and predestined her. God wills the God-man as a fullness of divinization and holiness. But this was to be a divinization and holiness coming to a sinful race and displaying all the greater excellence by the immense restoration to be accomplished.

The same is true of Mary. She is willed as the mother of this fullness and as a condition and an aspect of this outpouring of divinization. Accordingly she is willed in an order of absolute sanctity, and so, like all that is holy, she is meant to be immaculate. But she is also willed as joined by God to a sinful race, and hence as being in that race and associated with it, and therefore in solidarity with sin. What does this mean if not that the immense restoration willed in Christ was to be realized in her with unequaled fullness, that she was to stem from the sinful race although exempt from sin, and that she was to be wholly immaculate, though by way of preservation and exception? Thus she was willed with the will that willed the Son Himself and predestined Him as incarnate, and she was at the same time willed with the will that willed sinful humanity as the matter in which the Incarnation was to be effected. She was to be redeemed as befits one who is, in a certain real sense, the principle of redemption. "As the mother of the Redeemer, she is redeemed in a more sublime way." [20]

This is passive redemption in its perfection, because it is a perfect union with active redemption. At this point of decisive entrance, the Redeemer ought to produce a first, triumphant, absolute effect; otherwise we should have to say that, in a certain sense, He is unequal

[19] Epistle for the Common of the Blessed Virgin and a number of her feasts, the Immaculate Conception, the Nativity, and others. Cf. Ecclus. 24:14; Prov. 8:22.

[20] Pius IX, encyclical *Ineffabilis Deus* (*Collectio Lacensis*, VI, 839).

to His task. This is passive redemption at its origin, in its first and primordial realization; if it has any imperfection at that stage, it will be marred by imperfection throughout its course, and will not be worthy of God. If the redemption was decreed from the beginning, it had to assert its absolute primacy over evil from the outset; it had to be complete.

Therefore no greater purity than Mary's is possible, and Jesus Himself is no more exempt from sin than is she who is wholly exempt from sin. The difference between Him and her lies in the reason for the innocence, not in the innocence itself. He is without sin because He is who He is; she is without sin because she is His mother. If she is entirely sinless, the reason is that Christ's holiness shines forth in her and that His holiness is holiness itself. She is the mirror without stain and the image of His goodness.

Dogma is obstinately uncompromising in this matter. One would be a heretic were one to assert that she was sanctified later, or even at the second instant of her existence. The Church insists that there was not the slightest taint of sin in her for a single instant; an object touching the sun cannot be in twilight. In this purity we ought to be able to catch a glimpse of the pure divinity of Him whom it proclaims. For her, therefore, nothing is too pure.

In the same way the dawn has one glorious moment: the moment immediately preceding sunrise. Up to that time, only tentative glimmerings are discernible. First a faint pallor shows in the east, scarcely perceptible in the night. Then the light increases, slowly in the beginning, but later more and more rapidly. An instant comes when the radiance is so triumphant, the light so brilliant, and the brightness so dazzling for eyes accustomed to the dark that the beholder may imagine he is facing the sun itself. Yet it is not the sun, which, however, makes its appearance directly afterward, bursting forth like a ball of fire on the rim of the horizon. Only then we see what the sun is. Before this moment, deception was possible, so mighty did the sun appear in its herald, the dawn.

Thus it is with the Immaculate Conception. During all the preceding centuries the twilight of Christ was seen from afar, from the first beginnings of His purity and holiness, splendid even then in their effects on our race, although still most obscure in comparison with Him. But the Immaculate Conception is high dawn and the break of day.

This light rises for all men. The Immaculate Conception sets Mary apart from the rest of mankind, but only to unite her to Christ who belongs to all. It is the culmination of her passive redemption, enabling her to cooperate fully with the life of sacrifice that is the mystic continuation of active redemption.

In particular, it reveals the action of Christ even before the birth of Christ, and is a manifestation of the redemption which, emanating from the Redeemer, spreads out in all directions, ascending the current of the generations as easily as it descends. The Immaculate Conception is, in a way, the prototype of sanctification as it was operative during the Old Testament; so closely is Mary, the precise point at which God makes the race of men His own, linked to that race by God.

After the decree whereby God willed Christ, there follows the long preparation which is a remote realization of what is to come, and which permeates the whole of mankind's ancient history. All this preparation culminates in Mary, for in her alone it culminates in Christ. The preparation endures for countless ages. It is God's one work in this world. He puts all His love into it. With His grace He calls forth all that is genuinely good in the efforts of men. He fashions a human nature that is to be His own.

A day comes when all is ready. All things are gathered together in the Blessed Virgin, to be passed on to her Son. "With what praises I may celebrate thee I know not, O holy Mother of God." Heiress of all human holiness, flowering of humanity, she is the one estuary through which the waters of the earth flow toward the sea. These approximating sanctities do not make her formally holy, for holiness is something personal; but she is holy with the holiness of which they are a sketch and a sample, for they all have a part in forming Christ as man, and that formation is accomplished in her.

As the Old Testament with all that is holy in the history of mankind prefigured Christ, so it prefigured the Blessed Virgin. She is the one who is represented by the holy women and the sacred objects of the ancient covenant. She is symbolized by the Temple and the altar, by Sinai and the rainbow, by the burning bush and Gideon's fleece. All these signs point to her, because it is through her that He comes who was to come.

Finally, as the last step in the preparation, made by Christ who is about to appear, this human treasury of holiness is transmitted to her. Here too Mary is wholly united to Jesus, as she is to the race. As we have said, she is the flowering of all the figures; and we must now add that she herself is forever the absolute and complete figure, for, as mother of God, she is the bond connecting the God-man with mankind.

Motherhood, as we know, is not exclusively a physical function, any more than man is exclusively a body. The body makes one person with the soul. By producing the body, motherhood reaches the very soul through the body and implies a moral influence, and is designed to continue its influence in the education of the soul. The child's body receives definite features and a definite structure and temperament from its parents. These factors, in turn, conduce to a definite type of character and psychological attitude. And the latter calls forth particular shadings of supernatural holiness, for grace adapts itself to nature. Even in his holiness, a saint is the child of his parents.

This last adaptation, we should observe, had to be more perfect in the case of the Incarnation, because the two human natures in question, that of Christ and that of His mother, were wholly immaculate. There was nothing in them to prevent grace from being the full divinization of nature. In the Incarnation, moreover, the union between mother and Child is produced exclusively by the action of God, who alone brings it about that a human nature is the Word's nature. Hence the union must be very close and very perfect. In this case, lastly, the birth is virginal. With regard to the Blessed Virgin, the only human parent of Christ, the laws of heredity can apply with twofold efficacy, for she is the only one the Infant has to resemble. Indeed, we may say that the efficacy of these laws is more than doubled, for in this instance any possibility of a neutralization of opposite influences is ruled out. The Child may have borne some resemblance to St. Joseph; this seems fitting; but not as a result of heredity.

The Word did not repudiate these laws of heredity, especially as He wished to belong to the race that is ruled by such laws. We know more clearly now than in the days of Aristotle or St. Thomas that the role of the mother is no less active and influential than the role of the father: the child is a prolongation of the mother as well as of the father.

In willing to become incarnate, the Word wished to be such a prolongation of Mary, organically, psychologically, and morally. He who is a divine person because He is the perfect image of the Father, is also man, the Saint of saints among men, because by His incarnation He is the perfect image of His mother. What, then, must the Blessed Virgin be, in order to be such a model?

This relationship in soul is asserted in the Gospel. During the nine months preceding His birth, Jesus allowed nothing of Himself to be seen except the charity, humility, and piety of her who carried Him. In later years He who is the brightness of the Father's glory and the image of His substance,[21] revealed Himself progressively, growing in grace and wisdom before God and men by imitating her, as children do, by performing the actions she taught Him, and by repeating the words and prayers she suggested; He "was subject to them."[22]

In her memory as a mother, the actions and words of her Son, as also the words she heard about her Son, took root as in their natural soil, and there they lived their fruitful life. Twice St. Luke notes: "Mary kept all these words, pondering them in her heart."[23]

If we bear in mind that the first chapters of St. Luke report events from a point of view which must have been that of the Blessed Virgin and that, in all likelihood, they go back to her directly or indirectly, this observation is important. Luke, so careful in exactly recording the testimony of those who were eyewitnesses of what took place from the beginning,[24] enables us to hear Mary's own deposition. She told the Evangelist or those questioned by him about the years when Jesus was still living alone with her and Joseph. "The boy grew, He grew up so nicely in age and wisdom, and He was so obedient": is that not just the way mothers speak? Sometimes, as the recollections poured forth, she would interrupt herself to say that all this remained in her heart and that she never ceased thinking about such things. This remark has passed into the inspired narrative as the Blessed Virgin's signature to the Gospel of the infancy; it was a modest signature, as was suitable. Mary does not claim loudly that she is the one who is speaking. On the other hand she does not conceal

[21] Cf. Heb. 1:3.
[22] Luke 2:51.
[23] Luke 2:19, 51.
[24] Cf. Luke 1:1 ff.

the truth. She gives her testimony with utter simplicity, in the way she loves.

Thus Mary, Queen of the Apostles, is also the Queen of the Evangelists. When she tells about her Son's first thirty years, she makes known to the heralds of the word the good news of the hidden life, of the sanctification of all hidden lives, that is, of all human lives. In its universality this lesson is the great lesson of the Master, the lesson He taught, not in a few discourses alone, but in His whole manner of acting during almost His whole life. And she is the one who transmits it.

Before repeating this lesson she practiced it; in this again she is close to Jesus. As He is the hidden God, the Savior God, so she is the hidden Virgin. Nothing in the Gospel draws attention to her, except that she is His mother. She is never spoken of except in connection with Him. She worked no miracle during her life; later on, indeed, she multiplied them, but always in favor of her children. Christ, similarly, worked no miracles for His own advantage. But to mark their union unmistakably, He worked His first miracle in answer to her request.

We do not read that she engaged in any apostolate that won renown. Jesus, likewise, reserved the success of His preaching to His apostles.

She had His mentality so perfectly that, before His birth, she evaluated as He would have evaluated and judged as He would have judged. He had not as yet given forth His teaching on absolute purity, and the Old Testament had never had the idea of such a total consecration. But Mary already understood it; how else can we interpret her statement, "I know not man"?

Christ was to be the "servant of Yahweh" and claimed the title of servant; and Mary is the servant of the Lord: "Behold the handmaid of the Lord; be it done to me according to thy word." Is that not exactly the way Jesus would have spoken, Jesus who came to do the Father's will and who taught us the words, "Thy will be done," in the Lord's Prayer?

When we think of Mary's reminder, "They have no wine," at Cana, or her question, "Son, why hast Thou done so to us?" at Jerusalem, we may ask ourselves whether this delicacy of touch does not reflect exactly, with a feminine turn, the gentleness of Jesus as expressed in His query, "Wilt thou be made whole?" or in the parable of the prodigal son: "A certain man had two sons." When Mary found the boy Jesus in the Temple, she said: "Behold, Thy father and I have sought Thee sorrowing." Who taught her to put herself last? Whenever the ancients spoke of themselves and others, they invariably mentioned themselves first.

Or consider her *Magnificat*. It is her song, and when she composed it Jesus was not even born. Yet He made His presence felt to John the Baptist, and more so to her. In Mary's song, His thoughts are uttered: the greatness of the humble, the blessings promised to the lowly, the reversal of values effected by the Lord in exalting the poor and rejecting the proud, the joy of those whom the world ignores and who have the Lord with them; everything that the song proclaims is the same as the teaching promulgated in the Beatitudes and the Sermon on the Mount. The very prelude expresses the tone and accent characteristic of the preaching of Jesus; the mother's song foreshadows the hymn of thanksgiving uttered by the Son in the presence of God who showers the lowly and the humble with His favors. "At that time Jesus answered and said: I confess to Thee, O Father, Lord of heaven and earth, because Thou hast hid these things from the wise and prudent and hast revealed them to little ones. Yea, Father, for so hath it seemed good in Thy sight." [25]

As we hear Christ in His mother, we also hear in her the entire Old Testament, which is a prefigure of Christ. The *Magnificat* is almost wholly made up of biblical quotations.[26] The mother of the Savior, of the desired One of Israel, speaks as the daughter, or rather the queen, of the patriarchs and prophets. And this double relation with her Son, who is everything for men, depicts her so well that the *Magnificat*, echo of the Old Testament and prelude to the New Testament, is a very personal, unified, and spontaneous composition, as well as a prayer that was to become familiar to the Christian people. Thus Mary, the image of Christ, is a close bond of union between Christ and mankind.[27]

[25] Matt. 11:25 f.

[26] Cf. I Kings, 2:1–10.

[27] We may further note the remarkable decisiveness of reaction characterizing mother and Son: a sign of souls thoroughly attentive to themselves and to others. Recall, for example, how quickly Mary replies to the angel (Luke 1:38), goes to Elizabeth (*ibid.*, 39), and intervenes at Cana (John 2:3, 5); and how promptly Jesus goes to the heart of a question and gives a definite reply; this trait is made especially prominent in St. John (e.g., 1:38; 4:7; 5:6, 17; 7:6, 16, 28).

We hope we may be excused for adding a detail that is futile enough when the Mother of God is in question, but that has an interest for us ordinary children of men. Mary must have possessed a flair for poetry, just as Jesus did. Jesus had this gift of universal sympathy, this promptness of responding to a contact with anything, this facility and sincerity of wonder. We have but to recall, for example, His reverential and moving words about the flowers of the fields. "I say to you that not even Solomon in all his glory was arrayed as one of these. And if the grass of the field which is today, and tomorrow is cast into the oven, God doth so clothe, how much more you, O ye of little faith?" [28]

"God doth so clothe": we can see our Lord bending over these humble marvels, joyful and proud to be a man in the human universe of His Father's creation. We may well believe that Jesus wished to receive this very human gift from His mother, just as He received His human nature from her. She must have possessed it before Him. The proofs that she did are, among others, the special turn of poetry, delicacy, and taste found in the first chapters of St. Luke, in which her influence stands out so clearly. The same trait does not appear so strikingly in the rest of the Third Gospel or in the corresponding passages of St. Matthew. The abundance of poetic bits occurring in these chapters, and only in them, all have to do with her. But the *Magnificat* remains the clearest proof.

III. MARY AND THE CONTINUATION OF CHRIST

A third aspect of Christ, and hence of the relations between Jesus and His mother, remains to be considered: Christ as continued, Christ, as man, but because He is God, is continued in an organism which He vitalizes with His fullness and which, in the divine vocation, contains all men. Since He is man through His mother, she must occupy a special place with reference to all men.

We have already described certain aspects of this relationship when we were dealing with Christ Himself and His union with His mother; the head cannot be separated from the members. But we have still to bring out explicitly what is essential in it. If the Blessed Virgin is essentially the mother of the God-man, she is likewise a mother with regard to all men and their sanctification.

[28] Matt. 6:29 f.

Since men are the plenitude of Christ and are mystically He, and since, on the other hand, Mary is His mother, she must also be their mother, the mother of absolutely all men. In the words of tradition, she is the mother of the human race, the mother of the living, the mother of divine grace, the refuge of sinners, the comfort of the afflicted; she is the new Eve, the universal and catholic mother, type of the Church, perpetual advocate of all men.

Mary is the safest refuge and the most faithful helper of all who are in danger, and the most powerful mediatress and counsel of the whole world at the throne of the only-begotten Son. . . . With her motherly soul she interests herself in our salvation and is solicitous about the whole human race.[29]

Because she gave birth to the Redeemer of the human race, she is also the most loving mother of all of us whom the Lord Christ wished to have as His brothers [cf. Rom. 8:29]. As our predecessor of happy memory, Leo XIII, pointed out, "God gave us Mary and, by choosing her to be the mother of His only Son, filled her with maternal feelings that breathe love and kindness. Jesus Christ showed her to be such by His conduct, for He wished to be subject to Mary and to obey her gladly as a son obeys a mother. He declared that she was such on the cross, when He entrusted the entire human race, in the person of His disciple John, to her care and charge [John 19:26 f.]. And Mary gave herself to us as our mother when she generously accepted the burdensome inheritance left by her dying Son, and immediately began to discharge motherly offices in our behalf." [30]

Is not Mary the mother of Christ? Then she is our mother too. Everyone ought to bear in mind that Jesus, the Word made flesh, is the Savior of the human race. As the God-man, He received a body, just like the rest of men. And as the restorer of our race, He received a certain spiritual and, as it is called, a mystical body, which is the society of those who believe in Christ. . . .

In the womb of His most chaste mother He took flesh to Himself and at the same time joined to it a spiritual body made up of those who were to believe in Him. Accordingly Mary, who had the Savior in her womb, may also be said to have given birth to all whose life was contained in the Savior's life. Therefore all of us who are united to Christ and who, as the Apostle says, "are members of His body, of His flesh, and of His bones" (Eph. 5:30), have come forth from Mary's womb, like the body attached

[29] Pius IX, encyclical *Ineffabilis Deus* (*Col. Lac.*, VI, 843).
[30] Pius XI, encyclical *Lux veritatis* (Denz., 2271).

to the head. For this reason, in a spiritual and mystical sense, we are called sons of Mary and she is the mother of all of us.[31]

As we see, all this goes back to the divine motherhood and to the union of Christians with Christ. Christ is man because He is Mary's Son. As man He lives in Christians and causes them to live in Him. Therefore, too, in them He is her Son and the life He infuses into them is, with reference to her, a filial life.

This reasoning reproduces by way of adaptation one of the most ancient and authentic lines of thought in Christian teaching: that which establishes God's fatherhood over Christians by appealing to God's fatherhood over Christ. Tradition says that Christ is the Son and that He is one with us; therefore He makes us adopted sons in Himself, the only-begotten Son. Christian piety reasons in the same way about the motherhood of the Blessed Virgin. The whole Christ is Christ and Christians; to be mother of the whole Christ, Mary must also be the mother of Christians.

As the life of Christ is prolonged here on earth, the role of Christ's mother is likewise prolonged. The mysteries of Christ, the Annunciation, the Nativity, and the Crucifixion, are affairs of the past in their empirical aspect; but they are continued under a mystical aspect, and derive a mysterious completeness from that fact. The Blessed Virgin's motherhood is one of these mysteries: it continues, and takes on a mysterious totality in the totality of Christ.

Christianity is a new life, an eternal life, that is brought to men, and they are born to this life during the whole time of their earthly existence. But since it is their life, it is a human life, and human life requires a maternal principle as well as a paternal principle.

This is why God has created that marvel of marvels which is the heart of mothers. He has placed in it a deep, obstinate, and, we may even say, an unreasonable love, a love ready for all sacrifices, all eventualities, all favoritisms. What would become of us poor creatures if, during the years of our helplessness and misery, someone who is made for love did not bend over us, and if we did not have the certitude, anchored in our blood, that we are dear to someone?

Maternal love is so inseparable from life that we see it reflected in the very animals, to the extent that the human organism has some counterpart in them. But in man, rooted though it is in matter, it

[31] Pius X, encyclical *Ad diem illum* (*Acta Sanctae Sedis*, XXXVI, 452 f.).

reaches to the spiritual and moral life, to refinement of intellect, to the gifts of discernment, to generosity and heroism.

Conversely, recourse to one's mother is an instinct of life, as we gather from the first cry of the infant in the cradle to the last appeal of a wounded man in a hospital. At the same time, it is an important factor in religious and moral life; some things we ordinarily do not learn well except from our mother, particularly respect for woman.

God did not intend that supernatural life should be less human than natural life; quite the contrary. Nor did He wish the children He adopts in His Son to be left half-orphans.

So He created the Blessed Virgin. He who instills marvels of tenderness into the hearts of ordinary mothers could not fail to instill the same love into the heart of this pre-eminent mother, whose love for her only Son and for her adopted sons was to be in some fashion the counterpart of His own love. In her heart we shall find heaped-up miracles of affection and sweetness, something mysterious like the life of grace to which they correspond and like the Incarnation which is their inspiration.

For, to repeat, the Incarnation is everything; but its completeness is brought out by its gift of the Mother of God to men, so that she is their mother through a supernatural motherhood. If God Himself has made a virgin a mother, and if He has wished that she who is the mother of the God-man should also be the mother of the human race, He would not inspire her with motherly feelings of a tepid and reserved kind that would not be enough for even an ordinary mother.

The divine maternity, as St. Thomas says,[32] belongs to the order of infinite things; consequently the maternal love it expresses is in some sense infinite. Mother of the Infinite, mother in whom this infinite Son becomes the life of all mankind, she is to be, in a way, infinitely a mother, and God gives her a heart great enough to love correspondingly. We are here dealing with something that is meant seriously and sincerely, with all the realism of the Incarnation.

Therefore we can say that everything contributes to make her the worthy mother of men in their divinized life, just as everything contributes to make her the worthy Mother of God in His human life. The two are inseparable in the God-man.

The Immaculate Conception, which prepared Mary to be the mother of the All-holy, prepared her from the very beginning to be

[32] *Summa*, Ia, q. 25, a. 6 ad 4.

the mother of sinners. In freeing her from egoism, it freed her from that encumbering preoccupation with self that constricts the greatest loves: "If you, then, being evil, know how to give good gifts to your children, how much more . . ." [33] If ordinary mothers, in spite of sin which is in all, have such devotedness and self-forgetfulness, what should we expect of her that is all-holy?

Flowering of the race, the means employed by the Word to be more closely bound to men, how could she fail to be wholly bound to them? Reflection and model of Him who has loved us to the end, how could she fail to reflect His love? She was sanctified as a mother, and it is as a mother that she ought to have charity; and since this sanctification is without parallel, her motherly charity ought likewise to be without parallel. Since she has the fullness of grace as mother and is consequently all-holy, she also has the fullness of charity as mother, and therefore is wholly loving in her maternal love. As she is so closely associated with the Incarnation, she is carried along by the movement "diffusive of self" which is the movement of the Incarnation, by the fervor of divine love that burns in the Incarnation. This is a motherly way of loving; it is maternal love.

As she loves her Son with all the force of her body and soul and with all the power of her fullness of grace, she will love the members of this Son with the same complete love, with a love that is natural, we may say, so steadily does it burn without ceasing in that psychology which no evil has troubled. For He is in them: "that the love wherewith Thou hast loved Me may be in them, and I in them." [34]

Again, there is an aspect of the redemption, called passive redemption, which cannot be realized in Christ Himself, but is realized to the full in His mother, as Christ's honor demands. This is the Immaculate Conception. And there is an aspect of Christ's charity that cannot appear in Christ but can appear in Christ's mother; and Christ's honor requires it to be complete. This is the maternal aspect of that charity.

In this connection we should not think of a separate tenderness, of the fond indulgence of a mother that surpasses fatherly love. There is nothing in Christianity but God and His Christ; everything comes from Them and everything leads to Them. The Blessed Virgin manifests no goodness that does not come from Christ, just as Christ mani-

[33] Matt. 7:11.
[34] John 17:26.

fests no goodness that does not come from God. In comparison with
the charity of God which is infinite, all the created charity manifested in the humanity of Christ is but a trifle, because it is created;
just as, in comparison with the charity of Christ, all the charity appearing in the Blessed Virgin is small, because it is only a reflection.
But this reflection is so marvelously adapted to human nature and
is so revealing that in the designs of Providence there is an aspect
of Christ's love that men do not see clearly unless they look at His
mother, just as there is an aspect of God's love that men do not see
clearly unless they look at the God-man.

But in fastening our gaze on Mary, we see definitely Christ alone
and God alone. "He who hears you hears Me." Mary, like the
Church, leads us directly and surely to God, that is, to God as giving
Himself.

The Mother of God, as we have said, is the means employed by
God to enable Christ to be man in perfection. In the same way, as
we now see, she is the means employed by God to enable Christianity
to be human in perfection. The second consideration is important in
Mariology as well as the first, and is an aspect of the first consideration. Is Christianity not the continuation of Christ? This second consideration has a relation to spirituality, morality, and ecclesiology
that is similar to the relation the first consideration has to dogmatic
theology and Christology.

It helps us to perceive that the mystical body, a unity of greatness
and divinization, is also a unity of delicate and attentive adaptation; a
unity that takes men as they are, with due respect to their psychology
and their personal dignity; in a word, a human unity, such as it ought
to be if it is to be rooted in the hearts and being of men. Therefore,
as Christ took His individual human nature from His mother, He
takes, wins, and holds together all mankind through her.

To such a religion man will give himself with all his heart, and will
give himself to God all the more unreservedly. Thus in a new way
Mary exercises her mediation, which is but an aspect of Christ's
mediation. We need only to reflect that without her, prayers such as
the Hail Mary, the *Memorare*, and the *Salve Regina*, to say nothing
of countless hymns, would have no place in our lives, and that we
should have to suppress the Annunciation and the Mother of Sorrows
and, in some way, God alone knows how, supply for the Crib and
the Hidden Life.

Because of Mary, Christianity has a unique spirit of hope, joy, and human truth. Because of her, it remains a religion of freshness and youth for the aged. Because of her, it is a religion whose great mysteries are perfectly accessible even to little children. Indeed, these innocents are like kings, as everything centers around them: "the kingdom of heaven is for such." [35] Their mothers on earth tell them about the little Jesus and His mother, who is also their mother in heaven. All this belongs to their life, their thoughts, their joys. And that is just as it ought to be for their childish minds; and the same is exactly the Christianity of St. Augusine and St. Thomas, of Bossuet and Pascal.

After the children and their innocence come the sinners: the sinners who are more or less all men and the sinners who are monstrous criminals. For them especially Christianity would lack some of its goodness if the Blessed Virgin, the Mother, were not there. But because she is there, they can all know that there is someone who is a link with the whole order of grace, the "Mother of divine grace," someone closely related to the very Trinity, the Mother of the Word, someone who is on their side no matter what they may have done, for she is their mother. Indeed, she is their mother by a special title, because it is on behalf of sinners that Christ has come, and therefore it is for them that she is the Mother of God. The petition, "Holy Mary, Mother of God, pray for us sinners," reveals a logical inference rather than a contrast.

Mothers are mothers, and that is everything. They are mothers by their bodies and by all that they are. Mary is a mother in an even more profound sense, by the omnipotence of God: *per viscera misericordiae Dei nostri*. The more wretched men may be, the more merciful is her response; no matter how far sinners may have fallen, she knows how to change their hearts by the goodness of her own heart. They do not question her love and her readiness and promptness to intercede. Those who do not dare to face their own conscience, do not hesitate to go to her who is all-holy; and when they throw themselves at the feet of their mother, they have begun their reconciliation with God.

If we meditate on this confidence, we shall see that it is a form of faith in the redemption and the Incarnation. Not for nothing did the

[35] Matt. 19:14.

Redeemer, in willing to be the Redeemer, will that the Redeemer should have a mother.

The proof by contrast is also decisive. Where this sweet mother of grace is lacking, God Himself does not stand forth so convincingly as a Father, Christ is not so close to us, the Church is less of a family society, and Christianity loses much of its gracious charm. Without Mary our religion would come to resemble a Protestant temple that is without a living Presence and without altar, a sytem well ordered but cold: there is no longer a mother in the home. When a part of God's gift is rejected, the whole of His goodness and the realism of the Incarnation are laid open to doubt.[36]

In the order of love and donation which is Christianity, Christ glories in living for the benefit of all men. The same is true of His mother. Her high prerogatives do not cause estrangement, but open up possibilities of goodness and close union for all men; they are the expression of a Catholic function and a universal service. A service, to be sure; has not Jesus come to serve? Do not mothers have the great and sovereign right of being, in their touching way, the servants of their children? "Behold the handmaid of the Lord"—and of the Son, and of the Lord's sons.

[36] Pius IX, encyclical *Ineffabilis Deus* (*Col. Lac.*, VI, 843).

BOOK THREE
Christ

CHAPTER IX

CHRISTOLOGY AND THE MYSTICAL BODY

> "Through one of us, the Word has taken
> up His abode in all of us."
> St. Cyril of Alexandria, *In Ioan.*, I, 9

AT length the time was at hand. The gift that had been ready in
God's will from eternity was accomplished in mankind. This
gift is Christ, not primarily in what He did, but in what He is. As the
God-man, God gives Himself to all mankind and, in giving Himself
to men, restores them to themselves. For the Incarnation is not an
event that concerns the assumed human nature alone; it is *the* human
event par excellence, the universal and cosmic event; and that, not
only by its sublimity but by its efficacy. As St. Cyril says: "Through
one of us, the Word has taken up His abode in all of us. He dwells
in all in that one temple He took for us and from us, to have us all
in Himself and to reconcile all of us, in a single body, with His
Father."[1]

"Through one of us, the Word has taken up His abode in all of
us": this extension of the Incarnation, this supernatural unity, is the
mystical body.[2] And Christ, who possesses this extension and effects
this unity, is the mystical Christ, the whole Christ. This unity belongs
to the order of mystery; we can neither explain nor comprehend it
with the sole resources of the natural order. But once the mystery
is revealed and God has spoken, a certain understanding of it is pos-

---

[1] *In Ioan.*, I, 9 (*PG*, LXXIII, 161, 164). This, the saint declares, is the great
mystery.
[2] Like the Greek Fathers, Mersch sometimes uses the term "mystical body"
in a wider sense, as including not only actual members, but also potential members of the Church. The same doctrine is found in St. Thomas, *Summa*, IIIa,
q.8, a.3. See the Introduction.—Tr.

sible.[3] This understanding we must endeavor to acquire; the unity in question, more than anything else, will enable us to grasp the rest of the doctrine.

But the undertaking is not as simple as it may appear; the disagreements among those who have attempted it make this clear. To place ourselves in the best conditions possible, we shall do well to begin with the question of method: what line of thought should we follow, in what direction should we pursue our search, so as to advance toward an explanation?

I. THE METHOD

The question is easily answered. Indeed, we are surprised that no one has remarked the insistence with which Scripture and tradition point out where truth and light in this matter are to be found.

In the preceding pages authentic indications of this kind have enabled us to define the mystery of the mystical body, which is, as we have seen, the supernatural unity of mankind and of creation in the God-man. The same indications will now show us that this mystery, this unity, is closely connected with the Incarnation, and that it is an effect and a sort of prolongation of the Incarnation. Consequently, if a theory of the mystical body is to be constructed, the Incarnation must be studied and meditated. The connection is made clear in Scripture, although an explicit and reasoned presentation of it had to await tradition.

In the Gospel of St. John, which we may call the Gospel of the Incarnation, the passages that deal most clearly with the Incarnation present it as being somehow prolonged in a supernatural organism, which is the unity we are speaking of. This is the very theme of the book, as the author is careful to declare: "These are written that you may believe that Jesus is the Christ, the Son of God, and that believing, you may have life in His name." [4]

The life of God Himself in Christ, or the Incarnation, and the life of Christ communicated to souls, or the mystical body, the totality of Christ: these two things seem to be but one, the second being no more than the fulfillment of the first. The entire Gospel discourses in this sense, as we have shown elsewhere.[5] Here we

[3] Cf. the Vatican Council, Sess. III, cap. 4 (Denz., 1796).
[4] John 20:31; cf. 1:1–18; I John 1:1–4; 5:11, 20.
[5] *The Whole Christ*, pp. 151–81.

content ourselves with mentioning a passage of capital importance, the Prologue, which speaks more solemnly of the Incarnation than any other scriptural text. We shall see that it does not separate the Incarnation from the unity that is in question.

The perspectives are clearly established in the very first lines. The Incarnation is set forth not only as a grace that comes to an individual human nature, but as a gift destined by God for all mankind, or rather for the whole of creation. On the one side stand God and His Word, He who is plenitude of being; and on the other, everything that was made.[6] Between these two extremes, these two totalities, the drama will unfold. The Word who is life and light and the Son hovers over His creatures. He seeks them undeviatingly to communicate Himself to them and to make them glow with light and vibrate with life in Himself; His desire is to make them children of God.[7] Between the infinity charged with love and the unfathomable stupidity that shrinks back, the distance is continually narrowing.

At last the spark leaps: the Word is made flesh. The whole of the divinity is contained in that one spark. The result is the birth of the only-begotten, incarnate Word; but it is also the communication, in the only-begotten Son, of life, grace, light, truth, and divine sonship to the whole human race.[8] The Word has come to dwell in all of us through one of us.

This view, which is highly unified and at the same time most human and universal, does not differ from the one conveyed in the great Christological passages of St. Paul. The inspiring Spirit, we might almost say, fears lest an excessively narrow idea of Christ may be formed, and from the time He begins to speak of Christ, He depicts the whole human world as united to God in His only Son.

The resemblance with the Prologue of St. John is most clearly marked in the Epistle to the Colossians. As soon as the greeting placed at the head of the letter is finished,[9] Paul comes to Christ and immediately proceeds to exhibit Him as the Creator who holds together everything that was made, as St. John says, and who is before all and above all.[10] Here again we have two confronting totalities:

[6] John 1:3, 6, 7, 9, etc.
[7] John 1:4, 5, 9, 12.
[8] John 1:14, 16 ff.
[9] Col. 1:1–14.
[10] Col. 1:15 ff.

God and all creation. Then comes the forthright assertion: "And He is the head of the body, the Church," [11] reminding one of the sudden declaration, "And the Word was made flesh," on the first page of the Fourth Gospel.

At this point the accent is laid on the universal aspect, on the elevation, reconciliation, and pacification coming to all men through the God-man.[12] And the latter appears all the more unique and transcendental in the fullness He diffuses, "that in all things He may hold the primacy": [13] the Word dwells in all through a single one.

The parallel passage in the Epistle to the Ephesians [14] is even more emphatic in this respect, although it does not recall the Prologue of St. John so strikingly. The epistle opens with a grand hymn of thanksgiving in which the Apostle blesses God for having sanctified all things in Christ. The passage is well known. It treats, if we may use the expression, of the predestination of the whole universe, of the divine plan leading all to grace and adoption; and all this, in the fullness of time, is resumed in a single sanctity and in a single Man, in whom God recapitulates everything.

Reciprocally, too, almost every time the Apostle speaks of the unity of grace in which all Christians are gathered together and sanctified, he links it with the Incarnation.[15] He seems to have no technical formula to describe the exact nature of the relation. Sometimes Christ's humanity scarcely appears in this work of union; it is God who gathers men together and draws them to Himself, with some intervention on the part of Christ's humanity that is not clearly defined.[16] At other times the humanity of Christ appears as the great means employed by God to save men.[17] This latter case seems to be the more frequent. Because the entire fullness of the divinity resides in this humanity, it has such a profusion of life and grace that all men are flooded with life and grace, so that the abundance flowing to them shows forth the fullness contained in Christ's

[11] Col. 1:18.

[12] Col. 1:18 ff.

[13] Col. 1:18 f.; see the similar passage in Eph. 1:20-23.

[14] Eph. 1:3-14.

[15] Of thirty passages we have examined, only five depart from this practice.

[16] Cf. Rom. 3:24-27; 5:1-11; 6:23, 13:25 ff.; Gal. 4:4-7; Eph. 1:3-14; Col. 1:13-20.

[17] See Rom. 5:11-21; 6:1-11; I Cor. 1:30 f.; 6:15-20; II Cor. 5:14-21; 8:9; Gal. 2:19 f.; 3:26-29; Eph. 1:18-22; 2:4-10, 13-22; 3:1-10; 4:3-16; Phil. 3:14, 17, 21; Col. 1:26 ff.; 2:2-19; 3:1-4.

humanity. "In Him dwelleth all the fullness of the Godhead corporeally; and you are filled in Him, who is the head, . . . buried with Him in baptism, in whom also you are risen again by the faith of the operation of God." [18]

Tradition also proposes this scriptural teaching, but brings out its logical connections more clearly. Since we have developed the doctrine at some length in *The Whole Christ*, we shall treat it here rather briefly.

In the Eastern Church, the doctrine is best formulated by St. Cyril of Alexandria. He says that the Savior's humanity can give life because it is united to the Word of life, and that it can confer light, grace, and holiness, not because of what it is in itself, but because of what it is in the Word. This is clearly perceived in the Eucharist: the very flesh of Christ, which would be powerless and useless of itself, is a principle of life because it is united to Life. Christ's humanity is assuredly not His divinity; but from its union with the divinity it receives a new quality, it is altered and elevated to divine greatness.[19]

The most complete teaching in the Latin Church has been given by St. Thomas. According to him, the humanity of Christ possesses the closest union with the Godhead that is possible. Consequently it had to receive in the greatest degree the effect of this union, which is assimilation to the divine nature, or grace. Indeed, it receives grace that in a sense is infinite, and is sufficiently abundant to give of its fullness to all Christians. This humanity, taken by God into personal union for the purpose of sanctifying all mankind, possesses all the power and contact necessary for producing such an effect in all men.[20]

Under its different forms this teaching clearly exhibits the same structure. The Savior's human nature is elevated, divinized; it has this elevation and divinization from the divine nature; thereby it is made a principle of supernatural life, grace, and divinization, and hence a principle of supernatural unity in all mankind.

On all sides, then, the same teaching is given. The supernatural unity which is the mystical body is presented as a human effect and plenitude, produced in Christ's humanity by its assumption. This

[18] Col. 2:9 f., 12. Cf. 1:18 ff.; 2:6-19; Eph. 1:20-23; 3:1-19; 4:11-16; John 1:14 ff.
[19] See *The Whole Christ*, pp. 337-58, esp. 339-48.
[20] Cf. *ibid.*, pp. 451-530, esp. 472-78.

presentation makes the doctrine intelligible and explicable, and suggests a plan for a theory of the mystical body. It brings to our notice, first, the Incarnation and the supernatural perfection it conferred on the assumed human nature, and shows, secondly, how this perfection had to have the quality of a universal principle of supernatural life, unity, and totality in men, the quality of being "mystical," if we may use the term.

This does not exclude the part played by other considerations, or the function of the Holy Spirit, charity, the Eucharist, and the rest of the sacraments. But in the line of thought which seems to be imperative and which we shall follow, their place will be assigned and their true meaning will be brought out by the central truth of the Incarnation.

II. The Perfecting of Christ's Human Nature
by the Incarnation

Accordingly we must focus attention on Christ's humanity. All the divine decrees that sanctify the human race by making of it an organism of grace are included in the decree that willed the humanity of Christ, or rather are basically realized in the very way that humanity exists. It is God's own humanity, as the sacred document of Chalcedon proclaims.

Following in the footsteps of the holy Fathers, we all with one accord teach belief in one and the same Son, our Lord Jesus Christ. We declare that He is perfect in divinity and perfect in humanity, that He is true God and true man, composed of rational soul and body, that He is consubstantial with the Father in divine nature and consubstantial with us in human nature, "in all things like as we are, without sin" [Heb. 4:15]; that before all ages He was born of the Father according to His divine nature, and in these latter days was born of the Virgin Mary, Mother of God, for our sake and for our salvation, according to His human nature; that one and the same Christ, the only-begotton Son our Lord, must be acknowledged as existing in two natures unconfusedly, unchangeably, undividedly, inseparably, with no suppression of the distinction between the natures on account of the union, but rather with the individuality of each nature safeguarded and coming together in one person and subsistence, not parted or divided into two persons, but one and the same Son and only-begotten God the Word, Jesus Christ the Lord.[21]

[21] Denz., 148.

"One and the same": the Council repeats the words with majestic insistence; this man who is Christ is truly, strictly, identically God. The whole of Christianity is there. Even if one holds, contrary to St. Thomas, that the human nature in Christ has its own proper existence, one has to acknowledge or rather proclaim that this existence is incomplete and receives its ultimate reality only by being united to the divine existence. There are not two Christs, there is only one Christ; and in this Christ, consequently, the man is God, wholly God. "The whole God is man, and the whole man is God; whatever belongs to the humanity, God the man makes His own; and whatever belongs to God, the man God possesses." [22] "Just as God the Word, by taking to Himself what belongs to man, is man, so the assumed man, by receiving what belongs to God, cannot be other than God." [23]

This intimate union, this rigorous unity of person, implies a union in properties, a communication of idioms. "He who is true God is likewise true man; and although the lowliness of man and the sublimity of Godhead are conjoined, there is nothing contradictory in this unity. For just as God is not changed by His mercy, so neither is His humanity absorbed by divine majesty. Each of these natures, though in union with the other, performs actions proper to itself: the Word does that which belongs to the Word, and the flesh does that which belongs to the flesh." [24]

This interchange of properties does not involve their fusing; the natures remain absolutely distinct, and so do the properties. They are united in the person, not in the natures; and even when the person is designated by a term that represents only one nature, we can apply to the person the predicates of the other nature. This interchange is something truly ontological, and is not merely verbal or logical. The person is truly both man and God, and so the union of the two sets of properties is truly real in Him.

The divinity can in no way be affected by this union in the person; the divinity and its attributes are immutability itself. But the humanity is necessarily affected. To correspond to something real and objective, the communication of idioms has to correspond to something in the human nature. But this something in the human

[22] St. Gelasius I, tomus *Necessarium* (Denz., 168).
[23] *Libellus Leporii*, Cavallera, *Thesaurus doctrinae catholicae*, 669.
[24] St. Leo I, *Tomus ad Flavianum*, 4 (Denz., 144).

nature must be human, because the nature itself is human, and whatever is received, is received according to the capacity of the recipient. In the human nature, answering to something in it and fitted to it, this will be, not the predicates themselves, for that is utterly impossible, but the reaction and effect of these predicates, the union and adapting of the human nature to them, something that necessarily has some relation and proportion to them. This communication therefore, as we may term it, is not the communication of idioms properly so called, but is its result and, as it were, its prolongation in the interior of the human nature.

St. Robert Bellarmine, whom we have been following and commenting in this explanation, expresses the latter point as follows. "The Catholic teaching involves two things," he says. The first alone interests us at present.

> First, many created and infused gifts come to Christ's humanity from the hypostatic union, such as a most excellent grace and other perfections of the kind, which are not attributes of the Godhead except by a sort of participation, in the way in which we share in God's attributes through created qualities, although less fully than Christ's humanity shares in them. The communication of idioms does not consist in such gifts; for that communication is mutual, whereas the communication of these gifts is not mutual, since nothing accrues to the Godhead.[25]

This sharing in the attributes of the Godhead by the humanity of Christ must be determined more accurately. Theological treatises deal with this participation at some length and demonstrate its existence when they discuss the sanctifying grace Christ's humanity had to possess. Thus they come directly to the essential point. For our part, we wish to approach this subject less precipitately and to treat of it only at the end.

If this participation is Godlike and if it is a grace for the reason that it adapts the recipient to God, it is human because it is produced in a human nature and because, in its Godlike elevation, it is a more perfect way of existing for the human nature. Furthermore, it is conditioned by the limitations and potentialities—we do not say the virtualities—of the human essence. From the standpoint of the human nature and in the view of men who study the matter, the

---

[25] *Controversiae, II, De Christo capite totius Ecclesiae, III, 9.*

participation must therefore, in the first instance, appear as something human.

Undoubtedly the transcendental aspect that makes it a divinization and the human aspect that makes it an exaltation of the human nature are strictly inseparable; only the strict unity of the person with the two natures accounts for its existence. Yet the two aspects are distinct, with a distinction derived from that of the natures which are united. In these pages we wish to begin with the human aspect. Accordingly what is usually presented in theology as a divinization appears to be primarily a realization of the ultimate perfections human nature is capable of and, if we may say so, a transcendent "humanization."

This transcendence, however, becomes more and more the center of attention, and we shall find it increasingly difficult not to speak of divinization. When a drop of water reflects the brilliance of the sun, it is hard to see only water in it rather than the sun.

As is clear, the choice concerns no more than a detail in method and procedure. The procedure is imposed by the line of thought which the authentic teaching suggests. In considering Christ's humanity in itself, but as perfected by the hypostatic union, we may hope to gain an insight into the mystic totality of this humanity, or in other words, into the mystical body.

This detail in method justifies and even requires, on principle, corresponding details in formulas and points of view. When the same landscapes are looked at from different angles they appear different, precisely because they are the same. Yet the basic identity can be perceived. The line of thought, however different it may be, will issue in quite traditional theses, and in the course of the advance various crossroads that may not be overlooked will indicate junctions.

In the meantime the detour, if detour it be, will enable us to judge more clearly the extent to which the Incarnation and Christianity are human, and the extent to which grace, divinization, and the Gospel lay hold of man as man and become his chief necessity.

III. Intrinsic Perfection of Christ's Human Nature

The human nature of Christ, being the human nature of God, is evidently raised to a supernatural perfection. This perfection consists primarily and radically in the very subsistence imparted to it. As such, the perfection is not accidental or natural or essential, any more than the hypostatic union is.[26] It is substantial, or rather subsistential.

But this first perfection necessarily leads to a perfection that is accidental and intrinsic to the assumed human nature. For, since the union is accomplished in the person, the natures remain distinct, and the human nature remains distinct from the subsistence in which it subsists. Yet it does subsist there, truly, ontologically, and intrinsically; indeed, once the union takes place, this fact is the deepest and most intimate reality in it. Therefore the way the human nature exists is other than it would be apart from this subsistence.

Such is the perfection we are speaking of at present. It is a perfecting of a human nature and is therefore something human; but it is something by which a human nature possesses subsistence in God. It is a *mutatio*, says St. Thomas,[27] a change as compared with what the human nature would be were it not thus perfected, not as compared with a prior state that never existed; he also calls it a *perfectio*,[28] or, following the lead of St. Augustine, a *melioratio*, an amelioration.[29] Here we must rid ourselves of certain conceptions and imaginations which, by reducing this perfection to nothing, reduce the Incarnation to nothing. Such is a certain juridical cast of mind that would reduce this perfection to a right, a condition, a patent of nobility. A divine decree, in this view, would have conferred on the assumed human nature a sort of dignity in virtue of which God would consider it as His own and would enjoin on creatures the duty to regard it as such. Or again, a kind of gratuitous transfer and grant would have given to this human nature a title to divine attributes, the right to lay claim to supreme honors, the power to reign over all things, the ability to perform actions of infinite value and to make decisions having eternal ratification.

Complicated juridical theories of this kind do not compel us to acknowledge any ontological, intrinsic perfecting of Christ's human nature. Indeed, as they stand, they do not even allow us to perceive any reality in the Incarnation. We are given nothing but

[26] St. Thomas, *Summa*, IIIa, q.2, a.6.
[27] *Summa*, Ia, q.43, a.2 ad 2; IIIa, q.2, a.7 et ad 1; a.8; *Contra Gent.*, IV, 49.
[28] *In I Sent.*, d.14, q.1, a.1 ad 2.
[29] *Summa*, IIIa, q.2, a.6 ad 1; cf. St. Augustine, *De diversis quaestionibus 83* (PL, XL, 85).

certain acts of God that remain quite transcendent with respect to all finite being, including the human nature which is said to be assumed; and we do not see how this human nature exists otherwise than it would without any assumption.

We are told that it has a right, an ownership with reference to divine subsistence. But what meaning can such an assurance have? A right supposes a certain superiority. The Word is not a thing that can be appropriated. Subsistence does not consist in having, but in being. Moreover, rights reside in persons; the right conferred by the Incarnation would be a right over the Word given to the Word. In brief, all this externalizing, by identifying the Incarnation with shallow considerations and relations that are mere juridical entities, makes of it a superficial thing lacking solid truth, thus expelling it in some way from the assumed human nature and, by that very fact, from itself.

We beg to be excused for having set forth this juridical conception at such length. But perhaps our effort has some value in arousing attention to the matter. No one, of course, would admit the theory as we have put it; but aspects of it may easily worm their way into the mind that is accustomed to think in such a manner and to seek clarity of understanding in the realm of such ideas.

Assuredly a divine decree was necessary: Christianity, like creation, has no other origin. But divine decrees are efficacious. If God wishes a human nature to be His, it will be His, throughout its whole being, ontologically and intrinsically; for God attains being as being.

The divine action was efficacious. It consisted in an assumption, an attracting to the Word, a joining to a divine person, a union, an adhering, an elevation to God, a unifying action, as theologians variously put it. All this, surely, and nothing but this. But to be this, the divine action has to be received in the human nature, and *quidquid recipitur, recipitur ad modum recipientis;* it has to be received according to the capacity of the human nature. In the human nature, therefore, there will be something human, something called forth by the divine action, something that will be, so to speak, the received assumption, the passive attraction and joining, the *passio unitiva* corresponding to the *actio unitiva;* it will be the *terminatio ad Filium.*

The question is to determine what this something consists in; and this, we believe, is the great question in all theology. Theologians grapple with the problem chiefly in their commentaries on the *Summa*, IIIa, q. 2, a. 6–8.

We shall not follow them in their investigations; but at least we must insist on the truth that this attracting, this adhering, may not be envisaged as a sort of riveting or welding or dovetailing. This truth is quite evident; yet we shall have to be continually on our guard against the encroachments of the imagination. Nor may we fancy that some third entity slips in between the finite and the infinite, like cement or solder, to attach one to the other. Such is the connecting medium in which some Scholastics have sought the explanation of the Incarnation; but St. Thomas has triumphantly rejected it. It calls to mind the animal spirits that connect body and soul in Cartesian psychology. What could be a middle term between the finite and the infinite? And what would become of the union with God, if the human nature is only joined to this middle term?

The perfecting we wish to speak of is not and cannot be in the order of efficient causality that brings about the union, however slight the efficient causality may be; the union would in that case lose its transcendence. The perfection does not predispose to the union, does not prepare for it, does not facilitate it. The perfection comes into being through the union, not vice versa; it is the union that explains the perfection, not the perfection that accounts for the union.

We may say that the perfecting causes the assumed human nature to be the human nature of God and that it adapts the human nature for the union. It does so, however, not in the way of an efficient cause, but in the way of a quasi-formal cause. The union alone, the assumption alone accounts for everything. However, since the union is a work of omnipotence, it necessarily has an effect; so necessarily that, if this effect were not produced, the union would not take place. In the same way, when a rock falls on a cushion, the hollow produced in the cushion is the effect of the pressure of the rock, an effect so inevitable that, if it were not produced, the reason would be that the rock had not fallen, and an effect so immediate that it is but the passive aspect of the active pressure; it is an inseparable effect, an effect that accompanies the cause, but nevertheless an effect that in itself is not the cause.

Such is the perfection in question. It is not the assumption and it is not the subsistence of the Word; it is their result in the human nature. It is the accidental amelioration whereby the human nature in its own way—for it has no other—is truly constituted, in its interior, the human nature assumed by the Word, with an assumption that in itself is not accidental but substantial and subsistential; an amelioration that is in no sense an element or a determinant of the divine initiative, but that makes the human nature the beneficiary of that initiative.

Scholasticism insists that a thing truly is what it is by a form or by an act; otherwise it would be what it is by not being at all. Whatever it may be, it must realize in itself that by which it is. A form is required if a determination of being is in question; an act is required if being itself is in question. Since the assumed human nature is the human nature of God, it must have within itself that which makes it such. Undoubtedly, as we cannot repeat too often, it is such in the first place through the pure Act itself, which alone can be the principle of such a way of existing.

But the pure Act cannot itself be a change or an amelioration of a finite nature; it cannot be that which constitutes this nature, within itself, the beneficiary of the assumption. Although the Word's subsistence alone is the subsistence of the assumed human nature, the sole *id quo subsistit*, it cannot be the possession of this subsistence by the human nature and the latter's attachment thereto; for in the human nature that is something human. The personal unity of the God-man, which makes it absolutely impossible for the human nature to have the slightest personality of its own, nevertheless requires with no less absolute necessity that the human nature should have within itself that which establishes it truly and intrinsically in the unique personality of the Word.

With reference to the assumption itself, this factor will be neither a cause nor an intermediary, but an effect, and an effect so immediate and formal that it finds lodging only in the assumed nature, as assumed. It is the first effect of the assumption, the characteristic and formal effect, the effect produced in the only place where an effect can be produced, for the Godhead is absolutely immutable. We cannot really and seriously think of an attraction exerted by the Word, of a joining, a union, without having recourse to a corresponding change and perfection caused in the assumed nature by the union itself. It is a perfection that cannot exist or endure except in and through the union, and that expresses and actualizes the union in the nature receiving it, or rather actualizes according to the union, in the union, and through the union the nature which subsists only in the union. Consequently we can no longer think of this nature as it is in itself in virtue of the union without thinking of God to whom it is united.

Although the perfection in question is the product of the union and is received exclusively in the human nature, this does not mean that the human nature was wholly passive in receiving it. On the contrary, the human nature had to be intensely active in receiving it, even though this activity itself was received. The reception had to be accomplished in the deepest center, the very root of the nature, and hence had to be brought about in a suitable way, that is, through an act of immanent spontaneity; to lay hold of the human nature as it is, the reception had to take place in that nature's inner source of activity, which is liberty. Hence we should say that it implies an act of unreserved self-donation, consecration, and love, which is, as it were, a consent to the union. But the consent was given to the union as accomplished, and was called forth by the power of this union. The union raised the consent to the height at which the union itself was effected, for without such consent the union would in a sense be violent and would not be human in its term. Apparently we have to go so far as to say that the consent was elevated to such a height as, in its own way, to cause the union. It did not, of course, effect the union, but was needed in order that the union might be fully accomplished *in facto esse*. We can hardly exaggerate in asserting how perpetual and complete this consent to God had to be, and how intense a charity, a self-donation to God, to the work of God, and to all men, this immediate cooperation with infinite charity involved.

This consent had to be an enduring disposition of a special kind, expressing what was most deeply rooted in the human love that subsisted in the donation of God. It is expressed in a multiplicity of distinct acts, as is the case with all human acts; but through it they are all in communication, in the same humanity and the same divine personality.[30]

[30] We shall have occasion to come back to this disposition more than once, especially in connection with actual grace.

IV. Greatness of This Perfection

We must next point out the greatness of this perfection. Simply to be, for any creature, is not nothing, but is everything that the creature is. What, then, must it mean to be God? For that is what is in question for the man who is Christ: not to be with God or penetrated by God or bound to God, but to be God, literally, in person.

God is the transcendent totality of being, the hypostatic union is the closest of all possible unions, and the Incarnation is the unparalleled work in which God goes to the limit of His love and of man's capacity; and all this, at one stroke, bursts forth on the unresisting being that is the creature in the presence of the Creator. The entire being of the creature could not but be profoundly affected.

God becomes the creature's personality. And personality is the innermost center of a being, and God is most efficacious in His action. What will be produced by such an agent, that penetrates so deeply? United to fire, a log becomes a torch; united to God in unity of person, what will human nature become?

The Incarnation produces nothing new in the Word. The whole of the new effect called forth is in the assumed human nature,[31] and through it, in other human natures, while remaining in the assumed human nature. This new effect is, in the first place, the subsistence of the human nature in the Word. But to subsist in the Word, it needs something else than the subsistence of the Word Himself, who exists independently of the Incarnation. It needs, as the one new reality, the change we have been speaking of, the change that places the human nature in possession of such a subsistence.

The purpose of this change is to adapt the human nature to such a reception, so that it may be truly what God makes it to be; to establish in it a quasi-form or a quasi-act that corresponds, in the human nature, to the elevation coming from God and in God; to be, in the object affected by the Incarnation, the passio or quasi-passio in which the actio that is the Incarnation terminates; to place this human nature in the state of being and acting in a way that is henceforth required of it, to equip it intrinsically to be, in its attitude, its ontological bearing, and its activity, the human nature of the God-

[31] St. Thomas, Summa, IIIa, q. 1, a. 1 ad 1.

man; to express in itself the manner of being coming to it from God; to be the real foundation of the relation which is the hypostatic union so far as it unites two natures that remain distinct, a relation which is real and has its real foundation (not its efficient cause!) in the human nature alone.

The union we are speaking of is a certain relation that is perceived to exist between the divine nature and the human nature, according as they are conjoined in the one person of the Son of God. But every relation between God and a creature is really in the creature, and arises from some change in the creature; in God, however, it does not exist really, but only according to our way of thinking, because it does not arise from any change in God. Therefore we must say that this union we are speaking of is in God not really, but only according to our way of thinking; but it really is in the human nature, which is a creature of a sort; and hence we must conclude that it is something created.[32]

In the case of creation, the relation produced by the change is real only in the creature, and its foundation is the whole entity of that creature as brought into existence by God. The situation in the Incarnation is analogous. The relation brought about by the union is real only in the assumed human nature, and its foundation is the manner of existing and subsisting conferred on this human nature, causing it to be wholly referred to God; and this reference can be expressed in the human nature only in accord with its capacity. We should note that, as the relation imparted by creation is not an accident, so the relation imparted by the Incarnation is not, in the first instance, an accident: it is the conferring of subsistence and, in this sense, of existence. But, as we should like to point out, such a subsistential relation demands an accidental change of a highly special order in the human nature, and this change is the adaptation of the nature to such subsistence.

Therefore this foundation of the relation, this conformation, this adaptation, this expression, this effect produced, this received perfection corresponding to the active union, must involve a relation and proportion to the Word. The formula is audacious, no doubt. But how can we make any compromise? It is the sole reason for the relation's existence, and the cause producing it can have no lesser effect. The nature that receives the effect must be adapted to it.

[32] *Ibid.*, q. 2, a. 7; cf. ad 1 et ad 2; a. 8.

When God Himself lays hold of the creature that comes entirely from Him, He knows how to clasp it. The power at work is that which effected creation. But what is here accomplished is greater than creation. In raising up a being from nothing, creation raises that being to the level of a creature; the Incarnation raises a being above that being's level up to the heights of the infinite. If the change—and we understand the sense in which the word is used—that occurs in creation is complete, the unique kind of change which the Incarnation involves is infinitely more complete. But the nature that is affected is no less open to such a change. Indeed, it is more so; for could nothing be said to be open to a change throughout its whole being?

That this human nature may fittingly be what the assuming of it causes it to be, it must be divine, so far as it can; otherwise it would be a sort of negation of the union. This is the reasoning of St. Thomas. "Christ is true God in His person and His divine nature. However, since the distinction between the two natures remains notwithstanding the unity of the person, the soul of Christ is not divine by its essence. Therefore it must become divine by participation, that is, according to grace." [33]

"It must become divine by participation." Since the human nature is not divine in itself, it must become divine in some other way, through the union, by the participation it receives. We see how far the reasoning goes; or rather, we do not see, for the perspectives vanish in infinity. Since this man who is Christ is God, He must be God in His very humanity, so far as this is possible for a human nature.

"It must become divine." The human nature, in all the perfection it can have, is human. To be God's nature, it has to become divine. Being human, it cannot be divine except by being divinely human. But what can that mean? In any case, however great the amelioration may be, it cannot be an alteration, even a slight one; and, in this sense, it cannot be a change.

Natures are like numbers or definitions: the slightest addition or substraction makes them cease to be what they were. If you add one to ten, you have not got a more perfect ten; you have something else than ten. If the change called forth by the Incarnation were to modify the assumed matter in this way, if it were to add some

[33] *Ibid.*, q.7, a.1 ad 1.

properties lying outside the area of the extension, even though only virtual or possible, proper to the nature, it would make the nature cease to be human, and so there would be no Incarnation.

The documents of the faith are meticulous on this point. The human nature of Christ is a human nature, and nothing else than a human nature. It is exalted, glorified, bettered; assuredly. But is it only half human? Absolutely not. To speak more precisely, we can in no way question the consubstantiality of this nature with our own, and we may not imagine that it fuses more or less with the divine nature.[34] In the first case, Christ's perfect union with men would be brought to nothing; in the second, the true God-man would cease; in either case, Christianity would collapse.

Such a perfection should not be conceived primarily as an accretion of new qualities. The greater these would be, the more would Christ's resemblance to other human natures be obscured. In the case of the Incarnation, those qualities would have to be such that the resemblance would tend toward God. As the preceding pages have indicated, this perfection must be a transcendent actuation brought about by union with the pure Act; it can be nothing else than a pure adaptation, a pure assimilation and participation of one of the two natures with reference to the other. But only the human nature can be thus adapted.

Hence it must have both an absolute character and a relative character: absolute, because it is an intrinsic manner of being, which is a true foundation for a true union and truly establishes a state of union; relative, because it is there as an effect ever being actually produced by the union and as the expression in the assumed nature of subsistence in the other nature. Relative and absolute: it is the foundation of the relation, so far as the relation is real in one of the two natures; but it results from the relation, so far as the relation is the active assumption which is brought about by God, and which we conceive as a relation. Relative and absolute: it is the real and ontological reaction of one nature to the total and all-powerful communication of the other nature. Accordingly it exists only in the union.

We cannot conceive the union as a complete entity having the reason for its existence and its explanation in itself or in the human

[34] *Symbolum Epiphanii* (Denz., 13); St. Leo I, *Tomus ad Flavianum*, 4 (Denz., 144); Council of Chalcedon (Denz., 148).

substance it affects. In the man who is Christ we cannot stop with seeing only man; this would be absurd and contradictory.

The union of the two natures is unique and unparalleled; so is the perfection itself. The union is not comprised within the categories of natural reason; neither is the perfection. As the union is a union, so the perfection is an "entity of union," and we cannot say anything more adequate or basic about it; it is an entity that has neither meaning nor possibility except in expressing in one nature the union with the other nature and in formally causing the first nature to be a united nature. Either we think of it in thinking of the union, in believing in the Incarnation, and in envisaging the two natures, or else what we have in mind is not it at all.

We must familiarize ourselves with this new type of being. It is the type of being that is properly Christian and that is here realized in all its fullness, because it is here the first and total principle of Christianity. But it recurs throughout the whole of Christianity, because this sacred humanity we are speaking of is everything in all of us. We shall come back to it repeatedly; and so we have to show how it is rooted in Christ's divinity and humanity. Here we have its first appearance, its first assertion of itself. Ontologically, it is the human formula of the Incarnation; it is that which, on the human side, corresponds to the hypostatic union.

We must see how exact the correspondence is; how, as expression and effect of the union, it essentially supposes that the natures are closely and ontologically united and that, nevertheless, they are strictly distinct, thus avoiding both the heresy of Nestorius and that of Eutyches. The human nature, though completely dependent on the union, remains human; and this denies Monophysitism. But, while remaining human, it exists in a way which expresses the union and which is the reason why it exists and can exist only in the union; and this excludes Nestorianism.

To get an idea of this special type of being, of this "entity of union," we may think of what takes place in the human body when the spiritual soul animates it. The body is made up of bones and flesh, and yet it is quite capable of expressing thought and decision, or even virtue and holiness. The eyes are but blood and liquid, yet they sparkle with intelligence. The curving lips are but skin and muscle, and yet they reveal the thoughts of the intellect. But if the soul withdraws, the absence of all this is most impressive. Nothing remains but an inert mass over which for an instant, like a smile that vanishes, there flits a hint of expression and character. And that used to be the body: the body that manifested itself and acted in a certain way; but all this was perpetually being produced in the body by the soul, as being the work, the sign, the translation of the soul. In its substance the body was material, but nevertheless was spiritualized, because, united to the spirit, it had a sort of "being of union" with the spirit.

Of course the comparison, like all comparisons, is deficient, but it has roots in tradition.[35] There are others. We may think of a pinch of iron filings attracted by a powerful magnet and becoming magnetized in turn. Provided we do not dwell too much on the physics of the case, we may say that the filings now possess a quality that is in them only through their actual union with the master magnet: an entity of union, so to say. Other comparisons will be invoked in due course.

V. THE HUMAN NATURE PERFECTED IN ITS HUMAN AND SOCIAL CHARACTER BY UNION WITH THE DIVINE ESSENCE

The motive that underlies this perfecting determines its nature. The union with God realized in the Incarnation, the perfecting of the human nature that makes it divinely human, essentially depends on what God is and what the Incarnation is.

God is Being itself. He is "He who is," *purus actus essendi, ipsum esse subsistens*, as theology and metaphysics agree in defining Him. Through the Incarnation He unites Himself to a finite being.

A finite being, on the other hand, as envisaged by metaphysics, is something that shares in being. In terms of being, that is, according to what it essentially possesses in all that it is, it is defined by an affirmation of being within a negation of being: it is something that shares in being; it is what it is and is not anything else. But in any case it is something that shares in being; what else could it be?

Through the union which is the Incarnation this finite being is truly God. To give a scientific explanation of the union we could, no doubt, have recourse to various theological systems, but they all have to come to this central point: the man who is Jesus Christ is strictly God. This simple rendering of the mystery in terms of the

[35] Cf. The Creed of St. Athanasius (Denz., 40), and St. Thomas, *Summa*, IIIa, q. 2, a. 2 ad 2.

philosophy that is traditional in theology throws some light on the question.

God is Being itself; the human nature is something that shares in being, and absolutely nothing else. A priori, therefore, no opposition between the two is perceived that could prevent the first from uniting itself to the second, by taking it up into unity of being.

I profess the truth which is evident to spiritual souls that no nature can be contrary to God. If God is, and if this can be properly asserted of God alone (for what truly is, remains so unchangeably, since what changes was something that exists no longer, and will be something that it is not as yet), God has no contrary. If you ask us what is the opposite of white, we reply black; if you ask what is the opposite of hot, we reply cold; if you ask what is the opposite of fast, we reply slow; and so of other instances. But if you ask what is the contrary of that which is, we rightly answer that nothing is.[86]

God's absolute transcendence, which is the reason why He simply cannot have anything univocally in common with the finite, makes Him the first principle and necessary exemplar of all that is finite. Any being or aspect of being that would be completely lacking in analogy with Him who is Being itself, would be nothing. Everything that exists, in every particle of its being, exists only by having being from Him. Such a being is pure plasticity, capacity, complete receptivity with regard to influences emanating from that Being who causes being; for its existence is wholly owing to influences received from that Being.

Undoubtedly we can imagine some of God's actions which, when we think of His absolute power, would be in conflict with the very being of the finite; as for example, if God were to will that a man should be a tree. But in this case the opposition would come, not from God as God, but from the object to which the command is directed. But when there is question only of Being, and when God's will is simply that a being which in itself is finite should be Being itself, we do not see from what source a difficulty could arise. What could obstruct the action of the first on the second when the second is defined, caused, and constituted by the reception of that action?

Assuredly this does not explain in a positive way how a man can be God; for that we should have to have a positive and adequate

[86] St. Augustine, *De fide et symbolo*, 7 (PL, XL, 185).

idea of God, of Being itself. Nor do we deny that the positive possibility of the Incarnation is a mystery. But we believe we can perceive with certitude that the impossibility of the Incarnation cannot be shown.

The situation would be quite different if the hypostatic union were to join a finite nature to another finite nature, for example, a human nature to an angelic nature. At first sight, such a union would appear to be less astonishing; in reality, we think, it is unthinkable. For an angel exists in a definite way that excludes all other ways of existing, including the human way. The same is true of a man. In order to become an angel, a man would have to become what is a negation of himself, and so would cease to be himself: which is an evident contradiction and impossibility.

What is true of an essence is true of personality. However we may define personality, it is, in each essence, correlative to that essence. The illimitation, the totality, the absolute finality which personality connotes and which could exist without restriction if it were to exist separately in itself, actually exists only through the real existence of the individual in which it is realized, and hence with the limitations and exclusiveness involved in such existence. Therefore an angelic personality would be destructive of a human nature, and vice versa. Moreover, the unity of the person would require a real union of the natures and an adaptation of one of the two or of each of them to the other: that is, a union with what negates it and an adaptation to what excludes it; and this is resignation to death.

But to become God, to be God, is simpler; or rather, since the question at issue is the impossibility of showing the impossibility of such a supposition, it cannot but be simpler. God does not exist in a way different from the way man exists, for He does not exist either in one way or in another: He simply is. Or, if we insist on talking about a way of being, His way is to be without restriction or negation, to be entirely and eminently nothing but Being; to become God cannot in any way involve ceasing to be oneself.

Since all the positive ideas we form of God are unavoidably inexact and finite, they are opposed to other ideas. They admit of such opposition because of their limitations; their defect consists precisely in the fact that they have limits.

If anything were by nature opposed to God's fullness of being, it would be radically opposed to itself, to the very principle of its being. The rebellion of any being against God is truly insurrection against itself and its natural law. For the essential law and, we may say, the very substance of every being is to be in conformity with Being itself.

For the humanity of Christ, therefore, the assumption cannot but be in full accord with what is more essential to its being than it is itself, and must cause it to exist in God's Being in the most perfect way that is possible for it.

The simplicity of this union indicates how simple its effect will be. Union with Being itself affects being as being. A being is subject to other influences externally and passively. But this influence, which comes from Being itself, it receives by merely being. This influence, coming as it does from the first and eternal cause of its being, enters into it at the very inception of its own being. Since the subsistent Being is more interior to every being than any being is in itself, the influence can be more interior, more "natural" to such a being, than its own being. If that influence comes from the innermost life of the supreme Being, it will express itself all the more deeply in the innermost being of that which receives it. In the Incarnation, therefore, where the influence is total, it affects totally the being of the assumed humanity. The Man who has this humanity will be God. He will have no other ultimate being or personality than a divine personality; and the latter, although strictly belonging to God, will be no less easily and "naturally" the Man's personality. Thus affecting the very being of the human nature, this action of the supreme Being necessarily confers being; it gives being such as befits one who is very Being.

We have only to consider the assumed nature to perceive what the union produces in it. We call it being, not to suggest that it is something outside the union or that it has its own proper being, but because it is not nothing. This usage of the term is delicate; we require it for giving expression to our reasoning; we hope that the reader will allow the context to be its commentary. Hence we say that the union of a finite being with the absolute Being in personal unity can have no other immediate effect than to cause it to be in as absolute a way as possible.

To be, for a human nature, means to be human; and to be as absolutely as possible, can mean nothing else than to be human as absolutely as possible. Nothing else will do. The nature cannot receive some new, unheard-of quality; it is humanity, and can be nothing else than humanity. But it is such utterly and infinitely; does not theology point out that the grace which, in this humanity, is the elevation due to the union, is as infinite as it can be? In the same way existence lays hold of essence, not by causing it to be something else, but by causing it to be; not by adding to it an accidental perfection of any kind, but by giving to it as real what it had as possible.

With all the greater reason this is true of absolute existence when it assumes a human nature, to the point of becoming its most basic and incommunicable existence, as theology puts it, and to the point where we can truly say that the Man it constitutes is strictly God, as the whole of Christian dogma teaches. That existence causes the human nature, not to be something else, but simply to be, and to be in union and proportion with Being itself; not to receive some accidental perfection, but to have in a way that is worthy of God all that it would have in its own way if it were left to itself. The pure Act, communicated to the human nature, affects the nature in the manner of an act, in the manner, we may say, of its own act, but infinitely more perfectly, because it is Act in an infinitely more perfect way; it makes the human nature exactly what a human nature is, but with an intensity of existence that reflects and expresses Being itself, through a transcendent human actuation.

The human nature receives the Creator's action twice and in two ways. It receives that action, first, by a finite title and simply, in order to be a simple human nature. But it also receives the action on the score that it is assumed, in order to be a human nature, indeed, but a human nature that is one with the Creator. And it receives the Creator's action twice in its capacity as human nature, and hence in order to be a human nature; but the second time it receives the action in such a way as to be the human nature of God and therefore, to some degree, in the way of God, with an intensity and perfection that are, so to speak, divine.

God is not opposed to anything; therefore, in taking over all that is in human nature, He does not exclude or impair anything. The Infinite is everything, and is also everything with respect to the finite. God's action can be penetrating and incisive to the last degree, and has to be. But the nature thus permeated through and through remains intact and virginal, and clings all the more firmly to its being, just as a crystal ball penetrated by the sun remains transparent, but with a transparency that has become brilliant.

Tradition refers to all this as divinization, grace, fullness of grace; yet it is an accident inhering in the human nature, and hence is human. This is the point of view from which we must consider it here. The perfection is human, and therefore implies a human way of existing that is supernaturally perfect or even divinely perfect, since divinization is in question. But in the humanity there is nothing but humanity. That is the dogma taught at Chalcedon, and it must dominate all Christology; we are encouraged to see that our considerations come back to the dogma that was their point of departure. Christ is perfectly man, perfectly God, perfectly one; one and the same Son, our Lord Jesus Christ, is perfect in divinity and perfect in humanity.[37]

The human nature of Christ is an integral and perfect nature of a true Man who is complete in what pertains to Him and complete in what pertains to us.[38] His human nature does not differ from ours except in the intensity of its existence, and that but makes it the more human. This difference, consequently, is not at all a difference; it does not make Christ less consubstantial with us; it makes Him more consubstantial, perfectly consubstantial with us. Similarly the perfection produced by the union is undoubtedly a change, as compared with what the humanity would have been without it. At the same time it is not a change: it is the ultimate and absolute identification of the humanity with itself, which "is" infinitely more than it would be otherwise, and therefore "is" itself supernaturally.

Since this supreme perfection "is" supremely, and since it is supremely human, it can exist only in the manner of the human nature. But human nature has two essential aspects that are inseparable from each other: an individual aspect and a social aspect. Hence the supreme perfection here in question must have the same two aspects: individual and social. Scholastic theology holds that the grace of Christ, which is precisely this perfection as defined in function of the divinity and of assimilation to the divinity, is simultaneously individual grace and the grace of headship, that is, grace destined to influence all men; we may perhaps call it social grace.

The individual perfecting is not the object of this book. Yet we

[37] Denz., 148.
[38] St. Leo I, *Tomus ad Flavianum*, 3 (Denz., 143).

may say a few words about it, as it is correlative to the other and is necessary for a clear understanding of the other.

As the human nature of God, Christ's human nature is the splendor of humanity and the glory of our race. His unique personality, which is that of the Word, does not prevent Him in any way from having all the individual traits that in other men are so deeply rooted and so expressive of human personality. But everything in His human nature subsists in the Word in whom it has its ultimate complement, and is personal with the Word's personality.

The human nature of Christ is not *sui iuris* in the ordinary sense; that is, it does not possess the primary principle and the ultimate term of its acts in a personality of its own order. Yet it is not without dominion over all these acts; indeed, it exercises a more complete dominion over them, because it governs them by the power of the Word, who belongs to it. Being thus *iuris Verbi*, it is all the more *sui iuris*, but *iure divino*.

To appreciate the interior autonomy and the splendid detachment of conscience characteristic of Christ's human nature, we have to observe it in action, during the days of His mortal life, in its sovereign freedom, its simple spontaneity, and its perfect surrender. It does not have to be continually solicitous about playing a role, and is not wholly absorbed in an effort to preserve a listening docility, in fear of introducing a human element into divine conduct. God has come among us precisely to take over what is human. In His human nature He goes, comes, speaks, gives expression to human thoughts and feelings; He has human preferences and displays them, human indignations and utters them, human joys and fears which He allows to be perceived. God's human nature has a natural, human mode of activity.

It does not retire to the background; it has an unparalleled emphasis of affirmation and of self-assertion. We know the assurance with which this self is exhibited in St. John: "But I tell you; amen, amen, I say to you; I am the light; I am in the Father and you are in Me; everything is for man and for eternal life." This audacity is not less prominent in the Synoptics: "Moses spoke in the name of God; but I say to you." All morality, all the most absolute demands are founded on this self, without further justification; all aspirations and all finality, even the most exalted, lead to this self, without any necessity of further recourse.

At the same time Christ's human nature asserts its relation of complete dependence on the Father: God alone counts, God alone is good, God alone accomplishes everything. But it asserts this supreme excellence of God without ceasing to assert itself; the double assertion, expressive of the very mystery of the Incarnation, is for it a simple and obvious thing on which it does not have to reflect, for that assertion indicates its manner of being; to comprehend and proclaim it, Christ's human nature has only to exist and to live.

We may remark in passing that this is the way Christ's human nature understands the Incarnation; and hence this is the way its members will understand the Incarnation. Sharing in Christ's humanity and living their lives as earnestly as possible in their capacity as members, they will understand in virtue of what they are, by sharing in Christ's human understanding, at present by faith, later by vision. And this brings us to the social aspect found in Christ's humanity.

The social perfection of the assumed human nature is the main point of interest, as far as this book is concerned. This is what makes Christ, as man, head of a mystical body. Every man, as we said in an earlier chapter,[39] is social by nature: in a certain sense, man is universally human. Indeed, he is doubly social: first, he is a man by being consciously and internally what all other men are; secondly and chiefly—although this can hardly be expressed in human words —because the human form possesses its own act, really though imperfectly, and therefore, really though imperfectly, possesses its own illimitation.

This sociability, as we also said above, implies, besides an interior union with other men, an interior union with the whole human universe. This universe is needed in order that man may attain complete life and in order that the human form may manifest all its essential powers and relations. We do not intend to speak of this latter aspect at present, but we should not lose sight of it. The other aspect, union with men in general, is by far the more important factor in sociability.

This sociability exists in the human nature assumed by Christ, because it is a human nature. On this score God's donation which is realized in it and which, we may say, it is, is of concern to all men, by reason of the natural union it has with all. In the human race,

[39] Cf. chap. 5, sect. 3.

therefore, the sacred humanity is a principle of divinized life, a unity and a head with regard to the supernatural order.

But much more has to be said. Christ's human nature has this sociability, as it also has humanity, in an eminent way that befits a human nature belonging to God. The perfection that raises it above all men, also places it in all men. In assuming and divinizing a human nature, God assumes and divinizes all humanity, as the Fathers say so often. Therefore He assumes and divinizes its sociability. He assumes and divinizes human nature socially: the Word has come to dwell in all of us through one of us.

This supreme sociability is a property of Christ as mystical head. It involves a union of a Man with all other men, a possession of all human reality, and a splendid way of being Man, as is fitting for a Man who is God.

The fullness of humanity embraces all the varieties of psychology, character, and mentality, incompatible with one another but all deeply human in their limitless number, that are realized in different individuals. To be perfectly a man, one must possess them all; not by formally realizing them in one's concrete humanity, which is impossible, but in the only way that is free from contradiction, by being fully united to those who possess them. Such is the union, divinely perfect in a sense, that the humanity of God must possess.

Ens et unum convertuntur. In his relations with other men and with the universe, man has an indefinite number of human perfections which are truly his, although they are outside of him. In order that he may fully exist and may be fully one, he ought to possess them within himself, and therefore he ought to be united to all mankind and to the whole universe as perfectly as possible, since that is the only means he has of possessing them. Accordingly the human nature assumed by Christ, perfectly realizing its unity within itself, will realize within itself all mankind and the universe.

St. Thomas remarks that what a being possesses, it possesses more perfectly in proportion as it is able to communicate its possessions.[40]

[40] "Among things that are filled with any goodness or perfection, the one from which goodness or perfection flows out upon other things is found to be filled to greater repletion; for example, what can shed light on other objects, shines more brilliantly than they. Therefore, since the man Christ possessed supreme fullness of grace, as being the only-begotten of the Father, grace overflowed from Him to others, so that the Son of God, made man, might make men gods and sons of God, according to the Apostle's words in Gala-

When a social being such as man is in question, the principle is even truer. Man does not truly possess what belongs to him on the social level and by a social title, unless he is able to give what he has. Man does not attain his full human formation unless he also forms other men. Hence, to possess fully the supernatural perfection proper to a man, Christ's human nature must possess a perfection that is sufficient for all mankind, in a sort of universality and transcendent sociability.

As we have remarked, the form in every man has its illimitation in the same measure as it has its act. What, then, will the form be in this Man, who is illimitation and infinity itself? In the order of form the illimitation of His form will be more absolute, so far as is possible in a single individual.

In other human individuals, the reception of form in matter is the ultimate reason of individual subsistence, and the limitation it induces is also ultimate and hence definitive. In the humanity of Christ this reception also takes place and is real, and the individual character is marked; indeed, we have pointed out that this is much more the case. But such reception in this human nature is not ultimate, and the same is true of the limitations it induces. The subsistence of God is the sole ultimate, for it is the basis of everything in Christ. But God is pure infinity and unity, whereas matter is finitude and internal division. Accordingly the "ultimateness" coming from God will be altogether different from the "ultimateness" coming from matter. Individuation will be there, certainly, for individuation is essential to human nature. But this individuation will be through penetration into the infinite, and hence by "infinization," rather than an individuation through separation from others and by limitation.

But this "infinization" is on the human level, through the realization, in this human nature, of the Infinite and of all that can be infinite in humanity, so far as an individual human nature is capable of such exaltation. We have noted the doctrine of St. Thomas that grace, the supernatural perfection of this human nature, is infinite so far as it can be; it is infinite in its own line. If we reflect that grace

---

tians 4:4 f.: 'God sent His Son, made of a woman, made under the law, that He might redeem them who were under the law: that we might receive the adoption of sons.' " St. Thomas, *Compendium of Theology*, pp. 240 ff., Part I, chap. 214; cf. *Summa*, IIIa, q.8, a.5.

is an accident by which the human nature is made holy and divinized, we shall see what infinity in the assumed humanity is presupposed by the infinity of the grace received. Is not God infinite, and can anyone be divinized without being raised to the order of infinity?

We may add that Christ's soul does not receive the final seal of its union with matter and its restriction to a definite individuality, making it exclusively what it is and giving it its ultimately incommunicable existence,[41] except in its union with the Infinite and its subsistence in the unlimited Act. Consequently it is individual and even, in a sense, transcendent; but it is such with a transcendent illimitation: an illimitation that is proper to the human soul, but pushed to the extreme limits of its possibilities.

VI. PARTICIPATION IN THE DIVINE ATTRIBUTES

The passage from Bellarmine quoted earlier in this chapter pointed out that the hypostatic union produced in Christ's human nature a number of created and infused gifts which, without being the divinity's own attributes, are certain participations of them. We shall now consider these participations in the divine attributes. They will be a commentary on, and, if need be, a corrective of what we have said about participation in Being itself, that is, in the divine essence.

The Scholastics have affirmed such participation from the beginning, in a principle they wrongly attributed to St. Augustine or to St. Ambrose, that Christ's soul or His human nature possesses by grace all that God possesses by nature. We may illustrate this teaching by quoting a few lines from Hugh of St. Victor. "From the time that divinity was united to humanity, the humanity received from the divinity as a grace all that the divinity has by nature, so that, in this ineffable union, everything pertaining to humanity might belong to God in His humanity, and everything pertaining to divinity might belong to the Man in His divinity." [42]

---

[41] *Ut per se et separatim existat.*

[42] Hugh of St. Victor, *De sacramentis,* II, 1, 6 (*PL,* CLXXVI, 383). The principle is generally invoked in connection with Christ's knowledge. We meet it in Walter of Mortagne, *Summa sententiarum,* tr. I, c. 18 (*PL,* CLXXVI, 76), in William of Auxerre, *Aurea in quattuor libros sententiarum explanatio,* III, tr. I, q. 8, c. 1; and elsewhere. See also St. Thomas, *Summa,* IIIa., q. 10, a. 1, 3 et ad 3.

This principle is certainly in need of precision, and has not achieved the status of an axiom. The natures and their attributes remain distinct in the union, and it is inexact to say that the humanity has all that the divinity possesses, though by a different title; furthermore, a divine attribute possessed through grace would not be this divine attribute itself. The humanity possesses the divine attributes through the divinity's possession of them, in the sense in which we can say that it possesses the divinity; the humanity itself does not possess them. What the humanity possesses and has to possess is something which is on it own level and which, expressing the humanity as united to these attributes, expresses the attributes in a way that is conformable to the humanity.

As these attributes are modes of being, since they are Being itself, the something in question will be a mode of being. In their case, accordingly, the empirical concept of ownership has no sense. For example, God is the first cause. Therefore the Man who is Christ is the first cause. Accordingly His human nature will have to be adapted to this attribute, and must have a foundation proportionate to such a relation, that is, it must be the first cause in is own way and in its own order. This way, as well as the order established in it, is the divinized humanity. Hence Christ's humanity will be the first cause in this order, and indeed, we must say, in the order of divinization generally. But here we are speaking only of humanity; we dealt elsewhere with the angels.

Through the Incarnation, the first cause has become second cause. As second cause, however, it remains the first cause. Therefore it must be a second cause in a way befitting the first cause: by being, in the order of second causes, the universal principle for all that concerns divinization.

This assertion is traditional in theology. The humanity of Christ, as St. Thomas says, "is a certain universal principle in the order of those who possess grace, a certain universal principle of grace in human nature." [43] Since it is truly and wholly the humanity of God, it must be wholly divinized. Hence no divinization is possible unless it is a participation and an influence emanating from the divinization of Christ's humanity. For *quod est maximum* (and here we must add: *absolute maximum*) *in aliquo genere, est causa eorum quae sunt in genere.* If we could conceive a divinization produced independ-

[43] *Summa*, IIIa, q. 7, a. 9, 11.

ently of Christ's humanity, the latter would no longer be total, and we could conceive a greater, namely, the sum of the two.

To say that Christ's humanity is the first principle in the order of grace, is not to restrict its primacy but rather to explain it. Grace is not an epiphenomenon that leaves nature untouched; it is the divinization of nature. Therefore primacy in the order of grace is *eminenter* primacy in the order of nature.

Human nature essentially implies a first principle, a first ancestor, for it is made to multiply itself by generation. That ancestor differs from other individuals only accidentally and by the position he occupies; any man could have been the ancestor, and every man can be an ancestor with regard to an indefinite posterity. The species is like the individual in this respect, as it must be, seeing that it is but the multiplication of the form which is realized in the individual: it fashions itself and flows from itself to itself, just as the individual builds up an organism for himself and endows himself with his own moral value.

The Incarnation established a new human species, or rather effected a renewal of the species: divinized humanity. To be truly human, this new species too is equipped to flow from itself to itself and admits of a first principle.

However, since it is divinely human, it must spring forth divinely and have a first principle that is God as well as man. In the natural order this power, like humanity itself, reaches out and is divided into the vast multitude of individuals who are all equally men. In the divinized order the unity of mankind and its immanent power of issuing from itself receive a transcendent perfection, for humanity itself receives such a perfection, and *ens et unum convertuntur*. Hence this power is concentrated in a single individual, who is God as well as man. He will be the second Adam of the race, and the species proceeding from Him will be divinized. This does not mean that all others are excluded, for every man is essentially too social to be without influence on mankind. Indeed, men will be principles in a supernatural manner and therefore more excellently, because of their union with Him. He will be the first principle by the very power that they receive from Him. The glory of the first cause consists, not in destroying other causes, but in making them causes; and we read that Christ is the head, "from whom the whole body, being compacted and fitly joined together by what every joint supplieth, according to the operation in the measure of every part, maketh increase of the body, unto the edifying of itself in charity." [44]

"From whom the whole body . . . maketh increase of the body." The whole body is truly its own principle; but it is such through the head, and when it builds itself up, it is Christ alone who, within it, builds it up.

The humanity of Christ exercises its function of principle by an efficient causality which, really present in Him, has a definite way of operating in all His acts and states. "Whatever took place in Christ's flesh, even after the soul was separated from it, was profitable for our salvation, in virtue of the divinity united to it." [45] *Operari sequitur esse:* since Christ's humanity is a radical divinization of all humanity, its proper activity is the production of this divinization, and its supreme act, death, is this production in a supreme way.

However, since Christ's humanity possesses such divinization only by union with the divinity, it does not impart divinization except through its union with the divinity, in a dependent activity, by a participated and received power, which is properly speaking what Scholastics designate as its instrumental causality.

Instrumental causality: the notion of instrument is the best that experience can suggest, and we do well to have recourse to it if we wish to understand Christ's human activity. But its inadequacy is easily perceived. An instrument's cooperation with an action is external, material, passive; a painting requires something more than a brush. Christ's humanity, instrument of His divinity for the divinization of the human race, is the fullness of such divinization. When it divinizes, it communicates its own perfection, and hence it acts through its form, *per formam suam,* and the contact by which it acts is the contact of its mystic totality, *per contactum suum,* and not the contact of the divinity supplying for its own contact, as though by reversing the roles the divinity would serve the humanity as instrument. Therefore this action is its connatural action; [46] what else would God's humanity do except divinize humanity? But since

[44] Eph. 4:16.

[45] St. Thomas, *Summa,* IIIa, q.50, a.6; cf. q.48, a.6; q.49, a.1; q.56, a.1 et ad 2, 3; a.2 ad 1, 2, 4; q.57, a.6 ad 1; *Compendium of Theology,* pp. 231 ff., Part I, chap. 231; *Ad Rom.,* lect. 3, cap. 4.

[46] *Operari sequitur esse.*

it is what it is by God's gift, this mode of activity, to correspond exactly to what it is, has all the dependent and received characteristics that go with instrumental causality, just as, to be dependent in this way, the activity expresses clearly all that is intrinsic and proper to this humanity. The act by which God takes up the instrument is radically the act by which He makes it subsist; the act by which He employs the instrument is radically the act by which He fully divinizes it by giving it subsistence. The principal cause, the instrument, the material worked on, and the operation form but a single mystic totality.

Accordingly the notion of instrumental cause does not contradict the idea of first principle; in fact, it draws attention to the reason why the instrument is a first principle. A comparison common among the Scholastics helps us to understand that Christ's humanity has a kind of activity that is truly its own and is exercised *per formam suam*. They say that the humanity of Christ is a united instrument, an *instrumentum coniunctum*, as the body is with regard to the soul. When the body acts through the power of the soul, it acts *per formam suam*, and when it produces effects that are of a material nature pervaded by the spiritual, it communicates its own likeness.

Instrumentum coniunctum: the *coniunctum* is traditional; it merits examination. The sacred humanity has its causality from its union with God, from the new contact, immeasurably closer than any other, which it has with the first cause. Its proper action is to confer union with God by its mediation, and thus to communicate grace. Through this grace it brings about a union of all men with itself, with God, and with one another.

Consequently we may call it "causality of union," which corresponds exactly to the "entity of union" we spoke about in the fourth section of the present chapter. The word "union" recalls the word *coniunctum;* it implies that the causality in question is based wholly on the union which is the Incarnation, and that it is a properly Christological and Christian causality, no less than a supernatural causality.

To aid in understanding this, the construction of a metaphysic of causes is assuredly useful; but in working out the problem we have to keep the incarnate Word in mind, and we must think of such causality in the whole Christ.

After the attribute of first cause, we come to that of last end: this Man who is Christ is strictly the last end, because He is strictly God. In His humanity, therefore, He must be intrinsically adapted to this attribute; He must be the last end in the way possible for His humanity, in the proper order, the order of divinized humanity.[47]

Indeed, it is in this humanity, and more precisely in the transcendent perfection present in it because of the hypostatic union that God, the absolutely last end, makes Himself accessible to all mankind and to all creation. In this perfection, therefore, the sacred humanity is the expression of God in human terms, the manifestation of God in the sphere of human activity. It attracts all mankind and all creation with the very attraction of God; it is the last end, not of the order of grace, but in the order of grace. And such it ought to be; for in the order of grace it is the transcendent realization of humanity.

We have elsewhere brought out the fact that the end of man must be human, and that it implies a possession as perfect as possible of humanity—perfect naturally or supernaturally according as man is in the natural or supernatural state—and a possession of God in this possession of humanity. As concerns Himself, the Man who is Christ is not only in possession of the end but is, hypostatically, this very end. Hence He must be in complete and transcendent union with humanity, as He is with divinity. Relatively to other men, He is an end that is adapted to them: a fullness of humanity in a fullness of divinity.

This primacy, found in the order of efficient and final cause, exists also in the order of exemplary cause. Christ's humanity, being the humanity of Him who is the exemplary cause, must also be an exemplary cause in its own line, the line of divinized humanity. God, and more precisely the Word, is the universal archetype, in particular for humanity.[48] For humanity exists eminently in Him, in the way of an idea or rather of the Act: "Humanity," the idea of humanity which is God in God. This clarifies what we said above, that the Incarnation can be neither impossible nor natural, but must be supernatural with reference to the assumed humanity, and that the effect produced in the latter, designed to adapt the Man it con-

[47] Cf. Council of Trent, Sess. VI, cap. 7 (Denz., 799).
[48] St. Thomas, *Summa*, Ia, q.44, a.3; *Contra Gent.*, I, 54; *In I Sent.*, d.36, q.2, a.1; *Summa*, Ia, q.34, a.3; *In I Sent.*, d.27, q.2, a.3 et ad 3, 4.

stitutes as "Humanity," will be to make Him human with the individual and social perfection we spoke of before.

Humanity, the interior model which every man gropingly seeks,
will exist in Him transcendentally. He will be in humanity and within
range of humanity, the expression of the ideal "Humanity," so far
as it communicates itself; and the contemplation of His life will be
for every man the most sublime revelation of the interior law that
governs him.

First, last, and complete within regenerated mankind, Christ as
man takes all mankind to Himself, as He recapitulates it.[49] He fills
all things, *ut impleret omnia*,[50] just as God does. Christ is all in all,[51]
as God is all in all.[52]

A reflection of the divine omnipresence is found in Christ's human nature, as tradition records.[53] We must say a few words on this
subject to obviate the danger of reading into this truth a sort of
"panchristism" that would distort the genuine notion of Christ's
greatness, as pantheism distorts the genuine notion of God's greatness. Strict ubiquity or absolute omnipresence is a divine predicate:
God alone is present to the being of all things, because He is Being
itself. No finite nature, not even the humanity assumed by the Son
of God, can have this predicate.[54] Since the sacred humanity is not
the totality of being, it cannot be present to the totality of being.

Yet it is truly the humanity of this totality, and the Man it constitutes is the Omnipresent. Therefore, as has been said of the other
attributes, Christ's human nature must be adapted to the Omnipresent and must be omnipresent in its own way and in its own
order. This restriction is strictly necessary to avoid heresy and
absurdity. Christ's humanity cannot be present to all being except
through the divinity. But it must be present to the divinization of
man and of creatures, because it is the totality of divinization. This
is its properly human and supernatural immensity, through which
it shares in the divine omnipresence.

Human nature is indeed capable of a certain illimitation that may

[49] Eph. 1:10, 23.
[50] Eph. 4:10.
[51] Col. 3:11; 1:19 f.; Eph. 1:10.
[52] Cf. I Cor. 15:28; Eph. 4:6.
[53] For pertinent texts, see the index to *The Whole Christ*, s.v. Christ.
[54] Cf. the Second Council of Nicaea, actio VIII (Denz., 307).

be called an omnipresence, namely, that which is possessed, in its own order, by a form that has its act and hence its illimitation in human nature. Thereby the nature is capable of being assumed by illimitation in the strict sense, that is, by the divine omnipresence, and of being perfected, according to its capacity, by union and assimilation to that omnipresence.

In an analogous way we can speak of a certain illimitation of human nature in time. Because of his soul, man endures in the manner of a whole, with a duration which is not a part of temporal duration but which, being essentially superior, is capable of expressing all temporal duration. In Christ's humanity this purely human perennity subsists in the absolute perennity of eternity. Because it shares in and is assimilated to this absolute perennity, it has to be perfected in its own line. The sacred humanity lives with an eternal life, and so abundantly that men, by being joined to it, receive of the abundance of this life.

Thus Christ's human nature can be the unity of human history, as it is the unity of humanity. In the centuries preceding Christ's birth it can already have come, and in the centuries that follow, it can continue to live and to die. Similar considerations can be entertained regarding the divine infinity, unity, omnipotence, providence, etc. To avoid repetition, we shall not open up these subjects; they can easily be developed.

In the purely natural order all men exhibit a certain illimitation, and those whose external qualities or behavior more clearly reveal the human type quickly become the center and unity, and almost the soul, of the environment in which they find themselves. The point is not that they overshadow their fellow men, but that in their own persons they bring out the value of others.

The humanity of Christ possesses this superiority in a transcendent way, not only in some accidental qualities but in its very being: it "is" the humanity of Being. Accordingly it is the center and unity in a transcendent way, not simply by a certain psychological influence but by ontological efficacy, by truly causing men to be supernaturally more human.

To be a man, and not just a clod or a statue, means that one is open and receptive to the company of others, and is disposed to experience and live in oneself what others feel, to live their lives in oneself, if the thought may thus be expressed. How human, then, must that humanity be which God has made to be His own, with a respect that is in a sense infinite, for it is that which He has for Himself. To be a man is to have a power of self-donation, of recognizing oneself in every man. How human, then, must be the humanity which is that of absolute donation and which belongs to Him who is *infinite diffusivus sui*.

This is a transcendent humanism, immeasurably exalted above the terse rules of any classicism or romanticism. It is doubtless a humanism full of sorrow, for it is realized in a redemption. Yet it is truly humanism, and such as shows what man becomes when he is man in God and through God.

VII. Perfection in the Order of Personality

This totality of union, far from being opposed to the personal character of Christ or of Christians, is rather its consequence.

A person, according to the traditional definition given by Boethius, is a *rationalis naturae individua substantia*,[55] an individual substance of rational nature, or to be precise, an *incommutabilis*[56] *existentia*[57] or *subsistentia*.[58] This individual subsistence of rational natures, this separate and per se existence of primary substances in the rational order,[59] this *talis modus essendi quem circumloquimur per: esse per se separatum, ita quod repugnet ei esse in alio ut in quod, sive ut quo in quod, sive est pars in toto*, this *terminus ultimus, ut sic purus, naturae substantiae*,[60] this way of being a *substantia prima tota; substantia singularis et individua, integra et perfecta; ens, substantia per se subsistens vel existens; substantia discreta aut separata, vel per se ac seorsim posita*,[61] has been thoroughly investigated by theologians. In particular, they have taken great pains to isolate and define the formality that properly constitutes personality.

---

[55] *Liber de persona et duabus naturis*, III (PL, LXIV, 1343). Cf. St. Thomas, *Summa*, Ia, q. 29, a. 1: *Singulare in rationalibus substantiis;* IIIa, q. 2, a. 2, 3.

[56] Richard of St. Victor, *De Trinitate*, IV, 22 (PL, CXCVI, 945). Cf. St. Thomas, *Summa*, Ia, q. 29, a. 3 ad 4.

[57] Richard of St. Victor, *loc. cit.* Cf. St. Thomas, *Summa*, IIIa, q. 17, a. 2 ad 2; *De potentia*, q. 9, a. 3.

[58] St. Thomas, *In III Sent.*, d. 5, q. 1, a. 3; *De potentia*, q. 9, a. 3 ad 1.

[59] Cf. St. Thomas, *Summa*, IIIa, q. 16, a. 12 ad 2; Ia, q. 29, a. 1 ad 5; *In I Sent.*, d. 25, q. 1, a. 1.

[60] Cajetan, *In IIIam*, q. 4, a. 2, nos. viii, x.

[61] These are the definitions proposed and studied by Tiphanus; cf. *Dictionnaire de théologie catholique*, art. "Hypostase," col. 414.

This is a study of paramount importance for the scientific formulation of the great Christian dogmas. It is also an extremely delicate undertaking, and is so difficult that after centuries it has not yet been brought to a close, and no formula has yet, in all points, won unanimous adherence. It is, further, a most abstract study, and one that runs the risk, if it dominates attention for too long a time, of obscuring what is vital in this matter, which is the very heart of theology.

Accordingly, although we have our preferences, we wish to prescind from them, or at least to refrain from taking our stand on them, so as not to make our exposition dependent on them. We have already touched on this subject in earlier chapters, when we discussed the nature of persons, spiritual beings, and wholes, and on the other hand spoke of material beings, beings that are parts, things. Here we may content ourselves with recalling that these represent two types of being which differ in their very being, and that formulas of union which would be meaningless for things may not be impossible for persons.

Since man is not body alone or spirit alone or merely a thing or perfectly a person, he lacks a perfect idea of things as well as of persons. He naturally conceives of things as having some resemblance to persons; he regards them as objects that in a minor way are absolute, whole, complete, and interior to themselves, as though in themselves they were not mere parts relative to other parts and impossible outside the whole in which they exist.

Conversely, he conceives of persons as having some of the characteristics of things; this is the way he perceives them with sense experience. He comes to represent them as kinds of animals of superior nature, as tenuous bodies that are invisible and subtle, as counterparts of material bodies, constructed of what is nobler and more immaterial in matter. These tenuous bodies he endows with spiritual properties of which he has some experience in himself: intelligence, consciousness, will, freedom, and the like; and then he imagines he has an idea of person.

But the truth is that persons are essentially "other" than things. Things exist, but in a sense they lack existence; for they are exterior to themselves and to the whole in which alone they exist and which itself, throughout its extent, is exterior to itself; they exist with an existence that does not possess itself, that lets its own being escape.

On the contrary, persons, spiritual beings, exist by being what they are, by possessing their whole being in themselves.

Thus things are distinct from one another by being separate; they are distinct by the contours which, in marking their design, mark their limits. Persons are distinct by their inner fullness; contours and separation have no sense for them.

Therefore we should be wrong to identify separation and distinction. The incommunicability essential to persons is by no means the impenetrability that is a property of things. A person is incommunicable by being totally and definitively himself, so that a duplicate of this self is impossible. Yet a person is not incommunicable in the sense that he is imprisoned within himself and is unable to communicate anything of himself. On the contrary, the most perfect persons, the divine persons, exist in a complete communication of absolutely everything that they are.

From every point of view, accordingly, union among persons must be conceived on a different model. Things that are externally delimited are externally united. There is a contact of surface with surface, but clashes occur when they meet at the point they cease to be themselves; one thing does not encounter another except by repelling that other.

Persons, who are defined by their inwardness and totality (also, evidently, by their "ultimateness"), are united in this inwardness and totality. Propinquity, contact, superposition have no meaning for them. Such relations involve nothing but extension and external placing, and we are dealing with simplicity and immanence. In the case of persons, either there will be no real union, or the interior of one will become interior to the other; the distinction between them remains intact, but it asserts itself interiorly.

In fact, as we have said, the form in human nature, having its act in each individual, also has its illimitation in each. It has its act, and this is what accounts for personality, whether personality is proper to it or transcendent. It also has its illimitation, and this confers on it a certain universality. The two go together. By his personal life and by being present to himself, man has a certain presence of all humanity in him. Hence he will not exhibit himself as personal unless he gives himself and unites himself to the whole human race. Even on the natural plane we can truthfully say: "Lose thyself and thou wilt find thyself." In consecrating himself to all, he recovers himself. Morality declares this, experience demonstrates it, and arrival at the last goal will make it evident.

Accordingly a supernatural perfecting of personality, as conferred by grace, demands a corresponding perfecting of one's union with all.

This is why the transcendent perfection conferred by the hypostatic union requires a transcendent perfecting of the union. Undoubtedly the union does not perfect a human personality, for it consists in having nothing but a divine personality. Nevertheless it perfects the factors in the human nature which would have issued in a human personality if the divine personality had not been bestowed, and it perfects them in conjunction with the divine personality, which they have to express in their own fashion. Thus the fact of being a divine person, far from separating Christ from other men, transcendently unites Him to them all.[62]

For that matter, the most magnificent example of union that is possible is found precisely in the divine persons. There, where distinction is most complete, separation is strictly lacking. The divine persons are infinitely distinct, to the point of being defined exclusively by the relation that opposes them. But they are also infinitely united: not only because they are a single nature by their consubstantiality, but also because the very opposition that distinguishes them defines the origins and processions which place them in one another by circumincession: *semper in invicem, neuter solus*.[63] At this summit of all reality, the distinction among the persons implies not separation but union. This union and this distinction are communicated by grace to the mystical body.

VIII. Unification of Mankind by Trinitarian Unity

Here we are at the high point of the theology of the mystical body: this body has its principle in the life and unity of the Trinity. No doubt, as has been repeated often enough, this principle in the mystical body is the humanity of Christ. But we must go on to say that Christ's humanity has its mystic fullness and illimitation through union with God, and it has its union with God through union with the Word. Hence it is attached first and directly to the Trinitarian life as such; by sharing in this life and unity—for all

[62] St. Augustine, *De Trinitate*, VI, 9 (*PL*, XLII, 930).
[63] Eleventh Council of Toledo (Denz., 281).

life is unity—it is made the principle of life and unity for all mankind. In Christ's humanity, therefore, the Trinity is definitely this principle.

Jesus has clearly declared this truth. His main teaching on supernatural unity connects it closely with the mystery of the divine processions. In His teaching about these processions He includes Himself. In the eternal conversation among the divine persons, as translated into human words by one of these persons, He is one of the participants. We refer to the sacerdotal prayer, the last words of Jesus during His mortal life, words so solemn that He utters them to His loved ones in the form of a prayer to the Father; at this moment, infinite unity embraces all. He speaks of the absolute union among the divine persons, and of the union which those who believe in Him have with Him and these persons. The two unions together, the one deriving from the other and reproducing it, make Him the bond of the second and also the bond between the two. "That they may be one, as we also are. . . . That they all may be one, as Thou, Father, in Me, and I in Thee; that they also may be one in us. . . . That they may be one, as we also are one: I in them and Thou in Me; that they may be made perfect in one." [64]

The same affirmation occurs five times in a few words. How could He have insisted with greater vehemence? By participation and imitation Christ's loved ones are to be one in Him who is one of the divine persons, just as the divine persons are one. The desire that they may be in one of the divine persons is expressed three times; the prayer that they may be united as the divine persons are united is likewise repeated three times.

No one has the right to attenuate such a teaching to the point of suppressing it. The duty of theology is to devote its full energy to seeking an explanation that is in accord with the actual meaning of the words. We are deep in the very heart of mystery; no matter: at the bidding of Jesus, Peter boldly began walking on the waters. *Ingrediamur caliginem.*

The divine persons, as we have seen, are wholly distinct although they are wholly united. Men also, by nature and by the act which their form possesses, are at once distinct and united, though imperfectly and in their human way. Through the Incarnation, in the Man who is the Word, this double totality is joined to a certain

[64] John 17:11, 21 ff.

double totality of the Man.[65] The second totality, according to the reasoning that occurs throughout this chapter, will of course be elevated and divinized.

May we not say—surely the reader will not misunderstand—that the Trinity is in a certain sense a society made up of three persons united by consubstantiality and circumincession, and that this union is, so to speak, its sociability? We could then go on to say that in the case of Christ the human sociability, which is essential to every concrete human nature, subsists in this transcendent sociability. To express such a manner of being, the human sociability will become transcendent and supernaturally and divinely perfect. Thus Christ's humanity, through its union with the Trinity in the Word, will be able to admit the whole of humanity to a share in this transcendent "sociability," this union within distinction.

Accordingly the mystical body will be a reflection and a sort of sign of Trinitarian unity. On beholding the union of Christians with one another, men will perceive, by faith, the union of the divine persons: "That they may be made perfect in one; and the world may know that Thou hast sent Me." [66]

These considerations on the Trinity merely open up the subject. What we shall have to add concerns the relations of each of the persons with the whole Christ, and will come later, when we deal expressly with the divine persons. What we have to say here is that, as Christ is one of the Trinity, the unity that He builds up is a unity of the Trinity, and that this unity, which has its fullness and its existence through the Trinity ("I in them, and Thou in Me; that they may be made perfect in one"), has its fullness and intelligibility likewise in the Trinity, and hence in the mystery which is the origin of all mysteries. Consequently the mystical body is the mystical Christ.

IX. Corollaries for Christology and the Mystical Body

Thus we perceive that the mystical body is not an unthinkable entity. Indeed, we cannot think seriously of the Incarnation without thinking of the mystical body.

It is not an amorphous entity in which everything is mixed up, or

[65] Although Christ has no human personality, He nevertheless has this totality, which is a property of human nature, as we pointed out above.

[66] John 17:23.

in which personalities are blurred; it is a close union in which the composing factors remain distinct. The saints, the true Christians, thanks be to God, are not flabby non-entities afraid to be themselves just because they belong to God. We need but observe how they conduct themselves in their zeal and humility, their self-possession and ardent love, to perceive how fellowship in life has made them intensely alive. The only thing they have lost is isolation; their whole soul expands in catholicity. In a similar way the splendor of the noonday sun unites everything in a common brilliance of light, but at the same time enlivens colors, sharpens angles, and stresses contrasts.

The mystic Christ is likewise far from being an unthinkable entity; we cannot think seriously of Christological dogma without thinking of Him. We may define Him as Christ so far as He is perfected in the social aspect of His humanity by the hypostatic union. He is not a sort of fantastic being somewhat larger than a man. He is a man, truly, but a man who is God, and in the way that befits a social being.

The resulting union with the entire human race is extremely intimate; it may be called mystic identity. Does not St. Paul say that Christians are Christ? [67] Does not Jesus Himself say the same? [68] As the principle that makes them alive with eternal life, is He not, in the order of that life, more themselves than they are themselves, in the same way that God, in the order of being, is more each being than that being itself is?

But this mystic fullness, far from diminishing His distinction from others, increases it immeasurably. No man is so distinct from others as He is. First, because He is God; but also because He is united to them as no one else is. Universal principle of supernatural life and unity, He must be distinct from all as a principle is distinct from its consequences, as unity is distinct from the multiplicity it unifies, as plenitude is distinct from all participations. How could He unite them in Himself if He lost Himself in them? How could He make them one if He were not one? How could He diffuse His life through them all if He Himself were not superabundantly alive?

The mystic Christ is not a vague, abstract humanity which, to be all in all, would be nothing in itself. He is the Christ of the Gos-

[67] Cf. I Cor. 12:12; Col. 2:11.
[68] Matt. 25:40, 45; Acts 9:4 f.

pels, with steady gaze, determined action, clear-cut words. Indeed, it is precisely in asserting His incontestable individuality that He asserts His mystic universality; it is in declaring Himself judge of the living and the dead that He declares Himself affected by all that is done to His members; [69] it is in declaring His solidarity with the Father that He declares His solidarity with every man; [70] it is in daring to call Himself light and life that He presents Himself as light and life for all; [71] it is by having God in a special way for Father that He is the vine of which the faithful are the branches; [72] it is by being one with the Father that He enables His followers to be one in Him.[73]

Thus the Incarnation, by being the assumption of a human nature, that is, merely by being the Incarnation, is in a position to spread its effects to the very limits of the human race and of the universe. This it can do, not only because humanity is sociable by nature, but much more because the Incarnation makes it supernaturally and divinely sociable.

In this totality of Christ, therefore, the Incarnation forms a single whole with the divinization of all mankind, with the body of grace in which this divinization is effected, and with the supernatural life of all the members of this body: the mystical body is the fullness of the assumed humanity. When we say that there is nothing but the Incarnation, we do not exclude anything, but recapitulate all things. Accordingly the role of Christ with respect to mankind is onto-logical before it is operative. What Christ does, what He allows men to do with Him, is radically the full realization of what He is.

From the first instant of His existence—in fact, in the divine de-crees—God's union with all men is realized in Him. This is His es-sential mediation: not, primarily, to be a go-between effecting an alliance by perpetually traveling back and forth, nor an intermediary who takes a position at a halfway mark to expedite a journey, but to be at once, in the unity of a divine person, one of the Trinity and the unity of humanity, to be joined both to God and, in principle, to every man, and thus, by being what He is, to abolish the distance that separates man from God.

[69] Matt. 25:34 ff., 41 ff.; 10:42. Cf. Acts 9:3–6.
[70] Mark 9:37; Matt., 10:40; Luke 10:16; John 17:14.
[71] John 8:12; 9:5; 12:46.
[72] John 15:1–7.
[73] See especially John, chap. 17.

The most intimate thing in a man is his relation with God; this is what causes a man to exist. This is the relation which Christ, by uniting Himself to those who are His, influences first of all, and He influences it by making it infinitely closer in Himself. He comes to take His place, by union, in what is most intimate in a man; this is the mystery of Christ's interior presence in Christians. This presence and this mediation show how Christ is the substantial religion of Christians, their absolute and unique priest.

Because of its assumption, Christ's humanity presents three different aspects. It is a humanity hypostatically united to God, and so, by being suitably perfected, is intrinsically the humanity of God. It is a humanity closely united to all other human natures, and so is their mystic head. It is also an individual humanity. The first aspect designates its essential excellence; the second, its function; the third, its nature. The first aspect stresses the relation to the nature that assumes; the second, the effect of the assumption from the social point of view; the third, the assumed nature. But all three express the same unique human nature; they even show that it is more of a human nature than all others, for it is more perfect, as being united to God, and is in perfect possession of humanity.

All three aspects are closely united within this unity. Christ's humanity has its ultimate individual unity and its mystic plenitude by being united to God; this individual unity is perfected by the union to the point of becoming a principle of life for all men; and being thus united to all men, it communicates to all a share in the great perfections it possesses in its individuality through the union.

These three aspects of the sacred humanity are discovered in certain details which theology brings out and which sometimes seem hard to understand. As these aspects are immediately connected with the supreme principle of Christology, which is the dogma defined at Chalcedon, they show how such details are connected with it; and these details, in turn, by referring the three aspects to Christ, show that Christ is the origin of understanding in theology.

This is exemplified in the teaching on the threefold grace of Christ: the grace of union, the grace of headship, and the grace of the individual person. The latter two are a single grace.[74] At first sight, this multiplicity of graces is disconcerting. But if we think of

[74] Cf. St. Thomas, *Summa*, IIIa, q.7, prol.; q.8, a.5.

the three aspects of Christ's human nature, do we not see that it must be divinized in three ways, so as to be fully divinized? As God's human nature, it must be divinized with a transcendent divinization, "that it may become divine by participation, that is, according to grace." [75] This is the grace of union, the inner principle of all the grace in the sacred humanity. As united to all other human natures, Christ's human nature must be divinized with a divinization that can be imparted to all; this is the grace of headship. As an individual human nature, it must have an individual divinization. These three divinizations are evidently reducible to one, as Christ's human nature is but one; this is the individual divinization of the sacred humanity, so far as it is perfect as resulting from the divinization of union, which makes it the universal principle in all divinization, that is, which makes it the divinization of the head.

The same is the case with the teaching on Christ's threefold knowledge. If Christ's human nature has three aspects, must not His human way of knowing be characterized by those aspects? In order that His human knowledge may correspond to the position of the sacred humanity in the Word, it must embrace the Word, the Trinity, and the communication of the Trinity that takes place in the Word through the Incarnation. That this knowledge may correspond to what the sacred humanity is in mankind, it must attain to the whole of mankind and the entire communication of eternal life which makes mankind the body of Christ. And that Christ's human knowledge may correspond to His individual aspect, it must reach out to the objects that fall within the field of His human experience.

Without leaving the sphere of intelligence, we could pursue the same line of reasoning and say that Christ's human knowledge, which is joined to His divine knowledge through the union of the natures, must be a human knowledge divinized as knowledge by this union, that it must be transcendently perfected as social knowledge, and also as individual knowledge. And so we have the same three kinds of knowledge.[76]

Since there is only one human faculty of cognition, these three kinds of knowledge make up a single total knowledge; and this total

---

[75] *Ibid.*, q.7, a.1 ad 1.

[76] On this subject we may consult the instructive passage in St. Thomas, *Summa*, IIIa, q.9, a.2 ad 2, and compare it with q.7, a.1 ad 1.

human knowledge is united to the divine knowledge in the unity of a single knowing person, who is the incarnate Word. This latter union accounts for the perfection of the union of the kinds of knowledge with one another. We must not imagine that they interfere with one another; nothing could be more natural and smooth than their simultaneous exercise in Christ's human consciousness; they merely express what this consciousness is.

We can represent the matter more easily if we recall that, according to the data of science, knowledge depends on the vocabulary in which it is expressed to oneself and to others, and that this vocabulary itself supposes an activity occasioned by environment and a cooperation of the central nervous system. A miracle would have been necessary to supply Christ with such a vocabulary prior to all experience, and nothing in Christ's mission required that miracle. As far as His empirical consciousness is concerned, therefore, we can conceive that a real progress could have been made in the explicit formulation of the knowledge He had in His soul, and that His questions and expressions of astonishment corresponded to a very natural advance in His knowledge. Man is essentially a social being possessing knowledge. Christ is such a man; indeed, He is the supernatural unity of the race. However, as long as sin is rampant, mankind as it actually exists is opposed to union, and Christ is not able to extend fully to the whole race what He virtually is in Himself. Accordingly we can conceive that, as one equipped for social knowledge, and on the level of empirical and social knowledge, He did not have His perfection from the beginning; speaking, questioning, and listening were not a kind of sport for Him.

Christ's three kinds of knowledge are called by Scholastics beatific knowledge, infused knowledge, and experimental knowledge. The explanations they give vary slightly, especially as regards the second. They show that, as the term indicates, it is an infusion of mastered knowledge which expresses in Christ's humanity all that other men know by natural or supernatural knowledge, and which equips the sacred humanity for fulfilling its function.[77] Since this function is precisely that of being head, we perceive how their theory may be harmonized with the one just explained.

The Scholastics who speak of a threefold knowledge in Christ do not speak of a threefold love. Perhaps they preferred to confine

[77] Cf. St. Thomas, *Summa*, IIIa, q.9, a.3; q.11, a.1.

their attention to the speculative point of view. However, what concerns charity is not less esteemed in Christianity. To be consistent with the doctrine previously set forth, we must point out that three loves are found in the one human will of the Savior. Does not the action of the will have to follow the understanding? The will of a Man who is the Word does not love as it should unless it loves the Word, the Trinity, and the communication of the Trinity to humanity in the incarnate Word, that is, the whole of the divinized order as such. The will of a Man who is the head of mankind and of creation in the divinized order does not love as it should unless it loves all mankind and all creation that is divinized or to be divinized by incorporation into the God-man. Lastly the will of Christ as an individual Man loves in its own way by loving those who come into contact with Him.

We can discern the same threefold love if we think of what happens to a human love when it is joined in personal unity to divine love. This was our procedure in discussing Christ's knowledge. These three loves show how Christ is able to love men and God in every way. In the unity of the sacred humanity they are joined in one simple and complete attitude of will: the love of the Man who has loved mankind as no other ever loved it, the human love that is wholly human, as is possible only in the unity of a loving person who is God.

In the same way, apparently, we can speak of a threefold power in Christ's humanity. Since it is God's humanity, the unity and first principle in regenerated humanity, and an individual humanity, it must be able, as various occasions arise, to act in a suitable manner. It must possess the energy required for acting as an instrument of God, *instrumentum coniunctum*, but must have that energy as it has its ultimate existence, through the union that makes it personal. It must possess a power of incorporation and assimilation by which it can become the actual head of all creation; for this is how it realizes itself in fullness. Finally it ought to have, in its own right, the power that every man possesses. The first two powers coincide: God employs the sacred humanity as an instrument for the divinization of all creation by incorporating creation into it. Therefore both powers extend to the whole order of the Incarnation, including all that is miraculous; that is, "all the miraculous changes that are to be wrought, so far as they are capable of promoting the end of the

Incarnation, which is to restore all things in heaven and on earth." [78]
May we not say that this embraces all the miracles worked by God, and that the order of miracles has its unity and inner principle in this sacred humanity?

[78] *Ibid.*, q. 13, a. 2.

CHAPTER X

REQUISITES FOR COMPLETE REDEMPTION

"Man must save himself."
Cajetan, *In IIIam*, q. 46, a. 3

I. INTRODUCTION

A CHRISTOLOGY and a theology of the mystical body are incomplete without a soteriology and a theology of redemption. The authentic, familiar image of Christ is clearly the Crucifix, and the mystical body on earth is undeniably an organism that struggles and toils in the grip of sin.

The teaching of the Church on the redemption is set forth in the draft *De fide catholica* which we have already referred to in these pages.

God so loved the world as to give His only-begotten Son as a victim and to make Him, who knew no sin, a sin for us, that we might be made the justice of God in Him. Such ought our High Priest to have been, holy, innocent, unstained, set apart from sinners and raised above the heavens. Offering Himself, the immaculate One, to God through the Holy Spirit, with His own blood He entered once into the holies, and procured an eternal redemption. In the first Adam, the figure of Him that was to come, the human race fell in its first head; so in the second Adam, Jesus Christ, it was reconciled to God as in its second head. The man Jesus Christ, truly mediator between God and men, one man dying for all, satisfied divine justice for us; wiping out the handwriting that was against us and despoiling principalities and powers, He rescued us from our ancient slavery and restored us to the liberty of sons. For if by one man's offense death reigned through one, much more they who receive abundance of grace and of the gift and of justice, shall reign in life through one, Jesus Christ.

This true power of satisfying for the sins of all and of meriting for us the grace and inheritance of justification was present in the Redeemer's passion for the reason that His human acts possessed value corresponding to the dignity of the divine person who acted through the nature assumed by Him. Redeemed, therefore, not by corruptible things such as gold or silver, but by the precious blood of the unspotted and undefiled Lamb, let us make our souls chaste in the obedience of charity; and with faith in God's living Son, who loved us and delivered Himself for us, let us await the blessed hope and the coming of the glory of our great God and Savior, Jesus Christ.[1]

This doctrine was summed up and embraced in a single canon, the fifth of those that treat of the Incarnation: "If anyone denies that the Word of God Himself truly and properly satisfied for our sins by suffering and dying in the flesh He had assumed and that He merited grace and glory for us, or dares to assert that the vicarious satisfaction offered by the one Mediator for all men is opposed to divine justice, let him be anathema." [2]

These words, according to the report that accompanied the draft,[3] express the existence, the manner, and the efficacy of the redemption. Christ redeemed men by offering Himself in sacrifice for them; this sacrifice availed by way of vicarious satisfaction, that is, satisfaction offered in the name of the human race by the representative of the human race; and it had power to produce such an effect because of Christ's divinity.

The theology of this teaching developed slowly; heresy launched no offensive to precipitate the endeavor. But the way the doctrine is presented in Scripture clearly indicated the direction research was to take. St. John, who speaks at length of the redemption, exhibits it as a mystery of unity in Christ,[4] and St. Paul, who gives the most complete account of it to be found in Scripture, is perhaps even more emphatic in insisting that it is a mystery of unity. Christ is our salvation and our redemption [5] by taking us up into Himself,[6] by re-

---

[1] *Schema Constitutionis dogmaticae de fide catholica*, 4, Mansi, *Amplissima collectio conciliorum*, LIII, 290 f.

[2] *Ibid.*, 294 f.

[3] *Josephi Kleutgen relatio de schemate reformato*, c.4, no. 6, Mansi, *ibid.*, 304.

[4] John 11:52; 10:16; I John 2:2–6; 3:1–10; 4:9 ff.

[5] Rom. 3:24; I Cor. 1:30; II Cor. 5:21; Gal. 3:13.

[6] Eph. 1:3–10.

capitulating us in Himself through His blood,[7] by giving us life [8] and justice [9] and holiness in Himself,[10] by making us sons of God in Himself,[11] by gathering unto Himself the whole race like a second Adam and destroying the evil the first Adam had done to all,[12] by incorporating all men into the newness of His life through baptism.[13] As one of the Apostle's better commentators has clearly discerned, everything in this redemption is reduced to the great principle of solidarity,[14] to the truth of the mystical body.

Yet the first great soteriological synthesis proposed by Christian theology, the *Cur Deus homo* of St. Anselm (1098), leaves this principle in the background. The saint says that sin is an injustice that robs God of His honor.[15] Therefore it cannot be atoned for except by restoring honor, either by a just punishment or by a proportionate satisfaction freely accepted. God, who is justice itself, cannot be content with a partial reparation or a gratuitous pardon. On the other hand, the evil done is infinitely great, and man is too insignificant to remedy it by himself.[16] Nothing is left except that a God-man should come to restore the divine honor by a free and total obedience. This is what Christ did on the cross: "He gave to God His life, which was so sublime and precious that it sufficed to pay for all the sins of the whole world, and infinitely more." [17]

The idea thus expressed by the saint, the idea of vicarious satisfaction, has a secure place in theology. But the systematic form and especially the juridical cast he imparted to it do not possess the same value. Scholastic tradition has taken over the thought of the *Cur Deus homo*, but has perfected the theory.

St. Thomas in particular continues the work of St. Anselm on this point, but he goes farther than his predecessor. He resumes the notion of satisfaction conceived as a sort of juridical equivalence,

---

[7] Eph. 1:7; 2:13–22; 5:2–30.
[8] Cf. I Cor. 15:3; II Cor. 4:10 ff.; 5:14–21.
[9] Rom. 3:23–27; 8:1–11, 23.
[10] Cf. I Cor. 6:15–20; Eph. 2:3–10.
[11] Gal. 3:27—4:7; Rom. 8:3–39.
[12] Cf. I Cor. 15:44–49; Rom. 5:1–21.
[13] Gal. 3:26 ff.; Rom. 6:1–11; Col. 2:12–19.
[14] Fernand Prat, S.J., *The Theology of St. Paul*, II, 201.
[15] *Cur Deus homo*, I, 11 (*PL*, CLVIII, 376).
[16] *Ibid.*, I, 21, 23 (*PL*, CLVIII, 394 f.).
[17] *Ibid.*, II, 18 (*PL*, CLVIII, 425).

although he insists on it less and less.[18] At the same time he deliber-ately adds some ideas of his own, with an emphasis that shows how dear they are to his heart. These ideas form part of what is truly great in his theology, and are all connected with the doctrine of the mystical body.

First of all, as concerns the evil to be repaired, he shows clearly that it is not so much an infinite evil [19] as an evil of the group joined in solidarity, a sin of nature.[20] According to the reasoning he most often repeats, the universality of the sin accounts for the inability of a particular individual to make reparation; an individual does not equal the species. Someone who is equal or superior to the whole of nature is needed; and this can be only God, a God-man.[21]

St. Thomas also describes the curing of the evil as a work of solidarity. Christ is able to transmit His holiness and merits to men because He constitutes but a single person with them, a *persona mystica*.[22] The doctrine of the mystical body could not be set down in plainer terms; under this form it has a part in all decisive questions as their ultimate explanation. "Head and members are, as it were, a single mystic person; and therefore Christ's satisfaction pertains to all the faithful as to His members [23] . . . just as the works of any other man in the state of grace are referred to himself." [24]

[18] For example, compare the function of satisfaction in *In III Sent.*, d. 1, q. 1, a. 2; d. 20, a. 1 ad 5 and later, *Quodl.* II, q. 1, a. 1 with the place it holds in the *Summa*, IIIa, q. 1, a. 2; q. 48.

[19] The only passages that can be cited in this sense in the *Summa* are IIIa, q. 1, a. 2 ad 2; Ia IIae, q. 77, a. 3. *The Commentary on the Sentences* seems at first sight to contain a more decisive doctrine, but even there the saint regards this opinion as singular: "Or some say that a mere man is unable to satisfy even for actual sin unless we presuppose the satisfaction of Christ, whose satispas-sion gave efficacy to the satisfaction offered by those ancient fathers who were saved by faith in Him." *In III Sent.*, d. 1, q. 1, a. 2 ad 6.

[20] This point has not been sufficiently brought out by the saint's commenta-tors. It is often repeated in the earlier questions of Part III of the *Summa*.

[21] *In III Sent.*, d. 1, a. 2 et ad 6–9; d. 3, q. 2, a. 1 et ad 5; d. 20, a. 2 et ad 2, 4; a. 3; *Contra Gent.*, IV, 52 ad 12; 54; 55; *Summa*, IIIa., q. 1, a. 2 ad 2; q. 2, a. 11; q. 46, a. 1 ad 3; q. 48, a. 2, 4; q. 49, a. 5 ad 1. For a summary of the saint's thought on this subject, written during his last years, see the *Compendium of Theology*, p. 215, Part I, chap. 200: "The reparation of human nature could not be ef-fected either by Adam or by any other purely human being. For no individual man ever occupied a position of pre-eminence over the whole of nature; nor can any mere man be the cause of grace."

[22] *Summa*, IIIa, q. 19, a. 4; q. 48, a. 2 ad 1; q. 49, a. 1; *In III Sent.*, d. 18, a. 6, sol. 1 ad 2; *Ad Col.*, lect. 6, cap. 1.

[23] *Summa* IIIa, q. 48, a. 2 ad 1; q. 49, a. 1.

[24] *Ibid.*, q. 48, a. 1.

Christ has the power that enables Him to exercise so elevated and universal an action. It, too, is connected with the doctrine of the mystical body; it consists in the efficient action and instrumental causality we explained in the preceding chapter in setting forth the nature of the mystical body. We should note that St. Thomas speaks more and more of this power as his theological thought develops,[25] much more than of redemption, merit, or even satisfaction,[26] except so far as these aspects are reduced to the efficiency in question.

Thus in St. Thomas the theology of the redemption and of vicarious satisfaction tends to attach itself to the doctrine of the mystical body. But apart from the great Thomists of the sixteenth century, of whom we shall speak later, his school can scarcely be said to have followed him. Theologians were more intent on filling in the details of St. Anselm's theory and on making clear the power by which Christ satisfied and the measure in which His merit possessed a value in strict justice, than to discover, along with St. Thomas, how redemption was a work of unity, intrinsically efficacious and intrinsically universal in its application, as opposed to a sin of solidarity.

In our day, however, the tendency inaugurated by him is again prominent; truth, like life, is obstinate. The doctrine of vicarious satisfaction remains classical, but the endeavor has grown to present it less as a juridical process than as a mystery of vital solidarity enabling the head to satisfy for His members. This is undeniable progress; the goal is an explanation made possible by a more conscious possession of the original data and by an interpretation, in the light of such data, of elements gained during the advance of theological thought. This is the way a plant grows by thrusting its roots deeper into the soil.

[25] In the *Commentary on the Sentences* it is rarely mentioned. But in the *Summa* it is brought in on every possible occasion. Cf. IIIa, q. 1, a.6; q.2, a.11. See also the following note.

[26] In the *Summa*, IIIa, q.48, a.2 et ad 2, the chief passage on this question, he attributes only secondary importance to satisfaction and insists more on charity and on the unity of the mystical body than on equality of compensation. See especially a.6 ad 3: "The passion of Christ as compared with His divinity acts by way of efficiency; as compared with the will of Christ's soul, it acts by way of merit; as considered in Christ's flesh, it acts by way of satisfaction, inasmuch as it frees us from the debt of punishment; by way of redemption, inasmuch as it frees us from the slavery of sin; by way of sacrifice, inasmuch as it restores us to God's friendship." This is the summing up and conclusion of the whole question. We see how modest a place satisfaction occupies and how prominent efficiency is made.

In attempting to construct a soteriology according to the doctrine of the mystical body, therefore, we shall be merely following the movement of tradition and conforming ourselves to the line of thought that engrosses the attention of contemporary theology.

To carry out this plan we shall investigate, not what the greatness of God requires for an adequate reparation, but what fallen man needs for a complete restoration. We take it for granted that God makes such restoration possible. However, to remain within the plan drawn up for this book, we shall begin our study of the problem from the viewpoint of man and of man's sin. We shall eventually come to the God-man who recapitulates sinful mankind in Himself; in other words, we shall come to the whole Christ.

II. Theology of the Incarnation According to the Mystical Body: Reparation of Sin

Accordingly we begin with a study of sin. The greatness of creation is that God has nothing to work on; the greatness of the redemption is that God deigns to work on sin, which is opposed to Him. In creation He does everything alone. In the redemption He does more: He enables man to do everything along with Him; and His omnipotence, which appeared in the totality of the original production, appears yet more admirable in a totality of adaptation.

Grave sin, from the clutches of which God is going to aid man to escape, is opposition between a human will and the divine will. It is an act by which the human will renounces the last end to cleave to some secondary good. Thus the will acts against its natural law, which is the expression of God's will within man.

Consequently the act, like the state that follows it, is essentially interior: it resides in the free will and in the conscience, in the absolute interior. It consists essentially in a privation: a persons wills without willing the absolute good, which alone is absolutely worthy of being willed. Hence it is an act intrinsically mutilated, bereft of that which alone could give it a real value in God's eyes. The will despoils itself of its conformity with itself and with its true nature, and also despoils itself of the possession it could have had of the good that is supremely necessary for it.

In a certain sense, accordingly, the evil is infinite. The possession that was rendered impossible could not, of course, have been truly infinite; all that is human is finite. But the object of the possession is a good that is infinite in itself; the possession is *in ordine ad infinitum*, and is the culmination of all that man can desire; hence it is infinite in relation to man's powers. Therefore the infinity of the evil is negative and relative, such as is possible for man.

Furthermore the evil has something of the divine. Evidently it does not do any hurt to God Himself: the sinner harms only himself; but he harms himself in his relation to God, *in ordine ad Deum*. God is offended, not in the way a man is wounded or impoverished by the crime of another, but in the way the absolute Transcendent can be touched: by the violence done to His creature, by the injury the sinner does to himself.

In showing how sin is interior to man, we also show how its sanction has to be interior. Too easily sense experience deceives us and impels us to think of the punishment of sin under the form of human sanctions: imposed and arbitrary sanctions, that are linked to the transgression by another's will and that could have been different or not inflicted at all. The sanction for sin is contained in the sin itself; it is not, strictly speaking, the sin itself, but necessarily results from sin, by God's appointment. In the same way as God directs every being by the inner law of its nature, He also punishes sin interiorly. Whoever does evil breaks with the infinite Being and with his own nature; this is sin. Thereby he finds himself opposed to Being itself and to his own nature; and this is sanction. The sanction undoubtedly has an infinite and divine aspect, but only the same as the evil had: a negative and relative infinity consisting in the fact that it is a sanction *in ordine ad Deum et ad infinitum*.

God does not avenge Himself with all His might; rather man makes himself contradictory and absurd throughout his being. As long as the present life lasts man cannot perceive that this is so, because he does not perceive himself. But at death, when he will discover himself everlastingly, he will see how contrary to nature it is to be a sinner, at odds with himself and with Being.

This will be his hell, a hell that is far more the work of sin than of God. Indeed, we may say that God did not create it; if He had created it, it would be good in itself and for other creatures. Evil calls it forth, and brings it into being according to its own likeness; or, more accurately, God creates it in consequence of evil. Yet God does not thereby become malicious; if He did, separation from Him would be deliverance. God is and remains infinite goodness; and that is the basic reason why privation of Him is infinitely evil. He does not even hold back; indeed, He continues to offer Himself, supremely diffusive of Himself. The unhappiness is all the greater for being definitively shut off from such great goodness and for being the sole cause of its evil. In its essence, hell results exclusively from the goodness of God.

Everything else in hell stems from its essential nature, as a tree grows up from a seed. This is especially true of the mysterious fire mentioned in Scripture. The soul retains a relation to the body, although this relation is not the same as on earth; it becomes even closer, like a sort of imprisonment, through sin which is an enslavement to matter.[27] The soul remains what it is in virtue of its essence, the unity of the material world; it is such in a different way and more fully, for it has arrived at its final stage; but its condition is falsified and contradictory, because of its sin. The laceration afflicting the soul also enters into this relation to matter, and the suffering thereby caused will come, like a recoiling shock, from the outside universe which remains ever the human universe. Even in this respect, consequently, the punishment merely expresses what sin is, and is interior to the sinner as sinner.

In the supernatural order the good which sin deprives a person of is infinitely greater, because it is supernatural and much more deeply rooted in man, investing him with supernatural powers, but also because, being outside of man's nature, it is absolutely transcendent. Therefore the privation will be much more profound and extensive, but it will have an external aspect it did not have before, and will resemble a sanction inflicted from without.

This fact will reveal what the sinner was in himself and what he will have to remain; but, however great the privation may be, it will be human and finite like man. It will still be in ordine ad Deum, for God Himself had become interior to man. Yet the sin will not have touched God, for God no longer resides in the desecrated sanctuary, and the privation will be a privation only in the human measure in which the man ought to have possessed God.

The sins of just men are not like their good works. They perform their good works through grace, and the works thereby take on a divine greatness. But they commit their sins by rejecting grace,

27 Cf. St. Thomas, Contra Gent., IV, 90.

hence with nothing but their own powers; indeed, by sinning they diminish their own powers. The act is merely human, and besides is defective.

With regard to sin as actually repaired by the redemption, it is a sin of nature and of solidarity. To express the whole doctrine adequately and thus prepare the way for a complete soteriology, we should say that the sin in question is the totality of sin, that is, original sin so far as it has penetrated into each man and has been assimilated and actuated in different degrees through actual sins, or again, that it is the sum-total of sins joined to original sin and receiving from the latter the unity of grouping and disorder of which they are capable.[28] Here again, the privation is the continuation of the sin, and is human as the sinner is human. The universality of evil, as we have shown,[29] is the universality which the fault had in the supernatural unity of the origin.

As sin can be committed here on earth, it can also be repaired here on earth, with a reparation that is natural or supernatural according as there is question of a natural or supernatural order. The same changeableness of will that made sin possible also makes it curable.[30] We are speaking of complete reparation: reparation of the moral defection and of the damage it causes, of all the evil that sin entails and that, like the sin, is interior to man.

Therefore it is not sin as such, but sin committed in the order of grace and of the Incarnation, that requires the Incarnation for its adequate reparation. Why could not a merely human sin, committed in a purely human order, be removed by purely human powers in a way befitting human nature? Is man a creature so poorly made, so incapable of resisting when his life is at stake, that his life would be irreparably lost through his first sin that can, alas, occur so soon? "We live in extreme peril!" cries Boso in *Cur Deus homo*. Truly, in that case, God would be delivering men up to ruin by creating them, and His work would scarcely be released when it would often, and almost as a general rule, be fixed in evil before it is fixed in

[28] See St. Thomas, *Summa*, IIa IIae, q. 53, a. 1 ad 2.

[29] Cf. chap. 7.

[30] St. Thomas expresses the matter as follows: "As long as man leads a mortal life in this world, we know that his condition is such that he is neither immovably confirmed in good nor immovably obstinate in evil." *Compendium of Theology*, p. 214, Part I, chap. 199. For the case of original sin, cf. *ibid.*, chaps. 195 and 200.

itself. A person could always become evil when he is good, and could never become good when he is evil. How could we recognize the good Creator in such a primacy of evil?

Life is the time assigned to free will to develop a man and to make him good; shall the work become impossible when life has scarcely begun? Life is a time of change, during which union with the body prevents the soul from possessing itself completely and putting itself wholly forth in its acts; and evil is an attitude opposed to nature; could the will bury itself irrevocably in evil, sometimes with its first act, and forever? In that case what becomes of that *bonum naturae*, that good of nature, which constitutes man's very nature? "The good of nature, which is impaired by sin, is a natural inclination to virtue. This inclination is found in a man by the very fact that he is a rational. For it enables him to act according to reason, which is the same as acting according to virtue. But sin cannot entirely deprive a man of being rational, for then he would no longer be capable of sin. Therefore the good of nature cannot be completely taken away." [31]

This brings out the very essence of natural morality and of sin. Actually, no doubt, sin causes loss of grace which man cannot restore to himself by his own power. Hence it is truly a death. But it is not death in the natural order, at least not in the same sense. Freedom remains, and with it the sort of creative power it possesses. What has to be remade is only something human, and the essence of free will is to produce it. The so-called infinity of sin and of the ravages resulting from sin belongs to the same order as the will's infinity: it is an infinity in the order of inclination toward God; the will is free with regard to all the goods that attract it because it is a tendency toward being and toward God. Therefore everything needed for the work of restoration is at hand. The divine concurrence is evidently necessary; however, this is the simple natural concurrence that sustains in existence and operation the faculty producing natural moral value, not the supernatural concurrence that has a direct influence on supernatural moral value.

The sin that remains in the soul after the culpable act has been committed (that is, habitual sin, and in its own way original sin), is not like the ruin devastating material things after a collapse. A

[31] St. Thomas, *Summa*, Ia IIae, q.85, a.2; cf. *In II Sent.*, d.34, q.1, a.5; *De malo*, q.2, a.11, 12.

madman can demolish a cathedral which hundreds of skilled crafts-
men will never reconstruct. In the moral order the case is different.
The free will that has done evil is of itself outside of time. That
is why its act has a permanent aspect; and the permanent aspect is,
in essentials, habitual sin or original sin. But as long as the present
life endures, this very superiority over time is the reason why the
will, if it changes, will also change this permanent aspect.

We do not exalt God's transcendence by asserting that He alone
can fully repair a fault that is only too easy for the creature to
commit; such a view would reduce Him to a sort of gear necessary
for the stable functioning of His work. Sin in that hypothesis would
appear to be something enormous; man would appear to be tremendously important; and the Incarnation would lose its sublime character, to become merely the sole adequate remedy for a human sin.
Is all that well said?

If we must be careful not to make the supernatural a mere continuation of the natural order, we must also be careful not to make
it continuous with sin, which is the lowest degradation of that order.
The relations between grace and nature are not at all like this.
That which most closely approaches non-being in man does not
call for grace as the only adequate reparation; rather, such appeal
is made by what is most elevated in comparison with grace, not as
though grace were a necessary consummation, but because it is the
supreme perfecting of man and at the same time is absolutely inaccessible to his efforts.

If grace is conferred on sinful humanity, as it actually is in the
present order, the reason is not that there is a relation between grace
and sin, but that there is a relation between grace and the greatness
to which God calls mankind in spite of sin, a relation between grace
and the economy of grace that has original sin as one of its phases.

This conception is implied in the parallel between the two Adams
and in the whole of soteriology as set forth in Scripture. Scientific
soteriology at first lost sight of it; only a few allusions to it are
found in the *Cur Deus homo*.[32] St. Thomas restores it to its original
importance. In this connection he does not propose the distinction
which he clearly makes in another context,[33] between sin in the
natural order and in the supernatural order; but he insists on the

[32] Cf. II, 21, 23 (*PL*, CLVIII, 376, 393, 396).
[33] For example, *Summa*, Ia IIae, q. 86, a. 1.

social character of the sin effaced by the redemption and on the grace it ought to confer and does confer. The entire school follows St. Thomas in giving expression to the doctrine, although it stresses the second aspect more than the first. On the whole, however, we cannot say that it sufficiently draws attention to the difference that may exist between the two kinds of sin.

Restoration of the sinner by the sinner himself is not only possible but is indispensable, even though, in the present order, it cannot be brought about except by grace and indeed, as we shall explain, by the God-man.

Nevertheless we could quite naturally invoke an easier and more external economy. Daily life accustoms us to restorations, reparations, and pardons that come from without: a king may grant mercy to a condemned malefactor even though the latter does not repent, merely because he was born a minor princeling. Why could not God too be gratuitously kind, and respond to the most abject of miseries by the most generous of mercies? Assuredly we should be presumptuous to claim that such an economy of salvation is impossible; who knows the limits of divine wisdom? What we ought to say is that we do not see how it could be realized. Man is too interior to himself to be really affected by a work that remains exterior to him.

Of course God has the power to act on the free will and change it; in fact this is supposed in our reasoning. But the question is to perceive how this is done. And it is done, as is evident, in a way that befits God and is suitable for the will. God's way is directly to touch being as being and action as action, in what is most internal and essential; the will's way is to go first to what is first in itself, its own conscience. The will is a power of self-determination, it can cause itself to be; therefore God will touch the will in this very power, by causing it to cause itself to be and, if there is question of changing it, by causing it to change itself, by an act that is natural or supernatural according as the natural or the supernatural order is concerned.

The pardons granted by men do not demand so much as this, because they cannot accomplish so much. They are quite superficial and produce only superficial changes: some new relations, some slight new dispositions in souls, but nothing that renews a being.

But the pardons granted by God, being immense and radical, require that a man should yield himself up without reserve, that is, since the will is in question, in the very act of his will. This does not mean that less is given, for God gives this act itself by giving man the power to elicit it. Therefore more is given: along with the goodness that God's pardons bestow, there is given the power to be the principle of this goodness.

"Whatever is received, is received according to the capacity of the recipient." The free will is not changed in the way a piece of furniture is shifted from place to place. The will is a whole, not a part of a whole. Any change that occurs in the free will engages the whole of the will and hence its beginning (and primarily in God, assuredly), or else the will is not going to be changed. If the will is to be changed, it will have to be changed from within. The free will, if we may say so, is a being so far as it issues from itself to itself; any change it undergoes, to reach its essence, has to share in this proceeding and must issue from the will—under God's influence, to be sure.

Free will is given to man in order that he may perfect himself and, by continuing his creation through the power given him by the Creator, that he may make himself to be through himself what he already is through God: a first and dependent principle, a first principle in its own order, which is that of human perfection; *liberum est quod est causa sui*. The restoration conferred by God's pardon belongs to the order of this perfection, and therefore will have to have its first dependent and derived principle in man. Either the restoration will be accomplished through the cooperation of man and his liberty, or it will be contrary to nature and, far from repairing, will devastate.

Of course the reparation of the sinner implies other things besides a purely interior act. As theology points out, satisfaction is necessary, along with contrition. The two are distinct; the one is sorrow, detestation of sin, firm purpose of amendment,[34] the other is compensation, adequate if possible; the one is interior, the other is mainly exterior, and can sometimes even be supplied by someone else.[35]

[34] Denz., 897.
[35] St. Thomas, *Summa*, Suppl., q. 13, a. 2 et ad 1.

Yet the two go together. As man has an interior and an exterior aspect, so has his sin, and his reparation ought to have the same. Accordingly, in addition to the conversion of the soul itself, which is contrition, a reparation of all that was the effect and incarnation of evil is required, and this entails an interior healing, a mortification of the passions, an example to be given to oneself and others, restitution, and so on; and all this is satisfaction.[36] To be a complete detestation of evil down to its ultimate ramifications, contrition must imply satisfaction. Both together make up but one complete, human reparation, just as soul and body make up a single complete man; the first is a sort of form of the second, as the soul is the form of the body. Therefore, when we speak of the first, including everything that is in it, we speak also of the second; and when the repentance is sufficiently intense, God remits the punishment along with the sin. From both points of view, a human evil was done, and a human good must be recovered in man and in a human manner; human powers, by definition, are equal to the task.

This does not mean that in the present situation nothing else is needed. The point is that these two acts are also needed; humanity cannot be purely passive if it is to be truly restored.

The present order is an order of union; can we conceive that in the very act that restores this union God should wish to act in isolation, and that He holds man at a distance when He draws him to Himself? To save mankind without requiring mankind to cooperate in the saving act, is truly to act at cross purposes.

That is what St. Paul says in the texts cited at the beginning of this chapter. He who expiates our sins is the head of our family and He is one with us; therefore we ourselves "expiate our sins in Him and through Him." [37]

The Scholastics give the same explanation in their own way, when they contend that it is suitable for men to be redeemed by a man.[38] On this subject we shall quote St. Thomas, because of the

[36] Cf. St. Thomas, *Summa*, Ia IIae, q.87, a.6 ad 3.

[37] F. Prat, *The Theology of St. Paul*, II, 201.

[38] Prior to the Scholastics, St. Ambrose had written: "He took from us that which He might offer as His own for us, in order to redeem us by what is ours. . . . For what is the reason for the Incarnation except that the flesh which had sinned might be redeemed by itself?" *De Incarnationis dominicae sacramento*, 54, 56 (*PL*, XVI, 832). For the Scholastics themselves, see their commentaries on *III Sent.*, d.1 and d.20, or on the *Summa*, IIIa, q.1, or q.46, a.3.

commentaries written on the passage. The saint lists the following reasons:

First, by this fact man learns how much God loves him, and so he is induced to love God; the perfection of human salvation consists in this. . . .

Secondly, He gave us an example of obedience, humility, and constancy . . . virtues which are necessary for man's salvation. . . .

Thirdly, by His passion Christ not only delivered man from sin but also merited for him justifying grace and the glory of beatitude. . . .

Fourthly, the necessity of keeping sin at a distance is impressed on man. . . .

Fifthly, this manner of redemption redounds to man's greater dignity.

Our dignity! The word should be pondered whenever we think of our restoration.

It redounds to man's greater dignity that, as man was vanquished and deceived by the devil, so a man should overthrow the devil, and that, as man deserved death, so a man should vanquish death by dying.[39]

Cajetan knew how to comment on the passage without leaving the high plane of this magnificent humanism:

With respect to the reasons given in the text on the greater suitableness of delivering the human race by Christ's passion, note that they all seem to be reduced to two main heads: either to the delicacy of the divine disposition or to human dignity. The fact that we are brought to salvation by God's justly commended love and Christ's example, merit, value, and the like, regards the delicacy of God's disposition in procuring our salvation; and the fact that man saves and redeems himself, fights for himself, merits, conquers, satisfies, triumphs, rules, judges, and the like, regards our dignity, as is quite clear if we reflect on the matter.[40]

"The fact that man saves and redeems himself, merits, satisfies": as phrased by Cajetan, this is exactly the formula to which the preceding pages are reduced, and which perhaps has seemed strange: that mankind may be fully restored, it must restore itself, and this it has done in Christ. For the pure and simple Christian teaching is that Christ is redeemer through His humanity, not through His divinity, and that His humanity mystically contains all humanity. But Cajetan's formula was short-lived; so far as we know, it is not

[39] St. Thomas, *Summa*, IIIa, q.46, a.3; cf. a.1 ad 3.
[40] Cajetan, *In Illam*, q.46, a.3, no. 3.

found in later commentators of Part III. We should note that these commentators do not occupy themselves with the group of questions that are summed up in the formula; since these questions treat of Christ's life and death, the commentators left them to exegetes and preachers. Yet the thought has not disappeared; it is implied in what many Scholastics had to say on the intrinsic value possessed by the merits of Christians in the order of redemption. We shall soon have occasion to return to this matter.

We should add that this restoration of mankind by itself has to be a death freely consented to and desired, an act that consists in dying. But how can we speak of an act of dying? Death, as witnessed by sense experience, is rather the contrary of an act; dying is a sort of falling asleep from which there is no awakening. The psychological life of a dying person is like a lamp that is being extinguished; when it goes out, nothing is left. If we are spiritualists, we may add that it immediately springs up again on the other side; but on this side it ends up in a void.

However, if we take a large view of the matter, we may, without leaving this point of view, speak of an act of dying. In certain cases man feels himself departing, and he can and ought to acquiesce in his passing; in every case he ought to accept it at least in advance and implicitly, under pain of rebelling against God; and he actually does accept it by his daily submission to the laws of nature which premise the complete dissolution, to take place on the day these laws may require it. This is enough to justify us in saying that he dies by willing to die: he wills death in his feeble human fashion. And it is also enough fully to vindicate what these pages will bring out concerning the redemptive death, and to show that the soteriology they propose is not in solidarity with the philosophy of death that follows.

For our part we believe that death is something much more: that, while being an event in the body's life, it is a capital event in the soul's life. With regard to what death is in itself, we believe that scientific observation and sense perception have nothing to report. Even extraordinary experiences and the secrets narrated by those who may have escaped death or by certain saints give us no information. Such records do not bear on death, which did not yet take place; and besides, how could they express in concepts derived from earthly life that which is the cessation of such life? In certain cases they can perhaps enable us to surmise how the act of death is prepared for; they do not reveal what it is. We may read about a sort of clairvoyance that comes over the dying and empowers them to pass their whole life in review as on a screen; but these pages will not delay over that subject, and we shall do well to divest our minds of such thoughts, which can only distract us.[41]

Death, like man himself, is so essentially interior that it cannot be seen from the outside. The science we have to interrogate on this subject is philosophy, which considers the interior of beings. We shall conduct the investigation with more detail than the present chapter strictly requires, because of the importance of the notion of death for several other points of doctrine and for Christian life in general. In this way the reader will be able more easily to form a judgment on the idea of death we are going to suggest.

The philosophy of death, then, is a part of the philosophy of man, or rational anthropology. What we have to say about the matter is connected with what was brought out in chapter 5, sections 2 and 3, on the philosophy of man.

Man is composed of soul and body. Hence he is decomposable. Death is this decomposition: the separation of the soul from the body. As far as the body is concerned, death is dissolution; it is

[41] Of late years, a number of authors have written about this illumination. Some base their remarks on various experiences, narratives of the lives of the saints, and so on. In this connection we may mention P. L. Getino, in a study found in the appendix to his *Del gran número de los que se salvan y de la mitigación de las penas eternas* (Madrid, 1934). This work, vigorously attacked from its first appearance, was placed on the Index, March 5, 1936. The *Osservatore Romano* of the following day explained the condemnation as follows: "The aforesaid publication takes its inspiration from ideas that have been made popular for some time, especially by Protestant theologians. On the basis of specious arguments and arbitrary interpretations of texts of Sacred Scripture, along with phrases uttered by certain Fathers and Doctors, an attack was lodged against the clear and precise traditional teaching of the Church on the eternity and nature of the pains of hell. Besides, the volume expressly defends a bizarre theory that is current, about a pretended 'special illumination' which human souls receive from God at the moment of their separation from the body, thanks to which they may turn completely and perfectly to the Creator and may thus be justified and saved." We may conclude from this that what is repudiated is a theory according to which, owing to the illumination in question, everyone would be practically certain of going to heaven, and could thus dispense himself from working out his salvation with fear and trembling. No such view is advocated in our book. The act of dying we are speaking of, which is a part of life in the sense that it closes life, is not illuminated by the rays of the next life.

the end. By reason of its union with the soul, to be sure, the body is capable of rising again, exactly the same, because the soul remains the same; which would not be true of the body of an animal. Death is also the end for the soul, but only from a certain point of view, *secundum quid;* it is the end of the soul's union with the body, the end of the period of formation.

Accordingly we may present a definition of death as it concerns the soul, a definition that will dominate the rest of our exposition: death, for the soul, is the passage from a formative stage to a definitive stage.

The soul, in all truth, is affected by death. The soul was made to give to the body the delicate life that is exposed to death on all sides, a life that continues to exist in a continual progression toward cessation of existence and hence death, a life that terminates in detrition and death; in a word, to give to the body a life of death. The soul was made, moreover, to take its definitive form through this inner catastrophe. The body alone dies, assuredly; but the soul, as the actual form of the body, dies at the same stroke. It is mortal, if we may say so, with the body's mortality, just as the body is immortal with the soul's immortality.

We may even say that this death—not the illness that precedes death, but death itself—is more momentous for the soul than for the body. The body sinks into unconsciousness; the soul, on the contrary, awakens, but in a sort of lacerated condition, by ceasing to be what it was, in the suppression of the man it constituted. It is torn from itself to be restored to itself, amid an interior collapse and agony, a passing in the tragic sense of the term.

But above all, death is an act. The change that occurs in the soul itself, in its very consciousness and liberty, has to be an act of the soul, a conscious and free act. It consists in spontaneously willing, as spirit, what an unescapable necessity forces on man as body and part of the universe, in willing this event as such, with its unescapable necessity. This shows, we may remark by way of parenthesis, how starkly in opposition with the human act of dying is the attitude of soul which suicide supposes. Acceptance is what makes bodily death a human event. By it the will sums up and assimilates the totality of its being, and, at this supreme moment when human character is effaced in the body, stamps that character ineradicably on the soul.

Therefore death is an act; but, as we must note in order to fore-stall an inevitable objection, it is a very special act. It is a unique act, and has no more than an analogy with the acts of which we have daily experience, because the latter make up our earthly life, and the act which is death closes that life; also because our daily acts are done in union with the body, whereas death puts an end to that union. The body has its part in the act of death, but only to be left behind, and the contribution it has to make is only that of being no longer fit for the union. Whether the body is used, whether it is unequal to psychological functions, or whether it is torn apart or crushed, matters little; or rather this matters a great deal: it will the more easily be laid aside. It is no longer required to cooperate through phantasms or feelings in the ordinary actions of the intellect or will; the series of such acts has come to an end. The body acts, not to add one more such act to the series, but to close off the series by unifying it in its definitive stage.

The series was a progress toward a goal, by a simple *motus*. We cannot say of it: *quod movetur, movebitur, motus desinit per primum sui non esse*. The soul, being spiritual, possesses its own totality and hence its term; its duration must embrace the instant at which this term appears, and its dynamism must have the power to produce, and above all to receive, this appearance.

The act in question is not the new stage, but is the arrival at this stage regarded as connected with the progress toward it. It is an act of the present life and of union with the body, but so far as that life and union cease. It is an act of the complete man, body and soul, not an act of the soul alone, but an act in which the activity of the body ceases and the activity of the soul disengages itself. It is, as our definition indicates, the passage from here to there, but regarded from the standpoint of here.

This act has to be free, as its very essence shows; it is the passage of a free being to the definitive stage which its liberty has prepared. Otherwise the culmination of human life would be at variance with its structure. The value of life is proportionate to its morality; how could the moment that is supremely important for it be other than free and moral? The only thing that really counts in life is what is human, that which is somehow conscious and deliberate; could the moment toward which the whole of life advances, the moment that puts the finishing touch to man, fail to be human?

Without such liberty, furthermore, the whole life of the soul would be incoherent; a break would separate its two stages. Its stage here on earth is a simple preparation for its stage in the next world: it exists on earth only for the purpose of developing the attitude it ought to take as a spirit. Can the passage from one stage to another, the connecting link between them, have nothing in common with either of them? Can the emergence from the immateriality that disengages itself into the immateriality that is disengaged be wholly material? Can the transition from dawn to day be night? The soul is intended to determine the body; shall the body introduce into the soul its essential determination? Shall the body evoke what is the main thing or indeed everything in the soul and in man, although it is the less important part of man, and that at the precise moment when, in ceasing to exist, it ceases to have any importance?

The final failure of the body's life, which was always more or less feeble, is readily understood. But in the soul's life, which was in advance toward light and the acquisition of freedom, such a breakup and disappearance into darkness is meaningless. That the acts requiring the body's cooperation should become progressively difficult is easily explained; they can and should feel the approach of the end. But how can we conceive that the act which is the cessation of the body's cooperation should be implicated in the imperfections of that cooperation?

We can fall asleep unconsciously and actually do so, because falling asleep is an act within the series and has no effect on the series as much. But we cannot die unconsciously, because dying is the act that crowns the series of human acts and crystallizes it. These acts are free; a fortiori, the act by which they are crystallized ought to be free.

This, we believe, is a most decisive consideration. The essence of freedom is to determine an attitude for oneself, to achieve oneself. All the acts of the will tend to this. If no one succeeds in this while on earth, the reason is not only that man is not yet capable of being crystallized, but also that the acts themselves are intrinsically incapable of crystallizing him. Like man, they are still in process of formation; not having all their being, they do not have all their forces. Like the soul, they are still in time because of the body, and their superiority over time has neither its full act nor its full power. Some of them, for instance, acts of charity or mortal sins, are of such a nature that, if they endured to the end, they would fix the soul in good or in evil. But actually they do not and cannot, because they do not yet have sufficient being; since they exist in the man who is still in formation, they too are still in formation. Distended as they are in relation to one another, with some continuing in others, how could they achieve the soul that produces them, since they themselves are not fully achieved?

On the other hand, this achievement of the soul is the separation from the body which makes it possible; can we imagine that such separation, from this point of view, should have nothing voluntary in it? That separation crystallizes the soul; and free will is the power that crystallizes the soul; how, then, can we say that the separation is wholly without freedom?

Freedom was indispensable for the acts of earthly life, because they exercised some definite influence; surely freedom is indispensable for the act which definitely settles everything. The personal self was whole and free when it was confined to the body and shared in its servitudes; it must be so all the more at the moment of liberation. All the other acts were free because they were a certain escaping of the spirit from the exigencies of matter, and hence had something in common with death; the act which is a complete escaping and full death must also be free.

No one admits that freedom is determined from outside or that it can be forced to a definite line of action by outside influences. The acts that were simple phases in the attitude the will assumed were necessarily free; could the adoption of the irrevocable attitude be anything else than free?

The first act of the free will is rightly said to be of a special order and to be necessarily grave, at least objectively, because it bears on the end and not on the means, since the means cannot be chosen until the end has been willed. How can we deny that the last act is also of a special order? That last act also bears on the whole series, by bringing the series to a close, as the first did by opening it. The last act cannot have means for its object, any more than the first act could. There are no longer any means at this moment; there is nothing but the end which is imminent and which, at this very instant, must either be seized or rejected.

In the moral order, progress toward the end and acquisition of the end are sharply distinct, although joined. Ordinary acts were advances; the last act is the decisive acquisition or loss. Therefore it must be supremely moral and free, in union with the other acts but distinct from them.

Notice that I say: acquisition of the end, not fruition of it. The act that is merely the arrival of the term is logically prior to possession of the term. It is not yet penetrated with the light and saturation that the term implies; it has only made that penetration possible for the soul. Hence the act remains free with respect to this end, free with a liberty that is analogous to the liberty that existed in the series but is more perfect, because it gains full possession of itself.

If it is true that free will is the power to arrive at the end by its own efforts—with God's natural or supernatural aid, as the case may be—it must also be true that this act, the only one that arrives at the end completely, must be completely free, and that it is in a sense the only free act, not because it is the negation of all the other acts, but because it is the recapitulation of them all.

Accordingly these other acts preserve their undiminished importance, including their importance as the commencement of the last act. At all periods human life is formidable in its seriousness; but we should add that it is never lost before it comes to an end. For, since freedom is simple and undivided, the last act takes the lead over the acts that are performed throughout all the days of our life. When the last act comes, it will not be an absolute beginning relative to the other acts; it will sum them up. For the wicked, the last act is terribly hazardous; but for the good it is, so to speak, wholly prefashioned in good. Therefore it would be madness to live in evil, counting on a final change of heart, after everything has been done to render such a change impossible, just as it would be wrong to give way to senseless fears at that hour concerning dangers that have been, as it were, shunned in advance. The last act, being the culmination of the series, is influenced by the series more than any act within the series is; just as, by completing the series, it has more power of self-determination than any of the other acts has.

This act, the climax of life, is also the culmination of morality. It is full acceptance of the moral law, the most unreserved consent that is possible. When that moment comes, a man observes his human duty more perfectly than in any of his other acts; not only to the limit of his powers, but to the limit of himself. He casts himself into obedience as a sailor may cast a corpse into the sea: a few ripples are stirred up, and then nothing more is seen except the immense expanse of the waters.

Thus man realizes himself completely by his conformity to his duty and his tendency toward his end; nothing remains for him except to repose in this end. Why should he remain on earth any longer? His progress is achieved from within; the soul, which was the principle of his life, becomes the principle that causes this life to cease. This it does as the form of the body, in union with the matter from which it detaches itself, and in union with the operation of material forces that disintegrate the organism, so as to impart a human significance to this dissolution.

If death is like this, and even if it is only what appears to the outward eye, we can perceive what it ought to be in the restoration of man.

We arrive at the end by ceasing to become, by dying. For a man who is absolutely without sin, death could be very gentle. In the state of original innocence, as a result of a preternatural gift, the transition was not even death, but a simple passing from the formative state to the definitive state.

But for sinful humanity, especially if there is question of that total sin which we spoke of before, of that composite sin in which actual sins are associated with original sin in solidarity, the transition will be death in the fullest sense of the word. If a man wishes to save himself, he must not only get rid of himself so far as he is in process of becoming, but especially so far as he is evil. To be in a position to unite himself to God, he must divest himself of the sinner that is in him. But the whole of him is a sinner, even though he is not wholly a sinner; sin has laid hold of the very origins of his nature by finding entrance into his free will, just as sin came to defile the origins of his race by infecting the first man. Therefore the whole of him ought to be made to disappear, although not wholly; in other words, he ought literally to die, in order to die wholly to his sin.

Some slight, superficial act, some movement of contrition and a few brief penances are not enough. These may now suffice, because they are incorporated into the death of Christ and into the universal death that prolongs the death of Christ throughout mankind. Perhaps they would be enough to obtain a simple forgiveness. But God wishes much more and nature itself demands more, if full reparation is to be made; man is too valuable to permit of his being remade so cheaply.

Reparation for sin ought to be proportionate to the sin. Sin cannot be committed in the soul alone, for the soul is not alone; it is committed by the whole man. To efface sin, it is not enough for the soul alone to repudiate what it has become; the body also must be included in that repudiation. The whole man must rid himself of the sinner and withdraw entirely from himself; in a word, he must die. Only in this way can full human contrition and complete detestation of sin be realized.

But with regard to the sin as it actually stands, man's most strenuous effort, however indispensable it may be, is utterly insufficient. There is question of the sin of the race, of the universal solidarity of sin; the entire human race is to be restored. How could the death of a single individual produce so universal an effect? [42] We are dealing above all with a restoration which, to be complete, must restore grace, and therefore God, who alone produces grace in joining it to the soul. How could an act which is not God's act give God back to us?

Nevertheless man's death is necessary. To arrive so perfectly at his end, he must perfectly achieve his formation. To be united to God, when he is a sinner, he must be thoroughly emptied of himself. But this death of man will not be efficacious unless it is also a death of God. Accordingly the God-man and His redemptive death are required. Furthermore, the God-man is the mystic totality of the race. In His death all mankind will incur death, a death which is a going to God Himself.

The God-man, Redeemer: it is He whom we must now study. We shall see how His death magnificently meets the requirements of an adequate reparation capable of restoring the greatness we have lost.

[42] This idea occurs frequently in St. Thomas; cf. above, note 21.

CHAPTER XI

NATURE OF THE REDEMPTION

> "Through the redemption
> that is in Christ Jesus."
> Rom. 3:24

I. The Redemption from God's Viewpoint

THE preceding chapter has brought out, step by step, what the redemption ought to be. We must now consider what it actually is.

The first thing that has to be said about the redemption is that it is mainly, or rather exclusively, a gift of God. For redemption is granted in the God-man, and this is why it can restore to men their union with God. God has been pleased to love men, even when they are sinners; everything comes from that. In this fact is found the initial mystery, the unheard-of excess, of which all the profusions of goodness that follow are but consequences. The redemption is a work of divine love.

Christ is the unique and total gift of divine love; the redemption is likewise the supreme and complete gift of love. For it finds full expression in Christ, at the very moment He goes to the limit of His own love: "He loved them unto the end. . . . Greater love than this no man hath, that a man lay down his life for his friends." [1]

The most authentic exposition of this doctrine ever formulated begins with a reference to divine love: "God so loved the world." It ends with the same: "Let us make our souls chaste in the obedience of charity; and in the faith of God's living Son, who loved us and delivered Himself for us, let us await the blessed hope and the coming of the glory of our great God and Savior, Jesus Christ." [2]

[1] John 13:1; 15:13.
[2] This is the draft *De fide*, quoted at greater length p. 247 f.; Mansi, LIII, 290 f.

And Jesus begins His redemptive passion by reaffirming this love. "That the love wherewith Thou hast loved Me may be in them, and I in them," says our Lord as He enters the garden of the agony.[8] St. Paul describes the mystery of our reconciliation with God in similar terms. It is a mystery of mercy, of overflowing goodness, of excessive love: "But God, who is rich in mercy, for His exceeding charity wherewith He loved us, even when we were dead in sins, hath quickened us together in Christ . . . that He might show . . . the abundant riches of His grace, in His bounty toward us in Christ Jesus." [4]

St. Paul's words are echoed by St. John. God wished to show His love, and so He sent His Son, that we might live through Him. And God's love consists in this, that He loved us first, and sent His Son as a victim of propitiation for our sins.[5]

The entire Gospel, with the good news it brings, is full of the same truth: the excessive love,[6] the prevenient love,[7] the incomprehensible, generous love of God Himself.[8] God, if we may say so, conceived the idea of showing how He can love us. He wished to be nothing but love in His relations toward us,[9] and therefore sent His Son to die for us.[10] He wished to make clear just how far He would push His generosity, and so He gave His Son to be the life of us all.[11] Thus absolutely everything has been given to us. Who will be able to separate the men that God cherishes in this way in His well-beloved Son who dies for them, from the love that He bears for them? [12]

Love makes its appearance on all sides. Christ, whom love sends, is Himself love,[13] and is constrained to give His life for those whom He loves.[14] "He loved me," exclaims St. Paul; [15] He loved us, and delivered Himself for us, an offering and a sacrifice of sweet odor. He loved us with an ardent love, like that of a husband for his wife,

[8] John 17:26.
[4] Eph. 2:4–7.
[5] Cf. I John 4:9 f.
[6] *Nimia charitas*, says the Vulgate, Eph. 2:4; cf. 2:6 and II Cor. 9:14.
[7] John 4:9 f., 19.
[8] Rom. 5:6 ff.
[9] Cf. I John 4:8, 12, 16.
[10] Rom. 5:8 f.
[11] Rom. 8:28–32.
[12] Rom. 8:32–39.
[18] Rom. 8:35, 39.
[14] Luke 12:50; John 15:13; Luke 22:19; Matt. 26:28.
[15] Gal. 2:20.

and He wished to die for us.[16] St. Paul cannot sufficiently exalt this love that shines forth in our redemption,[17] he cannot say enough in praise of the glory of this grace that God has given us through the salvation we receive in His Son, for the remission of sins we receive from His magnificent grace; [18] he is unable to render adequate thanks for the immense benefit bestowed on us by the Father, who gives us a share in the heritage of the saints in splendor, who delivers us from the powers of darkness and transfers us to the kingdom of His well-beloved Son, in whom we have redemption and remission of sins.[19]

All this comes from God, and is like a second creation [20] that is as gratuitous as the first and is more glorious.[21] "If then any be in Christ a new creature, the old things are passed away, behold all things are made new. But all things are of God, who hath reconciled us to Himself by Christ, and hath given to us the ministry of reconciliation. For God indeed was in Christ, reconciling the world to Himself, not imputing to them their sins." [22]

"All things are of God." Everything comes from God in this lavish display of goodness and love, including all that comes from the sacred humanity, even the complete and bloody oblation of Christ's humanity, and even the satisfactions which the members of Christ offer in their degree. For it is God and God alone who, by a free gift, endows the sacred humanity with the power of mediation in so exalted a work,[23] it is the Father who sends His Son into the world to save the world,[24] it is the Father who gives His Son in order that they that believe may not perish,[25] it is God who flooded Christ with the charity that led Him to desire death for our salvation,[26] and it is God who associates men with the Savior's redeeming passion.[27]

All things come from God and, in a very real sense, all things were accomplished when God resolved to save man. From that time on,

---

[16] Eph. 5:2, 23–33.
[17] Cf. II Cor. 5:13–16.
[18] Eph. 1:5 ff.
[19] Col. 1:12 ff.; cf. 2:5–15; Eph. 1:15–20.
[20] Cf. Gal. 6:14 f.; Eph. 2:8 ff.; Rom. 8:18–23; 12:2.
[21] Cf. II Cor. 4:6.
[22] Cf. II Cor. 5:17 ff.
[23] Eph. 1:7, 19 ff.; 2:8 f., 13–22; Col. 1:20.
[24] John 3:17, and often.
[25] John 3:16.
[26] St. Thomas, *Summa*, IIIa, q.47, a.3.
[27] Phil. 3:10; Col. 1:24.

wretched mankind has become an object of God's tenderness. This is a mystery of God's prevenient kindness, of pure generosity, of love that is explained by nothing except itself; it results from the infinite bounty of the pure Act that creates everything without being determined by anything, and that does not await motives for loving but produces them. But once mankind has become the object of this inexplicable tenderness, everything is accounted for, everything falls into place naturally, indeed everything has already taken place in principle. Nothing remains but to transfer to time and to apply to mankind what has already been decided and hence is supereminently real in God's eternal omnipotence.

Therefore we should be falsifying perspectives were we to imagine that God remained angry up to the moment of Jesus Christ's death, and that He did not lay aside His wrath until He had beheld His Son's obedience, love, and sorrows. This may be an impressive way of representing the case, and may be useful from certain points of view, but it does not seem to us exact. God is first in all things; this does not mean that He deprives creatures of the primacy they may have on their own level, as rather He establishes that primacy. God is first in the order of act and of being, and He alone gives existence to things; God is first in the order of grace, charity, and mercy, and He alone repairs and elevates what He is pleased to repair and elevate. Who has first given to Him, so as to receive a recompense in return? [28] Is it not God's glory to show mercy without heeding any consideration but His will to show mercy,[29] and to have pity without being moved by anything except this pity itself? [30] If God is ineffably good to fallen man in spite of sin, the reason is exclusively the fact that He is good. But this goodness is not produced by Christ's death; rather it has produced Christ and the death of Christ.

What the death of Christ has produced is our own goodness. As we have pointed out, God did not remain angry up to the time of that death, although mankind remained culpable. God so loved men as to sacrifice His only Son for them and to have prepared this sacrifice in advance. But mankind, existing in time and entangled in its sin, cherished, along with the weight of its evil, a senseless

[28] Rom. 11:35.
[29] Rom. 9:22 f.; 11:33 ff.
[30] Rom. 9:15.

and distressing opposition to God. And God loved sinful mankind that it might cease to be sinful. In this cessation and in this restoration, brought about by Christ's humanity, the redemption, which is a work of love, is also a work of justice.

For it is a work of justice. All that man has ravaged in himself, in the depths of his soul, in his psychology and his body and his universe, he must rebuild, and he must consecrate and sacrifice all to the task. Justice that is rigorous, exacting, and perfect is required in order that perfection may return. Justice is needed; but a justice that is not opposed to love and that is not limited. For the redemption has no room for a plan of justice lying outside a plan of charity. There is room for nothing but love, and justice itself is a gift of divine love that brings back to a man a supernatural love of God.

This is not a justice that would give and restore something to God, but a justice by which God gives and restores men to themselves and God to men: "the justice of God, not that whereby He Himself is just, but that whereby He makes us just." [31] This is the justice which enables man to give himself to God and which God gives to man, even when He seems to demand something from man: "If thou didst know the gift of God, and who it is that saith to thee: Give me." [32]

God does not depend on His creatures for anything. In the beginning He fashioned man, not because He needed anything, but because He wished to have beneficiaries of His goodness.[33] Now that He accomplishes an even greater work, His independence is, if possible, yet more complete. He will repair mankind, not to recover anything that He has lost, but to manifest His full goodness and to have again children whom He may shower with greater benefits. Thus the redemption is designed, not to give anything back to God, but to give God back to man.

We would tarnish the splendor of the work were we to imagine that God's offended majesty is eager to exact a grim reparation of honor, and that He is appeased and satisfied because there "is presented to Him His Son who has died in protesting that not only the universe but this Son Himself ought to be destroyed in God's divine presence."

[31] These words are used in a similar sense by the Council of Trent, *Decretum de iustificatione*, c. 7 (Denz., 799).

[32] John 4:10.

[33] St. Irenaeus, *Adversus haereses*, IV, xiv, 1 (PG, VII, 1010).

I am conscious of a genuine veneration for Père de Condren, whose sentiments are expressed in these lines.[34] But I find myself unable to admit the concept of God that underlies them. Such haughty and destructive arrogance is at odds with what reason itself has to tell us of the pure Act and infinite Goodness, and is even more opposed, if that is possible, to what the Gospel teaches us of our Father in heaven.

We should also be in error were we to fancy that God's concern, in the redemption, is to be paid to the last farthing, and that He refuses to refrain from striking the guilty unless there is an innocent victim on whom the blows may fall. This sort of justice, that would keep a strict account of payments and receipts, but would be indifferent to persons, is truly a gross caricature; it is the justice of a tradesman, not of a magistrate. This is not the way Christ has become our justice. He did not satisfy in place of sinners, but rather, in Him and with power received from Him, sinners themselves render satisfaction and recover all that they have lost.

Sufferings and death were undoubtedly necessary. But God does not exact them, as a horrible satisfaction to which He had a right; the thought would be blasphemy. It is man who stands in need of them, in order to tear himself away from his sin. The justice that demands them is not some sort of divine vengeance; the natural law, inherent in man and even constitutive of man, in God's name fixes the relations and proportions among things. Speak of cruelty, if you will, as you stand before the cross of Christ and in the presence of mankind. But this is the cruelty of sin and of man in his sin. Sin has plunged evil into man's heart, so deeply that, to extract it, man must thrust the knife in, up to the hilt; sin has contorted man, in such a way that he cannot stand upright again without dislocating his bones.

By enabling man himself to satisfy, God does not pardon the less but pardons all the more, and with a pardon that is more gratuitous. For pardon, thus joined to human cooperation and incarnated in a redemption designed for mankind, enters more deeply into man and is more his own, more completely human.

Man's high station is respected even in the healing of his ignominy. Hence one of the aims of the Incarnation is to instruct man about the greatness of his dignity. Pardon does not fall on the sinner as

[34] D. Amelote, *La vie du P. Charles de Condren* (Paris, 1657), p. 42.

though it were a condescending alms, but rises from within, as an interior reconquest.

"The bruised reed He shall not break." [35] Do not the wounded have more insistent claims on gentleness, and does not fallen greatness call for keener sympathy, on the part of anyone who is unwilling to aggravate injuries? If God sets Himself to the task of healing, He does so with motherly tenderness, in a way befitting the absolute Good. Divine wisdom "ordereth all things sweetly." [36] Wretched man, who is but too prone to despise himself and to despair, is not disdainfully cast aside by divine goodness. Such an action would crush rather than lift up. On the contrary, God calls man and enables him to reinstate himself, at the value he has in his own eyes, at the value he sets on himself, and at the same time empowers him to recover his indispensable dignity as a man and a child of God. And God will perform the task with man, raising him up to a life that is the life of God, and inspiring him anew with a transcendence and a supernatural nobility.

Assuredly, this economy is more burdensome than a pure and simple pardon; it is more burdensome for man and above all is more burdensome for God in the God-man. But it is more respectful of man, more generous of God, more fitting and sweet; and a greater love is manifested in so exalted a union.

Therefore the justice in question is a justice that is the work of love, a justice that even needs love to be complete. Does not love desire union, and does not the whole supernatural order tend toward a union between God and man, toward the restoration of that union?

Can anyone conceive that God would realize this order in isolation? Can anyone imagine that when God holds out the invitation to draw near to Him in His interior and embracing presence, His first act would be to keep us at a distance and to negotiate through some intermediary? Can anyone suppose that when God comes to rescue mankind, to pursue man even in his sin, and to encompass him on all sides, He would begin by contemning man and acting as though he did not exist?

From the first step God has means of taking mankind with Him, of employing man as His instrument, of sharing His work with

[35] Matt. 12:20; cf. Isa. 42:3.
[36] Wisd. 8:1.

man: "What is thine is mine, and what is mine is thine." How then could He fail to do so, as though He who claims to love mankind should fear to be seen with man? Does divine love go to excess by cautiously weighing the matter? Does the divine unity hurl itself on the human race by being careful not to touch it too closely? Does God give an example of generous and total donation by holding Himself back? To set about saving man in this way, to act without permitting man to act, would, we may venture to say, be a very clumsy beginning.

This does not mean, as we see clearly, that the God-man is actually willed by God only for the sake of mankind. Nor does it mean that God wills mankind to be nothing but a sort of external appendage to the God-man. It means that the God-man is the totality and also the unity of mankind, and consequently His redemption is the totality and the unity of the redemption in mankind. When the God-man is willed, He is willed in His entirety, by a decree that is one even in its term, because in Christ it forms the unity of this term. But everything occupies its rightful place in this decree and in this unity. He who is totality and unity is willed by a total and unified will, and those who are Christ's members are willed by prolongation of Him and insertion into Him. But always in unity: the unity that love supplies and that God consecrates in Christ. The will that wills Christ, who is totality, may be conceived as a total will which includes all the special decrees that affect each man and cause each to save himself.

II. Redemption on the Part of Christ

If God, as God, is the one first principle of redemption, as He is of grace, Christ is the one first principle in redemption, as He is in grace. The absolute primacy that is proper to God passes into the humanity He assumes, in the measure in which this humanity is capable of receiving it, as has been explained in chapter 9. The sacred humanity, because it was produced for the salvation of all by God who saves and because it subsists in God, is salvation in its own way, just as it is life and holiness in its own way, because it subsists, for the life and holiness of all, in Him who is life and holiness itself. "Of Him are you in Christ Jesus, who of God is made unto us wisdom and justice and sanctification and redemption." [37]

"Of Him": everything comes from God, but everything comes in Christ: *in Christo Iesu*. Christ in His sacred humanity is the exact and only point at which the action that purifies mankind becomes a divine action, and hence is possible and efficacious. He is also the exact and only point at which God's work is fully in contact with human activity and renders it completely and divinely powerful.

In the work of redemption, consequently, the action of Christ's humanity is not a part, even though the greater; it is totality and unity, it is the first, unique, and universal principle: "the redemption that is in Christ Jesus." [38] "Neither is there salvation in any other. For there is no other name under heaven given to men, whereby we must be saved." [39] Christ alone is Redeemer and Savior. Of course God frequently receives this title in Scripture, especially in the Old Testament; but when the title is taken in its full force it refers to the incarnate God, to the God-man, as the New Testament makes clear,[40] for He it is who reconciles us to God and saves us in His blood. "And therefore Christ alone, so far as He is man, is directly the Redeemer, although the redemption itself may be ascribed to the whole Trinity as to its first cause." [41] To be Redeemer is proper to Christ as man, and is also essential to Him. For Him, to be Redeemer is quite the same as to be Himself.

Clearly all this has to be studied separately by us. Christology and soteriology are so vast that our intelligence cannot consider them separately or with a single effort. Still less can we set out to consider them both together. But the reason for this is the weakness of our minds, not any separation that exists in reality. In reality there was not an Incarnation that was later followed by a redemption; there was a redemptive Incarnation, and a redemption through the Incarnation. Christ was He who takes away the sins of the world from the very beginning, from His birth, from the preparation for Him in the Old Covenant, from the issuing of the divine decrees;

---

[37] Cf. I Cor. 1:30.
[38] Rom. 3:24.
[39] Acts 4:12.
[40] Col. 1:14; I Cor. 1:30; Rom. 3:24 f., etc.
[41] St. Thomas, *Summa*, IIIa, q.48, a.5.

and the body formed for Him and the soul infused into Him were a body and a soul made for sacrifice.[42] As the Incarnation was necessary to impart to this sacrifice the efficacy it possessed, the prospect of this sacrifice is necessary to give to the incarnate Word the true human physiognomy that was His.

To perceive the God-man as He really is, therefore, we must discern in Him a sort of inner ordination toward the redemptive death, a sort of exigence of death. This exigence evidently has its motive in us alone, not in Him who is holiness and life; yet it resides in Him, for we are in Him. Since He is God, that is, holiness and life, His sacred humanity mystically contains the whole human race, and hence all sinners, in order to make them holiness and life in Himself.[43]

He contains sinners in Himself; accordingly, in this strictly limited sense, He has something of the sinner in Him, and is a sinner because of our sin, so far as He is one with us and we are His body and His plenitude. If the formula is understood, it is seen to be free from blasphemy; there is question only of attributing to Him what really pertains to others, by an attribution that would be wholly extrinsic if He who is all in all were external with regard to all. He is the Holy One, surely, and is none other than the Saint of saints. But He is also man. Even an ordinary man is prolonged in all other men. He, the Man par excellence, is supernaturally and divinely prolonged in all men. He is the unity and the totality of the sinful race because He is God.

God and the sinful race: when we hear these words we perceive the sharp contradiction that is in Him and constitutes Him, and that ought to burst asunder and be dissolved. God and the sinful race: this cannot endure, evidently: "Let God arise, and let His enemies be scattered." [44] In God's presence, wickedness ought to collapse at once; on principle, it ought to give way on the instant; humanity, so far as it is sinful, ought to die, and is dead. And Christ is this death that enters into humanity urgently and hastily, and time exists only to express in a human way, but swiftly, what in principle is already accomplished from the moment the God-man begins to live.

[42] Heb. 10:5.
[43] Cf. II Cor. 5:21; I Cor. 1:30.
[44] Ps. 67:2.

As born Redeemer, He bears in Himself the exigency of the redemptive death from the moment of His birth. No one needs to take away His life; He Himself has already laid it down, in virtue of what He is.

The sinful mass cannot be incorporated into the Just One so long as it remains sinful. Precisely this is the reason for His interior distress and His inner ordination toward death. He includes this mass from the moment of His existence, because He is the head of mankind from that moment on. At the same time He does not include it, for it is sinful and He is holiness.

This explains His interior anguish—"How am I straitened" (Luke 12:50)—and the cause of death He carries in Him because mankind is His plentitude: the opposition of sinners, their opposition to Him, their opposition in Him, in that mystic organism that is theirs and that is His "body." How can we grasp the drama of the agony in Gethsemane and the appeals of the Sacred Heart? "His own received Him not"; [45] His own, His brothers, the members of His body who rise in their sins against Him and refuse to enter into Him except as thorns, nails, and hooks.

To be the God-man in the midst of an innocent mankind would have been unmitigated glory. But to be the God-man in the midst of sinful mankind is terrifying. For it means to be the meeting point of oppositions as radical as those set up by sin; it involves shock and clash. This is not formally the encounter between wrath and guilt, between hammer and anvil; not wrath but love is at work. The meeting is between the uncompromising exigencies of goodness and the abysmal misery that must be completely alleviated; application of the red-hot iron to the wound is needed.

More is involved than the deep peace of Christmas, the calm of that night in which heavens made sweetness and honey stretch out over the whole earth. Jesus is born and the Virgin prays. But if we listen we may hear in the silence the ticking, as it were, of an infernal machine. Sin is there, in that human race for whose sake Christ has come, and the Child is on the earth to join issue with it and to die of it. His birth is the beginning of death. "This day is born to you a Savior," the angel told the shepherds. And the Church sings: "To expiate on the cross the common crime of the world, Thou comest forth, an unspotted victim, from the sanctuary

[45] John 1:11.

of the Virgin." [46] "The common crime of the world." Death is
something that ought to come and that does come from the depths
of all history, and also from the depths of what Christ is in Himself.
Death is needed in order that the appalling collapse of man may be
repaired and that mankind may be flooded with eternal life which
the God-man possesses in superabundant fullness and, as it were,
under unbearable pressure, for the universality of sinful mankind.

Therefore His death will be the death of all, the death toward
which the history of each man and of all mankind is directed, the
death that corresponds to the sin of the human family taken all
together, the sin of the race, original sin.

This is the theory of the two Adams, the theory of the supernatural solidarity which, in a first man, has made all men guilty, and
of the supernatural solidarity which, in the new man, the God-man,
makes them all just. All that has been recalled or explained in the
preceding pages may enable us to set forth more clearly the great
figure of the two groups, and to bring out the speculative value of
the theory. We perceive the reason for the two solidarities and the
restorative action that the second exerts on the first. They are both
the result of a single supernatural elevation: *ens et unum convertuntur*. The second supplies remedies for the ills produced by
the first, and repairs those ills most magnificently.

The God-man, as such, is the reparation that thus takes place. In
virtue of what He is intrinsically, He takes His position at the head
of mankind to bring it all together in Himself, on the score that
He is the God-man. But on the score that He is the God-man in
a fallen mankind, He places Himself at the head of the universal
travail of suffering and death to gather it all together and make it
issue in His own death.

In each human life death is the point at which life is recapitulated
and gathered up for the passage into the next world. Such is the
death of Christ with regard to all mankind. At this point Christ,
dying Himself, gathers together all men, and all cast themselves into
Him, as rivers empty into the ocean. His death is the resumption
and the consummation of all deaths and of everything; it winds up
the history of the world even before it is finished, just as it winds
up the history of each man. All that ever happened here on earth
by the grace of God that is always and everywhere operative, all

[46] The hymn for Vespers, season of Advent.

that was ever done by way of renouncing evil and of effort more or less conscious to advance toward God, is found in this unique issuing, in this confluence of all truly human acts, and there achieves its totality, as it had its remote beginning. This emptying into Christ's death does not, to be sure, set our actions in motion, but imparts to them their movement toward Himself.

Thus Christ's redemptive death is an essential element in the theory of the mystical Christ and of the mystical body. Thus also, with regard to all human events and time itself which is the rhythm of these events, Christ's death is not a part but the whole. In other words, it dominates time by its inner power and is not confined within time.

Every human act contains something that raises it above time, because it is impregnated with spiritual life. This is even more the case with every human act inspired by grace, because it is impregnated with eternal life, and more so still with the human act of dying, which is the consummation of all the rest. How much truer is this of that human act which surpasses all others, of that act of grace in which grace operates at its maximum, of that death which recapitulates all deaths and is the supreme act of the God-man! As Christ is unity with respect to mankind, so this act is unity with respect to the whole unrolling of time, the unity that sums up all things by investing them with meaning and efficacy.

All this is a matter that the imagination cannot represent and that clear and distinct concepts, coupled as they are to phantasms, cannot adequately express; we are here in the presence of a totality which our means of cognition, designed for knowing parts, cannot utter sufficiently. But what of that? Is God's gift to be measured by our standards? We shall employ these means of cognition without being held back by their limits; we shall advance toward God Himself and the great gift He presents to us and the exalted idea we ought to have of it. But we shall not confine God's gift to them or smother it in them.

In the reality of the God-man, the very substance of the Infinite is inserted into the reality of the finite. Similarly, in the act by which the God-man dies and thus acts fully in His capacity of God-man, as we shall straightway show, the duration of the Infinite which is eternity installs itself in human duration, which is the succession of time. This duration of the Infinite suffers itself to become dependent on the point at which it installs itself; the event of events, the empirical event of the Savior's death is connected with all the facts that have preceded it and depends on them: the conspiracy of the Pharisees, the abandonment by the crowd and the apostles, the cowardice of Pilate, and so on. But it suffers itself to become dependent on these occurrences only to gather them all together and include them under itself. Transcendent as it is by its union with the infinite and eternal, it belongs to another order of things which dominates all that is flowing and successive, and eminently contains the latter. It is the entrance of eternal life and of eternity into our nether world. As the proper and characteristic act of the humanity assumed by the Word, it is, like that humanity, mystic and infinitely human; as the breaking forth of eternity into the sphere of time, it is not capable, in virtue of its inner nature, of being bounded and confined by time.

When we see this great event taking its place in history, we should not imagine that it depends on history; it is complete in itself, and depends only on itself and on God. Christ ought to have died; [47] but from within, owing to the goodness of God in encountering the sin of men, and owing to the interior nature of the God-man, Father of sinners.

Viewed from without, sin followed its criminal logic: "the love of self even to the contempt of God," [48] even to the point of putting God to death. That was its hour [49] and its seeming triumph. But divine love also followed its logic without deviating a hairsbreadth. "The love of God for man even to self-contempt," we might almost say: even to death, and the death of the cross; divine love has drawn everything along in its wake. It has utilized even the logic of crime for its own ends, so much so that what was the hour of sin was yet more its own hour.[50] Christ died only because He so willed,[51] and to be fully what He was: the Redeemer, the union of a sinful humanity with God. This is the interior mystery expressed by the *oportuit pati Christum.*[52]

The God-man, by being the God-man in sinful humanity, is in-

[47] *Oportebat Christum pati.*
[48] St. Augustine, *De civitate Dei*, XIV, 28 (*PL*, XLI, 439).
[49] Luke 22:53.
[50] John 12:23; 13:1; 17:1.
[51] John 10:18.
[52] Luke 24:26.

trinsically the Redeemer consecrated to death; conversely, by being the Redeemer who died on the cross, He emerges most clearly as the God-man in the midst of sinful humanity. This, as we have remarked, brings out all that He is, all the fullness of love, generosity, and obedience that makes up His unique character,[53] and also gives the impressive example of what the life of Christians, the life of His members, ought to be.[54]

But in that case—and this is what we should like particularly to stress—as man He fully takes the attitude which accounts for everything and acts wholly as God-man. For, as we tried to explain above, death is for every man the complete realization and the ultimate actuation of what he is, the crowning-point of his formation and his passage to a definitive state. It ought to be the same for this man who is God, but in a way befitting the God-man.

This means a way befitting a human nature that is already at the summit of perfection, *comprehensor*, for Christ is God; a human nature that has grace, charity, and holiness to such a degree that in their essentials they cannot receive any substantial increase. Yet this way must befit a human nature that is real, that is truly of our race and even gathers the whole race under itself. The incarnate Word wished to be like His brethren in all things; and for their sake, with them and in them, He is a *viator*, a wayfarer. He who submits to all the vicissitudes of human life and came among us in order to die,[55] surely wishes to submit to the great law of human life, which is self-realization through death. He who little by little incorporates mankind into Himself,[56] fully attracts men to Himself only at the end, by dying: "And I, if I be lifted up from the earth, will draw all things to myself. (Now this He said, signifying what death He should die.)"[57] In truth, as we have pointed out elsewhere,[58] everything in the authentic narrative of Christ's death shows it to be the summit and the climax of His life.

Christ was the God-man from the moment of His birth; His is a humanity that is wholly in God, and is also closely united to other

[53] John 15:13; 13:1; Phil. 2:3.
[54] John 14:31. Cf. St. Thomas, *Summa*, IIIa, q.46, a.3; *Contra Gent.*, IV, 55, 11-19.
[55] John 12:22 f.; 10:10, 17.
[56] Gal. 4:19; Eph. 3:15-36; 2:21; Col. 2:19.
[57] John 12:32 f.
[58] See above, p. 281 ff., and *The Whole Christ*, pp. 42 f.

human natures. But this humanity had not as yet acted according to its full power, neither as united to God nor as united to the species. It did not lack anything pertaining to either of these unions; however, so far as it was human and was operating in a human way, it had not as yet been able to put forth an action in which it released its full force. In a human way, I repeat: that is, in the way human actions are performed and according to the efficacy they have as human actions.

It had not yet given anything to God except transitory acts, by consecrating all its moments, activity, and powers to His love and service; these were but accidents. But now it can give everything and can transfer all to God in an act of submission, abandonment, and love. Up to now, furthermore, Christ's humanity yielded itself to the duties of human life, the service of mankind, and its function of devotedness and love for souls in this same transitory and accidental way: in preaching, journeys, fatigues, and the donations in which, in spite of everything, it had kept something of itself back. But now it can deliver itself entirely for us; it can cease to be a humanity so as to be wholly obedience to the laws of our universe and unreservedly at the service of our redemption.[59]

Now at last it is wholly with men and with God. It had been so even before, in consequence of the assumption brought about by the Word; but it had not yet been so by itself, by a human act that engaged it wholly and enabled it to enter fully, on the human level, into God and mankind. But now the deed is done. In His humanity Christ finally adopts the supreme attitude which reveals Him perfectly; He is wholly abandoned to God and to men, unreservedly on both sides; yet He remains one in Himself, and makes God and men one in Himself, despite the distance separating them; He is mediator in the act of a mediator, God-man in the full act of the God-man, of the union between divinity and humanity. In the same way that the traits of His countenance, like those of every man, took form little by little, we may say that the physiognomy of His humanity was fully etched only at the end of His life.

Operari sequitur esse. This summit of the God-man's human life is also the summit of His activity; and, as the God-man is

---

[59] This is to be understood in the sense that Christ, during the interval between His death and resurrection, was no longer a man but had a soul and a body separated from each other. Cf. St. Thomas, *Summa*, IIIa, q.50, a.4.

mystical and universal, His typical act, the act in which He reveals Himself fully, is likewise mystical and universal. In its most profound aspect, it is coextensive with all the multiplicity of mankind and with all time. This is why, although remaining one, He multiplies Himself over and over in Masses and Communions. Through them He comes to take possession of a numberless multitude of men, to make them pass over to God by incorporating them into Himself.

Accordingly this act is perpetual. As the unity of mankind, Christ ought to remain among men as long as mankind exists. And He will do so. But since He discharges in full the act of the God-man in this act, He will also remain in this act, that is, in the neverending continuity of hosts and Masses. Christ will remain among us; and this act, throughout the world of mankind, everywhere in the breasts and hearts of men, will be the great human act, the origin, the center, the culmination, and the support of all acts of virtue, of all works that are truly good, of all sacrifices, and of all immolations. Men have nothing else to do but turn to God and mankind, by giving themselves to God and men.

Christ's other acts could have been omitted; in that case He would have performed others that would certainly have been as good. But this act had to be done; it is His own; it is the act by which He fully realizes Himself; it is His act as the God-man in the midst of sinful humanity. Therefore this act alone is fully the act of the Redeemer. It alone is likewise, in the highest sense, the redemptive act, not by excluding but by including all the others.

The other acts assuredly shared in this redemptive function and significance. If we regard the infinite excellence imparted to them by the hypostatic union, any one of them would have sufficed for an infinity of redemptions; but if we consider their human structure, they would have possessed this excellence only in their own measure, which was essentially imperfect. For these acts were performed in a series of acts and were meant to be continued in other acts; they were not intended to be perfectly achieved human acts. And when they are regarded as acts of the God-man, their incompleteness is still more marked. As acts of the God-man they were undoubtedly more excellent than the acts of ordinary men, but they were so in their own way, as acts intended to be connected with other acts and hence incomplete in themselves. The life of the God-man and the love ennobling it were so unified that every event of that life was, in close union with all the rest, the preparation, the beginning, and the desire of the great act that was to consummate and crown the whole.

From its origin and conception, this sacred humanity had offered itself to God and to men: "Wherefore when He cometh into the world He saith: Sacrifice and oblation Thou wouldest not; but a body Thou hast fitted to Me. Holocausts for sin did not please Thee. Then said I: Behold I come." [60] The whole of Christ's life was directed toward the realization of this double oblation, but had not yet come to it. For the human soul is the form of a body, and this holds also for Christ's soul. So long as the soul is with the body, its action is dissipated and escapes forth into time; no matter how vehemently it may strive, the soul cannot throw itself wholly and definitively into one of its acts. Complete oblation, donation without reserve, is possible only at the instant when the transitory disappears along with the body that dies, that is, at the final act. Consequently Christ was not consummated—*consummatum est*—until this last instant, the instant for which, until then, He had been preparing. It was then that He became nourishment for men and the immolated God: Christ as He will appear on earth up to the end of time, God thus willing and He also thus willing.

In this death of Christ the essential aspect, the universal reconciliation with God and the consummation of all justice, is evidently the moral and religious aspect: the act of total love, of absolute donation, of unconditional abandonment, the act also of justice that completely restores mankind, whatever the cost may be.

Sufferings and the terrors of death are not the main thing; as we have pointed out, they are but the outer expression, in the body, of the work of reparation accomplished in souls. Yet they are the necessary expression of that reparation, and we must speak of them when we treat of the redemption, especially as they are its most visible element.

These sufferings, like the redemption itself, were enormous. But this enormity has to be understood. It does not derive directly from the divine infinity, as though there had to be sufferings severe enough to force the hand of God out of sheer justice, or as though they had to correspond to the infinity of the punishment of damnation, or

[60] Heb. 10:5 ff.

even of all the punishments of damnation incurred by sinners. This is the way Protestants, for example, have often represented the case,[61] interpreting in a forced sense and independently of the doctrinal context two verses from St. Paul which state that Christ became sin and a curse for us.[62] Christian preaching has sometimes veered in the same direction, for the sake of creating a more powerful impression. Christ, answering to God for all the sins of the world, is made to stand forth as an unmitigated sinner and as the foremost of the damned, crushed under the most absolute and complete wrath of God.

In actual truth, all this is out of the question; the work wrought by Jesus is diametrically opposed to hell. Hell is hate and opposition to God, to oneself, and to mankind; Christ's work is a work of love and union. The death it requires is the exact contrary of eternal death: it is a complete detachment from self and from sin and leads to attachment to good, whereas eternal death is a separation from good and from being and leads to attachment to self.

The work of Christ must be gauged by this detachment from self, this universal renunciation of sin, this universal return: by the totality of the return needed to separate the totality of mankind from the totality of sin. In this sense the death of Christ is infinite, with a human infinity corresponding to the particular infinity that can characterize human evil. It is the culmination, the climax, the totality of suffering. This is why Christ assumed a human nature, to empty the terrible chalice to the dregs, in order that the salvation of mankind might be fully achieved in His human nature.[63]

The severity of these sufferings is determined by their function. They sum up all human sufferings, with a view to making them efficacious. Christ's sufferings sum up all human sufferings, and so become the converging point of all anguish. "Save me, O God, for the waters are come in even unto my soul" (Ps. 68:2). They are complete human suffering, as can be known only by Him who is man, the Son of man, the head of mankind, by Him who alone is the union of the entire sinful race with absolute Holiness. This is the mystery of suffering and therefore a sorrowful mystery, which

[61] See Calvin, *Institutes of the Christian Religion*, III, 13; Luther, *In epistolam ad Galatas commentaria*, in *D. Martin Luthers Werke*, XLI, 432–38 (Weimar, 1910).
[62] Cf. II Cor. 5:21; Gal. 3:13.
[63] St. Athanasius, *Contra Arianos*, III, 23 (PG, XXVI, 369).

is an aspect of the total mystery of the God-man and receives its character from the latter mystery.

We should miss our road if we tried to show forth the greatness of the Passion by merely giving a description of it as it appears from the outside. Men have inflicted more abominable horrors than those inflicted on Christ. Moreover, excessively realistic depictions of the Passion are harmful; they distract our attention and keep us from meditating on what is essential. The whole course of Christ's sufferings should be described, certainly; this is doing very little, after all that our Lord has gone through. But always, and before all else, we should think of His love and of the work He accomplished in His passion: detachment from all sin, reparation of all malice, sanctification of all suffering, union and mystery of all human anguish.

We must meditate on the mystery of Christ, of the whole Christ, if we wish to grasp the mystery of His passion. Then its greatness and our union with it and the role it continually plays in our lives will clearly emerge; the reasons for meditating on Christ's sufferings and what we should contemplate in them will simultaneously appear. We have to understand Christ from within, because He has entered into us. We must also understand the redemption from within, for the only redemption we have is that which is now going on within us.

It is scarcely necessary to point out that the redemptive act thus conceived contains all the characteristics which theologians, following St. Thomas, are accustomed to bring to light: that it operates by way of merit, satisfaction, sacrifice, ransom, and also by way of efficient causality.

We have already spoken about the aspect of sacrifice, and we shall have occasion to speak of it again in connection with the Eucharist; to return to it here would be useless.

That the redemptive act operated by way of merit [64] is quite

---

[64] The question of the merit of Christ's death is extremely difficult. But the difficulty diminishes when we envisage all supernatural merits taken together as constituting but one in the total living organism that is the mystical Christ and in the sacrifice of this living organism. Merit remains a "right to recompense," but in the special way proper to this living being: a "recompense" that manifests what the mystical Christ is in itself, a "right" which is the beginning and earnest of the object of the right.

This merit, like the freedom it supposes, varies with the parts or aspects certain. Merit is a right to a reward, and the reward here is heaven and eternal life. Christ's death, as including and imparting value to the death of every man, has effectively restored the union between God and mankind. Therefore it has merited heaven and divine life, here below in grace, and later on in glory. This it has merited for all mankind, not only in virtue of the promises made by God, but through its own efficacy, by planting in mankind the seed of glory and by endowing mankind, in principle, with eternal life. By effectively destroying all that prevents man from receiving the divine gift, Christ's death brings it about, in principle, that heaven is on earth and that God is in man; man has in himself all he needs to possess God eternally, to merit God.

Ransom also must be considered, redemption and ransom. This is certainly the aspect hardest to explain, because the state of society from which the figure is taken has fortunately ceased to exist. The ransom is the price paid for our deliverance. To whom has it been paid? To the devil? But what right did he have to it? To God?

---

considered in the complete living organism. In Christ, who is the head and the whole, it is absolutely complete, but exists in the manner of a principle. From this point of view it is a super-merit. More than a right to a reward, it is a possession based on a unity of person with the ultimate end and the reward itself, a possesion that is essentially transferable, because Christ's humanity, through its union with divinity, is mystically united to all humanity. That Christ could merit secondary aspects of His glory for Himself must be admitted, since He was a *viator*, or wayfarer, as well as a *comprehensor*. As regards the essentials of merit, His unwavering attitude of will, His love, His self-donation to God and men, the spontaneous, free, and ardent submission with which His humanity acted in union with the Word, were evidently supremely meritorious. And through Christ's humanity the human race adapted itself as fully as it could to this union with God. As regards the essentials of this merit, however, it is formally merit only with reference to men; in Jesus Christ it is merit that is eminent, causative, or, so to speak, "capital." In the ordinary sense of the word it is merit in men alone, owing to the fact that they are influenced by it and that it becomes their merit in virtue of the good works they perform as members of Christ or by the reception of the sacraments.

We can admit that Christ's freedom, which was more perfect than the freedom of a simple *viator*, acted differently, and that it was not the freedom of a simple *viator*. Consequently, as is quite intelligible, Christ's merit was different from that of men.

In men the merit of Christ, flowing to them through the derivation that makes them Christ's members and increasing as they become more worthy members by their Christian life and in consequence of actual graces, will be merit in the strict sense of the term. But this is solely the result of their union with Christ.

But God is the one who pays, and besides, what need did He have of it? And what is this price?

From the point of view adopted in these pages, the following may be said. There is a ransom and a price, in the sense that a value which had been abstracted from God's work is again conferred on it by mankind that had abstracted it. The value is restored in such a way as to bring about an orientation toward God, and in this sense the price is paid to God. It has been restored by the suppression of evil, and in this sense the price has been paid, not to evil surely, but with reference to evil and in opposition to evil. Or, we may say, the work of reparation was a price paid to the order which justice and equity demanded in a mankind that had become deordinate; or again, to the order which mankind itself required before it could be re-established in order. By this means man has been delivered, or ransomed; he has been delivered from the bonds that shackled his liberty, from the powerlessness he had brought on himself of attaining the end appointed for him by grace.

Redemption has also been accomplished by way of satisfaction. We showed above how it compensated and repaired, with equality and superabundance, the damage caused to God's work, and how it was offered to God, although it was useful and profitable to mankind alone, to mankind in its orientation toward God.

What requires explanation is an adjective often appended to the word "satisfaction," an adjective that is traditional but that can be wrongly understood, as theologians warn. This adjective is "vicarious": vicarious satisfaction, that is, satisfaction offered in the name of another, satisfaction by substitution, by deputation. This notion might easily lead us to conclude that Christ has done everything in our stead; nothing remains for us but to receive, in a sort of quietistic way, what He acquired by the whole effort of His life. If we were to add that this receiving requires no interior activity on our part, but is a simple, confident abandonment, a fiducial faith, and that it brings about no internal change in our nature, we would be Protestants.

But such is not the case. Christ is our "vicar" only because, in a certain way, He contains us all in Himself: either morally, as some would put it, in the sense that God makes Him responsible for the race and that consequently the race has to follow the road of penitence He took; or really and mystically, as others would have it, in the sense that, being God, He is the unity of the race in His human nature, so that in Him the race has already begun its repentance in principle and germ, and that the life it receives imposes on it the duty of carrying out the work of penance. This latter conception is that of St. Paul, the Fathers, and St. Thomas; at least so it seems to us. This is the idea we have adopted.

But even in this conception there is a part of the work of redemption which Christ alone performs, which He performs for us, His members, and in which He is truly our "vicar." For He alone is without sin, and all men, so long as they are not yet incorporated into Him, are sinners. As such they are incapable of doing anything whatever for their supernatural welfare. Therefore Christ alone effects this first beginning. But this beginning is everything, for it sets the whole process in motion and sustains it. "Each of these natures, though in union with the other, performs what is proper to itself," we might say, applying to the whole Christ, head and members, what has been said of the God-man.[65] "What is proper to itself": the head alone is responsible for the fact that His members cease to be sinners and become just, that they cease to be a fallen race and become children of God. His death alone sanctifies all mankind.

But this way of regarding the matter does not bring out the whole truth, for it does not take into account the fullness of unity that is in Christ. It is this fullness of unity that allows the good acquired by the head alone to reach the members. The head and the members do not exist and act separately. They are distinct but not separate. Each nature does what is proper to it in union with the other. Even the part performed by Christ alone was done in view of this union, in the sense that it was meant to establish the union of men with Him. In an instant Christ's act, by its very nature, was one with the immense labor and death of all mankind, which it was to make possible and efficacious. It is the act of the head by being the beginning of the work of the members, or rather it is totality by causing the prolongation in which its fullness was to find expression.

When Christ dies for all and gives Himself to God and to all for the benefit of all, He dies not merely in the name of all but in all. It is not only "as though" mankind paid its debt through a delegate,

[65] St. Leo the Great, *Tomus ad Flavianum*, 4 (Denz., 144).

a "vicar" that is actually not mankind; the whole of mankind has paid the whole debt superabundantly, not as yet in the multiplicity of men throughout time and space, but in Him who is their unity and totality and who comprises in Himself, as in a principle and source, this multiplicity which depends completely on Him so far as it accomplishes its task. Accordingly this vicarious satisfaction is efficient by itself, like the merit, the sacrifice, and the ransom in which, as we have seen, redemption consisted.

Per efficaciam, per modum efficientiae: this way of effecting redemption, which is an aspect of the doctrine of the mystical body, has been mentioned above, in connection with St. Thomas, who proposed it. We need not repeat the exposition here. But perhaps we can suitably develop the explanation given above, profiting by ideas we have encountered since.

St. Thomas teaches that Christ's humanity, and in particular the passion and death suffered in this humanity, truly and efficaciously, *per efficientiam,* procures the reparation of the human race, in virtue of the power it receives from the hypostatic union and from the divinity employing it as an instrument of salvation. We may say by way of commentary—and it is scarcely a commentary—that every being acts according as it is in act: *omne agens agit per suam formam, in quantum est actu.* Christ is the God-man, with His humanity divinized to the maximum degree by the plenitude of grace. Therefore when He acts, and in the measure in which He acts, He makes men like to Himself; He makes them divinized men. And He acts fully in His supreme act, which is the act of His death; hence in His death He fully makes men divinized. Moreover, His death is the culmination of every death, of all the renunciation of the sinful self that ought to take place in all mankind so that it may disengage itself from sin and be saved.

Such is the action and efficiency of this death of Christ; it causes universal redemption in universal divinization. The only thing remaining to be done is to communicate the blessed benefit thus acquired to the whole multitude of mankind.

The view of divinization and redemption advocated in this realistic soteriology which is that of efficiency, is the same as the doctrine of salvation through divinization so dear to the Greek Fathers. It harmonizes well with the doctrine of salvation through reparation of evil, which is more often proposed by the Latin Fathers. For that matter, we realize perfectly that for all, whether Greeks or Latins, the Christian religion is essentially the religion of union with God in the God-man who died for all.

To perceive the convergence of these two theologies, we need do no more than contemplate them both in the God-man who unifies all things in Himself. In Him alone, on whom the whole divinity is poured out and in whom is enacted the whole drama of humanity, the two are joined in a single work in which He, the God-man, achieves complete self-expression. He is the God-man in a sinful race. That is enough. An economy of divinization which is also an economy of death is sketched out in Him, for death is a divinization of sinners.[66]

This efficiency is based on the activity of the pure Act Himself. Therefore it is tremendously active, and even imparts activity to those on whom it is exercised; they become active with its activity. And this activity is truly theirs, as Christ is truly their head. Hence it ought to find expression in them, in an activity that is theirs while remaining the activity of Christ the Redeemer, in whom they live and satisfy, as the Council of Trent teaches.[67]

Reception of the redemption will therefore be passive; but it will be passive in a special way, through an activity. For in ransoming His creatures, the Redeemer makes them His members; how could the latter, members of the Redeemer who is engaged in the act of redemption, fail to be active? How can the host, the sacrament nourishing Christian life, be anything else than a participation in the act of Christ's sacrifice?

Men receive this redemption, not as a gift coming from another, but as the grace incorporating them into that other. They receive it by becoming one with Christ who saves them and with the active redemption; they are baptized in His death. In their passive redemption they are persons whose existence has to be continued in union with the active redemption.

Thus we see how the act of ransoming, of saving, of restoring is transferred from the Son of man to mankind, from Christ to the Christian, from the head to the body. It is transferred along with Christ. Such is the way we must now regard this act; it remains the same as before, but we now see it in a different light. We must

[66] St. Thomas, *Summa*, IIIa, q. 48, a. 1 ad 2.
[67] Denz., 904.

regard it, no longer as it is in the head, but as it is in the members; men redeem themselves, but in Christ, who has first redeemed them completely.

III. Redemption Considered from the Side of Mankind

Christ alone is the Redeemer, as we have just said. But in communicating His life to His members, He communicates to them something of His quality as Redeemer. This quality He communicates especially to her who is united to Christ's members more closely than any other, that is, to His mother, who thus becomes the coredemptrix. This title which is attributed to the Blessed Virgin shows clearly that the fact of being redeemed does not prevent one from redeeming.

Indeed, all Christians have a share in this quality, and Mary, in this matter as in others, is the type of Christian life and of the Church. The members possess their share in a way that is received, diminished, dependent, participated, as befits members; theirs is a sort of "member redemption," we might say.

We will not go so far as to suggest that they are coredeemers, although St. Paul affirmed that they co-died and were co-crucified with Christ. It is better to leave words in the possession of their technical sense which has been fixed with such painstaking labor and which is so necessary for exact exposition. The notions of redemption, satisfaction, expiation, punishment, reparation, sacrifice, grace, merit, and justification are set off from one another by penetrating and important distinctions. These distinctions have been referred to in preceding pages as occasion demanded, and they should never be lost to sight. Even when we desire to pass beyond them, we have to suppose them, on pain of confusing the whole issue.

Yet we may go beyond them; after all, they are distinctions, not separations, and the analysis that determined them prepares the way for a synthesis that overshadows them without causing them to lose their sharpness. Christ's redemptive work, whose factors or aspects are indicated by these distinctions, may be multiplex from the point of view of the men for whom it was undertaken; yet it is one from the point of view of its origin, for it comes from God in Christ. Indeed, it consists in the production of this unity, for it brings men together in unity; Christ was to die "to gather together in one the children of God that were dispersed." [68]

The unity thus brought about by the redemption has to be found in the redemption itself. The redemptive activity, as we have pointed out, has to communicate something of its activity to those who are its recipients. It does not make them coredeemers; the word implies too great a participation in what belongs to the Redeemer alone. Rather let us say, if we may be allowed the term, that it makes them "co-satisfiers" or "co-repairers." The first of these words has its roots in tradition, as the following pages will show. The second indicates better, in our opinion, the efficaciousness proper to the operations of the redeemed. Both words imply that the Redeemer's action puts the Christian himself in a position to satisfy truly, to offer an authentic reparation, not side by side with Christ's action, but in and through that action.

Christ alone, therefore, is the Redeemer. But Christ is the head of a mystical body which, in the divine vocation, takes in all mankind. Christians are His members; they are mystically Christ. [69] So truly are they identified with Him that He, even together with them, still remains one. [70] Consequently, since the whole Christ is made up of Him and them, He Himself would not do by Himself whatever they would not be able to do along with Him. [71]

Christ is the first principle of all satisfaction. The unity, possibility, and efficacy of all satisfactions have their origin in Him. Therefore Christians truly satisfy in Him. Theirs is a satisfaction of members, a satisfaction that first affects what is secondary in sin, that is, actual

[68] John 11:52.

[69] "Therefore we too are He." St. Augustine, *Serm.* 133 (*PL,* XXXVIII, 742). Cf. *The Whole Christ,* pp. 431 ff.

[70] "No man hath ascended into heaven but He that descended from heaven, the Son of man who is in heaven" (John 3:13).

"If no man has ascended except Him who has descended, and He is the Son of man, our Lord Jesus: do you too wish to ascend? Then be a member of Him who alone has ascended. For He, the head, is one man with the rest of the members." St. Augustine, *Serm.* 91 (*PL,* XXXVIII, 570). Expressions like this occur frequently in St. Augustine and other ecclesiastical writers.

[71] In connection with the power of the Church over sin, Isaac of Stella writes as follows: "This power belongs no less truly to Christ by the fact that it belongs to the Church; indeed, it does not belong to the whole Christ unless it belongs to the Church. In like manner it is not less truly and solely God's power by being Christ's, and would not belong to the whole God, so to speak, if it were not Christ's." *Serm.* 11 (*PL,* CXCIV, 1728).

sins and the consequences of sin. It affects what is primary in sin, the guilt itself, only in Christ and through Christ.[72]

Christians are members of the Redeemer; they cannot be without some part in the redemption. Can we imagine that the Redeemer would achieve His fullness in a mystical body, and that the act of redeeming, which is His act par excellence, the act by which He gives existence to the mystical body, would fail to attain its fullness in the acts and satisfactions of this body? Since Christians are the fullness of Christ, is it not self-understood that they should fill out in their flesh what is wanting to the sufferings of Christ for His body, which is the Church?

Christ, as we said above, is essentially and intrinsically the Redeemer. Must not this mystical body also be essentially and intrinsically an immense redemption and an organism that satisfies? The reason is the same and ought to be the same on both sides, even though the manner differs. Christ, the head, is intrinsically the Redeemer, because He is intrinsically the God-man in a sinful race. But the mystical body is, in a way befitting a "body," the unity of grace by which, in the God-man, the whole of sinful mankind is united to God. It is a call to penance and death for sinful mankind, a sword "reaching unto the division of the soul and the spirit, of the joints also and the marrow" (Heb. 4:12). It is a redemption that is to come, a satisfaction that must be undertaken and that advances toward fulfillment, in order that the whole Christ may be Redeemer.

The Fathers have often pointed out that there is a sort of interchange of properties in the whole Christ, head and members.[73] This allows us to say, in the sense mentioned above, that something sinful is found in Christ, even though He is purity itself. Men alone are sinners; yet the whole Christ is one, and what is true of the members is true of the whole; but only by reason of the members. The inter-

---

[72] Certain distinctions might be introduced here, but we need not enter into them. Baptism remits all the sins committed by adults, as regards both guilt and punishment. Hence no satisfaction may be imposed. To impose such satisfaction "would be to offer insult to Christ's passion and death, as though the latter did not suffice fully to satisfy for the sins of the baptized" (St. Thomas, *Summa*, IIIa, q.68, a.5). Yet prior to baptism adults ought to be sorry for their sins, and after baptism they can and should repent of their sins, amend their lives, and rouse themselves to contrition and penitence. This is a sort of satisfaction, and in any case is a union with Christ's satisfaction. Cf. St. Thomas, *ibid.*, and q.69, a.2 ad 3; a.3.

[73] Cf. *The Whole Christ*, Index, "Communication of properties."

change of properties also justifies us in saying that the members truly satisfy, that they save and ransom themselves, even though they are sinners to be ransomed and Christ alone is the Savior; for the members are one Christ together with their head. This is not a figurative and unrealistic manner of speaking; it is the only mode of speech that takes into account the complete reality and the exact truth at issue. It is not a mere extrinsic attribution, any more than life is extrinsic to him who lives; and Christ is the life of Christians and their act of living.[74]

As the head is truly head only of the members proceeding from it, so the members are truly members only in union with the head whence they proceed. Similarly, the satisfaction offered by the head has its proper and unique superabundance only in conjunction with the satisfaction offered by the members proceeding from the head, and the satisfactions of the members have existence only in the satisfaction of the head.

For the sake of gaining a clear idea of the economy of the redemption, we shall find it worth while to reflect for a moment on this latter point. The satisfactions of the members we are now considering are not nothing. They are satisfactions of members informed, as by a first interior principle, by the satisfaction of the Redeemer as Redeemer.

If, as we have tried to make clear, God permits and requires mankind to restore itself, He will truly, really, ontologically place in mankind what it needs to do so. For this, mankind needs a God-man to be its center and its all; therefore it will have Him.

Therefore complete satisfaction implies that of the God-man. Hence, as the Fathers have often declared, there will be a sort of double passion. This is what St. Augustine brings out in the following passage.

How great must the surface of a man's body be, if he can be killed by all men? But here we have to understand that there is question of us, of our Church, of Christ's body. Jesus Christ is one man, head and body; the Savior of the body and the members of the body are two in one flesh and in one voice and in one passion; and when wickedness will have passed, they will be in one repose.

The passion of Christ is not in Christ alone; or rather, it is in Christ alone. For if you take Christ as head and body, the passion of Christ is in

[74] Phil. 1:21; Col. 3:3. Cf. Rom. 6:11; 14:8; Gal. 2:20; Eph. 2:5; Col. 2:13.

Christ alone. But if you take Christ as the head alone, the passion of Christ is not in Christ alone. If you, any person now listening to me, are among Christ's members, or even if you are not among my auditors (although actually you hear me, if you are one of Christ's members), whatever you suffer at the hands of those who are not among the members of Christ, was lacking to Christ's sufferings. This is why your suffering is now added, because it was then lacking. You are filling out the measure, you are not making it flow over. You are suffering as much as ought to be your contribution to the complete passion of Christ, who has suffered as our head, and who now suffers in His members, that is, in us. Each of us, in his little way, is paying into this common treasury what he owes, and we all contribute our share according to our means. The measure of suffering will not be full until the world comes to an end.[75]

St. Thomas speaks in like vein:

The passion of Christ causes remission of sins by way of redemption. The passion He endured out of love and obedience is like a price by which He, our head, delivered us, His members, from our sins, somewhat as a man might redeem himself from a sin committed with his feet by some good work he performs with his hands. In the same way as a natural body is one, though made up of various members, the whole Church, Christ's mystical body, is reckoned as one person with its head, which is Christ.[76]

This thought of St. Thomas is the same as that expressed by St. Augustine. The redemptive passion, taken in its totality, is the work of the whole Christ, that immense "mystical person" who is the head and body, and whom we also help to build up. This single mystical person is often mentioned by the Angel of the Schools, as the preceding pages have shown. But St. Thomas and St. Augustine and the other Fathers are not the only ones who speak in this way of the sufferings and satisfactions of Christians. The Church has given voice to the same expressions at the solemn sessions of Trent. The teaching it has promulgated on the subject is accompanied by a lengthy commentary contributed by leading theologians of the period. Indeed, the form in which the teaching is cast suggests a doctrinal commentary. We shall first quote the conciliar text, and then give a doctrinal commentary.

The words of the Council are as follows:

[75] In Ps. 61 (PL, XXXVI, 730).
[76] Summa, IIIa, q. 49, a. 1. See also q. 48, a. 1; In III Sent., d. 18, a. 6, sol. 1 ad 2.

A final reason [justifying sacramental satisfaction] is that, when we suffer and thus satisfy for our sins, we are made conformable to Jesus Christ, who satisfied for our sins (Rom. 5:10; I John 2:1 f.) and from whom we have all our sufficiency (II Cor. 3:5). Thereby we have a most sure pledge that, if we suffer with Him, we shall also be glorified with Him (Rom. 8:17). However, this satisfaction which we offer for our sins is not so exclusively our own as not to come to us through Jesus Christ. For we, who can do nothing of ourselves as of ourselves, can do all things with the cooperation of Him who strengthens us (Phil. 4:13). Thus man has nothing in which he can glory, but all our glorying is in Christ (I Cor. 1:31; II Cor. 10:17; Gal. 6:14), in whom we live, in whom we move (Acts 17:28), and in whom we satisfy, bringing forth fruits worthy of penance (Luke 3:8), which have their efficacy from Him, are offered to the Father by Him, and are accepted by the Father through Him.[77]

Our satisfactions are like this justice: they are ours and yet not ours; they are ours and belong to Christ. And the reason is clearly pointed out: it is the unity of the mystical body. This unity enables all the actions of the members, and hence their satisfactions, to share in the dignity that is in the head.

That such is the idea proclaimed in this passage can be shown also by the theological commentary furnished by sacramental theology. This commentary is suggested by the Council, for the passage occurs in an exposition of doctrine that has to do with the sacraments.

The Council teaches that in the sacrament of penance these satisfactions are an integral part of the sacrament, and that, along with contrition and confession, they constitute its quasi-matter. As we hope to show later, the sacraments are acts which Christ continues to perform in the Church and which, for this reason, are productive of grace. In any case, as is universally admitted, they are rites in which Christ and His grace are specially present and active. Human satisfactions are caught up in these rites and actions, which they require for their completeness. In other words, they are not simply our own, but are taken up into the very economy of the redemption, which is applied to Christians through them. Christ's action, which remits sins in the Church, lays hold of the good actions of wretched sinners, with the consequence that, because of Christ and in Christ, these actions have a part in the forgiveness of sins.

[77] Session XIV, c.8 (Denz., 904).

Moreover, this efficacy is found not only in the satisfactions imposed by the priest, but in all the actions and sufferings of this life, in the mortifications we inflict on ourselves as well as in those that come from without. All such sufferings can have the same power. *Quidquid boni feceris et mali sustinueris:* all these means, assimilated, informed, and actuated by the economy of the redemption and the blood of the Savior, enable us to satisfy in Christ.[78]

Therefore we may say by way of commentary that the satisfaction which is the first principle in the order of satisfactions is at work. It takes up, absorbs, and embodies all other satisfactions and in some fashion changes them into itself, so that all together make up but one complete satisfaction. Thus it displays its full power in the sacrament of penance, which is its efficacious sign.

This notion, which is contained in the teaching on the sacrament of penance, is also found elsewhere in sacramental theology. We meet it, for example, in the theology of the Eucharist; for the Eucharist is the redemptive act as prolonged and applied to all Christian life, to assimilate that life to itself.

It is likewise found in the theology of baptism, which imparts life to Christians by plunging them into the death of Christ. Baptism imparts life to them; but the existence in which it leaves them, or rather which it gives to them by consecrating the existence they already have, is full of trials and is subject to all the tribulations of earth. Theirs is not only the common lot of all men; the seal of Christ the Redeemer is on their entire sojourn here below, to bring about their progressive emergence from sin and their growth to the full measure of Christ.[79] By its inherent power the sacrament incorporates them into a satisfaction that seeks and finds its fullness in them, in their bodies and souls, in their life and death: "that you present your bodies a living sacrifice, holy, pleasing unto God." [80]

Baptism embodies all human satisfaction in Christ's satisfaction otherwise than the sacrament of penance does; it sanctifies the one who offers satisfaction, but does not take up his actions into the sacramental rite itself; it operates at the very base, we may say.

[78] Cf. Denz., 904 f.
[79] Cf. St. Thomas, *Summa*, IIIa, q.59, a.3; *In III Sent.*, d.29, a.3 ad 2. Cf. Eph. 4:13.
[80] Rom. 12:1; with regard to baptism, see 6:3–13.

Human actions and satisfactions are not its matter or quasi-matter.

Such is the lesson of the sacramental economy. *Omne agens agit sibi simile.* The sacraments are the actions of Christ performed today; [81] He communicates a likeness of Himself through them. The three sacraments we have been discussing are, in different ways, His actions as the Redeemer who makes reparation for sin. Consequently the likeness of Himself He communicates through them will be a likeness of Him as the Redeemer who makes reparation for sin. In redeeming and in granting forgiveness, He enables the faithful to become members of the Redeemer; and they in turn ought to have their part in effecting the redemption, in the derived, secondary, and participated way that is proper to members.

Theologians expound the lesson taught by sacramental theology when they treat of the intrinsic value possessed by the satisfactions of Christians in their capacity as Christ's members. This treatise, which we alluded to in the preceding chapter, stems from a brief passage in the *Summa*,[82] so far as we can judge; its development owes much to the influence of Cajetan [83] and Francis of Vittoria.[84] It is a section of the treatise *De Redemptione.* We have sketched its historical growth in *The Whole Christ*, pp. 513–28. There we gave Cajetan's clearly-formulated doctrine and reproduced characteristic passages from Hosius [85] and Nazarius.[86] We take the liberty of referring the reader to that work. If this teaching had been dealt with separately, it would very likely have cast new light on the whole treatise. But we must acknowledge that no one has studied it exhaustively.

In point of fact, the doctrine in question was too difficult for that period of theological development, however simple it may be in itself and however enlightened the masters of the time may have been. In those days the Spirit was guiding the speculative movement in another direction: the quest of clear notions, rigorously logical expositions, and well-ordered summas. For the mentality that

[81] Cf. chapter 18.

[82] *Summa*, IIIa, q. 1, a. 2.

[83] *In IIIam*, q. 1, a. 2.

[84] *Summa sacramentorum*, 201, *de satisfactione* (Salamanca, 1567), f. 158.

[85] *Confessio fidei catholicae*, c. 73, in *Opera omnia in duos tomos divisa* (Cologne, 1594), I, 282 f.

[86] *Commentaria et controversiae in IIIam Partem sancti Thomae*, q. 1, a. 2, controv. 7 (Bologna, 1519), I, 107–16.

was theirs and that the needs of the hour required, the idea of the mystical body could hardly have become easy and familiar.

Therefore the opinion that made its appearance in the works of the masters mentioned did not prevail. The attention of the Scholastics was taken up by current preoccupations, by the many theses that had to be established and the many texts that had to be brought to light, in a word, by the immense and necessary work they performed so well. They had neither the time nor the leisure to exploit the full value of this great idea and to bring out all the meaning that was in it; a meaning as yet half-hidden, though capable of bearing peace to Christians.

IV. Conclusions

In the midst of men who are supernaturally elevated or who are still to be elevated, the mystical body such as it is here on earth, the Church militant, is therefore a redemption which is still going on, not a glory that is manifest. On earth Christ lived a life of struggle, of misery, and of death; the Church here below, His "body," lives a similar life.

Christ is now in glory; the mystical body itself, as regards its nobler part, the saints, is likewise in glory; and no doubt life on earth, so dull in itself, is also a life of splendor and glory: the glory of the children of God. But for us who as yet remain behind, that glory is still to come, and exists only in germ and in hope: "in the hope of the glory of the sons of God." [87]

We may even go so far as to say that the Church militant is the victory and the glory of Christ, just as the grain of wheat has its glory in awakening from death in the profusion of the harvest. "But Jesus answered them, saying: The hour is come that the Son of man should be glorified. Amen, amen I say to you, unless the grain of wheat falling into the ground die, itself remaineth alone. But if it die, it bringeth forth much fruit." [88] But this glory in the Church militant is yet to come and, when it does burst forth, it will be in the Church triumphant, not in the Church militant. The victory is about to be gained, but at present the issue is hidden in the conflict that precedes it. The combat harbors victory and will surely

[87] Rom. 5:2; 8:18, 21.
[88] John 12:23 ff.

prove victorious for Christ; but the actual victory, like a seed, still lies concealed with Christ in God.

Our earth stands before God and men like a globe surmounted by a cross. Christ's blood has flowed over it, efficacious for all time, and continues to flow over it from the wounds of the martyrs.[89] Jesus often speaks of His "body" as though it were a suffering and dying organism,[90] and the only words He uttered on the subject after His ascension, as we read in the Acts of the Apostles, disclose that the body will always suffer the same persecutions as He Himself: "Saul, Saul, why persecutest thou Me? I am Jesus, whom thou persecutest." [91]

Our redemption in Christ was not accomplished until He had died. The same is true of the continuation of the redemption that takes place in the mystical body: it will not be finished for the whole body until that body has ceased to live here below, that is, at the end of time; it will not be completed for each member except at the death of each member.

Sin will not be suppressed until that comes to pass. As long as this world endures, there is time for sin, since we are in a time of trial. All this goes together. Therefore the work of redemption will truly continue, and trials will flow from their source; for sin has its part to play.

Sin caused the redeeming death of the Savior; sin will also cause the passion and death of the mystical body in which redemption is at work. In the Savior's death, however, the sin belonged exclusively to others; in the death of the mystical body, in the death whereby mankind redeems itself, the sin belongs, not to others, but to men themselves.

Accordingly the two pasions must differ. The passion of the head was spotless, and was submitted to with the innocence of a soul that was wholly filial and in which evil had no part.[92] Besides, Christ

[89] "From His whole body He sweat blood (Luke 22:44), because He displays the blood of martyrs in His whole body, that is, in His Church. . . . The flow of blood from the whole body is the passion of the martyrs suffered by the whole Church." St. Augustine, *In Ps.* 93 and 140 (*PL*, XXXVII, 1206, 1818).

[90] Matt. 25:31–45; 18:19 f.

[91] Acts 9:4 f. In the Apocalypse, too, the Church is represented as a body that struggles and suffers; glory, the nuptials of the Lamb, does not come till later.

[92] John 14:30; 8:46; Luke 23:46.

did not wish that His passion should seem to triumph over Him, and He let its inner disorder and moral collapse appear. The passion of the human race lacks this purity; it conquers; it supposes an interior sin from which we are disentangling ourselves but of which we are not yet free, and which dies in terrible convulsions. It is a passion of a sinner, a passion of sin, a lowly and inglorious passion. For redemption does not wait for sin to disappear before it begins to operate, but seizes and grasps sin while still alive to choke it to death. Or rather, the redemption allows sin to dash itself to death against it, first against the Savior, then against the Savior's body.

This occurs while sin is yet alive, for the law of sin rages malignantly in all men. And the "body" of Christ is designed for men, for all of them such as they are, to make them better than they are. This objective it accomplishes, in great part, by the quarrels and sorrows men cause one another and themselves, whether unconsciously or voluntarily or, as often happens, in a mixture of unawareness, malice, and good intentions. We must devote further consideration to this secondary redemption, the immense satisfaction offered by the body of Christ. We have already discussed the sufferings that come from natural laws and material causes, and we also spoke of this matter, at some length, when we gave our idea of what the act of dying may involve. What we are now going to say about sufferings inflicted by men may readily be applied to sufferings coming from the universe, which are much easier to understand.

Mankind is sinful. It bears the burden of its former crimes, and adds to it by its present crimes. Its infamies and atrocities, its pride and ferocious egoism, make it its own worst tormentor; what has unhappy mankind not essayed against itself!

Mankind is tormented not only by its malice but by a profound ignorance of itself which is the legacy of its sin and which causes it to suffer even in the good it possesses. Consequently an intense desire for justice and love, a longing for a better mankind in a better world, is formed and quickened in it, not without the aid of grace. But the longing is so vague in the obscure and incommunicable depths of conscience, and its manifestations are so incoherent, tentative, and divergent, that these divergencies often pass for antagonisms. The steps proposed for reaching agreement evoke challenges, and the latter multiply in the measure that the efforts are more numerous and deficient. Misunderstandings are added to misunderstandings, and a psychosis of insecurity and hostility develops. If certain unfortunate circumstances arise, if some more than ordinarily brutal display of selfishness occurs, disaster results. Men give way to terror and madness and passion, and wrath and carnage flare up, which no one desired before and which all the world desires now; and then we have the tragedy of a blind and raging giant who turns his own weapons against himself and rends himself to pieces in the night.

Such is the humanity that makes up the Church. We are dealing here with a delicate subject that is a source of dismay and scandal. We can readily understand that the Church should have its martyrs and that the innocent may be persecuted or succumb to illness. But that Christ's spouse, whom He has taken to make her holy and spotless, without defilement or blemish of any sort, that Christ's body, which God has chosen from eternity to adorn with the grace of adoption in purity and sanctity,[93] should be a body of sin, that it should be demeaned by pettiness and malice, and that its moral miseries should figure so largely even in its most characteristic activity, seems impossible to concede.

But it is so. The holy mystical body is a body in which redemption is accomplished and yet not accomplished; in which sin is ever present and active; in which each generation as it rises imparts renewed vigor to sin; in which, finally, sin has its necessary place: a place from which it has to be dislodged, a place in which occur most of the trials that will cast it out, a place in which redemption is at work.

Undoubtedly baptism, which applies the redemption to each individual, completely eliminates from the soul all the sin that was actually in it.[94] But baptism does not dry up the source of sin, as the Council of Trent clearly teaches.[95] The baptized person will have to struggle against the forces enticing him to sin, and also against himself, for he will often be his own chief tempter.[96] He simply cannot avoid all sin,[97] and a terrible possibility will always hover over his life: the possibility of losing his eternity.[98]

[93] Eph. 1:1-10; 5:25-28.
[94] Council of Trent, *Decretum super peccato originali*, 5 (Denz., 792).
[95] *Ibid.*, and *Decretum de iustificatione*, 9, 12, 13 (Denz., 802, 805, 806).
[96] John 3:5-16; Col. 2:20—3:3; Mark 8:34 f.; Matt. 10:37 ff.
[97] Council of Trent, *Decretum de iustificatione*, can. 23 (Denz., 833).
[98] *Ibid.*, 12, 13 (Denz., 805, 806).

Similarly, the source of sin remains in the Church militant in general,[99] for what baptism does in the individual, the death of Christ has done for the whole mystical body. The Church is made up of sinners; [100] hence its great prayers are the prayers of sinners: "Forgive us our trespasses"; "Holy Mary, Mother of God, pray for us sinners." Sin is in the Church, contagious and ineradicable, like the weeds in the field that are forever obstinately encroaching; and it will not be exterminated until the Church militant itself is no more, on the last day, the day of the harvest.[101]

The holiness of the Church is not less real for all that, but it is a realistic holiness, the sanctity of the Church militant. The Church is holy by reason of what God has placed and wrought in it; but it is not holy because of what men contribute of their own resources, or because of the activity they perform in it so far as that activity proceeds from them alone. Woe to those men who proclaim that they are just and better than their fellows: they directly oppose the work that is designed to save them. They are like the Pharisee who boasted of his holiness and departed from the Temple with his sins still unforgiven.[102] A profound similarity links the members of the mystical body to the most depraved of non-members; and those who try to be sincere are quite aware of this fact.

But then, if the members of the mystical body are sinners, they will have to act as sinners and, even when they wish to rid themselves of their sins, they will give many an indication, by the very way they rid themselves of their sins, that they are still laden with them. Exception must evidently be made for the actions of the Church that are the actions of Christ, for example, in the administration of the sacraments and the solemn proclamation of dogmas; there we find nothing but holiness. But everywhere else, wherever man acts as man, in all the deeds of even the best of Christians and the most exalted heads of the Church, human frailty and human malice and human traces of human sins frequently and inevitably betray themselves. The very saints do not wholly escape these miseries except at the instant of their full spiritual maturity, when

[99] However, we must remember that the Church, being the continuation of Christ, is indefectible, the source of holiness, and so on.

[100] The Council of Trent has defined that a person can be a Christian even though he is in the state of mortal sin. Cf. *ibid.*, can. 28 (Denz., 838).

[101] Matt. 13:24–30.

[102] Luke 18:9–14.

they come to die. We have to believe that grace tends to safeguard the pastors of the Church in proportion to the importance of their acts; but it does not suppress them; that would be to suppress man.

In addition to outright faults, there will certainly be impediments arising from egotistic views and worldly calculation even in the most apostolic aims, there will be prejudice and unconscious ignorance, vanity that obscures intelligence, sensitiveness that engenders unavowed grudges, haughty obstinacy that is mistaken for reverence toward the function one is performing; there will be inability to conceive and preserve a truly right intention together with a truly humble abnegation, and powerlessness to adapt oneself sufficiently to others to understand them. There will be all this mixture of evil in good that is the proper estate for mankind in need of redemption; there will be all the narrowness of mind and heart that begets misunderstandings and oppositions and conflicts and disagreements. By all these travails our human family is redeemed.

Such is the human wretchedness that makes us so indigent and evil even in the splendor of holiness that God bestows. But "where sin abounded, grace did more abound." [103] Here the omnipotence of divine mercy appears at its greatest. All these consequences of sin—not the act itself, of course—and the difficulties, even the moral ones, which it begets, the temptations and trials it calls forth, the sorrows it causes, all this is employed by God to restore the sinner by destroying the sin.

God is powerful and wise enough to avert the harm that could arise from sin in the soul of the sinner to be restored, although He does so in ways that often escape us. In particular He will see to it that those who, trusting in Him, are desirous of being fully obedient to the representatives He Himself has established in His Church, will not come to love Him less or work less effectively for His kingdom in consequence of the inevitable errors and faults of these representatives.

But why should God obstruct the painful, humiliating, and cleansing effects that arise in the Church from the sin that is in the Church? A redemption, a thoroughgoing and complete renunciation that demands sufferings, mortifications, and abnegation of self has to be accomplished, and the hardships in question are most fruitful means for reaching this objective. Let them remain, then, for in their own

[103] Rom. 5:20.

way they will contribute to the redemption. Without them the real mankind would not be taken into the Church, and a true death to self and to sin would not be effected. So let them remain; nothing can equal them in imparting to man a dislike of his baseness, personal and collective humility, patience, gentleness toward others, confidence in God, prayer, and, in a word, all the virtues man requires to renounce himself and have recourse to God. Especially at the moment he wins detachment from himself and his vanity, he needs to guard against attaching himself anew to himself in a more subtle pride: "that no flesh should glory in His sight." [104]

We must admit that collective humility is a virtue necessary for the Church militant. The Church may not for an instant doubt the work of glory and divinity that the Almighty accomplishes in it; but at the same time it may not doubt that this benefit is given to the unworthy and to sinners who have not yet completely broken with their sin, that is, with all that is most evil. "Because He hath regarded the humility of His handmaid; for behold from henceforth all generations shall call me blessed. Because He that is mighty hath done great things to me; and holy is His name. And His mercy is from generation unto generation, to them that fear Him." [105] All things serve God. Through Christ, God has taken humanity as His instrument. Therefore everything in humanity will be an instrument, including even the immediate consequences of sin.

Such is the return to God effected by the grace of redemption. It makes saints of sinners. In the interior of the soul, with the cooperation of man's freedom, it lays hold of the will and turns it about; this is contrition, which is necessary for the restoration of the sinner. In the outside world, it gains control of the consequences of sin and reverses them to make them remedies of sin; and this is satisfaction. It alters these consequences, which would have filled the measure of evil to overflowing, so that they may become means of advancing toward the culmination of all good.

Suffering becomes something to be treasured; it is a masterpiece of God's power and wisdom, in the mystery of Christ crucified, "who of God is made unto us wisdom and justice and sanctification and redemption." [106] The mystery of the redemption contains a

---

[104] Cf. I Cor. 1:29.
[105] Luke 1:48 ff.
[106] See I Cor. 1:30, 22–25.

wisdom and a philosophy: the Christian philosophy of suffering, the theology of suffering; and not only of suffering, but also of painful and humiliating effort, of mortification, defeat, and death; in brief, of all that seems least congenial to man and to human opinion. This theology is so beautiful, so human, and so comforting, that we shall do well to reflect on it for a moment.

In every age suffering has confronted man with a harsh problem, and the blows it inflicts are never gentle. Suffering is in man in spite of man, hostile, implacable, piercing. How can we explain this bitter oposition to our desire for happiness, this lack of harmony, this disorder, and what attitude shall we take before it? Faced with such questions, men have always experienced an urge to construct a philosophy of suffering.

Some philosophers have proposed the answer that suffering does not exist. In their view, suffering is nothing but an illusion which the body tries to impose on the spirit, and when it comes to us we must shout out that there is no such thing, that its claws tear only the flesh, and that the spirit remains beyond its reach, if we but so will. Others have insisted that we can suppress suffering, either by avoiding it through prudence and skillful management, or by distracting the mind by joyful memories when it assails us. In this way the wise man will live without adversity, just as, according to the first group, he can live without emotion, by drugging himself with apathy and insensibility. Vain efforts; suffering will soon force its presence upon our notice. The measures we take to avoid or deny it only serve to increase the torment, and the flood swirls so turbulently as to carry off all the dikes, and so powerfully as to smother consciousness.

What can we do, then, but admit that the undeniable exists, and that its vigor is undiminished? This admission is justified by natural philosophy, by the philosophy of ethics. In suffering, in the painful effort, and in death philosophy reveals an element pertaining to life itself, and hence one of the provisions of the divine plan for the world. The laws of nature, which God has designed for the construction of the universe and the constitution of the human organism, are also laws that, in certain circumstances, will wound or shatter that organism. No matter: these laws make man, and God has made the laws. The man who wishes to exist in conformity with his nature and God's plan for him, ought to wish the laws of nature to be as they are, since he is as he is. Even when they bring him suffering, man is so made as to welcome them, accept them, and ratify them, because they are still his laws, the laws that determine his structure, the laws of his human organism. His will, though it has its own natural law of freedom, has also its natural law in these laws of matter, for the will is a faculty of a soul that is the form of a body. The will imposes on itself, and God imposes on it, the obligation of eliciting its acts in harmony with these laws, of accepting them, and of ratifying them. The will ought to accept them first of all by heeding them in its free actvity, to the extent that they are involved in the organic processes of the body; it should attempt to fathom their secrets so as to control their forces in the interest of moral energies. By acting thus, it will make the universe more human and man more universally a man. But it ought to accept them even when it does not succeed in mastering them and when the bodily organism is trampled and bruised under their blind operation. For even then they are the laws of human life and the human universe; even then the will is so made as to elicit its acts in conformity with them.[107]

Such, in brief, is the natural philosophy of suffering. It is austere but reasonable. It holds that suffering is part of man's lot, and must be accepted along with that lot.

But faith penetrates farther, and we must now go on to consider the theology of suffering based on faith, the Christian philosophy of pain and hard effort and death. We shall see that theology's accents are more human, its doctrine more adequate and satisfying.

In the first place, this theology gives a fuller explanation of suffering, a theological explanation. It teaches that all physical evils, all sorrows and tears, come from a single moral evil, original sin, whose result and punishment they are.[108] Far from being chance accidents or clumsy failures of coordination among the wheels of a machine, physical evils form a system developed from a single origin. Hence we have unity, a situation that the mind can understand, a unity that stands self-justified. Undoubtedly it was possible for sin not to have occurred, and it ought never to have occurred. But its possibility was the condition for the existence of finite and imperfect beings. And its reality is the exclusive work of these finite beings. Once it

[107] Cf. chap. 10, pp. 262, 264 ff., 269.
[108] Cf. chap. 7.

was committed, it set off disorder at the center of the universe, in the human conscience that is the unity of the material world. From this center, which fixes the place of the universe, evil had to spread in all directions, no longer as moral evil, which is outside the susceptibilities of the world of bodies, but as the evil proper to these bodies, as physical evil. Evil had to spread, therefore, but this expansion is fully accounted for; the whole is reduced to morality and to the laws of the spirit, and converges toward an absolute intelligibility: an intelligibility not of sin, assuredly, but of the order in which sin is a privation.

To this explanation, which bears on the origins of evil, theology adds another that has to do with the goal to which evil actually leads. The first explanation makes clear how man caused evil to arise; the second shows how God makes it depart; this He does by using it to bring about the complete suppression of its cause which is sin, and thus to make it suppress itself.

The cause is suppressed in principle by God's goodness: God permits the man who has become a sinner to turn back against himself with a return that efficaciously divinizes him anew, in Christ. Suffering is precisely the best means for effecting this return, the best means a man can employ for dying to himself, for banishing complacent egoism, pride, and the spirit of rebellion.

The detaching of a man from himself is indeed pain. But justice requires that he undergo pain to extirpate evil. This pain is good for man; it should not be resisted or cursed; it should not be borne as though it did not exist, with an absent or stoic spirit. It can be understood, desired, and loved as pain.

This attitude is not strained or fanatic; it can be simple, patient, and human. Jesus suffered quite simply; His members need not suffer otherwise. For the miracle takes place in Christ alone. Only in Him, in His passion and death, human death and suffering are able to restore what had been destroyed and to effect a reconciliation with God.

Since Christians are members of Christ, their sufferings are, if we may be allowed the term, member-sufferings. And every man is a member of Christ, at least in God's invitation. These member-sufferings are joined to the complete suffering of the Redeemer, and are means of union with Christ. Therefore, as we perceive once again, they are means of union with God, and hence are good.

They take their place in the great passion of the whole Christ, and are therefore in some respect passive, not only because of the acts of virtue they call forth, but because of the initiative they leave to the Savior. No doubt, the more we resign ourselves to them, the more actively we will them, and the tighter is the bond they knot. But from the instant the will abandons deliberate revolt, a conformity is engendered in the depths of the soul and a union is formed, despite the protests of our feelings and the pangs of the flesh.

In any case, these member-sufferings do not have to be complete or be welcomed with whole-hearted acceptance. They were begun in Christ, and have also been sanctified and accepted in Him. Christians have only to continue them. The grace Christians possess and the charity that is in them make their sufferings acceptable in Christ. If the members supply what is lacking to the sufferings of Christ, they do so only in virtue of the power flowing to them from the head. The head abundantly makes up for the many defects found in the sufferings of the members, by enabling them to be member-sufferings, to which the head truly imparts what is needed to complete them and to attach them to God. All these sufferings together constitute a total and perfect suffering, in which Christ's suffering is, so to say, the form of the unity and meaning of the whole, as well as its sanctification and interpretation.

The sufferings of the members, however great they may be, are easier to endure in this unity, for they are borne up by Christ and His suffering. They do not have to be agonizingly painful, any more than they have to be wholly acceptable in themselves. Christ alone has suffered pain in its totality, for He alone is head. He alone, who is the unity of sinful humanity, has encountered the full shock of sin in the mystery of His passion and death. No one else can know a like fullness of suffering. Because of Him and His suffering, the sorrows of His members receive some comfort. Undoubtedly their sufferings will at times be more intense because of their share in Christ's redemption, and this will be the case in proportion to the Christian's holiness and the closeness of His union with Christ. But in the same measure they will become sweeter, because they are shared by Him. This greater sweetness is not necessarily the result of sensible consolations, but is rather the product of the forces that unite the soul to Christ and God through faith, hope, and charity.

Christ alone has suffered in solitude, without other support than God,[109] who sustained Him at that hour so that He might suffer more intensely.[110] He alone was engaged in the task at the moment when sinners were as yet no more than sinners, at the moment of unmitigated pain and pure redemption. Sinners come after Him, led and sheltered; and when they draw near to God they are already the redeemed who are united to God and to one another in the Savior. Hence they suffer as the regenerated, as the just who ought to grow more valiant, or as men who are now God's children, at least in vocation, and who ought to become such in reality or in more perfect degree.

This theology of suffering does not limit its discussion to man; it also discourses of the human universe and implies a philosophy of material creation, a Christian *Weltanschauung*. For material things have indeed cooperated in the redemption, and the death of Jesus Christ on the cross at once became manifest as a cosmic event, at a time when no other action of Jesus had made such connections clear. "And there was darkness over all the earth until the ninth hour. And the sun was darkened. And the earth quaked and the rocks were rent." [111] The creator has become Redeemer. Must not the whole of creation become a redemption?

The expectation of the creature waiteth for the revelation of the sons of God. For the creature was made subject to vanity, not willingly, but by reason of him that made it subject, in hope: because the creature also itself shall be delivered from the servitude of corruption, into the liberty of the glory of the children of God. For we know that every creature groaneth and travaileth in pain, even till now. And not only it, but ourselves also, who have the first fruits of the Spirit, even we ourselves groan within ourselves, waiting for the adoption of the sons of God, the redemption of our body.[112]

The economy of redemption is cosmic, for it is divine and also wholly human. The death of man, as a result of the death of the soul which is sin, has spread over the universe. If this death and the suffering that accompanies it are utilized by God for the destruction of sin, they are thus utilized throughout the whole expanse of

[109] John 16:32.
[110] Matt. 26:44; 27:46.
[111] Luke 23:44; Matt. 27:51.
[112] Rom. 8:19–23.

the universe. In order that the whole man may be restored, the material world, which is man's great body, must likewise be restored.

Consider this material world. Life is indeed at work there, but in the midst of struggle, destruction, and death. Death begins in the mineral kingdom, in the forces that act to neutralize and suppress one another, in the measureless loss of energies that go off in fruitless radiations through interstellar space. Death is even more widespread in the kingdom of the living. How many seeds have to be smothered in order that one may come to maturity; how many corpses are needed for the nourishment of a single organism! A thousand, ten thousand deaths for a life, and for a life that will end up in death. And this life, while awaiting death, is in conflict, competition, and combat with other lives; the roots under the soil snatch air and light from one another, animals fight and kill one another, devour and destroy one another. We might fancy that all this is disorder and the incoherence of parts that are badly arranged in an absurd work. But no; above all this and embracing all this stretch the magnificence of nature, the brilliance of the sky and the splendor of summer, the marvels of structure, ingenuity, and delicate adaptation. The order and the beauty are too stupendous to allow us to see in this nothing but disorder and bloodshed.

The explanation is that all this is the prolongation, the accompaniment, and the commencement of another death that is most meaningful and painful, but that issues in a breath-taking glory and resurrection. For man lives and dies with the rhythm of the universe, or rather the universe lives and dies with the rhythm of man. The two together make up a single complete being and life that are mortal and painful. In the human universe, in its catastrophes, its combats, and its splendors, all that is planned and begun is the tragedy of mankind, the long struggle in which man must detach himself from himself to cleanse himself of sin and mount up to God.

The tranquillity of death and resurrection, the magnificence of autumn, the rich calmness of dying nature, the reawakening smile of springtime in the winter that is still cold and menacing, all this is a sign, an accompaniment, and a prolongation of the vast human travail that is taking place and that absorbs mankind. This immense travail has been described elsewhere and need not be repeated here. Yet we ought to recall it, for it gives meaning to the yet greater travail taking place in the universe. By it, furthermore, the universe attaches and joins itself to the death of the Redeemer.

As the death that is in things culminates in the death that is in mankind, so the death of mankind culminates in the death of the God-man. Everything is recapitulated in Him, to find in Him its efficacy. In thus coming to climax all human death, which itself climaxes all human life, the redemptive death climaxes all that there is of death in this human universe. The redemption is the great event of the world.

This doctrine of suffering is one of the wonders of Christianity. The power of religion is perceived in the strength it imparts when the trials of life are on us; and its transforming energy appears most strikingly in this transfiguration of suffering.

Christ changes everything He touches, with a change that is not superficial but profound, and that affects the interior before it emerges outside. He took a human body, and at a stroke divinized in principle the whole human race. He also took to Himself miseries, sufferings, and human death; and behold, they are divinized in Him. The supreme terror has become desirable, and the very dissolution of the body is a goal toward which men aspire.[113] We must even venture to go so far as to say that evils have been divinized. Cajetan has explained the paradox in a few magnificent phrases which have won the approval of many theologians and which we have quoted elsewhere.[114] We take the liberty of repeating here the central thought: "Christ has taken to Himself all suffering, in order to divinize all the ills of the universe." [115] Here we see that Christian theology, in its Latin that appears so impersonal, is not afraid of bold formulas. The ills that make this earth a vale of tears are no longer ills. God has united Himself to them in Christ, and henceforth they are good things, divine things. "Just as the divine Word has in a sense assumed all the good in the universe by taking a human nature, seeing that all creatures are in some way to be found in man, as we stated in the beginning of this book, so by assuming the ills of men in all the sufferings of His passion, He has divinized all the

[113] Phil. 1:23.
[114] Cf. *The Whole Christ*, pp. 466 f.
[115] Cajetan, *In Illam*, q. 46, a. 5, no. 4.

ills in the universe; for all these ills are in some fashion found in the ills of man." [116]

Such an optimism, we may well say, is not without attractiveness: "Now that these ills have been assumed by the Word of God in His own person, they have undoubtedly been divinized." [117] This is not a petty and naive optimism that refuses to see evil, nor a shrinkingly modest optimism that allows a place for evil but is subdued by it. The optimism in question is courageous and uncompromising, and stares evil in the face, recognizing the work of reparation being accomplished by its means and successfully subjugating it. Nor have we here a philosophical pseudo-optimism which claims that the existing world is the best of all possible worlds; as though the very notion of a best possible world were not a contradiction.

The optimism is that of believers, a supernatural optimism. It asserts that this world, like mankind, is clearly not the best possible; quite the contrary. But it insists that God has wrought the best possible work: the divinization of man who had become evil, through man himself and by means of the very ills that man had brought upon himself.

Furthermore, it is an optimism that is not an easy good humor, but an attitude that has to be gained by God's grace, for it exists on a spiritual level which sinful man cannot reach and hold except by the utmost efforts of his fervor. It does not come of itself; we have to bring it forth in ourselves; and, since it involves suffering and pain, we can do that only at the price of pains and sufferings. It is an optimism of the redeemed and of redemption.

Finally, this optimism is a grace, and God Himself imparts it in conjunction with man's efforts. For it is the anticipation, through faith, hope, and charity, of beatitude. And all this is a grace and a gift.

SUMMARY AND REVIEW

By way of general summing-up, we may say that the redemption is wrought by Christ alone, in the act by which the God-man fully asserts Himself in His humanity as the God-man.

The preceeding pages were written, not to propose a definition

[116] *Ibid.*
[117] *Ibid.*

or a system regarded as superior to others, but to point to Him who is the explanation of all, because He is the totality, the unity, and the light of all. The redemption is not an abstract concept or theory. It is a Person who is intensely alive, in the act in which He lives most intensely. It is the immense and personal embrace by which God, in His incarnate Son, wrests sinful mankind from itself and from its sin, to press it to His heart. The entire divinity gives itself unreservedly; the whole of mankind is purged of its sin; the whole Christ is poured out in complete self-sacrifice on those who belong to Him. Who would venture to enclose this avalanche of totalities in a single concept or in a series of concepts? Concepts are only parts of our knowledge and express only parts of heaven.

Concepts are assuredly necessary, and the preceding pages have brought out all the meaning that, in Christ, is contained in the concepts of satisfaction, reparation, ransom, efficiency, and sacrifice. These concepts, as Christ Himself employs them for His teaching in the Church, convey a supernatural light that is indispensable for us. To have a clear idea and understanding of the redemption, we must cling to them with all our soul, study them, meditate on them. We must retain them because of the light they contain; yet our purpose must be, not to repose in them, but through them to go to the Christ they point out. They are like the rays of light we see shimmering among the clouds when the sky is overcast; the converging rays show where the sun is, but they are not the sun.

We ought to meditate on these concepts; but even more we ought to meditate on Christ and His redemptive act, and we should unite ourselves to this act by love, by receiving the Eucharist, by accepting sufferings, and by practicing mortification; in such association with Him who is redemption [118] and light,[119] we shall gain some understanding of the redemption. "Watch and pray an hour with Me during My agony": this request which Christ addressed to His apostles and which the heart of Jesus addresses to Christians, is not only or even chiefly a plea for consolation, but is an appeal for an exact and vivid knowledge of the mystery of redemption on our part, an invitation to an interior and positive understanding of soteriology.

He alone, the Brother of us sinners and the only-begotten Son

[118] Cf. I Cor. 1:30.
[119] John 1:4, 9; 3:19; 8:12; 9:5; 12:35-46; Phil. 4:7.

of God, means everything to us. He is the influx of the whole of divine life into the whole of mankind; He is the excess of divine goodness that, flowing from the Father through the Son to the Spirit, reaches down to mankind in the incarnate Word and, by the death of Christ, overturns the barriers of sin that were blocking its expansion.

This immense task is accomplished and brought to a close in Christ alone. From the very beginning, God's eternal decree of the redemption is Christ and nothing but Christ; for this decree envisages nothing else than Christ and the work in which Christ shows forth His plenitude; and He who makes this decree is also Christ, for Christ is God. Thus He, along with His whole redemptive work, was present in God, God with God,[120] in the very first instant of the economy of grace: "I was with Him forming all things."[121]

When the carrying out of the decree comes at the blessed fullness of time, Christ is still everything. He is this decree that is realized and, we may say, incarnated. For this decree, in God, is God, and Christ is God. Christ is the realization of this decree quite otherwise than He is the realization of the creative decree; for the created world is an infinitely lesser realization, whereas Christ is interior to God and is identical with God.

Likewise at the last stage, when the prolongation of the redemption is effected and its fruits are applied, Christ is still everything. To be redeemed is nothing else than to become one of His members, and no grace is given to men that is not designed to incorporate them into the Redeemer, while tending at the same time to separate them ever more from their sin.

He forever, and nothing but Him: in His divinity He is the source from which everything flows; in His humanity He is the center from which all activity is directed; in His mystic fullness He is the goal toward which everything tends. To know the whole work of redemption, we need know only Him: "I judged not myself to know anything among you but Jesus Christ, and Him crucified."[122] He alone applies, with terrible efficacy, God's im-

---

[120] In this sense likewise "In the beginning was the Word, and the Word was with God, and the Word was God" (John 1:1). Note also how the redemption is described in John's prologue as a conflict between light and darkness.

[121] Prov. 8:30.

[122] See I Cor. 2:2.

placable holiness to the sinful race. God acts in Him, not by His act, but by Himself; not by calling for some service or some supplementary deed in man, but by being a man, and a man of the sinful race.

Christ's action is powerful, like that of the first cause. But in this case the first cause does not act simply as first cause; the Incarnation was not necessary for that. It acts as second cause; that is exactly what the Incarnation is: God becoming man, the first cause becoming second cause. However, as is self-evident, the first cause becomes second cause in its own way; it does not take its place at the side of other second causes, but becomes the ultimate interior support of a second cause, the ultimate internal principle of its acts and their efficacy. The effects produced by this second cause, which is Christ's humanity, must therefore possess a powerful efficacy that is based on the efficacy of the first cause.

Consequently the redemption is objective; it does not consist, as liberal Protestants maintain, in a moral change which man brings about in himself after considering the example Christ has given. The change is wrought by God and is completely achieved, in principle, at the instant of Christ's death; so completely, indeed, that it goes on to transform men by its own inherent power. Since men are free, the change is not effected in them without their cooperation, and it necessarily implies a corresponding change that is the product of their free will and hence is subjective. But this subjective change is secondary as compared with the primary and complete change that is objective redemption; it is an effect, a prolongation of objective redemption, and, far from adding anything to the latter, receives everything it has therefrom.

The claim has been made, in a theory similar to that of the liberal Protestants mentioned above, although it is expressed in different terms, that the redemption is a self-saving, a salvation wrought by oneself, and not a salvation received from another. The whole of the preceding exposition proves sufficiently that our salvation is received from another: we are saved by God, and He has saved us even when we were dead in His eyes. Yet we hasten to add that this does not prevent the redemption from being a self-saving in the sense already explained, for God has saved us by uniting us to Himself and by giving us the power to save ourselves, in Him.

Salvation wrought by oneself, salvation received from another, subjective redemption, objective redemption, these are terms that are really not very satisfying, or at least are not exhaustive. They are employed to formulate the redemption in function of a dualism and a separation: on one side, God, on the other, man; on the one side a principle that is outside and above us, on the other our inner conscience. But redemption is precisely the action that suppresses the separation caused by sin and that restores unity. We have redemption and salvation because another, He from whom come salvation and life, makes Himself one, in Christ, with those He saves. Salvation is achieved in this union, in Christ, who is the first principle of the union: "the salvation which is in Christ Jesus." [123]

But the efficacy found in Christ's humanity comes from God, and the mystery of redemption is itself essentially a mystery of divinization, the divinization of the sinner. Sufferings and death are needed for this, and the divine will surrounds man with them on all sides in order to detach him from himself. From the point of view of man and sensation and conceptual experience, this is loss and destruction. But from the point of view that looks toward God, it is absolute gain. Sinful man must fall back, but only that God may advance. God's intolerant and exacting will requires the whole territory to be vacated, but only that He Himself may enter; He desires to take possession of body and soul, of the affections and the will.

And the divine will is God Himself, and God is love, and the Spirit is love, and love is the jealous and ecstatic force that unites. Therefore let God enter, let Him occupy the whole of us, let Him come to take us over; His desire is not to live in place of us but to live in us.

This is why we must welcome Him and His mortifying will with longing and love, with a reception that is spontaneous and joyful, filial and confident. This is the mystery of whole-hearted love and total transformation.

Love is at work and the Spirit of love is at work, relentlessly harrying sinful men to extricate them from their sins and to bring to birth in them, by the agony of a long travail, children dear to the Father and members of the incarnate Son. The purpose aimed at is that all may mount up to the Father through the Spirit and in the Son.

[123] Cf. II Tim. 2:10.

BOOK FOUR

The Blessed Trinity

CHAPTER XII

FILII IN FILIO:
THE LIFE IMPARTED BY THE TRINITY

AT length we come, through Christ, to the mystery of the Blessed
Trinity. We have seen that Christ's humanity means sanctification and redemption for the whole human race, because the race
is united to Christ. We now go on to show that, if the humanity of
Christ brings sanctification and redemption to all, the underlying
reason is the union of mankind with the divine Word and, in Him,
with the Blessed Trinity. Christ's humanity is the ultimate principle
in the order of grace and salvation; but the Blessed Trinity is the
ultimate principle of this order itself. All the grace that is ever
received by the mystical body of Christ comes from the Father
through the Son in the Spirit.

The transcendence of this sacred humanity sets it infinitely above
all men, but is also the reason for its immanence in all. Since the sacred
humanity is not separated from its transcendence, it becomes immanent in us along with its transcendence. Therefore it communicates its excellence to its members, just as it is the cause that makes
them members. As the Fathers say, the Son of God became the
Son of man in order that the sons of men might become sons of
God in Him.

I. The Mystery of the Trinity

The mystery of the Trinity is the greatest of mysteries. It is
the most mysterious of them all. Other mysteries contain at least
some aspect that is quite within the purview of man. In Christological
dogma, for example, the human nature of Christ is wholly similar to
other human natures, and the bread mentioned in the dogma of
transubstantiation is exactly like the bread we may encounter any-

where. But in the dogma of the Trinity everything is God and nothing but God; nature and person are identically the transcendent God as He is in Himself, and therefore completely elude our conception.

Everything that is mysterious in Christianity derives from this foremost mystery for it all comes from Christ who is the Son. Accordingly this mystery is the first principle in the order of mystery and, in this sense, is the unique and total mystery. For the same reason, the mystery of the Trinity is the source of all that is transcendent, supernatural, and life-giving in Christianity. Therefore, if the essence of the dogma is to reveal to us what is necessary and transcendent in God and also what God is pleased to become for us and in us, this mystery is the most essential of all dogmas. It is the "most majestic proclamation of the Church of God," [1] the dogma that dominates all the others, the "most authoritative teaching," [2] and that contains them all. In the phrase used by the Fathers, it is the truth that forms the very substance of the Gospel message.[3] The Trinity is the source of all life, of every gift, and also of the understanding of this gift: "the Trinity, origin of life." [4]

From the ontological point of view, the dogma of the Trinity holds the primacy in all Christian teaching. The same is true of Christological dogma, as this book supposes throughout. But this is because Christology implies the dogma of the Trinity. How can we proclaim Christ without identifying Him with the Son, and hence without referring to the Father and the Spirit? Christological teaching adds nothing but the way in which this Son, this Father, and this Spirit have given themselves to man and to man's knowledge. The dogma of Christology is the dogma of the Trinity as made known to men; it is a truth revealed to men in a giving of life to men.

Christological dogma, as we have seen, makes clear the religious character of Christianity, for it teaches us how men are brought into relation with God in the God-man. But in teaching how the God-man brings men into relation with the innermost life of God, with God as He is in Himself, it implies the dogma of the Trinity. Consequently we may also say that Trinitarian dogma brings out

[1] Dionysius of Rome, *Epist.* 1 (PL, V, 110).
[2] St. Basil, *Adversus Eunomium*, II, 22 (PG, XXIX, 620).
[3] Leo XIII, *Divinum illud.* Cf. Tertullian, *Adversus Praxeam*, 31.
[4] Third Council of Constantinople (Denz., 290).

the religious character of Christianity, for religion is a turning to God.

A religion is gauged by the notion of God it supplies. In the case of Christianity, this notion is furnished by the dogma of the Trinity, which therefore sets a stamp on Christianity as a religion. It may appear abstract, yet it regulates our whole religious attitude, including its most ordinary aspects, and does so even without our conscious advertence. A materialist conception of the Godhead inspires a materialist religion; a psychological or sensualist conception inspires a psychological or sensualist religion; a transcendent and mysterious conception inspires a pure, uncontaminated religion that leads us to adore God.

This affirmation has to be extended farther. The dogma of the Trinity reveals to the Christian what Being is in itself. Hence it perfects our idea of being, and this idea determines our whole spiritual and properly human attitude. Thus the dogma of the Trinity determines our entire human attitude. Once a relation with Being itself is elevated and transformed as it is in Christ, one's way of existing is elevated and transformed, and at the same time the activities that have to do with being, the activities of knowing and willing, are transformed and elevated. Through faith and vision, the Christian knows otherwise than the rest of men; and through charity, he wills otherwise.

Indeed, Christian life develops "otherwise"; the Trinity is like a vital atmosphere that penetrates it through and through. Christians are baptized in the name of the Father and of the Son and of the Holy Ghost. They are confirmed and receive forgiveness of their sins in the name of the Father and of the Son and of the Holy Ghost. When they come to die, the Church commends them to God by appealing to their faith in the Father, the Son, and the Holy Ghost: "Although he may have sinned, he did not deny the Father and the Son and the Holy Ghost . . . and while he was alive he was signed with the seal of the Holy Trinity." [5] With the sign of the cross they consecrate all their works to the Father, the Son, and the Holy Ghost; and the Church offers their worship to God the Father through the Lord Jesus Christ in the unity of the Holy Ghost.

Christians do not have to think of all this in order that such vital relations may have their effect. God thinks of these matters, and

[5] *Rituale Romanum,* tit. V, c. 7; tit. VI, c. 3.

Christ and the Church take thought on our behalf. From the moment Christians are in Christ, they are in the Son and hence in the Father; and eternal life springs up in them.[6] In the same way, the moment a piece of flotsam is caught up in the current of the stream, it sets out on its journey to the sea. The grace by which Christians live orientates them toward the Trinity; their last end, their beatitude, can be nothing else than the contemplation of the triune God as He is. Consequently their very being has to be properly adapted. In order that such a destiny may not be artificial, their life has to be raised to the heights of their eternal vocation.

When we dwell on these supernatural affinities we do not lessen the transcendence of the Trinity; we merely call to mind the transcendence of Christian life. If we keep perpetually speaking of the inaccessible loftiness of the three divine persons, we shall come to think of them as unknowable and absent. If we habitually represent the mystery of the Trinity as external to man, even to the Christian, do we not run the risk of barring God from our thoughts and our love? Undoubtedly, to avoid hell, a man will believe the doctrinal pronouncements that speak of eternal punishment, and he will force himself to regard these truths highly, as they deserve. But this will always remain an esteem such as one might have for the exit gate of a prison.

That has never been the genuine Christian attitude. Christians have never treated the dogma of the Trinity with the fear of some poor wretch condemned to handle explosives, or with the anguish accompanying a verbal orthodoxy that is solely intent on avoiding inexact formulas. On the contrary, they have pressed it to their heart, they have meditated on it over and over with the eagerness of a love that knows it is well regulated. They are God's familiars, and they hearken to God.

Notice how, from the very beginning, St. Paul or St. Ignatius of Antioch speaks of this mystery of the three divine persons. We might say that they spoke of it for the very pleasure of doing so. They did not keep a mistrustful watch over what they wrote, but let their pens run on to pour out the fullness of their hearts. Love is no less a profession of faith than the rigor of abstract language is.

The fire has not gone out in the Church. The great doctors of the early centuries did not recoil before long years of labor or

[6] Cf. I John 2:23 f.; 4:15; John 5:21-25.

persecution or exile, but at length drew forth from the documents of our faith the precise formulas of Nicaea and Constantinople. And once the formula was securely possessed, the labor continued under another form; the endeavor was to construct a theology on the basis of the truths that had been defined. That was the work of more than a thousand years; it was an immense collective enterprise, begun by the Fathers and pursued by the Scholastics, especially during the great ages of the thirteenth and fourteenth centuries. Its outcome in the Latin Church was the theory that is familiar: the metaphysics of relations, the psychology of the acts of thought and will, of saying and loving, the definition of the processions, of the rational, of the absolute.

This system may be judged imperfect, as inevitably it is. It may be found to be austere; how could it be otherwise? Human reason strained at it with its ultimate effort, and tried to go even farther. But he who contemns it as a tissue of idle speculations has completely failed to understand the magnificent tragedy. Faith parted the curtain, and the human mind caught a fleeting glimpse of the grandeur of something it could not hope to express. Forever afterward it was enthralled, and resolutely set itself to the quest of words and ideas that might represent in the least deficient way possible the mystery given to it, and the purpose for which the revelation was granted. What does it matter if the journey is endless in the harsh desert of abstractions? The pilgrimage was undertaken with a love that refuses to be rebuffed; the mind obstinately consumes and exhausts its powers in the effort to re-examine and correct its concepts, to plod on yet farther to the very limits of its resources, in order to express the inexpressible. This is neither rationalism nor Byzantinism. It is precisely the contrary; it is loyalty and consecration. Fire has fallen from heaven into man's intellect, and the intellect allows itself to be enkindled, and will burn itself out rather than relax its grasp.

We intend to take our part in this sacred search. But the point of view that dominates our expedition imposes a special itinerary. The sure explanation of the Trinity has to be sought in Christ. And indeed, do not men find it in Him before they express it in reasoned discourse? As St. Irenaeus said long ago, the whole Trinity gives itself in Christ: "In the name of Christ we may dimly perceive Him who anointed, and Him who is anointed, and even the ointment wherewith He is anointed. For the Father anointed, and the Son is anointed, in the Spirit who is the ointment." [7]

The Trinity contains its own intelligibility. When it gives itself, it also gives an explanation of itself, to the measure of man's capacity. Here on earth, while man is yet in process of formation, the knowledge is imparted in faith; in the next life, when man reaches his full stature, he will have vision of the truth. The main thing is to receive the Trinity as it gives itself in Him who is the Son of the Father, the Word, the co-principle of the Spirit; for, through the humanity He assumes, He is also the unity, the life, and the light of the human race. When we have Him, we have the ultimate explanation; and when we live and think in Him as He lives and thinks in us, we have everything we need to grasp this ultimate explanation.

Several ways of grasping the Trinity in Christ are open to us. Christ is the Son of the First Person; He is the Second Person Himself; He is the co-principle of the Third Person. When we are united to Him, therefore, we are, in Him and through Him, adopted sons of the First Person; with regard to the Second Person, we are members of the Word and share in His intellectual sonship; and with regard to the Third Person, we are associated in the work of love that has its terminus and its summit in the Holy Spirit.

These relations will be the subject of this and the following two chapters. They will show how our very life, which is a prolongation of Christ's life, is a vivid revelation of the mystery of the Trinity, an explanation well adapted to our powers and, at the same time, wholly derived from Christ. We shall begin with a study of the adoptive sonship and union given to us along with the Son; that union brings out most clearly the supernatural relation with the Trinity that is granted to men. We shall do well to recall first the information which Scripture and tradition impart on these matters, and then to reflect on this information.

II. Scriptural Data on the Sonship of Christians

In taking up the Scriptures, we need not go beyond the Epistles of St. Paul and the Gospel according to St. John. The important

[7] *Adversus haereses*, III, xviii, 3 (*PL*, VII, 234).

items to be found in the Synoptics are summed up in St. Paul and St. John.[8]

As regards St. Paul and his epistles, we may premise a general remark: all the passages in which the Apostle alludes or seems to allude to the Trinity exhibit the divine persons in the work of sanctification they exercise within men; and in these passages, as well as in the whole tenor of Pauline teaching, this sanctifying action is presented as something that takes place in Christ and in our incorporation in Christ.[9] The main texts will be quoted in the course of this chapter. They justify us in affirming that the Trinitarian teaching of St. Paul treats of Christian life in connection with the Trinity in Christ.

The same remark holds true if we reverse the terms: many passages that mention Christian life and life in Christ, present that life in connection with the Trinity in the incarnate Son. This aspect of the doctrine we shall consider in greater detail. We shall classify the texts in their chronological order, for a certain development in the teaching of the epistles on this point is noticeable.

The first passage to study contains the first unmistakable mention of the mystical body, and also the lengthiest description of it given by the Apostle: the whole of the twelfth chapter of the First Epistle to the Corinthians. The description is introduced by three verses that allude to the three divine persons: God (the Father), the Lord (the Son), and the Spirit. "There are diversities of graces, but the same Spirit; and there are diversities of ministries, but the same Lord; and there are diversities of operations, but the same God who worketh all in all." [10]

The "body" exhibits variety and multiplicity, which, however, find their unity in the one supreme Artificer who produces and

[8] In reading the Synoptics, the point to notice is the assertion of the Father's unique paternity, which is the same for Christ and for Christians, although the manner in which He is Father is wholly different. We find "the Son" and "the sons," "My Father" and "your Father."

[9] F. Prat, *The Theology of St. Paul*, II, 431, note S, gives a list of the passages that mention or seemingly mention the Father, the Son, and the Holy Spirit. They number twenty-six. All of them refer, some of them very strikingly, to the sanctification of Christians, grace, justification, or redemption. Half of them include a teaching on the mystical body, and in four cases insist on this teaching. Moreover, half of the remaining passages are closely connected with other texts that treat of our union in Christ.

[10] Cf. I Cor. 12:4 ff.

coordinates these attributes. Paul keeps repeating, "the same," and "one"; [11] and the supreme Artificer is throughout one and the same Father, one and the same Son, one and the same Spirit.[12] In a word, one and the same Trinity produces the organism in its diversity. On the other hand, this variety and multiplicity find their unity in Christ, and this same unity, which forms the whole aggregate into a single body,[13] is the one Christ, as the Apostle declares with emphasis.[14] Thus this body, which is one in Chirst, is also one in the Trinity, as we read in St. John's Gospel: "That they also may be one in Us" (John 17:21). This is brought out in two important verses according to which this body, identified with the mystical Christ, appears in the Spirit: "For as the body is one, and hath many members, and all the members of the body, whereas they are many, yet are one body, so also is Christ. For in one Spirit were we all baptized into one body, whether Jews or Gentiles, whether bond or free; and in one Spirit we have all been made to drink." [15] Indeed, how could Christians, called as they are to union with the Son,[16] fail to be in union with the Father and the Spirit?

This point is developed in the epistles to the Galatians and to the Romans, which complete the teaching on baptism we have just read. Paul desires to show the Galatians that the true sons of Abraham and of God are the Christians, not the Jews. For, he says, Christians are one with Christ, and Christ is the culmination of the Old Testament. "You are all the children of God by faith, in Christ Jesus. For as many of you as have been baptized, have put on Christ. There is neither Jew nor Greek; there is neither bond nor free; there is neither male nor female. For you are all one in Christ Jesus." [17] As Christians are one in Christ, they are sons in Christ; and not by any juridical attribution or by association with the ancient covenant, but by attachment to the same Father and through the action of the same Spirit. "When the fullness of the time was come, God sent His Son, made of a woman, made under the law, that He might redeem them who were under the law, that we might receive

[11] Ten times in twelve verses.
[12] Cf. I Cor. 12:3 f., 7-11, 13.
[13] See verses 12 f., 20, 25, 27.
[14] Cf. verse 12: "So also is Christ."
[15] See I Cor. 12:12 f.
[16] *Ibid.*, v. 9; cf. II Cor. 6:18; 13:13.
[17] Gal. 3:26 ff.; cf. 2:19 f., on union with Christ who is the Son.

the adoption of sons. And because you are sons, God hath sent the Spirit of His Son into your hearts, crying: Abba, Father." [18]

Although this sonship is received, it is of surpassing excellence, and gives us a relation to the Trinity. This is clarified in a similar text from the Epistle to the Romans, where St. Paul explains the nature of the new justice imparted to those who are in Christ.[19] He says that it is a life of adopted sons who are united to the only-begotten Son,[20] a life continually infused by the Spirit.[21] "Whosoever are led by the Spirit of God, they are the sons of God. For you have not received the spirit of bondage again in fear; but you have received the spirit of adoption of sons, whereby we cry: Abba (Father). For the Spirit Himself giveth testimony to our spirit that we are the sons of God. And if sons, heirs also; heirs indeed of God and joint-heirs with Christ; yet so if we suffer with Him, that we may be also glorified with Him." [22]

Therefore this is a sonship that comes from the Trinity itself, from the Father and from the Spirit; a sonship that comes down from on high to penetrate even into the material universe and hold out to it a painful hope looking toward the adoption of sons; [23] a sonship so sublime that for Paul it sums up the supernatural economy. "For whom He foreknew, He also predestinated to be made conformable to the image of His Son, that He might be the first-born amongst many brethren. And whom He predestinated, them He also called. And whom He called, them He also justified. And whom He justified, them He also glorified." [24] Everything is there; what could be added? God has given His Son so completely that the gift has entered into the substance of men, who thereupon are likewise made sons.[25]

The Christological epistles come back to the same thought, and give a further explanation of that predestination which makes Christians conformable to the image of the Son. They teach that this predestination flows out from Christ's predestination, that it is a

[18] Gal. 4:4 ff.
[19] Rom. 8:1, 10, 39.
[20] *Ibid.*, 8:1, 2, 3–10, 14, 16, 26.
[21] *Ibid.*, 8:9, 11, 14, 39.
[22] *Ibid.*, 8:14–17.
[23] *Ibid.*, 8:22; also vv. 19, 23.
[24] *Ibid.*, 8:29 f.
[25] *Ibid.*, 8:31 f.

sharing in His predestination; in Him who is predestined to be the Son,[26] those who are His members are predestined to be sons by adoption.

The first verses of the hymn of thanksgiving which opens the Epistle to the Ephesians express the same thought: "Blessed be the God and Father of our Lord Jesus Christ, who hath blessed us with spiritual blessings in heavenly places, in Christ. As He chose us in Him before the foundation of the world, that we should be holy and unspotted in His sight in charity. Who hath predestinated us unto the adoption of children through Jesus Christ unto Himself, according to the purpose of His will; unto the praise of the glory of His grace, in which He hath graced us in His beloved Son." [27] Everything comes to us from the Father of our Lord, and everything comes to us in Jesus Christ, our Lord, as these verses repeat over and over.[28] And the crowning gift, the summary of God's plans for Christians,[29] is our adoption by the Father through Christ and in Christ. This is the grace of graces, designed to be diffused over all creation; the Spirit is its seal and pledge. It is meant to incorporate us into Christ our head,[30] and to unite us in the Spirit with the Father.[31]

The same teaching, almost word for word, is found in the Epistle to the Colossians. The Apostle shows that Christ, the Son, is the prototype of all things and the image of the Father. He becomes the life, the unity, and the peace of regenerated mankind. He establishes the race in Himself, and by that very fact and grace, establishes us in sonship. Although He is the life of men and the only-begotten Son of the Father, He ever remains the same, as the passage repeats several times. How can our blessed God, who joins us so closely to His Son and transfers us to the kingdom of this Son of His love, do otherwise than admit us into the sonship that makes the Son what He is?

Giving thanks to God the Father, who hath made us worthy to be partakers of the lot of the saints in light; who hath delivered us from the power of darkness and hath translated us into the kingdom of the Son of

[26] Rom. 1:4.
[27] Eph. 1:3–6.
[28] A dozen times in fourteen verses.
[29] Eph. 1:5, 9.
[30] Ibid., 1:10, 13 f.
[31] Ibid., 2:18.

His love, in whom we have redemption through His blood, the remission of sins; who is the image of the invisible God, the first-born of every creature. For in Him were all things created in heaven and on earth, visible and invisible, whether thrones or dominations or principalities or powers; all things were created by Him and in Him. And He is before all, and by Him all things consist. And He is the head of the body, the Church, who is the beginning, the first-born from the dead; that in all things He may hold the primacy. Because in Him it hath well pleased the Father that all fullness should dwell, and through Him to reconcile all things unto Himself, making peace through the blood of His cross, both as to the things that are on earth and the things that are in heaven. And you, whereas you were some time alienated and enemies in mind in evil works, yet now He hath reconciled in the body of His flesh through death, to present you holy and unspotted and blameless before Him.[32]

The fullness that dwells in Christ and enables Him to reconcile all things in Himself, is explained more clearly a little farther on: "For in Him dwelleth all the fullness of the Godhead corporeally; and you are filled in Him who is the head of all principality and power." [33] His fullness and ours are set side by side: the fullness of divinity that He has because He is the Son, and the fullness that we have in ourselves because we have it in Him: "and you are filled in Him." What can this fullness be but a derivation of the fullness that belongs to Him as the Son? Christ's fullness becomes ours because we are in Him, the head from which all life flows down to the members. He is "the head from which the whole body, by joints and bands, being supplied with nourishment and compacted, groweth unto the increase of God." [34]

We can sum up the Apostle's teaching by making our own several lines written by one of his best commentators: "From the supernatural being received at baptism, special relations with each of the three divine Persons are derived: a relation of sonship with the Father; a relation of consecration to the Holy Spirit; a relation of mystical identity with Jesus Christ." [35] This last relation of "mystical identity" with the Son explains everything.

St. John is even more forceful than St. Paul. When he tells us about Christ, he generally adds that Christ, being the Son, places

[32] Col. 1:12–22.
[33] Ibid., 2:9 f.
[34] Ibid., 2:19.
[35] F. Prat, op. cit., II, 320.

the Christian in a relation of adoptive sonship with the Trinity. This doctrine is the thesis of his Gospel; the book was written with the purpose of inducing us to believe that Jesus is the Son, that by believing we might have life in His name, that is, a life proper to a son. "These are written that you may believe that Jesus is the Christ, the Son of God; and that believing, you may have life in His name." [36]

That this life in the name of the Son is a life in the Son, a life of sons, is clearly brought out in other passages that announce the same thesis and the same Johannine "testimony." [37] "This is the testimony, that God hath given to us eternal life. And this life is in His Son. He that hath the Son hath life. He that hath not the Son hath not life. These things I write to you, that you may know that you have eternal life, you who believe in the name of the Son of God." [38] "Eternal life," which is "life in the Son," belongs to those who believe in the name of the Son; [39] and this, according to a related text, is fellowship "with the Father and with His Son Jesus Christ." [40]

This fellowship with the Father and the Son, or with the Father through the Son, that is, with the divine life of the Trinity, is the message of the Gospel. John makes his meaning clear from the very first verses of the book. His intention is to speak about God who communicates Himself in the Word: "In the beginning was the Word, and the Word was with God, and the Word was God. The same was in the beginning with God." [41] The Word is the subject of the discourse. The Gospel is going to treat of the Word; not of God in general or in the abstract, but of Christ who is the Word that manifests the Father and gives the Spirit. "And the Word was made flesh." [42]

The Word is the divine person who was made flesh. He had always communicated Himself to men,[43] and from the beginning was a

[36] John 20:31.
[37] The Fourth Gospel was written "to give testimony." See John 19:35; 21:24.
[38] Cf. I John 5:11 ff.
[39] John 20:31.
[40] Cf. I John 1:3.
[41] John 1:1 f.
[42] *Ibid.*, 1:14.
[43] *Ibid.*, 1:5, 12.

life destined to be the light of men.[44] He now appears in the glory of His assumed humanity,[45] and this glory is a fullness of grace and truth that is diffused among all men. "And of His fullness we have all received, and grace for grace. For the law was given by Moses; grace and truth came by Jesus Christ." [46]

This fullness will have a filial character in men, for Christ's own fullness is such as He, the Son, receives from the Father; and men receive of His fullness. The truth that comes to them from Christ is primarily a knowledge of the Father, a way of knowing the Father that is proper to sons.[47] And the grace that will come to them will give them the power to become children of God in the Son,[48] for in the incarnate Word they are born a second time, not of men, but of God.[49]

"Children of God" is the phrase St. John invariably employs when he speaks of the sonship of Christians. Christ alone is the Son, the Only-begotten, and is never called "child." St. Paul prefers "sons" to "children" when referring to the faithful; John never applies the Greek word literally meaning "son" to any other than Christ. This is too sharp a contrast to be unintentional; the beloved disciple surely wishes to bring out the immense difference between our sonship and that of Christ. But this is not to say that he sees only the differences. Quite the contrary; even more than Paul, he insists on the union and similarity between the only-begotten Son and those who receive in Him the power to become God's children. Christ is of God; they too are of God; [50] He is born of the Father; they are born of the Father.[51] As He dwells in the Father, and the Father in Him, so they dwell in the Father, and the Father in them.[52] As the world cannot know Him, it cannot know them.[53] In a word,

[44] Ibid., 1:4.
[45] Ibid., 1:14.
[46] Ibid., 1:16 f.
[47] Ibid., 1:18.
[48] Ibid., 1:12.
[49] Ibid., 1:13.
[50] Ibid., 8:42, 47; 16:25. As regards Christians, see I John 4:4 f.; 5:19; III John, 11. Many similar expressions can be found.
[51] The same term serves in both cases. See John 1:13; 18:37; I John 2:29; 3:9; 4:7; 5:1, 18.
[52] John 1:18; 14:10 f., 20; 17:21 ff.; I John 2:24; 4:12 f., 15 f.
[53] Ibid., 1:10; 14:19 f.; 15:18 f.; 16:3; 17:14 ff.; I John 3:1.

they are God's children because they share in Christ's sonship; they are born of God by being reborn in God's Son.

The whole Gospel treats of various ways by which men are made adopted sons of God through their blessed union with the Son. We shall limit ourselves to a consideration of the great means by which this union is brought about and of the perfection to which is raises men.

This means is the Eucharist. For the Eucharist does not only unite us to Christ; it unites us to the Father in the Son and associates us with Christ's sonship. We should fail entirely to understand the Eucharist if we severed it from the mystery of the eternal genera-tion: "As the living Father hath sent Me, and I live by the Father, so he that eateth Me, the same also shall live by Me." [54] We perceive the continuity of the movement: the stream flows uninterruptedly from the Father to the Son, and through Christ to Christians. This flood, as we know from its origin, is the Trinitarian life itself. It catches us up in its embrace; and by eating and drinking Him who is the Son, the life that flows into us, which is His life,[55] cannot be anything else than a life belonging to sons.

And the Trinity, which makes us live in itself, will make us one in its own unity. This will be the summit of all perfection. Jesus Himself affirms this emphatically in the last discourse of the last Gospel, the discourse after the Supper. We may call it the Eucharistic discourse, not because it promises the sacred mysteries, but because it is a commentary on them at the hour of their accomplishment and expresses in words what they actually effect; these sacred mysteries give us life in Christ and make us one in Him, as He lives by the Father and is one with the Father. The discourse is a long exhorta-tion to union: union with God, union with Christ, union among Christians, union of love, confidence, and faith. But this union is not mere sympathy or harmony; it is the image and, as it were, the continuation of the absolute union among the three divine per-sons; it is an imitation and partaking of Unity itself.

That they may be one, as We also are one. . . . That they all may be one, as Thou, Father, in Me, and I in Thee; that they also may be one in Us; that the world may believe that Thou has sent Me. And the glory which Thou hast given Me, I have given to them; that they may be one,

[54] Ibid., 6:58; cf. 5:21, 26.
[55] Ibid., 6:53 f., 56; cf. 15:1-8.

as We also are one. I in them, and Thou in Me; that they may be made perfect in one, and the world may know that Thou hast sent Me, and hast loved them, as Thou hast also loved Me.[56]

These are but a few lines, and are full of repetition; yet they contain infinite riches which meditation will never exhaust. And the affirmation is so paradoxical and categorical that Christ could well afford to repeat it several times, to allow at least some of it to penetrate into the souls of His hearers. Mystery is latent in all its parts, but it is a mystery of love and generosity.

As Christ is in the Father because He is the Son, Christians will be in the Son and the Father because they will be in Christ. The unity which the Son has with the Father will embrace them in their own way. They will be one as the Father and the Son are one; they will be one in the Father and the Son; they will be one with a perfect unity: "that they may be made perfect in one." [57] Theology will have to explain and distinguish; it will have to discuss participation, grace, and the finite divinization that is inherent in the Christian. But it cannot blot out or minimize a word. If the divine gift were not integral, infinite, unheard-of, would it still be truly divine? Our own explanation will come later; for the moment we should note that Jesus Christ does not comment or restrict; He has not the slightest intention of toning down His expressions or making them more credible. At this hour He carries everything to extremes, and He makes no exception for unity: "He loved them unto the end," "That they may be made perfect in one." [58] As the Father loves the Son, He must also love Christians, and with the same love from which the Spirit proceeds: "That the love wherewith Thou hast loved Me may be in them, and I in them." [59]

Trinitarian life is indicated in this passage. Only the Father and the Son are named, and the Son speaks to the Father of their relations, their circumincession, and their consubstantiality.[60] The Spirit is not expressly mentioned, but reference to Him is implied; [61] it is He who is to achieve the work of love and union.[62] Consequently

[56] *Ibid.*, 17:11, 21 ff.
[57] *Ibid.*, 17:23.
[58] *Ibid.*, 13:1; 17:23.
[59] *Ibid.*, 17:26.
[60] *Ibid.*, 17:1–24.
[61] *Ibid.*, 14:17, 26; 15:26; 17:26.
[62] *Ibid.*, 14:16–20, 26–31; 15:26 f.; 16:12 ff.

this Trinitarian life enters into Christians; and it comes to them through Christ, the Son. They are one in the Father and the Son because Christ, the Son, is in the Father and is also in them. The four pleas for unity are introduced in a way to bring this out. In the first, the method of achieving this unity is not very clear.[63] In the other three, it is as plain as it could be. "As Thou, Father, in Me, and I in Thee, that they also, etc. The glory which Thou hast given Me, I have given to them, that they may be one, as We also, etc. I in them and Thou in Me, that they, etc." [64]

This announcement of unity is clearly contained in the announcement of eternal sonship; it is a sort of prolongation and application of that sonship to men. To explain how Christians are one, the Son first tells how He Himself is one with the Father; and men, in order to gain some notion of the intimate, living bond that unites them, must first believe in the generation of the Word and in the interior union of the persons of the Trinity with one another. Jesus does not of course say that these two unities are identical; the lower resembles the higher, shares in it, and is caused by it. But the resemblance and participation are real and far-reaching; Jesus cannot assert it emphatically enough. Accordingly, to understand this unity well, as also to possess it, we must believe in the mystery of Christ's eternal begetting; conversely, the unity among Christians will serve as a proof and sign of the mystery. This is what Jesus means to say: "That they also may be one in Us; that the world may believe that Thou hast sent Me. That they may be made perfect in one, and the world may know that Thou hast sent Me." [65] Thus the mystery of the life, unity, and predestination of Christians is rooted in Christ, the Son, considered in relation to the Father, that is, in His sonship.

III. Testimony of Tradition on the Sonship of Christians

The supernatural assurance that Christians are sons of God in the Son was not ignored by tradition. The new life that arises like a fountain of living water murmuring, "Come to the Father," [66]

---

[63] *Ibid.*, 17:9 ff.
[64] *Ibid.*, 17:21 ff.
[65] *Ibid.*, 17:21, 23; cf. 13:35 and I John 3:1.
[66] St. Ignatius of Antioch, *Ad Romanos*, VII, 2.

the "unction" which is received from the Father and the Son and which teaches us all things,[67] and finally the Spirit who suggests all truth,[68] will not permit Christians to forget the mystery on which their existence rests.

What tradition has said and meditated on this subject is too vast to be recounted here, especially as many texts have already been quoted in *The Whole Christ*.[69] The texts are the same as those that treat of our union with Christ, and with the Word and the Trinity through Christ. But the matter is so important that we cannot omit mention of some passages. They will help us in the indispensable task of following the line of development taken by tradition.

The Fathers who have most to teach us about our divine sonship are likewise those who speak most forcefully of our union with Christ. They also happen to be the most important figures in the history of Christian dogma. The doctrines go together; is not our union with Christ everything in Christianity? Each of the Fathers gives his testimony in his own way, insisting chiefly on that aspect of Christian truth which his mission charges him to set off in sharpest relief.

In the chronological order, the first to study is St. Irenaeus, the first of the great theologians whose works we still possess and the great teacher of the doctrine of salvation. As is well known, his teaching on salvation is summed up in his theory of recapitulation, of God's restoration of mankind that had broken away from Him; and this recapitulation is accomplished in Christ, the Son and the Word. The function of the Son, the Word, has to be brought out clearly; and Irenaeus sets to his task with energy. To his mind the recapitulation is essentially a return of creation to the Father who is the Creator; and this return is effected in the Son, by union and assimilation to Him. On this point Irenaeus is most explicit; he conceives Christian life in the Trinitarian scheme, as an ascent to the Father through the Son and the Spirit. "In His boundless love the Word of God, Jesus Christ our Lord, became what we are, in order to raise us up to be what He is.[70] . . . How could we share in the

---

[67] Cf. I John 2:27.
[68] John 14:26.
[69] See especially pp. 274–84; 311 ff.; 344–52; 431–34.
[70] *Adversus haereses*, V, preface (PG, VII, 1120).

adoption of God's sons unless we had received from Him a fellow-ship with Him through the Son?" [71]

For in Christ the Son Himself, the Word, is joined to the race of Adam, to gather it under His own headship; [72] thus He has brought into existence a new race, a new way of being man. Christ is "the Son of the Most High God, the Father of all, who effected the Incarnation and revealed a new birth." [73]

The first race of men was created in the beginning, when God united a breath of His mouth to the dust; the new race was estab-lished in these latter times when God united His Word and His Spirit to His original creature.

In the beginning of our formation in Adam, God's life-giving breath was joined to the work of His hands to animate man, and showed him to be a rational animal. But in a later age the Word of the Father and the Spirit of God were joined to the ancient substance that went into Adam's shaping to make man living and perfect, with knowledge of the perfect Father; so that as we all met death in the animal man, we might all be raised to life in the spiritual man. [74]

To the mind of Irenaeus the salvation brought by the Incarnation is a union with the Word and, through the Word, with the Father, in the sacred humanity assumed by the Word. Therefore heretics who deny that the Word assumed true flesh must also deny that they themselves are truly united to the Word. "They who say that He was only a man begotten by Joseph, persevere in their adherence to the original disobedience and die; for they are not joined to the Word of God the Father." [75]

"Joined to the Word of God the Father": this is one of the formulas used in referring to the Incarnation. We are at the root of all Christianity; as the saint explains in the same context, Christians are Christians because they receive the Word Himself into their souls. Then he goes on to show that the Word Himself announced the mysterious excellence of this grace.

Speaking of the gift of His grace, the Word says to them: "I have said: You are gods and all of you the sons of the Most High. But you like men shall die" (Ps. 81:6 f.). He is undoubtedly speaking to those

[71] *Ibid.*, III, xviii, 7 (*PG*, VII, 932).
[72] *Ibid.*, 1 (*PG*, VII, 932).
[73] *Ibid.*, V, i, 3 (*PG*, VII, 1122).
[74] *Ibid.*, (*PG*, VII, 1123).
[75] *Ibid.*, III, xix, 1 (*PG*, VII, 938).

who do not accept the gift of adoption but scorn the incarnation of the Word begotten in a pure birth by God. They defraud man of his ascent to God and offend the Word of God who became incarnate for them.

For this is why the Word of God became man; and He who is the Son of God became the Son of man in order that man, united to the Word of God and endowed with the gift of adoption, might become a son of God.[76]

This is the idea of the gift of grace we find in St. Irenaeus and his account of the reason why God became man: the Word was made man that man might be joined to the Word of God and thus in turn become a son of God. This is the chief aim and the whole purpose of the redemption. Before closing his work the saint repeats his teaching.

There is one Son, who performed the Father's will perfectly; and there is one human race, in which are accomplished the mysteries of God, whom the angels desire to see, although they do not presume to search out God's wisdom, by which His creature is conformed to His Son and incorporated into Him. God's Son, the first-born Word, was sent down to the creature of flesh and blood to be received by him. And the creature in turn was to receive the Word and mount up to Him, passing beyond the angels, so as to be wrought according to the image and likeness of God.[77]

The Fathers who came after Irenaeus during the Golden Age of Patristics treated the sublime history of man's salvation, in which the creature is embraced by the Word and also embraces Him, in a more speculative and systematic way, associating it with the dogma of the Trinity. Yet they always reserved room in the foreground for the union of the Son with the entire human race. We shall study this teaching in the two great champions of orthodoxy, St. Athanasius and St. Hilary. In the minds of both of them, the theology of the Trinity is connected with the theology of the intimate fellowship joining Christian life to the life of the Trinity.

St. Athanasius teaches this truth in his masterly work, *Against the Arians*. At the very outset he says that we become sons by our participation in the Word, who comes to us from the Father through the Spirit.[78] We become sons through the Son who is

---

[76] *Ibid.*, (PG, VII, 939).
[77] *Ibid.*, V, xxxvi, 3 (PG, VII, 1224).
[78] *Contra Arianos*, I, 9 (PG, XXVI, 29).

present in us,[79] and no adoption is possible apart from the true Son.[80] He could not make his point more clearly. He then goes on to explain how we are also taken up by the Word into the flesh He has made His own; [81] through our kinship with His flesh, we have all been joined to the Word,[82] and by our participation in the Son we receive a participation in God.[83]

We see what the Incarnation means for St. Athanasius, and how it embraces all mankind by the grace of adoption. He loves to say that to divinize men and make them children of God by adoption, the Savior had to be strictly God and truly the Son.[84]

The Father is truly the Father of the Son alone; nothing created, but only the Son, is properly God's Son. Therefore it is evident that we are God's sons not by nature, but through the Son who is in us; and God is not our Father by nature, but is Father of the Word who is in us and through whom we cry, "Abba, Father." Accordingly the Father declares that they in whom He sees His Son are His sons, and says: "I have begotten you"; and this verb "beget" refers to the Son, whereas the verb "make" designates creatures.[85]

"To make," "to beget": in Christian teaching these two verbs signify two ways of being that are quite different, but their union is effected in the Son, who is begotten, and who is "made" flesh. If we are careful to make our meaning clear, we can say that He is made, just as we can say that creatures are begotten, that is, in the Son. "Created things, by the very fact that they are created, cannot be said to be begotten, unless they are later made to participate in the Son who is begotten; then they may be said to be begotten. In this case they are begotten, not by virtue of anything in their own nature, but by being made to partake of the Son in the Spirit." [86] Therefore sonship enters creation in the Son. "As we all die in Adam because we are made of earth, so we are given life in Christ because we are reborn to a high estate by water and the

[79] Ibid., I, 39; III, 25 (PG, XXVI, 93, 376).
[80] Ibid., I, 39, 56 (PG, XXVI, 93, 129).
[81] Ibid., III, 34 (PG, XXVI, 397).
[82] Ibid., II, 69 (PG, XXVI, 293).
[83] Ibid., I, 16 (PG, XXVI, 45).
[84] Ibid., II, 70 (PG, XXVI, 296).
[85] Ibid., II, 59 (PG, XXVI, 273).
[86] Ibid., I, 56 (PG, XXVI, 129).

Spirit. Our flesh is no longer earthly but is taken up into the Word, because the Word of God was made flesh for our sake." [87]

"Our flesh is taken up into the Word": the Greek implies that the flesh of every man is "verbified" or made the Word; could the expression be bolder? If we reflect on the matter, does the statement mean anything else than that we are adopted and divinized, taking these words seriously? If He who is the Word and the Son in the literal sense united Himself to us in Christ, a resemblance to Him must be impressed on us. By becoming incarnate, the Son "ennobles all creation in the Spirit, makes men sons of God, and brings them before the Father." [88]

Such is the picture of the human universe as exhibited by Athanasius. It is an immense ascent up to the Father; an ascent of sons who, in the only-begotten Son, are orientated toward the Father by their supernatural life, by their "filial" existence.

St. Hilary teaches this ascent no less forcefully than St. Athanasius. But he insists more on the part played by the Savior's sacred humanity and on the union with it which all Christians have. He often remarks that all mankind was in Christ, and that Christ is present in all mankind. At the same time, in his opposition to the Arians, he is vividly conscious of the formulas that express the strict sonship of Christ. We observe that he frequently joins the two points of view in a synthesis; he speaks emphatically of the sonship found in all mankind and of all mankind in the state of sonship, through grace and adoption.[89] For in assuming an individual nature, the Son has in some way assumed all of us. How could we fail to be sons in Him? "The Son of God who was born of the Virgin did not indeed become the Son of God when He became the Son of man but, remaining the Son of God when He became the Son of man, took to Himself the nature of all flesh that the son of man might be the Son of God. Through this nature He became the true vine reaching out to embrace the whole race." [90]

"He took to Himself the nature of all flesh": this means, as we have pointed out elsewhere, the whole human race. The human race shares in Christ's sonship: "As long as the shoots remain in the

[87] *Ibid.*, III, 34 (PG, XXVI, 396).
[88] *Ad Serapionem*, I, 25 (PG, XXVI, 589).
[89] Cf. *The Whole Christ*, pp. 293 ff.
[90] *In Ps.* LI, 16 (PL, IX, 317).

vine, they necessarily retain the nature of the true vine." [91] And this nature, in the sense Hilary gives to the word, is the nature of Him who is born the Son of God. In Him, therefore, we too become sons through His sonship that is given to us by grace.[92]

The Incarnation reaches all the way to us, to "the sacrament of our assumption," as the saint says repeatedly. In commenting on the Epistle to the Colossians he says: "After mentioning the fullness of the Godhead that dwells in Christ corporeally, St. Paul immediately refers to the sacrament of our assumption: 'And you are filled in Him' (Col. 2:10). As the fullness of the Godhead is in Him, we also are filled in Him." [93] Thus we too are assumed; and by our "assumption" into Him we receive the crowning gift of His sonship, which raises us up to glory as it raised Him.[94] Assuredly this is a mystery that no man can fathom; but it is also a living reality that truly makes us live in the Word and the Son: "Let not the power given to everyone to become God's son turn out to be an obstacle to the weakness of anyone's anxious faith. . . . The Word who is God became flesh in order that, through God the Word made flesh, the flesh might be raised up to union with God who is the Word." [95]

If St. Hilary insists on the unique part played by Christ's sacred humanity in the union of all men with the Son and with the Trinity, St. Cyril of Alexandria is even more insistent. Although the holy patriarch is zealous for the dogma of the Trinity, he is particularly zealous for the dogma of Christology whose cause he champions. He undertakes to show that the sonship possessed by Christ's humanity is strict sonship through consubstantiality; but above all he wishes to show how this sonship exalts this humanity, this body and blood of Christ, and thereby the entire human race.

St. Cyril explains that the divine, eternal life which proceeds from the Father to the Son, as the pre-Arian Fathers had said, also comes to Christ's humanity and, through it, to Christians. The expansion continues and remains the same in the unity of the whole

[91] *Ibid.*, 17.
[92] Cf. *De Trinitate*, IX, 4, 7 (*PL*, X, 283 ff.).
[93] *Ibid.*, 8 ff. (*PL*, X, 287 ff.). The whole passage is instructive on the universal aspect of this "assumption."
[94] *Ibid.*, 9 f. (*PL*, X, 288 f.).
[95] *Ibid.*, I, 1 (*PL*, X, 33).

Christ, for the life received from the Father is also life in men.[96]
Are not Christians one in Christ as He is one with the Father? [97]
We may remark that this pattern of thought is that which the inspiring Spirit expresses in St. John; it is the mystery of the divine
life that is in Christ, the Son of God, and that comes to those who
believe in Christ, the Son of God.

St. Cyril states emphatically that the Spirit Himself is at work
in this work of life. And His activity tends wholly to make Christians
live in Christ and of Christ, with the life that is proper for sons
of God.[98]

The Son is life by nature, for He is begotten by the living Father.
His sacred body is also living, for in some way it is joined and mysteriously united to the Word that gives life to all. . . . Since the Savior's
flesh is life-giving, united as it is to Him who by nature is life, that is, to
the Word of God, we receive life when we eat it, for we become united
to it as it is united to the Word who dwells in it.[99]

Therefore, when we partake of it, it transforms us wholly into its
own excellence, that is, into immortality . . . that is, into life.[100]

In Christ and the Eucharist, accordingly, there comes to us a life
in the Word of life, the Son. Henceforth the Son Himself, through
the body He has taken, bears in Him all men,[101] the whole of
human nature,[102] as St. Cyril teaches, following St. Hilary. "Scripture tells us that He who was God, begotten of God before all ages,
is begotten today (Ps. 2:7), that in Him God might receive us as
His adopted sons; for all human nature was in Christ as man." [103]

The Word is united to us in order to unite us to Him and to
transform us into what He is, that is, to make us sons of God, not
by nature, like Him, but by grace; [104] to stamp us with His form

[96] The Father is a life-giving root, *In Ioan.*, IV, 3 (*PG*, LXXIII, 585), and
Christ is a new life-giving root for His whole race, *Homilia paschalis*, 27, 4, 6
(*PG*, LXXVII, 948); *Adversus Nestorium*, I, 1 (*PG*, LXXVI, 17).

[97] Cf. John 17:21 ff.

[98] Cf. *In Ioan.*, XI, 9-12 (*PG*, LXXIV, 512-71).

[99] *In Ioan.*, IV, 2 (*PG*, LXXIII, 577).

[100] *Ibid.*

[101] *Thesaurus*, 12 (*PG*, LXXV, 204); *In Ioan.*, I, 9 (*PG*, LXXIII, 164).

[102] *In II Cor.* (*PG*, LXXIV, 936).

[103] *In Ioan.*, V, 2 (*PG*, LXXIII, 753).

[104] *Thesaurus*, 24 (*PG*, LXXV, 400); *In Ioan.*, II (*PG*, LXXIII, 348); *In
II Cor.* (*PG*, LXXIV, 941).

and character of Son.[105] Thus through One, He has taken up His abode in us all.

"He dwelt in us" (John 1:14). These words reveal a profound mystery. We were all in Christ, and the common person of humanity is fashioned to new life in Him. . . . Through One, then, the Word has taken up His abode in all; and since this One has been constituted the Son of God in power according to the spirit of holiness, His dignity passes over to the whole human race. Through one of us, consequently, this word applies to us also: "I have said: You are gods and all of you the sons of the most High" (Ps. 81:6).[106]

This is the great Christian truth: the Son was made man that, in Him and through Him, men might be adopted as sons.[107] By our participation in the only-begotten Son we become adopted sons,[108] truly and "physically." [109] This shows clearly that He is the Son in the full sense of the term, that is, by nature.[110] "All paternity in heaven and on earth is derived from God the Father [Eph. 3:5], for He alone is supremely and truly Father. In the same way all sonship comes from the Son, for He alone is supremely and truly Son." [111]

Here is a last text. We quote it because it vividly expresses the saint's mind and also because it is really a summary of what we ourselves wish to bring out in studying the theology of man's adoption.

Christ is at once the only-begotten Son and the first-born Son. He is the only-begotten as God; He is the first-born through the saving union He has established between us and Him by becoming man among many brethren. He became man that in Him and through Him we might be made sons of God both by nature and by grace: by nature, in Him alone; by participation and grace, through Him in the Spirit.

Therefore, just as the attribute of only-begotten has become proper to the humanity in Christ, since that humanity is united to the Word according to the economy of salvation, so also to be the first-born among

[105] Dial., III (PG, LXXV, 837).
[106] In Ioan., I, 9 (PG, LXXIII, 161).
[107] Ibid., XII, 1 (PG, LXXIV, 70).
[108] Thesaurus, 13, 32 (PG, LXXV, 217, 472); Dial. III and IV (PG, LXXV, 837, 904).
[109] In Ioan., I (PG, LXXIII, 156).
[110] Thesaurus, 32 (PG, LXXV, 537); In Ioan., I (PG, LXXIII, 156, 180).
[111] In Ioan., II 1 (PG, LXXIII, 213).

many brethren has become proper to the Word, through His union with the flesh.[112]

"In Him and through Him we are made sons of God, both by nature and by grace." To the mind of St. Cyril, the incarnation of the only-begotten Son extends that far.

The Fathers of the East often assert, or at least implicitly suppose, that the Incarnation affects the whole human race. Indeed, objection has sometimes been taken to their stand, on the score that they teach a sort of collective incarnation in which the Word is united to all mankind, instead of the unique incarnation of Jesus Christ. We have elsewhere [113] given a list of the Fathers who seem to speak in this fashion: Athanasius, Hilary,[114] Gregory Nazianzen, Gregory of Nyssa, John Chrysostom, and Cyril of Alexandria among the great Fathers; others could be added. In view of such important, numerous, and harmonious testimonies, we find it hard to brush off the objection by saying that their expressions are infelicitous or inaccurate. On the other hand, the whole of Christianity, including these very Fathers, rises up against a collective incarnation that would replace the individual incarnation of Christ. Apparently, therefore, we have to interpret these texts in the light of the texts themselves and of the contexts supplied by the same Fathers, and also in the light of the doctrine taught by the whole Church on the relation between collective mankind and the one Christ in His individual humanity. This task we have already performed.[115] We have tried to show that the collective aspect of the Incarnation is nothing but the effect produced by the unique Incarnation in the countless souls that are made one by grace with the incarnate Son, who is their head and their all.

But even though we interpret all these passages in the sense which imposes itself naturally and which is the only one possible, we must agree that they closely associate our adoptive sonship with Christ's natural sonship, so that the former is the inseparable prolongation of the latter. According to all the texts in question, Christians are divinized and adopted by incorporation into the Son, the Second Person of the Trinity; in Christ and through His unique Incarnation,

[112] *De recta fide ad Theodosium*, 30 (PG, LXXVI, 1177).
[113] See *The Whole Christ*, Index, s.v. "Incarnation."
[114] We include Hilary among the Eastern Fathers, as his doctrine so closely resembles theirs.
[115] Cf. note 113 above.

our adoption has a real and special relation to this Second Person.

Latin thought, generally speaking, seems more concerned to make a clear-cut distinction between Christ and Christians in the economy of salvation, and to regard what is found in Christians only to the extent that it is really in them. This is undoubtedly a legitimate tendency and a necessary undertaking and a providential mission; but it does not greatly help us to perceive the bond existing between the adoptive sonship of Christians and the literal sonship of the Son. Hence it provides us with fewer texts—with the exception of Augustine who, as always, occupies a place apart.

As we come to Augustine, we must begin by referring to an idea he frequently mentions on the subject of grace. The grace possessed by Christians is a derivation of the unique grace which the hypostatic union with the Son has conferred on our head. Consequently the predestination and adoption of Christians is seen to be in a relation of vital continuity and organic union with Christ's eternal sonship.[116] The idea is most instructive; it anticipates what the School, following in the footsteps of the holy doctor, will have to say about grace in connection with the incarnate Word. However, we shall not tarry over it, for he himself does not make much of it, and besides he has far better things to say elsewhere on the point that interests us.

What St. Augustine teaches better than anyone else is the living, interior, and, as we should say today, psychological unity that brings Christians and Christ together in a single organism, a single man, a single Christ. And here his testimony becomes particularly valuable for our present purpose, for he adds: and a single Son.

Since we are He [117] and He is we,[118] and since we belong to Christ [119] and are Christ,[120] we must have His Father as our Father [121]

---

[116] "God calls many to be His sons, in order to make them members of His only-begotten, predestined Son"; De praedestinatione sanctorum, 30, 31. The same thought occurs in De bono perseverantiae, 24 (PL, XLIV, 981 ff.; XLV, 1033).

[117] St. Augustine represents Jesus Christ as saying: "I sanctify them in Myself, because they too are I"; In Ioan., CVIII (PL, XXXV, 1916), where the thought is repeated three times.

[118] "And we are He"; Sermo 133, 8 (PL, XXXVIII, 742).

[119] "We pertain to Christ"; Sermo 144 (PL, XXXVIII, 790). "We ought not to say that we are strangers to Christ, whose members we are, and we ought not to regard ourselves as a different person"; In Ps. 54 (PL, XXXVI, 629).

[120] In Ps. 26 (PL, XXXVI, 200); In Ioan., XXI (PL, XXXV, 1568).

[121] In Ioan., LXXV (PL, XXXV, 1829).

through the action of the same Spirit [122] who has brought about the birth of the Son in our midst. For the incarnation of the Word who is the Son continues on in the mystical body through the Spirit. "The Word incarnate is called the nuptials, for in the man who is assumed the Church is joined to God.[123] . . . In this man, the Church also is assumed by the Word." [124]

All mankind has been assumed in the single human nature that was assumed. This is just what St. Hilary had said when he spoke of the sacrament of our assumption in the Word. "That one man is assumed, whose head is Christ . . . he is the one assumed. He is not outside us; we are in His members. . . . Let us abide in Him and be assumed; let us abide in Him and be the elect." [125]

Assumed in Him who is the Son, we also shall be sons, each one in his own way. "We are called God's sons, but He is God's Son in a different sense.[126] . . . He is the only Son, we are many. He is one, we are one in Him. He is born, we are adopted. He is the Son by nature, begotten from eternity; we are made sons by grace in time." [127]

Accordingly there is a difference, yet union and unity. The two sonships become one in Him who is the source of everything. "In the Lord, therefore, redeemed as we are by His blood and washed clean by Him, we are sons and are the Son; for though we are many, we are one in Him." [128]

We are "members of the only-begotten Son of God." [129] The unity we have in Him and with Him is so close that, to love the Son completely, God must love us along with Him.[130] And on our side, to love God and the Son with all our heart, we must love those who, being His members, make up His fullness.

For God's sons are the body of God's only-begotten Son; and since He is the head and we are the members, the Son of God is one.[131]

[122] *Sermo* 71, 28 (*PL*, XXXVIII, 461).
[123] *Quaestionum Evangeliorum*, Lib. I, 31 (*PL*, XXXV, 1329).
[124] *In Ps.* 4 (*PL*, XXXVI, 77).
[125] *In Ps.* 64, 7 (*PL*, XXXVI, 779).
[126] *In Ps.* 88, 7 (*PL*, XXXVII, 1124).
[127] *Ibid.* Cf. the famous *Epist.* 140, 7, 9–12 (*PL*, XXXIII, 540–43).
[128] *In Ps.* 123 (*PL*, XXXVII, 1634).
[129] *In Ioan.*, CX, CXI (*PL*, XXXV, 1923, 1924, 1929).
[130] *Ibid.*, 1929.
[131] *In epist. ad Parthos*, X (*PL*, XXXV, 2055).

Therefore he who loves the sons of God, loves the Son of God; and he who loves the Son of God loves the Father. Nor can anyone love the Father unless he loves the Son; and whoever loves the Son, loves also the sons of God. Which sons of God? The members of the Son of God.[132]

Here we have clearly marked out for us the relation between vocation to grace and the life of the Trinity. The saint will come back to this point. But he continues: "By loving, a man becomes a member; and by love he fits into the structure of Christ's body; and so there will be one Christ loving Himself." [133]

This one Christ who loves Himself wholeheartedly is not precisely the whole of mankind, but is rather mankind joined in the incarnate Word to the Trinity: "If you love your brother, can it be that you love your brother but do not love Christ? How can this be, if you love Christ's members? Therefore, when you love Christ's members you love Christ; when you love Christ, you love the Son of God; and when you love the Son of God you also love the Father. Thus love cannot be divided." [134] Charity cannot permit dissensions, because the unity which God has in His indivisible Trinity does not permit them.

Choose the object of your love; the rest will follow. Perhaps you say: I love God alone, God the Father. You are wrong; if you really love, you do not love the Father alone; no, if you love the Father, you also love the Son. Very well, you may reply, I love the Father and I love the Son. But I love only God the Father and God the Son, our Lord Jesus Christ who ascended into heaven and sits at the right hand of the Father, the Word by whom all things were made, the Word who became flesh and dwelt among us; I love no one else. You err; for if you love Him, the head, you also love the members; and if you do not love the members, you do not love the head either.

Let no one bring in a distinction between love and love, for love is of this nature: as it is a joining together in one, it makes one and, as it were, fuses together everything embraced by it. Take some gold, melt the whole mass, and a single ingot comes forth.[135]

Thus the quality of the adopted son appears clearly in the perspective of real sonship. St. Augustine speaks of it as though he did not differentiate it from incorporation into Christ, the Son.

[132] *Ibid.*
[133] *Ibid.*
[134] *Ibid.*
[135] *Ibid.*

Many other Latin authors could be quoted. But we shall mention only one more, who cannot on any account be omitted, St. Thomas Aquinas.

Two series of texts on this subject can be gathered. In the first series, divine adoption is viewed as a certain greatness which God confers on the soul, whereby the soul receives, in a second birth, a likeness to the divine nature and a right to an eternal inheritance. This likeness and right are the characteristic notes of divine sonship and impart the quality of adoptive sons.[136] The donation is made by the entire Trinity. If we wish to give this doctrine a name, we may call it the juridical conception of divine adoption. It contains nothing that is especially mysterious or properly Christian, and does not fully exploit the great dogmas of the faith. In the second series of texts, divine adoption is shown to stand in special relation with the person of the Son; it is a participation in the Son. We may call this the theological or mystical or Trinitarian conception of divine adoption. The texts of the first series are more firmly linked to the abstract chain of theological conclusions, and occupy a more definite place, in the saint's speculative synthesis. As for the texts of the second series, we should be inclined to say that they have a more authentic doctrinal sound and that they fit in better with the great lines of tradition. But the reader may judge for himself. In general, these texts make an express appeal to Scripture, particularly to the words: "Whom He foreknew, He also predestinated to be made conformable to the image of His Son" (Rom. 8:29). However, as we hope to show, there is no opposition between the two series.

The texts of the first series ordinarily regard adoption from the viewpoint of the act producing it; the term that recurs again and again is *adoptare*. "Although the act of begetting in God is proper to the person of the Father, the production of any effect in creation is common to the whole Trinity, by reason of the unity of the divine nature; for, where the nature is one, power and action must also be one. . . . And therefore the adopting [*adoptare*] of men as sons of God pertains to the whole Trinity." [137]

According to its various aspects, the action is attributed to different persons; but in this case we have only appropriations. "Al-

[136] This reasoning is more developed in the early works than in the later; compare *In III Sent.*, d. 10, q. 2, a. 1, sol. 1 with the *Summa*, IIa IIae, q. 45, a. 6 et ad 1; q. 120, a. 1; IIIa, q. 23; q. 50, a. 2.

[137] *Summa*, IIIa, q. 23, a. 2; cf. *In III Sent.*, d. 10, q. 2, a. 1, sol. 2.

though adoption is common to the whole Trinity, it is appropriated to the Father as its author, to the Son as its exemplar, and to the Holy Spirit as imprinting on us a likeness of this exemplar." [138]

The list could be drawn out indefinitely. Whole pages of St. Thomas, of all the Scholastics, and of many Fathers could be adduced, all repeating the same doctrine, that adoption is a work *ad extra*, equally effected by the three divine persons. But what purpose would be served by such a heaping-up of testimonies? This detail of doctrine is quite familiar, and the little we have given is enough to recall to mind with sufficient emphasis what everyone knows. This view undoubtedly stands in contrast with the passages assembled on preceding pages; we may say that it is the antithesis following the thesis.

But this series of texts is not the only one at hand; St. Thomas himself provides us with another that is rich in many passages designed to show that adoptive sonship is closely related to literal sonship. Indeed, we must add—and the point is of great interest —that no other scholastic of note, so far as we are aware, has such a profusion of strong affirmations on this subject. Let us glance at several examples. "Adoptive sons are made to the likeness of the natural Son." [139] "The adoption of sons is brought about by a certain conformity of likeness to the natural Son of God." [140] "As a certain likeness of the divine goodness is conferred on all creatures by the act of creation, so a likeness of natural sonship is conferred by the act of adoption." [141]

The resemblance is produced in the soul by the Spirit.[142] Indeed, we have something more than a likeness; we have a participation, as the saint says, employing an idea he is fond of repeating in his later works. "Adoptive sonship is a certain participated likeness of natural sonship." [143] Accordingly, "since we have adoption mainly from the Son," [144] this adoption can come to us only through the

[138] *Ibid.*, ad 3.
[139] *Summa.* IIIa, q.39, a.8 ad 3.
[140] *Ibid.*, q.45, a.4.
[141] *Ibid.*, q.23, a.1 ad 2. See also Ia, q.33, a.3 et ad 1 et 2; IIa IIae, q.45, a.6 ad 1; IIIa, q.32, a.3 ad 2; q.43 ad 6; *In I Sent.*, d.16, q.1, a.3; *In III Sent.*, d.10, q.3, sol. 3; *In Ioannem expositio*, cap. 1, lect. 6; *Compendium of Theology*, p. 240, Part I, chap. 214.
[142] *Ad Rom.*, cap. 8, lect. 3; *Ad Gal.*, cap. 8, lect. 3.
[143] *Summa*, IIIa, q.3, a.5 ad 2.
[144] *Ad Rom.*, cap. 8, lect. 3.

Son and in the Son. "We are made adopted sons of God through Him who is the only-begotten Son of God by nature." [145] "The Holy Spirit makes us sons of God because He is the Spirit of the Son of God." [146]

To become sons in Him who is the Son, is the consummation of God's designs for us and of our predestination.

"Whom He foreknew, He also predestinated to be made conformable to the image of His Son" (Rom. 8:29). This conformity is nothing else than the adoption of sons. He who is adopted as a son of God is made conformable to His true Son: first, by the right of the inheritance shared, . . . secondly, by participating in the Son's brightness; for He is begotten by the Father as the brightness of His glory. And therefore, by enlightening the saints with the light of wisdom and glory, He makes them conformable to Himself.

"That He might be the first-born among many brethren" (Rom. 8:29). God wished to share His natural goodness with others by giving them a likeness of His goodness; for He is not only good but the Author of goodness. Similarly the Son of God wished to communicate a likeness of His sonship to others, so that He might be, not only the Son, but also the first-born among sons.[147]

St. Thomas expresses his thought even more strongly in his commentary on the Epistle to the Galatians:

"You are all the children of God by faith" (Gal. 3:26). Faith alone makes us adoptive sons of God. No one is an adopted son unless he is united to the natural Son of God and cleaves to Him. For faith makes us sons in Christ Jesus.[148]

This is why the Epistle says: "by faith in Christ Jesus"; and the Angelic Doctor comments: "That is: you are sons of God through Jesus Christ. . . . We are sons of God in Jesus Christ. You are adopted sons because by faith you are united to Christ who is the natural Son of God." [149] "And this adoption is especially associated with Christ, because we cannot be adoptive sons unless we are conformed to the natural Son. . . . Through the natural Son of God

[145] *Compendium of Theology*, p. 319, Part II, chap. 5.
[146] *Contra Gent.*, IV, 24.
[147] *Ad Rom.*, cap. 8, lect. 6.
[148] *Ad Gal.*, cap. 3, lect. 9.
[149] *Ibid.*

we are made adoptive sons according to grace through Christ." [150]

In truth, the idea expressed in these passages is exactly the same as that expressed in Scripture and the Fathers; it is the idea of adoptive sonship as a sharing in the strict sonship of Christ. This idea has survived. To show that this is so, we should like to quote a more recent document that may serve as an exposition of the ordinary teaching current in the Church on the subject. We refer to a section of the draft *De doctrina catholica* which we have already made use of several times. The selection deals with grace and good works. Adoption is the topic under discussion, and it is connected with Christ's sonship in a union that is close though not clearly defined. The opening lines set the tone.

God chose us in Christ Jesus before the foundation of the world and predestined us to be made conformable to the image of His Son, so that He might be the first-born among many brethren. Therefore the Father has given us this charity that, born of God, we might be called and might be the sons of God. By this adoption of sons we have restored to us that fellowship with the divine nature which is presently begun through grace and will one day be consummated in glory. Anointed and consecrated by the Son's Spirit, whom God has sent into our hearts, we are made a temple of the divine Majesty, in which the Most Holy Trinity deigns to dwell and to communicate itself to our soul, as Christ our Lord says: "If any one love Me, he will keep My word, and My Father will love him, and We will come to him and will make Our abode with him" (John 14:23).[151]

This eminent gift is again described a little farther on in the same chapter, in connection with the good works it enables us to perform.

These good works, which are performed with prevenient, concomitant, and consequent grace, do not avail for meriting eternal life without that gift of holiness by which the just are associated with Christ as members with the head, and as sons by grace with the natural Son of God. For our Lord says: "As the branch cannot bear fruit of itself, unless it abide in the vine, so neither can you, unless you abide in Me" (John 15:4); and the Apostle teaches: "And if sons, heirs also; heirs indeed of God, and joint-heirs with Christ" (Rom. 8:17).[152]

[150] *Ibid.*, cap. 4, lect. 2. Cf. lect. 3: through the Holy Spirit "we are joined to Christ, and are thereby adopted as God's sons."

[151] Mansi, *Amplissima collectio conciliorum*, LIII, 292; cf. 173, 234.

[152] *Ibid.*, 293.

"The just are associated with Christ as members with the head, and as sons by grace with the natural Son." This is what the documents of our faith say and repeat at every turn. In the Son we are sons, *filii in Filio*.

IV. THEOLOGICAL THEORY

1. **Introduction: the question and the method of solution.** These testimonies of Scripture and tradition raise a problem. How are we to conceive the existence of a special and real relation of adoptive sons with the true Son and, through Him, with the Father and the Spirit, without disregarding the solidly established principle of theology that divine works *ad extra* are common to the three divine persons? *In divinis omnia sunt unum ubi non obstat relationis oppositio*.[153]

In our opinion, scholastic theologians have not solved this problem, at least so far as we know, with the success that has crowned their efforts in so many other lines of investigation. They were not fully at home with the doctrine of the mystical body; and this is the doctrine that yields and even imposes the solution. If we study the Incarnation and reflect how it sanctifies the assumed human nature and the whole human race, we shall discover the relation it establishes between men and the divine persons.

2. **The subsistence of Christ's humanity in the Son.** The Incarnation can be considered from two points of view: as an action that produces a result and as the result produced by the action: *quasi in fieri* and *quasi in facto esse*.[154] In other words, we may regard it in its principle and in its term. This term, furthermore, can be the integral, total term, that is, the God-man as assuming the human nature, or else it can be the human nature as assumed and as intrinsically elevated by the assumption. This distinction between the action and the result will govern the exposition.[155]

Regarded as an action, the Incarnation is common to the three divine persons. It is a work *ad extra*, and every such work is common to the Three. However we shall have to come back to this assertion

[153] Council of Florence, *Decretum pro Iacobitis* (Denz., 703).

[154] Cf. St. Thomas, *Summa*, IIIa, q.2, a.8: "Assumption implies becoming (*sicut in fieri*), whereas union implies having become (*sicut in facto esse*)."

[155] Cf. F. M. Catherinet, "La Sainte Trinité et notre filiation adoptive," *Vie spirituelle*, XXXIX (1934), 113.

and clarify it; that task we reserve for the next chapter. For the moment, the best thing is to leave it as it stands.

But the Incarnation regarded in its term and result, the union of a human nature with a divine person, belongs strictly to the Son. The three divine persons have incarnated; the Second alone is incarnate. This result, however, is not an activity but a way of existing, the way of existing that is realized in the assumed humanity and that causes the humanity to subsist in the Word and accordingly adapts it to such subsistence.

A passage from the *De fide catholica* will help to fix this distinction. We have only to read the selection to perceive that it opens the door to the distinction in question and to the consequences that can flow therefrom.

> As there is one deity, nature, and substance in the three divine persons, so there is one indivisible operation by which the Most Holy Trinity establishes, disposes, and governs all things outside it. For the divine persons act *ad extra*, not individually, but so far as in their essence, will, and power they are one God, one source of all things.
>
> If anyone should maintain that creation or any other action of God that terminates in creatures, is proper to one divine person in such a way as not to be one, undivided, and common to all of them, let him be anathema.[156]

We observe that the doctrine concerns such of God's actions as terminate in creatures, *ad extra*. Consequently it does not touch something else that is quite different from an operation, especially an operation *ad extra*. Nothing is said about a subsistence in one of the divine persons *ad intra* or about the possible result of such subsistence, understanding this not of a result produced *ad extra*, but, if the case is verified, of a manner of existing that pertains exclusively to subsistence in one divine person *ad intra*.

Now the man Jesus Christ is the Son, and no one else than the Son; He is not the Father or the Spirit. This is the very essence of Christian teaching. Jesus Christ is literally the Son. We beg pardon for our insistence; but we believe that insistence is indispensable, just as we found it indispensable to insist, in an earlier chapter, on the reality of the union between the two natures. As truly as this man is God, He is the Son. And He is the Son, not by

[156] Chapter 1 and canon 1, 4; Mansi, *Amplissima collectio conciliorum*, LIII, 294, 298.

any mere figure of speech or by juridical imputation, not by a kind of possession or a grant of nobility, not by virtue of a simple decree or a contract of association.[157] He is the Son simply because He is truly and ontologically the Son. The proposition has to be taken in its full, realistic, and mysterious sense; otherwise the whole of Christianity vanishes like a mist. The pages to follow are based exclusively on this foundation.

Something more has to be said: Christ is God by being the Son. The truth is that He is God because He is the Son, not that He is the Son because He is God. And this too is essential to Christian faith; otherwise we should have to say that the Incarnation was accomplished in the divine nature rather than in a divine person, and consequently that all three persons became incarnate. Accordingly the God-man is truly and exclusively the Son. But the Son exists only in that relation to the Father which is the eternal, passive generation, and in that relation to the Spirit, which is active co-spiration. He exists only in the Trinity and with the Trinity. Therefore the God-man is God and is Himself only in the Trinity.

A conclusion universal in its bearing results from this truth. When the Incarnation took place, the Son as Son, God as revealed in the mystery of the Trinity, was given to a creature before God as considered in His nature was thus given; this priority is manifestly logical and not chronological. In other words, the God of the Incarnation is God as attained by faith alone, rather than God as known analogically by our unaided intellect. Therefore the Incarnation is a communication of the Godhead as Trinity rather than as simple Godhead, and the Christian as Christian knows God because he knows the Trinity, not vice versa; he knows God through the Son in the Father and the Spirit, and not in the reflection of God in the things he may reason about; he knows the living God in His life, and not merely the God of the philosophers. Of course this supernatural knowledge enables him to possess his natural knowledge of God more securely.

From the instant the Son was made flesh, the human race has included an individual who was a divine person, one whose existence is in relation to the other two divine persons. Beginning with this instant an instrumental cause of redemption, sanctification, and

[157] Council of Ephesus, *Anathematismi* 3, 8; Second Council of Constantinople, canons 4, 5 (Denz., 115, 120, 216, 217).

divinization has been within mankind and will always belong to mankind. The action of this cause was the action of the Word and of absolutely no one else than the Word. A single principle of eternal, theandric life has appeared in the midst of mankind, and this principle was the Son of God.

For the whole of Christianity contains Christ; the whole of humanity that is now regenerated contains Christ. It contains Him, not as a part properly so called, but as the source of its supernatural life, as the one through whom the whole "body" lives. And Christ is the Son. Through the Incarnation, therefore, humanity and Christianity contain the Son.

Such is Christianity in its source; must we not conceive that it remains the same throughout its growth? Must we not say that Christianity is "filial," if we may use the expression, and also Trinitarian? It is filial; that is, it has an essential and intimate relation to the Son, for Christ is its source and ultimate basis. It is also Trinitarian, for it is the result of a communication of the Trinity and is knowable only in function of the Trinity. The pages that follow will bring out this truth more clearly.

When we said, some lines above, that this communication of God was inaugurated at the instant of the Incarnation, we did not mean to imply that it did not take place before. For, as we mentioned earlier, from the time of the Fall mankind was intrinsically constituted the race of Christ by the divine promise, and by that very fact was made the race of the Son. If God, in His original creative plan, wished mankind to be the object of His infinite mercy in Christ, He thereby also wished it to be so in the Son.

If this is the case, God gave to the work at its inception a relation to the Trinity in the Word, and consequently faith and the supernatural life had a relation to the Trinity. Of course this was not known explicitly. Indeed, was it even known that there was a Son of God in the strict sense and that the Messias was to be God? But men believed in the one who was to come from God, and through this envoy, although men were unaware of it, faith bore on the Trinity. St. Gregory of Nazianzus says: "This is the way the matter stands: the Old Testament announced the Father clearly and the Son obscurely. The New Testament has openly shown us the Son and has given us indications of the divinity of the Spirit. But now the Spirit dwells in our midst and makes Himself known more clearly." [158]

For, as St. Gregory goes on to explain, men had to be prepared by gradual stages for a complete revelation. And in fact, progress in the revelation of this truth is manifest. Indeed, we should even be inclined to submit that the development is slower than St. Gregory suggests, and that the point of departure is more remote. For, to tell the truth, the Old Testament did not reveal the Father as Father; otherwise it would have had to reveal the Son. But we must recall that for the Greek Fathers, including St. Gregory, the word "Father" also designated God in general; and in this sense the Old Testament proclaims Him clearly. Since the object of faith is the living God, the mystery of God's interior life, which is the mystery of the Trinity, was implicitly contained in it. But Christ, who already numbered just men among His members, guided their human faith, which was as yet very indecisive in their minds, to the inner life of God.

3. **The resulting "filial" perfection.** Such, then, was the gift of the Trinity in Christ. Up to now we have considered nothing but its exterior aspect; we must go on to see how, in laying hold of the sacred humanity, it perfected that humanity interiorly.

God, who is Being, gives Himself by conferring being, not by causing this man to possess God but—we are inevitably led back to this point—by causing this man to "be" truly God.

Therefore let us study the Savior's human nature. A previous chapter showed that the subsistential amelioration which the sacred humanity receives from its hypostatic union with the Godhead requires a corresponding amelioration that is accidental and intrinsic to it and that divinizes it in itself, inasmuch as it is the human nature of God.

We perceive by now that Christ's human nature is united to the Godhead because it is united to the Second Person. The subsistential amelioration is primarily the dignity of subsisting in this divine person, and consequently the accidental amelioration it requires and evokes must be a perfection that corresponds to subsistence in the Son; it must be a "filial" amelioration.

[158] St. Gregory of Nazianzus, *Oratio theologica*, V, 26 (PG, XXXVI, 161).

To be literally and strictly the Son is something that concerns the subsistence, the personality which the sacred humanity receives, and not its nature. But we think that the fact of possessing such a subsistence must call forth a correlative amelioration and elevation in the human nature that receives this subsistence. Clearly, this elevation is not and cannot be the Son Himself or the Son's subsistence, for the Son is not a factor of the human nature; yet it is an adaptation of the nature to the subsistence thus received, an adaptation caused and required by this subsistence, hence a "filial" adaptation.

When a single word of God is launched forth into the void, it causes the whole universe to rise up in response; and the universe is exactly as God's word summons it to be. Can we suppose that nothing is produced when the very Word and Son gives Himself completely and forever to a creature? To become the human nature of the Son, must not the sacred humanity become "filial"? The perfection bestowed on that human nature is designed to fit it to be the Son's humanity, to equip it to act in a way that is becoming to the Son while yet acting in accordance with its own nature; how could such a perfection be other than "filial"? The divinization conferred on the human nature is produced exclusively by its union with God, which is exclusively a union with the Son; how could that divinization fail to be a relation to the Son and hence "filial"?

On the side of this human nature, the hypostatic union is a relation of personal unity with the Son alone. The immediate and real foundation of this relation in the humanity must be something that corresponds to the Son alone. Otherwise the union of the human nature with the Son alone would be purely extrinsic. This foundation is the "drawing to the Word" (*tractio ad Verbum*), the "passive conjunction with the Word" (*coniunctio passiva ad Verbum*), and is something that truly resides in the human nature. Consequently it must be a perfecting of the human nature, a new way of existing that the human nature takes on. In any case, this new way of existing is referred to the Son and is "filial."

The union of the sacred humanity with the person of the Son is neither the Son Himself nor the Godhead. As St. Thomas says, it is something pertaining to the humanity which is united to the Son. "The union implies a relation between the divine nature and the human nature, according as they come together in one person; but every relation that begins in time is caused by some change." [159] Either this change (*mutatio*) has no meaning, or else it is relative to the Son alone and is "filial."

St. John says, in a text previously quoted,[160] that the humanity assumed by the Word appeared resplendent with glory, and that this was a glory which such a Son ought to receive from such a Father. Is not this the same as saying that it was a "filial" glory?

What this "filial" character may be, can hardly be stated with precision. And that is understandable; is it easy to explain what the Son Himself is and how He was begotten? The first point to note is that this manner of filial existence, which is an adaptation to the union with the Son and the formal effect of subsistence in the Son, can be neither grasped nor explained except in terms of the Son. When men speak of Him, they are constrained to borrow metaphors from affairs that take place among them, in family life, between a father and his children. These images are as accurate as they can be in such matters, and they are authentic images suggested by God Himself. But they are no more than images. The prototype, the model imparting whatever value the imitation may have, is not human sonship but the eternal sonship of the Only-begotten. Jesus has given us an example of the way in which a human nature can express this sonship through the power of God. If we study His actions as recounted in the Gospel, especially if we meditate, in the light of His Spirit, on the dispositions of His heart and try to realize in ourselves the attitude of soul existing in Him, we can form some notion of what is involved in a human nature of the Son.

In the Trinity, the Son is a subsistent relation that refers the Second Person to the Father and the Spirit, just as the Father and the Spirit have reference to the Son. Therefore the "filial" character in the assumed humanity will be a participation of the relation to the Father and the Spirit. It will be a filial attitude, a reception of life, an attitude of envoy and of one who receives, a possession of the Spirit, an assurance of being led by Him and of being able to give Him, an interior and exterior life unfolding in a mission that is the mission of the Son in the mission of the Spirit.

This is a relative entity, indeed; but we should not think of it as we think of relative entities found on our earth, wholly superficial

[159] *Summa*, IIIa, q. 2, a. 8.
[160] John 1:14.

and almost external as they are. The relations implied in the sonship of the Word are identical with the infinity of being that is the Godhead; they express the ultimate depths of being. The "filial" character we are speaking about is relative in a way that calls these immensities to mind, because it is an adaptation to them and because, in its human fashion—for it is something human—it bears the stamp of greatness, since it is the pure effect of union with divine majesty.

To tell the truth, however, it is not so much a relation as an intrinsic union that conforms the human nature to the relations that are in Christ and the Son. It is that by which this particular humanity becomes the humanity of the subsistent relation that is the Word.

Nothing can be added to the relations that constitute the Trinity; there is nothing in the Blessed Trinity except them, and they are eternally unalterable. But one of these relations becomes the subsistence of a human nature, and in consequence this human nature is made to form a single person with it. Through the hypostatic union, therefore, this human nature has the same relations as the Second Person has. For the splendid simplicity of God cannot be tampered with; a reduced model of the Trinity, drawn to the scale of human convenience, is absurd and impossible. The sacred humanity possesses, in the Word, all the relations of the Word.

But the point to be stressed here is that, if the human nature possesses these relations because they are possessed by the Word, which is its person, it must be made subsistent in the Word and therefore must be subsistent in these relations. To possess these relations, the human nature must undergo a change; and this change is the effect wrought in the human nature by the hypostatic union and the adaptation of the human nature to this union.

This internal perfecting is not devoid of analogy with the quality of adoptive sonship that is given to Christians, as we shall see presently. It contains all that is implied in this quality, and in a far higher way. Essentially, however, it is not an adoption. For its essence consists in fitting this man who is Christ to be strictly and truly the only Son of God; hence it renders Him incapable of being an adopted son.

The supernatural excellence required for constituting adoptive sonship is not lacking; the perfection in question includes all the gifts, and much more besides, which adoptive sonship confers on us. But the subsistence proper to the assumed humanity absolutely precludes adoption. The only person who subsists in Christ is the only-begotten Son.

The case is different as regards divinization and grace. The perfection conferred by the hypostatic union is an attribute of nature, and the fact that the person in Christ is strictly God does not prevent the divinization of His human nature but on the contrary requires it. Sonship is a characteristic of the person; everything "filial" that the human nature can have, unites the nature to the sonship of the Son, so that Christ is exclusively the person of the Son by nature, and is not in any sense an adoptive son.

This observation has its own importance for refuting the adoptionist heresy in all its forms as well as the theological errors and rash opinions attaching to it. As truly as Christ is but one person, so also He is no one but the only-begotten Son. The same remark has the further value of preparing the way for the deductions to follow. This character that is found in Christ is shared by all Christians by their incorporation into this Man who is the Son. In order that this participation may impart to them their true character of sons and may produce in them a real adoption, that is, a union, wrought by grace, with Christ's literal sonship, this trebly holy Man must in all truth be the Son.

The "filial" character we are speaking of must first reside in what theology calls the grace of union that is found in the sacred humanity. The formula can bear several meanings; here we take it to mean the humanity's possession of the Son's personality in unity of hypostasis. This is an absolute consecration, a dignity flowing directly from the dignity of the Word.

However, since this grace of union is the principle that requires and produces the second grace of Christ known to theology, that is, grace in the ordinary sense of the word, or habitual grace and the internal, individual sanctification of the assumed humanity, this sanctification and grace, to be adapted to the grace of union, must likewise be "filial." As St. Thomas shows, the habitual grace possessed by Christ is the simple effect of the union and is "natural" to Christ precisely because He is the Word and the true Son of the Father.[161] Must it not, therefore, be a grace such as is fitting for

[161] *Summa*, IIIa, q.2, a.12 et ad 3; q.6, a.6.

Him who is the Son, a "filial" grace? "And we saw His glory, the glory as it were of the Only-begotten of the Father, full of grace" (John 1:14).

We have to go farther and say the same of the third grace which, according to theology, is found in Christ, the grace of headship. For this is nothing else than the habitual grace of Christ, so far as it is made supereminent and superabundant by the grace of union.[162] Since the grace of union and Christ's habitual grace are essentially "filial," the grace of headship must likewise be such. Accordingly Christ will influence the lives of Christians by a grace that is essentially "filial"; to all appearances, the grace thus flowing into us through our union and vital continuity with Christ will also be filial. But we shall take up this question later.[163]

If we contemplate the Incarnation, we can dimly perceive that a "filial" character of this sort is not impossible in a creature; anything that would remove impossibility from the one would remove impossibility from the other. What removes impossibility in the creature's case is, as we said above, the fact that creatures are only derived beings, whereas God is pure Being and the archetype of all being; consequently nothing is found in creatures that opposes or can oppose God's action, and therefore union with God can but perfect them according to their nature. What removes impossibility in the case of the Incarnation is the fact that the Son, even as Son, is also pure Being and the Creator and archetype of all being; indeed, God has created everything through Him, and the transcendent archetype of all things is found in Him. "Since God understands Himself and all things in one act, His one Word is expressive not only of the Father but also of creatures." [164]

Consequently nothing in any finite being is in any way opposed to God. Hence a finite nature—or at any rate a spiritual nature, for only such a nature is truly a whole—can bear the entire weight of the union and can be adapted to this union, without anything in it being destroyed or altered to the slightest degree. On the contrary, the creature will realize itself more perfectly according to its own type; if we may be allowed the expression, it will be supernaturally natural.

[162] Cf. St. Thomas, *Summa*, IIIa, q.8, a.5.
[163] Cf. *infra*, p. 369.
[164] St. Thomas, *Summa*, Ia, q.34, a.3; q.37, a.2 ad 3.

We should note that the amelioration in question is not a complete entity; it exists only through the power and perpetual support of the Son's personality which is given to the assumed humanity. It is the expression, in the humanity and its divinization, of the union with the Word from which this divinization flows; here we can only repeat, and with greater reason, what we have said in the same order of ideas about grace and divinization.

On this subject the Scholastics employ a comparison that is very apt, provided it is conceived in the way they conceived it, without complicating the issue with modern physical theories. They say that the illumination of the air by the sun, by which everything glows with light during the daytime, is a property of the air and is intrinsic to the air. But it exists only when the air is in contact with the sun and is, as it were, penetrated by the sun. The illumination in the air is a sort of diminished continuation and participation of the sun's illumination; it is, so to say, the brilliance of the sun as realized and expressed by the air in its own way. Although the brilliance belongs to the air, it is unceasingly caused by the sun, through a continuous self-communication.

Such is the "filial" perfection we are attributing to the humanity of Christ; it is the continuation in the human nature, adapted to the nature's mode of existence, of what the Son is in Himself. God alone, with the full efficaciousness of action proper to Him, unites this human nature to the only-begotten Son; and this union introduces the perfection in question, or rather necessarily calls it forth and sustains it.

It is a prolongation, continuation, derivation, participation of strict sonship; it is true and efficacious union; to be one with the Word is certainly not nothing. It is a new way of existing which fits the human nature for the union and is sustained by the union, and is impossible without the union of which it is but the expression in the assumed nature. It is a manner of being that makes this particular humanity the humanity of the Word; a manner of being, therefore, that has its cause in the Godhead alone and its internal determining principle in the person of the Word alone, but that is expressed as a new thing, as a reality truly produced in an ennobling and perfecting of the assumed humanity, to constitute it intrinsically as *tracta ad Verbum*. It is accordingly a special type of being, as we said in an earlier chapter and as we shall explain more fully later.

It exists only in the union, through the union, for the union; it is in truth an "entity of union."

All this is primarily verified in the sacred humanity of Christ; our next step is to extend it to all humanity, so far as we may. We must apply to the whole Christ what we have said of the individual Christ. Here more than anywhere else our argumentation is based on the close, supernatural, and very perfect union existing between Christ and Christians. This union does not prevent Christians from being distinct persons; but it does prevent them from being separated persons.

The Son alone among the divine persons has taken a physical body. Consequently He alone has taken a mystical body, for the latter is but a prolongation of the former. Therefore the mystical body is the body of the Son, not of the Father or the Spirit. The Father and the Spirit have been no less active than the Son in the production of the mystical body and its union with the Word, just as they were active in the formation of Christ's physical body and in endowing it with the hypostatic union. But the Son alone possesses the mystical body and makes it alive in Himself, in the same way as He alone possesses His physical body and gives it life, as He Himself has life from the Father.

Assuredly Christ is head of the mystical body through His human nature, and when Christians are incorporated into Him they are first incorporated into His human nature. But this human nature belongs solely to the Son and subsists solely in the Son. Union with it and incorporation into it mean union with Him who is the Son. Furthermore the sacred humanity mystically includes Christians because it is united to the Son, for it includes them because it is united to God; and it is united to God because it is united to the Son.[165] Hence Christians are truly received into union with the Son; how, then, could anyone maintain that they are not included in His sonship?

To state the case in a few words, Christians must be truly one with the Son to the same degree as they are truly one with Christ. Christ would not fully be the Son if the whole Christ, head and body, were not the Son. We have to add that, to this same degree, something "filial" must be found in them, as it is in the sacred

---

[165] On this conception of the character of headship, see *supra*, p. 242, and also what St. Thomas has to say about the *gratia capitis*, *Summa*, IIIa, q.8, a.5.

humanity of Christ. And this "filial" something has its cause and meaning in the sacred humanity's "filial" character which, in turn, has its cause and meaning in the sonship of the Son. Through the grace of the Incarnation, the Son, the assumed human nature, and the regenerated human race are all united.

The grace of divinization flows to Christians from Christ and hence from the Son. That is the constitution and essence of grace. Must it not, accordingly, be an adopting grace, a grace belonging to a son adopted in the only Son? We do not in the least deny that the usual teaching assigns a filial character to grace, for grace as ordinarily described gives a right to an eternal inheritance and confers a resemblance to the divine nature, and has also been merited by the Son. But we wish to restrict our discussion here to adoptive sonship regarded as sharing in strict sonship; this consideration excels and eclipses all other points of view.[166]

The filial character found in the sacred humanity of Christ has to be communicated to the members of Christ. We may recall what was said above: the perfection conferred on Christ's human nature, which is social, unites it supernaturally to all human natures; and since it comes from the union with God and the Son, it divinizes Christ's human nature by making it "filial." Consequently this "filial" character may be extended to all men; it is designed, by its structure, to be communicated and to express its infinity even in human nature, according to the capacity of human nature.[167]

Since men are divinized by being members of Him who is the Son, must they not have a divinization that is intrinsically related to the Son? This divinization can come only from their union with God, and they are united to God through Christ's humanity, which in turn is united to God by being united to the Son. Therefore the divinization possessed by men comes from their union with the Son, and in the Son with God. This divinization must have a "filial" character and must sanctify men by fulfilling its sole purpose, which is to make them worthy members of Him who is the Son.

Men possess this quality of sons and of divinized beings, not, like Christ, because of their persons, but because of their union through grace with the person of Christ and the Son. They are divinized by

[166] In this connection we should not overlook the texts quoted from St. Thomas on pp. 353–56.
[167] See what we have written about the grace of headship, p. 242.

grace and are sons by adoption. Yet they must be sons and must be Godlike as sons; otherwise their union with Christ and His sonship has no meaning.

As members of Christ they are members of the Son; we cannot escape this conclusion. We may and we must make distinctions; but we may admit no separation. Christ's divinity is not His humanity; person is distinct from nature, virtually in God, really in man; the person of Christ is not the person of Christians. Yet all these are united, without confusion or change but also without division or separation, not only in Christ but also, though in a different way, in the fullness of Christ which is the mystical body. Are not Christians one in Him, as He is one with the Father? If we separate them from Him, do we not rend Christ asunder? [168]

The objection may be raised that, although our adoption has a relation to strict sonship, this relation lies outside the adoption and is found in the person of Christ; consequently this relation is predicated of our adoption by a purely extrinsic denomination, according to a way of speaking that is far-fetched and open to misunderstanding. We reply that such would be the case if a body were extrinsic to its members and if life were outside the living person. If there were question of anyone else than Christ, if we were to say that all Frenchmen are emperors because Charlemagne was an emperor, our language would be pompous and absurd. But we are now dealing with the mystery of union. Branches are nothing, as branches, unless they are in the vine, and members, as members, are nothing unless they are in the body; likewise Christians are nothing unless they are in Christ, abiding in Him as He abides in them, according to the words He Himself addressed to them.[169]

There is an extrinsic aspect, certainly; all that we have, we have in Him. But there are also supremely intrinsic features; Christ is more interior to us than we ourselves are; He is the source of our life, He is our head and our all.[170] Our incorporation into Him endows our personality with its most intimate and supernatural depths. We are never so much ourselves as when we are in Him, and therefore nothing is so intrinsically ours as what is ours in Him.

[168] John 17:11, 21 ff.; I Cor. 1:13.
[169] John 6:57; 15:2-7; I John 2:24-28; 3:24.
[170] John 3:15 f.; Col. 1:18; 3:3 f., 18.

This is exactly what St. Cyril of Alexandria says in the text quoted and emphasized in the preceding section. "In Him and through Him we are made sons of God both by nature and by grace: by nature, in Him alone; by participation and grace, through Him in the Spirit." [171] This is what we have been contending. Christ alone is the Son; but we are united to Him. What He is in Himself, we must likewise be, but only through Him. In one sense we are He and in another sense we are not He; we are that which, left to ourselves, we could not be; we are He, but only in Him; yet surely, as members of Christ, we are truly in Him.

On the nature of our "filial" character we must here repeat, with proper adjustments, what we said about the filial character of Christ's humanity. Our filial character is an entity of a unique and special type. It is an intrinsic reality, but exists only through another's action. It is an amelioration, a change pertaining to the absolute order and is truly inherent in the soul, although it is only the consequence of a relation, namely, of our union with Christ and the Son, and has the sole function of being the real foundation of this relation. It is a perfection that is the simple prolongation in Christ's members of the personal union with God and the Son that is fully realized in the head and that affects the members according to the measure of their union with the head.

It is something that pertains to our humanity, resides in it, and perfects it, according to the humanity's capacity. But it proceeds from the Godhead and has no other source within the human race than the Son; for the Son alone among the divine persons is a man, just as, alone among men, Christ is God. Although it is wrought by the three divine persons together, it subsists through Christ in the Son alone; and in Christ it has its "filial" character from the sonship of the Son.

We must point out that expressions of this sort are not common in theology. The reason is simply that theology, in general, hardly treats of this particular subject, as specified by us. Theology considers adoption from the viewpoint of the action that produces it, and prescinds from any question of incorporation in Christ. But we have been regarding it from the viewpoint of the state it confers and the incorporation into Christ by which it exists. Since the

---

[171] *De recta fide ad Theodosium*, 30 (*PG*, LXXVI, 1177); see the preceding section, p. 348.

object of discourse is not the same in the two cases, divergence in the formulas need cause no disquiet.

As the Fathers repeat so often, we become by grace what Christ is by nature. Christ is the Son by nature, and He is God because He is the Son. The grace we receive ought to make us sons, that is, adopted sons, who are divinized because we are adopted. Our divinization comes from our adoption, and our adoption is no less sublime than our divinization; the excellence of both is derived from that of the sonship of God the Son.

If we understand the doctrine as thus proposed, we may, in our opinion, uphold along with all theology the incontestable axiom that divine works *ad extra* are common to the Trinity, and still say, following the suggestions of Scripture and tradition, that our adoptive sonship, as a state though not as an operation, has a real relation to the Son alone. Accordingly adoption is not simply and purely *ad extra;* viewed as we have described it, it is a share in a new way of being that was inaugurated by the Incarnation.

The Incarnation essentially consists in a union between a person *ad intra* and a nature *ad extra.* Hence the new order it establishes cannot be defined simply by the opposition between *ad intra* and *ad extra.* Regarded in itself, the sacred humanity in which the Word becomes incarnate is wholly *ad extra.* But the Incarnation causes it to subsist exclusively in the Word who is *ad intra.* Through its subsistence, therefore, the humanity ceases to be something *ad extra.*

In this respect the Incarnation differs radically from creation, with a difference that amounts to contrast. This is true unless, to be sure, we envisage creation as being, in God's designs, the first step in the preparation of a human nature for the Word and hence as the remote inception of the Incarnation. In itself, creation is the production of the order *ad extra.* By creation God produces the creature in its own subsistence, outside of Himself, and gives existence to a being that is not Himself. The Incarnation, on the contrary, is the taking up of a creature into the Word *ad intra,* so that it may subsist not in itself but in Him, and that through His subsistence it may be the human nature of God. As regards the distinction between *ad intra* and *ad extra,* the direction of the two works is diametrically opposed. The first has an external terminus, the second has an internal terminus; the first causes the order *ad extra*, the second causes, not the order *ad intra*, which would be an absurd conception, but the order of that which is "interiorized," if we may use the expression; that is, the order of what, left to itself, would undoubtedly be *ad extra* but which God causes to subsist in His Word *ad intra*, and which in this sense is *ad intra*.

We beg the reader to excuse the term, "order of that which is interiorized"; we have to express these notions as best we may. But does not the expression convey, with regard to the correlatives *ad intra* and *ad extra*, what the terms "assumed" and "divinized" denote in function of the terms "assumption" and "divinity"? Is there not some advantage in having a word to designate the way of existing called forth by God when He causes something that in itself would be *ad extra* to pertain strictly to one of the divine persons *ad intra?*

This order is inaugurated and summed up in the human nature assumed by the Son of God, and has its full meaning only in the assumption of that human nature. But it includes all that is contained in the assumed humanity.

The "filial" perfection found in the assumed nature, this same perfection that is extended through adoption to the members of the sacred humanity, would be wholly *ad extra* if it constituted a complete and isolated being, such as is human nature in itself. But if it is no more than an "entity of union," an entity that exists in a nature *ad extra* only when the latter subsists in a person *ad intra*, we should be guilty of defining it by a mere part of it were we to define it from the standpoint of *ad extra*. By its very essence, it exists only by taking root in the order *ad intra* through the personality of which it is the effect. How else can we conceive it except in the union of the two, in the order of the Incarnation, as belonging to the order of the "interiorized"?

Although different words are employed, the doctrine is the same as that set forth when we were speaking of the "entity of union" and of the perfection resulting from union. This entity is found in a nature solely as a consequence of union with another being, and has the purpose of adapting it to the union, of making it internally united, and of being the foundation of the relation which arises. To perceive that the term "interiorized" automatically becomes a commentary on the term "entity of union," all we have to do is to conceive that such a union with another nature is not realized except in the union with a person *ad intra*.

Thus we men, who used to be afar off, have been made to come near; [172] we who were strangers and outsiders have been brought inside and welcomed as members of the family.[173] Such is the superabundant riches of God's grace that is given to us in the bountiful generosity He has toward us in Christ Jesus.[174] He has made us His own beloved children [175] by sanctifying us in His well-beloved Son.[176]

[172] Cf. Eph. 2:13.
[173] Cf. *ibid.*, 2:19.
[174] *Ibid.*, 2:7.
[175] *Ibid.*, 5:1.
[176] *Ibid.*, 1:6.

CHAPTER XIII

REVELATION AND THE TRINITY

I. From God to Christ

THE subject of this chapter is revelation. We wish to gain some notion of its true nature as the knowledge about the Father that is imparted to Christians through the Son.

Revelation is a manifestation of truths by God who makes them known. It is a positive intervention on the part of God who discloses truths to His creatures by means of suitable signs. It is a communication of knowledge that is securely possessed, and is expressed in a divine language. Formulas such as these are quite correct, and we desire to show how perfectly they are verified in the case of Christian revelation, the revelation that actually exists, the revelation given in Christ. This revelation is indeed phrased in formulas; but the expression of revealed truths in formulas is contained in a greater gift that is indicated and unified in the formulas and that receives in them a fullness of meaning which well brings out the central thought expressed in the preceding definitions: revelation is a divine communication of knowledge.

The imparting of formulas is a necessary, although secondary, element in the communication of knowledge,[1] because it enables Christians to know as Christians. And this communication of knowledge is itself a necessary aspect of a communication of life, for, in the case of intellectual beings, true life is also a life of the intelligence. By making Christians members of Christ, this communication of life enables them to live an eternal life in the Son.

The divine language is made up of words and signs. But these words and signs are no more than an aspect of the one great sign

---

[1] Tanquerey defines revelation as a "manifestation of truth made to us by God through a supernatural illumination of our intellect."

that is the sacrament and the revelation of God Himself; and that is the Word. It expresses in syllables what He is in His living reality. It is a sort of translation that represents the divine Word in human words; and the translation has to be made because the Word has become flesh; but it receives all its forcefulness from the Word.

When we reflect on what the Christian revelation is in itself, in its deepest meaning and unique foundation, we see that it holds together in Christ. We have formulas, a language, and a positive communication from God. All this is true, all this exists; but in Him. These factors are reducible to one another because they are reduced to Him. As He is the donation of Trinitarian life, He is also its revelation. He is the very Word made flesh, the Word that has become perceptible, the Son in whom the Father appears and in whom the Spirit dwelling among us makes Himself known.

The Father appears to men in the Son; in fact, that is everything; the whole content of revelation is contained in that, and that is Christ. This is what we are going to speak of in these pages: the Father and the Son, the Father in the Son and through the Son.

We shall not at this point treat directly and explicitly of the Spirit. Thus we shall be following the example of Jesus, who did not speak clearly of the Third Person until He was drawing near to the end of His life, if we can judge from the Gospel according to St. John.[2] The Church, likewise, did not define truths about the Paraclete until after it had defined doctrines concerning the first two persons at Nicaea and Constantinople. However, the Spirit is virtually revealed in the revelation of the Son and the Father, for the Son is not the Son except as the co-principle of the Spirit; and the Father, in giving Him all that constitutes Him as the Son, gives Him the power to be, like Himself, the principle of the Spirit, in the way that befits the Son.

In the present chapter we shall not speak expressly of the other truths of Christian revelation; they are secondary, and are implied in this essential revelation. After all, there is only one gift in the order of being, the essential and total gift, the gift of God as He is in Himself, and this gift is contained in Christ. All things else in Christianity (the Incarnation, the grace of divinization, the Church, the sacraments, and the whole supernatural order) are incalculably precious

[2] John 14:16–27; 15:26; 16:7–16.

gifts; but this is so because they are the arrival and the reception of the first and unique gift. Their goodness is its goodness; this explains why their goodness is so great, and at the same time why it adds nothing to the goodness of eternal life.

What is true in the order of being is likewise true in the order of knowledge. The essential and total gift of knowledge, the full revelation, is the gift of the first truth as it is in itself and for itself, the gift of eternal light in the flash of its own brightness, the gift of the Trinity in the Word. *Toti infinito, et infinito prout est in se, non fit additio:* no addition to this infinity and absolute primacy is conceivable; and this infinity of revelation is made wholly in Christ, the incarnate Word. All the rest of Christian revelation, including Christology and ecclesiology, is truly an illuminating grace and a splendid light; not, however, because it adds any brilliance to what is light itself, but because it enables man to see this light.

A revelation that had as its object the Trinity alone would undoubtedly be full of light. But this light would be too pure to be perceptible to our eyes; to see the rays of the sun we need the dust particles floating in the air. The same is true of life and existence: the Trinity has always been eternal life. It does not become more so in Christ, the Church, and the sacraments; but through them it becomes eternal life for us.

The reason for this is that revelation is truly revelation only when it makes the acquisition of real knowledge possible for the intended recipient. Knowledge that would have as its object absolutely nothing else than the Trinity is strictly impossible for man, whether on earth or in heaven. Human knowledge has to be human knowledge even when it is evoked by God; and man can know absolutely nothing unless in the act of knowing something else he also knows himself. Such self-knowledge may be quite confused or even implicit, but it is strictly indispensable; and it has to be more perfect and explicit in proportion as the knowledge of another object becomes more perfect, more intimately present, and more vivid in the knower.

But we have already discussed this subject; neither man nor any other being can know anything unless he is aware, at least to some slight extent, that he knows, that is, unless he knows that he knows, that is, again, unless he knows himself. Were he to be entirely unaware of himself, he would be ignorant of himself as a knowing being, and hence he would be unaware of his knowledge, which in that case would not differ at all from ignorance.

Therefore, if a man is to know the Trinity, he must also know himself as knowing it, and must also be aware of the knowledge he has of it. All this is implied in the whole of Christian dogma, no part of which is intelligible if detached from the whole. Consequently the whole of dogma has to be known in order that the Trinity may be known. And therefore, if the Trinity is to be known with the full perfection possible for dogmatic knowledge of a revealed truth, the whole of dogma has to be known with like perfection.

Accordingly we are justified in studying the whole of revelation by concentrating on the revelation of the Trinity, and even by restricting our study to the revelation of the Father in the Son, that is, to Christ. "Neither doth any one know the Father but the Son, and he to whom it shall please the Son to reveal Him." [3] To begin, therefore, let us cleave to Christ alone. For the time being, let us not think of the formulas in which dogmas are expressed, although Christ Himself teaches them to us in the Church. We shall soon rediscover them, and in a better way; for we shall rediscover them in Christ.

In Christ, and in Him alone, we shall find everything. And, at the outset, to see what is most vital and central in revelation, we must turn our eyes to what is deepest in Christ, that is, His personality; and this personality is exclusively that of the Second Person in the Trinity, for Christ is one of the Trinity. In thus seeking what is most profound and immanent in the supernatural, we shall arrive at absolute height and pure transcendence. Yet we shall not leave what is within, for this transcendent person has become man; the interiora Dei and the interiora Christi coincide.

Therefore the first beginnings of the revelation made in the Church have to be sought in the Trinity. Hence we cannot be surprised if this revelation has to do essentially with the Trinity. If Christ, considered in His humanity, is life because He lives by the living Father,[4] He is also light, and we are light in Him,[5] because He proceeds from the light that is the Father: "Light of Light, true God of true God."

The three divine persons are consubstantial because all three are

[3] Matt. 11:27.
[4] John 6:58.
[5] Eph. 5:8: "Vos autem lux in Domino."

one and the same God. But the Son especially is what the Father is, by reason of the way He alone proceeds from the Father, for He proceeds unto similarity of nature, *in similitudinem naturae*. This similarity is remotely analogous to a similarity found among creatures, that which obtains between an idea or mental word and the thing expressed by the idea. This latter resemblance is called truth. Therefore the name "truth" is well adapted to express the perfect similarity that exists between the Son and the Father.

In a certain sense, of course, all the divine persons are truth; the divine nature itself is the first Truth and the principle of all exact knowledge. But if we mean by truth a resemblance to an exemplar, the concept no longer applies to the divine essence, for the divine essence is not relative to anything; it applies only to that one of the divine persons for whom to be is to resemble the person who produces His Word.

In the liturgy we chant: "Verax est Pater, veritas Filius, veritas Spiritus Sanctus, O beata Trinitas." [6] The Father is true, the Son is truth, and the Holy Spirit is truth; or rather, as Jesus Himself says in the very passages in which He teaches us about the origin of this Spirit, the latter is the Spirit of truth: He is the "Spirit of truth who proceedeth from the Father," the Spirit of truth who "will teach you all truth." [7]

In any case, as the light and truth of the Father, as the true light that gladly gives light about the Father, the Son is the person in the Trinity who expresses truth in fullness. By consubstantiality He is all that the other persons are: by circumincession He has all that is personal to the other persons; and, as proper to Himself, He is the Word, the Image. Therefore He is the whole intelligibility of the mystery so far as that intelligibility shines forth in the notional act of understanding; He is the absolute Truth which consists, not in resembling a model, but in being all that the model is. He is the eternally uttered Word who expresses everything and in whom is really and substantially contained all that there is to say. He is the manifestation without parallel, the unique and only-begotten expression in the fullest sense of the word. He is the apparition of God in God, and He is God.

May we use in this connection the word "revelation," divesting

[6] Second antiphon of the third nocturn for the feast of the Most Holy Trinity.

[7] John 15:26; 16:13.

it of any connotation of previous ignorance and imperfect knowledge, and say that the Word is the revelation of God in God? Certainly not, for we must avoid terms that too easily lend themselves to misunderstanding. Hence we merely hazard the term and withdraw it immediately; yet we wish to have pronounced it, for it ought to have been uttered. Although the eternal Word who images God in God is not revelation, yet revelation, when it is made later on, will be associated with this Word and this Image, and will prolong them. The truth that embraces Him in the glories of the saints is at the origin of all truth that has come to us. In Christ Jesus our Lord, there is no gap between this truth and the illuminating of the world by the light of Christ.

For the Word was made flesh. Jesus Christ is this Word made flesh; God comes to speak to us from the midst of mankind. As we have already noted, the relations of the Word are possessed by the humanity of Christ in the Word, through the possession of them by the Word who is the person of the humanity.[8] To subsist and to possess these relations is one and the same thing for Christ's human nature. In this human nature, no separation between what is most secret in God and what is most secret in man is possible. For what is more secret in God than the mystery of the eternal processions, and what is more secret in man than the personality that makes him man?

In Jesus Christ, these two secrets coincide: the secret of God becomes the secret of man, because this man is God. The veil of the temple that kept the holy of holies hidden is rent. The light is given, the light is united to men, and this union is not a philosophical system or an inspired book, but is Someone living, the man Jesus Christ. The unity of His person is the abolishment and annihilation of every screen and every veil between the human mind and the splendor of the Trinity. Therefore Christ is revelation. And the revelation in Him is not the less universal because of the fact that He is but one Man; is not this one Man the life of all mankind? To profit by the instruction intended for all mankind, we have only to let Him act and to let the living logic implied in His being develop and realize itself.

Therefore He is revelation, the removal of the veil. But in this phase of the divine economy the revelation does not yet consist in

[8] Chap. 12.

a knowledge or a teaching, that is, in a knowledge that is trans-mitted; it consists in a reality, in a real communication of realities. But what a reality and what a communication! He who gives Him-self is the supreme intelligible value, the term of the ideal act of un-derstanding, the Thought of the Thought that thinks itself. How could anyone ever suppose that in coming to our earth He would forbear to impart knowledge, to reveal? He who gives Himself is the Word; how could we imagine that He would remain silent? Jesus is the Word of God made man and dwelling among men. Should we not say that, in His person, He is the Word of God ad-dressed to the human race?

Thus we find the incarnate Word at the beginning of all revela-tion. There He is found, not outside of revelation, but forming a part of revelation, or rather comprising all revelation in Himself.

As all the divine persons have equally produced the Incarnation, they are all equally the author of revelation. But although the In-carnation was wrought by all the divine persons, it was wrought in only one of them. Likewise revelation, although made by all the persons, is made in only one of them, in Jesus Christ, the Second Person.

We said that Jesus Christ in His humanity is the first intelligible and the first truth in Christianity, just as, in His divinity, He is the first intelligible and the first truth of Christianity and of everything. Here we see, better than anywhere else, how well this title befits His humanity, which subsists in the splendor of the eternal Light and in the Word that expresses all the intelligibility of the mystery. Revelation begins in it; revelation burst forth at the moment the sacred humanity began to exist, and flows on without pause from the deep source where it is ever beginning to be, if we may say so, that is, to be the humanity of the Word. This humanity subsists in and through the appearance of the Truth on our soil.

In this way we may conceive that the sacred humanity, the first principle in revelation as regards the order of existence, that is, the ontological reality which is the origin of revelation, is also the first principle in the understanding of this revelation. To apprehend rev-elation as it is, namely, as it is intelligible, we have to see it make its ap-pearance in the God-man.

We must now examine how this real, substantial revelation be-comes formal revelation. As we considered it before, it is a communication of existence; it next becomes knowledge, and then a manifestation of knowledge. But it will remain in Christ; to see the whole of revelation, we have but to look at Him. Accordingly our next step is the investigation of Christ's knowledge. However, so as not to lose contact with Him who is the revelation, in studying His knowledge we shall consider what is most intimately "He," that is, His consciousness. Christ's consciousness is Christ Himself, as expressed by Christ Himself in Christ. Could we better speak of Him than by speaking of His self-knowledge?

Yet some precisions will have to be made. Actually Christ has a twofold consciousness, because He has two natures. In His first consciousness, the divine, He knows Himself as God; He knows Himself in a divine way, and knows everything else in knowing Himself. In His other, or human consciousness, He knows Himself as man; He knows Himself in a human way, and knows other things according as they are related to Him.

Therefore let us contemplate the human consciousness of Christ. He really has a human consciousness. The assumed humanity is complete; it has its intellect, and this intellect has its consciousness, just as the divinity has its own consciousness. And this consciousness, like Christ's knowledge, has various aspects: it is empirical, pure, infused, and beatific. But there is only one who is conscious, since there is only one person; and only one ultimate subject is expressed by the twofold consciousness, because Christ is one. In present-day terminology, "consciousness" may designate the conscious subject or the subject that is expressed by consciousness. In the second sense, we have to say that there is only one consciousness in Christ; whereas in the first sense, by which we understand consciousness to mean the faculty or act of self-knowledge, we have to speak of a twofold consciousness in Christ: the divine consciousness and the human consciousness; and the latter may be multiple.

The same is true with regard to the word "I." We must acknowledge that there are in Christ two interior expressions in which the conscious person utters Himself. In this sense there is a twofold "I"; and indeed, the human "I" in Christ is expressed in several different ways, and to that extent is multiple. But we must add that in Christ a single knowing person says "I" and is said by this "I"; in this sense there is only one "I" in Him.

These terms, as anyone may observe, are not those that theology has studied and worked out in order to give adequate expression to the dogma. We should do better to avoid them, if we did not, as at present, have to speak of the thing which they alone express. In employing them, however, we shall try to be careful and to watch out that the context may sufficiently determine their meaning.

Accordingly only one "I," only one total being is expressed; but this "I" which is uttered by the human consciousness, the only person who can be expressed, is the Word; and in Him the processions of passive generation and active spiration, and hence all the divine persons, are connoted. Moreover the Word is expressed as forming one with a human nature, in the mystery of the Incarnation and of superabundant grace, in the mystery of the whole supernatural economy; and that embraces all the revealed truths together.

Of course even the human mind of Christ could express the Word in a merely human and therefore inadequate way. But it had to express Him in some way, in order that the "I" it expressed might be truly its "I." Otherwise its subsistence in the Word of truth would have involved a lie; for if this "I" were restricted to what was human, Christ's human mind would not have expressed Him whom it would nevertheless have professed to express, because of the nature of this "I" which is that of the possessor of this intellect.

We can reason similarly if we consider the human nature itself, rather than the personality belonging to this nature. But then our reasoning will be based, not on the human nature as it is in itself, but on the transcendent perfection it possesses in Christ. Such a perfection cannot be the object of a purely natural consciousness; yet we do not for a moment suggest that Christ's human consciousness acts without the assistance of the divinity, and we shall show directly that the opposite is true. Furthermore, a supernatural perfection can escape the awareness even of a consciousness divinized by grace. That is the case with us, whose divinization is real even here on earth, but is not an object of a real consciousness.

We shall come back to this point in the following pages. In any case, we clearly perceive the difference between Christ and ourselves. In us, the supernatural is in process of formation, it is still in opposition to the remnants of sin in us, and is but a derivation and participation of Christ's supernatural excellence. In Him it is a plenitude so powerful that it dominates the essential human nature in which it is found. Moreover, He could not truly be said to know His human nature with His human consciousness unless at the same time He knew the supernatural perfection possessed by it. And this perfection, which is nothing else than an entity of union with God and the Word, cannot be grasped except by a knowledge that embraces God and the Word, and that extends to all union with God and the Word, that is, to all Christianity.

In whatever way we regard the matter, therefore, we are at grips with the very essence of the Incarnation, and are prescinding from all theological explanation. This man who is Christ is strictly the Word; He cannot truly know Himself without knowing the Word. We cannot conceive that the union of natures in Christ, which is so perfect in the order of existence, should be deficient in the order of knowledge, and that, since *operari sequitur esse*, this man who in *esse* is the Word, should be dissociated from the Word in that *operari* of His which is knowledge.

Must not the one call forth the other? The assuming of the human nature actuates that human nature in its innermost depths; must it not actuate also the depths of the human nature's spiritual and cognitive life? On the one hand, subsistence in the Word supplies the assumed human nature with its personality; on the other hand, the elements in which personality is most strikingly expressed in human nature and which most require personality (whether human or transcendent) are found in self-consciousness, in the placing of self completely within self. Does not the conclusion follow that the first place in which subsistence in the Word finds self-expression must be the consciousness of the assumed humanity? Consciousness underlies all human activity since it is present in all knowledge, since it is the reason why knowledge belongs to the one who knows, and since knowledge directs its tendency. It is through consciousness that activity is recognized to be truly the activity of the person who engages in it. Therefore must not the assumed humanity be conscious of the Word, in order that the human activity of the incarnate Word may truly belong to the incarnate Word in a fitting way, that is, in a human way? This consciousness of being the Word, which is the basis and fulcrum of all the human activity of Christ, is but the translation, in terms of knowledge, of what the hypostatic union with the Word is in terms of existence; for the Word is the ultimate support and the sole subsistence of all the human reality in Christ.

Does it not seem—we do not wish to use a stronger term—that if this humanity were conscious of itself without being conscious of the Word, it would represent itself in the order of knowledge as an independent personal reality, and that consequently, at the very origin of its intellectual life, the germ of the Nestorian heresy might be uncovered, notwithstanding denials that might be made later?

Human consciousness, yet true consciousness of God and the Word: these two aspects must be attentively considered. First, this is a human consciousness. For a human nature can have no other. The act of this nature, in Him who possesses the nature, folds back on itself and apprehends itself. Since this consciousness is human, it is essentially imperfect, with a human imperfection. Never, not even on the first Holy Saturday, not even in heaven, did the soul of Jesus cease to be the form of the material which it possessed or which it resumed; and never was its consciousness anything else than the act of an intellect that by nature was limited in its clarity of perception.

Therefore it does not express God adequately or exhaustively; no finite intellect can thus express God. Yet it must express God in a human way; it is the Word's human consciousness and therefore, even as human, it must be a consciousness of the Word. It is able to give expression to the Word because it was elevated for this purpose to a height which not even pure spirits can reach by their natural powers. As we showed in the preceding chapter, Christ's human nature is perfected and divinized because it is united to God the Word. Hence it is perfected especially in relation to God the Word; in the present case, this means that it is enabled to be internally conscious of the Word; it is equipped by the Word to be, so far as possible, a worthy consciousness of the Word who assumed the humanity.[9]

When we speak of the human consciousness of the Word, or of the ego which expresses the Word and the Trinity in the self-expression of a human intellect, or of the immanent human act of cognition which apprehends the transcendent God, we are quite aware that the formulas we are using go very far. But do not these formulas merely express in terms of knowledge what the Incarnation

[9] On this grace, this aptitude, cf. St. Thomas, *De veritate*, q. 20, a. 2, and the *Summa*, IIIa, q. 9, a. 2 ad 1.

is in terms of existence, and does not our faith rejoice that the Incarnation goes so far?

As God has let Himself be lodged in a human substance, He has also let Himself be apprehended in a human intelligence. Consciousness is the easiest knowledge of all; its movement is so gentle and quiet that it is not even noticed; it keeps pace with all the activity of the mind and with the mind itself. As it is present in all knowledge, it enables us to know our very knowledge; it is the unbroken thread and, as it were, the ultimate substratum of the intimate life of the mind. Nothing is so luminous, evident, and immediate as consciousness. Its light is quite proportionate and fully satisfying to the mind, for consciousness is the mind's proper act and its sufficiency.

The expression of God and the Trinity is found in the light which is the self-expression of Christ's humanity. The affirmation of what is innermost in God arises in the innermost act by which the Man affirms Himself. And the two proceed with the same movement: this Man who is the Word affirms the Word in the full affirmation of Himself.

The term "vision" is not too strong here; rather it is too weak; it calls up the idea of an exterior object, whereas consciousness is the vital act by which the human intellect simply folds back on itself. God lets Himself be apprehended in this act, to such an extent that the splendor of the Ineffable is joined without separation, as also without commingling, to the soul's own brightness.

This knowledge is in the highest degree human, by reason of the faculty that elicits it. But we must add that in the order of created things it is also in the highest degree a divine knowledge, by reason of its cause. A human intellect could not, by its own power, have given expression to the Word, any more than a human nature could, by its own resources, have come to subsist in the Word. On both sides there is the same strict impossibility; and on both sides there is the same bountiful grace and the same gift of God.

To understand the nature of Christ's human consciousness, we have to study this gift. Such considerations are but a continuation of the investigation already made in earlier chapters, on the Son's self-donation to the assumed humanity. We were able to show that Christ's human consciousness had to exist, by showing that God had to give it. Without it, the Savior's humanity, though completely divinized in its existence, would not have been completely divinized in its activity.

As is clear, we are still dealing with the perfecting of Christ's human nature, by considering the human nature relatively to what it would have been had it not been assumed; in other words, we are discussing the "entity of union" that has to be found in it. This "entity of union" necessarily implies a knowledge of the union, that is, a knowledge that can exist in a nature only because this nature is actually united with another nature.

As the perfecting of the human nature in the order of existence is truly a way of existing for the human nature, so the perfecting of knowledge is a way of knowing for it. But the perfecting in the order of existence is impossible without the hypostatic union, which alone can explain it. The perfection that is conferred adapts the human nature to the hypostatic union and is its effect, and is also the real foundation of the union, such as a real relation requires. Similarly the perfecting in the order of knowledge is impossible without the hypostatic union, which alone accounts for it. This perfection adapts the assumed nature to the union in the order of knowledge and is the effect of the union, and furnishes any real foundation for it that may be required.

In other words, although the perfection is on the side of the human nature, it is caused by the divinity that intervenes, not by way of a transcendent causality that would remain exterior, but by way of immanent union. In consequence of the divine influence, it does not exist in a humanity that is left to itself, but arises in a humanity that exists in God, and is given in order that the humanity may suitably subsist in God.

The act of consciousness would not be complete and true to itself unless it embraced God the Word, who is not, indeed, the nature that elicits the act, but is its ultimate substratum or hypostasis. The divinity is also necessary for other acts performed by the sacred humanity, as their first cause and to make them complete in themselves. But in the case of consciousness the divinity is necessary as an interior element, that the act may be within the divinity, as in the first principle from which it issues.

If, as we have brought out in the preceding chapter, the hypostatic union with the Son requires an amelioration in the assumed humanity to make the humanity intrinsically "filial," the hypostatic union with the Word must likewise, with the same necessity, require an amelioration in the humanity to make it belong intrinsically to the Word, to make it "verbal," if we may use the term.

"Filial" and "verbal" assuredly mean the same thing; the Word is identical with the Son, and is He whom the Father begets. But in our human way of conceiving, we believe that this difference may be noted: "Word" seems to indicate the relation which is the Son chiefly as it is found in Him, whereas "Son" indicates the same relation chiefly with reference to the Father from whom the Son proceeds (without excluding, as is evident, the Son's relation to the Spirit). This is the way we distinguish in our effort to grasp more clearly the unity of a pure, subsistent relation. According to this manner of conception, the "verbal" quality found in the assumed humanity will appear different from the "filial" quality, although in itself this quality is the same adaptation to the same simple subsistence. If we scrutinize the two qualities closely, we shall see very quickly that they are identical.

The Word is the Word of the Father. As a thought is impossible without a word, so the Father, who is eminently Thought, cannot subsist without His Word. To represent the Father without His Word would be tantamount to representing Him, according to the Greek Fathers, without intelligence, without reason, or "alogos," that is, irrational. As the Scholastics say, the Word is the interior Word in which the Father expresses all that He is, so exactly that this Word is a person like Himself, a whole that is absolutely similar to Himself, with the sole difference that the one is uttered and the other is uttering. Therefore the Word is begotten by way of intellection, as the supreme intellectual value and the supreme expression of knowledge.

We believe that these latter formulas, with the vagueness they entail, correspond to the element that is common in the teaching of the Greek Fathers and the Scholastics. They will be the point of departure for our own exposition. Such an exposition is undoubtedly best developed if it stays within the Scholastic framework, which lends itself to the most rigorous argumentation, and we cannot speak in all possible ways at the same time. Yet we hope that our reasoning will not become so dependent on the Scholastics as to depart from the thought of the Greek Fathers.

Accordingly, Christ's humanity is really and intrinsically the humanity of the supreme intellectual expression that is the Word. Therefore it must possess a perfection, an elevation, a new and supernatural way of existing that will adapt it to this condition and will make it truly and absolutely the humanity of the Word, the humanity of Him who is the term of supreme intellection.

This perfection is what we have called, when speaking of the "filial" perfection, an "entity of union." How could it adapt the humanity to the Word except by adapting it to the Son? The Son is Son because He is the supreme intellectual value and expression. To be adapted to Him, the assumed humanity must be endowed with a perfection that is related to intellection and that quite naturally flowers into knowledge. But what is a mode of existence that expresses itself in a mode of knowledge and has its act in this activity, if not a conscious existence? Is not consciousness the expression that a being gives of itself to itself in order to be in full possession of its existence, is it not existence itself as knowing and known? Moreover, if this consciousness adapts the human mind to the Word, should it not express the Word that is a relation to the Father and the Spirit, the Word that is not known unless the Trinity is known, and should it not utter the Word as united in personal unity to the humanity?

Therefore knowledge of the union that is the expression and even the proper act of an "entity of union" in the order of knowing, necessarily implies the union. How could a human nature be equipped to be the human nature of the Word, if it did not have its own word that expresses the Word? Thus this human nature is "verbal," that is, it is really and intrinsically the humanity of the Word, just as it is "filial," that is, really and intrinsically the humanity of the Son. But it is "verbal" as it is also "filial" through union with the Word; its typical knowledge is possible and conceivable only as a "knowledge of union."

The Word alone is the (passive) expression of Himself. A human nature cannot be fitted to express Him unless it is fitted to be united to Him. If the humanity is regarded as it is in itself, whatever can be thought of, conceived, or expressed in it is finite and human, and is not God or the Word. But this way of regarding the matter is equivalent to thinking of the Incarnation by prescinding from the Incarnation. If God remains aloof, He cannot evoke the knowledge we are talking about. God has to become one with the humanity;

and the humanity, as we have seen, is capable of existing in hypo-static union with the first cause. The knowledge it possesses in this union and the consciousness it expresses of itself will clearly be its own, but only because it is assumed by the Word and does not belong to itself. Only thus will it have a consciousness of the Word, a consciousness and knowledge of union.

Even when we devote special attention to the human element in this consciousness and distinguish it carefully from the full significance it receives from union with the Word, we may not separate the two; can we conceive one of two elements as joined to another without including the second element? Whatever may be the contribution of the human intellect in this knowledge, its own part is an interior conception, a mental expression that is surely splendid, unprecedented, indescribable, and supernatural since it comes from a most pure intellect and since God Himself fortifies it so that it may command a language in which God Himself may speak and be the word. But all this human excellence would not exist at all, would not be called into being, and would only imply a contradiction, if God did not unite Himself to the human nature, if the Word did not perfect it and take it to Himself. Considered in itself, this wonderful human intellect is incomplete in being and in knowledge, since it exists only in a union and can express nothing but a union.

We must study this union more thoroughly; then we shall understand better the knowledge of union it implies. For this purpose, we need to reflect more deeply on the nature of the Word regarded as knowledge and consciousness. This point raises a certain difficulty, because of the fact that the term "consciousness" and the closely related term "I" are not among the terms which theology has studied, refined, criticized, and made available for the technical exposition of the mystery of the Trinity. Yet we have to employ them; the point of view adopted in the present work requires them.

We called attention to this difficulty before, in connection with Christological dogma: the notion of "I" is one of those notions that may not be employed except with great care, since it is susceptible of several meanings. In using it, we have to make up by our own reflection for the lack of precision which only a long process of theological research can supply. According to the sense we give to the word, we have to say that there is a single or a twofold "I" in Christ: there is one subject who is this "I," yet He, because of

His two distinct natures, expresses this subject in two different ways.

Something similar occurs in the Trinity. On the one hand, we have to hold that there is only one consciousness in God, because He has but one nature. On the other hand, since there are three persons in God, we have to say that there are three ultimate and distinct subjects who know themselves and are conscious; in this sense the divine consciousness is threefold. For in ordinary parlance the word "consciousness" also means the ultimate subject that is conscious. Accordingly consciousness has two different meanings: first, it signifies the nature and its faculty or quasi-faculty; secondly, it signifies the ultimate subject who expresses himself and possesses this faculty. In the first meaning, as regards the Trinity, consciousness is considered as absolute and essential; in the second, it is considered as relative and notional. We may say that there are three conscious relations, or a triple consciousness of the relations, in the one absolute consciousness. As the relations in the Trinity are identical with the absolute nature, since they are relative only to one another, so these three conscious relations or relative consciousnesses are identical with the absolute consciousness, since they are relative, and conscious as distinct, only among themselves.

Hence we see that the notion and the word "consciousness" do not lend themselves to a simple and clear exposition of Trinitarian theology; and in employing them we must guard against possible confusion by referring frequently to traditional concepts and formulas. Nevertheless, given the direction of thought that has been marked out since the beginning as governing the present work and that imposes itself yet more imperiously in this chapter, we have no choice but to employ them. How can we do other than suit our vocabulary to the things we are discussing?

Moreover this change in point of view may enable us to glimpse the eternal truth under a new light and thus to perceive more clearly all the good contained in the traditional system. We scarcely need to remark that we have no intention of proposing a theory of the Trinity in these pages. We desire to make Christian truth more intelligible, not by devising theories, but by reducing theories to the whole Christ, to Christ living in us in the mystery of the life that comes to Christians from the incarnate Word, or rather from the Trinity itself, Father, Son, and Holy Ghost.

Accordingly we suppose that the reader is familiar with the ordinary theory, and we shall base our exposition on it as need arises. But to repose securely on it, we are compelled, if we may say so, to bring it within reach, to formulate it in function of the ideas we wish to speak of throughout, in function of Christ, His own interior life, and the interior life He gives to His members; that is, in function of the term and the idea of consciousness.

Man is undoubtedly somewhat audacious when he undertakes to speak of God with soiled lips and to translate the secrets of the Godhead into his human language. But has not the divine life itself come down to our human level and lodged in our poor hearts and our feeble intellects? If we made no effort to express that life with our faltering concepts and words, we should be guilty of contempt and presumption; we should be rejecting the light it attempts to shed and the cooperation it solicits. We ought to advance toward it, not in a spirit of cautious reserve, which would betray a lack of love for divine truth, but with docility, piety, humility, and eagerness. Such is the way of speaking we propose to follow, in order to express the truth in function of the notion of consciousness, which is so well known to us.

God is conscious, because He is a spirit. He has one absolute consciousness. But this consciousness is so perfect and so indescribably one, that it is triune; that is, it has its interior, eternal act and its immanence in a threefold relative consciousness (in the sense explained above). If the divine nature is considered, the activity of this consciousness is one; but if the divine persons are considered, it is carried out in two notional operations, the second of which is not an activity of consciousness, but an activity that follows conscious activity.

God who knows Himself in His divine essence is, within His inner life, identically knowledge that utters and that is uttered, consciousness that expresses and consciousness that is expressed, the Father and His Word. The Father knows Himself, and the immanent term of this knowledge is the Word. Hence this consciousness is notional and "originating," not absolute.[10]

[10] We may say that the generation of the Son resembles an act of consciousness. However, a difference should be pointed out. In the case of human consciousness, he who knows and he who is known are the same nature and the same person, whereas in the notional act we are speaking of they are, indeed, the same nature, but not the same person. But if we understand the mat-

The Word, on the other hand, exists in relation to the other two divine persons and in correlation with them. To give expression to the Word, the assumed humanity must also express the other persons and the whole Trinity; but it does so, if we may thus formulate our thought, from the point of view of the Word, by union and adaptation to the expression that the Word has. By grace, therefore, the sacred humanity must form in itself a knowledge and a consciousness that, through union with the Word, may express the whole Trinity.

Now the Trinity is Being as it is in itself and for itself, in the pure immanence of its transcendence. And knowledge, which is a function of being, is characterized by its power to attain to being and by the being it can attain to; the two are correlative. In consequence, the knowledge and consciousness possessed by Christ's humanity constitute a special kind of knowledge which is most sublime and quite different from all natural knowledge, and which inaugurates here on earth a new way of knowing. In the same manner, as we showed in the preceding chapter, the assumed humanity, through the ontological amelioration it receives, inaugurates on earth a new way of existing and of being man.

We have employed the term "entity of union," that is, an entity that is possible only when a man is God and subsists in God. We must now use the term "knowledge of union," a knowledge that is possible only when a human knowledge is found to be a knowledge of God, inasmuch as the man possessing it is God and has to act and know accordingly.

This knowledge is not the product of abstraction, the agent intellect, and reasoning. The contact with being is quite other than that which is effected in sensation and which manifests the intellect to itself by introducing into it something else than itself, that is, the phantasm. Rather it is a contact by way of union, within the very unity of this being itself. There is no question of a progressive ascent toward a cause starting off from sensation and never arriving at any-

---

ter aright, this difference and this fecundity do not prevent us from likening the first of the divine processions to an act of consciousness; in fact, this is the best means natural speculation has of imparting some understanding of it. We are thus enabled dimly to perceive how the person of the Word, who springs forth in the divine "consciousness," may also, through the greatest of graces, but without violence or difficulty, spring up in the human consciousness.

thing but a negative knowledge of the absolute; there is a direct union with the Absolute and in the Absolute.

As this contact with being and intelligibility is achieved in a different way, the object thereby attained is also different; it is a different aspect of being. As the contact is effected by way of union, the object attained through it is Being in its union with itself, in the mystery of the Trinitarian union. Natural knowledge attains being only in the external works of God, as a reflection of God and in relation to God; but the knowedge we are speaking of attains being in its interior life, in the relations which that being is in itself and for itself alone. God is known to others as inaccessible and *tamquam ignotus;* but as regards the sacred humanity, God is attained as the first thing known and as always known; for the knower knows everything else by being conscious of himself and of who he is— at least in an implicit way.

Therefore this knowledge should not be classed among other kinds of knowledge as a special and singularly privileged case, or as a consciousness that is more penetrating and religious, or as a belief that rests on higher and more certain testimony. It is radically different, with a superiority that derives from the infinite Godhead, for it is a knowledge possessed by a man who is God; it is the knowledge which God evokes in a man by causing that man to be Himself. As compared with all created knowledge, it is absolute knowledge. Although it is finite and human, it shares in the divine way of knowing, because, by attaining to infinite Being itself, it embraces all being, and especially because, by attaining to God, it attains to intelligibility itself.

Yet it is human; it is a man's consciousness. Moreover, it is human with a transcendent perfection, for it is divinely human. In the order of existence, the fact that the humanity belongs to God, who is Being itself, means that the assumed humanity is more perfectly, supernaturally human; similarly, in the order of knowledge, the fact that a consciousness belongs to God who is Being and the Word, means that this human consciousness is more perfectly, supernaturally human.

To make this clear, we have only to repeat and adapt what we have said about the possibility of the Incarnation. The Word is God, He is Being itself, and not a determined, limited mode of being. Thus, in becoming God's humanity, the assumed human nature does not become something else, it is not altered; on the contrary, it becomes itself in a higher way, for it is united to its cause, to its exemplar, to its end, to Being itself. The same is true of this humanity's consciousness, so far as it is a knowledge of being; by containing the Word who is Being, it is more closely united to its principle, to its exemplar, to its end; it is more perfectly itself.

The fact that the Being it grasps is precisely the Word, involves nothing that would incapacitate or alter it; we have said enough in the preceding pages about the analogy between the Word and Christ's human consciousness. Indeed, the faint insight we have into so profound a subject leads us to wonder whether the admirable harmony between the two was not decreed from the beginning, either before or after the prevision of original sin; whether God did not make man's consciousness so that in the God-man it might become the sanctuary in which the Word uttered by the Father alone would be expressed in a human fashion.

In any case a new knowledge finds its way into mankind, a knowledge that comes from God Himself to man, and springs up in the deepest center of mankind, in the heart of this Man who is the heart of the whole race. This is the way the sun casts flowers upon the earth, by causing them to spring up from the soil. The soil alone sends forth the flowers; but God gives this knowledge, and it is formed in the God-man; it is human and at the same time truly divine. It is what we call revelation.

We have already seen how this revelation was inaugurated: the Word, the expression of God by God, became present among men because a human nature began to subsist in the Word. At that moment, however, the revelation existed only *in actu primo remoto;* it was as yet confined to the order of existence, and would not find expression in the order of knowledge until later. But we are now going to speak of knowledge properly so called, knowledge at the point where it first burst forth in mankind.

We read: "Truth is sprung out of the earth." [11] Truth, the absolute truth about the absolute intelligible, arises from our race. "The seed is the Word of God" (Luke 8:11); the divine seed fell on our earth, and that is enough. By this one great grace, which is unceasingly at work, the gift that comes down from heaven mounts upward from within man.

[11] Ps. 84:12.

When we are taught by the Word, we are taught by Him who has been sent to dwell in us. The gift and the teaching are more perfect because of the fact that He who gives and teaches is given to us and especially, to speak correctly, because He has become what we are. His message is not less divine on that account, but becomes more splendidly and divinely human.

He is a man who is also the Word of God and one of the persons of the Trinity, and at the same time is the supernatural unity and life of mankind. And that is everything. He expresses Himself within Himself; but, because of all that He is and because of God who makes Him all that He is, this interior Word is the source of all divine truth in all of regenerated mankind. This truth is the whole of revelation, faith, and the beatific vision; and it does not pass beyond this one man who is the Word of God. But it manifests His fullness: "There will be one Christ knowing Himself."

This knowledge, this consciousness is an unparalleled grace. It is the supreme grace in the order of knowledge, and the first universal principle in the order of intellectual graces, just as the grace of the assumed humanity that possesses this consciousness is the first principle in the order of grace in general. For the consciousness of being the Word can be possessed only by Him who is the Word, who is God. No greater union with God or assimilation to God is possible than that which comes to a man from the fact that He is God, and grace is the divinization in which this union and assimilation are expressed.

Grace or divinization of knowledge, adaptation of a man's intelligence to the Word, is the complete intellectual grace. It is also perfectly one. Everything is contained in it; the object to be known, the way in which it is known, and the act of knowing are closely connected with subsistence in the Word. Once this subsistence becomes a fact, everything else necessarily follows and yet is a free gift; for such subsistence is a free gift.

Therefore this is the revelation of revelations; but it is not a doctrine that comes from outside or a teaching that is wholly exterior. For it is primarily the voice of consciousness, the voice that is even more intimate to the human consciousness of Jesus than His own human nature, the voice by which this humanity, that is one with the Word, expresses nothing but what is in continuity with the act of the Father who utters the Word.

The harmony between Christ's two natures is so perfect, His human psychology is so guileless, and everything is so exactly aligned, that the sacred humanity was completely enlightened from the first instant of its illumination by the Word. The Word's brilliance enkindles the brightness of the human consciousness; yet the latter remains what it is, and the brilliance of the Word remains the splendor of the Word, the light that proceeds from light, *lumen de lumine.*

Accordingly this is a grace, and is no other than the grace of the hypostatic union, which primarily affects being, but flowers into knowledge from the root of being, at the point where knowledge is in contact with being, in the consciousness that affirms being as it is in itself. This grace comes from the Father in the Word. Consequently, when Christians receive it from the Word, they receive it from the Father. They are instructed by Christ the Word, they hear His words, they believe His message, they think as He does with all their heart, and they desire to have no other teacher. Yet they are taught by the Father.[12] In Christ and through Christ they are admitted into the stream of light that flows from the Father, and are thus given a place in the movement of the eternal generation. As a result of their docility, by grace they become children, not of the Son and the Word, but of the Father alone, in the only-begotten Son to whom God in His goodness has united them by faith.

II. From Christ to Christians

A. Interiorly, through consciousness. "And the light shineth in darkness" (John 1:5). The sun rose in the heart of one man to enlighten all mankind. We could immediately proceed to contemplate this enlightenment in the incomparable words in which Jesus proposed His teaching. If we were to do that, however, we would cut it off from all intermediaries, and so would not see it radiating out from the sun itself. To perceive the vital expansion in its continuity, we must first observe it emerging from the interior of Jesus, in that supernatural perfection of His humanity which makes Him the head of the regenerated race.

The same union with the Word that perfects the assumed humanity to such a degree that it is completely and supernaturally

[12] John 6:45.

human, also perfects the consciousness of this humanity and invests it with its full, supernatural character of human consciousness. As we said before, this is mainly an individual perfection. But it is also social and universal; and this is the aspect we must now consider. Everything human is social; and what is human in a way that is worthy of God must be divinely and infinitely social, so far as is possible for anything that is human and individual. Christ's human consciousness is a consciousness belonging to God; therefore it must be as divine and infinite as a human consciousness can be. It must possess itself and its humanity in such a way as to include all humanity; it must be so interior to itself as to coincide with the supernatural "interiorization" of consciousness that is found in every human consciousness united to it.

Let no one object that consciousness must be self-enclosed; that is only a defect and imperfection of consciousness. The immanence of our human consciousness is so precarious that it has to be sheltered within ramparts; in the same way certain animals have to enclose themselves within shells because they lack skeletons. To reflect on itself it has to shut out other beings, because it is not complete being; it has to shut out what is human, because it is not fully human.

Men are not completely men, for the matter that individuates them limits their form and their humanity. Moreover, so long as they are on earth, they are not men to the full extent of their capacity. The law of their morality is one of growth, and the commandments it imposes on them oblige them to foster union with other men; to assure ourselves of this we have but to recall the natural law, or the Master's precept as brought out at the sentence of the Last Judgment and in St. John's Gospel.[13] What does this mean, if not that a closer union of men with one another, a greater fellowship of all with humanity, ought to be achieved here on earth, during the period of our probation? Man will not be fully man until that goal is reached; at the present time he is not far along the road. Likewise the human consciousness he has at present is not yet a fully developed consciousness of man, but only its beginning. Full human consciousness, while remaining interior and personal, is a consciousness that is inwardly linked with every other consciousness.

But this is something that awaits the future. In the meantime, our tightly-shut compartments remain. But this imprisonment, instead

[13] Matt. 25:34 ff.; John 15:12.

of warding off contamination from our possession of ourselves, merely deprives us of light. Our lack of understanding, our power-lessness to express to ourselves all that is deeply human in others, far from helping us to comprehend our own humanity, hides it from us. These deficiencies are not the cause of our consciousness, but on the contrary make it less human.

We are convinced that the human consciousness of Jesus did not suffer from such limitations; the reasons that place them in us do not exist in Him. We do not perfectly grasp our union with mankind, because we are not yet perfectly men; but He, the God-man, the *comprehensor*, is man in perfection. We are unaware of others be-cause we are only individuals on a par with them; but He, the head of the race, is all in all.

In the order of human knowledge, Christ's human consciousness is what Christ Himself is in the order of humanity. It is the supreme and transcendent realization, the most human consciousness of all, because it expresses a humanity that is more perfect than all others; it is also the most divine consciousness of all, because it "expresses" the divinity in a way that is more penetrating; and it is the most con-scious of all, because it is adapted to the personality of the Word. Hence it must be conceived as the first principle in the order of hu-man consciousness, by reason of its supernatural perfection that is the source of the supernatural light shed on others. To be infinite in the manner that befits God and to be unlimited in the manner that befits such a human consciousness, it must manifest God in a way that is human but unlimited, so that of its superabundance it may illuminate the whole human race. If we will, we may represent it as a sacred contemplation in which all thoughts converge on the Word who is within; but we should also represent it as a rising of the sun.

"How am I straitened!" (Luke 12:50.) To be the light of the world, the human light which makes God visible for all mankind, involves more than a timid desire for communication and an ex-change of confidences; it means an unreserved, ardent, anxious, im-passioned need, like the fervor of a love eager for self-sacrifice. St. Paul, who was not Christ, nevertheless cried out: "Woe is unto me if I preach not the gospel" (I Cor. 9:16). John the Baptist existed "to give testimony" (John 1:8). Jesus is the light, whose life, whose very nature, is to give forth light. The good news He comes to bring begins in Him, the revealer *in actu primo*. He is revealer, as He is mediator, by His substance before He is so by His actions. He is mediator because, as God-man, He is the union of God with men in His person; He is revealer because, as man and the Word, as the unity of mankind and pure divine light, He is in His person the expression of God and the Trinity for all mankind. When He preaches and teaches He is Himself in act: "For this was I born," by His eternal birth as well as by His temporal birth, "and for this came I into the world"—this is the office that belongs to Him as head in the order of intelligence—"that I should give testimony to the truth." [14]

His inner superabundance is like the pressure that makes the blood circulate and the heart beat to fashion and nourish the members of the body; this is what makes His consciousness the head's consciousness, and gives Him the power to raise up members and to awaken in them the consciousness of being members. This superabundance, however, is something that is received. The action or causality belonging to the sacred humanity is an action that is received and is dependent on the divinity, yet received in the subsistence without which it would not be received. Consequently it is reduced to what the Scholastics rightly call instrumental causality, to a sort of "causality of union."

God's plan for the diffusion of light as well as for the communication of life is magnificent in its simplicity and unity; it unfolds wholly in Christ, that is, in the whole Christ. Christ Himself comes first; He has all the gifts. Through His consciousness of Himself and through subsistence in the Word, He has an intuition of the Trinity. What others receive is not something that has been refused to Him, but what has been given to Him in superabundance.

After Christ come His members. His consciousness is united to the consciousness of all men because He is conscious of the Word. The conciousness of all men is in Him, because He is in God; and every consciousness that is in Him is in the vision of God (now by faith, later by the light of glory). Since their supernatural consciousness cannot be illuminated except by sharing in His light, they have a sort of received consciousness of the Blessed Trinity and the work of salvation.

[14] John 18:37.

Each of the members has his own interior knowledge and consciousness; no other kind of knowledge and consciousness is possible. But each member has knowledge and consciousness through incorporation into the "body" in consequence of Christ's influence; otherwise they would not be members. If Christians are truly Christ's living members, they cannot but have a consciousness, or rather an elevation of their natural consciousness, of being members of Christ; and that makes them conscious of their membership. As Christians, they are intellectual beings; the grace and quality of membership affect what is most spiritual in them; He whose members they are is the Word, the supreme intellectual value.

We have said and we shall repeat that the consciousness of the members cannot be formed or expressed without a teaching proposed in words, dogmas, and mysteries, and that here on earth, during the period of formation and Christian gestation, as we may call it, this consciousness never loses its obscure and externalized character; in brief, it exhibits the traits which theology recognizes in faith. But its existence appears certain to us. Christians are truly and intrinsically members of Christ, they are adopted sons in the true Son, they are internally divinized and united to one another in the Church, and through a sacramental economy they are in contact with eternal life. All these gifts are received in the substance of their supernaturalized souls. But this could hardly be so if their consciousness, the voice of the soul, were not influenced by these truths and if it were not able to express itself in expressing their true state. If we were to maintain that conscious beings are Christ's members but that they lack awareness of such membership, we should have to hold that they are not Christ's members to the extent that they are conscious, and that their ego, whereby they are most themselves, does not share in their membership.

To be members of Him who is the Son, Christians have to be "filial," that is, they have to be adopted, and their divinized life and existence must be a life of adopted children. Similarly, to be members of Him who is the Word, the term of absolute intellection and the supreme intellectual value and expression, they have to be "verbal," if we may speak thus, or "verbified," as St. Athanasius says.[15] Their divinized life and existence must be orientated toward understanding and reflection, a life that reaches its summit in an

[15] *Contra Arianos*, III, 33 (*PG*, XXVI, 396).

interior expression that shares, in a way suitable for members, in the expression of the Word by the Father in their head.

What we have said of the head we must now say of Christians, making due allowance for their position as members. Christ's humanity had to be supernaturally perfected in its way of existing, so that it might be adapted to be the Word's humanity. This perfection had to be such that it could immediately pass over into the realm of knowledge, for the Word proceeds by way of intellection. But the knowledge in which being is expressed is consciousness; and the consciousness that is adapted to be the Word's consciousness must, in its own way, express the Word Himself. Therefore Christ's human consciousness has to contain the Word. It does not utter the Word to itself alone; that is evident, and we have explained the matter; nor does the Word utter Himself in it, for the Father utters the Word. But because of its union with the Word, Christ's human consciousness expresses an interior marvel which would be impossible outside this union and which adapts it for union with the Word uttered by the Father; the Word is uttered divinely in the human consciousness by the Father alone.

All this has to be applied to Christians in their capacity as members of Him who is the Word. They have to be elevated in a way that is proper for members of the Word who is the refulgence of the Father's splendor and thought. Such an elevation in the order of existence has to pass over at once to the order of knowledge, for it is associated with a procession by way of intelligence. And this knowledge, which directly expresses existence, is consciousness. Therefore, since Christians are members of the Word, they must be conscious of their membership in the Word. To express all that they are and have in the Word, their consciousness must include an expression of the Word.

This expression would be impossible were it not for the mystic union they have with Christ's assumed humanity and the hypostatic union the sacred humanity has with the Word. In the consciousness of the Word and of the assumed humanity, the Word is expressed by the Father; the same must be true of the consciousness of Christians. This consciousness comes from their elevation as members of the incarnate Word, and particularly from the elevation of their knowledge. Their knowledge is elevated by a "verbal" divinization of their being and their faculty of cognition which enables them to acquire, through grace, a knowledge that is supernatural, noble, divinized, and infinitely greater than any simple human knowledge. It is so exalted that it surpasses the range of natural consciousness, and can be acquired only by one who is, in Christ, a member of the Word. Its dignity appears in the fact that it is designed for mystic union with the human knowledge which the incarnate Word has and which is the Word's human consciousness. Through this union, which makes it possible and for which it is ordained, it becomes a consciousness that expresses the Word, a consciousness belonging to a member of the Word.

The Father alone utters the Word. However, since He adopts us as His children by grace, He utters the Word in us. As we are men, the Word is uttered humanly in us, in a human knowledge which we acquire through grace. The Father sends His light into this knowledge of ours, and indeed has called it forth for the purpose of receiving such a light. "This is eternal life, that they may know Thee, the only true God, and Jesus Christ whom Thou hast sent." [16]

B. Exteriorly, through teaching expressed in formulas and signs. We have seen how Christ's consciousness, in expressing the mystery of God, expresses it for all men. On His part, that is enough to make Him our first truth. On our part, that will be enough when we achieve our full stature as men and Christians, in heaven; then, without need of anything else, we shall see the absolute light in His interior light. But at present, so long as we remain in our condition of sinners and our state of formation and growth, that does not suffice, for the ears of our heart are too deaf to catch a wholly spiritual message. Accordingly He who has come to help the weak and the wretched has spoken a different language; He has put into words and phrases the message that He brought and that He was. This is the message found in the discourses which the Twelve heard and which all succeeding generations in turn hear proclaimed in the Church.

These discourses are magnificent in their simplicity and grandeur, in their clarity and mystery. But their graphic lucidity comes from the light we have spoken of, from the consciousness of Christ that is interiorly communicated to us, and from the grace that accompanies all these words. The oral teaching clothes the truth and

[16] John 17:3.

makes it perceptible. The words are the body, the grace is the soul; the words are the lamp, the grace is the flame without which the doctrine would be a dead letter and an empty sound.

When an ordinary man speaks, the similarity between his psychology and ours and the natural sociability that begets a sympathy between him and us empower his words to evoke in us thoughts which become ours and which we understand. When Christ speaks, the communication is established by the supernatural resemblance of our psychology of grace with His, by the sociability, or rather unity, that links head and members. And the thoughts which His language arouses and which proceed from us are truly ours; but they are even more a vital influx flowing from the head to the body, from the vine to the branches: "yet not I, but the grace of God with me" (I Cor. 15:10).

Christ speaks of the mystery of God, of the Trinity in Unity. He speaks in syllables and formulas. Definitions of the Councils, sermons, catechisms, theological systems, the prayers taught by the Church, the *Pater noster*, the *Gloria Patri*, the liturgy, the attitude of a child in the presence of its Father, are all channels conveying the divine secrets to us.

But there is more to all this than appears on the surface. We sometimes see trees whose wrinkled trunks and dry, brittle branches give them the appearance of dead wood, though in reality they teem with sap and are conveyors of fecundity and growth; they have inner reserves of power that will some day be manifested in the shape of leaves, blossoms, and fruit. The same is true of doctrinal formulas. They are truly imposing in their clarity and precision; yet this outer beauty is nothing compared with the treasures within. Through them the mind of Christ, the spirit of Christ, the thinking processes of the incarnate Son, are brought to us.

"I know Him, because I am from Him and He hath sent Me." [17] In all His words Christ teaches us about the Father and the life of the Trinity. He habitually speaks of the Father; and if, at first sight, the relation between what He says of the Father and the life of the Trinity does not always appear clear to our myopic eyes, other passages reveal the divine generation that is the basis of all He has to tell us.

He talks about the Father on every possible occasion. As soon as

[17] John 7:29.

our attention is drawn to this point, we notice how strikingly the
Father is proclaimed and proclaims Himself, either explicitly or implicitly, in all that Christ has to say. Of course Christ also speaks of
Himself. But we should observe that when He speaks of Himself,
and the more He speaks of Himself, He also announces the Father.

The revelation of the Trinity occurs frequently in the Gospel according to St. John. Everything else in this book is, by comparison,
an abbreviation, a summary, or an introduction. If we read these
sacred pages with our minds on the dogma of the Trinity, we shall
be astonished to see how it is mentioned or referred to at every turn.
Often, and with remarkable emphasis, it is brought in for its own
sake (John 5:20 ff.; 10:29 f.; 14:7–13; chap. 17), but more often it
is mentioned as the teaching that constitutes the importance or, if
we may say so, the main content of other doctrines. Baptism (John
3:58), the Eucharist (6:58), Christ's entire task in the world (5:17;
10:25, 37 f.; 14:10), His obedience to His Father (4:19, 34; 5:30,
36; 6:38 ff.; 10:17; 14:31; 15:10), the glory He receives from the
Father (5:23; 8:49, 54; 12:26; 13:32; 14:13, 28), the Father's love
for Him (3:35; 10:37; 15:10), the life He gives (5:22, 26), the
redemption He brings (10:24, 27), the judgment He pronounces
(5:22–27), all this is seen to reflect the first great truth, the Son of
God who is born of God in the Trinity.

That is the very theme of the work, and the Holy Spirit wished
it to be clearly expressed (John 20:31; 1:14–18; I John 1:3; 5:13,
20). The book was written that we might believe that Jesus is the
Son of God—hence the Second Person of the Blessed Trinity—and
that we might have eternal life in this Second Person of the Blessed
Trinity. What the Author wishes to impress on us, what He keeps
repeating, is not exactly that Jesus is the Messias (John 1:19, 27, 41;
4:25), nor even the simple fact that He is God (10:33), but that He
is God (1:32 ff.; 10:25, 30) by being of God (1:8, 18), by coming
from God (1:15–18), by being the Son of God 1:14, 18, 34; 17:1).

Jesus Himself insistently presents Himself in this light, in this
movement of the divine processions. If the Fourth Gospel is characterized by the fact that Jesus frequently speaks of Himself in it,
it also has the further characteristic, which is the same as the first,
that He does not refer to Himself except when mentioning the Father (John 3:16; 16:22; 20:21) who sends Him, as He says over and
over (3:7, 34; 4:34; 5:30, 37; 6:38–44) and who is always with Him

(8:29; 16:32). The Father and the Son are inseparable and are in each other (14:10; 17:21, 23); and this circumincession is such that Jesus can propound all His teaching on the Father and the Trinity without ceasing to speak of Himself.

He Himself declares that He is not His own absolute origin (John 5:30, 36); He is begotten (1:14); His career is a mission (17:18; 20:21); His life is received (5:39; 6:58; 8:29). "If any man will do the will of Him, he shall know of the doctrine, whether it be of God or whether I speak of Myself" (John 7:17). St. Augustine asks: "What is the teaching of the Father, if not the Word of the Father? If Christ is the Word of the Father, He Himself is the doctrine of the Father. But the Word cannot be the Word of no one; He must be the Word of someone. Therefore He said that He Himself is His doctrine, and yet that He is not His own doctrine, because He is the Word of the Father. For what is so much your own as you yourself? And what is so little your own as you yourself, if all that you are belongs to another?" [18]

If Christ is the teaching of the Father because He is the Word, He is this teaching in all that He is. His slightest gestures speak of the Father from whom He comes (John 5:17, 19). All His works are so clear a testimony that, if people will not believe Him, they must at least believe the works and realize, on seeing them, that He is in the Father and the Father in Him (10:38; 8:28). At His touch everything becomes an intelligible sign: the evening breeze (3:5–8), the loaves of bread at Capharnaum (6:27, 55–58), the vine and the living water (15:1; 4:10–14), the flock following the shepherd (10: 25–31). All these humble incidents, when He speaks of them, become instruments for revealing the Trinity.

But His person is a message even more than His words and actions are. As the Word, He is Truth and, as He Himself says (John 14: 6 f.), He is the truth about the divine processions in His very being. To teach, He does not even have to open His mouth; He manifests the Father merely by letting Himself be seen. This is what He declares during the discourse after the Last Supper, in a few words that are very gentle but inexhaustible in meaning. Philip has pleaded: "Lord, show us the Father, and it is enough for us." And Jesus answers: "Philip, he that seeth Me seeth the Father also" (John 14: 8 f.). Words and sights are no longer needed; He Himself com-

[18] *In Ioan.*, XXIX, 3 (PL, XXXV, 1629).

municates the whole truth to the souls of those who cleave to Him.

As the truth is whole, in the sense that it expresses everything, His revelation is whole, in the sense that it leads to a full comprehension of Him. In itself, the mystery is above our understanding (John 1:18; 5:37; 3:12; 6:46; 17:25); but in Christ it draws near to us and becomes something familiar. Jesus never speaks of it as a cold and distant truth made known to us to humble our minds. On the contrary, He exhibits it as a light (1:9; 3:19–22; 12:32 ff., 44 ff.), as a life (1:4; 3:16), as a vision that God grants us (6:44; 14:7, 17, 19; 15:26; 16:13). Our part is to open our minds to the light that is offered (1:6, 10; 3:19, 32; 5:34, 38), to believe (20:21), to love (8:42; 14:20–23), to obey the commandments (7:17; 15:10), to make ourselves docile (5:24; 6:37, 40, 44, 65; 8:47), above all to attach ourselves to Christ (7:28; 8:19; 14:6, 20; 17:2, 3, 7, 8, 24); then we shall acquire a certain understanding of the incomprehensible. This understanding is not the fruit of an accumulation of concepts, but comes from living contact with the living truth, "because I live, and you shall live" (14:19).

For He is the total explanation of the mystery no less than He is the one who reveals it. And He comes to clarify it in us, as the Gospel says with insistence (John 1:16 f.; 20:31), and as He repeats so often (3:15 f.; 4:14, 36; 5:13). The entire Trinity comes with Him to dwell in each breast (14:23, 26; 6:45; 15:25). In consequence of this indwelling, we have in us all that we need in order to understand; but in Him and through Him. But if each of us possesses Him, we possess Him even more perfectly in the unity which all of us together form. Jesus Himself gives this unity as a reflection, an image, a participation of the unity of the divine persons (17:11, 21 ff.). The Church, and each Christian in the Church, lives with the unity that is an explanation of the Trinity, because each lives a life received from the Trinity.

The mystery of the elevation which God effects in the soul of each man and in all mankind taken together, is just what is needed to supply the key to the mystery He reveals about Himself. The mystery is the inner life of God; the explanation is the communication of this life. This is a very special kind of explanation, as we see. It is not found in a system of abstract concepts which we have to penetrate at the cost of great effort; rather it is one with the life we receive, as the mystery itself is identical with the life God lives.

The explanation is not so much an object of study we force our-selves to contemplate, or a source of casual, passing satisfaction; it is an explanation that is living and that has to be lived. It is rooted in the principle of our will and intellect, and cannot be detached so as to be scrutinized from without, but unites itself to our soul in order to strengthen, enlighten, and confirm our intellect and will from within.

This revelation proceeds from Christ with a movement that is quite natural. We must now examine how it enters into Christians with essentially the same natural movement. The revelation reaches us in a continuous flow. Christ who conveyed it with His lips of flesh during the days of His mortal life, has never ceased to diffuse it and adapt it to the new intellectual needs of mankind during the centuries of His mystical life. This He does through the ministry of the Church.

When we regard His teaching as expressed in words, formulas, conciliar declarations, and abstruse and difficult theological texts, we may be tempted to think of constraining bands imposed from without. It is nothing of the sort. These formulas have a necessary and vital part to play in Christian life. In Christ and in the conscious-ness He has as head there are found a superabundance and a kind of pressure of fullness that flow into His members through doctrines and formulas. Corresponding to this there are found in Christians and in their consciousness as members a need and a kind of appeal to be filled; and so they turn toward these teachings and formulas. The interior life of members consists in being in a state of perpetual reception and request.

For, as we showed above, these members are conscious that they are members, and their consciousness flows to them unceasingly from Christ. But a consciousness that would be nothing but an in-tellectual entity would not be a true human consciousness; it would be imperceptible and indivisible. Without words to express it, men would not be able to release it, and so it would be unconscious for them. Human consciousness does not come into existence without sensible signs, any more than the human soul comes into existence without a material body. The human consciousness cannot exist without the sensible signs; the one implies the other; and all together make up God's true donation.

The gift of formulas necessarily remained imperfect and incomplete during the period of the Old Testament. But now, during the period of full grace, we need formulas that are as exact as they can be made. Such are the formulas which Christ has given and which He continues to give in the Church.

They may come from without, but their effect is within; they permit the faithful to realize what they are through the gift that came from without. The formulas speak of the pure, transcendent Being and His gift; but this transcendent Being has given Himself and has become immanent in Christ. To express what they are in their immanence, Christians must express this transcendent Being; are they not divinized, adopted sons, and members of the Word? What need have they of a consciousness that would represent to them nothing but what is ordinary and human? They have entered into a new creation and a new being, the theandric being, who, through the Incarnation, communicates to them the inner life of Him who is Being itself, and admits them to the Trinity.

The formulas that convey this knowledge to them are not a dead letter. By revealing God to them in precise terms, the formulas make them aware of their best and most essential possession. The only way they can be known as Christians who live in the Son as He lives by the Father is through a revelation that comes from the Father.

To correspond exactly to the life lived by Christians, the message has to be received, as this life has to be received; it has to come to them with the advent of this life; it has to come to them from God, in Christ, as a formula that is imposed, as a dogma. But this transcendent aspect adapts the message to the interior life it announces and, far from making it something external to Christians, renders it more internal. For Christ who teaches these formulas in the Church is identically He who is more interior to Christians than they are themselves. He is the interior principle of the life they have as sons of God. His voice, which comes from outside, also comes from within, from those inner depths where He gives them to themselves. The voice is exterior but possesses an inner force; it follows the same course as the life and consciousness of the members and is their voice, for it is the voice of Him through whom they exist.

As long as we regard Christians apart from the Church and Christ, the revelation that is expressed in words seems to come to them from outside. But if we regard Christians in Christ and the Church, and consider them precisely as Christians, this outer aspect disappears. Then we behold but a single organism in its entirety, the whole Christ, head and body. It is He who builds Himself up in unity, by imparting to the whole the unity of the head; it is He, too, who develops Himself as knowing and as conscious, and who reveals Himself to Himself, by the power He has as head, by the knowledge that flows from the head. As the head is spirit and body and as the members are spirit and body, so this knowledge that comes to the members from the head is spirit and body, inner light and material formulas. But the two make up one knowledge and one consciousness, just as body and spirit are one person. Both factors in this unity come from the same origin, but each in its own way, in order that everything may come from Christ and that Christians may be perfect members of Christ and faithful members of the Word.

Accordingly the acceptance of formulas is quite different from the docility of children in elementary school, and belief in dogmatic pronouncements implies much more than a mere verbal enrichment. Such acceptance or belief is the outer, corporeal aspect of a fellowship with pure eternal light and with the Word of God who was made flesh. Without these formulas, the Word would not have become flesh and a man in the most complete sense. Through them, as through the sacraments, the Word of the Father enters into us.

When Christians, by the grace of God, profess belief in these truths, what takes place in them is in continuity and union with what takes place in God. Flesh and blood do not reveal these words to them; the Father Himself begets His Son and His light in Christians; and the Son is God of God, light of light. The first principle of this profession of faith and of the words expressing it is not found in them; strictly speaking, this principle is not even the Son, but the Father. As the Father is He who begets the Son, as the Son is begotten by the Father, as Christ is the Son and has a mystical body, so Christians are begotten by the Father as adopted sons in Christ, the only Son. The Son is Word and expression; and they too, in Him alone, are begotten as word and expression, that they may be perfect as their Father is perfect, in Him who is their brother and their all, the Word.

We have to repeat here what we said about Christ's human consciousness. The head's consciousness does not utter the Word, but the Word is uttered by the Father in it, for Christ's humanity subsists in the Word Himself, and His whole humanity, including its consciousness, has to be intrinsically adapted to this subsistence. The same is true of the whole Christ and of the consciousness of the Son's members. Their consciousness has to be in harmony with the head's consciousness and has to receive influence from the head's consciousness; it possesses a similar, though deficient and derived, expression of the Word. Hence we must conclude that this expression comes from the Father and is begotten by the Father; its origin is the same as that of the Word Himself, for only one origin is possible; it is connected with the Word's origin by title of membership in Him who is the Word.

Consequently the knowledge thus possessed by Christians is not wholly the work of their cognitive faculties. It is not produced, like the rest of their knowledge, by the abstractive processes of the agent intellect or by some reaction of their intellectual life in response to the stimulation of sensation. The consciousness of the Word's members is dependent on the Word, and the Word is begotten and uttered by the Father. Without this Word begotten by the Father, their knowledge would be engulfed by obscurity, just as the air would lose its illumination were the sun to be extinguished.

Yet the members' knowledge is not the Word Himself and is not uttered by the Father. Such a fancy would betray ignorance of the distinction between the two natures in Christ and also of the distinction between Creator and creature. This knowledge is expressed by man, for it is human. Faith, like the vision that will come later, is truly an activity of man and, in this sense, is truly human and can convey only what is human, as we showed above. If the Trinity is expressed in man's knowledge, it is expressed in a human fashion, in its union with man through Christ alone, throughout the economy of salvation that is described in Christian teaching. The Trinity is expressed by man, and his consciousness is truly a human consciousness that expresses something related to it as the natural ego is related to natural consciousness; and this something is the Trinity, Father, Son, and Holy Ghost, as united with mankind in Christ, head of mankind and of the Church. The consciousness of Christian men truly expresses all this; but what it expresses is possible and has meaning only because God unites it to the Word uttered by the Father, in such a way that it is adapted to the Word by sharing in the adaptation that perfects Christ's humanity.

Although this knowledge is truly human and is effected by man, it is also given and produced by God in those who, being members of Christ, are members of God. But God does not produce it merely as first cause, in the way He produces everything, nor as sole cause by creation, in the way that, for example, He could produce a perfectly mastered knowledge of Latin in the mind of a child. He produces it by union, by becoming really and hypostatically one with a man who is really and mystically one with all Christians. Hence He produces it by way of union, not by way of creation.

Undoubtedly we can rightly say that God creates or con-creates this knowledge, in the sense that He is its supreme cause. But He does not create it in the sense of calling it into existence in beings wholly separate from Him by a simple command, in the way He brings other things into existence. It cannot be created in this way; it exists only in union with God and His interior light. Production of it by ordinary creation would imply the creating of God Himself; and what other creator is there to create the unique Creator?

God creates this exalted knowledge by creating that filial character of which it is the expression, and which we discussed in the preceding chapter. He creates it by the gift of Himself, by the unceasing bestowal of Himself. In the order of knowledge, therefore, it corresponds exactly to a filial way of existing in the order of being. It proceeds from this filial character by the power of the Father, in Christ the Son, for that power produced the filial character; but it proceeds from the humanity of the man Christ, in whom this filial character is fully realized.

The outburst of light that is the generation of the Son in the Trinity and the faith that ardently embraces the sacred dogmatic formulas go together. We may not stop with looking at the exterior; we must contemplate the interior. When we know and love a person we recognize him in the sound of his voice, in the way he chooses and accents his words; we catch the vibration of his soul in the vibration of his speech. In the same way they who believe in Christ and love Him and receive His word in charity, also receive Him, together with the Father and the Spirit. "The words that I speak to you, I speak not of Myself. If anyone love Me, he will keep My word, and My Father will love him, and We will come to him and will make Our abode with him. And the word which you have heard is not Mine, but the Father's who sent Me." [19] He who is uttered by the Father and spirates the Holy Ghost enters along with His words into the heart that opens itself. In Christ the entire mystery of the Trinity comes to take possession of mankind.

The words, the revelation cast into formulas, are the sensible manifestation of the substantial revelation that is Christ, the incarnate Word; they are rays of the divine light that searches out the depths of the human race; they are a source that is the welling-up of a subterranean pool of water. They are spirit and life, not because they are syllables and sounds, but because they are the outer, corporeal aspect of the life that communicates itself interiorly, the life of Christ, light of light who sheds light over those who belong to Him.

For Christ's members are indeed light, in Him and through Him. The life that comes to them from Him is designed to make known to them what He is and what God is in Himself, as well as to acquaint them with what they are.

In His sacred humanity Christ was a living revelation of the Trinity, not only by His words, but by His very being, His slightest gestures, and even His manner of speaking and acting. In Christ and through Him, the same must be true of Christians. They will reveal the Trinity, assuredly, by repeating the sacred formulas that come to them from Christ and the Church, but also by their mode of life and action, by all that they are. By acting, thinking, and willing in harmony with the grace that inspires them, by being always and in all circumstances adopted sons of God in the true Son, they will be some sort of revelation of the Trinity for themselves and their brethren. They will be a revelation of the Trinity in their conduct, for the revelation of Christ is perpetuated in His members. Christ's humanity was able to reveal the Word and the Trinity because of its union with the Word and the Trinity. This union is continued in Christ's members by their incorporation into Him, and carries the same weighty meaning.

To gain a clear understanding of the Trinity, therefore, Christians ought to conduct themselves more and more as members of Him who is the Son, that is, as adopted sons. They ought to have more and more confidence in the Father, and an ever more perfect spirit of abandonment to Him, dependence on Him, and zeal for Him. Then,

[19] John 14:10, 23 f.

as theology points out, they will acquire a living appreciation and an experimental knowledge of the Trinity.

The spirituality of divine adoption, the "little way" of spiritual childhood, is far from being a matter of no consequence; it is a psychological and ontological adaptation to the message brought by the Son, and it is an approach to an interior knowledge of this message, a knowledge by sympathy and connaturality, or rather by an inner incorporation into the Son and a deeper understanding of themselves; the two come to the same thing.

Revelation has by no means sunk into silence; it remains here on earth, because the Word remains here, as encompassing, as interior, as powerful as ever. Revelation remains, and is always the same; nothing is added or modified. The Word is perpetuated in His mystical body, and His teaching is contained in it.

CHAPTER XIV

THE HOLY SPIRIT

INTRODUCTION

WE come at length to the Holy Spirit, through whom we are made adopted sons of the Father in the Son. The function of the Holy Spirit is extremely important in the lives of Christians; theology, in our day as in former ages, rightly insists on His part in the sanctification of souls. St. Paul attributes almost as much to the Holy Spirit as he does to Christ.[1]

Indeed, the powerful influence exercised by the Holy Spirit gives rise to a difficulty. How can we say that the Holy Spirit accomplishes the whole task without denying that Christ accomplishes the whole task? We can readily understand how some have succumbed to the temptation of regarding the work of the Holy Spirit as the completion of Christ's work, which in that case is thought of as being imperfect. In different ways this temptation has successfully assailed the Montanists, the Fraticelli, the Joachimites, and all those who have imagined three successive reigns of increasing perfection: the reign of the Father in the Old Testament, the reign of the Son in the New Testament, and the reign of the Spirit in a future epoch that is being made ready by the New Testament. How could they have missed the truth that God's work, after the Fall and even before, is summed up in Christ the Son, and that it consists in bringing the whole of creation to the Father, in the Son, through the Spirit?

Hence we believe we should be in error were we to search for the place of the Spirit outside that of Christ, and to say, for example, that He comes to contribute the finishing touch, that it is

---

[1] Cf. J. Lebreton, *History of the Dogma of the Trinity* (London: Burns Oates and Washbourne, 1939), I, 316 f.

He who inspires and evokes all that is most exquisite and heroic in Christian fervor, or that His domain is the reign of the perfect. This is at once too much and too little. It is too much, because the Spirit of union does not occupy a private reserve and because everything, absolutely everything, has been given to us in Christ. It is also too little, because the Spirit of the Lord fills the whole earth and the entire work is His.

In reality, no separation may be made. The Spirit is all and accomplishes all in His own way, just as the Father and the Son are all and accomplish all in their way. But everything is summed up in the Incarnation and in the incarnate Word, and the explanation of the Spirit's work has to be found within the totality of Christ. Mankind has no access to the Father as Father except in the incarnate Son; neither does it possess the Spirit as Spirit except in the Son. If we wish to know how mankind possesses the Spirit, all we have to do is know how the Son possesses Him, or more accurately, how the humanity assumed by the Son possesses Him. Once this point is fixed, the possession possible for regenerated mankind is likewise fixed: it will be a mystical extension of the sacred humanity's possession of the Spirit, just as all regenerated humanity is the mystical extension of the humanity assumed by Christ. Since the Incarnation may be regarded in two different ways, this possession may likewise be regarded in two different ways: as an action that unites humanity to divinity, or as a state induced in united humanity by this action.

I. The Holy Spirit and the Action That Incarnates and Sanctifies

Regarded as an action, the work that effects the Incarnation is attributed to the Holy Spirit, although it is common to the three divine persons. The same is true of every work of sanctification which fashions the mystical body of Christ and which is a prolongation of the work of the Incarnation, as this body itself is a prolongation of Christ; that is, it is undoubtedly common to the three divine persons, but is ascribed to the Holy Spirit by appropriation. The reason for this has already been given: all divine works *ad extra* are common to the three persons, and the Incarnation, no less than sanctification regarded as an action, is a work *ad extra*.

However, as we have seen, the Incarnation is not *ad extra* in the same sense as the other works of God. It is *ad extra* by logical priority; in the mentally conceived instant that precedes it, the humanity, regarded in itself, is exterior to the divinity. But the Incarnation consists precisely and formally in causing the sacred humanity to cease being exterior. Therefore the Incarnation is *ad intra* by reason of its effect, by the personality it gives to this humanity. Of course the Incarnation does not produce anything in the person of the Word, but as a result of it the assumed humanity has no other personality than this person.

If creation is the production of the order *ad extra*, the Incarnation is the taking of a creature to the Word *ad intra* so that it may subsist henceforth not in itself but in Him; it inaugurates what we have called the "order of what is interiorized," the order of that which, left to itself, would be *ad extra*, but which God has caused to subsist in His Word *ad intra* and which, in this sense, is *ad intra*.

Obviously this action is mysterious. We would be incapable of describing it further if God Himself had not given us information on the subject in Scripture and tradition, which attribute it to the Holy Spirit. The Incarnation, as we have noted, is attributed particularly to the Holy Spirit. Our justification is likewise attributed to Him. He who formed the head also forms the members. He who fashioned Christ's physical body also fashions His mystical body, for the one may not be cut off from the other. The same Holy Spirit who was sent to Nazareth was sent to the Cenacle; and the Church was born on the day of Pentecost, as Jesus was conceived on the day of the Annunciation, *de Spiritu Sancto*.

This birth of the Church extends over the centuries. New regions are Christianized, new Christians come into the world, Christian life grows unceasingly in souls. The Holy Spirit is continually being sent, and Pentecost never comes to an end. The book of the Acts exhibits Him as ceaselessly coming down into the world, no longer under the form of fiery tongues, but through the intermediary of the apostles and their preaching. He directs their journeys, He opens up new roads to them and brings others to a close, He inspires their words, fills them with courage, gives them joy, wisdom, and authority. And He pursues the same course in all Christians, by an activity that is similar though quite hidden, until Christ is formed in them. He gives them the spirit of Christ (Rom. 8:9, 11), the mind of Christ (I Cor. 2:11–16), the spirit of adoption that cries out to God in our hearts, "Abba, Father" (Rom. 8:14–18; Gal. 4:6), He pours charity into their hearts (Rom. 5:5), He brings them all together in Christ to be a single organism of salvation (I Cor. 12:11 ff.). He instills the first stirring of faith into the soul (I Cor. 12:3; Rom. 8:27) and, on our entrance into glory, He will endow our bodies with eternal life (Rom. 8:11).

Briefly, God who once before created the world takes it up into His creative hands a second time. In creating it the first time, He gave existence to things; but the second time, He places His own existence in it. And this loving action that proceeds from the Father through the Son to the Spirit is so eminently a work of love that it is attributed to the Spirit.

What is the meaning of this attribution? Certainly, as we have already remarked, there can be no question of an action that belongs exclusively to the Third Person. Although the work of the Incarnation and of sanctification has some connection with the order *ad intra*, as we have tried to make clear, it is not purely *ad intra*.

Yet the attribution of this work to the Holy Spirit is so evident in the documents of our faith and it has so solid a basis in the partially *ad extra* character of the active Incarnation, that it has to mean something real and important. What is this meaning? Theologians propose various explanations. Such lack of agreement is often an indication that a problem is not yet solved; in any case their suggestions are valuable signposts for those who are in search of a solution.

Among other attempts at clarifying this point, they say that the Holy Spirit, who proceeds by way of love and as the terminus of the unity of the Father and the Son so far as they are a single spirating principle, is holiness, love, a kiss, a gift, union, consummation, and perfection. But the work that is accomplished in Christ's humanity and, through it, in all humanity, is a work of love.

We may add that the Holy Spirit is the only person who comes after the Son in the Trinity. But the work of the Incarnation also comes after the Son, for it joins a human nature to this divine person who is eternally anterior to such union. We may conclude that there is some correspondence between this work and the Holy Spirit; and the Spirit seems to occupy the right place in the Trinity for its accomplishment. Or again, we suggest that the Holy Spirit, who has no proper action in the life of the Trinity, has one by appropriation in the extension of this life which is the Incarnation.

II. The Holy Spirit and the Incarnation: Christ the Spirator even as Man

The preceding exposition is no more than an introduction, in which the Incarnation is regarded in the act that produced it, not as it is in itself and in the new manner of being it confers on the assumed humanity. We must now consider it from this latter point of view. This study will enable us to fill out the explanations that have been given on the role of the Holy Spirit in the act that incarnates the Word. These explanations have been incomplete up to now, and should be so regarded. They have been given priority out of respect for logical procedure, in which the act of the cause precedes its effect. Furthermore, we possess traditional formulas on this subject, and we had to take them into account, especially as they furnished us with an excellent point of departure. Unfortunately, consecrated formulas are lacking for the aspect we are now going to discuss, namely, the Incarnation and sanctification regarded as achieved; and this is a difficulty. On the other hand, as we have noted, a satisfactory theological explanation of the part we have already considered is hardly available, whereas in the further development we are now undertaking our course of reasoning is clearly marked out by the central dogmas of Christianity.

The earnest endeavor to gain some knowledge of the Holy Spirit is a real way of adoring Him. The Spirit of truth comes in the name of Christ to speak within our hearts, and He does not draw near to us for the purpose of hiding Himself. In thinking about Him with all our energy, while preserving complete docility to the data of revelation and full adherence to the truth He suggests, we do not consecrate ourselves less to Him than by keeping silent; indeed, we consecrate to Him our very activity.

This is the attitude we wish to maintain when speaking of Him with the bold and humble simplicity of God's children, who are truly at ease, however awkward they may be, when they are occupied with the affairs of their Father. They have within them the Spirit of God's children, the Spirit of divine adoption, the Spirit of truth, and He informs them about all the blessings they have received; and God has told them over and over that they have received the Spirit.

In the preceding chapter we remarked that the resemblance between the Father and the Son, which is the resemblance between the Speaker and the Spoken, between the "consciousness" that expresses and the "consciousness" that is expressed, is such that it necessarily implies unity. The perfection of this consciousness requires unity; but it also requires a real distinction between these two persons. Hence the unity exists between two who remain two; it does not consist in their identity of nature, but results from their distinction as persons, the distinction between the perfect exemplar and the perfect image, between the Father who is exclusively the Father and the Son who is exclusively the Son.

Therefore this unity, of which we may catch at least a glimpse, cannot be identical with the persons, for they remain two. Consequently it must have a term that is distinct from them, and also, to be perfectly their unity, it must have a term that is as perfect as they are, and hence is personal like them in its very relation to them; in God, the persons are relations. Accordingly the unity must proceed from them and be distinct from them, because they are its principle and because it has its origin from this principle. With respect to it, the two others must be one, but one in a way consistent with their distinction as Speaker and Spoken, as two persons entirely alike in their very distinctness; theirs is a unity that exists only in duality. Therefore the Spirit, in His very relation to such a unity, must be connected with these persons as distinct in themselves, as Father and Son, while being in Himself their unity regarded in its term.

So far, all we have said involves no more than procession by way of intellect and the consequence of such procession. We must now come to procession by way of will and love, which is the procession of the Holy Spirit. The action of the unity we have been discussing, which follows the action of knowing and the uttering of the Word, is an action of the will and of love. The will is the power of withholding oneself and of distending oneself; love is the force that unites; and the movement of the two follows the movement of knowledge.

However, we are not going to give a complete theory of procession by way of the will, and still less are we going to refashion an accepted theory; such an undertaking would be too vast and too naive. We intend to do no more than treat of it briefly, as we did in the case of procession by way of the intellect, so as to accomodate slightly the course of traditional theology to the lines of thought we have made our own in this work.

Love, then, by which we mean spiritual love, is an act of the will, of the soul. If this were the place to treat the matter philosophically, we should say that its object is being as being, or rather as Good, and also the ego of the one who loves. As the act of a rational appetite, its object is being as good; as the act of a particular rational appetite belonging to a particular subject, its object is the ego of this subject. Being and the ego are two necessary objects, although they are not necessary in the same way. The first, that is, being, is absolutely necessary, for the rational appetite as rational, and hence every rational appetite, requires such an object; the other, the ego, is only relatively necessary, that is, it is necessary for the subject in whom this appetite is found, and hence for this particular appetite. These considerations naturally stand in need of further amplification, but that would take us too far afield, and after what we said earlier about the intellect, the course of the development may be surmised.

At any rate every love, however disinterested it may seem to be and actually is, is a self-love, and nevertheless every spiritual love, however self-centered it may be, is by an exigency of nature a love of being itself and passes beyond the lover's own limitations. At present we are more interested in love of self than in love of being, but we should not forget that the one implies the other, as the knowledge of oneself supposes the knowledge of being, and vice versa.

In God alone the two are strictly identical, for God alone is pure being. His love of Himself is the love of all the infinity of Being, and His unrestricted love of being is nothing but love of Himself. God loves Himself, and all the infinity of His love consists in that love of Himself. He loves Himself as He knows Himself; He cannot love Himself except by knowing Himself, and this love is His essence by identity. The same love is found entirely and identically in each of the divine persons.

Like God's knowledge, this love is so perfect that, while ever remaining undivided, it entails an interior procession, that of the Third Person. For love has an immanent fecundity. To love and will oneself is a certain manner of being in oneself and for oneself, a way of being possessed and embraced as an object of complacence, of self-donation to self, of placing oneself in oneself in a recognition of the interior unity which one has in oneself. A being must exist for himself in his very being, just as he exists for himself by his knowledge; he must exist in himself as loved and willed by himself, just as he is known by himself.

The existence of such an immanent term is evidently less clearly known in the action of the will than in the action of the intellect, precisely because the will and not the intellect is in question. But we believe we can vindicate its reality by observing how every love, even the love for external objects, is more charmed by its own inner dream, more captivated by an ideal it sets before itself, than it is held by the thing that is regarded as its object. This ideal is not something conceived or reasoned, except in the sense that within the unity of man the intellect comes into play and is aware of what the will experiences; it is rather something that urges and attracts, a finality that stimulates and beckons. Its existence is manifested in the very illusions love cherishes, in the demands of perfection it inspires, in the severities, the blindness, and the clairvoyance it calls forth. Every man realizes that he bears within himself a highly flattering portrait of himself, and he would gladly judge himself by it; we say "portrait" in lieu of a better word, for what we are referring to is not an image or a representation, but an obscure aspiration.

Thus love forges for itself its own object and its own motivation. In its own way it is fecund; it moves itself and inaugurates itself, and is free in the sense that it establishes a place for itself and causes its own act. As soon as someone begins to love, he exists in himself and for himself; he is in himself as that which is loved because he is engaged in the act of loving; without this, he would not love.

This immanent process helps us to understand the spiration of the Holy Spirit. God loves Himself. This love, being mysterious and perfect, mysteriously and perfectly issues in this sort of production, this placing of oneself in oneself.

God knows Himself in a consciousness that expresses and in a consciousness that is expressed, and subsists as knowing in the distinction between the Speaker and the Spoken. In the same way He loves Himself in a love that "spirates" and in a love that is spirated, in an active love and a passive love, and subsists as loving in this distinction between the love that proceeds and the love from which the latter proceeds.

Such is the procession of the Holy Spirit: spiration of love, sigh

of love, kiss and gift, union and communion, charity and inner consummation. But this love is so infinite and efficacious, and also so
simple and self-enclosed, that the term arising within it is as powerful, as real, and as personal as the love itself: *unus amor spiratus, qui
est identice id omne quod est unus amor spirans.*

This procession necessarily presupposes procession by way of
intellect, which is the procession of the Word, and in a sense is a
continuation of the latter; the two are quite distinct but nevertheless
connected. The Word, being the perfect image of the Father, is a
person distinct from the Father; here we have procession by way
of the intellect. But we must go on to say that, because the Word
is the perfect image of the Father, the Father and the Son necessarily
love each other and are united to each other in this love and union,
which has as its term the Holy Spirit; and here we have procession by
way of the will.

The procession of the Holy Spirit has only one principle. The
Council of Florence has defined this truth: "Let all profess that the
Holy Spirit is eternally from the Father and the Son, and has His
essence and His subsistence equally from the Father and the Son, and
proceeds eternally from both as from one principle by a single spiration." [2] The Father and the Son in their unity are the principle of the
Holy Spirit, and each of the two, as distinct from the other, is a co-
principle: *duo spirantes sunt unus Spirator.*

The Holy Spirit proceeds from the Son, not so far as the latter is
distinct from the Father as Son, but so far as the Son, while being
distinct from the Father, is identically what the Father is. Thus the
Son is no less the principle of the Holy Spirit than the Father is, although He is the principle of the Holy Spirit by His own procession
from the Father. Accordingly, when we say that the Father is the
principle of the Holy Spirit, we say the same of the Son, for the Son
receives from the Father the power to be the principle of the Holy
Spirit. For this reason we should do better to avoid saying that the
Son is the principle of the Holy Spirit unless we add that He is such
along with the Father and by reception from the Father; the Son is
principium de principio. We state here once for all that this is what
we have in mind in these pages, even when, for the sake of brevity or
emphasis, we say that the Son is the Spirator.

It is well to observe that the unity of spiration does not come to

[2] Denz., 691.

the Father and Son from the Holy Spirit. On the contrary, the Holy Spirit proceeds from this unity. Furthermore, the Holy Spirit is not the reason why the Father and the Son love each other; this love of the Father and the Son is the origin of the Holy Spirit. The Holy Spirit is not in any sense a principle with respect to the other two persons; but they are a principle with respect to Him.

Consequently the unity of spiration is not a unity of reciprocal love, for such a love implies two principles of love. Love in the Father and the Son, regarded as notional, is so intense and perfect that reciprocity is presupposed by it, but is not found in it; this love is the realization of that perfect unity toward which created loves can only aspire. This is the unity that has the Holy Spirit as its term, *in unitate Spiritus Sancti.*

Moreover, as is quite clear, this unity of spiration is not the unity of a love which the Father and the Son would have separately each for Himself, for they are not distinct in their love; they are distinct only as Speaker and Spoken. Nor is spiration the act of the divine essence for itself, the term of the love which the Godhead as such has for itself. Regarded as pertaining to the divine essence, such love is common to all three divine persons, and is one in all of them; hence it has none of them as a term distinct from the others.

This essential love subsists in three divine persons, just as the divine essence subsists in three persons. The absolute consciousness that is the divine essence is identical with three conscious relations, which actually are this one consciousness, each in its own way, that is, as expressing, as expressed, and as the unity of the two taken in its term. In the same way the absolute and eternal love of God for Himself is identical with three relations of love, of which two are spirating love or love that is a principle of an immanent term, their duality being prerequisite to this love, while the third, the spirated love, is the love that is the term of this spirating love. Each of these three relations is wholly love, as each of the three is wholly the divine consciousness; yet each is this love in a particular way, in a special relationship to the others.

The conclusion of all this is that the Word who is Christ is spirating love, the co-principle of the Holy Spirit; He is love, as the Holy Spirit is love, but in His own way, in the relationship of principle to term. To be thus the Spirator or principle of the Holy Spirit is as essential to Him as to be Son. When we say that He is Son, we indicate His entire origin; when we say that He spirates the Holy Spirit, we indicate His entire activity; and the two together designate Him in His entirety. He is nothing but Spirator as He is nothing but Son, for in their absolute simplicity the two are strictly identical.

Undoubtedly there is a certain kind of distinction, that is, a virtual distinction, between Spirator and Son. For, abstracting from all mental consideration of them, the two, taken in themselves, admit of contradictory predicates, as the Spirator is by identity the Father, and the Son is not the Father. Yet, in the mystery of the Trinity, the identity between the two is nevertheless absolute, like the identity between this Spirator and the divine nature, although here too the same virtual distinction obtains, since the Spirit is by identity the divine nature, whereas He is not in any sense the Spirator. We may even say that the person of the Son is identical with the Spirator before He is identical with the divine nature (with a purely rational priority, as is evident), for the Spirator pertains to the notional order, which is intermediate between the orders of essence and person.

Accordingly, as it is true to say that the man Jesus Christ is God because He is the Word, and, in this sense, that He is the Word prior to being God (with a priority of reason), it is true to say that this man is the Word prior to being Spirator, but also that He is Spirator prior to being God.

The man Jesus Christ, as we have just said, is the Spirator together with the Father, *principium de principio*. This is the point we must next consider.

Although the assumed humanity is not the divinity nor spiration, it subsists in Him who is the Spirator of the Holy Spirit and is truly and intrinsically the humanity of Him from whom the Holy Spirit proceeds. These are not approximations to the truth or pious exaggerations or even theological appropriations that remain mere appropriations in spite of their exactness. Our statement is an accurate declaration of great Christian dogmas. Hence we need not debate the matter; we have only to believe. We should also meditate, for the whole of the revealed message, with its original vitality, is found in these great truths and supreme principles.

What we have to say on this subject is the counterpart of what we said earlier in treating of the work of grace given to us by Christ. This work, as we pointed out, is accomplished by the Holy Spirit; Christ was conceived and born of the Holy Spirit.

The Gospel often represents Jesus as having a special attitude toward the Holy Spirit which He does not take with respect to the Father. "The Father is greater than I," He once said; [3] but He says nothing of the sort about the Holy Spirit. On the contrary, the Spirit receives from Him; [4] the Spirit will perform the task previously assigned to Him by Jesus Christ. Jesus promises Him, sends Him, and gives Him, for the Spirit is His: He is the Spirit of Jesus, as we read in the Acts [5] or, what comes to the same thing, the Spirit of the Lord.[6] Of course this power comes to Jesus from His divinity; but, as we gather from reading the Gospel, the sacred humanity is no more excluded from it than from the person of the Word. With His human lips He declares: "It is expedient to you that I go [by His death and ascension, hence in His humanity]; for if I go not, the Paraclete will not come to you; but if I go, I will send Him to you." [7] Later on, He breathed on His disciples with His human breath and said to them: "Receive ye the Holy Ghost. Whose sins you shall forgive, they are forgiven them, and whose sins you shall retain, they are retained" (John 20:22 f.). Briefly, His human nature has its part in His divine relations with the Holy Spirit, for it was assumed precisely for the purpose of divinizing the human race, that is, of giving grace to men, and this purpose is realized through the invisible mission of the Holy Spirit.

The witness of tradition is the same. For example, this is what St. Athanasius says:

The Word as Word and Wisdom is not anointed by the Spirit whom He Himself gives, but the flesh assumed by Him is anointed by the Spirit and in the Spirit, in order that the holiness conferred on the Lord as man may flow out from Him to all men.[8]

Later the saint comes back to this idea and gives it stronger expression:

As the Word, prior to His incarnation, gave to the saints His Spirit as something of His own, so also, once He had become man, He sanctifies all men by the Spirit, and says to His disciples: "Receive ye the Holy

[3] John 14:28.
[4] John 16:14 f.
[5] Acts 16:7.
[6] Acts 5:9; 8:39.
[7] John 16:7.
[8] St. Athanasius, *Contra Arianos,* I, 47 (*PG,* XXVI, 109).

Ghost." He also gave the Spirit to the seventy other men; for it is through the Spirit that David prays to the Father in these words: "Take not Thy Holy Spirit from me" (Ps. 50:13). And when He had become man He said: "I will send you [the Paraclete], the Spirit of truth" (John 15:26); and the Word of God, who cannot lie, has indeed sent Him. Therefore "Jesus Christ, yesterday and today and the same forever" (Heb. 13:8), who never changes, is the one who both gives and receives: He gives, as the Word of God; He receives, as man. For the Word as Word does not profit by the gift; He always had everything and He always will have everything. But men begin to receive good things in Him and through Him. Accordingly, when we are told that He is anointed in His human nature, we are to understand that we are the ones who are anointed in Him.[9]

Let us note well the course of the thought: the God-man, because of what He is, possesses the fullness of the Spirit and has it in His humanity, not assuredly by reason of this humanity, but by reason of Him to whom the humanity belongs; and He pours out this fullness over the whole human race. This mysterious communication, this participation in Christ's humanity, is an earnest of what our own humanity is to become, and anticipates what we shall say in the last section of this chapter. Likewise the texts which we shall then adduce will provide a forceful commentary on the texts from which we have just quoted a few examples. The whole of Christian teaching holds closely together.

But we must proceed. Christ's humanity possesses this relationship to the Holy Spirit in the most intrinsic way possible, that is, by the personality that is its own. Although quite distinct from this personality, the humanity is so united to it that the man thus constituted is this very person, not by juridical imputation or by something equivalent to grace, but by strict ontological subsistence. The man *is* the person.

This course of reasoning is unescapable. It is the reasoning that has been employed to bring out the "filial" and "verbal" perfecting of the sacred humanity, and that has always been employed in theology to bring out the grace and divinization which the humanity has to possess in fullness. The humanity must likewise have an elevation that truly makes it the humanity of the Spirator, that is the real foundation of the real relation with the Spirator which is the hypo-

[9] *Ibid.*, I, 48 (*PG*, XXVI, 112).

static union, that fits it for the exalted position it now occupies, and that enables it to act in a way suitable for such a humanity.

Active spiration in the infinite Word is not nothing; it is the whole of His personal activity. And the humanity of Jesus subsists in this pure source of eternal life. How could anyone imagine that the humanity is not affected thereby! Let such a one observe how an explosion of a dynamite charge affects the dust lying about. "Each of these natures, though in union with the other, performs functions proper to itself: the Word does what belongs to the Word, and the flesh does what belongs to the flesh." [10] This is exactly what we are trying to say; each nature exists in its own way, and this existence expresses itself in its own way of acting; but each acts in union with the other. The Word does what is proper to the Word. To Him belong the miracles and works of sanctification, as the holy Pontiff goes on to explain as he seeks to illustrate his doctrine with concrete examples; and to these examples we may add that work which belongs to the Word as Word, namely, the co-spiration of the Holy Spirit. This latter activity clearly differs from the others, since the humanity is not employed as an instrument therein, as it is in the operations that are properly theandric, such as the various healings and the redemption. Indeed, the humanity cannot have any part in the spiration of the Spirit, although it does truly cooperate and is made to cooperate in the work of the Incarnation, which is the divinization of the universe. But we may not conclude that the humanity remains outside this spiration. How could that be, seeing that it is not outside the Word whose whole activity consists in this spiration, and that the Word is one with His humanity and does not at any time or in any of His actions lay aside the hypostatic union? Even in spirating the Holy Spirit the Word is He who has become man and who makes the sacred humanity His own; consequently He spirates in union and communion with His human nature. Although Christ's human nature has no part in the spiration in virtue of its nature, it does have a part through the hypostasis that is ontologically and absolutely its sole subsistence. The distinction between the human nature and the Spirator is indeed infinite; yet the human nature is united to Him.

We may add that the formal effect produced in the human nature by this union, the real and interior foundation that makes this union a real relation, the intrinsic adaptation that keeps the union from

[10] St. Leo the Great, *Tomus ad Flavianum*, 4 (Denz., 144).

being violent and contrary to nature, are likewise inconceivably sublime. A humanity that in itself, though not by itself, becomes the humanity of the Spirator, is not left unenriched.

A little farther on in the document we have quoted, St. Leo remarks:

Although in our Lord Jesus Christ there is only one person who is both God and man, the source of the lowliness predicated in common of both natures [as when Christ said: "The Father is greater than I"], is different from the source of the glory common to both [as when He said: "I and the Father are one"]. For from us men He has the humanity in which He is inferior to the Father, from the Father He has the divinity in which He is equal to the Father.[11]

"The glory common to both": although the two natures differ infinitely, the reality of the union requires that the glory of the one should be shared by the other, in the degree possible to the latter. No glory belongs more immediately to the divine person of the Son— for the divine nature is united to the humanity in His person—than the glory of being Spirator. Consequently none can be more fully shared by the sacred humanity.

At bottom this effect must be the same as the divinization and sonship we spoke of earlier, for the Spirator is God and the Son by identity. Yet it has to have some special feature corresponding to what is special in spiration. But what is special to spiration and makes the Son the Spirator is love, the love that unites Him to the Father and constitutes Him principle of the Spirit, for the spiration of the Holy Spirit is accomplished by way of love.

Consequently love must also adapt the assumed humanity to be the humanity of the Spirator. This is a human love, for it belongs to a human nature; yet it is a love that surpasses the resources of human nature left to itself, since it is called forth by union with divine love. This love is theological charity, such as it existed in Christ. Love such as this has to be found in Christ's human nature. Human nature necessarily admits of spiritual love, for it is a spiritual nature. In Christ, this love has to be love of God and the Spirator. Therefore it has to be a divinized love, so as to be worthy of God who is the Spirator.

[11] *Loc. cit.* (Cavallera, *Thesaurus doctrinae catholicae*, 681).—To make the context clear, a little more of the passage is given than in Mersch's quotation. [Tr.]

The Word is love, for He is spirating love. He is all the love that is God, but in His own way as the Word, in the way of the spirating love that is the principle of spirated love. A human nature and a human love divinized by union with the Word must be divinized in a way befitting spirating love, in a way that conforms this human nature and love to the love of the whole divine nature, yet in a way befitting spirating love.

This is necessary in order that the assumption of the human nature may not be incomplete and defective, in order that the love of this human nature may receive subsistence in the subsistence which the assumed humanity receives in the Word, and, if we may say so, that its first point of departure and personal principle may be the love that is proper to the Word, spirating love.

The assuming of the human nature produces its effect only in the assumed humanity; and it is an action in which God gives Himself so unreservedly (for He gives all of Himself) and acts so intimately (for He acts there by the union of Himself and not by distant production), that it evokes results which are in some sense infinite. All the effects it produces in the order of love are received in human love; and this love alone experiences the weight of the infinite love that presses down on it; how can it fail to take form, down to its deepest constituents, from this infinite love, as from an all-powerful seal?

Actus sunt suppositorum; the very acts of Christ's human nature are acts of the Word, the Spirator. They are strictly and ontologically His acts, not because God regards them as such, but because God has made them such. They are intrinsically the Word's acts, because God's will produces all that is most constitutive and interior in things. Hence these acts must be constituted accordingly. But all human acts derive from love, and in Christ's humanity, which is divinized in its unity as in its being, they derive from love in an even stricter sense. Therefore His human love must be made intrinsically capable of eliciting acts that are true acts of the Spirator. Only thus will it really be the human love of the Spirator, a human love so intense, so perfect, and so powerful that it would be impossible were it not united to the Spirator Himself in hypostatic union, so as to be sustained and divinized by the Spirator's own love.

This love is human; but its "spirating" quality does not come from the fact that it is human; that would be absurd. It has this quality from the spiration of the Spirator and subsists in Him. But we may say that the perfection which it receives and which makes it "spirating" is its conformation to spirating love; because of this conformation it is the human love of the Word as Spirator, and of no other. It is a human love and charity so intense, so perfect, and so powerful that its basis can be nothing else than the Word's spirating love.

Let us never suppose that this human love is left to itself. Christ's human love is not isolated. It is united to the love that is God, and it is personal love because it is the Spirator's love. Its ultimate source (*principium quod*) is the Spirator. Let us think of it in its union with the Word from whom the Spirit who is Love itself incessantly proceeds. The assumed humanity, considered in itself, cannot account for the perfection of the love that is nevertheless its own. The explanation is to be sought in Him who took it to Himself as only He can, who loves with intensity and a sort of ecstasy and fecundity, and who, not having any other personal activity, expresses the excesses of His love in this activity.

Accordingly we have here a new love, an expression in man of God's own love; it is new with a transcendent newness, like the eternal and Trinitarian life that flows into Christians from the Son. Although it is new, it reveals something of divine love, love taken at its source. It is not a love embellished with some external ornament; it is created love intensified as love, by union with infinite Being and Love. It is new because God evokes it otherwise than He evokes all other created loves, that is, by hypostatic union with Himself; and in it He lives the mystery of love.

Therefore it is an "entity of union" and a "love of union" that continues the series of theandric realities discussed in earlier pages. It is a state in which human love rises above its essential limitations and has a supernatural perfection, and in which it subsists in the love that is the co-principle of the Holy Spirit. Such dignity and ardor are impossible except in actual union with the divine person who spirates, and are inconceivable unless they are thought of in conjunction with this person.

This love is theological charity in its perfect realization, the supreme theological charity from which all charity derives. And indeed, when we reflect on Christ's charity, we see that it bears a certain likeness to spirating love. For this charity is the mainspring of all the actions of Christ and of all that He was and suffered. All this was voluntary in Him and was offered up out of love. On the other hand, all His activity and sufferings and states are the great instrumental cause of salvation, and the sole instrumental cause, for other instrumental causes operate through its power.

Thus Christ's charity is the source, within the human race, of the divine life that is diffused throughout mankind, just as spirating love is the principle of the Holy Spirit in the Trinity, and in this sense is the principle of the personal divine life of the Third Person. But the two go together, and Christ's charity is the principle of our divine life because it is the human love of Him who is the principle of the Holy Spirit's divine life.

Perhaps a consideration of the divine missions will contribute some light to this discussion. We said that the love issuing from Christ's humanity is a principle of divinization on earth. And divinization, as we showed at the beginning of this chapter, is brought about through the mission of the Holy Spirit. Therefore, if Christ's humanity divinizes us, it must have some connection with the mission of the Holy Spirit. But how is that possible unless it is united and conformed to the Word who sends the Spirit? And does the Word not send the Spirit because He is the co-principle of the Spirit, and hence spirating love?

Accordingly, if Christ's human love divinizes, and if its whole activity among creatures is taken up with that function, the reason is that it is united and conformed to the Word's spirating love. We have tried to explain this conformation by pointing out that Christ's human love is essentially, by the supernatural elevation it receives from the union, a love belonging to the Spirator, to Him who spirates and sends the Holy Spirit.

Of course the active mission as such belongs only to the Word. It does not belong to the assumed humanity. But this humanity subsists in the Word who sends the Spirit, and in virtue of this subsistence, which is intrinsic to it, also sends the Spirit, although only in conformity with the Author of the mission. And this conformity is likewise intrinsic to the sacred humanity, not by reason of the latter's own nature, but by reason of Him to whom the humanity belongs.

In this way we may explain how the entire work of divinization is effected by Christ and His love, while it is also effected by the Holy Spirit and His sanctifying action. These are not two separate causalities of which one could not operate except by encroaching on the other. The efficacy of Christ's charity depends on the hypostatic union with the Spirator, and the Spirit's action, regarded as a mission, is attached to the spiration of the Spirit by the Spirator; from either point of view, our whole sanctification is wrought in the Son, the incarnate Son.

We may add that the charity found in Christians is exhibited as a participation in the Holy Spirit and an assimilation to Him, and that the same must be true, in a far higher sense, of the charity found in Christ. But we shall speak of this point later, when we treat of the relations existing between Christians and the Holy Spirit.

However we may envisage Christ's charity, it always has the appearance of being a way of loving that is proper to a man who is the Spirator. This is the mystery of His love: the love of the Sacred Heart. The whole of Christ's human love wells up in His heart; all human love is one, and Christ the man, who is also God, is one in a higher sense than other men.

This is a human love, yet a love belonging to God and the Spirator, a love that translates the mystery of eternal love into human terms and expresses it, so to say, in human psychology. Christ shows us this love entering and penetrating into mankind, and He wishes it to be a source of answering love in us, a love that embraces Him as He is and mounts up in Him to God, until it reaches the very heights of the divine processions. This is what St. Paul writes: "For this cause I bow my knees to the Father of our Lord Jesus Christ . . . that He would grant you . . . to know the charity of Christ which surpasseth all knowledge, that you may be filled unto all the fullness of God." [12] "The charity of Christ which surpasseth all knowledge": this love excells any idea we may form of it, and God alone can make it known, as He alone can make it subsist in Himself.

III. THE HOLY SPIRIT AND THE INCARNATION: CHRISTIANS AS MEMBERS OF CHRIST THROUGH LOVE

Having considered the head, we now go on to consider the members. Since the head has special relations with the Holy Spirit, the members must likewise, in their own way, have special relations with Him.

We perceive, at least dimly, that we have reached a climax; and

[12] Eph. 3:14, 19.

what we have to say now surpasses all limits. We shall express our thoughts as best we can with our sluggish and awkward human words. But we shall speak our mind to the glory of God and His Christ, without seeking to make the gift more credible by belittling it. Christian thought has long been familiar with the excesses God takes pleasure in when He wishes to manifest His love. Love is wont to go to extremes. Divine love also goes to extremes, and does so divinely. And, we may say, it goes to the utmost extremes in the very matter we are now going to take up. On the cross, divine love passed all bounds in a sensible and empirical manner, in a sort of human way; here it passes all bounds absolutely, in a divine way.

To accustom our eyes to such brilliance, we must first look at the light as Jesus uncovers it to us; it is He who teaches us how to see the Spirit.[13] He Himself, as we saw above, displayed in His human nature an attitude of astonishing familiarity with the Holy Spirit; and He Himself, by His instructions as well as by His example, has suggested a like attitude for His disciples.

He has declared the transcendent greatness of the Holy Spirit.[14] But especially He has spoken of the Spirit as a gift. Indeed He describes the Spirit chiefly as a gift,[15] a gift that imparts interior power,[16] even a gift we have a right to in consequence of divine promises.[17] "Receive ye the Holy Ghost," said Jesus;[18] possess Him, hold on to Him, He is yours. And the faithful have received Him. He is theirs [19] as truly as He is the Spirit of Christ. He is their very own Spirit,[20] and a person possesses Him from the moment he becomes a Christian.[21] "But Peter said to them: Do penance and be baptized every one of you in the name of Jesus Christ for the remission of your sins; and you shall receive the gift of the Holy Ghost." [22] "The gift of the Holy Ghost," that is, the gift that is the Holy Ghost; the phrase occurs elsewhere [23] and it reveals a definite mentality. The

---

[13] Cf. John 14:9–20.
[14] Matt. 10:30; 12:31; 28:19; John 14:16 f.
[15] Luke 11:13.
[16] Luke 24:49; Acts 1:8.
[17] Luke 24:49; Acts 1:8; 2:33.
[18] John 20:22; cf. 7:39; 14:16 f.
[19] Acts 5:32; 8:15, 17, 19; 10:47; 15:8; I Cor. 12:13; II Cor. 2:4; I Thess. 4:8.
[20] Gal. 4:6; Rom. 8:15 f.; cf. II Cor. 2:10–16.
[21] Acts 10:47; 19:2.
[22] *Ibid.*, 2:38.
[23] *Ibid.*, 10:45; 11:16 f.

Church feels secure in her possession of Him who has truly been given to her; she is so sure of Him and of what we may almost venture to call her "rights" over Him, that she in turn gives Him to whomever she pleases.[24] She looks upon offenses committed against her as sins committed against Him,[25] discerns His active presence in her own conduct,[26] and recognizes His decisions in her own: "It hath seemed good to the Holy Ghost and to us," [27] say the apostles and elders at Jerusalem quite simply, without seeming to be aware of the enormity of their assertion.

For the first Christians, as is clear from the Acts and from St. Paul's epistles, the Holy Spirit is literally what Jesus had announced: a pledge deposited in their hands,[28] a good they possess in consequence of irrevocable promises,[29] an inner guest on whom they depend and who is infinitely great,[30] but who yet is theirs so completely that they can grieve Him, expel Him, and extinguish Him.[31] The gift has penetrated so deeply into their souls that this Spirit of the Lord is, as it were, the light that guides their steps and the life that animates them; in Him they are holy, just, and strong.[32] They possess Him so perfectly that the profound distinction between Him and them, between the Spirit of God and the life of grace they live, is hardly marked, so that we are not always able to discern in St. Paul's epistles whether "spirit" designates the Third Person or the manner of thinking and acting characteristic of the Christian spirit.

From the very beginning the Church has given adoration and obedience to the Holy Spirit.[33] But she does not take the attitude toward Him which she has, and apparently dare not lack, toward the Father and the person of the Son. The Church prays to the Father and the Son; but we do not observe that at the beginning she prays to the Holy Spirit. Thus we notice in the Acts that the apostles implore God to support them against those who had slain His Son

[24] *Ibid.*, 8:17, 19.
[25] *Ibid.*, 5:3, 9.
[26] *Ibid.*, 9:17; 10:19 f.; 20:22 f.
[27] *Ibid.*, 15:28; cf. 6:10; 21:11.
[28] Cf. II Cor. 1:22; 5:5; Eph. 1:13; Rom. 8:16.
[29] Acts 1:4; Gal. 3:14; Eph. 1:13.
[30] Cf. I Cor. 3:16; 6:19 f.; II Cor. 3:17; I Thess. 4:8.
[31] Eph. 4:30; I Thess. 5:19.
[32] See the texts cited p. 417 f.
[33] Acts 5:3 f.; 10:19 f.; 20:23. Add to this the references to the Trinity in St. Paul.

Jesus and to give them strength to preach in His name; and "they were filled with the Holy Ghost, and they spoke the word of God with confidence." [34]

The sight of such freedom arouses in us, we believe, the dispositions requisite to understand the doctrine about the gift of God in the Spirit, the gift that is the Spirit. The man Jesus Christ, as we have said, is the Spirator of the Holy Spirit in literal truth. He is also an individual of the human race in literal truth, and indeed the individual who is most closely united to the human race, since He is its supernatural head. From this fact we may draw a first consequence that is still somewhat external to the subject, but that prepares us to regard it from within.

It is, then, strictly true that the human race includes the Spirator of the Holy Ghost, and that all men have the Spirator of the Holy Ghost as their fellow man, their brother, and the closest of their neighbors. Therefore it is also strictly true that the mystery of the spiration of the Holy Ghost which takes place within the Trinity now takes place also within mankind. From the time of the Incarnation we have to speak of this transcendent activity if we wish to draw up a description of human activity that does not omit what is essential, just as we have to mention the Word if we wish to count all men without overlooking the most important among them.

But there is more to be said, and this is the second consequence, which envisages the truth from the inside. Christians are members of Christ in the most intimate part of themselves, for they are incorporated into Him by grace, which affects the substance of their souls. And this Man is a real person who spirates the Holy Ghost; He is this person in the depths of His humanity which is united to the Word and subsists in Him. Furthermore, this Man is united to all men and is the source of grace and of the supernatural life throughout the whole order of grace by the exaltation of His human nature which subsists in the spirating Word.

This is an interior union, if ever there was one; it is a union in the absolute interior of being. Hence this union has to affect the interior of being by expressing itself therein and by adapting it to itself.

Christians are members of the co-principle of the Holy Ghost, and this co-principle of the Holy Ghost, regarded in His totality, as He who has become man, as the whole Christ, head and members,

[34] Acts 4:24-31.

is He and they together. If the whole Christ is the Spirator, we have to conclude—dare we say it?—that the members are the Spirator along with Him; if they are to exist and love in the way that is right for those who are members of Him who is the Spirator, they must love as members of the Spirator, with a love that is derived from the Spirator.

When we say that the Son is the Spirator, we should recall what we are supposing throughout, that He is such together with the Father and that He receives from the Father the power to be the Spirator: *principium ex principio, qui, cum principio sine principio, est unum principium Spiritus Sancti.* We showed in an earlier chapter that Christians, as members of the Son, must share in the Son's relation to the Father, and that they must be "filial" by sharing in Christ's sonship. In the same way we should like to show here that, as members of the Spirator, they must share in the Son's relation to the Spirit and be "spirating" with a participated spiration that is communicated to them by Christ.

We have purposely desired not to tone down the formulas; if a judgment is to be passed on the truth and orthodoxy of these ideas, they must first be enunciated with uncompromising boldness. Only a false prudence would introduce corrective modifications; if correctives are needed, they will be inserted by the inherent logic of the ideas.

In the present case, a corrective is implied in the notions of participation and member; but not in the notion of spiration or of relation to the Spirit. There everything or nothing must be said; the only real and conceivable relation to the Spirit that Christ has to give is the relation of Spirator; if we may not speak of this relation, we may not speak of any. The whole point is to determine how we may speak of it; that is where we find any needed corrective; there is question only of a participation in that relation, or, more accurately, of an incorporation into Him who is the Spirator even as man, and of the effects that must flow from this incorporation. The "spirating" character will be found in Christians only so far as they are members, and in a way belonging to members; it will be found in them by way of participation, because of their union with the incarnate Word and their participation in Him.

This, then, is what they are as Christians; Christ is the Spirator, and the members of Christ are members of the Spirator. That is all;

absolutely nothing more than that is asserted, and no other restriction need be added. But that much has to be said. The two expressions, "members of Christ" and "members of the Spirator" are true with the same truth and real with the same realism.

Christians are members of Christ, they come to a head in Christ, they are intrinsically and supernaturally incorporated into the Spirator. Hence their activity must be the activity of members. Its worth is greater than if it were the fruit merely of their own powers. As the members are incorporated into the head, so their activity is in continuity with the activity of the head, that is, of the sacred humanity which, because of the hypostatic union, is closely associated with the activity of the Word in the spiration of the Holy Ghost.

These distinctions are important. On the other hand, the union is very great, for it is an intrinsic union, the most far-reaching of all unions and, in a real sense, the closest and most necessary; it is intrinsic and necessary for the assumed humanity, which otherwise would lack the personality of the Word; it is intrinsic and necessary for the members, who otherwise would be deprived of their membership. In virtue of the unity of the whole Christ, the activity of the members is in continuity, through their supernatural life, with the activity of the head.

Accordingly a principle of union is necessary, an "entity of union" of the sort we described when speaking of our adoption and filial character, but with the shade of difference that is required by the fact that what is now in question is an activity and a source of activity rather than simple existence. In Christ, the head of the members, something of this kind is found, an excellence flowing from union with the Spirator and adapting to this union; and it is found in such abundance that it can be communicated to the members. This is charity.

We have already spoken of Christ's charity and of the mystery of Christ's charity. We may well say that it is a divine mystery, for Christ's charity is such as to indicate that the sacred humanity is truly the humanity of the co-principle of the Holy Spirit. It is also a human mystery, for this charity was given in such abundance that it could be the source of charity for all those who live the supernatural life.

Here we must apply to the order of activity what we have said, when speaking of the orders of being and knowledge, about the mystic perfection that ought to be found in the sacred humanity because of its assumption.

The charity in question is human, for it is a perfection of human nature. Yet it must be supernaturally infinite in a human way, because it is truly and literally the charity of Him who is the infinite God. It is the charity of Him who is the first principle, the charity of Him who is the Spirator, of Him who is present in all being and is the transcendent unity and perfection of all being. Hence this charity must be abundant in a way suitable for the first principle in the order of charity, of the first principle that is interior to all supernatural love and that perfects such love.

Besides, if Christ, as considered in His very humanity that is united to the Word, is mystical and is the unity of grace in mankind, He must be the same in His supernatural human will and love, for they belong to the Word; they too must be mystical, so as to be able to fill all men from their abundance. By its very nature love is self-diffusive, and its first gift is itself; and eternal Love, with which Christ's created charity is in communication, is surely a gift. Hence Christ's charity must be able to communicate itself to the highest degree.

Moreover, Christians, regarded as members and Christians, need to have a way of willing and loving that is suitable for members and that, like their supernatural existence, is infused into them by Christ. As members of the God-man, they are divinized in their very being; they must also be divinized in their willing and living, otherwise their inner nature would be inconsistent. They are divinized in Christ and the Spirator; and in Christ the Spirator they must likewise be divinized by an elevation of their love and will. They will thus, in Christ, be associated with the spiration of eternal love.

Then they will be divinized in exactly the right way, as members of the Spirator associated with the God-man's active spiration. Each of them will have his own charity, as each has all his virtues; willing and loving are attributes of intellectual life, and all intellectual life is personal. All these charities will be profoundly distinct from one another, because, being supernatural, they will be supernaturally distinct.

In particular they must be distinct from Christ's charity, on account of its transcendence, which makes it the universal source in the order of charity. But this very transcendence is a source of union;

since the very excellence that distinguishes Christ's charity from all other charities is the reason why it is so closely united to them all. These other charities, though distinct from one another, are likewise united to one another by the supernatural deepening of their being and their distinction from one another, because this supernatural deepening comes to them from their common union with the charity of Christ who incorporates them into His charity and makes them all members of one another.

This charity, as we may well consider the point here, has all that is needed to be an "entity of union," an adaptation to union with the Spirator. Catholic theology has always taught that charity is a special relation to the Holy Spirit, an assimilation to the Spirit, a participation in Him who is love, charity, and gift.

Charity, and hence every virtue, is internally active, in the sense that it produces its own act, its own love, just as spirating love is the principle of spirated love. It is not, as some of the Scholastics thought and as the Quietists later maintained for a different reason, a sort of holy impassiveness in which the Spirit acts directly, causing inert strings to vibrate with His sovereign breath and eliciting acts of charity without the cooperation of any created habit. It is essentially active and fecund; it makes Christians active principles with regard to the divine life that is in them, as we shall have occasion to show when we come to the question of grace. This is just what occurs in the life of the Trinity: spiration is what constitutes the Son a principle.

May we not see here a resemblance that implies a relation and a participation, especially since, according to the Council of Trent,[35] this quality of being principle belongs to the charity of Christians by the fact that they are living members of Christ who is the co-principle of the Holy Spirit? Of course the divine life which charity produces is not that whereby God lives in Himself, but is the life He grants us to live in Him. It acts only on its own level; as the supreme actuation of Christian life, it is a cause of Christian life; just as God acts on His own level in the mystery of the immanent processions.

The distinction is clear, but the union is even clearer. Charity develops only in the members of the incarnate Word; what it does on its level is in continuity and union with what the Word does on His level, since the Incarnation, which joins the two natures in the God-

---

[35] Sess. VI, cc. 3, 7, 16, can. 32 (Denz., 795, 800, 809, 842).

man, also joins the two activities: hypostatically in the head, by grace and participation in the members.

The resemblance goes even farther. Charity is not a principle of divine life except in union and cooperation with actual grace, that is, with an aid given by God. In other words, it is a secondary co-principle, for grace always has the main initiative. Likewise the Son is not a principle of the Holy Spirit except with the Father; He is a "secondary" co-principle, in the sense that He receives from the Father the power to be equally and identically the same principle as the Father Himself.[36]

Furthermore, charity does not constitute a principle that is separate from grace in the order of divinization; the two are a single principle, and the effect produced comes wholly from the one no less than from the other.[37] Similarly the Son is not a principle that is separate or even distinct from the Father in the spiration of the Holy Ghost; the two are a single principle, and the Spirit proceeds from them both. Thus charity, which unites Christians among themselves and which even, in God's designs, unites all men together, is joined in Christ to the action in which the Father and the Son are united in the spiration of the Holy Ghost. Here, too, Christ's faithful are one, as the Son is one with the Father: "As Thou, Father, in Me and I in Thee, that they also may be one in Us." [38]

We believe that these reflections on charity explain a number of

[36] This difference stands out among others, that the Father, with the Son and through the Son, is the principle of the Holy Spirit, whereas grace, which is given by the whole Trinity and especially, in the sense of attribution, by the Holy Spirit, is the principle of charity in Christians. Yet we should note that, if the production of grace, particularly actual grace, comes from the Trinity and the Spirit, the whole of the supernatural reality which all grace tends to establish in man is a life of adopted sons, and that adopted sons receive everything from the Father in the only-begotten Son who receives everything from the Father. The state of glory, which is the order of grace arrived at its culmination, shows this clearly: adopted sons will have existence and knowledge and will from the Father in the only-begotten Son, through the participation coming to them in Christ from the eternal begetting. In this life and knowledge infused into them by the Father in the Son is found the source of their eternal love which will express their consummated union with that love which, in the unity of the Father and the Son, spirates the Holy Ghost, seal of their unity.

[37] St. Bonaventure says tersely: "Meritorious works, which proceed wholly from grace, likewise proceed wholly from our free will, yet mainly from grace." *Breviloquium*, V, 2 (*Opera omnia* [Quaracchi, 1891], V, 255).

[38] John 17:21.

texts which exhibit charity as the main bond of unity, and sometimes as the only one, existing in the mystical body. But above all they reveal the close connection between Christian life and the life of the Trinity. That is clearly the most important meaning they have. If Christ is the Word and if Christians are truly members of the Word, the first principles regulating the conduct of Christians are the sacred formulas that define what the Word is and what His activity is.

Some dogmatic phrases, such as *ab utroque*, *Filioque*, *per Filium*, *unum principium*, and *unica spiratio*, may seem at a first superficial glance to be abstract formulas without meaning for our daily lives. Yet, as we have seen, they are the foundation of Christian morality. We may say that they alone allow Christian life to develop fully, for they alone, considered in their ultimate implications, enable us to define the true attitude of him who believes, loves, and acts in Christ.

Conversely Christian activity, the life of faith and charity, contributes efficaciously and graphically, even though obscurely and implicitly, to disclose to the faithful the exact, profound meaning of these formulas. The dogmas that declare what the Son is to the children of divine adoption, are not a burden encumbering the memory but a light revealing what their life and its ultimate origin are; and this life in turn helps them to understand the dogmas better.

Perhaps we will not be exceeding the bounds of propriety if we point out that the Churches in which the doctrine of the procession of the Holy Ghost from the Father and the Son alike is denied or relegated to the shadows of uncertainty, are also the Churches in which Christian life is observed to be less active, less fervent and zealous, less devoted to the apostolate and to missionary work, less careful to guard their full independence of action and to avoid the enslaving protection of Caesaropapist states. Indeed, if we admit that the Son is purely receptive and passive in the life of the Trinity, do we not suggest a passive and receptive attitude to the sons of adoption, to the members of this Son? How are they to receive an influx of activity and zeal from Him who has no activity within the Trinity? These remarks should not be understood in a simplist sense; we would sin against truth and reverence were we to ignore the supernatural life and fervor found among our separated brethren. Christian life is nowhere given over to indolence, and the point we are touching on in passing is extremely complex. We are also aware that Christian teaching, which in itself is so unified, may admit of alternative expressions. But to safeguard the honor of this unity and the importance of Trinitarian dogma, we must, without intending to offend anyone, make clear that the conception one has of the activity of the Son cannot but affect the norm one assigns for the activity of the adopted sons.

Besides, is it not significant that these Churches, in their very conception of Christian conduct, have, in varying degrees and manners, a tendency to exalt the sacramental economy and a sort of passive sanctification by the liturgy, not with a view to making these means a principle and stimulus of supernatural activity intensely personal in character as well as intensely dependent on God and Christ, but rather to find in them a kind of substitute for personal activity? Here again, to focus attention on these matters and to save time, we have to use blunt words; certain reserves and distinctions might well be made; and especially we could say that their liturgy may be understood in a sense that, in spite of profound differences, reveals points of similarity with Catholic liturgy. But to speak in general terms and to remain within the limits of our criticism, do we not see that this way of thinking betrays the same conception, namely, that the Christian, as member of Christ, is not a true principle of divinizing action, just as the Son is not the principle within the Trinity of the love that is the Spirit?

The doctrine of the epiklesis is, in this respect, no less important than the doctrine of the procession of the Holy Ghost from the Son. As is well known, the Oriental Church considers as necessary, indeed as the only thing necessary, for the consecration of the Eucharist an invocation to the Holy Ghost that usually follows the words of institution, "This is My body." This teaching can be presented in various ways which we need not describe here. But what we have to point out is that it is closely bound up with the doctrine of the procession from the Father alone. The latter doctrine declares that Christ is not the principle of the Holy Spirit; the former doctrine teaches that Christ's words, pronounced in His name by His minister, do not suffice to bring down the Holy Spirit.

What we have said about our participation in Christ, the Spirator of the Holy Ghost, may be applied, with the same restrictions, to our participation in Christ regarded as the one who possesses and gives the Spirit. Christ possesses the Spirit otherwise than He possesses the Father; He possesses Him as His Spirit, not as His Father. The same is true of Christians. They are to possess the Spirit truly by possessing Him in their head to whom they are united.

As they are made fit by their adoption and divinization to be members of the Son who is God, they are made fit to be members of the Son who possesses the Spirit, by a possession of the Spirit and an indwelling of the Spirit who makes them "spiritual" [39] in the strongest sense of the word. A sort of interior affinity and aspect of their Godlike elevation adapts them intrinsically to this Spirit and to the reception of His presence, touches, and gifts. Is not this, or an awareness of this, what the mystics try to say when they speak of the soul's espousals with the Spirit? Is not this what theology teaches when it refers to souls interiorly disposed to be united to the Spirit and led by Him, or when it speaks of the connaturalness of the gifts of the Holy Ghost in Christian life? [40]

But we have more than the Spirit's gifts; we have the gift that is the Spirit Himself. Christian grace, by its very nature and by the union it confers with Him who is the principle and possessor of the Holy Spirit, also gives us a possession of the Spirit through our union with the possession which Christ the possessor has; it makes us fit to enjoy the Spirit, *frui persona divina*, as St. Thomas says,[41] to embrace the Spirit within ourselves as a sacred treasure or a holy object in a temple,[42] to own Him as one owns a gift. St. Thomas writes about the error of saying that only the gifts of the Spirit are given, but that the Spirit Himself is not given.[43] "The Holy Spirit is possessed by man and dwells within man by the very gift of sanctifying grace. Hence the Holy Spirit Himself is given and sent.[44] . . . Many special gifts are distributed to Christ's members by the gift which is the Holy Spirit." [45]

But if He who is essentially a gift [46] is given so generously to men, we may confidently expect that He will continue to be a gift in those

---

[39] Cf. I Cor. 2:13–16; 3:1.

[40] Cf. St. Thomas, *Summa*, Ia IIae, q.68, a.1, and often elsewhere.

[41] The expression occurs several times in the *Summa*, Ia, q.43, which treats of the divine missions.

[42] Cf. I Cor. 6:19.

[43] St. Thomas, *Summa*, Ia, q.43, a.3 et ad 1, 2, 3; cf. a.5 ad 1; q.38, a.1, *sed contra*.

[44] St. Thomas, *Summa*, Ia, q.43, a.3; cf. q.38, a.1, 2.

[45] *Summa*, Ia, q.38, a.2, quoting St. Augustine, *De Trinitate*, XV, c.19, no. 34 (*PL*, XLII, 1084).

[46] St. Thomas, *Summa*, Ia, q.38.

who receive Him, and that in some way, in virtue of the very bestowal of Him on them, He may be given by them. This does not
mean that men of themselves, no matter how high they have been
elevated by grace, can give the Spirit; only God can do that.[47] At
most they can act as instruments and ministers in the economy of
grace in which God alone makes this donation.[48] But the point is that
men are not left to themselves if they have grace; in Christ they are
one with Him who gives and sends the Holy Ghost. When we consider them in this unity—and that is the only correct way of regarding them as they really are—we must acknowledge that they too give
and send the Holy Spirit, by the fact that Christ their head gives
and sends Him. In its general outline the matter is settled; a Christian,
acting as a Christian, efficaciously influences the degree of holiness
present in all mankind.

How this may involve a giving of the Holy Spirit is obviously a
delicate point and is hard to conceive and express, for we must be
careful to leave intact the absolute transcendence of the Third Person. To preclude all misunderstanding, we should like to repeat our
views once more.

If the activity of Christians were considered from their standpoint alone, as though they were separated from Christ's humanity
and the latter were separated from the Word, any talk of such a donation would be blasphemous; we should then have to be satisfied with
saying that God sends His Spirit out of consideration of the good
works of Christians and His own promises. But if this supposition
itself is impious, if the members exist in actual union with their head
and if Christ's humanity is not a person removed from union with
the Word, we have to say that men, who of themselves have at most
a moral and occasional causality respecting the mission of the Holy
Spirit, are one, in the totality of the supernatural organism in which
they live, with Him who in all truth is the co-principle of this mission.
Thus their activity, regarded as an activity of members of this co-
principle and, if the term may be allowed, a "member-action" in
relation to the action of this co-principle, cannot be adequately envisaged except in terms of the action of this co-principle. Since the
latter action gives the Holy Spirit, their action also gives Him, but

[47] *Ibid.*, q.43, a.8; St. Augustine, *De Trinitate*, XV, c.26, no. 46 (*PL*, XLII,
1093).

[48] St. Thomas, *In I Sent.*, d.14, q.3, ad 1, 3.

only in Christ and through the donation He alone makes; yet we must add that He makes the donation in the fullness of His whole body. In Himself, as the head who is the unity and the whole of His body, He makes the complete donation; in the Church, when it acts as the Church, continuing His very gestures, He makes the same donation, to which nothing new is added, for it merely extends the donation already made; in His members, lastly, He makes the donation in a way consonant with the nature and position of the members. The action of the members would have no meaning and would have nothing to do with the giving of the Spirit, if it did not share in His action by being incorporated into it and by becoming a donation in Him; regarded only in itself, any action of a member would be no more than a good work of a Christian. But we should understand well that union with the head is not something superficial or accidental for the members; it makes them members and turns their own activity into an activity of members.

If this is the truth, the Holy Spirit has a role in Christian life that is analogous to His function in the Trinity. He is "the seal of charity and the bond of the Trinity." [49] In the Trinity He is the supreme bond, the ultimate seal expressing the perfection, the culmination, and the immanence of divine life; in this last divine person, who is the term of the unity of the other two persons, the procession of divine life comes to a close. [50] In Christian life, likewise, He is the one who consummates and seals all in unity, for He is the beginning and the end. Everything begins in Christ through the work of the Holy Spirit who forms Christ and Christians: "conceived of the Holy Ghost." And in Christ everything culminates in this work of charity that is connected with the giving of the Holy Spirit and that furnishes the supernatural organism with the principle of its own growth through the power of the head. [51]

After this discussion, we may complete what we said at the beginning of this chapter about the phrase "conceived of the Holy

---

[49] St. Epiphanius, *Ancoratus*, 7 (*PG*, XLIII, 28).

[50] Cf. Pseudo-Dionysius, *De divinis nominibus*, II, 4 et paraphr. 7 (*PG*, III, 641, 672); St. Basil, *Hom.* 24 (*PG*, XXXI, 609); Council of Toledo XI (Denz., 275).

[51] Cf. Eph. 4:16: "From whom the whole body, being compacted and fitly joined together, by what every joint supplieth, according to the operation in the measure of every part, maketh increase of the body, unto the edifying of itself in charity."

Ghost" and the attribution to the Holy Spirit of the divine action that forms the Church and Christians.

We mentioned there that the mystical body, like Christ Himself, is unceasingly born of the Holy Spirit. The reason for attributing this to the Holy Spirit is now clearer. The Spirit is the sole divine person who may be represented as given to this body as the cause of its growth. To some extent this principle of growth is at the body's disposal; and, although it comes to the body as a pure gift, the body can draw on its power for the intensification of its own life. This organism, conceived as a single reality, is produced by God alone; at the same time, however, it builds itself up through Him who is its head. We may even say that, regarded as pre-existing in the Word from all eternity, it builds itself up from the first beginnings. Accordingly, with this general view in mind, to explain how this organism, which is produced by God, is also produced by itself, we must conceive that the divine action proceeds from Him who is at once the head and the totality of the organism. But within the Godhead only the Spirit has such a relationship to the Son. Therefore, to put all the factors together, we must conceive that this organism is formed, made, created, augmented, and perfected by the Spirit. This is the only way of conceiving that at the same time it is Christ who forms Himself in the mystical plenitude of His body.

Such, then, is the significance of the Holy Spirit for the mystical body. He is the power that brings it to birth and causes it to grow, the power the body possesses yet receives, the energy that invests it,[52] that rises up within it,[53] and that can almost be said to emanate from it, since in Christ the force can be set in motion. Yet this power comes from on high,[54] and is supremely free and all-powerful. These predicates assuredly differ, even to the point of contrast; but their union should not surprise us, for it is but the continuation of the union that is in the God-man.

With regard to the soul of the mystical body, we incline to the theory that this soul is grace as present in all Christians and indeed, according to the divine vocation and the first movements of grace, in all souls; for union with Christ is offered to all men.[55] Or, what

[52] Luke 24:49.
[53] Cf. John 14:17; 15:26 f.
[54] Luke 24:49; Acts 1:8.
[55] The theory that sanctifying grace rather than the Holy Ghost is to be regarded as the soul of the mystical body was a view freely debated by theo-

comes to the same thing, we may say that the soul is Christ who, in His humanity but by His divinity, is the first universal principle within the order of grace, that is, the first interior principle that infuses the supernatural life of grace into the whole organism. When we speak of "soul" in connection with man, do we not mean a spirit that has its own act and that, notwithstanding its transcendent spirituality, is the form and interior principle of the whole body? The soul is what makes the body a living and human body.

Whether we regard grace as an influx emanating from Christ or as Christ who infuses grace, it is present in all parts of the body and communicates to each part its own share and degree of life. Although grace is multiplied according to the number of men who possess it, it remains one throughout the whole body, and therefore the life it imparts is a single reality, an exigence of union, and a unity that increasingly develops and forms itself.

We have elsewhere studied the texts that suggest this point of view; [56] they indicate that the mystical body is the continuation of Christ, the fullness of the mystical Christ. They do not expressly teach this doctrine; but in our opinion, the conception they reveal of the spiritual organism and its unity lead to our theory.

Besides, our way of representing the doctrine does not imply a denial that the Holy Spirit is the soul of the Church. Since the Spirit is in the Son, He is an interior power incessantly infusing a life that has not yet reached its full perfection and forming an organism that is not yet completely constructed. But in this view the soul seems to be regarded as a quasi-efficient cause that acts by contact and vital union, without being in any way a constituent of the living being in question. On the other hand, when the soul of the mystical body is conceived to be the grace of Christ, in the sense we have just explained, the soul is regarded as the formal or quasi-formal principle which makes the organism what it is.

However, we do not wish to insist on this way of envisaging and expressing the matter. The choice of words is secondary, for it con-

---

logians up to the appearance of the Encyclical of Pius XII, "Mystici Corporis Christi," of June 29, 1943, which states that the Holy Ghost is the soul of the mystical body. See *Acta Apostolicae Sedis*, XXXV (1943), 219 f. In the paragraphs that follow, Mersch endeavors to reconcile the apparently conflicting doctrines.—Tr.

[56] See *The Whole Christ*, Index, under entries "Soul," "Spirit," "Christ," "Mystical Body," "Grace," "Church."

cerns only our human way of conceiving the role of the Spirit in terms of a metaphor. However real the union of all Christians in Christ may be, the figure of the body that represents the union remains but a figure. The employment of this figurative language may have its advantages, but it also has disadvantages. If the allegory is pushed too far, it becomes inexact; if we concentrate on it unduly, it distracts the mind from the reality which the comparison is meant to clarify; if we develop it with excessive subtlety, it casts a suspicion of unreality on the doctrine it is supposed to explain and risks becoming distasteful to many minds, especially in our time.

The true question and the great problem is to determine precisely what, in actual fact, the role of the Spirit is with respect to the "body" of Christ. This is the point we have desired to study in these pages, and we believe that a reconciliation of views on this detail is possible; for, at bottom, only a slight difference of emphasis is noticed between those authors who hold that the soul of the mystical body is the Holy Ghost, and those who consider that it is grace or Christ's proprietorship.

The mystical body as such, in the unity of the whole Christ, has special relationships with the divine persons, and these relations derive from Christ's relations, which are those of the Son. No others are conceivable. The only real relations that can be predicated of the persons of the Trinity are those which are these persons themselves.

Consequently the mystical body has God the Father for Father, through the sonship of the Son. This sonship is merely participated in adoptive sonship. The whole body comes from the Father, proceeds from the Father, and is begotten by the Father, but only in the Son from whom it has its totality. And we can say that it proceeds from the Father only if we envisage it in its union with the Son and suppose that this union is already effected. Its essential attitude, in time and eternity, is to receive from the Father. Here on earth this attitude finds expression in the virtue of hope, the virtue that makes us desire and expect all we are and shall be. In heaven our good will no longer be an object of hope but will be an eternal and assured reception, coming from the Father in Christ; there we shall see God and shall be an expression of God in the beatific vision.

The preserving force and ultimate interior subsistence of this body is the Son, who causes it to be all that it is. It does not come from the Son; it "is" the Son, hypostatically in the God-man who is its head, and mystically in all His members; yet in its own way it "is" the Son, and its supernatural, proper, mysterious character is based on that fact. Therefore that which best expresses its nature is something basically intellectual, a reality of the cognitive order that conforms it to the Word, that is, faith here on earth, and the beatific vision in heaven; but in any case, some sort of knowledge.

Lastly, as its interior efficient principle, as the vital energy which causes it to take shape and grow and which also enables it to concur in its own growth, the body has the Spirit. This way of existing finds expression in the virtue of charity.

The three theological virtues of faith, hope, and charity correspond to three aspects in the divinization of the God-man's "body," for in Him the body shares in the relations which the humanity of the God-man has with the divine persons. In no sense is it all of these persons, but it possesses them all and is relative to them all in the God-man, the Son. First of all, it is related to the Son as to Him who is the hypostasis of the assumed humanity, and through that humanity, the divine person who is the head of the whole human race. Next, it has relationships with the Father and the Spirit, since, by title of membership, it shares in the Son's relationships. Thus the theological virtues fall into their proper order: first comes faith, then hope, then charity.

Conclusions with Reference to the Trinity

We are now in a position to appreciate the nature of the explanation the present work proposes about the Blessed Trinity. We have no ambition to supplant the explanations put forward in the various theological syntheses; our explanation does not even come into contact with them, for it moves on a different level. We are trying to give a positive explanation of a living thing, not an interpretation of formulas. A positive explanation of a thing has to be sought in the thing itself. The positive explanation of the Trinity is the Trinity itself. That is its own explanation; and this explanation filters down to us through the Incarnation. The whole Trinity is found in Christ, because He is the Word; the Trinity is expressed in this person, and is made known to us in its relation to Him.

And Christ lives in us and we live in Him. In the measure of our living in Him, we shall have the explanation of the Trinity in ourselves, and especially in the measure in which we live this life in relation to the Trinity; such a life is a life of the Word, of the Son of the Father and of the co-principle of the Holy Ghost.

Therefore let us live intensely our life of faith, hope, and charity; let us live this life intelligently, reflecting on it with an eagerness to learn. Let us develop in ourselves, to the utmost power of our will, the consciousness that we belong to the Word and the divine Thought; let us develop confidence in the Father and zeal for Him, and docility, love, and fervor in the Spirit. Then we shall come to some understanding, not in words and concepts, but in growth and life-giving light, of the mystery of the Father, the Son, and the Holy Ghost. In the "little way" of spiritual childhood, in adherence to the Church, and in devotedness to our neighbor, many a treasure of theology will be found.

Christ Himself, we may well judge, taught the mystery of the Trinity by His actions even more than by His words. Trinitarian formulas are rare in the Gospel, and there is hardly one more explicit than the formula of baptism in St. Matthew. The other passages that teach this truth, numerous though they may be, are accounts Christ gives of His conduct or of the conduct He requires of others. Such conduct is the main theme of His message. In the presence of the Twelve He always acted in function of the Trinity, if we may put it that way, that is, in a way that presupposed and implied the Trinity. In His dealings with God He always took, quite naturally and recognizably, the attitude of a Son in the presence of His Father, the attitude of one who receives everything he has and is, the attitude of one who relies on another for absolutely everything.

By the influence of His example and the power of His grace, far more than by His words, He has gradually instilled into the souls of His followers a similar attitude, an attitude of reference to the Father, of confidence in the Father, and of a wholehearted, supernatural, mysterious love. Under the action of the Spirit, this attitude enabled the disciples to understand the sense of His words, although their lives were already manifesting it, and also brought Christ's revelation to the dogmatic formulation given by the Church.

The same is true for the Christian. Meditation on the formulas of Nicaea and Constantinople, on the theological syntheses of St. Gregory, St. Augustine, and St. Thomas, and on all that tradition has said about God's interior life, undoubtedly ought to impart to us a vivid understanding of the dogma of the Trinity. But that under-standing is also, and particularly, fostered by acting in the way the Church recommends, by taking the attitude of adopted sons, and by living the life of faith, hope, and charity which, in Christ, unites us to the Word and, through the Word, to Him who is our Father and to Him who is our Spirit.

BOOK FIVE

In Christ

CHAPTER XV

THE SUPERNATURAL

> "We are His workmanship,
> created in Christ Jesus."
> Eph. 2:10

I. INTRODUCTION

IN Christ and in the new union that is given to mankind in Him, a new way of existing is inaugurated. A new way of existing that is the supernatural. Fully realized in Christ, it spreads from Him over the whole vastness of His mystical body; and this is the mystery of the Church. Through the Church it flows into each soul; and this is the mystery of grace.

The scientific notion of the supernatural did not achieve separate formulation until rather late, and we have to await the sixteenth and seventeenth centuries to find explicit and methodical treatises on it. This is easy to understand. Such a notion supposes reflex judgment on the realities we call supernatural; before such a judgment can be made scientifically, the realities have to be known scientifically.

But spontaneous Christian thought did not wait for erudite speculation. From the very beginning Christians had at least a confused intuition that the order of things to which God was leading them was above everything in nature, that it was at once new and transcendent, that it was a new life, a new creation, a fellowship with God, a divinization, a heavenly life. Does not all this, almost to the very terms used, express the idea of the supernatural? For that matter, the word itself was designed and proposed quite early; St. Cyril of Alexandria speaks of things above nature, *supra naturam*, which God gives to us in Christ.[1]

[1] For example, *In Ioan.*, I, 9; II, 5; XII, 1 (PG, LXXIII, 153, 348; LXXIV, 700).

All these aspects were soon grouped around a single idea, that of something which was strictly, absolutely, intrinsically, and substantially supernatural. All genuine questions about the supernatural are proposed in connection with this central reality, and we have to comprehend it if we wish to understand what Christianity purports to be. This is the subject we are now going to study.

As the name suggests and as theologians unanimously teach, the supernatural is that which absolutely exceeds every finite nature, whether real or possible, created or capable of being created, and which surpasses the entire range and all the resources and exigencies of nature, even though it is realized in nature.

The program of the Vatican Council, to mention one document, describes the supernatural as follows; and first, such as it was at the beginning when it was conferred on Adam.

The supreme Creator and Lord, whose power is not subject to the properties and laws of created nature, in His inexhaustible goodness wished to raise the human race in its first parent to a state in which it would share in divine good beyond the condition of its nature. Therefore, in addition to the endowments by which the first man was perfected in his own nature, God imparted to him the wonderful gift of sanctity and justice, so that he who was a servant by nature but a son by the gift of the Holy Ghost, might carry out the divine commandments and perform works of virtue, not only by the power of nature but also by the grace infused into him, and thus merit an eternal inheritance. . . .

This is that elevation of man which Catholic teachers, following in the footsteps of the holy Fathers, have rightly called supernatural. For it transcends the exigency and powers of created nature, and therefore is not due to the condition of nature or to man's merits, but is a sheer benefit bestowed by God's generosity. . . .

If anyone should deny that there are divine gifts and institutions which surpass the exigency and powers of created nature and perfect it beyond its own order, let him be anathema.[2]

Such a gift clearly cannot be a complete, self-existent substance in creatures; it can be, as the Council says, only an elevation, an enriching, a perfecting of something already existing. To be supernatural,

---

[2] Schema *Constitutionis dogmaticae secundae de fide*, cap. 3 (Mansi, *Amplissima collectio conciliorum*, LIII, 288 f., 294).

however, it must be a transcendent perfection, that is, it must possess an excellence more exalted than anything the existing creature can in any way give to itself or procure by itself. It must be something that touches the order of creation, for it perfects a creature; but it must be beyond the creature's range, for it surpasses the creature. Only the infinite Creator, only God, thus absolutely surpasses every finite being, real or possible, created or creatable. Accordingly Christian teaching, as exemplified in the document just quoted, says that the supernatural is a "participation in the divine good, in a good that naturally pertains to God alone." [3]

Therefore the supernatural can be defined only in terms of God. This is not the way the natural is defined. Things are what they are by nature, and only they need be considered when the question of defining them arises. God is indeed their necessary cause, and we have to think of God if we are to think rightly of creatures and render them intelligible. But God is their transcendent cause, and when we think of Him in this connection, we have to think of Him as infinitely remote.

We wish to insist here that the supernatural is of a different order. To define it in its internal structure, we have to look to God, for God Himself determines its essence. Do we not, in fact, say that the supernatural is a divinization? And how can we say that it is a divinization unless we include a reference to God? Is it not true that the supernatural has actually been established on earth through the mystery by which God Himself has entered into the world and into humanity? We do not mean to imply that the supernatural can be God as He is in Himself. God is natural to Himself, for He is His own nature; and, since He is the Absolute, He cannot be a perfection of a relative and finite being.

Therefore the supernatural cannot be anything else than a union with God, a relation to God that perfects a finite being. This union and this perfecting require clarification, for at first sight they seem to be impossible. How, in fact, are we to envisage a perfection that is so exalted as to surpass all the natural powers of a being, yet remains so distinct as to leave intact the limits that mark out and define that

---

[3] See, in addition to the passages quoted above, the *Relatio* of J. Kleutgen (Mansi, *loc. cit.*, 298). The text is borrowed, in part, from St. Thomas, *Summa*, Ia IIae, q. 110, a. 1.

being? Too heavy a load crushes the bearer; and a being's essence is like a number which the slightest addition does not reinforce but changes specifically.

The natural order is made up of all those things which creatures require to be fully themselves and all they can attain or expect by their own efforts or their receptivity with respect to other things of their own kind; and the history of these gropings, of these thrustings, of this universal growth, is the poem which nature sings as the world unfolds. It is a splendid poem, a progress without end, for the most perfect of all possible worlds is impossible and no swallow will ever be the perfect swallow. But the progress is limited by the plane on which it deploys, for no swallow will ever become a nightingale without ceasing to be a swallow, as in general nothing will ever surpass its nature without losing its nature. But then, what becomes of the notion of the supernatural?

The supernatural, you will say, is union with God, a union that perfects a nature. And you are right. But here too a difficulty thrusts itself forward, and it is at bottom the same difficulty appearing in a different guise. For nature itself is nothing but a union with God and a relation to Him. Is not creation a relation to God in the creature? Since God is Being itself, He is the last possible cause, the ultimate and exclusive reason for being, and the sole necessary exemplar of everything. To be is nothing else than to resemble Him, to receive from Him, to depend on Him, and to share in Him with regard to everything that the creature is. To receive a further union, especially one so great as to exceed all natural capacity, implies a supplement of interior reality, an addition to the essential components of nature; and do we not perceive that such an addition borders on the inconceivable?

This is the important lesson brought home by the objection that is annoying us: the supernatural cannot be conceived as the natural plus something else, as though the sole difference between the natural and the ultimate perfection to which it may be raised is to be found in the quantity of being or the number of qualities possessed. This is the sort of difference that distinguishes one nature from another. It involves no more than a modification of form by the addition of new notes, and exemplifies specific differences: thus ten becomes eleven, and the plant assimilated by an animal becomes that animal. Changes of this kind imply too much and too little: too much, because they

alter the nature in which they occur; too little, because they remain
within the sphere of nature in general.

We have to go much farther than this before we arrive at the
supernatural. The supernatural involves a change of a different order,
a change that is at once far more radical and more delicate, a change
that affects a being by causing it to be the very thing it was but in a
different way.

But can a thing be "in a different way" without being something
else? And can we conceive that one and the same thing may have
two ways of being, two ways of imitating God? We perceive easily
that this is impossible unless we have some means of distinguishing in
God, or more accurately in man's knowledge of God, two aspects
that are unequally internal, according to which God can communicate Himself in two ways that are unequally perfect and can cause
beings to be what they are in two ways that are unequally adequate.

This is actually the direction in which theology has pushed its
search. To determine what the supernatural is, it distinguishes two
aspects in God and, consequently, in our union with God.

The first of these aspects is God such as He is known in philosophy; God as the cause and exemplar of everything; God as imitated
and expressed in His works; hence God as conceivable to some slight
degree in function of His works, plus the simultaneous denial of any
relation on His side with these works, since He is the Absolute. Envisaged in this way, God is "known as though unknown," He is God
such as He appears in the mirror of creation, in something that is not
He, God in His external effects. As such, God is the foundation of
the natural order.

The second aspect is God as He is in Himself, within the Godhead:
the inner life of God, not merely the external effects; *Deus prout est
in se*, not merely *Deus prout relucet in creaturis*.

Of course God is one and the same under both these aspects.
Through the infinite fullness of His being, He who is the first cause
and sole exemplar of every creature, also has an infinite life in which
He is infinitely above all creation. For this reason, He whom every
being must imitate in order to exist, is not really imitable by anything;
everything has a relationship toward Him, but He is not in relation
to anything. He simply is, He is Himself and nothing else. In His
absolute transcendence over all that is not He and in His absolute

immanence in Himself, He can be known and loved by Himself alone and by him "to whom it shall please the Son to reveal Him." [4]

If the relation to the first of these two aspects is the foundation of the natural order, the relation to the second aspect must be the foundation of the supernatural order. As soon as we represent the matter in this way, the difficulties that seemed to make the notion of the supernatural inconceivable melt away. One of these difficulties is framed thus: How can God give Himself to a thing more thoroughly than through the entire being of that thing, and how can a being receive an increase of being that exceeds its limits without disturbing the frontiers within which its nature is contained? The difficulty is not hard to solve.

The answer is apparent. When God has commuunciated Himself to a thing by the being that is interior to the thing, He can still communicate Himself by the being that is interior to Himself. The resulting enhancement will be less an addition of being than a deepening and an interiorization of the being that was already there. As first cause, God has already acted on the thing by causing it to exist; now He acts by uniting His own perfect being with the being of the thing, thereby causing it to exist in a more perfect way. As God is not numbered along with anything else, and as the Trinity is not numbered along with the divine essence, this new perfection is not numbered along with the perfections which the recipient had before. Therefore it has nothing in common with a specific difference added to constitute a new nature. It is rather the elevation of all previous perfections to a new order, somewhat as the promotion of a merely possible essence to real existence is the passing of all its perfections from the stage of possibility to the stage of actuality.

A spiritual being, at any rate, is open to such a perfecting of its nature. As we said when speaking of the Incarnation, when union with God is at stake, there is no question of union with a determinate type of being which, as it is partly constituted by the negation of all other being, is also constituted by the negation of that being to which it is to be united. We perceive that such a union would be fatal. But God, who is the pure act of being, is not the negation of being, but is rather the cause and exemplar of all being. Therefore a more intimate union with Him, far from entailing destruction, is essentially a fulfillment. A closer union with pure Being must bring to the creature a more perfect identification with himself, that is, a

[4] Matt. 11:27.

more adequate realization of himself. The being that is admitted to such a union will become a "super-being" and will acquire a "super-perfection"; and that being's nature will be elevated in an exact but transcendent prolongation of its own specific perfection, thus entering into a state of "super-nature."

Should we not add that nature, as nature, is quite susceptible of this supernatural perfection that is so super-perfectly natural? We may say that just as there are two aspects in God, regarded as Being itself, there are two aspects in every being regarded precisely as being: the aspect by which it is itself, an image of God who is the first cause of all, and a pure relation to this aspect of God; and the aspect by which it is in possible relation to God as He is in Himself and exists only for Himself. Without the second aspect, the creature would not imitate being at all and hence would not be a being; but, on the other hand, this aspect supposes no more than a possibility in the creature, for the union and real relation with this aspect of God can come only from God's personal initiative. Although this is a simple possibility, it is essential, and does not imply an accessory and fortuitous perfection; it is the possibility of existing more perfectly, and therefore of being oneself more perfectly and of existing according to one's essence. As soon as the divine offer is made, the simple possibility passes to a stage of supreme exigency, flowing from the creature's attachment to its own being and from the very nature of things. But until the offer is made, the exigency is merely possible, for it is possible only as supernatural, and until the supernatural becomes accessible, only nature is in question.

We shall not tarry longer over this point. It has been sufficiently studied elsewhere, and we know how many excellent works have been written on the orientation of nature toward the supernatural, the natural desire for the beatific vision, and the possibility of the supernatural order.

The question that will detain us for a little while has to do with a different detail. Cannot our conception of the supernatural be pushed farther? Christian teaching has given us many particulars about the second aspect of God, which regards the interior things of God or God as He is in Himself. It informs us that God Himself has explained what He is by revealing to us the mystery of the Trinity, of the inner mysterious life the three divine persons live within the unity of the divine substance. Should we not, then, adapt to this truth of faith the clarification that has been made of the supernatural in function of natural truths, and should we not say that the supernatural consists in a relation and union with the Trinity as Trinity?

Theology does not ordinarily answer this question in the affirmative. All that it has to say about the subject may be reduced to the following few points. The first point is of capital importance; faith teaches definitively that all the supernatural excellence possessed by the sacred humanity of Jesus Christ is owing solely to the hypostatic union, which unites it to the Word, who is one of the persons in the Trinity. Secondly, as regards all the faithful, the act of faith and even more the beatific vision, charity and especially glory, and hope, too, in its way, attain God as He is in Himself, and therefore the Trinity of divine persons; therefore, in some way or other, the supernatural life of the faithful must have some relation with the Blessed Trinity.

That is about all. Further developments have of course been attempted. The movement of dogma is straight toward the Trinity; theology moves in the same direction. The synthesis it tries to fashion would be successfully achieved if it could show that, as Christ is perpetuated in the Christians who are His members, the relations He has with the Trinity are also perpetuated in them, and that the supernatural, which finds its supreme and total realization in Him through union with the Word and the Trinity, is prolonged in Christians through a prolongation of the same union with the Trinity.

But an obstacle blocks the path: the certain principle that God's external works are effected by the three divine persons, and not by one of them as distinct from the others; and also the certitude that the supernatural, as found in us, prescinding from Christ and the subsistence in the Word that is personal to Him, is a finite thing and quite *ad extra*.

However, if what we wrote in the course of the preceding chapter is correct, this obstacle does not exist on the plane of thought pursued in this book. As regards both the incarnation of the Word and the sanctification of Christians, we beg leave to distinguish between *operari* and *factum esse*, that is, between the act of God who gives Himself and the situation in which the finite is found as a result of that giving. Further, we submit that Christians as Christians are so really and intrinsically united to Christ that they cannot be more adequately described than in terms of Christ and their participation in Him. In that case, nothing prevents us from considering the imposing organism of the eternal life of mankind as the expansion and plenitude of the unique grace that is in Christ because He is one of the persons of the Trinity.

Once this is granted, we must push on to the conclusion. The movement of theology presses us, and the synthesis is so beautiful, so specifically Christian, and so "theological" that we may not shirk the task. Indeed, does it even have to be undertaken? May we not rather say that it is so imperative that it performs itself?

II. Thesis and Demonstration

Let us say, therefore, that to conceive the supernatural clearly we must first turn our attention to God as He lives within the Trinity. We do not mean in any way to suggest that God's unity is less essential or profound than the Trinity; unity and Trinity are necessary to God, as they are necessary to each other. God's unity, to be one with the total perfection He requires, has to propose itself and be grasped—we are but struggling with our poor human words—to know itself and to embrace itself; and this knowledge and embrace constitute the Trinity in the mystery of the immanent processions. Likewise the Trinity, to be the Trinity with the perfection that is indispensable to God, requires to realize itself in three terms which are pure relations to one another and which, subsisting in these relations, are identically the same unity.

But with reference to us the divine unity represents something less profound in God, for to some extent it appears in God's works and is knowable, although imperfectly, to simple natural reason; whereas the Trinity, which does not express itself in creatures and hence is unknowable except through revelation, represents God as He is in Himself and for Himself alone.

This brings us back to the *interiora Dei*, the *profunda Dei, Deus prout est in se*, mentioned in preceding pages. There we spoke of God's relation with Himself alone; now we can speak more exactly of the relations that are in God and are God, relations of the persons, who are one and the same God, with one another. We also mentioned strict immanence and transcendence; we may now say that the immanence is the summit of life, and that the transcendence is such that God suffices fully for Himself, that He is one but not alone. We further said that God is knowable and lovable for Himself alone;

we may now add that God is knowledge and love that produce strictly consubstantial terms which subsist in persons so united to one another and so exactly correlative that they are fully received into one another, and are so completely involved in one another that they exist, not by title of distinct persons, but because they are one God. Lastly, we spoke about God as He is in Himself and as personal; we may now say by way of commentary that the personal God is three persons, for such is His way of possessing personality.

Personality in us men is the deepest thing in us and the good that is most completely ours. It is something that we do not communicate except in the measure we wish, if indeed we can speak of communicating it at all. All other things belonging to us are, so to say, external possessions which are exposed to expropriation by others; but this last stronghold, this strictly interior life, is so exclusively ours that no one knows anything about it or has any part of it unless we make it accessible: "For what man knoweth the things of a man, but the spirit of a man that is in him?" [5]

The same, if we may make the comparison, is true of God. His *exteriora* are the fringe of His cloak which creatures may touch, and have to have permission to touch, in order to exist. But the mystery of His life in which three persons are one God is for Him alone and in Him alone; that is His secret, and no other being, if left to itself, can touch or divine it. Therefore the communication of it exceeds all that any finite being, any created nature, can desire and attain on the level of its own development and its particular perfection.

Accordingly, when we describe the Trinity and think of what the creature is in its presence, our mind is automatically supplied with a formula which is the description of the strictly supernatural in its highest perfection. Thus this august mystery, which expresses the transcendence of eternal life as found in God, its principle, also expresses the transcendence of this same life as found in mankind after men receive a share in it.

The divine actions and communications in which everything is given without anything being created, take place in this life of the Trinity; these are the generation of the Word and the spiration of the Holy Ghost. Does not logic suggest that in this same life are found the origin and explanation of that other action and communi-

[5] Cf. I Cor. 2:11.

cation which also give everything without creating a new nature: divinization, divine adoption, and the supernatural?

This mystery specifies Christianity as metaphysics, as a conception of life, and as a religion; it describes Christ as a person and as a mediator, that is, as He is in Himself and as He is for us. To be consistent, should it not also describe the reality and the new way of existing which Christ and Christianity have brought into this world, that is, the supernatural? The natural order is defined as a relation to the God of reason, to the Pure Act of the philosophers; we submit that the supernatural should be defined as a relation to God such as faith and the supernatural order show Him to be, namely, God who is the Trinity.

We believe that this sort of language is by no means an innovation. The most ancient and most authentic Christian teaching has expressed its thought in this fashion, although implicitly.

Jesus Himself does the same. The Master does not employ the abstract term, supernatural. But He often speaks of the thing signified by this term. Most often He designates it as eternal life, and He associates this life with the Trinity. This is the life which the Word has in Him because He is God and in God; it is the life which the Father possesses in abundance and communicates in its totality to the Son, the life whereby the Son lives of the Father and proceeds from the Father. His sacred humanity possesses this life in profusion and diffuses it throughout the human race. He Himself is wholly from the Father; all that He has, His doctrine, His works, and His holiness, comes to Him in the eternal begetting, and He shares it all with His followers, through their faith, their acts, and their union with God. Therefore all the grace and the gifts they receive, all that they have of the supernatural, come to them from the eternal processions and from the Trinity. If we undertake to read the Gospel of St. John according to this point of view, we shall find to our astonishment that the Master hardly ever speaks of the new reality that comes to Christians and transfigures them, that is, of the supernatural, except when He speaks of the mystery that is in God and is the Trinity. "As Thou, Father, in Me and I in Thee: that they also may be one in us." [6] *Ens et unum convertuntur;* as the unity among Christians is characterized by a relation to the Trinity, so their existence as Chris-

[6] John 17:21.

tians or, in other words, their supernatural reality, must be characterized in like manner.

What Christ taught has been taken up and repeated by tradition. In an earlier chapter we showed how pointedly the Fathers and ecclesiastical writers present Christian life as an adoption that is nothing less than a participation in the very filiation of the Son. By expressing their thought in this way, they say equivalently that the supernatural, which is this life, is a participation in the Trinity and a union with the Trinity.

This sort of reasoning merits fuller development and closer study. At present we wish merely to call attention to the researches that still have to be made. We have not at all pushed our own investigations to the limit. Yet the little we have done permits us to suggest that, if they are pursued farther, they will lead to a conclusion of this kind. At first, as was natural, the doctrine was viewed as a whole, and no explicit distinction was made between God from whom the divine and supernatural gift came, Christ in whom it came, and the supernatural itself. Regarding this whole and the supernatural comprised within it, writers could say and did say that it was a relation to the Trinity, a divine adoption, and a possession of the Spirit. Distinctions had to be introduced; and this was the work of succeeding generations.

Then grace and the supernatural were viewed apart, in themselves; and since they are accidents modifying man and are things *ad extra*, their real but not exclusive character as finite things was placed in the foreground, and nothing further was said, along the lines of this conception, of a relation with the Trinity as Trinity; at the time no one looked in the direction pointing to such a relationship. Of course no one denied the connection between grace and the supernatural on one hand, and Christ and God on the other; we are all familiar with the relations St. Thomas describes between uncreated and created grace, between glory and grace; but these bonds were much less an object of study than the supernatural considered in itself. Those bonds might eventually have been lost sight of, if the course of Christian thought had not been charted by God Himself, as it actually is. Thanks to God's beneficent providence, we now see them better than ever.

In our own day, our study induces us to perceive that grace and the supernatural are a union with Christ and an incorporation into

Him, and hence to understand more clearly how the bonds linking them to Christ are intrinsic and essential to them. But if grace and the supernatural unite us to Christ, how can they fail to unite us, in Him, to the Trinity? If, therefore, we now take up again the original formulas we can understand them in a more precise sense and ascribe to them a greater value. This is owing to the labor of later ages which, in their criticism of the formulas, have brought us to the point where we can fix the exact source of that value. On the assumption that the historical abridgment given earlier was objective, this represents true progress, *in eodem sensu, ad eumdem sensum.*

In any case, the notion of the relation between the supernatural and the Trinity did not disappear during the long centuries when the supernatural was mainly conceived as something perfecting man. A proof of this is found in the texts from St. Thomas we quoted along with others when we were trying to ascertain the connection between the supernatural adoption of the Christian and the generation of the Only-begotten. Further witness is provided by other texts in which the same saint, when proposing his theory of the divine missions, establishes a close relationship between sanctifying grace and our possession of the divine persons. "The power of enjoying a divine person necessarily implies sanctifying grace." [7]

So far as we know, Zumel is the only one of the Scholastics who proposed a definition of the supernatural as a communication of the Trinity as Trinity.[8] He discusses "the action of God according as God is imitable by creatures, that is, according as He is one. . . . Secondly, God may be considered as triune, and as such He cannot be substantially imitated by any creature . . . yet the creature may be elevated to a supernatural end (that is, to the vision and love of God as triune). . . . But those creatures which are ordained and which ordain to God as triune, that is, to some participation and attainment of God as He is, are said to pertain to the supernatural order." [9]

With greater persistence than in earlier days, modern theologians

[7] St. Thomas, *Summa,* Ia, q.43, a.3; cf. also ad 1, 2; a.4 ad 1; a.5 ad 2; q.38, a.1.

[8] F. Zumel (or Cumel), 1540–1607; he became professor at Salamanca, 1580. Cf. *In primam secundae S. Thomae commentaria,* q.110, a.4, disp. 5 (Salamanca, 1594; II, 243 f.); *In primam divi Thomae partem commentaria,* q.12, a.3, disp. unica (Venice, 1597; p. 199).

[9] *In primam divi Thomae partem commentaria* (Venice, 1597; p. 243).

endeavor to discover how the theological virtues can have one of the divine persons as the term, exemplar, and principle in which they share, and how grace, which is the root of these virtues, and glory, which is the flowering of grace, may exhibit some affinity with the Trinity as such. They are not sparing in their labors or in lengthy, abstract, and involved argumentation, thus bearing splendid and touching witness to the yearning that runs through Christian thought of finding some mysterious and intimate bond with the Trinity itself.

The theme of our own book constrains us to say that, in our opinion, the difficulty and imperfection of their endeavors come from the fact that they do not sufficiently bring into the foreground what we consider to be the central truth: Christ the incarnate Word, and the incorporation of men into Christ. They continually run the risk of saying too much or too little: too much, by attributing to mankind some union with the Trinity other than that of Christ; too little, by not assigning to Christians a share in that union.

The explanations they give are difficult, subtle, laborious. Is that not an indication that their explanations are not the only ones or even the main ones? For in so essential a point, which deals with what is most exalted in Christian life, the explanation should seemingly be within the grasp of all minds, at least in its basis if not in its technical elaboration. "Thou hast revealed [these things] to little ones." [10] The most divine and the most vital mysteries have been revealed also, if not mainly, for the benefit of the lowly.[11] They too, in their own way, no less than others, have to grasp enough to be able to think as believers.

We hold that one explanation is imperative; it is imperative in all parts of theology, but here more than anywhere else. And that is Christ. This explanation may not be easy to express scientifically, but it is easy to possess and to live, since Christ lives in us and we live in Him. We may formulate it by saying that He, with His sacred humanity which subsists in the Word, is perfect union with the Trinity, and hence the supernatural in its full sense. The rest of the supernatural is assuredly not nothing; yet it is His, not by identity, which would be equivalent to suppressing it, but by derivation and participation.

[10] Luke 10:21.
[11] When Jesus gives thanks to the Father for having revealed these things to little ones, He is speaking precisely of the Trinity; cf. Matt. 11:25, 27.

Therefore let us lay down as a principle that the supernatural, at least as it is found in the present order, is a mode of existing that is fully realized in the sacred humanity of Christ, by a unique and perfect union with the Trinity as Trinity. The union of the sacred humanity with the Trinity is perfect, for it is the strict unity of a divine person; and personality is the ultimate, both in humanity and in divinity. It could not be more perfect. Even if several divine persons were united to several distinct human natures, the union would not be greater; it would be multiplied without being augmented.

Toti non fit additio. Nothing outside such a totality could conceivably be numbered with it or could augment it by being added to it. Consequently every lesser union must be thought of as comprised in it and, not being identified with it, as derived from it; a ray of light is not added to the sun, for it emanates from the sun. In the order of union with the Trinity, in the supernatural order, the hypostatic union is a maximum, a summit from which everything flows, an infinity from which everything proceeds; it is a totality and a unity. It is a sort of first principle *in* that order, though not *of* that order: "a sort of universal principle in the genus of beings that have grace," [12] a kind of fullness of exhaustive realization that eminently includes all other realizations, a kind of fullness of form whose supereminence explains and supports all others, whose superabundance replenishes all others, and which, simply by being what it is, is also what all others are without suppressing their integrity; for it causes them all to be what they are.

Thus Christ, who sums up in Himself the gift of God to men and the whole order of grace and glory, "who of God is made unto us wisdom and justice and sanctification and redemption," [13] thereby also sums up the whole of the supernatural. His sacred humanity, in its subsistence in the Word and in its mystical union with men, does more than possess the supernatural; we may say that it is the supernatural; for it is defined, because of the hypostatic union, by what is supreme in the supernatural, and is the maximum in that order, summarizing it completely.

Therefore we have to regard the supernatural in Christ's humanity if we wish to see it whole. Christ's humanity, the first principle of the supernatural in the order of being, is also the first principle of the

[12] St. Thomas, *Summa*, IIIa, q.7, a.9.
[13] I Cor. 1:30.

supernatural in the order of understanding. It is the primary intelligible object, the center and the unity to which the supernatural must be traced back if it is to be understood. St. Augustine had indicated this line of thought in his study of predestination, which is precisely the mystery of the supernatural considered in the divine election that brings it into being. "There is no more striking example of predestination than the Mediator Himself. If any of the faithful wishes to gain a clear idea of predestination, let him study Christ, and in Christ he will find himself." [14] "Let him study Christ." We must scrutinize this sacred humanity. In Christ's humanity the Creator acts on His creation in a new and more powerful way; and from this contact with Being a new type of being emerges that is greater, more excellent, and more unified than the first. This is the supernatural. A new type of being, we repeat, and new as being; this is what we must examine more closely.

God produces this being otherwise than He produces beings by creation. He produces it by the subsistence He communicates to the humanity He assumed. The action whereby the three divine persons together effect the Incarnation is not in question here, as we see clearly. What is at stake is rather the new relation caused by this action, and the effect it necessarily has on the assumed humanity. This effect is everything that adapts this humanity to such a situation: sonship, divinization, and grace.

This divine intervention, like the divine action that produces grace in us, could, indeed, quite fittingly be called creation, or rather concreation or something similar, since it issues in a complement of being rather than in complete being. The result produced exists in a creature as an accident of that creature; hence its existence must be like that of the creature. Moreover, the complete and exclusive cause of its existence is found in God alone; of itself it is nothing, yet God unceasingly gives it existence. Or else, if we prefer, we may say that it is produced from nothing, in the sense that, although it is educed from the creature's obediential potency, nothing of the same order previously existed in the creature.

But even if we use the word creation, we must not forget that the two actions are quite different. Indeed, the difference is so great that the employment of a different word is desirable. We should like to suggest a term that we shall use from time to time: "causality through

[14] St. Augustine, *De dono perseverantiae*, 67 (PL, XLV, 1033).

union," an intervention by way of union that produces, as we shall explain in the course of this chapter, a special type of being, the supernatural, which may consequently be called an "entity of union."

By creation God establishes beings in themselves, outside the Godhead. By the Incarnation considered *in facto esse*, God establishes a being in the Godhead and above the being's own nature, by suppressing all distance and by becoming strictly immanent in that being. Creation, in the thing created, consists in having the cause of being outside the being; the Incarnation, considered in the assumed nature, consists in having the cause of being in the being itself, as its sole personality. Hence this is a new kind of action, in which God, who always and everywhere is pure Being and the source of all being, acts with all His being by giving Himself; God acts by causing this man to be truly God, truly Being, and to have within him all that is needed for being; God acts not from afar, but as an internal constituent in the order of subsistence.

This is action by union, by the most intimate of unions; a union consisting in the unity of a divine person. In the assumed humanity this union is effected at the very point where personality would be found, that is, it is the union of this humanity with itself, its ultimate center of convergence and its first principle of activity, for this is what God prolongs in some fashion and further concentrates by fixing it and making it subsist in Himself. We may also observe in passing that the union is effected at the point where the sacred humanity is united to all other humanities, since, if what we said above is correct, the same spirituality of soul that accounts for man's personal character, at the same time accounts for the human universality that is found in every soul and joins it to all souls. Lastly, God brings this union into being by the mystery of union in Himself, for the mystery of the Trinity is certainly a mystery of union. In the Incarnation, therefore, and in the subsistence He communicates to the assumed humanity, God acts not only in a way that is different from creation, but by a different aspect of Himself.

We find ourselves at a loss when we attempt to express such truths, for anthropomorphism inevitably slips in; yet they must be expressed, for they alone lay bare the root of the mystery. We beg the reader, here even more than elsewhere, to have the goodness to try to understand us, and to seek rather the truth we are endeavoring to enunciate than the inaccuracies of language we have not managed to avoid.

After this consideration devoted to the causes of the order of things which was inaugurated by the Incarnation and which is the supernatural, we now go on to study the supernatural as it is in itself. We are inquiring into the perfection that results directly in the assumed humanity from its union with one of the divine persons. We are not concerned here with the simple fact of being united to this person, but rather with the Incarnation *in facto esse*, the Incarnation considered from the point of view of the assumed humanity, in which it produces an effect that would have not existed without it and that exists only because of it and in it.

As we have already remarked, the Incarnation does not produce anything new in God. Therefore, unless it is to produce nothing at all, it must produce something in the human nature that is assumed. Since it is a relation, and a relation that is real only on the side of the human nature, it must have a real foundation; otherwise it would be no more than a legal fiction or a figment of the imagination. And since this nature becomes God's human nature, it must be intrinsically conditioned for this purpose. If the Incarnation is not to issue in a monstrous disproportion, the human nature must be adapted to its new dignity, or more accurately, to its new manner of existing.

This adaptation will not constitute a substance or a complete being, but a quality, an accident, for it is a perfection of human nature. The only "substances," to use the theological vocabulary of the ancients, or, as we may say more precisely, the only natures in Christ are the divinity and the humanity. The union between them is not a third nature, but merely joins them in a single person. Yet this union is so real that it produces a corresponding elevation in the human nature. Since this elevation resides in something that is not itself, it is an *esse in*, an accident.

But in qualifying it as an accident, we express only that aspect of it which regards the human nature in which it is realized, not the aspect which regards the divine nature for which it exists, although this latter aspect is by far the more important. Accordingly the term "accident," which qualifies the elevation well, does not qualify it adequately. Considered adequately, the elevation passes beyond the limits of an accident; it is like the new wine that can be poured into old bottles, but then proceeds to burst them. Aristotle's categories are too narrow for this mystery of the Most High that comes to elevate and enlarge infinitely the natural universe which is partitioned into these categories; how could something that is greater than the whole be compressed into forms designed to measure the parts? Besides, being as such does not enter into these classifications; a fortiori the Being that is very Being cannot be comprised within them. And the effect produced by the Incarnation is a new type of being, a new way of existing; it is an assimilation to Him who is Being itself. How could a mountain range be set on a fragile platform?

When we think of the reason for this new being, we see that its difference from all created entities is not to be explained solely or mainly by the order that separates accident from substance; for it pertains, by derivation, to the order that separates the finite from the infinite. This is what distinguishes a humanity that truly belongs to God from what it would be were it not God's humanity.

Since we are dealing with a new kind of being, we shall do well to designate it by a new word. To express the action producing it, we have suggested the term "causality of union" or "causality through union," and to represent the type of being thus realized, the term "entity of union." By this we mean an entity, a reality that does not exist and cannot exist in a given being except in and by actual union with another being. In the former, it is pure adherence, pure *esse in*, and all its reference and assimilation is to the latter. It is but the expression and result, in one being, of union with another, and is impossible and inconceivable outside such union.

In all truth, it is a new type of being; to have a new and infinitely closer relation with a different and infinitely more intrinsic aspect of Being itself cannot be without consequence for any being. Such a relation must cause the latter to "be" otherwise and more perfectly, and must make it in some sense a "super-being," as we said above; that relation must cause it to realize the nature it possesses in a higher way, that is, in a way that is ontologically and absolutely "supernatural." Thus the notion of the strictly supernatural is again described in function of the Trinity and of union with the Trinity.

A being is characterized by its relation with God; this and nothing else measures its internal greatness and its nobility. If this relation changes, the being will change, and will be something else. If, as in the Incarnation, the relation changes by becoming infinitely more intimate, the being will change by becoming infinitely more intense; it will be itself, but will be so infinitely better and more than it has a right to be; it will be absolutely supernatural.

A correct conception of this being may require a revision of the very notion of contingent being. If this being is contingent, it is contingent in the way demanded of a contingent nature that belongs to a necessary divine person. A new treatise *De ente* needs to be written on this subject, a *De ente supernaturali*. This treatise should not have the scope aimed at by Ripalda when he composed his monumental work, and should not be a description of all that concerns the supernatural, its extension, and its history, but should rather be a study of its essential comprehension and a sort of ontology of the supernatural.

Such a metaphysics can be quite simple. We believe that it is indispensable in order to scotch the notion that the supernatural is a special type of nature. As the supernatural is a kind of being unique in its class, it needs a unique ontology. This ontology cannot, of course, be opposed to natural ontology; the supernatural is not opposed to the natural. This ontology supposes natural ontology but goes beyond it, as the supernatural itself lays hold of the natural and elevates it.

As this ontology treats of an "entity of union," its first principle must formulate all that is essential to this being, and must also bring out the fact that it is an entity of union. This principle will be the sacred dogma of Chalcedon, the dogma of the hypostatic union: two natures and one person; a perfect man who is truly the perfect God. It will also be the verse of the Gospel: "That you may believe that Jesus is the Christ, the Son of God." [15] Or it will be the formula that defines the supreme and most excellent supernatural elevation: a being, a man, who is what He is by being God. Or, if preferred, it will be the declaration, not that the pure Being is inaccessibly transcendent and all other beings are analogous, but that the pure Being is truly man, that a man is identically this Being, and that through Him other beings, other men, are made one.

This is the formula that defines Christ. Accordingly we may say that the first principle in this ontology is Christ in His sacred humanity. This humanity is not merely a particular case in which the supernatural has been splendidly realized; it is the acme of the supernatural, the supernatural in all its perfection. It is the supernatural in a sense that remotely recalls the ancient physical conception of the sun as light. This is what Scholasticism intended to bring out

[15] John 20:31.

when it taught that Christ's grace is infinite, not as being, but as grace, "in its specific nature as grace." For Christ's grace "has whatever can pertain to the nature of grace . . . as it is a universal principle for bestowing grace on human nature. . . . In a similar manner we might say that the light of the sun is infinite, not indeed in being, but in the nature of light, since it has all that can pertain to the nature of light." [16]

The first characteristic assigned to such a being by its own ontology, which is an ontology of union (and not of creation), is the fact that it brings together predicates that of themselves are infinitely distant. It can and, in a sense to be determined presently, it must be finite and infinite, created and uncreated, human and divine, temporal and eternal, contingent and necessary. It can harmonize these pairs of predicates because they involve no opposition, whatever the distance between them may be. The infinite, the uncreated, the divine is Being itself; the finite, the created, the human share in being; their union with Being cannot be impossible; [17] and if this union is actually realized, it must somehow be expressed in the nature that receives it. The entity in question has to admit of these predicates, because its very essence is to adapt intrinsically a finite, created, and temporal nature to be strictly the human nature of the Infinite, the Uncreated, the Eternal; but this it could not do unless it pertained in some way to the order of these attributes. Its essence is to be the expression of the divine nature and attributes that are impressed on the human nature so deeply as to become one with it; how could the human nature be the expression of them unless it expressed them?

We should clearly understand that there is not and cannot be a middle term between the infinite and the finite. Everything finite is equally distant, that is, infinitely distant from the infinite, and consequently cannot truly be an adaptation to the infinite or an expression of the infinite. If there is such an adaptation—and that has to be admitted because the Incarnation is real—it must pertain to the order of the infinite itself. It does not pertain to that order by identification, for then it would no longer be an adaptation of the finite; nor by a simple quality that would be no more than an accident of the finite like all other accidents, for such an accident could never adapt any-

[16] St. Thomas, *Summa*, IIIa, q. 7, a. 11.

[17] This is a repetition in very brief form of what we said above, pp. 460 f., along with the necessary explanations.

thing to the infinite. Rather it is an entity that depends on the two united extremes, that corresponds to a new type of being, the "entity of union" we spoke of; it is that by which the finite, as united to the infinite, expresses this union and is adapted to the union by the power of the union lodged in the finite substance.

Since it is an "entity of union" it must religiously respect the integrity of the natures it unites, for it is exclusively an "entity of union." But on the same score it must adapt one nature to the other sufficiently to permit of a true and interior union. It respects the divine nature by leaving intact the divine nature's immutability; it respects the human nature by completely and divinely perfecting the human nature. The adverb "divinely" need not dismay us; St. Thomas dared to say: "Christ is true God by reason of His divine person and nature. Yet, since the distinction of natures remains along with unity of person, Christ's soul is not divine in essence; hence it must become divine by participation, which is by grace." [18]

To entertain such a conception without experiencing shock, we need a rejuvenated line of thought; for we are dealing with a new ontology, and our concepts bear on being as being. "Be renewed in the spirit of your mind." [19] We must be divinely renewed in the deepest center of our minds, at the very source of thought. As this entity exists only in Christ and through Christ, it can be conceived only in Christ; this is true both of the supernatural that is in Christ and of the supernatural that flows from Christ into men. This entity exists in its own way, and therefore cannot be conceived except in its own way, and that is the way inaugurated by the Incarnation; it is conceivable in the distinction between the humanity and the divinity and hence in their union in the Second Person of the Trinity. The distinction and the union are found in the Son, and at the same time; and all this is conceived in a single act and believed with a single faith, for all this makes up Christ and is the reason why Christ's humanity is all that it is both in itself and for us.

What we should chiefly notice about this entity is its ontological excellence, and hence its intensity and infinity of being. The original creation is a magnificent thing; but with reference to this second creation that takes place in Christ,[20] it is but a point of departure;

---

[18] St. Thomas, *Summa*, IIIa, q. 7, a. 1 ad 1.
[19] Eph. 4:23.
[20] Eph. 2:10.

if we may venture to say so, it is that which nothingness was for the first creation; and the greatness of this second creation is measured, not by what is suitable for the creature, but by what is suitable for the Creator.

When we contemplate this truth, we should give up our spatial categories, our quantitative calculations, and even our very concepts, which represent nothing but finite realities such as the parts of the human universe. They are too restricted even to represent man so far as he is spirit and the unity of his universe. How much less adequate are they to represent the interior elevation by which a human nature becomes the humanity of God!

Jesus Christ is everything, just as at the beginning the Word was everything. But all things were made by the Word, and through Him all things are unified in their origin. Likewise in Christ, in the excellence His humanity received when it was made the true humanity of God, all things are remade in principle. The totality of men, unlimited as it is, is one, and is a single Christ in its origin. The very unity of the Word enters into men and finds expression in their unity which is an interior adaptation to, and a perpetual participation in, the Word's unity: a unity which shares in the Trinitarian unity and the union of the Three: "that they may be one, as We also are one" (John 17:22).

When viewed by the eyes of the body, Christ and His humanity take up so little time and occupy so little space; that is, "in the sight of the unwise" (Prov. 3:2). But to the eyes of the soul, to the eyes of faith which are able to perceive interior vastnesses, Christ and His humanity are a mystery of grandeur and unity. "We behold something which is glorious that can know no end, something which is sublime, lofty, boundless, that is more ancient than heaven and chaos." [21]

Sacred Scripture says of this humanity that subsists in the divinity: "In [Christ] dwelleth all the fullness of the Godhead corporeally, and you are filled in Him"; [22] Christ is "full of grace and truth . . . and of His fullness we have all received"; [23] He is "the head from which the whole body . . . groweth unto the increase of God"; [24]

[21] Hymn for First Vespers of the feast of the Transfiguration.
[22] Col. 2:9 f.
[23] John 1:14, 16.
[24] Col. 2:19.

"If, then, any be in Christ a new creature, the old things are passed away, behold all things are made new." [25]

Thus this second creation, which recapitulates all things in the God-man, does not shrink into itself, but takes firm root in the Necessary, to spread out thence to infinity. All mankind, the whole human universe, and even, in its own way, the whole angelic world, are blessed and exalted in Him. The good flowing into all of us is the very good that was first brought forth, in plenitude, in Him alone.

[25] Cf. II Cor. 5:17.

CHAPTER XVI

NATURE AND NOTES OF THE CHURCH

I. Nature of the Church

THE ordinary procedure followed in studying the Church is to consider it as it appears in itself. But we can also study the Church by considering it in the light of Christ. This is the procedure we shall adopt in these pages. Such a study of the Church will not expose us to the danger of losing sight of it as it is in itself, but will rather lay open to us its inner principle and cause. The Church is the continuation of Christ, for it is His mystical body.

A remark seems to be in order here. Although we may nearly always regard the terms, Church and mystical body, as interchangeable, it does not follow that the two expressions have exactly the same shade of meaning in every case and from every point of view. We believe that we would be forcing the sense of the Pauline text, "the Church, which is His body," [1] and of several similar passages, [2] if we claimed to find in them an affirmation of such identity. However, some authors are of this mind, and they even go so far as to declare that the mystical body in the strict sense of the word is exclusively the Church militant. [3]

In this contention they are quite orthodox. Yet we are of the opinion that the Apostle's doctrine is not completely decisive on this point, [4] and tradition has taken a wider view of the teaching. [5] In the

[1] Eph. 1:23; Col. 1:18, 24.—On the divergence, more apparent then real, between Mersch and the encyclical *Mystici Corporis Christi* of Pius XII, see the Introduction. Throughout the present chapter Mersch regards the Church and the mystical body as coterminous. [Tr.]

[2] Cf. I Cor. 12:12–30; Rom. 12:4 ff.; Eph. 5:23–30.

[3] Thus, for instance, J. C. Gruden, *The Mystical Christ* (St. Louis: Herder, 1936); cf. especially p. 160.

[4] See especially the context of Eph. 1:23 and Col. 1:18, 24.

[5] See *The Whole Christ*, Index, s.v "Church," "Mystical Body," "Christ."

ordinary language of the Church, "mystical body" connotes the entire multitude of those who live the life of Christ, with a life that admits of degrees,[6] whereas the word "Church" represents the society of the baptized faithful as organized under their lawful pastors.

The two realities are closely related, and the present chapter will show how the one necessarily involves the other. But the two are not absolutely identified on this earth. A person can be a member of the visible society of the Church without actually living the life of Christ as a perfect member of the mystical body; this is the case with a Catholic hardened in sin. Likewise, one can truly live the life of Christ without being actually attached to the visible society that is His Church; an example is a pagan who would have received grace and charity without being aware of the Church, or a fervent catechumen.

It is quite true that the Church visible alone, as established over the entire earth, fully represents what Jesus Christ desires. But it is also true that the visible Church is far from having achieved that position, and Jesus Christ foresaw this. Accordingly the great number of souls effectively living the life of Christ is one thing, and the visible Church is another; in a matter so delicate, dealing with such important objects, we shall find it useful to have two different words to designate two realities that differ *de facto*, however closely they may be related *de jure*.

As we perceive, the two notions, while involving the same truths, line them up differently and stress different points. These notions are the product of different thought-processes and theological elaborations; they correspond to different questions and preoccupations. By forcibly reducing them to each other we should be renouncing a traditional heritage of meditations and studies, and the apparent simplification resulting might turn out to be an impoverishment; instead of having two shades of thought, we should have nothing more than two synonymous terms. This would be the more regrettable inasmuch as the particular notion of the mystical body, in spite of a certain indefiniteness which detracts from its maneuverability for purposes of controversy, has a special tonality and resonance that fit it for some theological expositions, for example,

6 Cf. St. Thomas, *Summa*, IIIa, q.8, a.3.

those that undertake to make clear to Christian people the nature of their life and its mysteriousness.

Besides, it has the advantage, which is often important, of being but slightly weighed down with Latin or juridical terms, and of having preserved almost the same meaning for many of our separated brethren as for ourselves. By safeguarding its particular significance, we keep alive the possibility of conversations, of exchanges of views, and even, perhaps, of formulas of union. Providence cannot but have some reason for preserving it and for thrusting it into the foreground in our day.

In any case, to return to the subject of the present chapter, our purpose is to study the Church regarded as the body of Christ and its continuation here on earth. Our aim is not to construct a treatise *On the Church* for its own sake; many excellent ones are at hand. Our wish is rather to see, at least in bold outline, how an ecclesiology that is nothing but a continuation of Christology would take shape. If the Church is the continuation of Christ, should not the science that describes it be a continuation of the science that describes Christ?

Christ continues Himself in the whole of mankind that is susceptible of salvation, that is, mankind as living in heaven, in purgatory, and on earth. This threefold continuation corresponds to a threefold Church: the Church triumphant, the Church suffering, and the Church militant. With regard to the earth in particular, Christ is continued—if we can speak of continuation in this connection—during the centuries that preceded Him as well as during those that have followed Him.[7] Hence there is a Church of the Old Testament and a Church of the New Testament.

During the centuries that preceded Him, Christ pre-existed as a man pre-exists in the human line that prepares and announces him. However He pre-existed not only as an effect issuing from its causes, but as a principle giving rise to this whole line regarded as progressing toward the God-man and presaging His holiness. This pre-existence is the community of Israel which we may call the Church of the Old Testament,[8] and in a wider sense is all that is truly religious in all the religions of ancient times.

During the centuries that follow Him, Christ is to perpetuate Him-

[7] Cf. *ibid.*
[8] *Ibid.*

self in a new form, which is the new way of existing He gives to the human race. This is the life of the Church in the strict sense, the Church militant properly so called—the Church that is the object of discussion in this chapter.

Every man survives himself to some extent in the wake he leaves behind. This wake is the more clearly marked and enduring the more intensively the man himself has lived and acted. It will have supreme intensity for the sacred humanity of Christ, for He lived and acted with supreme intensity. In other words, it will derive its most characteristic traits from Him and will be closely connected with His humanity. To be the continuation of Christ's humanity in this way, it must be constituted as the sacred humanity is constituted, and must, so to speak, be the continuation of the sacred humanity's constitution.

But Christ's humanity was both an empirical thing and a mysterious reality. Viewed from the outside by the eyes of the body, it was a humanity like all others, carried along by the same tides, lashed by the same winds and rains, subject to the same laws of the universe with their ordinary lack of concern for the individual. It was a humanity as visible as all others and open to the same processes of observation. From within, this empirical humanity was mysteriously divinized with a superabundant fullness, so as to possess, in the manner of a universal source, the supernatural life and divinization of all mankind.

The second of these two aspects, divinization, exists only in the hypostatic union with the divinity; it comes from this union and exists for this union. Hence the temptation may arise to say that this second aspect is the divinity. The formula would evidently be inexact; the divinity is not an aspect of the humanity. Yet we would be able to interpret it in an acceptable sense.

As these two aspects are found in Christ's humanity, they will also be found in the mystic perpetuation of that humanity which is the Church. The Church will likewise be an empirical thing and a mysterious reality.

First, it will be an empirical, concrete, visible, tangible thing, like all human realities that prolong themselves in some form of continuation; for it is a human institution, a human society. And it is a society quite visibly and tangibly; its sociology and canon law can be written down; it has its clearly defined members and its definite seat: it is the

Church of Rome, as Jesus Christ was Jesus of Nazareth. As a society it is perfect in its kind, with a firm and well-delineated structure, as befits a thing that is the perpetuation of the God-man.

Secondly, the Church will be an invisible reality: a life of thought, love, and grace that is infused into souls, a divinization and adoptive sonship which, in the unity of the only-begotten, incarnate Son is diffused throughout all mankind so deeply as to be inaccessible to natural consciousness, and which, in the depths thus reached, unifies mankind in itself and attaches it to God.

Through this second aspect, that is, the divinization conferred on it, the Church is a theandric reality, a divine-human reality, as many authors aptly put it. The reason is not that the Godhead is one of its elements or aspects, or that the Church has its own union with the Godhead independently of Christ and His hypostatic union, but only that it is the perpetuation of the theandric humanity, the humanity fully divinized and subsisting in the Word, the humanity of the God-man.

This second aspect is what makes the Church the new mankind, the mankind that exists otherwise and more perfectly, by a new and more efficacious contact with pure Being, and with a new and more intimate aspect of Being than that which constitutes simple mankind. This mankind is not the result of the impress of the divine hands, but exists in its divine head, in the most interior of unions with the divine life.

We call it the new mankind, for in it is realized, like a new human form or a new human act, its supernatural, "filial," Trinitarian form. It is mankind par excellence. It is not a replacing but a renovation of the old mankind, and is henceforth the only admissible form of mankind, the form to which all mankind is directed by the divine vocation and by the work which grace begins to perform in it. For this reason the Church, like mankind, will have two aspects, one external and visible, the other internal and invisible. But these two aspects are joined and make up a single new mankind.

The two aspects of the Church, the visible and the invisible, are often called the soul and the body of the Church. This manner of speaking may have disadvantages, and they are brought out in our day; but it greatly facilitates certain explanations. Hence we may profitably devote some consideration to it.

The body of the Church, as we see at once, is the external aspect, the empirical society which is the Church of Rome. The word "body" does not have here the precise sense it has in the term "mystical body." For the expression "mystical body" designates the mysterious and interior element of the Church; even for those who identify the Church militant with the mystical body, it does not designate the external aspect, the "body," except so far as it is the outward manifestation of the interior soul, which consists in such a mystery.

The soul of the Church must clearly be the factor that makes this society a living organism; it is the first general principle of a collective and unified life in all the members. This factor can be nothing else than the grace which causes all these members to be living members of Christ, the divinizing grace that is infused into all by one and the same Christ.[9] Or else we may say that it is Christ, the Son of the Father, regarded as the principle of life in the whole supernatural organism because of this infusion: "a certain universal principle in the genus of such as have grace," as St. Thomas says, "a universal principle for bestowing grace on human nature." [10]

Christ's humanity cannot be such a principle in the Church unless His divinity is an interior source of supernatural fullness and teeming life in it. In this sense we may say that the divinity and in particular, by appropriation, the Holy Spirit, is in some way a soul with respect to the grace and divinization of Christ's humanity, and hence that it is also a sort of soul, the soul of the soul, the life of the life of the Church. We can be still more precise and say that the divinity, as possessed by the person of the Son, has this function by a causality of union, that it is a sort of quasi-formal cause, or rather a quasi-actuating cause imparting subsistence, and also that the Godhead and the Trinity and in particular the Spirit have the same function by way of efficient causality or production. These considerations, which we propose in passing, may serve to round out what we said in chapter 14 about the soul of the mystical body.

In any case we should note well that the soul of the Church, together with the body, forms a total entity, a single Church of Christ, just as soul and body constitute a single man or as the empirical aspect

---

[9] The infusion will be actual and complete or only partial (faith and actual graces) or even merely postulated by the baptismal character, in the case of Christians living in the state of sin.

[10] *Summa*, IIIa, q.7, a.9; a.11.

and the fullness of divinization make up a single Christ. Christ's divinity and humanity are united *inconfuse et incommutabiliter*, though also *indivise et inseparabiliter*; [11] in an analogous way His humanity and the transcendent divinization of it that is brought about by union with the divinity are united without confusion but also without division; they are distinct but inseparable. This union existing in this distinction passes on to the Church. Because of Christ, the two aspects that perpetuate the two aspects of Christ's sacred humanity, the aspect of empirical society and the aspect of fellowship in grace and divinization, are indissolubly united in the Church, without on that account being identified.

The Church knows only too well that they are not identical, for she is aware of the presence of sin, and that she herself, the sacred body of Christ, is in exile, "absent from the Lord." [12] The empirical organism which is the outer aspect of the Church has not yet fully assimilated the grace, the unity, and the holiness whereof it lives and whose totality is found in it germinally, truly possessed but not yet completely realized. Just as the life of grace in each Christian depends on union with God, so the unity, the substance, and the essence of the Church regarded as an empirical society depend on union with Christ, with His grace, and with God who gives grace in Christ; yet the Church is not formally this grace nor Christ, for they are not empirical.

But this way of regarding the Church is nothing more than a mental precision. In reality, the main thing is the union we have been speaking of; although the united elements are distinct, even as elements they exist through this union and in this union. When our view of the visible aspect of the Church comprises it as it actually is, we perceive perfect intercommunion and inseparability: "what God hath joined together, let no man put asunder." [13]

Some say that this union is the most marvelous trait of the Church; others say that it is the scandal of the Church; in any case it is the mystery of the Church. In the same way the union between the divine nature and the human nature is the characteristic feature of Jesus, a fact that spells ruin for some and resurrection for others; but in any case it is a sign of contradiction. That the divine nature is

[11] Cf. the Council of Chalcedon (Denz., 148).
[12] Cf. II Cor. 5:6.
[13] Matt. 19:6.

a mystery, will be readily conceded. But that a reality which is of this world and is even, at times, too much of this world, should be a mystery, appears irritating. The Church is a society like other societies, granted; or it is an ideal entity, a fellowship in love of God and one's neighbor, granted again; but its claim to be both together, to belong to time and to eternity, to possess the qualifications needed to administer its property and to have the mission of dispensing divine life, this is what bands idealists and positivists against it—and is also the very thing that enables it to gather both these parties within its embrace. The Church does indeed make this claim and has to; otherwise it would be false to itself and would cease to be the perpetuation of the God-man.

This is a paradox, if you will; assuredly it is a mystery—the Christian mystery par excellence, the mystery of the Incarnation. Therefore Christians, who are what they are by their membership in Christ and their connection with the Incarnation, must understand this mystery; indeed, they do not have to understand anything else. It alone explains them to themselves, and it alone is the adequate object of their knowledge. This will become clearer in the light of what we have to say about the notes of the Church.

II. THE NOTES OF THE CHURCH

A. Theory of the notes in the mystical body. The two aspects we have been discussing are so closely united that details of the one are reflected in details of the other, and that the exterior of the Church is an indication of its interior nature. This leads to a theory about the notes of the Church, a subject interesting to consider at this juncture. Our point of view is not that of apologetics, and we shall propose no explicit apologetic. Our concern is with the theological significance of the notes, especially as viewed in the light of the theology of the mystical body.

If the Church is actually the mystical continuation of Christ Himself, its method of making itself known and of proposing itself for men's belief, will be a continuation of Christ's method. Accordingly if we wish to know what the Church and its notes are, we have to consider Christ and the credentials He presented about His mission. Therefore we shall study Jesus Christ at some length; this will also afford us an opportunity for getting to know Him better.

The great proof Jesus Christ gave of His mission and teaching is He Himself. This is as it should be. That which is first in any genus does not depend on that genus for anything whatever. Christ is the first in the order of grace and of the new mankind, in the order that sums up and transfigures the whole of the ancient order. Nothing in the new order or in the old order was a proportionate authentication or proof of Him.

He was a man who was a person and an empirical individual by being the Word; and that was enough. Appointed by God for the salvation of all men, He took part in their misery and intervened in their tendency toward God. He is the sanctuary in which the Trinity gives itself to mankind, the precise point of direct passage from the human to the divine, the living way, the entrance that beckons, the path that leads to the heart of God and lies open to the heart of man. He is the road that lifts and carries those who travel on it, and which therefore invites and attracts with the attractiveness of God Himself.

If the assumed humanity was to be this offer of the invisible even in its visible form, if it was to subsist in this donation of the necessary even in its flesh and blood, it had to reveal some outwardly perceptible reflection of this invisible and necessary, this imponderable but intensely meaningful property, which to this very day it retains in the Gospel narratives like some quality that endows a countenance with living expression and that is everything or nothing according to the will of each observer. Although this property is phenomenal and empirical, it exists only through a mystery and in a mystery, and is not really perceptible except in the perception of this mystery. It is something that leads the beholder to faith and blesses his eyes with faith; for, although it appears in the domain of natural vision, yet it is profoundly rooted in the supernatural, that is, the domain of faith.

Between this vague something and the grace that is everywhere offered and everywhere active, there were harmony and proportion; indeed, there were even affinity and continuity. Did not Christ's sacred humanity, empirical as it was, contain the transcendental totality and the visible form of grace, and did not something in it have to reveal this excellence that constituted it? Between this something and the life of grace which God in His universal goodness formed or sketched or tried to sketch in every soul, there were always this proportion and participation that could be discerned as though by intuition and connaturality.

Since it existed in the experimental domain, this quality was necessarily perceptible in some degree by natural knowledge. But it was open to natural knowledge in a very restricted and imperfect fashion, like an insoluble problem and a sign of contradiction. Because of the total divinization it expressed, it pertained essentially to a different order and required a different kind of knowledge: supernatural knowledge, the knowledge that belongs to grace and faith.

If we desire greater precision, we may say with St. Jerome that the quality we are speaking of must have been a certain radiance of mien, a certain majesty of attitude; [14] or we may recall what some of the Fathers have said of Christ's beauty. In our opinion, however, we shall do better to leave to the supernatural its ineffable character.[15] Let us confine ourselves to the assertion that this visible man was God who was giving Himself, and that those to whom the Father gave the grace that "drew" them [16] could in some way discern immediately the glory of God shining in the face of a man,[17] the glory which the Father sheds over His only-begotten Son: [18] "Philip, he that seeth Me seeth the Father also." [19]

Accordingly Christ was His own sign, His own proof, His "note." He is the way, and needs no other way to lead to Him. He is the perfect mediator, and supposes no other mediator to introduce men to Him. The truth is the judge of itself and of falsehood. As the truth is its own criterion, and as light is its own demonstration, Christ presented Himself through Himself: "He signs Himself with His own light." [20]

This is the way we see Him teaching in the Gospel, without basing His words on anything but Himself, without proving anything, without appealing to authorities; He is content to manifest Himself and to live most nobly the message that is really He, the gift of the Trinity to mankind. This procedure is particularly striking in the

[14] *In Matt.*, I, 8, 9; III, 21 (*PL*, XXVI, 53, 56, 152).
[15] Cf. John 7:12, 46 f.; Matt. 7:28 f.; 27:63; Mark 1:22.
[16] John 6:44, 66, and elsewhere. This grace is offered to all, as we said above.
[17] Cf. II Cor. 4:6.
[18] John 1:14.
[19] John 14:9; cf. 12:45.
[20] St. Ambrose, *In Luc.*, II, 45 (*PL*, XV, 1569). Cf. St. Augustine, *In Ioan.*, XLVII, 3 (*PL*, XXXV, 1734).

case of His moral teaching, which is not a set of rules deduced from certain principles; it is not even a system that prevails because of its coherence or its appeal to the lofty sentiments of His hearers. It is He, the God-man and the incarnate Son, who is the living formula of all divinization and access to the Trinity. He has only to be Himself without keeping anxious watch over His words or restraining Himself, He has only to act and react frankly and simply in the presence of the Twelve and the multitude, to voice His preferences, His indignation, and His approval, in a word, to express Himself, in order to formulate the code of supernatural perfection for all mankind.

To be sure, He appeals to His miracles [21] and prophecies [22] by way of authentication. But these miracles are He, so strongly does He assert Himself in them; [23] and the prophecies are also He, for He is the key to them and their fulfillment.[24]

He presents His miracles more as a mark of His spirit, as a revelation of His mission, His goodness, and the gift of God in Him,[25] that is, as the sign we spoke of before, than as an external guaranty designed to overpower all rationalist explanations.[26] Does not He Himself reprehend the evil and adulterous generation that demands miracles as a condition for faith? [27] In any case, His great argument, the essential motive on which He bases faith and for which He exacts so much confidence, is He Himself,[28] His word, "But I say to you," [29] and His works: "Believe the works." [30] The supreme sign He gives is He Himself in His love for the Father and His obedience to the Father,[31] that is, He Himself as the Son. He is there, He is God,

[21] John 5:20; 6:26; 7:31, 11:47; 14:12; Mark 16:17.
[22] Matthew, *passim;* Luke 24:25; John 5:46.
[23] Luke 7:13-16; John 5:6-9.
[24] Cf. Luke 24:27, 45 f.; 4:21; John 5:46.
[25] Matt. 11:3-6; Luke 4:3-9. Cf. Matt. 9:8; Mark 2:6, 12.
[26] Matt. 16:1; 12:39.
[27] Matt. 12:38-42; John 4:48; Mark 8:11 f. See also the passages in which Jesus requires silence of those who have been the beneficiaries of His miracles, Mark 1:43 ff. (cf. v. 38); 3:12; 7:36 f.; Matt. 9:30 f. Thus the adulterous generation had a ready pretext for rejecting the miracles, by ascribing them to the devil (Mark 3:22), by denying them (Matt. 28:13), or by suppressing the wonder-worker (Mark 3:6; John 7:31 f.; 12:47).
[28] John 3:11, 18; 7:37 ff.
[29] Matt. 5:22.
[30] John 10:38.
[31] John 5:36; 10:25, 38; 14:10 ff.

and He gives Himself to the world; no need to seek outside of Him for an authentication of His message.

What He thus was in Himself, He is also in the Church; and the Church is the same in Him. Like Him and because of Him, the Church has its miracles and prophecies; does not St. Augustine say that the prophets foretold the Church even more clearly than they foretold Christ? But the miracles of the Church are not its chief argument. May we not even say that they are not in the front rank of arguments? These miracles of goodness, mercy, and kindness seem rather designed to exalt charity, to foster love and devotedness toward others and generosity toward God, than to furnish an irrefutable minor for a syllogism to be used in controversy.

The great argument of the Church, as of Christ, must be the Church itself in Christ and Christ in the Church; for in the Church Christ continues to be God who gives Himself, and in Christ the Church continues to be the point at which God unites Himself to men and the emergence of the divine in the human. The Church cannot be all this in its empirical exterior, in its outer aspect as a visible institution, without some of its inner nature becoming manifest to the eyes of men.

In Jesus Christ, as we have said, this external appearance had the character of a sign and a note. According to the well-known text of St. Leo the Great, each of Christ's two natures, acting in conjunction with the other, revealed the other by its own way of acting; and therefore the incarnate Word manifested His divinity in His risen body when He exhibited His pierced hands, "to induce us to acknowledge that the divine and the human natures remained each in its own individuality, and thus to perceive that the Word is not the flesh, but rather to confess that the one Son of God is both the Word and the flesh." [32]

The same, by analogy or rather by continuation, must be true of the Church. The Church continues Christ even in its visible exterior; hence this visible exterior must be modeled on Him, so that they who are able to read the delicately drawn but eloquent signs may discover Christ when they look at the Church. The Church, like Christ and in Christ, is an empirical reality and a transcendent mystery; yet it remains one; in the Church, therefore, as in Christ, a close

[32] St. Leo the Great, *Tomus ad Flavianum*, 4 f. (Cavallera, *Thesaurus doctrinae catholicae*, 681 f.).

union between the two must obtain. Since the Church, in its empirical aspect, is truly the body and the exterior of a divinization that diffuses itself, something in the empirical aspect must reveal this divinization.

As the redemption is still going on and as the persons to be divinized are sinners, this trait will ordinarily not be brilliant or glorious, and will not be completely decisive on the experimental level; on the contrary, it will be humble and hidden, though captivating. To the extent that it exists in the empirical order, it will be an object of natural knowledge, and can be fashioned into a science; this science is apologetics.

Yet its empirical exterior reveals only half of what it is, for it is essentially the expression of a transcendental divinization. It will not be wholly perceptible unless this divinization is also perceived; hence an act of faith elicited with the help of grace is needed. Generally speaking, therefore, it will be a path leading to faith. It is a perpetual offer of the grace of faith, for in Christ it is the body and the expression of the divinization that is perpetually being given. In itself, when taken in its totality, it is a complete and sufficient sign that needs no other sign or introduction, a sign suitable for every soul. Such is the teaching of the Vatican Council:

The Church itself, by reason of its admirable extension, its eminent holiness, and its inexhaustible fruitfulness in all good, its Catholic unity and unshakable stability, is a great and perpetual motive of credibility and an irrefutable witness of its own divine mission. And therefore, like a standard set up before the nations,[33] it beckons to itself those who do not yet believe, and assures its children that the faith they profess rests on a most secure foundation. And a power from on high confirms this testimony. For our most gracious Lord stirs up and helps with His grace even those who wander astray, that they may "come to the knowledge of the truth" (I Tim. 2:4), and strengthens with His grace those whom He has brought "out of darkness into His marvelous light" (I Pet. 2:9), that they may persevere in this light; and He never deserts those who do not desert Him.[34]

This passage describes the double action of Providence, internal and external, that gives an outer sign and grants interior grace for the understanding of the sign. The two matching gifts, or rather the

[33] Cf. Isa. 11:12.
[34] Vatican Council, Sess. III, c.3 (Denz., 1794).

single but twofold gift, is suited to the twofold nature in man and is like the twofold action exercised by Christ's humanity: the action of His word without and the action of His grace within.

Thus the Church itself is a sign of itself, perpetuating across the centuries the witness that Christ gives of Himself and of His prolongation in mankind, and continuing also the witness given of Christ by the Father. "The Church itself," says the Council; the Church itself is seen in its own light, in Christ; the Church itself attracts those who are as yet its sons only by divine vocation; the Church itself retains its children, and confirms and consolidates their faith.

The science of apologetics, which considers the Church from outside, from the point of view of those who as yet remain beyond its doors, can discern the notes only from without. Accordingly these notes appear only on the surface, not in their essence, as marks sufficiently proclaimed by Christ and sufficiently discernible in themselves to set the Church apart from all other Christian confessions. But these marks, as such, are arbitrary, without a necessary connection with what they indicate; Christ could have chosen others, or could have made them express something else.

But in the theology of the mystical body, which considers the Church from within, the notes are also considered from within. This does not diminish their visibility; do we see the windows of a cathedral less clearly when we look at them from inside? The notes remain decisive signs and unimpeachable witnesses; they are such intrinsically, for they contain what they express, and they also contain Christ, who expresses the same thing; for they are ways of making known the presence of Christ in the Church. Once we perceive them distinctly, we need no longer speculate about Christ's past intentions or about the meaning He wished to give to these characteristics; they speak for themselves. Moreover, what they manifest in the interior of the Church is identical with what grace accomplishes in the interior of souls. At one stroke they teach the necessity of the Church for the inner life of Catholics and the essentially ecclesiastical nature of this inner life.

The list of the notes is well known. The Vatican Council gives it in the passage quoted above, even while insisting on the interior character of the guaranty which the Church is in itself. In the details mentioned by the Council, the "unshakable stability" may be taken as corresponding to apostolicity, for it signifies that the Church still is and always will be what it was at its origin at the time of the apostles. Thus we have the four traditional notes: unity, holiness, catholicity, and apostolicity.

And in fact, as we should observe, these four notes are exactly what we would expect of the society of grace in which Christ and His characteristics are perpetuated. Christ's humanity receives its complete holiness and divinization directly from its union with God. This unparalleled perfection makes it the unity that contains, as in a source, the entire supernatural work accomplished by God among men over the surface of the earth and throughout the duration of the centuries. These four characteristics, unity, holiness, universality throughout space, and duration throughout time, are possessed by Christ's humanity regarded as the head of a mystical body. Therefore Christ's humanity will possess them in the society that is His body, and this society will likewise possess them. And these are the four notes of the Church regarded as the perpetuation of Christ: unity, holiness, catholicity, and apostolicity.

We may comment on this group of four notes by referring to what we have said about the Church, the new, supernatural mankind. Mankind has a certain unity by its very nature, an imperfect unity that gropingly seeks self-realization here on earth. It has a certain moral value or holiness, of which it possesses the norm in its natural law and which it must work out in detail. It also has a certain universality of its own, so that it finds self-expression only by spreading out indefinitely in space and time.

Mankind must likewise have unity, holiness, and spatial and temporal universality in its new, supernatural form, but in a new way and under a supernatural form; it must possess these properties in Christ, as it has its new form in Christ. And thus once again we have the four notes mentioned in the Creed: "one, holy, catholic, and apostolic Church."

One, holy, catholic, apostolic: these are the four traditional notes with which we associate the characteristics possessed by the Church as the body of Christ. But we repeat that we need not envisage them here formally as notes, as apologetic proofs. We can find elsewhere all the discussions of this subject that may be desired.[35] We wish

---

[35] See, for example, J. A. Moehler, *Symbolism;* translated by J. B. Robertson (London: Gibbings, 1906); R. H. Benson, *Christ in the Church* (St. Louis: Herder, 1913); *Paradoxes of Catholicism* (New York: Longmans, 1913);

rather to present a theology of them in function of the doctrine of the mystical body. We are not concerned here with what the exterior of the Church is *de facto* or with the reasoning processes for which that fact can furnish a foundation; our purpose is to examine what this exterior is *de jure*, what it means for the faith, and accordingly what exactly we may expect to find there.

B. Unity. The first of the notes, unity, is perhaps the one that appears to be most prominent to the outside world and that best makes the Church known.[36] It is also the note that is most explicitly brought out by Christ's words.[37] Hence we shall have to consider it attentively.

Even infidels have been struck by this unity and by the marvelous organization that builds up the new Jerusalem into a unique whole so solidly cemented that neither the inevitable clash of human self-interests nor earthly or infernal forces have been able to make a breach in the impregnable structure.

However, he who sees nothing but this exterior has not as yet seen anything; such a unity is but the unity of a machine. If that is all we extol, we run the risk of repelling those who believe in life and its spontaneous freedoms. The unity of the Church is something much more and much better; it is the visible expression and the social body of an interior unity that is its soul and life, the visible side of a great invisible deification by which God in Christ unites all men with one another and with Himself. As the soul is the living principle and the explanation of the body, this invisible unity gives meaning to the visible unity; to understand the latter we have to understand the former.

We have already spoken of the soul and the body of the Church. Here we need but apply these notions to the idea of unity, especially of social unity. Every society may be said to have a soul, a collective soul, which makes it a living organization and is the form by which the multiplicity of members receives the collective unity that consti-

---

E. Mersch, *Morality and the Mystical Body;* translated by D. F. Ryan (New York: Kenedy, 1939).

[36] Leo XIII, encyclical *Satis Cognitum* (Cavallera, 272).

[37] St. John Chrysostom thus accounts for Christ's prayer, "That they may be one" (John 17:22): "Nothing so scandalizes people as dissensions. . . . Therefore Christ wishes all to be one . . . for harmony attracts more converts to the Church than miracles." *In Ioannem,* hom. 82, 2 (*PG*, LIX, 444).

tutes it a society. This soul is neither a complete substance nor a spiritual substance; its only reality consists in the social activities of the individuals it unites in the common end, means, and aspirations that bring them together. The more perfect a society is, the more perfect its soul will be. If the society has a supernatural perfection, as the Church has, its soul will likewise have a supernatural perfection. In the case of the Church, as we said before, this soul is the humanity of Christ regarded as a universal principle of divinization.

This soul of the Church which is the humanity of Jesus has an absolute unity, for it is one with the unity of a divine person, and at the same time, by reason of this divinity, it is the interior source of life, unity, and supernatural inwardness of each member. Hence it is simultaneously transcendent and immanent. In the same way, we may point out as a comparison, man's soul is one in itself because it has its own act and is a spirit, and it is also one with all parts of the body, imparting unity to all, because it is the form of the body.

We shall first consider the attribute of transcendence. Through Christ, the unity of the Church has its ultimate principle in one of the divine persons. This ultimate unity and nothing less is what Christ desired for His followers: "That they may be one, as We also are one," He repeated over and over. He conferred this ultimate unity on them by incorporating them into Himself, and no other ultimate unity is found in Him than the person of the Word. As His followers are one in Him, He Himself is one in the Word. Hence they must be one in Him, the Word, and therefore in God as triune.

Accordingly this is a sacred unity, an essentially supernatural unity. To get some idea of it, we may have recourse to natural analogies, such as comparison with well-regulated states or with families or the organism of living beings. Nothing is more legitimate; yet we must go beyond such figures. We are dealing with a fellowship that is infinitely above all this, a fellowship with the mystery of absolute unity.

In the preceding chapter, when discussing grace, we spoke of a new kind of being, supernatural being, that exists through union with the very interior of Being. We must speak in similar fashion of supernatural unity. The Church is one with a unity that no finite being can bestow on itself or receive from the Creator by way of creation; a unity that cannot exist except by interior union with the inner unity of Being, that is, with Trinitarian unity. In the humanity of Christ, this is the hypostatic union; in the rest of mankind, it is mystical union with Christ's humanity.

This union cannot be known in itself alone, any more than it can exist by itself alone. Either we do not see it as it really is, or else we perceive in it Him who, through union, makes it what it is: Christ who is present in His members, the Son whom the Father sends to all mankind, the Trinitarian unity. This, and nothing less, is what Jesus desired for His members: a unity that comes incessantly from the Trinity and that incessantly carries those who contemplate it toward the Trinity. "That they all may be one, as Thou, Father, in Me and I in Thee; that they also may be one in Us; that the world may believe that Thou hast sent Me. . . . I in them and Thou in Me; that they may be made perfect in one, and the world may know that Thou has sent Me." [38] This unity is a note, a sign, and we do not see it fully unless we believe in Christ as He is in the Trinity and in His humanity.

The primacy of such a unity is evidently absolute. It is not the product of the members it joins together, in the way that the unity of natural societies is a product of the tendency toward union found in men, whether such union is imposed by nature or sought by free choice. Rather the members are the product of it, and it makes them one in itself; for Christ by His influence causes Christians to be Christians, and they cannot live unless they are all united to Him. Thus the Church exists more truly in Christ, its unity, than it exists in the multiplicity of His members; for in Christ it exists in its source.

Yet that is the very reason why it exists so perfectly in each of Christ's members; it is as immanent in them as it is transcendent over them. For Christ, in whom it resides perfectly, resides deeply and supernaturally in each member. Compared with this unity, the unity of natural societies is superficial and external, and consists in a certain common end and means, a certain imitation of nature that cannot have full self-consciousness or take full possession of itself; for it is not in contact with the root of being.

The Church alone is so perfectly one in Christ that it has all its unity in all its parts, in the way that the human soul is present whole and entire in every part of the body. St. Peter Damian says that every Christian soul is the whole Church, and that the Church is also every

[38] John 17:21, 23.

human soul: "The Church of Christ is held together by such a strong bond of charity that it is mysteriously one in all men and whole in each man. Deservedly, then, the whole universal Church is regarded as the one spouse of Christ, and through the sacramental mystery each soul is considered to be the whole Church." [39]

The unity of the Church is not a fitting together of parts, but a union of persons; and since these persons are wholes, they are united to one another as wholes, by an interior bond. The Church is one in this way because it is a society of men, but much more because it is a society of men sanctified in that Man who is the person of the Word; and therefore, as we said above, this Man supernaturally brings all the others together in Himself as persons.

We cannot argue from this totality of the Church in each of its members, that it exercises all its functions in each. "If the whole body were the eye, where would be the hearing? If the whole were hearing, where would be the smelling?" [40] A unity that would suppress variety would no longer be a multiplicity, and if differentiated organs were lacking, the organism would cease to exist. [41] Specialization and distinction must always be present, as we shall show later at greater length. But this specialization is for the benefit of the union; the various members, though not possessing the totality of functions, will perform their respective tasks, each in its own way, for the life of the whole and through the life of the whole. [42] The very variety of operations bears witness to the unity of the Spirit and of Christ, as St. Paul declares. [43]

What we have to conclude from this totality is that the principle of ecclesiastical unity may not be taken in too narrow a sense so far as it affects each Christian soul. Otherwise the supposition would have to be denied. Christ is the bond of inner unity in each member, as He is the bond of collective unity in the whole assemblage. Is Christ divided, so that we may ask if a member situated on one side is better than a member situated on the other side? In a very real sense, there is no more in the whole Church than in a single member of the faithful, as there is no more in heaven than in a person who receives Holy Communion. The difference is that Christ is in the

[39] *Opusculum* XI, 5 (PL, CXLV, 235).
[40] Cf. I Cor. 12:17.
[41] Rom. 12:4 f.
[42] Rom. 12:3; I Cor. 12:18, 25.
[43] Cf. I Cor. 12:4-14; Rom. 12:5.

Church for certain functions, and is in the believer to make him live and act. He is the same in one and the other, and we should explain the mystery of unity very badly were we to split it into sections in order to compare the fragments.

Unity of this sort will find its clearest expression in love or charity, the great unifying force. Is not this unity the perpetuation, in the limitless human race, of that loving embrace that was and forever is the Incarnation? This is an infinitely close and efficacious embrace, because the love poured out in it is infinitely ardent; it is the embrace with which God, in His incarnate Son, presses mankind so strongly to His heart in love and for love that He makes men one among themselves and with Him.[44] "God so loved the world as to give His only-begotten Son, that whosoever believeth in Him may not perish, but may have life everlasting." [45]

This is the way the Fathers regarded our unity; for them it was a sweet and good unity, a gentle and motherly unity, a unity of love, charity, and devotedness.[46] This is also what Jesus wanted. He had no use for a unity expressed in overlordship and flattery. He said quite unmistakably: "The kings of the Gentiles lord it over them; and they that have power over them, are called beneficent. But you not so!" He required a unity of mutual service, respect, and love.[47] In the discourse in which He spoke at greatest length and indeed exclusively about unity, His theme was restricted to love. This is the discourse after the Last Supper, and was uttered after the institution of the sacrament of unity and charity. In His thoughts unity and charity are linked, and He speaks of them together; they are equally His sign,[48] His commandment,[49] His supreme concern. In His eyes, unity and charity are identical.

That is exactly what our unity is: "One Christ, loving Himself." [50] The one Christ gives Himself unreservedly to all His members by giving them to one another and to God. This unity proceeds from eternal charity. Consequently it must not only be anchored in charity but must also inspire and vitalize charity; it must make each man look

[44] Eph. 1:5 f.; 2:4, 6.
[45] John 3:16.
[46] See the Index to *The Whole Christ*, s.v. "One," "Unity."
[47] Luke 22:25 f.; John 13:1-17; I Pet. 5:3; II Cor. 1:23.
[48] John 13:37; 17:21, 23.
[49] John 15:4-7, 12; 13:34; 17:12, 21-26.
[50] Cf. St. Augustine, *In epist. ad Parthos*, X (PL, XXXV, 2055).

upon all other men as being one with him, as the pupil of his eye, as being one in calling and in fact with God and Christ, as those whom he must save at all costs in order to save himself.

We need scarcely remark that such a unity differs to the point of contrast from a simple centralization. Of course a certain centralization is indispensable in the Church, as in every human society. But its importance should not be exaggerated; indeed, it is the product of a gradual formation, and varies with different epochs. At the Vatican Council, for example, a certain bishop could maintain without heterodoxy that centralization was excessive in the Church; he could not have said the same of unity without offending against the faith.[51]

Unity in Christ is life and a condition for life. Centralization is an abstract formula that can lead to death if carried too far. By forcing life too much to the center, it runs the risk of lopping off members and of killing the organism. Two things so different cannot be identified.

Ecclesiastical unity, moreover, exhibits seeming paradoxes at some essential points of its structure which clearly mark out its originality as compared with other kinds of unity obtaining among men. For instance, the inequality resulting from the duty to command that is found in some and the duty to obey that is found in others, leaves intact the equality that levels them all in the eyes of the one supreme Pastor, whose sheep they all are.

Ecclesiastical superiors exercise their leadership as public personages, and their superiority, which is genuine as regards their office, vanishes when their private life is in question. They interpret the law of Christ with authority deriving from Christ, and they alone have such power; but the law they alone interpret has to be observed by them in common with all the rest. True, they dispense the means of sanctification; but, like all the others, they need the sacrament of penance if they sin, the Eucharist if they wish to have life in them, and extreme unction when they come to die. From this point of view they are part of the faithful, no less than their subjects. The pope, like any other Catholic, has to go to confession, and he needs a priest to administer the sacrament. As a private person he too is one of the sheep of the flock he leads in his capacity of public person.

[51] Cf. Mansi, *Amplissima collectio conciliorum*, L, 409–19. Some of the words uttered by Bishop Melchers verged on the extreme.

I may be mistaken, but this combination of radical equality with radical inequality seems to me to indicate the point at which the Church differs from natural societies. Natural societies fluctuate between absolute monarchy that always threatens to degenerate into a despotism incompatible with the multitude's personal autonomy, and an unsociable egalitarianism prone to deny the unity that ought to organize the masses in a hierarchical order. The Church speaks with an authority which it receives from its head and which is stronger than that of any king, for it is the authority of God and is always exercised under God's direction. No account has to be rendered to anyone on earth, and no one demands an account, for all are persuaded that what that authority does it does well. At the same time, the Church speaks with perfect equality; all have sinned and have the same need of a Savior and a Teacher, for all alike are children in His eyes.

The center of each soul and the center of the whole organism coincide in Christ. The formulas that may seem to imply centralization actually signify reverence for the interior life, and formulas of supernatural personalism become formulas of interior Catholicism and union.

That is the theory. In practice, it is carried out imperfectly, at times very imperfectly indeed. But even this has its foundation in theory: the Church and its unity are still in formation, and this formation progresses in an order of redemption, that is, in the midst of sin and evil. Unity is realized only little by little, in the neverending struggle against its contrary that is ever springing up within the growing unity.

We shall come back to this point in a moment. Indeed, we could come back to it at every moment, in connection with each noble attribute we shall have to extol in the Church. To avoid repetition, we may here emphasize the matter once for all, so that we shall not have to say the same thing over again whenever important occasions demand reference to it.

One of these occasions occurs precisely at this juncture. While discoursing on unity, we have to consider the contradiction which a divided Christianity offers to Christ's prayer, "That they may be one." The scandal has its explanation, and the explanation touches the essence of Christianity: the unity of Christianity is the unity of a redemption that has to be achieved step by step. Sin remains in

the world and in the Church, and sin is a breaking-away and secession, the source of narrow egoisms, of suspicious individualisms, and
of shattering lusts. The work of unity has to be accomplished in a
process of separation and disintegration; it is a struggle for unity in
the Church militant; a struggle against a multiplicity that, from
within and without, is ever springing up again with resurging sin.

For the evil that makes its appearance in schism is found in all
mankind and in the heart of every believer. In the matter of unity,
neither the world nor Christianity nor each soul realizes the ideal.
The world is rent apart in a profusion of religions when there should
be but one; the hosts of those who cleave to Christ and sincerely
desire to cleave to Him are divided among a great number of Christian confessions, although Christ founded only one Church; and the
faithful keep aloof from one another in various ways, although they
ought to foster union and charity in Christ. These three gaps are
connected; the cleavage showing up in various places comes from
the same evil, the same practical forgetfulness of the immensity, the
catholicity, the charity, and the unity of Christ. The fissures will not
be repaired at their base unless we are sharply aware of this evil.

Any attempt to seek the source of this evil in others is fruitless.
We have no more right to judge them than we have power to change
them. We perform a salutary work if we ferret out the evil in ourselves and in our own people, for we have the duty to be humble and
the power, God aiding, to become better. Catholics especially, who
can make no concessions in the matter of doctrine, ought to be eager
to make concessions about their persons. Their Church, their leaders,
and they themselves enjoy so many privileges that are the good of
Christ in them, that they ought to be happy to emphasize their personal shortcomings as wretched sinners; no one, certainly not they
themselves, should be tempted to look on these privileges as personal
glories.

God Himself teaches them in Sacred Scripture to make such
acknowledgments. Scripture narrates how the first bishops, but
recently consecrated, were all guilty of defection through fear:
"The disciples all leaving Him, fled." [52] After this example, Catholics
need not be afraid to avow that in the course of the centuries, at
times of persecution, bishops have led their people into heresy and
schism. In the apostles' desertion, Scripture focuses its inexorable

[52] Matt. 26:56; Mark 14:50.

light on Peter's abandonment,[53] and so strongly stresses his denial, his break with unity, and his failure to make a public profession of faith that, as we behold the foundation stone crumbling, we are bound to realize that the firmness it will have later on is not a quality of the rock itself. And with reference to this same Peter, Scripture reports the altercation at Antioch.[54] Peter, invested with the full power of the papacy after the Ascension and Pentecost, in the seeming opportunism of drawing back from the wearisome task of dealing with a separatist clique, holds himself aloof from the great Church and thus furthers secessionist tendencies. This harsh fact is found in the sacred text. And Paul, under the inspiration of the Holy Spirit, insisted on relating this weakness on the part of him who ought to have been the pillar of the Church,[55] just as he wished then and there to reproach Peter to his face; for Peter was pulling away from Christian life and unity.[56]

What Scripture does, Christians can do without treachery to piety, and indeed with the joy of humility. They can acknowledge that they themselves and their pastors have carried God's treasure in a fragile vessel. They should glory religiously in all that God has wrought through their Church; but they should be even readier to proclaim that they have contributed precious little, and should add that, if God has in all essentials preserved the bond of unity in their leaders, personal shortcomings have counteracted the miraculous work of unity by many an act of petty selfishness. Let them fear to put their hopes in any man or even seem to do so.

All this was inevitable, and Jesus foresaw it; the human heart is so easily duped and so quickly befuddled. There had to be and there has been the sort of pride that identifies august functions with banal personalities; there had to be and there have been opportunist insincerities, abuses of power, and inability to understand; and in such human constrictions the splendid unity of Catholicism could not display all its grandeur and attractiveness. The astounding thing is not that egoism and narrowness have entered the sanctuary, for Jesus has opened it to men, but that they have not penetrated farther.

In turning such matters over in our minds, let us guard against

---

[53] Matt. 26:69–75; Mark 14:66–72; Luke 22:54–62; John 18:16 ff., 25 ff.
[54] Gal. 2:11–21.
[55] *Ibid.*, 2:9.
[56] *Ibid.*, 2:16–20; 3:27 f.

the conceited and sordid joy of finding our superiors at fault. Under pretext of exalting unity, this would degenerate into a spirit of secession. "Hypocrite, cast out first the beam out of thy own eye" (Matt. 7:5). The evil is a human evil; all men, whether they are priests or religious or laymen are soiled by it, and the first task of the grace that heals it is to show to each man the center of infection in him.

Do we not have to confess, to our shame, that in many religious environments the faithful abandon Catholic practices, piety, life, and even religion, because those in authority make these matters so exclusively their own affair that private individuals no longer see what part is left for them? In many places is it not true that defections, secessions, and petty schisms are owing to the imperious airs of the clergy, whether secular or regular, to their perpetual interfering, their perfidious opportunism, their mania for identifying docility to grace with respect for the soutane, in a word, to the egoism and the vanity that make some churchman instead of Christ the center of religion and substitute an odious vaunting of self for the witness that ought to be borne to the unity of all mankind?

Do not the faithful, who are likewise men, as all priests are numbered among the faithful, have to admit that they are quick to believe in their own superiority and the bad faith of others—a trait hardly calculated to attract these others—and that they scarcely show the rest of men that the unity whereof they live, Catholic unity, is the unity of the whole human race? How many of them care, if only a little, about the union of the Churches and the conversion of the world? And yet Christ who is in them has ardently desired and still desires such unity; and countless of their separated brothers long for it with passionate weeping.

If that unity does not come, may not the reason be, in part, that we obstruct it? If it does not appear attractive, is not the reason that we defile it under our leprosy? And if upright souls do not discern it, is not the fault also in us who keep it hidden? That is what we have to recognize before we can apply a remedy; it is not our job to weigh the responsibilities incurred by Photius or Henry VIII. We need collective humility, ecclesiastical humility, the humility of sincerity and love that cries out its deficiencies in the public squares for fear lest men saddle them on the unity of Christ, humility that is the mark of Christ and the true service of unity.

If Catholics, the faithful and their pontiffs, would let Christ display in them all that He is and all that the Church is in Him, the path leading to the union of Christian Churches would soon be smoothed. And if other Christians would let Christ show forth in them all that He is and all that Christianity is in Him, all the love, the sincerity, and truth, the unity that He is, the religious unity of the earth would soon come to be a reality.

But if man's sin does not allow this supernatural unity to display all its glory in the redemption that is still going on, sin cannot keep it from existing, for it is indefectible, and even in the divisions caused by sin, cannot prevent it from being a seed, a force, an inception of the perfect unity it actually is. Although the Catholic Church is made up of men and hence of divergent individualities, it is not on that account less but rather more a magnificent spectacle of unity for those who have eyes to see. In spite of everything, ourselves included, the unity of all mankind in Christ is found in us. Little by little it will make us less unworthy of bearing witness to Him.

The unity of all mankind and of all Christianity in Christ is found even in the divisions of the Christian confessions. More deeply than human lack of understanding, Christ with His unity lives in all His followers who have not sinned against the light and against charity; and such followers are numerous, and Christ's life is in them. As we write this we are thinking respectfully of the Christians of the Russian Church and of the Protestants of the German confessions who, during the Second World War, remained faithful to Christ even at the cost of life. The faith that they all have, despite the faulty formulation they give to it, is a participation in the God-man's knowledge; their hope is a longing anticipation of the unity of all men with God in Christ; their charity is a communication of the love that embraces all mankind in the incarnate Son; their grace is the same eternal life that flows from the same source and is diffused over all, bringing them all together by the very principle that gives life to them as individuals. Hence unity exists in all Christianity; it is disfigured on the surface, but is real at the center. It exists, and therefore the effective and visible union of all, which otherwise would seem utopian, must be said to be capable of realization. Unity comes at the first springing up of all Christian life, for Christ sends it along with all His love. In our efforts to achieve it outwardly, we have an invincible ally within.

To dedicate themselves to the realization of this aim in the way open to them, Catholics have only to be Catholics, or rather to become ever better Catholics. They must rid themselves more and more of an ever resurging individualism, nationalism, and of all particularist pride of culture, temperament, and mentality. To the greatest extent possible, they must be living witnesses to God's gift to all mankind in Christ.

Those men who remain outside as well as those who are inside may fail to perceive all that is implied in the one true Church. But that does not make its lines less clear. In desiring to draw near to God, they really desire what the God-man alone has to give and what His Church, which has a particular pope and a definite canon law, unceasingly holds out to them.

When God delivered Himself up to mankind in Christ, He drew no limits; the believer who has eyes to see, knows that the Savior's human nature is mystic and catholic: "Christ is all and in all" (Col. 3:11). Likewise, when Christ delivered Himself up to His Church, to Peter and the apostles, He did so without reserve or restriction, and His Church is a mystical and universal "body." Wherever He may have gone after that, to take His place at the right hand of the Father or in the depths of souls, He remains the Christ of His Church and of Peter; and the first steps of His approach to any heart and the first touches of His grace that is never idle in any part of the world, is also the first moment of His residence in men.

The vast extension which the body of the Church receives from its soul is comparable to the extension which the human body receives from the human soul. As the form of the body, man's soul is limited in time and space, for the body is thus limited. As a spirit, however, the soul is so superior to time and space that, far from being contained in them, it rather contains them, as is evidenced by its power to give intelligible expression to them. But this soul, this spirit, constitutes with the body a single being that is man. The soul imparts existence to the body and is its act, its ultimate interior principle; and the body is the realization and expression of the soul on the level open to experience. Accordingly, if the body on its part limits the soul in time and space by its own limitation, the soul, on its part and because of its own illimitation, confers on the body a certain independence of time and space. We may ponder, for example, the boundless expanses attained by certain of man's acts that in themselves depend on his animal life, such as the act of imagining or the act of seeing. They take place in the organism and through the organism, and yet they reach objects at the immense distances where these objects are located, and at will bring forth in interior vision vast regions with their limitless spaces. And in an act such as this man sees also himself: an infinitesimal speck, almost indiscernible, clambering up a mountain or losing itself in a crowd. This clearly brings out both the smallness of the body in itself, and the greatness it has as an instrument and as the body of such a soul; it is a limited body of an unlimited soul, and hence is in its own way unlimited.

We may say that the body of the Church presents an analogous case. It likewise is the body of something unlimited, the body of a soul that is the universal gift of the Infinite to men in Christ. In its own way, therefore, it must share in this illimitation. The body realizes and expresses such illimitation on the empirical level, as we have said. And this illimitation in turn impresses itself on the body, conferring a certain illimitation on it as an empirical thing, but with reference to the supernatural attitudes entailed by such illimitation. However, the body's illimitation is only a sharing in the soul's illimitation, and is discerned only when the latter is apprehended by faith.

Nevertheless the Church is a society with a limited exterior. But when we contemplate the infinite gift which God offers to all men in this Church, we may discover, discern, or conjecture some influence exercised by the Church whenever some effect of this gift allows itself to be discovered, discerned, or conjectured; we may apprehend certain derivations or coincidences that are sometimes extraordinary, sometimes quite natural. Such presages and inklings are found wherever grace works and man cooperates, however little, with the divine advances. Even non-Christian religions, to single out those that seem farthest removed from the body of the Church, may be regarded, by what is essential to them as human religions, as the collective responses which mankind, left to itself and without special graces, but still in the grip of sin that continues to wreak havoc in it and all its works, even the fairest, has given as best it could to the divine vocation that takes in the whole race of men after the Fall. But the Church is not that same response, for it is the absolute and last response, the blameless, sure, integral response that a special Providence has called forth, the response made by God Himself and subsisting in God Himself, although made also by men and by a man who is the God-man.

May we not say that the Church is great with all the extension of those religions, that is, with all the extension of the religious phenomena in mankind, though with an expansion that is still to be achieved and still to be freed of the encumbrance of matter and of sin? May we not say that the Church is one in their immense multiplicity? Thus we may behold the one Church in them all, just as, when we know how to look, we can discover the one sun in scattered rays, or the full glory of the opened flower in the midst of the drooping leaves that surround it.

If the Church is thus the "body" whose soul is Christ, and if it is union with God and the vehicle of the universal salvific will, it must be necessary with the necessity of Christ, of God, and of God's universal will to save. Therefore we must insist that salvation is not to be found outside the Church, and that submission to the Roman Pontiff is necessary for the salvation of every human creature.

This does not mean that adherence to the Church is just one more condition to fulfill in order to achieve salvation,[57] but that the Church is salvation such as it is offered today; not that the Church is an added intermediary between God and man, any more than Christ is such an intermediary, but that it is the pure gift of God to men which is always present in the way that is needed for men. Christ is mediator, not as a third person placed between two conflicting parties, but as God who lives with man in the unity of His unique divine person. In like manner the Church is not a mechanism placed between Christ and the faithful, but is Christ Himself who has come to live in mystical union with the faithful.

Thus the Church, which is necessary as Christ is necessary, is intolerant as Christ is intolerant. Christ is essentially intolerant; since He is the way, the truth, and the life, whatever is cut off from Him is deviation, error, and death. And in Christ, the Church is also essentially intolerant. Christ continues to be in the Church what He is in Himself, the way, the truth, and the life; outside the Church, consequently, men can only lose themselves, deceive themselves, and die.

Although this intolerance is essential to the Church, it is not dis-

[57] Cf. chap. 8, p. 175, on the Blessed Virgin's mediation; the one is a type of the other.

dainful or arrogant, any more than Christ's intolerance is. Christ readily admitted that a man might be upright, holy, and acceptable to God before knowing Him and becoming His disciple. He admitted this and rejoiced at it: "I have not found so great faith in Israel"; "I say to you that the publicans and the harlots shall go into the kingdom of God before you." [58] But He was the union of God and man, and He regarded all such reconciliations of man with God as reconciliations with Himself. The Church does the same. It does not pretend that the persons of whom it is composed, whether they are its visible heads or its members, are of themselves a road to God; it says that Christ is in them fully enough that, although they may be less noble than their task, He is never unequal to His mission. The Church does not say that no holiness can come to light outside its visible frontier; but it claims that holiness, wherever it may spring up, is always hers. Any degree of holiness that may be realized, is found fully in the Church alone. Hence the Church can admire such holiness, without ceasing to believe in its own unique excellence. Without in any way abating its intolerance, and even when pushing its intolerance to the extreme limit, the Church can be free from all aggressiveness and can ever throw open its doors in warm welcome.

Every source of saintliness on earth, even in schism or paganism, belongs to the Church, for holiness springs up only from a seed that has retained something of the Church or is linked with the Church in virtue of the grace of God whose visible form is the Church. The Church is still fertile in those separated fragments. As St. Augustine points out, it sometimes happens that a vine has pushed its way into brambles, and that a traveler sees a bunch of grapes hanging in the tangle of briars; he gathers the fruit but avoids the thorns: "Pluck the grapes, avoid the thorns, but notice the root"; the traveler knows well from what root the cluster comes. [59]

This teaching does no violence to souls, and it is not an irking imperialism usurping power to regulate the torrents of grace or imprison its flood within alien banks. Life itself gives notice of its exigencies in order to develop its greatness, and requires full attachment to the body in order that the blood may richly nourish all its parts.

Therefore, when the Church declares that men must have her for their mother, as otherwise they will not have God for their Father,

[58] Matt. 8:10; 21:31.
[59] St. Augustine, In Ioan. XLVI (PL, XXXV, 1730).

she merely expresses in words what grace silently urges in the hearts of those who have received grace but have not clearly understood its demands. The Church does not roar with the haughty tones of a martinet, but pleads with the anguished insistence of love. Her intolerance is exacting but sweet; it is the intolerance of unyielding truth.

C. Holiness. After unity comes the mark of holiness; we believe in "one holy Church." As we have already spoken of holiness in various connections, little remains to be said. The holiness of the Catholic Church as expressed in its moral code and its cult, its sacraments and its teaching, is well known. Everyone is acquainted with the schools of sanctity, similar in the midst of variety, that are the religious orders nurtured in her bosom: missionary and hospital congregations, Carthusians and Little Sisters of the Poor. We observe the magnificent procession of saints whom the Church sends forth to meet the Lamb; and we should note that they are saints because they belong to the Church and have lived the teaching of the Church with love.

We should like to dwell on this truth. What makes the saints heroes? This has to be understood, and we would miss their meaning were we to pay homage to them by turning aside from the masses of their fellow men. The saints manifest what the people are, and point out the treasures of holiness found among them, somewhat as miracles, according to St. Augustine, have the purpose of drawing attention to the marvels that daily occur throughout the world but that become commonplace because of their very frequency: *assiduitate viluerunt.*

The saints repeat this lesson often. Their humility, their occasional deficiencies, a certain lack of achievement, even the perfections that are found in them but are received from others, bring the truth home to us. They are saints because of the environment in which they live and because of Christ from whom everything comes to them and who continues to live on in the whole Church. Their holiness was rooted in the common soil before it became their own. Therefore it bears witness to the Catholic holiness of the Church and not, properly speaking, to their own sanctity.

This common holiness is the outstanding as well as the greatest miracle wrought by the all-holy God. It is a human holiness, prosaic like ordinary human life; a holiness suited to every man and even to every sinner, since every man is a sinner. This miracle is more striking and significant than any other, for, being the message of divinization for all men, it is more precisely the pure message of the God-man, the message addressed to all mankind. The message gains a hearing from every man, for every man perceives that it describes a perfection meant for him; it tells of a holiness, a divinization he can actually possess, and grace operating from within informs him of his need of it.

We need not demonstrate the existence of this miracle in these pages; we have only to give the theological theory, which in turn will effectively aid us to ascertain its existence. The principle in this theory is the Christological dogma, which also governs ecclesiology, that Christ is perfectly God, perfectly man, and perfectly one; and hence that He is the type and ideal of divinized man, who is man as he actually is, Adam's progeny. The conclusion arrived at is the formula of common, universal human holiness: to be divinized in Christ, man, whoever he may be, is exactly as he ought to be; his sluggish heart, his intermittent courage, and his barely awakened intelligence are just what are required; even his sin, with all the miseries it leaves in its wake, is so far from being an obstacle that it is precisely what a continuing redemption presupposes.

This description of man in Christ's redemption and in the holy Church which is a redemption indicates how man ought to unite himself to God's will and freely to let himself be formed by this will. With man's free cooperation and even through such cooperation, in all that man can do and suffer, God will beget him as His adopted son in His incarnate Word. Everything can help toward this. Our very difficulties and past faults will teach us patience, humility, filial dependence, prayer, obedience, and adherence to God in love. The poor human effort, so short of breath and power, is exactly what God needs in order to insert His own all-powerful effort that can make sons of Abraham out of stones and children of God out of wretched men, by utilizing their very miseries.

This holiness can always be realized, because the precept to be holy is measured by one's inner capacity and light. It is universal, because all men, with their human resources, have all that is needed for receiving it. It is transcendent, because it is inserted as a member into the holiness of the God-man, the Redeemer, and because it makes Christians perfect as the heavenly Father is perfect, thus imitating Christ who is the consubstantial image of the Father. And it is a collective holiness in which the holiness of each individual combines with that of all the others to form a single holiness of the whole body, and in which each is begun, developed, completed, explained, influenced, and supported by every other; like the Christian life and the quality of membership in Christ, each man's holiness is interior to each, yet is connected in solidarity with the holiness of all. Such sanctity may not seem very remarkable when regarded in its apparent isolation, but is magnificent when regarded in its connection with the whole, for then it is splendid with the splendor of the whole.

To see it thus we need grace, the *gratia redemptoris* that corresponds to the holiness. This grace is precisely the grace which holiness makes manifest and of which it is the outer body, the grace contained in the reserves of holiness under pressure, so that it is always ready to gush forth. And in order that no one may distractedly and indifferently wander past the sight of holiness and grace that are so near, a more striking holiness breaks forth at points, posing in an inescapable way the perpetual question: "What think you of the Church?"

The holiness in question is conferred by the redemption. We believe that we have to meditate deeply on Christ the Redeemer if we wish to understand the universal holiness of His work. The great wonder is not that God raises up saints, but that He makes saints out of the poor sinners that we are, by means of the consequences of our sins and in an environment continually ravaged by sin. The task is earthly and humble; it is the march of rational animals, heavy-footed and soiled, toward God. But that makes it all the more splendid and moving; it is the work of repeated repentance and forgiveness, of a cult that is partly material and is always accompanied by the letter that weighs down the spirit. But in general this magnificence remains invisible even to those in whom it is realized, and the glorious image that is slowly formed in the souls of the just will not be seen until the day when all veils are parted.

For God, who assists His holy Church to be the Church militant on earth, does not assist it to be the Church triumphant on earth. He helps it to fight aganist the sin that still remains in the heads as well as in the members, the sin that keeps it from being what it ought to be and what it already is in seed and hope, in Christ.

The holy Church humbly proclaims this fact in her prayer and teaching. In the liturgy and the psalms the officiating priest who speaks in the name of the Church unceasingly avows his guilt; and in her teaching the Church affirms with all her might that sinners are indeed her members, and her priests and pontiffs, though laden with faults, are nevertheless priests and pontiffs. "No flesh should glory in His sight." [60] Neither the faithful of the Church nor the hierarchy may appropriate to themselves the glory that is due to God alone. They do so to some extent; that seems to be inevitable for poor human nature. Yet no man ought thus to glory; the genuine holiness which is dogmatically defined must be universally human and truly catholic.

D. **Catholicity.** In the ordinary sense, the catholicity of the Church means its universal diffusion. Universal diffusion belongs rightfully to the Church, for the Church is the message of salvation addressed to every man; universal diffusion is also a fact, for the Church is established everywhere or almost everywhere. The Church has always been aware of its vocation to cover the earth; scarcely was the Church born than it set about its duty of converting the Roman Empire, and even spread beyond that Empire's frontiers. It has always returned to this work, and after the persecutions and reversals it suffered, began again both to repair its ruins and to invade the universe.

Even more astonishing than this expansion are the resistance of the Church to the disruptive influence of distension and the fact that, while ever spreading, it remains intrinsically one.

Though spread over the earth, the Church everywhere carefully guards the same faith, as if it occupied but a single house. It believes the same dogmas, as though it had but one heart and one soul. It announces this teaching with a single voice, and transmits it as though it had only one mouth. The languages spoken over the earth may vary; but the power of tradition remains the same. The Churches founded in Germany do not differ from other Churches in their beliefs or traditions; nor do the Churches that are in Spain, or those found among the Celts or in the East or in Egypt or in Libya.[61]

[60] Cf. I Cor. 1:29.
[61] St. Irenaeus, *Adversus haereses*, I, x, 2 (PG, VII, 552).

Space does not conquer the Church, but the Church conquers space. The whole universe, and it alone, is big enough for the Church.

We have only to scrutinize this catholicity with attention to find in it the particular truth that is the theme of these pages. The paradox of this immense extension is that it leaves the unity of the Church intact. Over the whole earth the Church remains a single entity, the one mystical body of the Savior. The universality of its expansion corresponds exactly to the central characteristic of its constitution. Besides having a positive commission, it has a need to expand in order to be itself, just as a tree, in order to live, has to spread its branches over the surrounding land.

Jesus commanded the Church to teach all nations. This order merely expresses the structure He gave it. And this structure in turn is merely the expression of Jesus Himself in the society where He continues to live. Thus we come back again to the Incarnation, the point of departure and the orientation of all Christianity. As we said before, the Incarnation heightened the perfection native to Christ's humanity by endowing it with the personality of the Word; yet it remains human, or rather becomes fully human, so far as a human nature can be made fully human in God and by the power of God. Therefore it is universally human and the principle of life for the whole human race.

Christ does not change. In the Church, which is His body, He retains His fullness of humanity. Because of Him, the Church is perfectly, transcendentally, surpassingly human; and all mankind is needed to express concretely the human perfections contained in the Church, the mystical body of Christ.

In consequence, the property of catholicity does not merely prove that the Church is endowed by God with powerful forces, or that it is supported by God's all-powerful assistance. It is the sign that the Church is human with a divine perfection, and that it is the mystical body of Him in whom all mankind can and ought to be recapitulated. It is a "note" informing us, by God's grace, that the Church is even more than a society founded by Christ; for it is Christ continued.

The observable fact that the Church fills the earth is a strong argument in its favor. But the thousand indications demonstrating that it remains the same in this immense expansion, and that this appropriation of the universe is the act by which it achieves its full growth, giving to Christ all mankind that is His plenitude and to mankind the supernatural physiognomy it can receive from Christ alone, is a more decisive proof that it is the Church of the Lord; for thus it is His body.

The Greek word for Church, *Ekklesia*, is derived from a root meaning "call." May we not interpret the name as the great call, the limitless vocation God offers to the whole human race which in principle He assumed in Christ?

The catholicity of the Church is an inner catholicity, a radical and constitutive catholicity, of the whole Church and of each of its members. The external catholicity is but the expression of this internal catholicity. The external catholicity expresses the internal catholicity, first, as we have said, in a certain universal adaptability. The religion of the God-man is suited to every man in the formula of universal holiness it proposes and the universal realism in which, as the continuation of the redemption, it admits and can admit the multitude of sinners, that is, the multitude making up actual mankind. Everything in this religion is to be theirs, not by sufferance but by right.

Sin is obviously the reason why the Church has not yet been able to impress its catholicity on all mankind. Too much sin bars its expansion. Even so the internal catholicity finds expression, though only in a sort of anguish and torment and in the ardent pressure that impels the Church to attain its true size and to become in fact all mankind.

To be true to itself, the Church must become completely universal. So long as it has not yet arrived at this goal, it does not outwardly correspond to what Christ is within it. There are certain kinds of union with God and types of sanctity which are genuinely human and truly belong to the Church, but which the Church has not yet presented to God or the world because they are peculiar to some particular nations, races, and cultures that have not yet entered the Church.[62] In other words, certain genuinely religious attitudes have been drained off by other religions; we are not referring to other Christian sects, in which this truth is quite evident. Yet such attitudes properly belong to Christ, as we have tried to show.

All this variety of temperaments and mentalities is needed to bring

[62] This is well brought out by P. Charles, *La prière missionnaire* (Louvain, 1935); cf., for example, p. 83.

out the unique holiness possessed by the Church as the mystical body of Christ. Catholicity, holiness, and unity are not mutually exclusive but rather mutually complementary. Since the Savior's holiness is transcendent, it requires the universality of men to display in detail all that it contains in unity. The Church will not have its full perfection until the peoples of all the nations have entered its doors. Meanwhile it possesses only by right and in compressed energy the power for good that cannot operate at full efficiency except in the totality of the human race. In the same way we cannot see all that a child is capable of until he becomes a man.

As a universal society and the unity of mankind, the Church cannot realize the perfection of its unity save in a magnificent variety. Man, always essentially one, is also essentially diverse according to the various epochs, environments, climates, and circumstances in which he lives. Since the Catholic religion is the religion of man and of the God-man, it does not have to be uniform to be unified. In its teeming life, every shade of humanity, every people, every race, and every century has its own peculiar, rightful place and its particular, individual Catholic luster.

This unity in variety, this living catholicity can be only the work of centuries and of a long, patient labor that assimilates everything without suppressing anything. In the beginning, missionary effort is geographically restricted and inevitably establishes a certain uniformity that is the product of centralization. But time passes, and the Spirit who peoples the Church over all the earth has in our day made more clearly manifest the divine commission of supernatural universalism, and so we have native clergies, hierarchies, languages, arts, and outlooks. The Spirit suggests more and more unmistakably to the Church the variety, the flexibility, the adaptation, and the multiplicity of human preferences it can allow. The unity of the Church is a living unity, like the Spirit's own unity, for its unity is that of Christ; it is a unity so immensely human that it cannot well find expression except in the immensely variegated unity of mankind. To tell the truth, a different kind of unity, a unity achieved by rigidity, monotony, and conformism would be clearer, easier to conceive mathematically, and to organize juridically; but it would be dead and inhuman; it would not be a unity vitally organized to form a living thing; it would not be the mysterious, catholic unity of the Church. The day is coming, and we see it approaching, when the catechism will be thoroughly Indian in the Indies, Malaysian in Malaysia, and Russian in Russia, as it is Latin among the Latin races; and it will be all the more profoundly one on that account. We need not add that, although such a work can be begun by missioners, it cannot be carried through to completion except by the indigenous Churches themselves.

Faced by these bold initiatives of the Spirit and also by threats of deep cleavages among the peoples, certain cautious souls entertain misgivings about unity. As if the unity of the Church, that has to have external expression, had its source in externals! As if, in itself and its inner principle, it were in any way a product of external regulations! All the bishops and all Christians might be walled off from one another in unconnected reservations; nevertheless Catholicism would be one; they might all speak different languages; yet Christ, the life of them all, would still be one. There are neither Jews nor Gentiles; all men are one in Christ.[63] And the inner unity would reproduce outer unity by adapting it to circumstances; for men do not make this inner unity; it makes itself, and Christ makes it by making Christians His members. Such is its life and energy that man can oppose it by trying to force it into his own categories as well as by rising up against it to cleave it; strangling causes death no less efficiently than dismemberment. The unity of the Church is not a formula but a life, the life of Christ, first principle of the new humanity, who makes it more supernaturally one in its very humanity, and hence more supernaturally varied, by bringing it into living unity.

God can intervene as He pleases; but in the Christian economy which He has made His own, He performs His actions through men. Men are responsible for the coming of salvation to all mankind for whom it is destined, and men set the limits of this salvation by the degree of their cooperation. External activity, the departure of missioners, and even financial resources are needed in this collaboration; but they are not the essential thing. The essential thing is the source of all this, which is charity, love and devotedness toward others, ardent concern for the salvation and happiness of all, inner zeal for the kingdom of God; the main thing is intense living of the true Christian life, that is, the life of Christ; not the life He lives in Himself, but the life men let Him live in them; both the full life He lives

---

[63] Gal. 3:28.

in the Church, and the mysterious, inceptive life He endeavors to live by grace everywhere in mankind.

That is the inner fire; and it is Christ present here on earth in His members and in the charity of men. The irradiation of the heat that is to spread over the world depends on the flames of this fire.

E. Apostolicity. The Church exists everywhere and always. Its life resists time as well as space, or rather dominates time and space, and from so high a vantage point that it takes in all the successive generations of men as it comprises their geographical expansion.

The thing that is now the Catholic Church began with Adam. The first to be a member of Christ was Adam, or else Abel, as is said more often, to preserve the parallelism between the two heads of mankind. The Church endures forever, and is always the same since its origin. But at this first beginning the Church was in a preparatory stage; it was not fully established until after the life and death of Jesus, or, more precisely, after Pentecost. As Christ, head of the whole mystical body, is not, properly speaking, a member of that body, according to the ordinary teaching of theology, we must hold that the Church, as the mystical body, began with the apostles. In this sense it has the characteristic, or note, of being apostolic.

This note has been emphasized from the origins of Christianity. The Fathers declare that Christian preaching is true because it is the same as the preaching of the apostles; the demonstration of a truth is its connection with the teaching of the apostles. The vindication the Church gives of itself is that which we still, in our day, mention when we address God Himself: "Peter the apostle and Paul the teacher of the nations are they, O Lord, who have taught us Thy law."

In the works of the Fathers as well as in modern controversial treatises, this vindication takes the form of a historical argument: the point is to establish lists of bishops. Such lists are our guaranty that today's teaching is the same as that of the beginning.

This establishing of identity that continues throughout all the passing centuries in spite of the variations and lapses that occur everywhere, is also a sign of God's assistance. It is an unmistakable mark of a unique life that is tremendously resistant and that wears out time itself. The latter point of view is the one that specially interests us in this book. As we see, it is a particular and partial way of regarding apostolicity. We believe that, if it does not comprise all that is implied in the note, it at least allows us to perceive more clearly, from the point of view of these pages, what this note signifies.

When we discover in the Church of today the same life, the same reactions, the same beliefs, and the same attitudes as in the apostolic Church, we are manifestly confronted with a life that is unequaled in its kind and is more excellent than any human life. Such a mystical, living being, that gathers to itself the centuries, bears its own witness that it is more man than man himself, if we may so express our thought; we mean that it is man, but man with a superhuman perfection received from the divine assistance and from union with God.

This Man, who is man to the limit of human capacity, is Christ, the head of a mystical body, the God-man. Furthermore the Church, whose continuity is clearly contemporaneous with all the centuries, bears witness that it is Christ continued. Its note of apostolicity flows directly from the thing signified, that is, the close relation existing between the Church and Christ whose body it is.

To convince ourselves that the Church remains always the same, we have only to study its doctrine at different periods, its cult, and its history. We shall speak of its doctrine when we come to investigate its teaching office.

The cult practiced in the Church likewise gives testimony to a perpetual identity. It remains always the same, and always consists in conferring a sort of perpetuity on the actions of Jesus. The cross is unceasingly raised up at Mass; the Savior's death and resurrection are continually being renewed in baptism; the Redeemer's blood still flows in the sacrament of penance. In a word, Christ is the one who continually confers the sacraments through the ministry of His priests. The life of Christ is the perennial inspiration of the liturgical year. Advent, Christmas, Lent, and Easter are His own history that is perpetually unfolding among the Christian people.

Moreover, when we meditate on the history of the Church, we see that it presents striking resemblances with the history of Jesus. Benson has brought them out clearly in a very suggestive book. We shall not undertake to perform a task which he has rendered superfluous. Let us merely recall that the thought is by no means new, and that Athanasius based his apologetic works, *Against the Greeks* and *On the Incarnation of the Word*, on this view of the notes of the Church. The vitality of the Church is proof that it lives a superior life, a life that flows into it from a risen Savior, a life of resurrection. Indeed, from the very beginning, Catholicism has had the destiny of going from agony to agony and from resurrection to resurrection. There have always been Herods and Pilates, executioners, and also, alas, Judases, as well as apostles and holy women. What happens in the Church is the continual renewal, or rather the continuation, of what took place in Christ.

Christ's history, consequently, unfolds in time, because, like us who are still living our mortal life, He is in time. But as it unfolds, this history bears witness, with numberless signs, that it remains unchanged, whereas time is nothing but change. The history of Christ is still today what it was at its origin; we observe the same actions, the same events, the same life, whereas time exists only on the condition of ceasing to exist.

CHAPTER XVII

THE FUNCTIONS OF THE CHURCH

WHEN we were considering the notes of the Church, we saw
that Christ abides and lives in the Church. We now go on to
show that Christ thus remains in the Church to act in it.

He continues to exercise the activity He exercised in former times.
During His mortal life He acted in His physical body; He now acts
in His mystical body. Then He was the way, the truth, and the life.
As the way, He guided us toward the Father; as truth, He taught
us the things of heaven; as life, He was the source of eternal life. He
still carries on this triple office of head, teacher, and sanctifier in the
triple function which the Church carries on in His name, of teaching,
governing, and sanctifying. We shall first discuss the office of teaching.

I. THE TEACHING OFFICE

Christ's teaching career was too important to come to an end with
His mortal life. Can we conceive that the Word was made flesh with
the purpose, as He Himself declares, of giving testimony to the
truth,[1] and that His voice should die away in silence after three years?
As we pointed out in the pages that treated of revelation, Christ's
humanity, subsisting as it did in the Word, was in itself a human
teaching without limits, and was so great that it could not express
itself fully except in the totality of the human race. Regarded as
teaching, therefore, it had to spread over the whole world to be in
all mankind a principle of knowledge, just as, regarded as life, it is
spread over the whole world to be in mankind a source of grace. In
the same way as Christ's humanity fashions for itself a living body
out of mankind, a body vigorous with eternal life, it makes out of

[1] John 18:37.

mankind an intelligent organism that has knowledge of eternal truth.

This living body, like Christ's humanity, is both visible and invisible. Consequently the life of knowledge perpetuated in it must be at once visible and invisible, and likewise the influx of knowledge by which the sacred humanity produces and maintains this life must be visible and invisible. But the knowledge communicated to the mystical body must be the same as that possessed by Christ the head, for in the unity of Christ the life of the whole Christ is one and the same.[2]

The invisible communication of this knowledge is accomplished in the souls of Christ's members. It is a donation of life and thought, a sharing in the mind of Christ in the life of Christ, enabling us to judge and evaluate in a way suitable for members of Christ. It is a participation in the consciousness Christ has of Himself as head of mankind, a consciousness so human yet so penetrating that it can enlighten the consciousness of every man from within.[3] This interior illumination is not a simple elevation of the faculty of knowledge without any bearing on the new objects to be known. As a sharing in the consciousness of Christ it is related to every Christian dogma that imparts instruction about Christ. It is meant to express Christ; it conveys a kind of preliminary sketch of Christ that is not yet filled in. Since this knowledge is possessed by a member of Christ, it expresses Christ who has members in a body that is the Church, and who, being God the Son, is able to unite members to Himself.

An illumination of this kind is not a passive reception of light-rays. To live is to act and, for a spirit, to know is to live; even material things do not shine in the rays of the sun without vibrating in turn. To receive light in any true sense, Christians have to cooperate with it by letting it penetrate into the deepest reaches which the soul can lay open to it. They have to think out their faith with loving docility; they have to meditate on it with eagerness and continual adherence to Christ, so that, through the power of the head who is Christ, they

[2] This visible influence and magisterium will be to the invisible influence and magisterium what the body of the Church is to the soul of the Church, and what the formulation of dogma in words and phrases is to the supernatural knowledge present in souls.

[3] "The Word was . . . full of grace and truth" (John 1:14); "Every one that is of the truth, heareth My voice" (John 18:37). "Christ is the master who teaches secretly in the school of the heart," says St. Augustine, *Confessions*, IX, 9 (*PL*, XXXII, 773).

may develop in themselves a mentality suitable for Christ's members.

The mention of a member implies an organism. Christians do not belong to Christ unless they are all joined together in Him. They would not live their life of knowledge in Christ unless they all lived together, in a common reception and a universal collaboration; this is a phase of the communion of saints. Their collaboration must be both interior and exterior, because the nature of man has these two aspects.

This is the work of the immense collective life of the Church, so far as that life is intellectual. Every Christian has the ability and the duty to take part in it in his own way, either by expressing it in his life or by scientific investigation, according to his vocation, his talent, and his condition. His baptismal character, and particularly the character he receives in the sacrament of confirmation, invest him with the ability and the duty to render public and social testimony,[4] to teach, if not by authoritative instruction at least by his solidarity and fellowship in charity, and to engage in that communication of life, conviction, and thought that marks the adult.

But the work would not be entirely human if it were purely invisible; such an influence on thought alone is too delicate and imperceptible to suffice for the sluggish minds of men and the rigorous precision required by supernatural truth. That is why Christ lives on in the Church not only by an invisible continuation in souls, but also by a visible continuation in social authority. In this authority Christ is prolonged as the exterior principle and visible, efficacious unity of the society that owes its existence to Him. And by the visible teaching office He exercises in this authority, He is prolonged as the exterior principle and efficacious unity of the propagation of knowledge and light that come to us from Him.

The interior teaching, the growth of each member in truth for his own benefit and that of others, is not in full union with Christ and does not share in absolute certitude or infallibility unless it is in union with this authority. In this authority Christ still continues to teach externally and audibly; when we hear it, we can still hear Him. His human word reflects the eternity He has as the Word; He does not cease to be uttered either in His divinity or in His humanity. His human word is the decisive word that judges every generation, and the act that announces it never ceases to function.

Such is the mystery of the teaching Church. "Peter has spoken

[4] Cf. *Decretum pro Armenis*, Denz., 697.

through Leo, and Christ has spoken through Peter." This accounts for the superior character of this teaching authority; it is the superiority of Christ Himself. The doctrines proclaimed by the Church are heard outside. Men may be struck by the firmness, the flexibility, and the time-resisting quality of this teaching. But no one can perceive from outside why it always remains the same.

We may approach an explanation by considering the divine Omnipotence that from heaven invisibly guards the deposit of revelation. But, in our opinion, we have not yet arrived at an understanding so long as we represent this assistance as a distant aid guaranteeing an invariable fidelity that is merely material. When Jesus Christ promised to remain always with His Church, He was not speaking of any such remote aid. He does not dwell in us, nor we in Him, from the heights of heaven; He is within us and in our Church. The Church is His body; when the Church teaches, it lends Him its lips, its voice, and its effort; but He is the one who speaks.

We hear the Church, but "he that is of God heareth the words of God." [5] We hear the words spoken by the Church, but what we hear is not the Church. For the Church is the continuation of Christ. Just as the words uttered by the sacred humanity of Jesus did not have their first starting point in that humanity, so the doctrine of the Church is not its own doctrine. Jesus has given to the Church the words He Himself received, and the Church speaks the words of God and the word of Christ.

The Father gave to Jesus the words He spoke, and the Father spoke them in Him. [6] Our Lord's teaching existed in the flood of light that issued from the Light, *lumen de lumine,* just as He Himself subsists in Him who sends Him. [7] Such is also the Church and the teaching of the Church; this teaching comes from the Father and has its origin in the brightness of eternal light.

Accordingly this teaching is essentially Trinitarian in its content, in its origin and support, and in the mission of those who announce it. For this mission is connected with the eternal processions: "As the Father hath sent Me, I also send you." [8] When we stand in the presence of the teaching Church, we are in the presence of absolute

---

[5] John 8:47.
[6] John 7:16 f.
[7] Heb. 1:1 ff.; John 10:37 f.; 14:10–13.
[8] John 20:21; 17:18.

mystery. Therefore, to grasp the message of the Church and to know what its teaching authority is, we need a revelation from the Father; only the Father can reveal the Son,[9] and He alone can tell us where the Son's voice is to be heard today.[10]

"The Church is the pillar and the ground of the truth"; [11] and "it is the Spirit which testifieth that Christ is the truth." [12] The Church truly takes the place of Christ; yet we cannot say that the Church pilfers anything that belongs to Him; He alone is the truth in the Church. Therefore we may say that the teaching of the Church is not less infallible than the teaching of Jesus, and yet that Jesus alone is infallible; He is infallible in the Church. The dignities are equal here, for they both are one dignity; on the one side it is personal, on the other it is mystically communicated; but on both sides it is the dignity of the uncreated light made flesh.

Human individuals do not count on these heights. The theological formation of the pope and the learning possessed by bishops gathered in a council are not important; in themselves they know nothing, they can do nothing, they serve no purpose. Even their deficiencies, however great we may suppose them to be, do not count. Jesus Christ is in them; can the insignificant clay that we are dam up God's omnipotence? We can say of their teaching office what we may say of their governing authority: in themselves and of themselves they have no power.

Yet they are Christ's vicars. They must tend flocks that are not their own with a care that is not their own in pastures that are not their own. But they alone have the duty of tending the flocks, and the sheep have but to hear, not the voice of these shepherds, but the voice of the one great Shepherd.[13]

Never, perhaps, did Christ so boldly place His reliance on men as when He said, "Feed My sheep." [14] When He said over the bread, "This is My body," He knew that the bread could not play Him false, that it could never resist transubstantiation, that it could never give poison to souls instead of life. But when He told Peter, "Feed My flock," He knew well that man would always retain the power

[9] Matt. 11:27; 16:17; John 6:45.
[10] Cf. John 14:29.
[11] Cf. I Tim. 3:15.
[12] See I John 5:6.
[13] John 10:16, 27.
[14] John 21:17.

of going back on Him. He was fully aware that man's mind is dull, often harried by blameworthy prejudices, and even by excessive eagerness to do well. Yet He dared to commit Himself completely to one among us; He put His signature to this man's decisions and definitions before they were issued, so that, if this man were to fall into error, He Himself would be in default.

A sort of "Real Presence" is found in the pope and the episcopate. The Son of man is sure enough of His mystical undertaking in our race to give us His pledge that He would reside in the pope and bishops until the end of the centuries, and that their shortcomings in knowledge would not keep Him from being the truth in them, any more than the commonplace triviality of bread would keep Him from being our life in the consecrated host. In the pope as well as in the episcopate, we repeat; both make up the teaching Church, and both are infallible. Catholic doctrine is characteristic on this point, and for my part I do not see how it can be satisfactorily understood without appealing to the truth of the mystical body.

The power to teach is said to be twofold; it is truly found in the bishops and it is truly found in the pope. And the full teaching authority which is in the pope does not prevent the same power from being really in the bishops when they act as a body. Anywhere else such a regime would be impossible; what can a parliament do when the monarch is absolute? But the two are perfectly compatible in the Church. The pope's power is the power, not of his person, but of Christ who teaches through him. The same Christ also teaches in the assembled bishops, and has the same power in them. Yet there is only one power, because there is only one Christ; and although the two organisms are not identical as organisms, they will always be found to be in agreement, because they have but a single power.

A Christian is someone who refuses to see anything else than Jesus Christ. His docility to the bishops is the same as his docility to the pope, for it is the docility he has to Christ. The definitions of a council and the declarations of the incarnate Word are absolutely equivalent for him. They are, indeed, identical in the unity of the mystical body; the council continues Christ, as the voice that strikes the ear continues the voice issuing from the speaker's mouth.

Obviously the teachings of the magisterium do not all have the same doctrinal value. What we have said applies fully only to the cases in which the Church acts in the plenitude of its power, that is, in the totality of its incorporation in Christ, to define revealed truth. Other cases admit of correctives and explanations; theology treats of them, and we need not enumerate them here. We need only to point out that in these other cases human thought acts to some extent on its own responsibility, and that consequently the mystical Christ informs the teaching office less completely. However, the teaching office is always the organ by which Christ acts, and His action remains always a powerful preservative against error, even if it does not manifest itself in the infallibility that properly belongs to it. And therefore, whenever the Church speaks, an internal assent is to be given. But this assent can be based on the absolute competence or on the relative competence of the Church, as the voice through which truth speaks, according as the Church acts with the fullness of its authority or employs that authority only partly.

From this point of view, the teaching activity of the Church resembles the sanctifying action of the sacraments. The words pronounced at the consecration by the least worthy of priests in the most distracted of Masses are no less efficacious than the consecration pronounced by Jesus Himself at the Last Supper. Similarly, the teaching of the Church is no less sure than that of Jesus.

This teaching of truth has its own proper efficacy. "The word of God is living and effectual." [15] Of its very nature it is incisive and penetrating; such it was in Jesus Christ, and such it remains in the Church. Christ spoke as one having authority. His teaching possessed the power of helping His hearers to understand and to believe. His miracles were no doubt numerous and impressive; but they were not indispensable; His bare assertion was enough to give a firm basis to faith.[16] On His testimony God has erected the whole economy of salvation; [17] and this testimony is valid for all those who are of the truth, for no other reason than that it is His.[18]

Christ's testimony has not ceased to be given; it is found in the teaching of the Church and constitutes the efficacy of that teaching. In former days His voice was heard across a few yards of space; now it is heard through the Church; such media cannot in any way cut down the power of the word. The people of Samaria once said to

[15] Heb. 4:12.
[16] John 4:19; 20:29; Mark 13:22.
[17] John 1:18; 8:14; 12:44; Apoc. 1:5.
[18] John 18:37.

the woman who had announced Christ to them: "We now believe, not for thy saying; for we ourselves have heard Him." [19] The situation is exactly the same for us Christians of the twentieth century; we believe, not because of what our priests, our parents, and our books have told us, but because we ourselves have heard Him through the organs by which He Himself speaks.

The Vatican Council declares that the Church is the custodian and teacher of revealed truth. The Church exercises this office with supernatural perfection, not only by transmitting and authentically interpreting the truth or by enjoying the constant assistance of Him who is the author of the truth, but mainly by being, in a mystical sense, He who gives the truth and who sums up in Himself all truth. Since He is there, His witness of the Church is not less cogent than was His witness of Himself. Therefore this testimony, like the Savior's own affirmation in other days, can penetrate the soul and, if the soul's will cooperates, can rouse it to give the assent of faith.

Consequently we may say that the teaching of the Church is more than a rule and guaranty of the faith; it is also the ultimate foundation of the faith. This statement, of course, has to be rightly understood. We do not say that explicit submission to the external teaching authority is the only condition that makes an act of supernatural faith possible; if this were so, the souls of good will that are outside the Catholic Church could have no faith. Nor do we say that attachment to the bishops and the pope, regarded as persons who exercise an external office, is enough to establish us formally on the immovable rock of truth. What we are trying to bring out is that this point of view is not adequate. The Church is Christ, and Christ is God. When the Church as such speaks, we need not pursue our investigations farther. All we have to do is believe; and the one we believe is God.

Some may object that God is only the invisible protector who assists His ministers from without. That is true, if we are looking only at the surface of things or at the body of the Church. But it is not true if we consider the true reality. Since the time of the Incarnation, God is not other than Christ; and since Pentecost, Christ is not other than the Church. On the one side, hypostatic unity; on the other side, mystic unity; but in both cases the unity is real. The Church is the word of God addressed to all the nations; the Church

[19] *Ibid.*, 4:42.

is the eternal Truth that has drawn close to us in order to become ours. When we believe in the Church, we believe in God.

The teaching of the Church begets faith; it is like the sacrament of the Eucharist, which is not only the sign of the life that is given, but is this very life in its source. And that is the case in the various ways of conveying this teaching as provided for in the structure of the Church, for example, in the teaching of simple priests or in the instruction Christian parents give to their children. Christ speaks everywhere, as He speaks always.

As the superiority of the teaching authority is that of Christ Himself, its "interiority" is also that of Christ. The mystical body is a unique kind of entity; it is a single, living, supernatural being. Its life, which it receives from Christ, is expressed in a knowledge and love that also come unceasingly from Christ. As Christ is living, so this knowledge and love are living; as Christ lives more intensely than we do, this knowledge and love live more intensely than we do; and as Christ lives in us, they too live in us, and more ardently than we. The essential requisite of doctrinal progress is found in this fact. The formulas we succeed in expressing outwardly are vague and confused; but every living man knows what life is, and every Christian who lives in Christ by faith and love knows, by his faith and love, what this life in Christ is.

As the centuries pass, men in whom Christ dwells come to know Him more and more perfectly. Through grace, the teaching of the Church, and their own reflections, men express and comprehend Him better and better. The doctrine is not new; it is old; but it becomes better understood. The reality is not new; it is the same as it was in the beginning; but it is more explicitly possessed. The identity is complete; since the time Christ began to exist, no entirely new light has shone or will shine in His humanity. What we understand is the mutual gift; better still, the gift itself makes itself ever better comprehended by continually giving itself. Yet there is advance and growth. New jewels are brought out of the ancient treasury. But this development merely accentuates the living identity; the better we come to know Christ and Christianity, the better we perceive that we now possess more fully the gift that was unreservedly handed over to men at the beginning. The very acknowledgment of this fact shows how rich in definitive doctrine the origins were.

In this point, as in all others, the progress of doctrine surpasses any progress of which we have experience as much as the supernatural surpasses the natural. For the goal to which the progress of doctrine is to lead was realized from the start, since this goal is the beatific vision. Christ had this vision from the instant of His conception. Doctrinal progress wholly consists in communicating to the members what pre-exists in the head.

In this progress of dogma, the only thing that can account for its structure and internal coherence is union with grace. Here we are thinking of all our supernatural activities, particularly of faith. Faith is a union of the mind with Christ and His knowledge. Therefore it confers a special competence on our supernatural knowledge. This trait should be clearly brought out. Too often faith is represented, even by those who have the best of intentions, as an intellectual timidity, as a fear that keeps a man from thinking for himself and that induces him to accept the ready-made ideas of another. It is like that only when it is badly exercised. In itself, union with light tends to make vision more piercing and luminous. Submission to the teaching authority of the Church as such, that is, as representing the incarnate Word, ought to impart to the mind a new boldness and a sort of rapture. We think, but not alone; we think in Christ, with Christ, through Christ. Truly we are the ones who think, and we think with all our heart and soul; but even for us our act of thinking is a rich and splendid mystery. And when Christ lends to our thinking His cooperation, His light, and His thought, our concepts are bathed in eternal light. Let us think, then, for when we reflect we let the rays of this brilliant light penetrate our souls. Let us think, out of love for Him who is the Word and Thought and Truth; let us think, for our reflections are the only love our minds are capable of when they are in the presence of the truth that charms them.

But we should think with Christ, in Him, and in dependence on Him. He stands before us, very near, real, and attentive, in the magisterium of the Church. He is there to deliver to us the data of our undertaking, to sustain our effort, to correct our wanderings if need should arise, and to approve the result. What more could we desire? If we approach the work with a craven or irresolute spirit, the fault is none of His; for we ought to perform the task in Him.

The part played by man in the vitality of Christian teaching is very great, and we do well to assure ourselves on that point. To appreciate the fact better, have we noticed how important it was in the very founding of the Church? Jesus came to establish the Catholic Church on earth; but the ones who actually established it were men. Christ Himself hardly preached to anyone except the lost sheep of the house of Israel; and during His mortal life He sent His disciples nowhere except to the villages of Palestine, directing them not to travel the roads of Samaria or to cross over to the pagan districts. He Himself apparently wished to do no more than train the apostles and to make ready the seed that later, under His hidden action and His bidding, would be sown to spread the Gospel over all the earth. In point of fact, truly Catholic preaching, the diffusion of the true doctrine, is the work of the Church, not of Christ; or better, it is the work of Christ in the Church. The body of Christ has built itself up; as St. Paul says, it has achieved its own construction and growth; but it was able to do so because it was attached to the head and possessed the real though invisible power of the head.

Can we not say the same with regard to Christian teaching? Jesus has given us the whole doctrine; yes, indeed, but as a seed rather than as something fully formed. He spoke under the form of images, practical counsels, occasional lessons, parables, and especially examples. He never declared explicitly, in the precise formulas of defined dogmas, that He was one person with two natures; that He was one of the Trinity, consubstantial with the Father, and, along with the Father, the principle of the Holy Spirit; that He came to expiate, by vicarious satisfaction, an original fault and numberless actual sins; that His second coming, which was at hand, would be His return in the Church. In a word, He hardly gave any exposition of Christian doctrine, if by that we mean an orderly collection of propositions. What He taught was rather the sketches or first drafts or, so to speak, the seeds of formulas. In general He was content to be Himself, to be the summing-up of all truth in Himself. He conducted Himself as a man and as God, He acted toward God as a Son with His Father, and also as someone able to give God and to pour out the Spirit. He acted as a hostage coming to free all men, and as a founder coming to establish a society in which He Himself would live mystically. But the formulation of the truth in words, the reduction of these realities to a body of doctrine, has in large part remained the task committed to the Church. The apostles had to piece Christian teaching together from what He said, displayed in His own person, and suggested; what has been accomplished is His work, but it has been performed by them. He would ever aid His Church, but from within; His Spirit would bring all truth to mind, and would also see to it that not so much as a superfluous comma would be added.[20] Yet the Church would draw up its Creed, its councils, and its theological summas in Him; for the head and the body are inseparable.

A Christian is a member of the mystical body, not by his own effort, but through Christ. On the other hand, the act of knowing, which is a function of being, is construed as the being that knows. Consequently, although the Christian truly knows, he knows, not of himself, but through Christ. But Christ, who lives in souls by His "anointing" and His living truth, does not express Himself outwardly and authentically except in the teaching authority of the Church. Therefore this "anointing," this living truth, in a word, this Christian life, appeals to the teaching authority when it appeals to Christ, and its voice is lifted up in the councils: "Peter, teach us; you have the words of eternal life, and you have them for me."

Thus entreated by Christian life, Christ proceeds, not to restrain it or to supplant it or to suppress it, but to call it forth and to complete it. The theologians who keep silent for fear of attracting notice and are content merely to criticize or to treat of subjects that are safe and lacking in vital interest, are not those of the strongest faith; Christians who leave to ecclesiastical superiors the task of thinking out their religion for them, resigning themselves to a passive faith, are not the most fervent. As though the internal act of thinking were the exclusive prerogative of the external magisterium as such; or as though God had not fortified His Church with an unfailing authority for the express purpose of enabling men to think without fear!

The union between the authority of Christ in pastors and the life of Christ in souls is perfect. It springs up from the spontaneity of Christian life. What is outwardly submission, is inwardly supreme autonomy. Let this word frighten no one; it is necessary to bring out the glory of our faith. But such autonomy clearly implies that the faithful are united to Christ. As long as we dwell on their distinction from Christ, the case is different; but is the branch of the vine a branch merely because it is distinct from the vine?

The faithful are in Christ, and Christ is in them. Living faith brings

[20] *Ibid.*, 14:26; Matt. 5:18.

Christ to dwell in His members. When the believer surrenders himself to Christ in faith, Christ is no longer a stranger; He is the believer's life and his all. And when Christ entrusts His truth to a believer,
He entrusts Himself along with it. From the instant of its coming,
faith is no longer faith in someone extraneous and remote; it is faith
in Him who is more interior to us than we ourselves are; and from
then on, we may say, it is faith in oneself, and is autonomous rather
than heteronomous. However, it is autonomous, not with reference
to the Christian alone or to Christ alone, but with regard to the unity
of the whole Christ; outside this union there is neither Christian nor
Christ. A man believes in the mystery of unity only from within this
unity.

In this mystery of unity, that is, in the true reality, the life of supernatural knowledge, or faith, is spontaneous and interior, like all life;
but it is such in the same way as it is life, that is, in Christ. In His
mystical body, Christ forms Himself as the one who knows: *et erit
unus Christus noscens seipsum.* On the empirical level, the magisterium appears to teach the faithful; in reality, Christ teaches Himself, *Christus docet Christum,* as St. Augustine says in a passage of his
Tractatus in Ioannem which expounds the ideas dealt with in this
section, although the method of treatment is somewhat different.
The saint there explains how Jesus can say, in St. John, that the
Father will show Him yet greater things, so that the disciples and
not He will marvel, as though, in showing these things to Him, the
Father had really shown them to the disciples.

The magisterium of the Church is not the exaltation of a few
individuals above masses kept in tutelage; it is the means God uses
to elevate the whole populace. The office of the popes and bishops
will pass away, and it is not because they have taught that they will
see the Light in heaven, but because, like any of the faithful, they
have believed. And everything else will pass away, *ex cathedra*
definitions and infallibility in teaching. But infallibility in believing
will remain, in the sense that the belief of the faithful will become,
century after century, infallibility in seeing, the certitude of vision.
Hence the greatness is shared by all, and all alike are illuminated; and
this resembles a democracy. But the greatness comes through the
ministry of some, especially of one; and only some, especially one,
hold the torch; and here we have the monarchical principle. But this
one and the others and all are illuminated because they are in the

house; [21] and here we have the synthesis of both aspects. In reality, there are not, on the one side, those who teach, and on the other, quite separate, those who are taught; there is but one life, one mystical body, one complete Christ, head and members. When the head communicates light to the members, a single mystical man grows in knowledge: *et est unus Christus docens seipsum.*

Like all the others, and as much as the others, pope and bishops need to be taught by Jesus Christ. But Jesus Christ teaches them by means of the function they discharge. As private persons, they are subject to the power which, as public persons, they wield in the name of God. This is very revealing for the exact nature of the magisterium, for it shows that teaching is an action of Christ performed through men, and not an action of men. They can teach and they must teach; but the truth they teach comes from Christ, and is greater than they. As a priest effaces himself before the host he has just consecrated, they ought to efface themselves before the doctrine they proclaim. Their faith ought to be just as absolute as that of the priest at the consecration, and we may seemingly add that in all likelihood it is more meritorious. We of the general body of the faithful behold the arbiter of our faith in the majesty of liturgical functions; but they who hold this office know themselves in their workaday lives, and they appreciate better than anyone what imperfect and feeble instruments the Master has deigned to use. No matter; they have the strict duty of regarding their pronouncements as excluding all doubt, even to martyrdom if need be. They have been but a channel of truth; and their pronouncements are not the product of their own reflections but come from the mind of Him who, in the flesh hypostatically united to the Word, has brought us the doctrine of truth.[22]

II. THE GOVERNING OFFICE

Christ, then, is the way, the one way that leads to the one goal necessary. He is not only the Redeemer in whom we ought to have confidence, but also the Legislator to whom we owe obedience. The Council of Trent says that if anyone maintains the contrary, let him be anathema.[23] The grace by which we live in the supernatural order

[21] Matt. 5:15.
[22] St. Augustine, *Epist.* 105, 16 (*PL*, XXXIII, 403).
[23] Sess. VI, can. 21 (Denz., 831).

has its first origin in Him; the decisions which we make ought no less to have their first principle in Him.

Accordingly Christ is head and legislator, not only by the Father's appointment, but in virtue of His person. That office is an adjunct of His sacred humanity, coming to it from the hypostatic union with the Word; it is the one bond by which our will is linked to absolute rectitude. In His humanity, Christ is forever the head.

Being regulates action, and the head's existence regulates the existence of the members. Therefore Christ's existence, His very substance, is the first rule for the activity of Christians and legislates for them. Just as Christ does not merely teach truth but is the living truth, so He does not merely propose His moral code but in His concrete existence is that moral code; He "is" the way and the formula of supernatural goodness. Wherever and however He may perpetuate Himself, He is always the same formula and the same guide.

Christ is the first principle in supernatural life; He must also be the first principle in supernatural conduct. However, He is so in His own way, not as a cold axiom that entails consequences, but as a life that has its energies and its fruitfulness in love. The Son's humanity, which introduces a new life, a theandric life on our earth, brings us a new love, a theandric love, the love that burns in divinized man and that turns toward God and man with all its inner thrust. In its tendencies, aspirations, and exigencies, this love has its law preformed and virtually existing in itself. Therefore, in infusing this love into us by making us His members, Christ infuses into us an interior law, a living guide of life, that becomes our law as fully as it is His.

That is the first way Christ directs and continues to direct mankind. He has also another way. Christ is so essentially and radically a law of Christian activity that He is present in all its manifestations. Action follows being; [24] He is a principle, and He acts like a principle. His slightest gestures reveal Him, and therefore show men what a child of adoption ought to be in the presence of the Father; and His words, discourses, and parables, which disclose His way of thinking, evaluating, and feeling, are the rule of perfection that befits His divinized members.

Man has a deep need of practical precepts and norms of conduct

---

[24] *Operari sequitur esse.*

set forth in words. Christ gave us such during the days of His mortal life; and He continues to give them, for they are always necessary. Hence Christ gives us two kinds of moral directives, the one internal and invisible, the other external and visible.

Likewise in the Church, the continuation of Christ here on earth, there are and have to be two directives that are always set before us, two legislative functions, two kinds of moral guidance, one interior and invisible, the other exterior and visible. The reasons for this may here be given briefly; they have been developed at length in connection with the teaching office, which has the same two aspects.

The interior and invisible directive is the great and mysterious love that is propagated in the soul of the Church, the charity of Christ. This charity is a driving force and a law both in the whole Church and in each soul, for Christ is life wherever He may be. This law, more than any other, is interior to the members, and has its exigencies, aims, and orientations for itself and for them. It is also a law that is always new and that flows unceasingly from Christ and the life He lives in His members; hence it has its own way of directing.[25] This is a "member-charity," if we may suggest such a term, for it comes to the hearts of men by means of a ceaseless communication from the head; it is a charity that enables us to evaluate, judge, will, and love in the way that is fitting for members who have been raised to the supernatural life, and also in the way of Christ and God; for we are members of Christ who is God.

In Christ, God may be said to lay hold of our every action, whether internal or external, by its root and source, for in the last analysis it is love that guides and acts. At the same time He causes this action to be more intensely ours, by implanting deeply within us the supernatural principle of our action. He does this simultaneously in each member and in the collective unity of them all which is the Church; for the same Christ incorporates the one and the other into Himself. He gives a law by giving a love, which is the gift of a life.

This giving of a law, this interior direction is effected by interior lights, by the attractions of grace, by the instigations of the Holy Spirit, by the very unfolding of the supernatural life, and, since all life is activity, by the earnest efforts which all Christians make, with God's help, to acquire uprightness and perfection. The unction of

[25] See what we said in the preceding section, pp. 520–23, on the interior light given by Christ.

Christ, says Holy Scripture,[26] teaches those in whom He resides, not only regarding truth but also regarding charity.

This invisible guidance, as we have said, does not remain alone; it is accompanied by a visible guidance. The latter is given in the visible Church, by visible superiors in whom Christ continues His visible government; it is given by the teaching, guiding Church. It consists in the commandments of the Church, in canon law, in the various schools of spirituality and religious life, in the admonitions of superiors and directors of conscience, and the like.

St. Thomas treats of these two kinds of guidance, or of this double aspect of Christian law, in a series of instructive questions "On the Law of the Gospel, called the New Law." [27] He starts out with the principle that the Christian law is instilled into our hearts before it is written down, and says that it consists primarily and essentially in the grace of the Holy Spirit: the New Law is chiefly the grace of the Holy Spirit inscribed in the hearts of the faithful, and is secondarily a written law containing precepts which dispose us to receive grace or which pertain to the use of that grace.

The first of these two aspects of the New Law requires the Christian to be docile to grace; the second exacts obedience properly so called. These two virtues, like the two aspects of ecclesiastical guidance to which they correspond, are distinct but also connected. By means of these two virtues a single complete adherence to one Christ and a single love is achieved; in the same way the connection of limbs with the body involves a sharing in the life of the body and an insertion into the body through nerves and muscles. Thus the two virtues imply each other as a condition for the full exercise of each; to be completely docile to grace, we must be willing to hearken to it as uttered by its authentic voice, the visible authority established by Christ; and to be fully obedient to the external orders issuing from Christ and the principle of grace, we have to be responsive to the slightest interior movements of grace. Both are required for the effective exercise of Christian activity. The more intense, ardently willed, noble, and free this activity is, the more eager it will be to be guided and sustained by Christ, both outwardly and inwardly.

The visible direction given by Christ through His visible representatives is the main topic to be here discussed. We wish to show

[26] Cf. I John 2:20–27.
[27] *Summa*, Ia IIae, q. 106–8; cf. q. 91, a. 5; q. 98, a. 1.

that this guidance is very special in nature and that the authority through which it is exercised is unequaled. For the authority possessed by ecclesiastical superiors is that possessed by Christ in His sacred humanity, whose directive office is perpetuated in them.

Christ's authority has two essential characteristics relative to the human race: it is above men and within them. These two characteristics are closely connected and have a certain quality not to be found elsewhere. They result from the fact that Christ's humanity is hypostatically united to God, that it is consequently the unity of regenerated mankind and the first principle in the life of the supernatural organism, and that, like a soul, it is superior and interior to the whole human race.

This, and no other, is the authority that is perpetuated in ecclesiastical superiors. They are fully invested with it when they act in the plenitude of their office, which occurs rather seldom; in all other cases it is more or less attenuated. But there is no other authority in the Church.

According to outward appearances, ecclesiastical superiors are individuals, and the faithful are other individuals, quite separate from those placed above them. As individuals, however, ecclesiastical superiors are private persons and are not superiors.

All their power comes to them from the invisible Christ who assists them and issues orders through them. But the invisible Christ establishes a mystical unity between the superiors and the body of the faithful, for He is the life of the whole Church as well as the greatness of the governing authority. As long as we do not see Christ in our superiors, we do not see their right to command; but as soon as we see Him in them, we can no longer discern any line separating them from the multitude. In any organism, the members are interior to one another because of the unity of their life. The same holds in Christ; the members of the Church, in spite of the diversity of their functions, are so closely united in the same life that they are interior to one another. Some lead and others are led, but all together form one Christ who is all in all of them and leads them all Himself.

This is the second aspect, the interior characteristic that marks the authority received from Christ over the faithful. The two aspects are complementary; and the second shows how the first is possible, and how such authority can have real power over man's conscience. For, if it is false to say that ecclesiastical authority lacks essential superiority and that it can only confirm the decisions of conscience, it is also false to say that it is an absolute power falling ready-made from heaven, without any root in the interior life of souls. How could we believe that anything coming from heaven and from the Creator Himself in His supreme gift should be so ill adapted and so extrinsic to the very nature of creatures?

Even in the natural order, authority is intrinsic to the members of a society; for authority is the function that imposes on each member the condition of social life, that is, the way of acting which each member, within himself, requires of himself as a member. It expresses what each member confusedly seeks or ought to seek, and therefore prescribes what each one should require of himself or of others, though often it commands in vain. For, in the last analysis, in our inner nature we are social beings; nature leads us to exact of ourselves what is needed for the whole group. By enacting appropriate measures, authority formulates what our conscience has already pre-determined in an uncertain and vague fashion, so that we may say that it is to some extent within all the members, even while it is above them.

The same holds true of ecclesiastical authority, except that here the question takes on a supernatural profundity, because of the deeper unity and the supernatural life of the members. Authority is the visible organ of this unity. What does this mean, if not that authority is the visible organ of the principle of the most profound, personal, and supernatural life of souls? In the measure that Christ is more interior to souls than their need of reconciliation with Him or their nature itself, ecclesiastical authority, in Christ who confers authority, is more interior to souls than any natural authority. One and the same Christ is the source of the interior supernatural life found in Christians and the principle of all the authority possessed by superiors. In Him, the two exist within each other; and the Church, by all that it is, is the same whole Christ, everywhere interior to Himself and superior to His members.

Therefore, when ecclesiastical authority sets before Christians the will of Christ and the duties of charity, it gives expression to the will that arises in them and the duties that Christ prescribes within them. In the human body, similarly, the spoken word issues from the mouth, but expresses the life of the whole body. In this matter the Church differs from natural societies or states; citizens have a certain natural competence, inadequate perhaps yet real, with regard to the common good which authority has to promote, whereas Christians have no such natural competence with regard to the supernatural good which ecclesiastical authority has to formulate. Whatever competence may be theirs, they have in Christ and in the new life He gives them. But having that, they have full competence, for Christ has it. However, they have it in their own way, as members who receive all that they possess; and the established authority has the same in its own way, as the means by which Christ legislates for us in the person of ecclesiastical superiors.

Yet we repeat that what Christ thus proposes is what He thinks and wills within souls and what His members likewise will in their capacity as members. When the members obey their superiors, therefore, they obey themselves and the life they have as members. True obedience is not separate from true supernatural sincerity with oneself. And this explains how the New Law is a law of freedom and love. "The New Law, which derives its pre-eminence from the spiritual grace instilled into our hearts, is called the law of love; and it is said to contain spiritual and eternal promises, which are the objects of virtue, especially of charity. Therefore men are attracted to such objects, not as to something alien but as to something of their own." [28]

These great perfections show that Christian authority, like Christian obedience or the Christian social organism, is a thing apart, a thing that is new with all the newness of Christianity. When we think of these truths, therefore, we should avoid trying to fit them into ancient concepts or the simple notions of natural ethics. Such narrow naturalism would so constrict these qualities as to destroy them. We have to use natural concepts, to be sure, but we also have to surpass them. This is particularly true of ideas that connote a pagan juridicalism too prone to disrespect human dignity, such as those expressed by the words domination, *imperium*, subjection of persons, good pleasure, and so forth. We must carefully purify such ideas before enclosing sacred things in them. "The kings of the Gentiles lord it over them . . . but you not so" (Luke 22:25). We should be mindful of prudence even when dealing with the best of such terms, those which we have to use most frequently. Whatever good may be found in any type of government, is sure to be found

[28] *Ibid.*, q. 107, a. 1 ad 2; q. 108, a. 1 ad 2.

in the Church of Christ. But the Church possesses such good qualities in a different way, for the goodness of Christ is pre-eminent.

Accordingly ecclesiastical government has all the advantages found in monarchies, such as unified power, continuity of tradition, and the absence of clashes resulting from disagreement. But it has these advantages differently; the unity of the Church is transcendent, for it is founded on the God-man. In Him it is more perfect, more necessary, and more absolute; we may say that the Church is more monarchical than a monarchy. We may also say that it is more democratic than a democracy. It does not stop with giving the people an element of sovereignty, but gives them the whole sovereignty, for it declares that the Master is possessed wholly by each of the faithful. It gives sovereignty not only to the entire corporate body, but to each individual. Each one can say in Christ, "*L'Etat c'est moi.*" Each one carries in his soul the whole of Catholicism and all its life.

In an ordinary society, such a formula would spell the ruin of the society; what collectivity could withstand so absolute an individualism? The prospect of unity crumbling to pieces before the onslaughts of particularist tendencies that escape governmental control, is the peril that threatens democracies. That danger does not exist in the Church. True, the head is in every member of the Church; but the head does not issue commands in each one. That presence of Christ which makes the greatness of every Christian and deepens his personality, also brings about the submission of each one to the officially constituted authority that legislates.

Thus the Church is at once more democratic than democracies and more monarchical than monarchies. Strictly speaking, it is neither monarchy nor democracy, but is only the Church. The Church is unique, without parallel; if it has traits similar to those exhibited in states, it has them in its own way. The several states, lacking the life by which the Church lives, would perish if they tried to imitate the Church too closely.

Ecclesiastical superiors are Christ's vicars; their own personalities should retire. They best display their authority, which is that of Christ, when they efface themselves and let themselves be forgotten. This requires humility and abnegation. They should never think, or allow others to think, that the slightest part of the obedience due to them is based on their virtues, their foresight, or their wisdom; by so acting they would cheapen the principle of their authority and would be fostering schism.

Let them efface themselves, yes; but they should not withdraw into hiding. They must devote all their resources, all their intelligence and sagacity in instructing and learning, all their wisdom, firmness, and strength to the exaltation of Christ's authority. Harmful and insidious as is pomp about their person, a certain magnificence should surround their office. Yet prudence must be consulted; the splendor should be such as befits Christ.

Their authority is so much His that it must be exercised as He would exercise it, with sweetness and charity, with devotedness and humility, in a spirit of service, self-sacrifice, and consecration to others. The aim is not, as it might be in the hypothetical case of a natural order or in the Old Testament, to act for a God remote in His transcendence, but to represent God who does everything possible to be near, small, close by, accessible, and without ostentation: "He emptied Himself" (Phil. 2:7). Haughtiness in ecclesiastical superiors would be a betrayal of the charge laid on them.

The office of teaching is particularly delicate and onerous. The service of truth requires absolute attachment to the truth of Christ, and must be at the same time an ardent love of all truth and also a complete confidence in it. Christian truth is precious because it is supernatural. Any lack of reverence for intelligence, for its precision and even its scruples, toward its efforts and even its gropings, would be a depreciation of that special attitude of mind that is faith. The Church knows and practices this intellectualism, and we need not point out what it has achieved in the sciences, the arts, and philosophy. But what we have to call attention to is the intrepidity of faith it demands, the certitude that all expeditions into the world of the spirit have but to follow a straight route to advance toward Him who is the truth.

To desire nothing but the truth, to cling to it at all costs without being wedded to one's version of it, to be an authentic witness to it— a "martyr" in Greek—requires a whole-hearted integrity and loyalty before which personal interests no longer count. Such an attitude supposes a sort of eagerness to acknowledge one's own errors and past mistakes, that the pure truth may be disengaged (evidently this does not touch points which God Himself guards from the contamination of error), even if some scandal should result. The opposite scandal, occasioned by the eventual discovery of more apt procedures, would be much greater. Intellectual leaders should not be troubled by the fear that confidence in their persons may suffer a setback; what importance attaches to their persons, when Christ and the integrity of truth are at stake?

The teaching office requires even more than that. Ecclesiastical superiors must lead, to be sure, but in the name of another; and this other never ceases to lead in the interior of souls. His leadership is exercised on a plane of boundless range, in accord with His exhaustive knowledge of mankind, its resources and its growth through the centuries, and also in accord with His comprehensive knowledge of God. Human superiors guide us for a few days only, with the few dim rays with which Christ has enlightened their narrow human minds. From every point of view and at every instant the task is greater than they, because of the unfathomable riches of its eternal present, the immense developments it potentially contains, the delicacy of its perpetual adaptation to the changing history of men, and the indescribable energies and overwhelming love at work in it. The task is greater than they, in its initiatives, bold aims, and splendid variety coupled with unity, whose formula is beyond their grasp; yet they have to direct the work without forcing or compromising it. Christ undoubtedly aids them in their labor, but only in that slight part of the action He assigns to them during the days He makes use of them, and without revealing to them the whole of His plan or guaranteeing any more than bare essentials. The future is coming upon us like a vast problem, and the present is full of countless questions; our leaders would like to ask, as Peter did on the shore of the lake: "Lord, and what shall this man do?" [29] Lord, what is to become of the ship I am steering, and what will the unrolling of the centuries bring hereafter? The taciturn reply is ever the same: "What is it to thee?" Why busy yourself with what is not your affair? Do your own job today, another will do his tomorrow, and after that another and another. And through the ministry of them all one alone will achieve the undertaking, and that is Christ.

As they face their task, therefore, superiors have to be unpretentious, reserved, and submissive to Christ who works in them. That is also the attitude they must take—and this is a new requirement—

[29] John 21:21 f.

even before those whom they direct, without ever ceasing to direct them; for Christ resides also in their subjects. Christ who is present in superiors to lead through them, is likewise present in the faithful to live in them. Indeed, we must go so far as to say that Christ dwells more deeply in the faithful, and hence also in superiors regarded as among the faithful, than He does in superiors in their capacity as superiors. He is in the faithful to live in them, to sanctify them interiorly, and to divinize their persons; and He is in superiors to direct the people through them and to exalt their function. If superiors were all in the state of mortal sin, they could still perform the essentials of their office; but if their subjects were all in the state of mortal sin, what is essential to them would be wholly lost for a time. The grace of superiors as such is a *gratia gratis data*, that is, a grace given for the benefit of others; the grace of the subjects as such is a *gratia gratum faciens*, or sanctifying grace; and the latter, as St. Thomas says, is far more excellent than the former.[30] In both cases the dignity is that of Christ, but in different ways: on the one side it exists as in a channel; on the other, it is shared in.

Thus understood, obedience is a guaranty against all heteronomy and all enslavement. It has never been perfectly practiced among men, and therefore cannot produce all its effects. This is also true of ecclesiastical authority, which is not infallible except in definite circumstances, and hence rather rarely. The rest of the time it enjoys God's special assistance, which has modalities and a measure known to God, but which does not necessarily exclude error. To spare it every false step and every mistake, God would have to multiply miracles to an extent that would continually interfere with the order of providence He has chosen, and which would moreover replace by His own activity the activity He has decided to leave to men.

But this is secondary. On principle, if God's plan is faithfully carried out, if superiors really act as Christ's representatives, and if subjects really act as Christ's members, the latter may rejoice in their certainty that by obeying they will never be doing the will of other men. If this marvelous freedom, love, and divinization are seldom realized in daily life, is the fault to be ascribed to Christianity or to Christians?

Besides, even if those who take the place of God assume a haughty air and thus at times prove unequal to their task—and for that, who

[30] *Summa*, Ia IIae, q. 111, a. 5.

could blame them?—obedience can still retain all its freedom and autonomy. That is certain. From time to time at any rate, owing to fatigue, distraction, the burdens of personal cares, or to any other reason, superiors will inevitably, instead of endeavoring to express God's will and of actually expressing it, utter what occurs to their own minds which are always limited in many areas. On the practical question of the attitude to take in such a case, or on the question of representations to be made or the recourse to higher authority that may be legitimate or even obligatory, we need say nothing here. All we have to say it that even in this case obedience to superiors, carried out with the dispositions we have indicated, is accomplishment not of their will but of Christ's will; they have only been intermediaries and instruments.

Christ was well enough acquainted with our poor race to know that imperfections are inevitable. If He nevertheless wished to employ men as His vicars, He was sufficiently wise and powerful to lead us to God even through ill-advised commands. All this was foreseen, permitted, and willed. He still retains the same knowledge and the same will; and therefore He makes the orders of superiors His own. Otherwise He would be giving up His redemptive economy, which consists in saving and guiding men by men. Consequently, even when superiors are wrong, and even, as can happen, when they are responsible for their own error, the subject does the will of Christ by obeying them. When Christ chose them as His vicars, He made room for their shortcomings in His supremely perfect plan. What may not be His will in their decisions, is His will if the over-all plan of the Savior is considered; and the man who obeys in such circumstances submits to no one but to Him who alone is all our life.

Accordingly, if anyone should maintain that authority requires an absolute separation between him who commands and him who obeys, he is ignorant of the nature of authority in the Church. Christ is the only one in the Church who guides His members; and because they are His members, He does not shove them around like pieces of luggage, but guides them and nourishes them and surrounds them with loving care; "for no man ever hated his own flesh." [31]

Obedience of this kind is the task of Christian people. Such obedience is no less difficult than commanding, and involves the same central problem: the difficulty of acting in Christ as members of

[31] Eph. 5:29.

Christ, when we are poor sinners. We shall say only a few words about this difficulty, for we have touched on it repeatedly in the preceding pages.

To obey as a member of Christ, one has to obey with faith and charity, with a magnificent independence of men, in complete attachment to Christ and God. Effort is required to reach these supernatural heights where great freedom reigns in total self-donation to God, where obedience is nobility and exaltation, where we welcome the will of God who has come to divinize the will of man.

To obey as a member of Christ, a man has to will with Christ; and that means that he has to will intensely. Distinction of functions is not division of life; in unity and obedience each member must do his utmost to promote the life of the entire body.

Catholic Action seems to be the providential means of inspiring Christians more and more with this manly attitude and full living of Catholic life. By sharing in the apostolate of the hierarchy, they will become convinced that the task of the Church is their own task, and that Christ has not come down on earth to supplant the activity of His members by Himself or through His representatives, but that on the contrary He wishes to call it forth more and more. Assuredly the whole "body" grows through His power and by following the directions He issues through ecclesiastical superiors; in general, however, this growth is brought about by the activity of the members. "From whom [Christ] the whole body, being compacted and fitly joined together, by what every joint supplieth, according to the operation in the measure of every part, maketh increase of the body, unto the edifying of itself in charity." [32]

"In charity": the work of unity is achieved by the virtue of unity, which is charity. The Church has often been said, during these latter years, to be the school of reverence. That is true. But even more truly, it is the school of charity. In the whole Church there is but one Christ who Himself directs His own growth in charity: *unus Christus aedificans seipsum.*[33]

[32] *Ibid.*, 4:16.
[33] *Ibid.*

CHAPTER XVIII

SANCTIFYING OFFICE OF THE CHURCH:
THE SACRAMENTS

> "He it is that baptizeth."
> John 1:33

THE office of sanctifying is the most important of the functions of the Church. If we speak of it last, the reason is that it sums up and fittingly concludes the whole discussion. It also introduces the subject of grace, which we shall treat of in the following chapters.

Like the other functions, the sanctifying office is a continuation of a corresponding function exercised by Christ in His sacred humanity. This entire chapter will investigate the nature of this continuation. We shall show how the Church which sanctifies is a continuation of the Savior's humanity which sanctifies.

I. THE SACRAMENTAL ECONOMY

The sanctifying power of Christ's humanity is so great that it continues to sanctify throughout the whole expanse and duration of mankind, and therefore continues to function after the Savior's mortal life.

The sacred humanity is holy with the perfect holiness that is suitable for a human nature which is literally the human nature of God. This man who is Christ is truly and really Holiness itself; consequently He must be Holiness itself even in His humanity, though in a way that is proper for a human nature. Therefore His human holiness must be perfect with a perfection that requires all mankind for its full manifestation. Like the sacred humanity itself, Christ's human holiness must be a totality and a first principle in the holiness of the regenerated human race.

Grace was conferred on Him as on a universal source of grace in the genus of those who have grace.[1]

Grace is bestowed on Christ's soul as on a universal source for communicating grace to human nature . . . in the same sense as we may say that the light of the sun is infinite, not indeed in existence, but in the nature of light; for it has all that can pertain to the nature of light.[2]

The grace of Christ has an infinite effect; for it extends to the salvation of the whole human race.[3]

The very excellence of Christ's holiness is an indication that it was meant to embrace and divinize all mankind. And that brings in the Church. The Church diffuses holiness, thus building up for the Saint of saints a social body designed to include all men. The purpose of the Church is to make clear what the hypostatic union of one of the members of the race with Holiness itself signifies for all mankind, and to manifest what is involved for Holiness itself by the fact that, in assuming a human nature, it took to itself the entire race of men.

This diffusion of holiness has two aspects: an interior or spiritual aspect, and an exterior or sensible aspect.[4] The reasons underlying this distinction are the same as those we brought out when discussing the teaching and governing office of the Church. We have little to say about the first aspect here, as we treat it at some length when we come to speak of grace.

The human holiness of Christ was chiefly interior, in His soul, in the mysterious depths of His divinization where His human nature subsisted in the Word. Similarly the diffusion of this holiness is accomplished chiefly within men, in their souls and in the soul of the Church. It is the product of the silent work of grace and of the Holy Spirit. It requires of men an interior docility and cooperation that rises to the surface from within. Each of the faithful, by his zeal and charity, and through the communion of saints, contributes to the growth of all the brethren and of the Church in holiness, through the power of Christ and the union He establishes among them all: "That

[1] St. Thomas, *Summa*, IIIa, q.7, a.9.

[2] *Ibid.*, a.11. We should here think of the sun as it was regarded in the physics of the Middle Ages.

[3] *Ibid.*, obj. 2 and ad 2; and often elsewhere, e.g. *Contra Gent.*, IV, 56.

[4] Cf. St. Thomas, *Summa*, Ia IIae, q.108, a.1. This passage is very instructive concerning the relations between sanctification through charity and the economy of grace and the sacraments. See also *De veritate*, q.27, a.4, part of which we quote in note 6 below.

there might be no schism in the body, but the members might be mutually careful one for another." [5]

In the ordinary sense of the word, the communion of saints is a union of life among the members of the visible Church, thanks to which the sacraments are common, and the prayers, good works, and merits of each redound to the benefit of all. At present we are taking the term in a wider sense, as a union of life among all those who, sharing in Christ's life in any degree, are to that degree united among themselves. Just as the visible Church is the external realization of the mystical body, the communion of saints in the ordinary acceptation is the realization and "body" of the communion of saints as we are now considering it. We believe we must bear the latter meaning in mind if we wish to form an idea of all that is implied in the former.

The second aspect of the diffusion of holiness in the Church will have to be studied at greater length; for it explains the sacramental structure of the Church and the communication of spiritual grace by material media.

We should note that the sacred humanity of Jesus acted in a similar manner. One man influences another by his actions and words; and the Holiness of God became man to influence men in a human way. From the time the humanity of Jesus began to exist, there has been found in the world an empirical reality which, bringing other beings into contact with itself, brings them into contact with holiness; and there are also sensible procedures that produce eternal life, and human words that cause eminent purity and sanctity.

We may say, consequently, that the sacred humanity is the great sacrament, the sacrament par excellence.[6] It is the expression and type, as well as the propagating principle and the overflowing full-

---

[5] See I Cor. 12:25.

[6] This excellence of Christ's humanity as the first and greatest sacrament is implicitly taught by St. Thomas. In *De veritate*, q.27, a.4, he says: "The humanity of Christ is the instrumental cause of justification, a cause that is applied to us spiritually by faith, and corporeally by the sacraments. For Christ's humanity is both spirit and body, in order that we may receive the effect of Christ's sanctification." One of these sacraments, the Eucharist, contains Christ's humanity; and "the other sacraments have some share in the power by which Christ's humanity acts as an instrumental cause of our justification." Cf. the *Summa*, IIIa, q.62, a.5: "The principal efficient cause of grace is God Himself, compared with whom the humanity of Christ is as a united instrument, and the sacrament as a detached instrument. Therefore the power of saving must flow into the sacraments from His humanity." Cf. *ibid.*, q.60, a.6; q.62, a.3; Ia IIae, q.114, a.1 and ad 1, 2.

ness of divinized humanity. It is a sign and a cause of divinization and grace; hence a sacrament. It is the symbol of the work of consecration which God performs on earth, and the visible form taken by divine love and by the life of grace He infuses into man: "a symbol of a sacred thing and the visible form of an invisible grace"; [7] therefore it is a sacrament.

It is such in its substance and in itself; but only by virtue of the divinity and the hypostatic union. Therefore it acts sacramentally through the received and dependent causality which is known as instrumental causality, the properly Christological and theandric causality we spoke of in an earlier chapter. This causality is found in all Christ's human acts, for it pertains to the very substance of the sacred humanity; and that is why the sacred humanity effects the salvation and divinization of the world by all that it does as well as by all that it endures.[8]

Since this causality is found in a human nature, it goes into action in a way appropriate for the human nature to which it belongs, and therefore acts more fully in those actions that are directed to the end of the Incarnation, such as the actions of remitting sins, conferring grace and peace, and the like. But especially, if what we wrote above is correct, it acts with supreme power in the supreme act of Christ's humanity, that is, in the act of dying.

All the sacraments operate with the power of Christ's passion; [9] therefore the sacrament par excellence is the one that unceasingly perpetuates the sacrifice of Calvary. Christ is enduringly present in His Church through the sacrament of His death, as the fountainhead of the whole sacramental economy.

The visible Church, as the continuation of Christ's humanity, perpetuates the sacramental character of the sacred humanity as the sacrament par excellence. Like Him and in Him, it is a sacrament essentially and in its very structure; it is the appearance of the divine in the human, the visible form taken by grace to be more easily and always within reach of men, that is, to be given to them more abundantly and hence to be grace in a more available way. The Church is a sacrament in all its acts; its life is sacramental, its worship, its dogmas, and the example of the faithful are sources of sanctifying

[7] Council of Trent, Sess. XIII, c. 3 (Denz., 876).
[8] St. Thomas, *Summa*, IIIa, q. 48, a. 6.
[9] *Ibid.*, q. 62, a. 5.

power. "You are the salt of the earth. . . . So let your light shine before men, that they may see your good works and glorify your Father who is in heaven." [10] The Church is fully sacramental in certain acts that express it best, in certain acts entrusted to it by Christ to be His own acts in the Church. This is especially the case with regard to one of these acts, which is pre-eminently the act of the Church and at the same time is literally Christ Himself and His sacrifice.

Christ, indeed, always acts in the Church, for the Church is His body. Ordinarily, however, He acts in the Church with an action that belongs to His members and is shaped and limited by their peculiarities and miseries. But in the acts we are now referring to He acts with an action that is exclusively His own, an action which shows that He alone is the first principle and the giver of life in the organism of grace. In the other acts, the sacramental power of the Church is somewhat attenuated; in these acts, that power is exercised in its pure state and is concentrated. These acts are the seven sacraments.

Accordingly the sacraments must be defined as the main acts of the Church, the acts it performs with its full power as the continuation of Christ the Sanctifier. Or, if we prefer, they are the acts by which the Church, the body of Christ, fully actuates itself as the body of Christ, the body of holiness, the body of grace; or again, they are the actions of Christ the Sanctifier living in the Church.

The sacraments are truly signs and causes of grace, as we shall soon explain. But according to the line of thought we are pursuing, this is a consequence, and the definition expressed by this function is a conclusion to be arrived at. In this book, which is a study of the mystical body, the primary feature of the sacraments is the fact that they are the perfect actions of this mystical body. Theology teaches that in themselves they are rites having a matter and a form. We may add that these entire rites are in turn a sort of matter that receives its dignity, its power, and its ultimate sacramental "form" from the fact that they are effected by the Church and according to the intention of the Church; and this is what makes them what they are.[11] This ultimate form, this appropriation of these actions by the Church,

---

[10] Matt. 5:13, 16.
[11] Council of Trent, Sess. VII, *De sacramentis*, can. 11; *De baptismo*, can. 4 (Denz., 854, 860).

can be said to be expressed in one way or another by the sacramental formula, that is, by the form of the sacrament in the usual sense of the word.

When a sacrament is administered, the one who acts is the Church, and is also Christ who continues to be an efficient cause of holiness on earth. The minister of the sacrament steps forward only to efface himself, by lending his hands and lips to another who acts through him; for it is this other who acts in the continuation of Himself among men. This other is the only one who interests us here; in fact, He is the one who consecrates and baptizes, as the Fathers repeated so often.[12] We have nothing to say about the powers the ministers may have; mention of such powers would be absurd. Even the Blessed Virgin, the saint among saints, does not figure in the sacramental formulas. We pray to her before, we pray to her afterward, we pray to her on all occasions; but not just then. For then we do not pray; someone acts; Jesus acts. Even the deprecative formulas which are sometimes found are recited with an absolute assurance; He who then speaks authentically in His "body," in His members, speaks with authority,[13] knowing well that He cannot fail to be heard by the Father.[14]

A sacrament is not, in the first instance, an action of God; it is an action of Christ who continues to live on in the Church and who continues His redemption and His ascent toward the Father in His mystical body. This fact permits us to see immediately what the sacraments chiefly accomplish. *Unumquodque agit in quantum est actu; omne agens agit sibi simile:* everything acts so far as it is in act, and every agent produces an effect similar to itself. Since that which acts is the Church as fully actuated, the product of its action is this same Church, this Church in its members, the incorporation and attachment of members to the Church. The main activity of the mystical body effects the propagation, preservation, and growth of this mystical body, according to the various aspects and organs through which that activity is exercised. In truth, how could its action fail to produce such an effect? It produces the Christian as Christian, as a genuine member of that reality in the order of grace which is Christ continued.

[12] See *The Whole Christ*, Index, s.v. Sacraments.
[13] Mark 1:22.
[14] John 11:42.

That is the first effect of a sacrament: to admit a man into the Church absolutely or to perfect his union with the Church in some particular manner, to confer a state of the Church, a condition, a way of being that is membership in the Church or an aspect of such membership. And the sacraments produce such an effect really, not merely according to outward appearance; for the Church is not merely an external thing. Its exterior is but the expression and the body of its invisible life, which is grace and divinization in Christ. A purely external link would not link anyone with the Church. As the Church is essentially a thing of the soul, the link joining one to the Church has to be a thing of the soul; as the Church is the organism of grace, the link has to be forged in the depths of the spirit where grace resides. We can belong to other societies by an external bond, for they themselves are external; but we cannot belong to the Church unless we are united to it by an internal bond, for the Church is a living organism.

We believe that this is what theologians have in mind when they speak of the "adornment of the soul," of the "real or intentional disposition for grace," of the production or the further actuation of the baptismal character as the first effect of the sacraments.[15] A link with such a thing as the Church has to have all these traits.

This union, this "adornment" is not produced in the same way by all the sacraments, as we shall point out later. Three sacraments in particular confer it absolutely, causing it to exist where it had not existed before. These are baptism, confirmation, and holy orders. Baptism and confirmation bring about the incorporation of the member into the body, either as an individual or by title of social competence. Holy orders empowers a member to admit other members; it does not admit the member who receives it (as he is already a member), but through him provides for the future admission of others, for it confers on him the power to insert them into the body.

We believe that incorporation in such definitive form is the character which these sacraments impress; it realizes all that is implied in the notion of character. In the first place, it is a sign or mark distinguishing those who belong to the Church from those who do not belong. Whatever outward manifestation it may involve, it is, like the Church, an interior thing, a thing of the soul. And, like the Church, it is not formally grace, but is necessarily connected with

[15] Cf. St. Thomas, *In IV Sent.*, d. 1, q. 1, a. 4, quaestiunc. 1.

grace. Furthermore, to be truly a link with the Church, it must be indefectible, perpetual, and definitive, as the Church is indefectible and ultimate. Thus it is a spiritual and indelible sign imprinted on the soul, and is distinct from grace; these are precisely the properties of the character, according to the Council of Trent.[16]

The notion of the character given by St. Thomas seems at first sight to be somewhat different. He says that the character is "a certain sharing in the priesthood of Christ, derived from Christ Himself," a participation that empowers one to receive the action of this priesthood and to exercise its functions.[17] But when we reflect that Christ continues His priesthood in the Church precisely as the cause of our sanctification, we see that connection with the Church involves connection with Christ's priesthood.[18] However, we are insisting more on the social aspect of our union with the Church, as that is more in accord with the point of view governing our discussion. The Angelic Doctor also insists on this aspect when he shows that the character is like enrollment in an army [19] or fellowship in public worship.[20]

The first and immediate effect of the sacraments is union with the Church, a definite position in the Church, and eventually the character. The actual production of grace follows, and is more important in the order of dignity, even though second in the logical order of becoming. For this production is not the essential effect. The proof is that some of the sacraments can really exist, that is, can be validly conferred, even though they do not produce grace because of some obstacle. That would be impossible if their essence consisted in the production of grace. On the other hand, these sacraments cannot truly exist unless they produce the respective characters that confer definite positions in the Church.

Although the Church to which the character joins a man is not formally and from every point of view identical with the life of grace and with the continuation of Christ in mankind, it is truly and ontologically the body of this life and grace, and the external form

[16] Sess. VII, *De sacramentis*, can. 9 (Denz., 852).

[17] *Summa*, IIIa, q.63, especially a.3.

[18] This point of view avoids the difficulty that the greatest effect of Christ's priesthood is received in baptism, when the prospective recipient has as yet no character.

[19] *Summa*, IIIa, q.63, a.1; a.3 and ad 2, 3. The comparison is quite traditional.

[20] *Ibid.*, a.1–3.

of this continuation. Consequently union with the Church leads of itself [21] to union with Christ, with the Son, and with the Trinity. The position in the Church to which one is assigned is a state that of itself brings holiness and grace. By conferring this state and this union, the sacraments *ex opere operato* confer grace, holiness, divinization, and divine adoption. Just as the most excellent thing in the Church is the soul and the divinized life, with which everything else is compared as a body, so the most excellent thing in the sacraments and that which almost obscures everything else in them is this power of conferring grace.

Thus the definition we proposed at the outset comes back to the traditional definition, which is the best. The sacraments are signs and causes of grace; they are signs which cause the grace they signify. A sacrament is:

a symbol of a sacred thing and a visible form of invisible grace; [22] a thing falling under the senses, which by God's institution has the power both to signify and to effect holiness and justice; [23] a sign of a sacred thing that makes men holy.[24]

If anyone should say that the sacraments of the New Law do not contain the grace they signify, or that they do not confer grace itself on those who set up no obstacle, and therefore should imply that they are only outward signs of grace or justice received through faith and certain marks of the Christian profession by which believers are distinguished among men from unbelievers: let him be anathema.[25]

The digression we have made enables us to see how the sacraments produce grace and how their salutary action fits in with the general plan of salvation. They produce grace by bringing men into this general plan, and by connecting the soul with the genuine and secure channel of grace.

We spoke above about sacraments that are truly conferred yet do not actually give grace, "sacraments validly received but unfruitful," as they are called. We may now examine how their functioning is to be explained. The dispositions strictly necessary for being joined

---

[21] *Ex opere operato.*
[22] Council of Trent, Sess. XIII, c.3 (Denz., 876).
[23] *Catechismus Romanus*, II, c.1, q.11.
[24] St. Thomas, *Summa*, IIIa, q.60, a.2.
[25] Council of Trent, Sess. VII, *De sacramentis*, can. 6 (Denz., 849).

to the visible Church are less perfect than the dispositions strictly necessary for receiving grace. It may happen that the first set of conditions is met while the second is not. Then, in virtue of the sacrament, only the first effect will be produced; the soul will be admitted into the Church or will be given a definite position in the Church, but will not receive grace. Such a situation is abnormal and even violent: union with the body of grace without the accompaniment of grace. As long as this state of affairs lasts—and it will last forever if a character has been imprinted—it will be a title to grace and an exigency for grace. Therefore, as soon as the obstacle is removed, grace will be released. Grace will flow in virtue of the sacrament, without the necessity of a new rite, through the intermediary of the position in the Church to which the soul has been admitted.

The action of the sacraments is patterned on the action of the visible Church and has a similar structure. Therefore a sacrament is the proper act of the sanctifying Church. The Church is a body that has a holy soul; a sacrament is an action that unites one to this body and therefore, by way of consequence, to this holiness. God has sanctified all mankind, not by an invisible decision but by a visible Man and His visible actions. Similarly the sacraments sanctify each individual person in the visible continuation of this Man, not by an invisible action of God but by a visible action of the Church.

Sacramental grace, the grace conferred on the soul by the sacraments when a person is inserted into the Church, has the essential trait of being a grace of the Church. It is a grace of union with all men and has social implications. It is a grace, sanctifying or actual, that sanctifies by incorporating one into the Church and that disposes one to action in collaboration with the whole of regenerated mankind. It is an ecclesiastical grace.

In the present order, every grace is a grace of the Church, because every grace unites the recipient to God who has united Himself to men; in other words, it unites man to God in the God-man and in the continuation of the God-man that is the Church. By an inherent tendency it gravitates toward the Church to which it is linked by an invisible bond, and that tendency is not at rest until the bond is also visible.

The grace of the sacraments, sacramental grace, not only moves in the direction of the Church, but also comes from the Church; it is connected visibly as well as invisibly with the Church; it owes everything to the fact that it belongs to the "body of Christ," just as the holiness of Christ's humanity owes everything to the hypostatic union. Hence it is more perfectly a grace than non-sacramental grace. It is not necessarily more intense, but through its double connection, visible and invisible, with Christ, it shares more fully in Christ who is still living on earth, and therefore better verifies the notion of *gratia Christi*. Consequently all grace, by the very fact that it is grace, is related to sacramental grace, as it is related to the visible Church.

In content and nature, sacramental grace is primarily and essentially sanctifying grace, for it is primarily the grace that makes one a living member of the God-man, and that is what sanctifying grace does. But this sanctifying grace, being a grace of union with Christ and the Church, varies according to the degrees of union and the positions in the Church the several sacraments give. This point will be developed in the sections devoted to the individual sacraments.

Yet, we must add, *prius est esse quam esse sic;* though union may vary, it is still union. Consequently all the sacraments, even the sacraments of the living, are able in certain circumstances to produce first grace. Moreover sacramental grace includes actual graces, which correspond to the special end of each sacrament and to the modalities of the state it produces.

Actual graces are given by God at suitable times, and we can conceive that the sacraments have only a moral causality in conferring them, by investing man with a sort of juridical title for receiving them at the moment appointed by God in His generosity. But the procedure will appear more unified if we bear in mind the attachment to the Church and the state which are the first effect of the sacraments. The Church is a living organism in which actual grace is an interior energy and a sort of power of growth. This grace comes from God, as the Church comes from God; but it comes through the Church. By inserting a man into the Church, the sacraments put him in contact with the source of actual graces, and make available for him the graces that correspond exactly to the union the sacraments confer. In the same way the insertion of a member into a physical body does not place that member in the blood stream, but enables it to benefit indefinitely by the circulation of the blood in the manner that best suits it.

When we speak of the essence of the sacraments and their effects, we are inevitably led to touch on the kind of causality they exercise. In technical language, this is a causality *ex opere operato*, a causality that resides in the sacraments, and not in the subject who receives them or in the minister who confers them.

In point of fact, as we have said, the sacraments are the actions of God and Christ and of Christ in the Church; the actions of God who united and still unites Himself to men; the actions of Christ who is present on earth today to sanctify the men of today. Therefore they contain all that is necessary to unite us to God in Christ and to Christ in the Church, and hence to bestow ecclesiastical life, Christian life, divinized life. They cannot but sanctify and give grace. Accordingly we have to recognize that their causality is fully as real, efficient, and physical as any natural causality.

They possess such power in virtue of their institution by God. But this institution is not a mere decree belonging to the past; it is somehow continued in the very structure of the sacraments. They are the actions of the God-man in His continued life, and perpetually actuate for the benefit of men God's will to divinize them in the God-man and in the Church, which is the continuation of the God-man.

Their causality is perpetually dependent and received; it is an instrumental causality. But when we reflect that they are actions of the mystical body and of God who gives Himself to us today, we perceive that the attachment to God which makes them instruments is essential to them and gives them in Christ the power to produce their most sublime effects, union with God and deification. The instrumental quality found in Christ is perpetuated in them, and retains the same excellence and the same properties. To understand their action, we have to consider it in Christ.

Surely we do not have to point out that when their action is envisaged in this way, it has absolutely nothing in common with magic. Magic is an idle claim to control divine forces and make them work in man's place; belief in the sacraments is faith in God who has given Himself to us unreservedly, and an overwhelming sense of gratitude, humility, and love in the presence of such unparalleled generosity.

When the sacraments are regarded in this way, their connection with human action becomes clear. If we were to think of nothing but their administration, apart from every other consideration, we might fancy that they are incompatible with the idea of human cooperation, making it useless in the measure that they are efficacious. But if we regard them in the humanity of Christ, the first and total sacrament, we see that quite the contrary is true. By taking this humanity to Himself, God has made it the great active principle of the supernatural order, the living and free instrument which He uses to accomplish His work.

Throughout the entire process of its development, the supernatural has to remain what it was at its origin, the assumption and exaltation of human energy by divine power. The Almighty comes among men in a continuation of Christ's coming to us, not so much to accomplish great things by Himself as to enable mankind to accomplish them; and that is the greater achievement.

If the sacraments united us directly to God, we might be led to fancy that they transport us to our last end through the activity of God alone, thus leaving us in repose. But they unite man to God by uniting him to Christ and the Church, to Christ who is still striving and toiling in the Church. Consequently they engage us in action, an action that originates in God but is performed by man; and the real sanctification they impart has to be freely and laboriously assimilated by man who receives it; for man must achieve self-realization in action and suffering, by the power which God confers in the sacraments.

The sacraments are the means granted to man for taking part in the divine action and receiving grace; they are also the means God employs for enlisting human action and cooperation. When man administers them and makes them minister to him, he lays hold of God, indeed, but of God as He is in Christ; and God, in turn, lays hold of man, arouses him to supernatural works, and makes him capable of divine activity.

As the sacraments are the perfect and typical acts of the Church, they are the type of Christian activity. Far from being a suppression of Christian activity, they are its summit, the high point at which Christian activity shares abundantly and quite humanly, and hence spiritually as well as empirically, in divine action. By their means Christian activity is adequately and authentically joined to the activity of Christ and therefore of God. Like the water that flows down from snow-capped peaks into valleys, the life and power of Christ flow down from these lofty heights into all Christian conduct, and there become fervor, zeal, charity, and good works. We have to witness this flowering of activity to appreciate the reserves of energy and the incitements to effort that are conveyed to the soul by these sacred rites, and to realize how false we would be to them were we to hold aloof from toil and sacrifice.

True Christian life has apparently never yielded to such a temptation. The Church has sanctioned modes of life that allowed little room for the sacraments, as, for example among certain fathers of the desert.[26] But it has never approved modes of life that would make little of charity, zeal, and sincere love for God and one's fellow men, in order that one might spend the whole day in receiving the sacraments, going to confession and Communion, and celebrating Mass after Mass. The positive law of the Church has always guaranteed the good order of Christian life. If the sacraments, by themselves alone, were the most abundant source of sanctity, a man would do the best thing possible by receiving them with maximum frequency, and the Church would never dream of restraining so salutary an eagerness.

By giving the sacraments to men, God has conferred on them the principle of their supernatural activity. Possession of the source of activity is essential to man in the natural order; what is freedom if not the power to determine one's activity for oneself, to have the *causalitas sui actus?* God has designed the same procedure for the supernatural order, that this order might be perfectly human and that divinized mankind might be no less provided for than simple mankind. God has carried out His design by giving man the sacraments, the means of starting the flow of grace which is the beginning of every supernatural act, the means of awakening and arising in response to the call of God, who initiates every good movement.

Why are there seven sacraments, and not more or fewer? God and Christ have decided this matter, and nothing proves that they could not have decided otherwise. What is certain is that these seven sacraments correspond beautifully to the various functions Christian life is called on to perform.

St. Thomas brings this out in the *Summa* when he discusses the

[26] This resulted, not from contempt of the sacraments or exaggerated reverence for them, but from sheer impossibility. In these cases, which are after all rare, the saintly hermits were in contact with the sacraments through the communion of saints.

life of grace that animates every Christian, the sin that threatens this life, the virtues that should adorn it, and the vices that oppose it.[27] Our own task is to bring out this same truth in relation to an idea we have shown to be essential to the definition of a sacrament, that is, the fact that it joins us to the Church. Our development will involve several very slight modifications of the theory proposed by St. Thomas: we have to insist more on the social aspect of the sacraments.

Union with the Church may be regarded either as a process that is being effected in various ways, or as a fact that is already accomplished and that endures thereafter. This suggests the first division to be made; it places six sacraments on one side, and the Eucharist on the other.

Among the sacraments that produce union with the Church, some have to do with the individual union of each Christian, and others with the union of other Christians, that is, the power to bring other men into union with the Church. The latter are the two sacraments of matrimony and holy orders. The former, those which effect the union of the individual, can join a person to the Church on earth regarded as it is here on earth, or regarded as a preparation and entrance to the Church in heaven. The sacrament of extreme unction finds place in the second category; the first category contains the sacraments of initiation, the initiation of the individual as such, and the initiation of the individual into the sphere of social action and influence; these are baptism and confirmation. This category also contains the sacrament of restoration, which is penance.

We shall come back to these characteristics of the various sacraments when we treat of each in turn. For the present, it is enough to have seen how the very notion of sacrament suggests the reason for their numbering and grouping.

II. Six Sacraments

A. BAPTISM

Baptism is the sacrament of the successive production of the Church, the sacrament by which the Church, the sacrament par excellence, provides for its own existence and extension, the act by

[27] *Summa*, IIIa, q.65, a.1; cf. *In IV Sent.*, d.2, q.1, a.2, 3; *Contra Gent.*, IV, 58.

which the Church acquires members and creates Christians. The most ancient documents we possess insist on this social aspect.

As the body is one and hath many members, and all the members of the body, whereas they are many, yet are one body, so also is Christ. For in one Spirit were we all baptized into one body.[28]

As many of you as have been baptized in Christ, have put on Christ. There is neither Jew nor Greek; there is neither bond nor free; there is neither male nor female. For you are all one in Christ Jesus.[29]

The Creeds bring out the same aspect, generally by mentioning baptism after the Church. Thus the Creed of Nicaea-Constantinople declares: "And [I believe] in one holy, Catholic, and apostolic Church. I confess one baptism for the remission of sins." [30] And the Council of Florence asserts in the decree *Pro Armenis:* "The first place among all the sacraments is held by holy baptism, which is the door of the spiritual life; for by it we are made members of Christ and of His body which is the Church." [31]

To unite one to the Church, to make one a member of the Church, to place one in a state of belonging to the Church, is, we should say, the primary, necessary, and essential effect of baptism; the sacrament cannot fail to produce this effect as soon as it is conferred. But before it can join a person to solidarity in justice, the sacrament must rescue him from his previous solidarity in evil. In the order of logical succession, the first effect of baptism will be the destruction of original sin and all other sins. By joining a man to the Church, the sacrament joins him to Christ in His union with men, that is, to Christ who gives Himself to mankind in His passion and in the Mass.[32] And Christ who thus gives Himself is Christ who destroys original sin and all sins. By uniting us to Christ, finally, baptism unites us to the Son, to God, to the Trinity; it incorporates us into Christ

[28] See I Cor. 12:12 f.; cf. 1:12-16.

[29] Gal. 3:27 f.; cf. Eph. 4:3-16; Col. 2:12-19.

[30] Denz., 86. The same is found in certain forms of the Apostles' Creed (Denz., 3, 9); likewise in the Creed of Epiphanius, of the Eleventh Council of Toledo, and of St. Leo IX (Denz., 14, 287, 347).

[31] Denz., 696.

[32] The connection between baptism and the Mass is brought out in the liturgy of the vigils of Easter and Pentecost, and also in the ceremonies of adult baptism; cf. *Rituale Romanum,* tit. II, c.4, no. 52; *Codex iuris canonici,* 753, 2.

and confers on us divine adoption, grace, the supernatural life, and the indwelling of the whole Trinity.

Therefore the grace that is given, the grace in which the Christian is born anew and is made a Christian, is a grace of redemption, a grace of death to self, of abnegation, and of conflict; it makes one a member of the Church militant, of the redemption that is still going on. "All we who are baptized in Christ Jesus are baptized in His death. For we are buried together with Him by baptism into death; that as Christ is risen from the dead by the glory of the Father, so we also may walk in newness of life." [33]

This grace is our entrance into the supernatural order, for it is our entrance into the Church, the great sacrament. Hence it is essentially social. Baptism is God's act because it is the act of Christ and of the Church, and it is the act of the Church because it is the act of the whole of Catholicism, a liturgy, a public cult. Even the private baptism of a new-born infant that dies immediately thereafter is administered in the name of all Christianity; and in the solemn ceremony of baptism on the vigils of Easter and Pentecost we can observe how the entire assemblage of the faithful welcomes the new member into their society through the ministry of the celebrant.[34]

B. CONFIRMATION

According to the Roman Catechism, confirmation is the sacrament that completes baptism; it makes perfect Christians out of those who are already Christians. We are of the opinion that its primary effect is to unite one to the Church as an adult, to confer the status of adulthood and of social value in the Church.

Since confirmation joins one to the Church, it gives grace: a grace of maturity and hence of fruitful activity, which acts and diffuses itself through faith, hope, and charity; especially charity. Baptism had given this grace radically; confirmation gives it formally and directly. It qualifies the recipient for a personal apostolate, assigns

[33] Rom. 6:3 f.

[34] Baptism is so essentially public that the older Scholastics did not even believe that infants could be baptized before their entrance into human society, that is, before their emergence into the world; how could they who had not yet been born be reborn? In later ages moral theologians have declared that when circumstances warrant, such infants, in danger of death, must be baptized, even if the validity of the baptism is doubtful; so necessary is this sacrament. And they are right; there is only one economy of salvation, and it has its visible form and means in the visible Church and the sacraments.

him the mission to render public testimony of Christ,[35] and empowers him to cooperate with his fellow Catholics for the diffusion of the interior life. A person is confirmed to propagate, defend, and teach his religion, not through the exercise of authority, but out of the superabundance of his own life, by the fervor of his charity, the contagion of his intimate convictions, his hope, and his enthusiasm, and by the communication of life that characterizes adulthood.[36] As this fervor, zeal, and maturity of individual and social life are attributed to the Holy Spirit, we must say that the Holy Spirit, bearing His rich offer of gifts and graces, confers confirmation.

Briefly, through the sacrament of confirmation a man becomes a perfect Christian on the level of personal life, in all that he is and can accomplish by his personal supernatural life.

The priesthood also confers a universal sanctifying mission, but in a different way. The ordained priest exercises ecclesiastical priesthood, the priesthood of the whole Church and of Christ Himself, priesthood in the strict sense of the word. Confirmation involves a mission to be carried out by the so-called priesthood of the laity, a derived priesthood that is a sort of membership in the strict priesthood, and that is related to the latter as a Christian and a member is related to the whole body and the whole Church.

The priestly office is a delegation to offer sacrifice, to present the people's worship to God, and to bring back graces from God. Its integral exercise requires duly appointed ministers. In the natural order, such ministers merely perform publicly what each man is obliged to do in his private life; they are the outward expression of a universal, interior priesthood. In the supernatural order, everything is brought under the headship of Christ. In this order, the priesthood is more exalted, and the external priesthood is more fully authorized; internally and externally, in the way suitable for it, it is the priesthood of Christ.

The priesthood of Christ, like His grace and His sacrifice, was a perfection [37] that was to be perpetuated in mankind to bring men to the full realization of their human capabilities; as St. Thomas says, it was a sort of first cause or principle in the order of priesthood, "the source of every priesthood." [38] Christ's priesthood is perpetu-

---

[35] *Decretum pro Armenis* (Denz., 697).

[36] See St. Thomas, *Summa*, IIIa, q. 72, *passim*.

[37] *Ibid.*, q. 22, a. 1 ad 3.

[38] *Ibid.*, a. 4.

ated in two ways that correspond to the structure of the Church which is the continuation of Him. It is perpetuated, first, in a priesthood that is the prolongation of Christ's priesthood, that has all the power of the latter, and that performs certain sanctifying actions as effectively as Christ's own priesthood could. This is priesthood in the ordinary sense of the term, and is conferred by ordination. Secondly, Christ's priesthood is perpetuated in certain deficient participations by which His members share in His sacerdotal power in a measure suitable to their position; their participation varies with the degree of their membership, and therefore depends on the intensity and the particular conditions which the supernatural life has in them.

Omne agens agit sibi simile; all life bears a resemblance to him who gave it. Since Christ as priest gives life to His members, their life will have a sacerdotal quality. The members cannot reproduce the acts which their High Priest performed with all His power; only the sacrament of holy orders confers such power. But they can perform similar acts in the lesser fashion that is within the competency of the members. Therefore we may say that the sacrament of confirmation invests Christians with a universal power of santification that is truly their own: the power and the duty of Catholic prayer, of Catholic edification, and of intercession for all men by way of merit and supplication.

Therefore this sacrament equips men for Catholic Action. This apostolate must, of course, be under the direction of Christ through the hierarchy. But Catholics are fitted and qualified for it by divine law and by a quasi-natural ecclesiastical law. The confirmed Catholic is responsible for his part in promoting Catholic holiness, in redeeming the world, and in evangelizing the earth. He must contribute his effort, not by usurping the functions of the head, but by collaborating in a way suitable for a member who is fully formed and who shares in the life of the whole. To live his own life, he must make the well-being of the whole his own affair, for the two are inseparable. His life comes from the Church; likewise his fellowship in the life of the whole and his part in Catholic Action come from the Church; thus his work is officially authorized.

We said above that the Church and Christ are the great sacraments, in a wide sense of the word. Since the Christian is a member of the Church, especially after he has been confirmed, he also is a sacrament in a similar wide sense, though in a lesser, derived way. He ought to be a sign and a witness of grace, which is Christ's life in the world; he ought to assist in the propagation of this life; he ought to be a living sermon of the hidden mystery that makes him alive. All this means that he is to be a sign and cause of grace, a symbol of a hidden reality, a visible form of invisible grace, that is, a sacrament. Yet, we repeat, he is a sacrament only in a wide sense of the word, a sacrament that acts not *ex opere operato* but *ex opere operantis*, not through the administration of an impersonal rite but through the influence of an energetic inner life.

These comparisons may seem to be a trifle forced, and they would be harmful if they led us to overlook certain necessary distinctions. But they serve a purpose if they make clear how the organism of the supernatural life is one in the multiplicity of its parts.

The three characters imprinted by baptism, confirmation, and holy orders differ, yet all three involve union with Christ in the Church. Baptism is the basic character; the other two may be regarded as an enhancement. Confirmation reinforces the baptismal character to the maximum degree on the level of personal life and activity; holy orders reinforces it to the maximum degree on the level of functional operation, or rather raises it to that level.

To perceive more clearly the greatness of the character imprinted by confirmation, we need but recall the general teaching of theology that this sacrament was instituted at the promise of Pentecost [39] and was first conferred on Pentecost itself,[40] that is, at the great outpouring of the Spirit that was like a universal baptism, the baptism of the whole Church, and the inception of a universal priesthood: the inauguration of the work of sanctification, and the establishment of the apostolic and episcopal body. This outpouring is what animated the mystical body; the Holy Spirit, the Lord and Life-giver, is bestowed on everyone who is confirmed. On Pentecost the Holy Spirit was given to the whole Church that then existed,[41] and not to the apostles alone.[42] The Holy Spirit made real apostles of those who were already priests and bishops. The perfection that comes with confirmation makes him who receives the sacrament a fully-formed

[39] Cf. John 14:16, 26; 15:26; 16:7–12; Luke 24:49; Acts 1:4–8.
[40] Council of Florence, *Decretum pro Armenis* (Denz., 697).
[41] Acts 1:13 ff.; cf. 4:23–31. Christian piety has always represented the Blessed Virgin in the midst of the apostles.
[42] Yet the apostles are mentioned emphatically. Cf. Acts 1:13, 25; 2:7, 14.

member of Christ and animates him fully with the Spirit: that is, as we repeat for the last time, in the order of personal life, not of public office.

C. PENANCE

Living union with the Church, which is effected by baptism and confirmation, is restored by the sacrament of penance, provided that it needs to be restored; and penance restores it integrally. In consequence, the sacrament of penance restores our union with Christ and God, and completely recovers grace for us.

Penance supposes that a preceding union has been impaired. The severance can never be absolute, for the character imprinted on the Christian is indelible. But it can more or less closely approach an absolute break. It comes closest to an absolute break in the case of those sins which the ancient penitential discipline regarded as capital and canonical, and, in our own day, in the case of sins involving infamy or excommunication. In these cases, too, the sacrament of penance displays its full power and best manifests its range. Such are the cases we have mainly in mind in the following exposition.

However, we shall speak of all cases subject to the tribunal of penance. For all sins, even the slightest of venial sins and the traces of past sins that leave intact the bond with the visible Church, tend to weaken this bond, which ought to be a bond of charity; sins have the effect of destroying charity, of cooling its fervor, or of facilitating its loss.

Every sin is in some way a departure from God who has drawn so near to men. But God draws near to man in Christ, and Christ is now dwelling among men in the Church. Therefore every sin is a withdrawal from Christ and the Church; it is an offense against the body of the Church, because it is an offense against the soul of the Church.

If it is true even in the natural order that no one sets himself in opposition to God unless he is in opposition with himself, the same is yet truer in the supernatural order, in which union between God and man is closer. Every sin in a baptized person is an offense against his baptism, a violation of his character as a member of Christ, and hence an attack on the whole body which is the Church.

As God is offended in the Church, He also grants pardon in the Church, and the priest who absolves the sinner represents God by representing the entire Church.[43] We should not be surprised to see the Church intervene in the deepest recesses of the consciences of its members, in their most secret relations with God and their own supernatural life. Nothing is more the affair of the Church regarded as the body of Christ and the union of all souls with God in Christ, than these sacred intimacies.

God and Christ are visibly present in the Church alone; hence they visibly grant forgiveness in the Church alone. This is the way they wish to forgive, for this is the way established by the Incarnation. God and Christ also grant pardon in other ways, as is clear; the whole supernatural order, along with the natural order so far as it is caught up in the supernatural, is in fact an immense pardon, for it is an immense redemption. But to give this pardon more efficaciously to man, God has made it visible in the man Christ; and this sacrament is no other than Christ who, with a visible action, grants forgiveness yet today. He is the authentic body of complete forgiveness, because, though God, He has placed Himself for all time and in a human way within the reach of man. All divine pardons granted by God tend by their inherent dynamism in the direction of complete forgiveness; they all lead to union with God, and this union is effected in the Church and in the sacrament of penance. And therefore all those who, in response to grace, sincerely wish to be forgiven by God, turn to the Church, even though they may not be aware of it. When the Church declares that no sin is remitted without the desire of the sacrament, it declares what it is, and what the sacrament and divine forgiveness are.

The Church is a body, and the faithful are its members; is not the restoration of a member chiefly the work of the body? As a member is a member through the body, he cannot regain the status of a living member except through the body. The life of a member is a continuous influx received from the Church; restoration of this life must also be an influx. This life is a fellowship in the whole of Catholic life; it can be restored to a fallen member only through the initiative of Catholic life which again takes hold of the member and reincorporates him into itself.

Yet the member's own efforts are strictly necessary. Although

---

[43] This is brought out by many ancient writers, beginning with the famous passage in Tertullian, *De poenitentia*, 10 (PL, I, 1245). Some of these texts may raise difficulties, but they are very instructive.

the restoration of a member is mainly the work of the body, is it also the work of the member. What takes place is not the creation of a new member, but the repairing and reanimation of an old member. The member regains life and truly lives anew, but in dependence on the organism. Hence the member must be active and do his share; he must do what is required on his part to recover life. Yet his efforts would avail nothing toward the recovery of life without the whole body. Baptism, which gives the member his initial existence as a member, presupposes the lack of membership; all the prerequisite conditions are external to the sacrament itself. But the sacrament of penance is a restoration, and therefore supposes membership, as well as a certain activity on the member's part, as a preliminary condition before it can be administered. The member's acts dispose him for the effect which the sacrament is to cause, and are a sort of reparation striven for by the member himself, corresponding to the restoration which the body will effect.

Since the member is a free agent, he must regret and detest his sin, resolving never to commit it again. That is his indispensable part in the action, and of its nature tends to promote the member's reinstatement. The grace that comes to fruition in the sacrament is at work in the member's efforts.

But the member's part in the action has a necessary relation to the body. The sinner must exhibit his contrition to the Church, and therefore must confess his sins. He must present himself for reinstatement as a member in good standing, and must manifest his desire to be such a member in his very opposition to the sins that cut him off from living membership; in other words, he must be willing to perform, and subsequently must actually perform, the penance which the Church enjoins on him for these sins. Accordingly contrition, confession, and satisfaction are required. From this point of view satisfaction is regarded, not as a sort of restitution made to God, but as a restoration of the sinner in his relations to God and as a restitution made to the Church and the Christian community through works of edification, though always with reference to God.

These acts of the penitent are a sort of judgment he passes on himself,[44] a judgment of blame and an appeal for rehabilitation, a judgment he manifests to the Church that the Church may pass an efficacious judgment which condemns the sin and purifies the sinner.

[44] Cf. I Cor. 11:28.

They are a kind of matter submitted to this definitive act on the part of the Church and a request for restoration presented to the Church with the confident hope that the Church will effectively grant it.

The Church accomplishes this restoration by the sentence its minister pronounces, and in this sentence "the power [of the sacrament] chiefly consists." [45] Such an act of decision, judgment, and rehabilitation is public and social in nature, and supposes public power, that is, jurisdiction. If we may compare it with human procedures, as we should, we can do no better than liken it to judicial processes: "The Father . . . hath given all judgment to the Son." [46] St. John Chrysostom comments: "This is true, but I observe that the Son has turned all this judgment over to the Church." [47]

The judgment is of a very special kind. In a certain sense, Christ does not judge; He Himself disclaimed the office: "God sent not His Son into the world to judge the world, but that the world may be saved by Him." [48] He says that He judges and yet that He does not judge; [49] His judgment is so far above men,[50] so penetrating,[51] and so efficacious within them that His very judgment is the act of a Savior: "I came not to judge the world, but to save the world." [52] His judgment does not stop with ascertaining that crime has been committed or even with declaring that conversion has been effected, but destroys crime, induces complete conversion, and re-creates innocence.

The judgment exercised by Christ is continued in the sacramental judgments. To understand the latter, we must think of Christ rather than of sentences passed by human magistrates. The judgments pronounced in the sacrament of penance are primarily judgments that save, and are an aspect of the great work of redemption that is always going on. They create justice, and are not limited to establishing the fact of wickedness; they penetrate souls and raise them up from within, and are not purely external judgments that confound and crush; they are an aspect of Christ Himself, who offered Himself for condemnation that we might not be condemned.

[45] Council of Trent, Sess. XIV, c.3 (Denz., 896).
[46] John 5:22.
[47] *De sacerdotio*, III, 5 (PG, XLVIII, 643).
[48] John 3:17.
[49] John 8:15 f.
[50] John 5:22, 30; 8:16, 50.
[51] John 3:19 ff.; 12:48; cf. 8:1-11.
[52] John 12:47.

The first effect of the sacrament is to rejoin the sinner to the Church as a penitent, to assign him the status of penitent in the Church. By uniting the sinner to the Church, the sacrament gives him the grace of a penitent, of one who is forgiven and restored to favor. This grace is essentially medicinal; it causes adherence to good by opposing evil; it arouses charity that involves hatred of sin and egoism, as well as reaction against tepidity, sloth, and lust.

The actual graces accompanying sanctifying grace of this sort are those that suit the condition of the forgiven penitent. They are graces of humility and sorrow, of prudence and confidence in God; they induce respect for one's neighbor and unwillingness to judge anyone except oneself.

These important effects manifest the usefulness of those confessions that are called confessions of devotion. Such confessions do not restore habitual grace, which has not been lost, but intensify the Christian's penitential attitude, and bring our struggles against self-love, our purification from sin, and our asceticism into closer harmony with the Church.

D. EXTREME UNCTION

The sacrament of penance, as well as the whole Christian life, which ought to be a prolonged repentance, receives its consummation in the sacrament of extreme unction.[53]

This sacrament also joins us to the Church. In former times it was administered by a number of priests.[54] As the "sacrament of the departing," [55] it joins to the visible Church the person who is about to quit this visible Church; it attaches him to the visible Church regarded as the passage to the invisible Church, the Church triumphant. The proper object of this sacrament is the bodily, psychological, and moral state characterized by the fact that the organism is failing and giving way under the pressure of evil, the state in which death makes its appearance in the sphere of visible experience, the

---

[53] Council of Trent, Sess. XIV, *De extrema unctione* (Denz., 907).

[54] D. Martène, *De antiquis ecclesiae ritibus* (Paris, 1700), II, 105 ff.; M. Jugie, *Theologia dogmatica christianorum orientalium* (Paris, 1930), III, 474. St. Thomas writes in *Contra Gent.*, IV, 73: "A number of priests may fittingly be present at the administration of this sacrament, and the prayer of the whole Church shall contribute to its effect. . . . But if only one priest is present, he is understood to confer this sacrament with the authority of the whole Church, whose minister he is and which he represents."

[55] Council of Trent, Sess. XIV, *De extrema unctione*, c.3 (Denz., 910).

state of dying. Its effect is to bring this state under the power of the Church, to make it a state of the Church, that is, a special way of being a Christian for one who is ill and dying. It enables this state to be a state of a member of Christ, a state of dying in Christ and of being conformed to the dying Christ.

All the sacraments apply the death of Christ to the life of Christians; extreme unction applies Christ's death to that climax of their life which is death. Born at baptism of the death of Christ and nourished by His death in the Eucharist, they live a life of death. The death of Christ, that universal death which was universal deliverance from sin and universal admittance to God, has long been their own death.[56] From their birth they were dead in Christ's death, they were dead in principle, mystically dead.[57] Now they have to die in actual fact, in Christ and in the death of Christ; theirs is the death of members, for their head died before them. Truly, the state of dying is a Christian state.

Extreme unction sanctifies, "sacramentalizes," this state. This sacrament is the death of Christ that comes to Christians at their own death, that they may die in the Lord.[58] It is the sacrament that unites them to the dying Christ, by a visible rite accompanying their death which is a visible extension of the of the action of the dying Christ. The sacrament incorporates their death *ex opere operato* into the vast sacrifice of mankind, in the great elevation of the human race which Christ on Calvary and in the Mass offers up to God in Himself. Thus extreme unction, which is closely connected with penance, is also closely connected with baptism and the Eucharist and holy Viaticum. The whole sacramental order is one in Christ.

By making the dying state a state of the Church, a way of being in Christ, extreme unction makes it a state of grace, that is, a state which brings grace if no obstacle is interposed. If such an obstacle blocks the way, extreme unction confers grace as soon as the obstruction is removed; and if grace should happen to be lost, the sacrament leads to its recovery, by facilitating the necessary acts of attrition and contrition.

This sacramental grace, the grace of advancing to heavenly glory, fully verifies what is required of all grace. It is a beginning of eternal

[56] Cf. II Cor. 5:14–21; Rom. 6:2.
[57] Col. 3:3.
[58] Cf. I Cor. 15:18; I Thess. 4:16; Apoc. 14:13.

life, a grace of steadfast courage and everlasting security, a grace that turns man's fall into the arising of an elect soul. "The prayer of faith shall save the sick man," the Epistle of St. James assures us emphatically when indicating the effects of this anointing.[59] Theology explains that the sacrament disposes so adequately and directly for glory [60] that, when the Christian receives it with all the requisite dispositions, "nothing remains in him that can prevent the soul from receiving glory at its departure from the body." [61]

The grace of extreme unction exerts its power when the recipient is in a condition of extreme weakness, and introduces the dying person into a state of eternal peace and security, which it prefigures. Hence it is a strengthening and alleviating grace; "The Lord shall raise him up," says the Apostle.[62] Lastly, this grace leads to complete deliverance from the life of sin and to the holiness of heaven. Therefore it is the complement of the sacrament of penance and a perfect cleansing of sin and its remnants, if the dispositions of the dying person are favorable; "and if he be in sins, they shall be forgiven him," St. James adds.[63]

The nature of the actual graces conferred by extreme unction is easily perceived. They are graces suitable to the condition of the dying Christian; they are graces of strength, constancy, patience, confidence, faith, and hope in the midst of the physical and moral hardships that mark this condition; graces of tranquillity, peace, longing for heaven, and detachment from the world; graces also of bodily relief, if that is profitable, and even of healing, if a postponement is useful for procuring later a better entrance into heaven.

We may be permitted to extend the exposition a little further by applying the reflections on death we engaged in earlier. This hypothesis lies outside the scope of the development, which should not be thought to depend on it.

Every theologian will agree that, since extreme unction has the purpose of sanctifying death, it also has the purpose of actually conferring the grace of final perseverance. It is not the only means designed to obtain this effect and does not produce it infallibly; but of itself it tends directly to confer such a grace.

[59] Jas. 5:15.
[60] St. Thomas, *Summa*, suppl., q.29, a.1 ad 2; q.32, a.2 et ad 2.
[61] St. Thomas, *Contra Gent.*, IV, 73; the phrase recurs twice.
[62] Jas. 5:15.
[63] *Ibid.*

Here our hypothesis comes in. The grace of final perseverance is more than the simple coincidence of the state of grace and the last instant of life. It is the culmination and crystallization of the whole life of grace, on the side where grace can still touch the becoming process that belongs to this earth; it is the summing-up and the consummation of all grace.

The starting point and the goal of the life of grace are supremely important, like the seed and the fruit of a plant that explain the whole plant. They are the two extremities of a vital growth that, like everything vital, is a unit. The beginning is everything, because it is the start of everything; and the end is everything, because it is the recapitulation and the climax of everything.

Therefore the final grace and the initial grace must both be conferred by a special action of the organism of grace, by a sacrament that is exclusively their own: baptism on the one side, extreme unction on the other. In this sense extreme unction is pre-eminently the sacrament of grace, for it is the sacrament of definitive grace, of settlement in grace, of eternal glory. However, it does not by itself confer eternal glory or transfer us simply to the Church triumphant, but merely prepares the way, so far as that lies within the power of the Church militant. Therefore we cannot say that it imprints a character.

E. MATRIMONY

The four sacraments we have reviewed unite us or reunite us to the Church. Before such a union can be effected there must be men to be united and a visible organism to unite them. The two sacraments of matrimony and holy orders are designed for this purpose. The former supplies candidates for the reception of the sacraments, the latter provides ministers for the administration of the sacraments.

The sacrament of matrimony is the sanctification of a natural institution. It elevates the contract and union that are the unfailing source of human nature to the level of a Christian thing, an affair of the Church, and thereby equips the Church with the means of perpetuating itself. Such a means is needed in a perfect society, and is the element that puts the finishing touch to its organization.

This sacrament does not formally sanctify children, although it does bestow on them a juridical holiness and an inception of formal holiness; for, as St. Paul seems to indicate, it gives them, through their parents, a relation to the society of saints and hence to holiness.[64] Children are persons, and therefore cannot be sanctified except by a sanctification that affects them personally; such sanctification is the effect of the sacrament of baptism.

However, the sacrament of matrimony sanctifies the union and the state in which children are brought into the world. It joins the married couple as such to the Church, so that their marriage itself and the free act by which they definitively and perpetually give themselves to each other becomes also an act of the Church performed by the Church, and the state of married life becomes a state of the Church and a way of Christian living.

This sanctification is necessary. Because of the God-man, man's condition needs to be divinized and actually is divinized by baptism; in a similar manner the state that gives origin to man must be divinized by a special sacrament. The very nature of matrimony requires it to be given a place in the sacramental economy. For it is the state in which mankind finds its supreme fulfillment on the empirical level, and in which the individual is actuated and exalted within the human sphere to the point of coinciding, in a certain sense, with the species and of becoming a cause of man.

In the present order, this unity and full realization of humanity do not remain where nature established them, but are transcendently perfected in the mystery of the whole Christ, that is, of Christ and the Church. In this order, consequently, matrimony is related to the mystery of Christ. It does not fully achieve its purpose unless it is rooted in this mystery and is, so to speak, informed, actuated, and elevated by the mystery, and unless it becomes through such actuation a reality of grace that in its own way imitates the Incarnation, the first principle in the whole economy of grace. Briefly, it has to be a sacrament in order to be the function of human unity and perpetuity in the way that is fitting for Christians. Therefore matrimony itself, the contract as such and the state of married life that flows from the contract, is a sacrament.

Thus the union of man and woman becomes, on its lower level, what the mystery of human unity in its final phase is on its higher level: the mystery of the union of the triune God with all mankind in the God-man and in the mystical extension of the God-man. Through the sacrament of matrimony the Church communicates

[64] See I Cor. 7:14.

to its members a participation in the mystic espousals by which God becomes man and the Church itself becomes the body and the flesh of Christ.[65] By its union with the Word, the Church becomes the ideal form and type of conjugal society, and this society, like a cell that has its life from the whole organism, is formally a reproduction and a participation in the ecclesiastical society, which in turn is a participation, through Christ, in what we may call the absolute society, namely, the union of the three divine persons with one another. As the Christian, an individual member, is related to the whole Church, so the union of husband and wife, who are members, is related to the union of the whole Church with the whole Christ in the supreme unity of the Trinity: "that they may be one, as We also are one" (John 17:22). In the supernatural order, the basic human society is, in an elementary and derived way, what the perfect, human, supernatural society of the Church is in fullness. The entire mystical body is one, and the life of the whole flourishes in all its parts.

Union with the Church implies union with grace. Therefore Christian matrimony confers grace. But this is a special grace, a sacramental grace whose properties correspond to the properties of the union with the Church which the sacrament directly produces. It formally sanctifies husband and wife in their souls; but it also sanctifies each of them in function of the other, as they have to live in function of each other; it makes their very union a sacred and eternal thing.[66]

Through this grace the family, that essentially human reality, becomes a reality of the theandric order; it becomes an affair of the Church militant on earth, and also, we may add, of the Church triumphant in heaven. What God has joined together, God will not put asunder, and in the city of the saints He well knows how to preserve, in a way that is mysterious [67] but real, the ties He has forged in Christ, the ties of kindred that build up the city of men.

This special way of having grace entails a special way of having the theological virtues. Husband and wife are to love each other with charity through God and in God, with a divine and changeless intensity; and we may dare to suppose that they are to have with re-

[65] Eph. 5:23, 29.
[66] For necessary explanations and restrictions, see E. Mersch, *Morality and the Mystical Body*, pp. 216–22.
[67] Cf. Matt. 22:30.

spect to each other a confidence and fidelity that represent some degree of participation in the virtues of faith and hope.

The sacramental grace of matrimony is a source of actual graces. United to the Church, the very fountainhead of graces, husband and wife are placed in a state and condition of receiving graces suitable to their particular function, graces that will make them worthy members of the mystical body as spouses and parents.

These graces will sanctify them through the duties of their family life and will equip them for these duties. They are graces of mutual support, aid, and edification, graces of strength, perspicacity, and adaptation, graces helpful for the education of their children, graces that will sanctify them in the happy hours that will be theirs and also in the hardships and anxieties that will not fail to come to them.[68] We may not forget that the grace which causes the splendor of their state and the beauty of their love was merited by Christ's passion, and that it inserts them, as husband and wife, into the redemption of suffering. This is indicated in the Council of Trent: "Christ Himself, who instituted and perfected the holy sacraments, merited for us by His passion the grace that perfects natural love, confirms the indissoluble unity of matrimony, and sanctifies the married couple." [69]

We said above that matrimony makes the family a cell of the Church and a sort of Church in miniature. Within this little world, parents have a kind of priesthood and teaching authority, *vi muneris et quasi potestate ordinaria*. By divine and ecclesiastical law they have the right and duty of having religious exercises performed in the family and of presiding at them, as also of teaching the children God has entrusted to them to pray, believe, and love. This right and duty are assigned to them by their state and by the sacrament, which endures in its effects. They possess their right and duty in dependence on the Church, for conjugal society as realized in them is derived from the Church. We may say that they have this right and duty by delegation from the Church; but the delegation comes from the very structure of the Church, from the sacrament of matrimony, and from human nature; hence it is prior to the positive law of the Church.

Mention of the priesthood in connection with the sacrament of

[68] Cf. I Cor. 7:28.
[69] Council of Trent, Sess. XXIV (Denz., 969).

matrimony is traditional. St. Thomas compares the two, and the comparison is not to the disadvantage of matrimony. "There are some who propagate and preserve spiritual life according to spiritual administration alone; and this is the function of the sacrament of holy orders. And there are others who propagate bodily and spiritual life together; and this is the function of the sacrament of matrimony, by which a man and a woman cooperate to generate and educate children for the service of God." [70]

The sacrament of orders has its own points of excellence, and they are more sublime; yet they do not suppress those of matrimony. Is it not true that the strongest religious influence a man undergoes is that of his parents, and that the most important teaching in the Church, to which every believer, even the pope, owes so much, is that received at a mother's knee? Indeed, this teaching is given by Christ through those who represent Him and have received His sacrament, the sacrament of fathers and mothers in Christ.

By sanctifying husband and wife, matrimony creates the atmosphere in the home that is most needed for their baptized little ones. The union of these little children with their family is their union with the Church; they belong to the Church by belonging to their parents. The parents are even more qualified than the parish priest to judge whether their children are ready to make their first Holy Communion. [71]

F. HOLY ORDERS

Holy orders, like matrimony though in a different way, is essentially a social sacrament. Matrimony sanctifies the causality which man receives from nature over the natural existence of other men. Holy orders imparts a causality, which no one has by nature, over the supernatural existence of other men.

This power is what distinguishes holy orders from all the other sacraments. The other sacraments make men members of the Church; holy orders makes a man a representative of the whole Church. The other sacraments join members to the body that they may perform the actions of members, and these sacraments, by what they are intrinsically, determine the nature of such actions. Holy orders joins a member to the body that he may perform the actions of the body,

[70] St. Thomas, *Contra Gent.*, IV, 58.
[71] *Codex iuris canonici,* can. 854.

without specifying or affecting these actions by what it is intrinsically.

This fact reveals its excellence, and also what we may call its inferior quality: its excellence in the order of the function it gives, its inferiority in the order of the holiness it confers.[72] In other words, the sacrament confers the power to administer all the sacraments, but does not confer a holiness proportionate to this universal power.

That it confers holiness is immediately evident. It joins a person to the Church and therefore to Christ and God. The character it imprints, the character proper for a dispenser of the sacraments, is a state of the Church which is the body of grace. Hence it gives a state of grace and a way of existing that calls for grace. But this holiness has no proportion with the function that is conferred. This is beyond question; for such a holiness would have to be a holiness of God, the total holiness of Christ, holiness itself.

Indeed, we are taught as a truth of faith that the validity of the function does not in any way depend on the holiness of the person. Undoubtedly the prayers that accompany sacramental rites or the Consecration of the Mass have greater value if the minister is a holier man, as is the case with any prayers. But the sacraments and the sacrifice in themselves, and whatever is formally and exclusively the work of the priest, do not have greater value if he is holier: "the effect of the sacraments is not greater if they are administered by a better minister." [73]

The other sacraments sanctify action by sanctifying a being, and sanctify the two equally; the sacrament of orders sanctifies action directly, assuring the validity of sacerdotal functions and their efficacy; and this is essentially independent of the being who discharges the functions. Accordingly we avow that do not clearly understand the purport of the considerations proposed by Pseudo-Dionysius, which have so greatly influenced Christian speculation, on the eminent holiness, so Godlike and perfect, of pontiffs and priests.[74] We are inclined to see here traces of the Platonic emanentism and the Monophysitism that have been remarked in him. In fact, we should

[72] Cf. St. Thomas, *Summa*, Ia IIae, q. 111, a. 5 ad 2.

[73] *Ibid.*, IIIa, q. 64, a. 1 ad 2.

[74] *De ecclesiastica hierarchia*, esp. 5, paragr. 5 ff. (*PG*, III, 505 ff.). We may see how in the *Summa*, suppl., q. 34, a. 1, St. Thomas is influenced by this doctrine, and how he disengages himself from its consequences, *ibid.*, ad 3; q. 36, a. 3.

say that he regards the persons of ecclesiastical superiors, and not their instrumental mission, as constituting a sort of intermediary between pure divinity and the human world, or as a sort of higher angelic order possessing, by virtue of its inherent excellence or its closer natural proximity to God, the means of illuminating and sanctifying lower orders. For the Monophysites, Christ was some such sort of middle term between God and men, with a mixed nature, half divine and half human.

But the notion of an intermediate being between God and man is an illusion that must be dispelled. Christ is strictly God, and He sanctifies by His own power because He is holiness itself. But that is not the case with priests; they do not bestow sanctity out of their own resources, and they have received no holiness that sanctifies them in their persons in such a way as to entitle them to be called sanctifiers in their own right. In themselves, as persons, they are members of the Church like other Christians, and they need only to be made holy like other Christians, with a holiness that is proper to members.

This and no other is the holiness to which their ordination raises them in a special way. The particular turn it gives to the grace they receive is, as we have mentioned above, a special grace of function, of self-forgetfulness, of consecration to the service of all. This is what they need to be representatives of Christ without arrogating any credit to themselves, and to be channels of santification that transmit everything and add nothing: *in obsequium plebis Dei*, as the *Roman Pontifical* puts it: "By their consecration may they change bread and wine into the body and blood of Thy immaculate Son, for the benefit of Thy people." [75]

Charity and humility are the two essential aspects of Christian grace. By conferring this grace, ordination but accentuates in Christ's members their quality as members. We should say that the character of holy orders, so far as it tends to sanctify the person who bears it rather than to sanctify other persons, may be regarded as an accidental perfecting of the characters of baptism and confirmation.[76]

Christian priesthood, in addition to its proper sacerdotal powers and because of them, has a special place in the duty that devolves

---

[75] Prayer said at the ordination of priests, after investment with the chasuble.
[76] In the liturgy, priests are ranged alongside of laymen among confessors who are not pontiffs.

on all Christians, that is, in the witness to be rendered to Christ and His teaching, and in the vital activity which the members exercise in the unity of the body. And this is yet another reason why the personal holiness it requires and confers is a holiness belonging to a member, to one who is confirmed in his membership.

III. The Eucharist

If holy orders is so great a sacrament because it gives the power to confer all the sacraments, the Eucharist is much greater, since it contains Him who has instituted the sacraments and accounts for all their power.

Its greatness is such that, to explain it adequately, we should have to make a survey of the whole of Christian teaching; we should have to review all that touches on Christ and the gift of Christ to the Church, and all that, from one end to the other, this book is trying to express. The reader will understand that we cannot think of undertaking so long a repetition, and that we must be content with a summary.

But such a summary is needed; according to the whole of tradition, the Eucharist is the sacrament of the mystical body. Discussion of it cannot be ommitted in a theology of the mystical body. The precise aspect of the Eucharist that has to be brought out is the fact that it is the sacrifice of Christ as still being offered and diffused throughout the entire mystical body, in order to assimilate all Christian life to it.

1. THE SACRIFICE OF THE CROSS

The Eucharist is Christ's sacrifice. We believe that sacrifice may be defined as the supreme act of religion, the act in which religion is most completely expressed. If the action is interior, we have an interior sacrifice; if it is exterior, we have an exterior sacrifice that incarnates the interior dispositions. The word "sacrifice" is ordinarily reserved to designate the exterior act. This definition is given here without any attempt to justify it; the exposition that follows will enable us to judge if it accounts for all the rites that are brought forward as sacrifices, and if it shows how all these point to Christ's sacrifice as their supreme fulfillment.

In general, religion is a conscious and deliberate straining of the creature toward the Creator, an aspiration toward God, a desire of nearness and union with Him, so far as all this is possible for a creature.[77] The most perfect act of religion is the most intense aspiration toward God, the strongest effort to pass beyond the level of the workaday life of sense to mount as high as possible up to God. Therefore religion has a negative aspect, that is, a separation, and a positive aspect, that is, an oblation, an ascent, a consecration. The two aspects can unite perfectly, and the separation can be illuminated with all the splendor of the consecration.

When mankind is sinful, as is actually the case, religion and religious activity include yet another factor that tends to intensify the negative aspect. By becoming a sinner, man makes himself incapable of achieving union with God; something in him—or rather the whole of the sinner, though not wholly—is opposed to this union and resists it. Therefore religion, the ascent to God, implies detestation and suppression of the sinful self, and the supreme procedure in this order, fully actuating this disposition, is the effective suppression of man. This is not a ritual murder or suicide, for such a thing is incompatible with morality and religion, and religion is at stake here; furthermore, how could the destruction of all human tendency by the destruction of man be a progress toward God? Rather it is the voluntary and positive acceptance of death, at the hour appointed by the decrees of Providence. In point of fact, death is precisely the punishment inflicted by God for sin; and death, as we have tried to show, is man's supreme moral act, and therefore ought to be his supreme religious act. In the meantime, interior sacrifice is a disposition of opposition to self and of mortification, and the external action, the external sacrifice expressing the interior disposition, ought to involve a suppression and a destruction. Taken as a whole, therefore, the external sacrifice will include, beside the positive aspect of oblation and consecration, a negative aspect by which, in one way or another, the separation becomes immolation. All this, along with several other points yet to be brought out, has already been touched on in connection with the redemption and the redemptive sacrifice.[78]

We must go a step farther. In the supernatural economy, the only one that exists or has ever existed, neither religion nor its highest act can be exercised by man alone. Sacrifice is indeed offered by

[77] We have explained our mind on this subject in *Morality and the Mystical Body*, chap. 1.
[78] Chaps. 10 f.

man, but God inspires man to offer it, and God's causality is stronger than in any other act; for this is the supreme act. Such is the adequate notion of sacrifice. We shall see how fully it is realized in the God-man and in His death.

The God-man, regarded in His substance, is the perfect realization of human religion and the virtual supppression of human sin, for, in His personal unity, He is the union of the human race with the inner life of God. This is true most of all in His supreme act, which is His act of dying. We have dealt with this sufficiently when treating of the redemption. In any case, this act is the supreme religious act, the sacrifice par excellence. It is also a universal sacrifice, summing up all other sacrifices and giving them their value.

By actuating Christ's humanity to the highest degree, this act also actuated to the highest degree the character of mystical head possessed by the sacred humanity. Thereby it became the act of all mankind, not as yet in the multitude of men, but in Him who is the source of supernatural life for all. Dying as our representative, with a death that crowns His office as our representative and our unity, He died a universal death, in the death of the entire sinful race; and when He returned to God, He brought back with Him the whole of regenerated mankind.

Christ's sacrifice is the universal sacrifice because it is fully His sacrifice; it is the sacrifice of all mankind. He who is the recapitulation of the whole race, gathers together in His sacrifice the sacrifices of the whole race, and, in addition, all the religious activity of the race that culminiates in the sacrifices men offer.[79] He sums them all up in one act that embraces mankind and includes it in this final achievement and consummation. Therefore this act is the climax of everything, and puts the finishing touch to all activity, especially to all the sacrifices that have ever taken place in mankind, so that at the end Christ could say: "It is consummated." [80]

The sacrifice of Christ is the goal to which the sacrifices of the Old Law were directed by God Himself. It is also the goal, though in a different way, of all other sacrifices offered in good faith, no matter where or when. If we are able to perceive that the whole ancient religious history of mankind turned toward the Redeemer, in response to the grace operating in it and the efficacious promise

[79] John 3:14–17; 12:32.
[80] John 19:20.

made by God to the first sinner, we must also perceive that all the activity and sacrifices occurring in it turned toward the redemptive sacrifice. In all these peoples, with the exception of the people of Israel who were under a special providence, such aspirations and tendencies, with the divine help at work in the sinful mass, found the meager expression they were capable of. In this way the sacrifices of ancient times arose. They were imperfect, awkward, and sometimes horrible and criminal; yet some noble or appealing aspect was usually observed in them. Gropingly, in response to the divine stimulus, mankind was searching for God and for the Savior whom it had briefly glimpsed at its origin and who was slowly drawing near to His race. What mankind was unconsciously trying to do, was accomplished solely, but perfectly, in Christ's redemptive sacrifice.

Thus His sacrifice takes its place at the head of these aspirations, like the summit of a pyramid that commands the whole structure. The God-man recapitulates all mankind, and His sacrifice unifies all religious activity, at least whatever is truly good in it. All these sacrifices, multiple when viewed from the side of the men offering them and of their innumerable sins, are seen to be one when viewed from the side of God who gathers them together in the God-man.

This is the mystery of the total sacrifice, the mystery of the dying God-man, in the mystery of the whole Christ. As it appeared outwardly, the death of the God-man was only a fragment of human history, a momentary event in the duration of time; but when viewed from within, it is perceived to be the fullness, the unity, and the climax of all history and time.

Indeed, any human act is above time, for it is partly spiritual. Far from being measured by time, a human act is able to express time by knowledge and to measure it. The supreme human act, the act of quitting time to enter eternity, is eminently above time. And the supreme act of the man par excellence who is the God-man, His act of dying, is even more perfectly above time, for it is supernaturally superior to time. As the God-man is the racapitulation of mankind, His act of dying is the recapitulation of mankind's superiority to time.

The divinization of Christ's sacred humanity assimilated it to the divine eternity, and therefore produced in it a sort of human permanence, a possession of all human duration, to the extent that such a thing is possible in an individual human nature. This quality has

584 THEOLOGY OF THE MYSTICAL BODY

to be found at its highest in the act by which the sacred humanity achieves its supreme human realization, that is, in the act of dying. In this act, therefore, the sacred humanity has to be present to all mankind, for at that moment it definitively incorporates the human race into itself. Accordingly we would miss the true nature of this act if we were to see nothing more in it than a tragedy of a few hours' duration. All history and the whole secular development of mankind are summarized in this instant as in an interior principle; and to perceive it aright, we must observe it as it unfolds, in its central meaning and its full importance, throughout all the history of all the centuries.

This unfolding affects mankind interiorly and exteriorly, for mankind, Christ, and His act of dying itself have an exterior and an interior aspect. It affects man interiorly. It causes men's life, in the most secret recess where grace incorporates them into Christ, to grow in detachment from self and from sin, and to become an enduring aspiration and approach to God. It turns their life into a long oblation and immolation, that is, a sacrifice that lasts until their death and definitive passage to God. This is the great sacrifice being offered within mankind, repeating endlessly the first great sacrifice, the sacrifice of the head.

But Christ's death also affects man exteriorly, and indeed reaches man by his outer nature, for the Word became flesh and founded a visible Church to act on men from outside. In His supreme act, which best expresses and communicates Him, Christ remains faithful to this economy, whose acts reveal its character.

At the moment of making His complete oblation, Christ enclosed it in an efficacious sign that could be renewed and multiplied indefinitely and could render the oblation present to all mankind. On the eve of His death, He took bread and wine and said: "Take this, and eat and drink; this is My body and My blood, My sacrifice and My immolation. Do this, everywhere and always, in memory of Me." Thus the sacrifice was offered in advance, and the cross became inevitable; but thus too the cross, even before it was set up, became the Mass, the sacrifice of Christ ever present among men.

2. THE SACRIFICE OF THE MASS

The Mass is the perpetual expression and realization of the universal aspect found in the sacrifice of the God-man. It is the sacrifice of Christ, not as originally offered by Christ, but as communicated to Christians in an empirical rite. It is the immolation of the head sacramentally continued in the members, in the way that the head Himself is continued. It is the sacrifice of Christ that takes possession of all mankind in a visible manner, to make its riches available for all. It is the perpetual pouring out of Christ's life that enters unceasingly into souls and therefore issues unceasingly from Him.

Or we may say that the Mass is Christ's sacrifice, which is the regeneration of mankind, coming to take its rightful place in the heart of mankind; it is Christ's sacrifice, the supreme human act, installing itself at the origin of all human activity. Or again, we may say that it is Christ's sacrifice endlessly summoning forth, in a visible rite, the sacrifice of the mystical body; for, in St. Augustine's terse formula, it is the sacrifice of the mystical body. "Christ is the priest; He Himself is the offerer, and He is the oblation. He wished the sacrifice of the Church to be the daily sacrament of this event; and, since the Church is the body of Him who is the head, it learns to offer itself through Him." [81] This last formula needs a commentary. The Mass is the sacrifice of the mystical body only so far as this sacrifice is one with that of the head, or rather is contained in the sacrifice of the head as in its source and model.

The life of Christianity and the life of every Christian ought to be a sacrifice and a sort of prolongation of the redemption. It cannot be such except in the redemption and sacrifice of Christ. Therefore Christ's redemptive sacrifice is operative in all Christianity, both visibly and invisibly. The visible communication, the body, the sign and the efficacious means of the invisible communication, is the Mass.

The Mass is the visible coming of the sacrifice of the Cross to the whole of Christian life, in the vast sacrifice of regenerated mankind which it calls forth. It is the immediate action which the absolute sacrifice exercises, in an empirical rite, on all derived sacrifices. Therefore it is essentially a sacramental sacrifice, for it is a sign and a cause: a sign that really contains the sacrifice of the Cross in its supra-temporal aspect, and that causes what the sacrifice of the Cross was designed to produce, that is, the sacrifice of the mystical body. It is the presence, the representation, and the activity of the sacrifice

[81] *De civitate Dei*, X, 20 (*PL*, XLI, 298; *Corpus Viennense*, XL, 480; see the variant readings).

of the Cross in the visible and sacramental Church, under a visible and sacramental form.

The two aspects of the sacrifice of Calvary are distinct, but not separated; we may say that they constitute a single sacrifice that is *the* sacrifice. Likewise the sacrifice of the Mass and the sacrifice of the Cross are distinct in the way several Masses are distinct; but they are not separated; they form one sacrifice, which is *the* sacrifice.

These formulas are proposed not as mere pious phrases, but as the strictly scientific statement of what the essence of the Mass is. If they are somewhat mysterious and vague, the reason is that this essence consists in a mystery that transcends nicely marked-out concepts, just as the supernatural in general transcends all natural categories.

We believe that they automatically impose themselves, without any need of searching them out, once we admit the doctrine of the mystical body in its full realistic sense. But they are valid only in this case. Christ must be one in Himself as well as united to all men, while remaining distinct from them as they are distinct from one another, in order that His immolation may be made present over and over again among men without ceasing to be unique and completely self-sufficient. Otherwise we cannot conceive that there are many sacrifices while yet there is only one sacrifice, and that an act now taking place is a sacrifice because of its union and relation (a relation that is intrinsic and constitutive) with a sacrifice offered nineteen centuries ago and completely finished so far as its exterior aspect is concerned.[82]

This relation to the sacrifice of the Cross is highly important in faith and religion whenever the question of the Holy Sacrifice comes up. We are not surprised that the same is true of speculative theorizing about this sacrifice. This is clearly seen in the embarrassment theology experiences and in the many solutions it proposes when it attempts to define the essence of the sacrifice without stressing the relation to the Cross and the doctrine of the mystical body. When theology engages in that sort of attempt, it must be satisfied with an extremely vague and indeterminate notion of sacrifice, seeing that Christ is now established in glory; furthermore, such a notion corresponds poorly with what the faithful have in mind when they

---

[82] *Munus aeternum, redemptio aeterna*, says the liturgy with reference to the Holy Sacrifice; thus in the secret for the feast of the Holy Trinity, the Postcommunion for the fourteenth Sunday after Pentecost, and elsewhere.

speak of the Sacrific of the Mass. Or, if theology is unwilling to rest content with so attenuated a notion, it must relax the application of the notion to the Mass. The notion then retains the elements of real offering, consecration, and immolation, but the explanation given is that the Mass is all this only because God considers it as such; or that Christ would be really immolated if He were not in a state of glory, and therefore incapable of being immolated; or that He is placed in a condition which has the outward appearance of an immolation and in some sense is equivalent to an immolation; or that something else that is not Christ, but is closely connected with Him, such as the matter of the sacrament, is really offered and virtually destroyed. In all such ventures we see how difficult it is to conceive that the Mass is really, truly, and substantially the sacrifice of Christ, which is what the proponents of these theories wish to make clear. Such difficulties are bound to come up when a theologian undertakes to determine what is essential to the Mass, and then begins to empty it of this essential element, that is, of its mysterious and constitutive relation to the sacrifice of the Cross.

We have still to point out what enables the Mass to be the sign and continuation of the sacrifice of the Cross. As St. Augustine says, "if the sacraments did not in some way resemble the things of which they are sacraments, they would not be sacraments at all." [83] Theologians have carefully studied the question, and have clearly brought out, among other points, the importance of the separation of the species. We can do no more than summarize their teaching; but we wish to lay special emphasis on the fact that the two species are articles of food, and that in the Eucharist Christ is our bread, as He Himself declared; the total oblation made by Him who delivers Himself up in this way is admirably expressed. It is a complete oblation to God, reminding us of libations, and also a complete oblation to men, reminding us of the purpose of food.

If that is what the Mass is, the Christ of the Mass is formally the Christ of the Cross. The latter is undoubtedly identical with the historical Christ; and Christ is undoubtedly no longer on the cross but in glory.

On the altar, however, He is present neither as historical nor as glorious. He is present as the body delivered up for us and as blood poured forth for us, as dying and communicating His death to His

[83] *Epist.* 98 (PL, XXXIII, 363).

followers. Death is assuredly His passage to glory, and is therefore a glory; but from the standpoint of earth, this glory is manifest only in the immolation leading to it. On the human level, the glory of this immolation consists in the fact that the immolation is diffused among men; it is a passing to God that contains mystically and procures sacramentally the passing of all humanity to God. This is the sense in which the glory of the Cross is the Mass.

Accordingly the Mass is no less sublime than the sacrifice of the Cross. It is not merely *a* sacrifice; it is *the* sacrifice, the absolute and total sacrifice, the full sacrifice of mankind. It has the same efficaciousness as the sacrifice of the Cross. Like the latter, it is a sacrifice of adoration, thanksgiving, satisfaction, and impetration. It does not deprive the sacrifice of the Cross of any of its importance, but rather fully brings out all that importance. Consequently the veneration we have for the Mass does not in the slightest detract from our veneration for the Cross.[84]

The Mass adds nothing to the Cross. God is no more glorified than He was before, and no graces are merited beyond what had already been merited. The fruits which the Mass distributes are those of the sacrifice of the Cross.[85] But the Mass does distribute them; what it adds to the Cross, by the power of the Cross, is the universal expansion of the Cross. The sacrifice of Calvary becomes the sacrifice of mankind and the glory it gives to God ascends from mankind; holiness, abandonment of sin along with the sinful self, and union with God enter into mankind's possession.

This is the new element contributed by the Mass, and it applies even to the worship due to God. The Mass enables mankind to offer to God the supreme worship offered by Christ. Therefore the Mass must pervade mankind, and it does so through the action of mankind, by the active participation, both interior and exterior, of the faithful at Mass. Most of all the Mass pervades mankind by its own action; this is why it was established, and it has power *ex opere operato* to accomplish its purpose. The Mass lays hold of the faithful more than they lay hold of it, through Holy Communion.

The sacrifice of Christ is made present to us under the form of nourishment, and enters into us and is assimilated as a Communion intended for us. The priest's Communion is necessary for the essential

[84] Council of Trent, Sess. XXII, c. 2 and can. 4 (Denz., 940, 951).
[85] *Ibid.*, c. 2 (Denz., 940).

integrity of the sacrifice; this is a public and Catholic Communion, required by the public cult. The Communion of the faithful is necessary that the sacrifice may have all desirable perfection; this is private Communion, but is also Catholic, and is required by the interior cult. The Communion of the faithful is continued in their spiritual communions and in all their Christian life.

3. HOLY COMMUNION

The sacrifice is not Holy Communion. "If anyone should say that a true and proper sacrifice is not offered to God in the Mass, or that the offering means nothing else than that Christ is given to us to eat: let him be anathema." [86] Yet Holy Communion is the culmination and crown of the sacrifice. Great insistence is laid in our day, and quite properly, on the importance of the Mass as a public sacrifice. But this preoccupation should not lead us to lose sight of the immense importance, indeed, we would say, the greater importance of Holy Communion.

In the Synoptic Gospels, no less than in St. John, Jesus Christ spoke more of the Eucharist as a sacrament than as a sacrifice. We have only to read His address at Capharnaum, the words He uttered in the Cenacle, and His discourse after the Supper, to perceive that what He left to His followers is indeed His sacrifice; but such reading informs us, above all, that the nourishing food He gave His disciples is what makes them abide in Him, and Him in them, to unite them all together in Him within the Trinity, to embrace them in His love and His sacrifice.

St. Paul speaks in the same vein, and all the early patristic tradition is with him. They put more emphasis on the sacrament than on the sacrifice. Hence we are in agreement with Scripture and tradition if we make Communion the center of our lives. And by doing so we best bring out the true greatness of the sacrifice, for its greatness and its essence consist in gathering all Christian life into the redemptive sacrifice, which was and ever remains the climax of Christ's life.

The two are inseparable. The Eucharist is a sacrament because it is a participation in the sacrifice, and as a sacrifice it constitutes a covenant, a Communion. Communion is the reason why there is a Mass, but the Mass is the explanation of Communion. We have no way of communicating except by sharing in the Mass, nor of com-

[86] Council of Trent, Sess. XXII, can. 1 (Denz., 948).

municating well except by sharing in the spirit of the Mass. The nature of the Mass is such that we unite ourselves more closely to it by communicating, even outside of Mass, than by being present at Mass without communicating. The best way to exhort the faithful to communicate, so far as possible, along with the priest's Communion, is to get them to understand this truth, rather than to dissuade them from communicating at other times.

The greatness of Communion and its connection with the sacrifice appear clearly in its effects. The effect of the Eucharist, as of the other sacraments, is to unite us to the Church and thereby to Christ, and to give grace. The Eucharist does this in a different and much more perfect way than the other sacraments.

It unites us to the Church in Him who is forever the center, the unity, and the whole of the Church. The Eucharist joins us to the Church which is so truly the continuation of Christ that at will it causes Christ to appear in the midst of its gatherings; and this is Christ who gives Himself to the Church. And the Eucharist unites us fully to the Church by granting to each of the faithful the possession of Him who is the source of all the life and unity of the Church.

If the Eucharist thus unites us to the Church, need we add that it unites us also to Christ? The two are so completely one in the sacrament of unity that we can hardly say that one is the consequence of the other. The Eucharist unites us to the Church by uniting us to Christ, and unites us to Christ by uniting us to the Church. This is so true that a man who does not belong to the Church is incapable of such union with Christ; he might receive the body and blood of Christ, but this would be the same as not receiving Christ at all—except, of course, for non-sacramental graces, which Christ can give at any time.

This union with the Church and Christ is something quite different from spatial union. The very splendor of the sacramental rite can keep us from seeing the even more dazzling splendor of the *res sacramenti*. The eating of the sacred species is but a sign, and can take place without producing any effect; is not Christ inclosed within the ciborium, and does not the ciborium remain cold? The action of the Eucharist goes much farther. It is a food,[87] and union with food is effected in a mysterious exchange of life, in an assimilation by which one becomes the other. But in the Eucharist, the more vital of

[87] Council of Florence, *Decretum pro Armenis* (Denz., 698).

the two is the bread we receive, the "bread of life." [88] This bread consumes and changes into itself the one who eats it. "Partaking of the body and blood of the Lord does nothing less than transform us into what we eat." [89] Consequently it imparts an interior likeness to Christ, a participation in Him, an incorporation into Him, and the quality of membership in His body.

This assimilation is what we call grace. The Eucharist gives this grace primarily as an assimiliation to Christ and a fellowship of life with Him in His mystical body, through a union with Christ that is at once visible and invisible, and also in a union with the visible and invisible mystical body that is the Church. As we shall see, this is also the main function of grace.

The Eucharist assimilates us to Christ, not because it is such or such an act or particular state, but simply because it is Christ Himself. Consequently it perfects incorporation into Him and confers grace, not from this or that point of view, but simply as grace. Similarly, it unites us to the Church simply as the Church, the indefectible body of Christ. It is the sacrament of permanent union and it produces the permanence of our union with the Church, with Christ, and with grace. It gives grace, not by causing grace to arise in the soul, but by sustaining, nourishing, and increasing the grace already in us.

Therefore the Eucharist is pre-eminently the sacrament of grace, as it is also pre-eminently the sacrament of the Church and the mystical body, the sacrament of the Christian and of Christian life. Every sacrament is a sacrament of grace, of the Church, and of the Christian; but the Eucharist is the sacrament par excellence, *the* sacrament, the Blessed Sacrament.

If Christ assimilates us and transforms us into Himself in this sacrament by making us members of His body, the reason is that He has a higher life than our natural life. This is the life of divinization and grace; in a sense it is infinite; it is the life which Christ's human nature receives because of its union with the Son.

"As the living Father hath sent Me, and I live by the Father, so he that eateth Me, the same also shall live by Me." [90] The Eucharist divinizes us by uniting us to Christ. The grace it confers is divinization, divine adoption, and union with the whole Trinity. In Christ

[88] John 6:35, 48, 51.
[89] St. Leo, *Serm.* 63 (PL, LIV, 357); cf. *Epist.* 59 (PL, LIV, 868).
[90] John 6:58.

and in the mission of the Son, its sacramental action is connected with the Trinitarian processions. This shows how the Eucharist, sacrament of grace, imparts grace and accurately represents its functioning: it unites us to God and uncreated grace, by incorporating us into Christ in fellowship with the Church; by virtue of a causality exercised through union, it enriches us with an inner, accidental perfection. All these characteristics can only be mentioned here. They have been or will be studied in their proper place, especially in the chapters on grace.

We can be somewhat more specific. In this sacrament, Christ assimilates us to Himself such as He is in the moment of His supreme act, that is, His redemptive death. In other words, He assimilates us formally and directly, not to His transfiguration and heavenly glory, but to His conflict against sin. The sacrament was instituted, not for the saints in heaven, but for poor sinners who are struggling against sin that is always oppressing them. Its effect is not the instantaneous production of fervor in its highest pitch, as we should expect if we thought only of Christ and His holiness, but the launching of redeemed sinners, still burdened with their weaknesses and sluggish minds, on their journey to God. The effect is not immediate admittance to eternal triumph, but persistent progress along the road that leads to victory; for the Eucharist is our viaticum, our Pasch, our passage; it is our glory also, but in hope and pledge, not yet in actuality.

The act by which Christ likens us to Himself in the Eucharist is His sacrifice. The Eucharist has the tendency to make the lives of Christians a sacrifice, so that the Cross may take possession of mankind. Christ offered full reparation for sin; the faithful also offer reparation, both for themselves as individuals and on behalf of the whole mystical body; theirs is a reparation proper to members, and continues Christ's reparation, on which it depends and from which it derives.

Christ the Redeemer, who assimilates Christians to Himself, is Christ in the greatest act of His love.[91] His love impels Him to perfect obedience to the Father and to the offering of Himself as a holocaust for men. This love permeates Christians and transforms them into itself.

Therefore the Eucharist gives us charity; it is the sacrament of

[91] John 13:1; 15:13.

charity, no less than the sacrament of grace. We honor it more by devotedness to our fellow men than by an ornate ceremonial, although the latter is also indispensable. The love it engenders for God and our neighbor, by assimilating us to Christ's integral love and incorporating us into Him, is in turn integral love, the love that cannot stop short of the complete gift of self.

This donation, by which Christ makes His members like to Himself, has given the final human perfection to His union with all men. He brings His followers together in a universal union, that they may all be perfectly one in Him, as He is one with the Father.

In this unprecedented way the Eucharist is the sacrament of the Church that is one and Catholic in Christ. It makes Christian life Catholic from within, and unites the life of each to the life of all by uniting the lives of all to itself.

We perceive that the Eucharist manifests Christ more than it hides Him. It conceals only His external features, which remain inaccesibly remote from us, however close He may draw to us. Yet it gives us Him who wishes to do away with remoteness, who wishes to dwell within those whom He loves. Christ comes among us to be taken and eaten by us; and there are some who would say that this has no meaning!

What external manifestation could better show what Christ is and better declare what He does? The act by which He gives Himself unreservedly to God and men crowns His life's activity and reveals all its nobility. With this act He enters lovingly and deeply into the heart of every man, that it may be the dynamic principle of every action man performs. His desire is that men may tear themselves from their egoism and may ultimately come to learn what it means to live in the God-man.

The consecrated host, reclining on the paten, is motionless and silent; it seems to be the perfect ideal of calm recollection and reposeful intimacy. Yet the truth is far different; this living bread represents humanity's supreme effort to leave its lower self behind and, in its head, mount up to God. In this same effort the strong embrace of infinite love clasps all the children of adoption to itself in God's well-beloved Son, to make them enter somehow into one another as divine love itself enters into them to transform them and their love into the image of itself. This is the perfect human act, and it is diffused throughout the whole Christ.

CHAPTER XIX

SANCTIFYING GRACE

> "The grace of God, life everlasting
> in Christ Jesus our Lord."
>
> Rom. 6:23

THE sacraments, the visible Church, and the empirical aspect of Christ's humanity delineate the external structure of a supernatural organism that is interiorly animated by a supernatural life. This life is grace. We now turn to a study of this subject.

I. INTRODUCTION

In a general way, according to the definition universally received, grace is a gift presented to rational creatures with a view to their eternal life. The gift implies a special intervention of God, a wholly gratuitous generosity, and a new union with Him. This is the topic we wish to treat in the following pages. We shall develop it in line with the idea dominating the whole book, that is, the idea of our incorporation in Christ.

We may say that all grace found in mankind is, in one way or another, the divinization humanity receives because it is either the humanity of God Himself in the God-man, or the humanity of the members of the God-man. For the moment we prescind from the question whether the grace possessed by Adam prior to original sin or the grace of the angels corresponds to this conception. We have already touched on this matter and shall come back to it. We do not assert that grace is necessarily such *de jure* rather than merely *de facto*. Personally, however, we do not see how grace would be possible without an Incarnation under some form or other; but we are also aware that God can do many things that lie beyond our comprehension.

Grace is of many different kinds. We have uncreated grace and created grace, grace that is supernatural in the way it is conferred and grace that is supernatural in its substance, sanctifying grace and actual grace; and these graces, particularly the latter, are very numerous and diverse. Yet we believe that this variety is reducible to unity, the unity of Christ and of God who gives Himself in Christ. The variety is but the adaptation of this unity to the multiplicity found in man.

If this view is correct, grace at once becomes more intelligible, for it exhibits greater unity. Since, moreover, this unity is the unity of Christ, grace will appear more clearly to be *gratia Christi* rather than merely *gratia Dei;* it will be seen to be an intrinsically Christian thing that is definable in the light of the Christological, Trinitarian, and ecclesiological dogmas of Christianity, and will depend less on metaphysics or natural ethics.

Is it not strange that many treatises on grace, some of which are beautifully written, make but little mention of Christ and the Church, although the life they describe is nothing else than the life which flows from Christ into the members of Christ? Is it not true that the gift of God, as they present it, seems to be a highly individualistic and abstract entity, although it is the very thing that makes all men one in the Father and the Son, as the Father and the Son are one in each other?

II. The Plan

The first point that emerges when grace is regarded as the divinization flowing from Christ to the whole body of Christ, is the distinction and union between sanctifying grace and actual grace. As the body is still in process of formation here on earth, its divinization is also in formation. Hence it must include both a power of formation and growth, and an initial level of life that truly exists but has yet to increase. The power of divinization, and divinization as already present though still imperfect, consist in actual grace and sanctifying grace, as the following pages will show.

In this chapter we shall consider sanctifying grace; but many of the details that arise involve actual grace, and when they come up we shall not omit reference to them, for these two graces are at bottom the same reality. However, the questions that pertain properly to actual grace will be reserved for the following chapter.

We may mention in passing that the full realization of this divinization is glory, for glory is also a grace.[1] St. Thomas teaches that glory is grace arrived at its goal and final consummation,[2] just as grace is glory itself, though only in germ, preparation, and inception.[3] Glory is to grace as a definitive state is to a preparatory state, or as man fully formed is to man in formation.[4] Again, glory and supernatural beatitude are to grace as natural beatitude is to natural moral goodness; in putting the matter thus, however, we must clearly understand that the supernatural embraces and elevates the natural.

III. THE DOCTRINE

With reference to sanctifying grace, which we are to study in the present chapter, let us begin with an exposition of the Christian teaching on this subject. We shall propose the doctrine, as we have done on other occasions, according to the draft *De fide catholica*.

The Catholic Church teaches that grace, which is given through the merits of Christ the Redeemer, is of such a nature that by it we are not only delivered from the slavery of sin and the power of the devil, but also, renewed in the spirit of our mind, we recover the justice and sanctity which Adam lost for himself and us by sinning. This grace does not merely repair the powers of our nature, so that by its help we may fully conform our habits and actions to the norm of morality, but it reaches beyond nature and transforms us into the image of the heavenly Man, that is, Christ, and regenerates us to a new life. For God chose us in Christ Jesus before the foundation of the world, and predestined us to be made conformable to the image of His Son, that He might be the first-born among many brethren. Therefore the Father has bestowed on us this charity that, born of God, we should be called and should be the sons of God. This adoption of sons has restored to us a participation in the divine nature that is now begun through grace and shall one day be consummated in glory. Anointed and consecrated by the Spirit of the Son, whom God has sent into our hearts, we are made temples of

---

[1] St. Thomas, *Summa*, Ia IIae, q.114, a.3 ad 3.

[2] *Ibid.*, q.111, a.3 ad 2.

[3] *Ibid.*, IIa IIae, q.24, a.3 ad 2.

[4] *De veritate*, q.27, a.1 ad 5.

the divine Majesty, in which the most holy Trinity deigns to dwell and to communicate itself to faithful souls, as Christ the Lord has said: "If anyone love Me, he will keep My word, and My Father will love him,, and We will come to him and will make Our abode with him." [5]

Wherefore this also has to be held and professed by all of Christ's faithful, that sanctifying grace does not consist only in the favor by which God accepts man as pleasing to Him and is prepared to give the helps of actual grace, nor in mere passing acts, but is an enduring supernatural gift that is divinely infused and inheres in the soul, both in justified adults and in infants regenerated by baptism. This renovation of man by the incarnate Word is that mystery hidden from ages, whereby God more wonderfully re-establishes in the second Adam what He had established in the first Adam.[6]

A. UNCREATED GRACE

"This renovation of man by the incarnate Word": this grace, this supernatural gift, is what we have to consider now. To gain an idea of its nature, we shall examine it in Christ. The first thing to say about this grace is what the fathers of the Vatican Council affirmed in the words just quoted, that is, that it comes to us in the incarnate Word and, indeed, with His very advent.

The origin of grace is the decree that determined the Incarnation. In deciding on the Incarnation, this decree decided to attach mankind, in one of its representatives, to the principle that is eternity itself, to the very generation of the Word, in such a way that the sacred humanity assumed by the Son would live by the living Father whose life is to beget the Son, by the Father who sends His Son into the world. In this way those who were to be joined to the Son and to receive His life through faith and the sacrament of bread, would live by Him, as He lives by the Father; in Christ, they were to have life from the Father and the eternal generation. Thus grace is the eternal life that comes to mankind in Christ, for no other reason than that Christ exists.

The decree that settled the Incarnation has settled everything in principle. It willed Christ alone; but in willing Him, it willed Him in His entirety, along with His fullness that is His mystical body. All things are divinely unified in these divine origins, and are the

[5] John 14:23.
[6] *Schema de fide catholica,* final redaction, cap. 5 (Mansi, LIII, 292). We may note that the very first paragraph, which deals with grace in general, describes sanctifying grace.

unified effect produced by the One; and the eternal predestination of the one Mediator between God and men, the man Jesus Christ, is so great and complete that it is also the predestination of all men who were to be His members.[7]

This is the way Jesus Himself spoke: "God so loved the world as to give His only-begotten Son." [8] God loved the whole world when He gave His Son. Thus also Scripture presents the Incarnation in the Gospel according to St. John, when it exhibits the union of the Word with flesh as the union of God with His creation, as an expansion of life and light by which God, in His only Son incarnate, communicates His life and light to the race of men.[9] Lastly, this is the way Scripture sums up the entire Christian message when, in St. Paul, it reduces the "good news" to a single proclamation, the preaching of the "mystery," the secret of divine goodness and love.

God unites Himself to all men as well as to the angels. He gives Himself to all, even to pagans and sinners, in Christ in whom all are to become saints, pure and spotless before the sight of God. All are elect and chosen in Christ, because He is all in all.[10] This supreme act of God's love, goodness, and power is the ultimate source of the Incarnation and the first cause of grace.

We may call it the first uncreated grace, or uncreated grace in its unity and totality. This term, uncreated grace, can be understood and is understood in different senses, somewhat as in the case of the formula, "grace of union." In other words, the divine approach that constitutes this grace of God may be regarded, so to speak, according to different degrees of nearness to man. At its summit, uncreated grace is God Himself who decides to give Himself and actually does so. It is also, in a sense that is more pertinent to us, this decision and donation of God regarded in themselves and, as it were, in the abstract. Or again, and closer to man, it is the dignity investing the man who possesses God. This dignity itself may be considered simply

---

[7] St. Thomas, *Summa*, IIIa, q.24, a.3, 4. The idea finds frequent expression in St. Augustine.

[8] John 3:16. This is a gratuitous love that causes the lovableness of its object, and is not caused by it; cf. John 17:26.

[9] John 1:1–17; cf. I John 3:1; 4:7–16. See above, chap. 12.

[10] Eph. 1:3–10. Cf. *The Whole Christ*, pp. 89 ff. The relation between grace and the "mystery" announced by St. Paul is noted in the final draft of the *De fide catholica*, quoted above. "This renovation of man by the incarnate Word is that mystery hidden from ages, whereby God more wonderfully reestablishes in the second Adam what He had established in the first Adam."

in the relation it gives with so august a term, or in the human better-
ment that must serve as the foundation for such a relation. In this
latter sense, uncreated grace no longer differs from created grace
except in the point of view from which it is regarded.

This uncreated grace is everything in the order of grace, as God
is everything in the order of being. Nothing can be added to it, but
everything else is derived from it. Grace has its fullness and its
gratuitousness from it. Nothing can require or demand such generosity; in fact, reasons are discernible that tend to keep grace at a
distance, for mankind has sinned. But God, in His goodness and
mercy, has chosen to love us; and His goodness cannot be accounted
for by anything extraneous to it. God "is rich in mercy" (Eph. 2:4).

Once this initial gratuitousness is understood, all other gratuitous
gifts are comprehensible. They are implied in the first gift, from
which they flow as a result or a continuation or a necessary consequence that may be truly due in justice because of preceding graces;
for the whole order of grace is strictly one. But later graces share in
the absolute gratuitousness of the initial gift by reason of this very
unity; for example, the reality of merit, which we shall speak of in
its proper place, confirms the strict gratuitousness of the gift regarded as a whole.

In the course of these pages we should not lose sight of the double
role of unity, which explains both how every other gift is given in
consequence of the first gift, and how all that comes after this pure
gift, though not a pure gift with respect to a preceding gift, is nevertheless a pure gift because the original gift was such.

As for the unity of grace, it is complete from the first moment, just
as the grace itself is complete, and, like the grace itself, it resides
wholly in God. The kind of unity peculiar to grace is most perfect.
What the following pages will bring out concerning the ontological
character of grace and the perfection of its nature, holds equally for
the perfection of its unity, for *ens et unum convertuntur;* grace has a
transcendent unity that is based on the divine unity itself. The divine
character of this unity helps us to understand that merit and the almost necessary ties existing between one grace and another, ties that
are possible in the order of grace because of this unity, come from
God and His divine goodness.

The completeness of this gift accounts for its absolute character,
its abundance, its prodigality,[11] and even, as some of the saints have

[11] Eph. 1:4; 2:4; Rom. 5:5–11; II Cor. 9:14 f.

said, its extravagance. Indeed, we could have been sure of this a priori; if God gives Himself, He is not satisfied with half-measures. Parsimony has no place in God or in love. God's love leaps forth from the mysterious depths of His Trinitarian life. Poor sinners though we are,[12] we are loved with the same love with which the Son is loved; [13] we are loved in a divine person who has become man to be as we are. Why has He done so? God has kept nothing back; whatever He possesses, He has generously made over to us in Jesus Christ.[14]

Grace has an essential relationship with the Trinity.[15] Our meditation on grace has to begin with meditation on the Trinity. Grace is unintelligible unless we think of its absolute commencement, which is the matchless, incomprehensible, infinite love which the Father has for men in the Son through the Spirit.

Grace preserves this transcendent and excessive quality throughout the course of its development in us; and the same quality is found in the indescribable generosity of Christ. The extremes to which the Savior went, His death on the cross, the institution of the Eucharist, the solicitude with which He served us — for He did serve us — are truly amazing. But their roots lie deeper, in the depths of Christ's subsistence; they represent an attempt to make known to us in human fashion the divine act in which the Trinity went so far as to give itself in the Word.

These excesses scarcely appear on the outside; mankind remains miserable, and the Church remains terrestrial. But they still occur in the redemption; God's work is still going on in the midst of sin, and even utilizes the consequences of sin.

Gratia redemptoris, gratia redemptrix. Grace is called the grace of the Redeemer, not only because it was merited by the Redeemer, but because it is structurally a redemption that is being accomplished, a union of God with creatures whom sin still assails.

B. CREATED GRACE IN CHRIST

The Blessed Trinity is the ultimate transcendent source of all grace, and the humanity of the Word is its first interior principle. "Grace was conferred on Christ as on a universal principle in the

[12] Rom. 5:6 ff.
[13] John 17:26.
[14] Cf. Titus, 3:6.
[15] See chaps. 12–15 above.

genus of those who have grace . . . as on a universal principle for bestowing grace on human nature." [16] To see what grace is in us, therefore, we must first consider it as it is in the Blessed Trinity and in Christ's humanity; our grace is a sharing in the grace possessed by Him. St. Augustine observes: "The brilliant light of grace is the Savior Himself. . . . If any of the faithful wishes to acquire a clear understanding of grace, let him contemplate Christ, and in Christ he will find himself." [17]

The preceding pages have shown that Christ's sacred humanity had to have a new mode of existing that divinized it transcendentally, since it is truly and literally the humanity of God's Son. We also pointed out that this mode of existing is accidental as compared with the constitutive factors of Christ's human nature, but that nevertheless, through a quasi-formal rather than efficient causality, it enables the nature to exist in a way befitting the humanity of Him who is Being itself. Lastly, we showed that this accident is an "entity of union"; it exists only in the hypostatic union; it exists by virtue of and for the sake of this union, as a response of the human nature to the enfolding and assuming embrace of uncreated grace, so that it has no intelligibility apart from this assumption. It is like the flash of intelligence that can appear in the eyes; the eyes are nothing but flesh and fluid, yet the expression of the soul is reflected in them, and the reflection dies away instantly when the life of the soul is stifled. The entity in question is like the message, so rich in meaning and expression, that is apprehended in a musical phrase; the music is nothing but motion and vibration, but a message is conveyed by it because a man hears it, and the message vanishes as soon as the attention wanders, for it is there only for those who heed it. Or again, to employ a traditional comparison, it is like the heat and light of incandescent iron; by nature the iron is a drab and chilly thing, but heat and light break forth in its heart when fire invades it. In some such way this accident, existing in the assumed humanity and adapting itself to the humanity, is the expression of the divinity in which the humanity subsists. On its own level this humanity, which is truly God's humanity, has to be divinized. Indeed, it is divine. The word may seem audacious, but it is the term chosen by theology.

[16] St. Thomas, *Summa*, IIIa, q. 7, a. 9, 11.
[17] *De praedestinatione sanctorum*, 15; *De dono perseverantiae*, 24 (PL, XLIV, 781; XLV, 1033).

Here we have something we must ponder. Otherwise, in thinking about the subsistence of the assumed nature in the Word, we show that we are content with traditional formulas without searching into their meaning. That which unites this humanity to the Son is said to be the *tractio ad Verbum*, the *elevatio ad Deum*, the *coniunctio* or *adhaesio Verbo*, the *unio recepta et passiva*. Quite true; it is nothing but that, but it is that. In the order of efficient or quasi-efficient causality all this is brought about by God and the Word alone; yet it is real because it is received in the sacred humanity and in a way befitting the humanity: *quidquid recipitur, recipitur ad modum recipientis*. Unless we wish to reduce this union to nothing, to a local juxtaposition, to a mechanical juncture, or to a juridical fiction, we have to admit something in the assumed humanity that makes it an assumed humanity, something that is human because it pertains to Christ's humanity but that is also divine because it makes that humanity the humanity of God. Whatever this something is, it is not strictly the assumption but rather the effect of the assumption.

Christ's humanity is truly divine, but by union, *per participationem quae est secundum gratiam*. It is divine as a being may be said to be divine which in itself is not God, but which God, with all His power, truth, and self-donation, makes His own. Without being God, such a being is nevertheless God's.

Therefore Christ's humanity must be divine. Nothing in the human nature as such can be an exigency for so sublime an attribute, which consequently is a grace, a wholly gratuitous gift. In fact, it is the summit and the very type of every gratuitous gift, as St. Augustine well shows.[18] Yet, as the saint remarks, it is required by the subsistence of this nature; according to this point of view, therefore, while remaining wholly supernatural, it is natural to Christ's human nature.

We have judged it necessary to bring out this transcendent "naturalism" of grace at the very outset; for, as grace develops in a man, it is observed to arouse a special sort of opposition in nature that may become extremely violent, as is to be expected in an order of redemption. Moreover, this "naturalism" shows how closely the successive steps of the coming of grace to mankind are linked together. The gift that descends from heaven does not fall on the race to crush mankind; it rises up within the race and elevates mankind; it comes from

[18] Cf. *The Whole Christ*, pp. 403-8.

God who gives it by appearing among us as one of us. Accordingly, while it springs forth entirely from God, it also springs forth from our race.

C. CREATED GRACE IN THE MYSTICAL BODY

The unity that is found in Christ passes to all mankind that is united to Him. We explained at length the reasons for this transference, when we discussed the universal aspect of Christ's assumed humanity. Here we need only to add several considerations by way of applying these reasons to the present subject.

Humanity is essentially social. By divinizing Christ's humanity, the Incarnation made it supernaturally and divinely social, and gave it a social efficacy, a power of universal expansion. In the single human nature that was assumed, the deification of the whole race was really and radically accomplished. The grace given to Christ resided in a nature that was to carry it to the limits of mankind, and supernaturally and infinitely intensified the power and the movement that were to propagate it.

The magnificent unity of the divine plan is apparent. The whole work is wrought in Christ, by reason of the hypostatic union, which essentially makes Him what He is. Through this union His human nature subsists in the first principle of all things and in the first principle of all grace. Consequently, by a sort of assimilation and communication of properties, the sacred humanity is the first principle in its own order, that is, in the order of divinized humanity and of grace. In a certain sense Christ is "the principle of all grace according to His humanity, as God is the principle of all being." [19] The hypostatic union, which causes Christ's human nature to subsist in God, the uncreated grace who gives Himself, likewise empowers it to be in its own way the donation of God and the communication of this uncreated grace to all mankind. Thus the sacred humanity itself is enabled to be grace, created grace, the visible form and the overflowing profusion of grace; it is the high point in the order of divinization, the universal source of whose "fullness we have all received, and grace for grace." [20] Christ's human nature subsists in God who is eminently *diffusivum sui;* in its own way it will be *diffusiva sui,* by being *diffusiva Dei.*

[19] St. Thomas, *De veritate,* q. 29, a. 5. Cf. *Compendium of Theology,* p. 248, Part I, chap. 216.

[20] John 1:16.

Its union with God, perfecting all that is essential in it, and hence also its social aspect, is a union with men; otherwise it would not be a human union. Therefore its divinization, which is unique and without parallel, is a unique and unparalleled principle of communication.[21]

When the essence of grace is adequately perceived, it is seen to be a deification, not of an isolated man, but of humanity. There is no such thing as an isolated man; the grace that comes to a man unites him supernaturally to all men. This truth merits attentive consideration, for it is the key that opens up all the consequences that result for the Catholic aspect of all Christian life and all interior grace. Christ alone is the full divinization of the race; alone, but not separated. The distribution of graces and their multiplication in the many individuals of mankind are based on our unity in Christ and are recapitulated in this unity.

When our vision penetrates far enough into grace such as it is actually found in mankind, we see that it is one in its very multiplicity. Grace is the unique union with God brought about by the Incarnation; and the Incarnation extends to the totality of Christ, to the whole human family which grace endeavors to fashion into the mystical body of Christ; and the whole body reacts to grace by an intrinsic conformation to it and a godlike elevation.

Evidently, as we are about to show, grace comes to persons, for the human race is made up of persons. But for the moment, true to the order of ideas governing these pages, we wish to dwell on the fact that the universal character of grace overshadows its personal character. Grace effects the deification of the *Christus universus*, of the whole mystical body, and transforms regenerated mankind into the "body" of this grace.

This body, being the fullness of Christ, will have the history and the successive stages of Christ's life for its own history and successive stages. Before actually coming in the flesh, Christ was on the way all during the long advent that is the story of the Old Testament. We may even put forward the conjecture that He was on the way long before that; we may suppose that He was decreed as soon as creation was decided on, as the priceless gift which God in His goodness

---

[21] Therefore we see how truly St. Thomas says that in Christ the grace of union, the grace of headship, and His individual grace are one single grace. *Summa*, IIIa, q.8, a.5 ad 3; *In III Sent.*, d.13, q.3, a.1, sol 1 and 3; cf. *In Ioannem*, cap. 3, lect. 6; *De veritate*, q.29, a.5 et ad 7.

wished to present to men who were in no way worthy of receiving it.

We scarcely have to change the terms or modify the exposition to show that these stages in the coming of Christ find their counterpart in the whole organism which is the fullness of Christ and the "body" of grace. The decisive stage is reached when this organism is constituted by the Incarnation, although the organism still has to be constituted and to grow in its members until the end of the world. The preceding stage is the whole life of mankind subsequent to the promise made in Eden. For God's promise is efficacious; it was entrusted to the race as a "seed of God," as an active power that turns men's souls toward Christ and makes mankind the progeny of the Savior, the race of God, the lineage of the Holy One. Prior to this stage we can conceive another: that in which mankind was first envisaged as the recipient of a great pardon and the object of gracious mercy, as the race of Him who is divine Pardon and reunion and mercy.

If we may represent matters thus, the human race is a family that requires grace, not by its nature but by the vocation God destined for it from its remotest origin. Speaking in this sense we may make bold to say that grace, wholly supernatural though it is in itself, is natural to the race; grace is needed, not to constitute mankind formally as such, but to make it the "body" of this Man whom God had in mind from all eternity. Certainly, the destiny to become this "body" and to possess such a Man is a wholly gratuitous gift for the race; but from the time the race began to exist, grace was included in this gratuitous gift, and mankind ought to possess it.

D. CREATED GRACE IN EACH INDIVIDUAL

The main point yet remains to be considered; we refer to what is ordinarily known as sanctifying grace, that is, grace as personally affecting every regenerated man. The mystical body of Christ is made up of persons; if the mystical body is to be animated by grace, these persons must receive grace, and, since they are persons, they cannot receive grace except in a personal way.

Since the members are elevated in Christ and through Christ, their elevation must be an influx, a participation of Christ's elevation. Hence we shall gain a better idea of the members' elevation if we examine Christ's elevation. To pass from one to the other, all we have to do is realize that the latter is related to the former as source and totality are related to derivation and member.

The supernatural elevation intrinsic to Christ's humanity comes from the hypostatic union. It is an accidental perfecting of His humanity owing to the hypostatic union and expressing this union; it is an "entity of union," a perfection resulting from union. The successive phases—successive only in logical analysis, not in time—which we have to bear in mind when considering the human nature thus perfected, are the following. The supernatural perfecting of the human nature affects both its individual and its social aspect. This perfection adapts the nature to the subsistence which it receives and which is subsistence in the Son; hence it is a "filial" perfection, as we showed when treating of the Son. Finally, the perfection that adapts the nature to be the Son's humanity, adapts it to be God's humanity, and therefore divinizes it. But we should note that the human nature is divinized because it is made filial, and not contrariwise; for this humanity belongs to God because it belongs to the Son, not vice versa.

All this comes to Christians from their membership in Christ, and is theirs in the participated and derived manner that is proper for members; yet it comes to them in the same logical order and internal dependence as are found in Christ. In their elevation, consequently, as in the elevation of the assumed humanity, we have to consider that the union with God which Christians enjoy as Christ's members is their participation in the union which Christ as head has with the uncreated grace of Christ. The perfection which flows to them from this union is their created grace.

The successive phases of this perfecting grace, in Christians no less than in Christ, are the following. First, it confers a supernatural elevation on their humanity by incorporating it into the new humanity or "body" of Christ. Moreover, it embraces all that is essential in humanity, the individual as well as the social factors. Further, it is essentially a "filial" perfection, an adoption, because its very essence and purpose is to unite men to the Son in Christ. Lastly, it divinizes those who receive this adoption, for the Son to whom it unites men is God. In the order of genesis, divinization logically follows adoption, just as the character of divinization found in Christ's humanity is subsequent to its filial character.[22]

[22] See the *De fide catholica* of the Vatican Council, quoted above.

In meditating on these aspects, the best order to follow is that just indicated, the order of logical succession. This is the order we intend to follow. The various aspects, however, are not separated, although they are distinct; interactions take place among them, and some of the assertions we shall be naturally led to make about the earlier ones will not be fully intelligible except in the light of the later ones.

In the first place, then, all the just are in Christ and He is in them. Furthermore, they are justified persons and are Christ's members precisely as persons. Therefore they have a personal title to share in the special union of His humanity with God, in the transcendent presence of God, and in His uncreated grace.

This uncreated grace is what accounts for the presence of God which Christians enjoy, namely, the indwelling of the Spirit and of the Trinity. It is true that such presence and indwelling are not fully intelligible except in the light of the adoption and divinization that are their effects. But we have spoken sufficiently of these effects in the preceding pages, and so can now go on to consider the particular mystery of God's supernatural presence. That it is a mystery cannot be questioned; for it is connected with the mystery of God's presence in Christ's humanity and with the mystery of the Incarnation that is God's loving gift to us. The first principle in the science of Christianity, here as everywhere, is Christ and the Incarnation.

Therefore we should not think of the kinds of presence suggested by sense experience; they are too lowly, and we mention them only to drop them. The contact between two objects placed together, or the compenetration of a body by air, by space, or by the ether, is no more than the juxtaposition of two things that remain foreign to each other; and since they are foreign, they are outside each other and even absent from each other. Their nearness and so-called presence only emphasize their distance.

Indeed, we have to go beyond the idea of presence that philosophy or metaphysics can supply, such as the presence of two persons who know each other intimately and imitate each other, the presence of every being in all others, and even the presence of the absolute Being in every being as demanded by the analogy and participation of being. The latter is the most perfect of such comparisons, but is still not enough.

In the mystery of Christ's humanity, God's presence is far more sublime. He is present by what He Himself is, not merely by what the sacred humanity is. He is present by way of union and personal unity. He is present in such a way that the ultimate depths of this Man are those of God Himself, and the inward reality of this Man is that of God Himself; for this Man is a divine person. The presence of God that we Christians enjoy is a sharing in that presence, and is a sort of membership in it; for we are members of Christ.

In the mystery of the Incarnation, the united natures remain distinct; and in the mystery of incorporation into Christ, the persons of Christians remain distinct from Christ and from one another. They likewise remain distinct from God who unites Himself to them in His Son. But they are not separated from God in anything that He is. He is present within them by His being, and not merely as their cause.

Indeed, the most secret life of God is the most notable feature of His presence in Christians. Through their union with the incarnate Son, their union with the mystery of the eternal generation and of the Trinity is logically prior to their union with the divine nature of God such as He is known by reason. God is present to them in His very inaccessibility; they are admitted into the intimacies of the Trinitarian life and are equipped to know it and to adapt themselves to it before they have such relations with the abstract Godhead of the philosophers. God is present to them as He is present to Himself, by the sequence of the divine processions and by His interior circumincession. He is united to them by the inner union of the three consubstantial persons. "We will come to him and will make Our abode with him." [23] "As Thou, Father, in Me and I in Thee: that they also may be one in Us." [24] "That the love wherewith Thou hast loved Me may be in them, and I in them." [25]

This self-giving of God, this uncreated grace, is what calls forth created grace in Christians, and it operates in them as it is present in them, through their union with Christ. Hence their grace is a derivation of the grace that is found in Christ; it is an accident of a sort, an "entity of union." When we say that it is an accident, we mean that it exists in the human nature of Christians as in a subject of inherence; without it, their nature would still be a true human nature. It is an

[23] John 14:23.
[24] Ibid., 17:21.
[25] Ibid., 17:26.

intrinsic accident, a quality, a *habitus*, as we shall show later. But it is a very special accident and is unique in its kind, a supernatural, divinizing accident. Such a specific difference necessarily modifies the generic notion; we are here dealing with a singular mode of being, which likens a creature to the Being that transcends every modality.

We have said enough about this divinizing entity in connection with Christ; and since we shall have to come back to it, we need not insist on the matter here. The point we have to bring out is that this divinizing entity is an "entity of union," and "accident of union." But we may be brief, as we are merely employing ideas already developed.

The entity in question makes man the beneficiary of the uncreated grace that comes to him in Christ; it is the reaction of his human nature to God's gift; it is the possession of God by human nature, corresponding to God's donation of Himself; it is human nature's way of expressing, through a sort of formal causality, the new mode of being that is bestowed on man. It is the adaptation of human nature to this mode of being, and the reception of a real foundation for the new relation that has been granted.

Such an accident cannot be conceived as something existing alone. As it is an "entity of union," we have to think of it in its function of uniting and in connection with the man who receives and God who gives; we must associate it with the donation that is epitomized in the God-man. Accordingly we cannot represent grace as something set apart or isolated, any more than we can define a knot by stating what severance is. Yet the temptation to do so is strong. Man, enamored of conceptual and mathematical clarity, is always trying to picture grace along the lines of things familiar to sense experience, as though it were a little entity complete in itself, a sort of spiritual crown which God selects from His treasure-chest, and which He may give, take back, return, embellish, or leave as it is, according to man's merits.

This translation of grace into empirical terms satisfies nothing but our imagination; it conveys nothing to the mind except insuperable problems. Even on a lower plane we strip intelligibility from various metaphysical realities, such as mind, freedom, or existence, as soon as we make "things" out of them. These entities belong to another order and are essentially wholes; they cannot be adequately expressed by conceptual knowledge, which is only a part of our whole knowledge, and expresses only those entities that are parts.

When grace is conceived in this way it becomes a nature; it may be eminently noble, but it is still a nature. How, then, can it be something essentially above nature? How can it become one with him who receives it, and how can the nature of him whom it affects avoid being denatured?

Consequently grace is not a complete entity, a substance existing in itself. It is the change that comes over a man when he is united to God. It is that by which the gift that God gives in a divine way exists in man in a human way; it is that which makes man formally what the coming of God makes him effectively. It is at once more and less than a self-enclosed entity; it does not exist as a thing, but rather causes man to exist in a new way.

Therefore grace is not a thing that can be isolated. Although it is neither God, who gives it, nor man, who receives it, it is inseparable both from the self-donation of God who produces it, and from us whom it makes Godlike. We may say that it is the entrance of God into us, so far as this entrance changes us intrinsically and conforms us, to the degree that this is possible, to God who draws near. It is our very soul as internally ennobled and elevated by the indwelling of God and for this indwelling. Or we may say that it is the union of God and man, so far as this union produces an "amelioration" that perfects man's nature with a perfection that is transcendent and supernatural, for it confers on us a sort of intrinsic proportion with God Himself. Thus understood, this perfection may be regarded as a divine way of being man, as is right for the God-man and His members.

The perfection conferred on Christ's humanity by the hypostatic union makes that humanity, as it were, universally human, so that Christ can reach out to all men, contain them in Himself by grace, and raise them to the supernatural state. This mystic fullness enables His humanity, which was made the unity and the head of the race, to be the instrument that is perfectly equipped to purify and sanctify all mankind.

Men are gathered together and incorporated into the sacred humanity thus perfected, to be conducted by it into the supernatural order. Whenever an instrument is used for any purpose, it must first be applied to an object before it can shape that object into the finished article that is envisaged.

But if anyone is taken up and incorporated into Christ's sacred humanity, he is given a part in the new way, the supernaturally perfect way of being man. He receives a sort of new nature, a supernature which is the divinization of simple nature, and shares in the way of being man that is proper to Christ and that is His with so great an abundance that He can enrich every man with it. In other words, he is perfected with the supernatural, human perfection we have been discussing. He receives it in the way Christ's humanity receives it, and shares in that reception. As found in Christ's humanity, this perfection arises from the fact that, being united to Being itself by uncreated grace and the hypostatic union, His nature is adapted to this union by existing in a more perfect way. As Christ's human nature is a human nature and nothing else, the perfection it thus receives makes it more perfectly and completely human; yet it is human as only a nature can be that is the humanity of God.

A participation in the same union is found in us. Therefore the union ought to bring us the same results or, more exactly, a share in the same results. As members of Him who is Being itself, we are admitted to a new and infinitely closer contact with Being, and must in consequence exist more perfectly and intensely; moreover, since the existence we have is human existence, we must be more perfectly and thoroughly men, in Him who is man par excellence.

God is pure Being. When He gives Himself, the recipient truly possesses Him, not so much by having as by being. Such a one is what he was before, as he can be nothing else; but he now exists with a richness of life that is impossible except as a result of the gratuitous donation of Being itself, and that in its own way reflects this donation. If such a second creation is not to turn into annihilation, it must firmly seize and reinforce the first creation.

An ancient theological adage expresses a profound truth when it affirms that grace does not destroy nature but perfects it. The Godhead is not a limited essence with determinate characteristics incompatible with those of the nature to which it gives itself; it can communicate itself without altering the essence receiving it. If an angel were to unite himself to a man, he would communicate his own attributes to the man, because the angel has his own particular way of existing. The man would then exist in a different way than before, and, so far as we can reason about such matters, would cease to be a man. In other words, such a union is impossible.

But if "angelization" is impossible, divinization is not. God is not a limited being, with contours that would clash with the contours of a finite thing. His way of being is simply to be, fully and eternally, with all the necessity, perfection, and immensity that pertain to being. When He unites Himself to a finite nature, He does not change that nature's way of being, for His own way of being is not alien to it. He does not make it different, but causes it to be more thoroughly, more infinitely and divinely what it is. Therefore divinization, or created grace, is not an alteration of ourselves. It is a full realization of ourselves: grace does not destroy but perfects nature.

Accordingly grace respects nature, and meets nature as God's assuming act met Christ's humanity, with consideration, reverence, and love. Grace accommodates itself to the slow and heavy gait of clumsy rational animals. It adapts itself to the play of our natural laws, and inclines them to its own ends without doing violence to them.

This does not mean that grace is not exacting, for its function is to lay hold of all to perfect all. Yet its exactions are tempered by the helps it imparts, and therefore can be more insistent, because they never cease. It has soothing remedies even for the wounds left by sin, but also makes great demands. Grace has to work on man such as he is, and strives to make him better; it has to work on the sinner and the consequences of sin, as otherwise it will lack the proper matter for its operation. For the grace we are speaking of is the grace of the Redeemer; it is essentially redemptive grace.

To be sure, grace is incompatible with sin, for it is the expression in man of union with God, the absolute Good. But it is also the transfiguration of sinful humanity, and this is not the least of its beauties and its victories. This perfect adaptation, this realism, and even, if we may use the term, this "naturalism" of supernatural grace, does not at all overshadow its transcendence, but rather sets it in relief, and brings out the ontological perfection and the noble task of grace.

Since grace perfects nature, which is a principle of operation, it also perfects the faculties by which nature operates. Since it perfects being, it also perfects the faculties of being. In particular it perfects the specifically human faculties of intellect and will in a way that is suitable for men who are united to Being itself and who, in Christ, are members of Him who is. Thus grace has an inherent tendency to invest the soul with faith, hope, and charity.

As grace is a divinization and a special relationship to the Trinity, this perfecting of the faculties must have God as its object, principle, and motive. We perceive, consequently, that it is theological, and that each of the theological virtues has a special relationship to the Trinity. Yet, as it comes to sinners through a redemptive grace, we also perceive that these virtues, however victorious they may be in themselves, have a tincture of the banal, the soiled, and the ordinary in man. Our faith, hope, and charity operate in the midst of a redemption that is still in process of accomplishment. We have no reason to feel surprise at the obscurities, the anxieties, and the vacillations that creep into our faith, hope, and charity.

On earth, grace is still achieving itself, and will not attain its full development short of the glory of heaven. Hence the virtues of faith, hope, and charity are in an imperfect state. Charity will reach its full stature only in triumphant love; faith and hope will not realize the perfection found in them until they are transformed into vision and possession. The imperfection of this stage is the reason why the bonds between the virtues and grace are so fragile, so that a person may have faith and hope without charity and grace. These fatal separations will no longer be possible in heaven, where glory, vision, possession, and love will all be one.

Since man is individual as well as social by nature, the perfection he receives in Christ must likewise be individual and social. Grace is personal in each man. In each individual it has traits that correspond to peculiarities of race, nation, age, contemporary civilization, temperament, and character; it has its own unique quality that makes it quite distinct, though not separate, from the grace of all other men.

This is a capital point of doctrine in the theology of grace: the justice of each man is not the justice of Christ or of God as imputed to him, but is strictly his own.[26] The supernaturally personal character of grace is what causes the supernaturally personal character of holiness, of the theological virtues, and of the whole eternal life of each Christian, and, *mutatis mutandis,* of each saint in heaven. Each has his own virtues, and has them in his own way. The individual, and especially the person, is indescribable and unique; and these proper-

[26] Council of Trent, Sess. VI, cc. 7, 16 (Denz., 799, 809).

ties, this irreducible originality, in the best sense of the word, are what grace divinizes.

The cause of this variety is not a multiplicity of divine decrees assigning to each man his own vocation and particular characteristics. It comes from the single volition that willed Christ so powerfully that in Him it embraced the divinization of the multiple, diverse, restless thing we call humanity. The cause, therefore, is to be found in God and Christ and in their unity, and also in humanity and its structure and the direction grace gives it toward God and Christ.

Accordingly each manifestation of Christian sanctity is sharply distinct from others by clearly marked individual features and by the roots it has in the very heart of personality and in the very substance of the soul. Holiness is distinct in proportion to its excellence. Hence it is unique in Christ. The sanctity of Christ is distinct from every other holiness, for it is the source and model of every holiness, by the very fact that it is united to every holiness. This distinction, whose intensity implies a corresponding intensity of union, is communicated by Christ to His members in a degree that is suitable for members.

Theology has discussed at great length the personal aspect of grace, the interior contact all regenerated souls have with God, the elevation they receive in their nature, and the economy of aids by way of illumination and protection that guide all men in their very freedom of action toward God who is their end. We are aware of nothing we can add. Truth is a common possession, and we make all this our own.

It seems to us, however, that theology has not said everything, or rather that it has said very little, about the social aspect of grace. Yet this social aspect is what makes it the grace of Christ, not only in its meritorious and exemplary causality, but in its very essence and structure, and in the personal divinization it confers on each soul within the God-man's mystical body.

We claim no credit for stressing this aspect. In the designs of providence, the doctrine of the mystical body has advanced until it now occupies the foreground. This progress greatly facilitates our understanding of the nature of grace and its relations with life and personal will. The doctrine also makes clear that the Christian religion is not an isolated relationship of each man to God, but the catholic and universal union all men have with God. Each person is united to God by the union which all have; each one is united by the supernatural structure of his nature which, in the unity of Christ, is made for this union with God in fellowship with all.

In its inner essence, in its personalism which makes it the supernatural crown of personality, the divinized life of grace finds itself opposed to individualism. While grace is a personal and interior thing, it is also a thing of union and fellowship. These two aspects are essential to the grace of Christ, to holiness, and to Christian virtue, as they are essential to the quality of a member of Christ, a Christian. There is distinction here, and it deepens as man advances in supernatural perfection. But there is no division, for every growth in being is growth in unity. Immanent life, interior liberty, spontaneity, and intimacy are present; but there is no isolation, separation, independence, or severance from mankind. Even on the natural plane mankind is a unified thing, and man, in search of full life, seeks union with his kind; and he would find it abundantly in natural beatitude if he were not destined to find it much more perfectly in the supernatural state. But in either case, particularly in the second, union is human, and it unifies men as they are, as persons interior to one another, as units that require all the others to realize fully the capacities of all.

These two characteristics of grace, its essential personalism and its no less essential social and ecclesiastical aspect, are really but a single divine life that is infused into men. We should not say, without further qualifications, that the Christian is for the Church but not conversely, or that the Church is for the Christian but not conversely. Such comparisons suggest divisions, and the Church and Christ are meant to exist in unity. The unity that interiorly perfects each member by intensifying his personality, and the unity that gathers all together by animating the whole body, are one and the same unity, that of Christ and His life; and Christ is for us, as we are in Him and from Him and for Him.

As regards the second phase in supernatural elevation, the "filial" perfection that fits Christ's members to be members of the Son, we have dealt with it sufficiently in speaking of the person of the Son; we need not return to it. Therefore we can proceed immediately to the third step in this elevation, the divinizing perfection that adapts Christ's members to be members of God.

The two phases are not really distinct, since the person of the Son is not really distinct from His divine nature. The distinction between them can be no more than a mental distinction, which, however, is sharply marked in this class of distinction, and corresponds to something real. It is based on the virtual distinction between the divine nature and the divine persons.

Supernatural elevation is a conformation and assimilation to the divine nature, inasmuch as it divinizes. As such, it receives the name of grace, and verifies the theological definitions of grace. Consequently we have to say that grace is formally a union with the divine nature as nature, rather than a union with one of the divine persons; and yet, if our previous exposition is correct, the reality we call grace is materially a fellowship with a divine person before it is a fellowship with the divine nature.

Christian teaching has long been explicit on the subject of this divinization. Christians receive an elevation in the very substance of their souls, and this elevation makes them truly Godlike; they are made "partakers of the divine nature" (II Pet. 1:4). It makes them inherently agreeable to God, objects of His love, and worthy of His heaven. God alone counts in the eyes of God; if Christians are to have any value in His mind and are to find favor in His sight, they must first have been made like to God.

This assimilation to the divine nature has often been brought out by scholastic theologians, especially by St. Thomas. But the Greek Fathers have taught it with greater force and amplitude of development than anyone else.[27] They seize every possible occasion to show that all Christianity is summed up in it; God, they repeat, became man that man might become God.

In our day the term "divinization" is often used to designate our supernatural elevation; many even prefer it to the word "grace." They believe that it is richer in meaning, and even more concrete; it directly calls a number of familiar realities to mind. Is not divinization somewhat like illumination or heating? Has not everyone observed how crystal glows when it is held up to a light, or how an object becomes warm when it is placed on the hearthstone? Similarly, everyone can grasp how a man becomes divine when he is brought close to God.

That is quite true. Yet we must bear in mind that assimilation to God is beyond all conceiving, just as God Himself is. Indeed, we

[27] See *The Whole Christ*, Index, s.v. Deification.

may say that it is even more so, because, in addition to the impossi-bility of conceiving God, we have the difficulty of conceiving how lowly man can receive a likeness to infinite excellence. When we think of heating or illumination, we can readily understand how a low degree of heat or light may make a thing resemble a great heat or light. The nature is the same, only one is smaller; they are com-pared as one to a thousand. But what can a "low degree of divinity" be? How can a mode of being make a man resemble God, since God is not similar to anything?

Furthermore, how can a man in any true sense put on a form that will divinize him? He already has his form, and that is what makes him man. How can he receive another form that will make him divine, without ceasing to be human? And how can he introduce into his form the modifications that are needed to make it divine and that have to be so great as to be almost infinite, without stretching it well beyond the necessarily narrow limits capable of admitting accidental changes, and without bursting it asunder? Is it unseemly to recall the fable of the frog that endeavored to blow itself up to the size of an ox?

We believe that this difficulty may serve as a convenient starting point for an inquiry into the nature of divinization and grace. We have to appreciate the full force of the difficulty if we wish to bring to its solution the effort of mind needed to represent aright this new type of being, supernatural being, which has no more than a remote analogy with any being we know. We have to turn our thoughts to a new ontology, for that is the goal we now have to reach.

We have already touched on this subject when discussing the supernatural, and also when treating of the effect produced in Christ's humanity by the assuming act. Here we shall find it enough to indicate the connections which link that event with the idea of divinization and grace.

The first point we wish to mention is our own opinion that divini-zation is unthinkable apart from the Incarnation. We do not maintain that God could not have called it forth in any other way; such a contention would suppose an adequate comprehension of God's power and of the supernatural order. Nevertheless, in the absence of data to the contrary, we do not see how we can conceive the matter otherwise.

In any order, what is derived and secondary can be understood only through what is primary and per se. In the order of divinization generally, and more particularly in the order of divinized humanity, the God-man is primary. Therefore the order of divinized humanity, the order of divinization, is comprehended in and through the God-man. In the God-man alone God has become accessible and has given Himself in a communication that cannot be natural to any creature. Hence the idea of a true gift of God requires Christ for its intelligibility.

The God-man exists. Therefore, as we have said, His humanity must be truly, intrinsically, and objectively the humanity of God. In the order of efficient causality, that humanity receives existence from God alone. But it does not have existence from God in the order of formal or quasi-formal causality, for the natures are distinct. To have existence in the order of formal causality, a change must take place in it that makes it the humanity of God, "not in the way of an efficient cause, but in the way of a formal cause"; [28] and the change must be such that the man it constitutes is truly God. This is the change previously described, the perfection so tremendous, so sublime, and so perfect that it is impossible unless it rests and terminates in Being itself.

We assert that this perfection, in union with the divinity to which it is necessarily united, is the formal or quasi-formal cause of the divinization of Christ's humanity. We can also say that the perfection by itself alone is the quasi-formal cause, since it necessarily implies this union.

This, we believe, is the right idea of total, ontological, intrinsic divinization. It is not the Godhead itself, for the natures remain distinct. It is a new way of being that arises in the humanity; a way of *being*, we repeat, and such as befits a human nature; but it is so excellent, so sublime, so exalted, that a man could not have it unless he were God, in the strict sense of the word.

Such is the divinization of Christ's humanity. We shall do well to contemplate it, for it is radically the divinization of all humanity. Since it is divinization in all possible profuseness, it spreads to all and becomes interior to all, just as Christ's sanctifying grace flows forth from Him to produce the personal grace of every Christian.

Can one truly become a member of Christ's humanity without

[28] St. Thomas, *Summa*, Ia IIae, q. 110, a. 2 ad 1; cf. q. 111, a. 1 ad 1; a. 2 ad 1; *De veritate*, q. 27, a. 1 ad 3.

sharing in its divinization, without receiving from Him a divinization cut to the measure of a member? Christ's humanity incorporates all regenerated humanity into itself precisely because it is so exalted and so perfectly divinized. Must we not say that it divinizes all humanity by infusing into regenerated humanity a share in its own divinization?

This excellence of Christ cannot divinize by itself alone, for it is something finite and is a quality of a finite humanity; such a hypothesis makes no sense. The condition of its existence is the fact that it does not exist by itself alone, for it is an "entity of union," the result, the expression, and the insertion of a union, by a union, for a union, in a union. To conceive it correctly, we have to think of it in connection with the divinity to which it unites the humanity, that is, we have to think of it by believing in the Incarnation, with that special form of thought which is faith.

This is also the way to represent the divinization of the Christian. We should not think of it as an independent entity having of itself the power to sanctify, but as an "entity of union" that joins us to Christ and His divinity, and that has no power to divinize apart from such union and divinity. This does not mean that of itself it has no power to divinize, for it is a uniting force; a member is a member because of its bond with the body, and a Christian is a Christian because he belongs to Christ. The thing to do, then, is to represent it as it is, in connection with Christ, by believing in the whole Christ, and to trace it back to Christ. The union between God and man that is found in Christ and is something human in Christ's humanity, is what enables us to understand the divine in humankind.

Accordingly grace, as far as its mode of existing is concerned, can be nothing else than an accident in man. Yet it is truly divine, because it is an "entity of union" modeled on the hypostatic union.

This idea of divinization opens up many avenues of thought, as we realize as soon as we examine it carefully. God is the absolute Being. When He divinizes man, He bestows on him an "entity of union," a union with His own most intimate life, His Trinitarian life, with God's own inner mystery of union. Therefore divinization, and consequently grace, is something essentially ontological. It does not merely confer this or that new perfection, but makes the recipient exist in a different way, by actuating the remotest capacities of finite being.

In a preceding chapter we showed that every finite being included, beyond its natural existence that likens it to God regarded as the first cause of the finite, a possibility of existing in an immeasurably greater and better way, that places it in a possible relationship with God as He is in Himself, with the Blessed Trinity.[29] "The power of receiving grace is always measured by the receiving subject, and is caused by the principles of that subject," says St. Thomas.[30] The two aspects we can conceive in God (according to our way of knowing), that is, God as pure act and the cause of everything, and God as the Trinity in His interior life, enable us to conceive, on the analogy of Being itself, the two aspects we just said are present in every being. The second of these two aspects can be actuated only by a wholly gratuitous intervention of God's interior life. Prior to that, it is nothing but an obediential potency. Nevertheless, when it is made possible or real by the divine goodness, it becomes the supreme and complete mode of existing of the creature thus gratuitously endowed, and is the creature's supreme necessity; henceforth it is necessary in order that the creature may truly "be."

We see, therefore, that the science of grace is not a sort of edifying psychology or a pious exhortation, but is literally an ontology, a metaphysics; we might say a "meta-metaphysics." Its principle is being such as it is in its inner mystery, and such as it is made known to sinners in Christ the Redeemer; hence its principle is dogma: the dogma of the Trinity, of Christology, of Ecclesiology. Its content is the description of this mode of being which is more than natural being, and is above the oppositions that characterize natural being, the oppositions between created and uncreated, temporal and eternal, finite and infinite. It rises above these oppositions because it is an entity of union.

Thus we can conceive that nature and grace are perfectly united to make up a single thing, with a unity that is so perfect it surpasses every unity which nature could realize; for it is produced by God Himself. Undoubtedly this unity is still insecure here on earth. But this instability is not owing to any ontological imperfection discoverable in the unity, nor to the eternally immovable Being who gives it, but solely to the natural fragility of the being in which it is realized. So long as the latter is in course of formation, it can be false

[29] Cf. chap. 15.
[30] *In II Sent.*, d. 26, q. 1, a. 2 ad 2.

to itself and rise up in rebellion against its own being, that is, its natural law. It retains this power even when it possesses the source of eternal life, and this mutability found in man is alone the reason why participation in the immovable Absolute is changeable in man. Grace itself is not affected by the downfall of the person it resides in. It no longer continues to exist, for it had existence only in him; yet in itself it is not touched, because its existence resulted from the self-giving of the changeless God. And when it returns after man's repentance, it is restored essentially intact as though no disaster had occurred, for God gives Himself as He had given Himself before.

Because of its ontological essence, grace affects the innermost nature of a person when it first comes to him, and goes on to take ever deeper root in him. In this it resembles the hypostatic union, which reaches down to the deepest recesses of the assumed humanity, and lodges in what would have been its personality, that is, in the very source of its existence and operation, thus making the human nature subsist in the personality of the Word. Similarly grace resides in a man's innermost center, in the very substance of his soul, below consciousness, the human faculties, and the information of the body by the soul, thus setting the whole on the bedrock of Being itself and divinizing man from within.

This ontological aspect, viewed from the point of vantage we have taken, opens up the full meaning of the scholastic teaching that grace is an entitative habit. God is pure Being; to possess Him truly a man must exist otherwise than by his natural existence; he must receive and possess a new way of existing. From the same standpoint grace, regarded as an assimilation to God, is a new act rather than a new form, for God is act, not form. However, in accord with the point of view that regards grace as something in man, we may admit that it is a form; but we should add that it actuates more than it informs, and that it imparts fuller being rather than another kind of being.

We conclude, therefore, that grace is less a change than a gift that turns over to a person the perfect possession of himself. In this light it is seen to be the exact opposite of a change, at least of a change that would alter a man. Since the principle of identity is the principle of being as being, and since grace is a supreme consummation of being, we may say that grace is a supreme identification of a person with himself.

CHAPTER XX

ACTUAL GRACE

"We are God's coadjutors."
I Cor. 3:9

I. INTRODUCTION

We shall begin our discussion of actual grace by giving the Catholic teaching on the subject. The lines we here quote from the draft *De fide catholica* come after the passage we transcribed in the preceding chapter to convey an idea of sanctifying grace.

Any virtue or morality resulting from the exercise of merely natural faculties is far removed from the Christian justice and sanctity that lead the person who engages in good works to the kingdom of heaven. For, although the rational soul has a natural power of perceiving and doing what is lawful, which is not only free from blame but is rightly deemed praiseworthy, nothing of this sort, if performed without faith and grace, pertains to the holiness that brings one to eternal life. The disposition fitting one for beatitude, no less than the life of beatitude itself, comes as a free gift from the merciful God, for it surpasses nature. Therefore the powers of nature are not sufficient for any salutary act either in the just, so as to make them more just, or in sinners, so as to dispose them for justification. Our Lord assured us of this when He said: "Without Me you can do nothing" (John 15:5).[1]

This passage and other documents that describe actual grace may be summarized by saying that actual grace is a divine influence added to natural energy, a passing aid or help given to the human act as such, that is, to the act of knowing and willing, enabling it to operate in a

[1] *De fide catholica*, 5 (Mansi, *Amplissima collectio conciliorum*, LIII, 292 f.).

way conducing to the possession of our supernatural end. St. Thomas says that it is "a divine aid whereby God moves us to will and to act aright." [2] The liturgy, the Fathers, and the theologians make use of the following terms: *illuminatio, illustratio, instinctus, aperitio voluntatis, suasio, inspiratio, adiutorium, desiderium, cupiditas boni, motio.*

As something passing and not permanent, as a strengthening of the faculties and not a state, actual grace is seen to be clearly distinct from sanctifying grace. Ordinarily, in fact, as we know from the authentic description of the process of justification given by the Council of Trent, the initial actual graces are given when as yet sanctifying grace is absent from the soul. Nevertheless actual grace is closely associated with sanctifying grace. Actual grace is wholly designed to introduce sanctifying grace into the soul, to further its growth, and to enable it to act. We cannot speak of the one without speaking of the other.

Jesus Christ presented them both in this association. The passage in which He speaks most of the one is the very passage in which He speaks most of the other, and the two are joined in a single teaching. This passage is the discourse after the Last Supper, especially the allegory of the vine, which is a summary of the doctrine of the Fourth Gospel on this subject. The Savior there tells us about the new life, sanctifying grace, by which His members will live in Him and therefore also in God; they are to be one with Him as He is one with the Father; they are the branches and He is the whole vine. To make clear the nature of this life and this sanctifying grace, He speaks about the fruitful activity of those who live in this way. He explains that this fruitful activity comes from Him and His Father; in other words, it depends on actual grace. "Without Me," He says, "you can do nothing." The entire energy of the branches, all their works and fruits, are those of the vine and have to come to them from the vine. Without the inspiration and help of God and Christ, Christians are powerless. This text may be said to be the basic principle in the theology of actual grace, and, as we have seen, it describes sanctifying grace. This is the text that has dominated all that the Fathers and Scholastics have had to say about the matter.

[2] *Summa*, Ia IIae, q. 111, a. 2.

II. Dialectic of Actual Grace

1. **Uncreated grace.** To grasp the nature of actual grace we must trace it back to Christ and find its place in the general economy of grace. Therefore we must turn our thoughts to Christ's subsistence and to God, the author of all grace. When we were studying sanctifying grace, we remarked that every created grace is based on uncreated grace. As is quite evident, we have to say the same of actual grace. And first of all we may observe that there is something that may be called uncreated actual grace.

This is God Himself who, having decided to unite Himself to man in Christ, likewise decided to enable man to unite himself to God in Christ. God did not wish to bring about this union by His own action alone. He wished it to be effected by man as well, in order that from its very origin it might be a union adapted to the spontaneous and free nature of man. For this purpose, man was to be aided by God, that is, by actual grace.[3]

God's desire to help man to enter into union with God in a way that surpasses human powers, has no explanation except in the divine goodness. It is wholly a grace and pure generosity. Yet the aid was due as soon as God willed sincerely—and He never wills otherwise —to unite Himself to man and to raise him to the divine plane of sanctifying grace.

In the order of grace considered as a whole, the gratuitous character of grace is verified in sanctifying grace rather than in actual grace, which is subordinate to sanctifying grace in its essence as well as in its properties. Sanctifying grace is gratuitous because of the spontaneous and mysterious act of liberality by which God decided to give Himself. We should say the same of actual grace; it is gratuitous because of God's decision to aid man with an assistance that would operate interiorly and universally. Everything else, however multiple, remote, and intimate it may be, is a consequence of this attitude taken by God, the source of all being.

2. **Created grace in Christ's humanity.** The effect of this uncreated grace is the production of created actual grace in mankind. Actual grace is produced first and fully in the recipient wherein it is first and fully applied, in the sacred humanity which God assumed

[3] God decreed the redemption in the same way, for the whole plan is one.

in order to accomplish the grand work of divinization and of union with Himself.

This humanity was united to God in such a way that only one person acted in the two natures, divine and human. Hence the action of the human nature had to be reinforced and elevated so as to be, in the most worthy manner possible, the action of God who gave Himself to the creature. Christ's actual grace consisted in this reinforcement. The statement needs a fuller explanation, but we prefer to postpone it until we come to treat of the actual grace that is given to individual Christians.

We can see clearly enough that Christ's actual grace raised His human activity to the supreme summit of perfection in the order of divinizing human activity.[4] It not only enabled Christ's human activity to tend toward divinization, but caused it to be an activity suitable for a human nature already so fully divinized that it was a universal principle of divinization; for this human nature is the human nature of God Himself.

The actual grace of Christ was seemingly different in kind from that of simple Christians here on earth; the same cannot be said of sanctifying grace, whatever may be the differences between the sanctifying grace of Christ and that of Christians. Of course it was a grace; human nature, left to itself, is never able to act in the order of divinization, any more than it is able to supply itself with adequate aids. Yet, if we regard the human nature of Christ not merely as a nature but as this particular nature in the hypostatic union, we have to say that actual grace was strictly due, and that, coming as it did from God, it came from Christ's interior. "This aid comes to Christ's human nature from within Him and is due to it because of the union, so that it cannot be refused even by God's absolute power."[5]

3. **Created grace in the mystical body.** Such is the inner unity of the grace we have been speaking of. It is present fully in Him who has the plenitude of grace. This unity and gratuitousness flow from Christ into His whole mystical body, where it is present in a participated and derived way.

[4] In particular it raised Christ's act of dying, the crown of all His human activity, to the supreme peak of perfection. Hence this act is the principle of all grace given in the sacramental economy; all the sacraments derive from the Passion and the Eucharist.

[5] Suarez, *De incarnatione,* disp. 17, sect. 4.

The abundance of actual grace in Christ's humanity enables it to flow into the mystical body from one end to another, and so its fullness becomes manifest. As the head has the fullness of grace, the body has the universality of grace. Because of the Incarnation, humanity numbers among its members a true man who is literally God and who unifies all mankind in Himself. Therefore humanity contains in profusion whatever it is in need of to carry it forward to God and to divinize it; it possesses the universality of grace virtually and in principle.

The whole Christ, the mystical body, as a living body joined to its head, has its transcendent dignity and realized divinization in Him. It also has the power of preserving itself and of growing, as is necessary for every living human being; that is, it has the power to achieve its divinization. This power comes to it by way of union, just as the body itself has life through union. The power flows continually from God, who is already in the body through Christ, by a gift that is already given, since the Giver Himself is given. This gift is intrinsic to the mystical body, for it constitutes the mystical body. Coming from God, therefore, the power comes also from the body; and in coming from the body, it comes from God.

Considered in its totality, the body of Christ in which Christ lives possesses in Him the totality of grace. No grace is given except what Christ has merited and brought to us by being the union between God and men. We should like to suggest, further, that no grace comes without the cooperation of Christ's mystical body. Since Christ has manifested the fullness of His life in the mystical body, He also manifests the full extent of His activity in it. The superabundant merit and efficaciousness of Christ has as its effect and prolongation and full manifestation a corresponding efficaciousness in the whole body. As a general rule, no grace is given to the human race that has not been implored, begged, merited, and in some way brought down by the human race, by the Catholic Church, and by the action and love of the mystical body.

In this immense unity and vital continuity, the economy of grace is unified and continuous. It is quite gratuitous from the initial gift to the ultimate prolongation, with a gratuitousness that is everywhere actual and active, and is a gift that comes without interruption from an ever spontaneous love. And it is all the more gratuitous for the reason that it freely imparts a power to merit it in some degree.

4. Actual grace in each individual.

a) Reasons for grace. Man is moved by God by means of something that is in man. In the order of efficient causality, the movement comes from God and has its source in Him alone. But in the order of formal or quasi-formal causality it is realized in man, and must be something that perfects man, a transcendent strengthening of human energies.

However, the term "formal cause" is far from being satisfactory, for we are dealing with a perfection resulting from union with God, who is not a form but is pure act, a perfection in the order of activity issuing in the actuation known as divinization. It is a new and essential perfection, rather than something which invests action with new modalities and determinations. It is a perfection in the order of action regarded as a being, rather than as informed by this or that quality: it does not endow human actions with a different sort of efficacy, but imparts greater intensity to their own efficacy, giving them greater entity, activity, and efficaciousness through their transcendent union with the pure Act.

If God calls man to a divinization of his nature by union with Himself, He also calls him to a divinization of his activity by cooperation with Himself. Divinization must always be based on God who gives it by giving Himself. The divinization of activity cannot be the simple effect of the divinization of nature, for, although the latter comes from God who gives Himself, it is not the principle that induces God to give Himself. To be truly divinizing, therefore, activity must be actually based on God who gives it by giving Himself, that is, it must be the product of an actual grace that equips it intrinsically for such action.

b) Genesis of actual grace. Any explanation of the order of grace must take into account a certain interior, ontological character arising from within a being, as required by union with Him who is the source of reality and the principle of everything found in beings. This necessity, which is never absent, can be brought out in several ways.

One way to consider the matter is to point out the necessity of a real foundation for the relation of union and cooperation. Or we can call attention to the necessity of an interior adaptation making the human act truly efficacious and cooperative, so that God may make use of it in the work of divinization. Or again, speaking in terms of the mystical body, we can recall the adaptation that gives efficacy to the human act in a way befitting a member of this body, an efficacy that is incorporated and assimilated into the total efficacy of the body, an efficacy by which the member shares in the efficacy of the body of Christ, the Only-begotten. Further, we can apply the same reasoning to a consideration of the internal communication of activity which Christ the head exercises in His members. Lastly, we can speak of the real, ontological effect which the fact of being thus taken up by God must produce in the activity that is allowed to collaborate with God. If an infinitely remote contact with the divine creative power constitutes the creature's inherent natural power, what power and strengthening must be imparted by the intimate contact which God has with human energies when He associates them with His own activity in Christ and in the "body of Christ"? The efficient or quasi-efficient causality by which God associates man's acts with His own, must evoke, in the fashion of a formal or quasi-formal cause, a corresponding elevation of these acts in their own order, a divinization of their activity and their efficacy. This is precisely what we mean by actual grace.

c) Nature of actual grace. Thus regarded, actual grace is an "entity of union," that is, it is a new kind of being, called forth in a being by union with another being. Therefore it is neither God and His omnipotence, nor man and his natural energies, nor some third sort of absolute entity.

We need not fully expound these conceptions here. To be fair to all parties, we should have to encumber and qualify the exposition by reviewing the various explanations and corrections that have been contributed, and the different ways of comprehending them on the part of true and admirable Christians. In any case, most theologians are aware of the facility with which certain theories can degenerate into misanthropy, passivism, and quietism. Some of the explanations proposed involve a separation between the work of God and the work of man at their very point of departure, and the breach goes on widening. Any such separation is diametrically opposed to the basic principle of all Christianity, which is the union of God with man in the whole Christ, and hence a union of God's action with man's action.

No one doubts that God can act alone; and assuredly the first foundation of the order of grace as a whole is an act of God alone, the indivisible act that decreed and effected the Incarnation. But this act intended a union, and indeed willed that union more intensely and divinely (according to our way of conceiving) than it willed creation. Thereafter an order of union gradually developed; and the union was intended by the uncreated grace. In union Christ finds His plenitude.

As represented in some theories, actual grace does not even have enough entity to be studied by metaphysics, and falls shorter still of what is required for a supernatural entity. The nature of man and that which absolutely excels man and human nature cannot be adequately expressed in an idea which is only a part of man's knowledge and which man can master and surpass. Yet the temptation thus to regard actual grace is so natural that it can slip in unperceived; and even after stating that grace is transcendent, mysterious, and supernatural, one may easily and unconsciously come to identify it with a sort of charge of energy that is invisible and ethereal, but nevertheless of the same type as sensible energies, which God can give, take back, offer once more, or hold in reserve. One may come to represent it as a sort of spiritual impulse which God couples on to man's will, or as a dynamite cartridge which God entrusts to the feeble human workman.

We have already pointed out, in connection with sanctifying grace, that such a conception is quite untenable. How can anyone fancy that a created and finite entity is able, by itself alone, to empower man to cooperate with the Infinite and to act effectively in the order of divinization? To be so powerful, an entity would have to be God Himself. Only God can act on God; only He can give God. A finite entity cannot do so by itself alone. The very supposition involves a flat contradiction.

Accordingly, if grace, which is finite, is endowed with such power, the reason is, as we said when speaking of divinization, that grace is essentially a thing that does not stand alone, a thing that exists only in union and in consequence of union, to equip for union and to express union in the being that is united; it is an "entity of union," understanding the phrase as we have explained it. We may go farther and say that it is a "reinforcement of union," for it acts forcefully and effectively; it is a reinforcement that exists only in union, results from union, and is designed for union. It arises in Christ's humanity, because that humanity belongs to God through the hypostatic union;

and it arises in Christ's mystical body and in His members as soon as they become members, in order to make them fully members. For, either in fact or in the efficacious divine vocation, they are members of Christ who is God, and therefore are members of God.

Consequently, if grace can act in the sphere of divinization which comes from God, it cannot be something that stands by itself alone. The condition of its existence is that it does not stand alone; it is a reinforcing of union. Union with God and Christ is essential to it. Within this union, its divinizing power is conceivable; in fact, lack of that power would be inconceivable.

Such a process of activity would be unthinkable in the natural order. How can anything truly act in a sphere that is infinitely above its own sphere? *Operari sequitur esse; unumquodque agit in quantum est actu; propter quod unumquodque tale et illud magis.* In the natural order, man would be but himself, and his activity would be limited to what he himself could do; God would intervene only as the transcendent first cause.

The case is different in the supernatural order; the same principles, applied to another set of realities, are applied in another way. Assuredly, *unumquodque agit in quantum est actu;* but that which is in act is man united to Christ, and in Christ to God. The complete explanation is to be found in the whole agent; and this explanation is found in the man who acts. At least in vocation, he is united to this whole agent, and the actual grace with which he acts has no other finality or essence than to bring about an actual and accomplished union.

God's employment of human energies by means of a reinforcement of union turns our thoughts to the kind of causality that is called instrumental causality. God is truly the principal cause. The human agent acts with a power that is received, to perform a work that is chiefly the work of the principal agent, since it is a divinization; and man acts thus because God lays hold of him for His own work.

With regard to this work, theology is fond of saying that the sacred humanity, whose fullness is constituted by Christians, was an instrument used by the divinity as an instrumental cause for the divinization of the world. As theologians explain, this instrumental quality was an aspect of the fullness of grace possessed by the sacred humanity. Christ's humanity was made a fit instrument for the divinization of all humanity, because it was assumed by God through the hypostatic union, because of its "entity of union" and its "reinforcement of union," that is, its grace. It was an *instumentum excellens, instrumentum animatum et liberum, instrumentum coniunctum.*

Since Christians are members of Christ and have grace as members of Christ, they are made instruments by grace as Christ was, by an extension to them of the instrumental quality found in Him, a quality they possess in their own way, as members.

The "reinforcement of union" with God which is actual grace appears at its greatest where union is realized at its greatest, that is, in the humanity of Christ. Based directly on the hypostatic union itself and on Christ's sanctifying grace, it impels the sacred humanity to accomodate its activity faithfully to the Word and to God, to every action of God and to the divinization of the world.

This accomodation is manifested in the perfect charity with which the sacred humanity energetically ratifies and ardently desires its union with God and dependence on Him. Consent is given to the union which already exists, and is the product of the union. This consent is elevated by the union to the heights on which the union itself is effected; without such consent the union would not truly be a union, for it would not be truly human in its term. Perhaps we should go so far as to say that the consent is elevated even to the point of causing the union, not to accomplish the union, but that it may continue to be an accomplished and consummated fact. We find it impossible as well as useless to declare all the charity, all the loving self-donation to God and to the whole work of God, and hence to all men, that is implied in this perpetual and complete consent that flows from the plenitude of actual grace.[6]

Continuing along these lines, we may apparently say that one act, or rather a single active disposition, is at the basis of all Christ's activity. This was love and charity, the unitive virtue, the total donation of self to God and men, a donation that was voluntary, joyous, unyieldingly firm, and eager for sacrifice. Since mankind and all human activity are multiple, Christ's charity is manifested in countless different acts. But at bottom they are all acts of charity and freely willed union.

This disposition and activity Christ imparts to His members. Or,

[6] Cf. St. Thomas, *Summa*, IIIa, q. 34, a. 1 and 3.

what comes to the same thing, we may say that the grace which is personal to each Christian, though emanating from Christ, inspires every Christian with a like disposition and activity.

Actual grace, then, is an "entity of union," a "reinforcement of union." Consequently, as it comes to us *in facto esse* from Jesus Christ in whom the union is fully realized, it comes to us *in fieri* from Him who brought about the Incarnation, that is, from God and, more particularly, from the Holy Spirit.

That it comes from God Himself is clear, for it is a reinforcement that results from union with Him who is absolute force and omnipotence. The force we are speaking of is not that with which God endows creatures at their creation, for that is essential to them, although it is a participation in His power and hence a union with Him. What we are now speaking of is a force which no creature can have from its own nature, and which therefore cannot be the product of simple creation, for it confers a power of acting on the Creator Himself and on the gift He makes of Himself. It is a force that can arise in the creature only from union with the Creator.

Indeed, we should say that it comes from union with the interior life of the Creator, that is, from union with the Trinitarian life. For every created force by its very nature is a relation and union with the Creator regarded as the cause and archetype of all that is outside Him. To get an idea of an increase of force that is supernatural and above all creatable being, we have to think of God's interior life, of the power which God has in Himself alone, and which is active in the immanent processions within God.

When we reach such lofty heights, we find that the light is too rarefied, or rather too pure, to permit of our seeing with clearness and comfort. What we are trying to say turns out to be a hesitant stammering; yet the glory apprehended in a single ray escaping from the Godhead is more illuminating than all the brilliant spectacles of earth. "Better is one day in Thy courts above thousands." [7]

In any case, we should not overlook the special mention of the Holy Spirit in the words used by the angel to announce the Incarnation, or in the words chosen by Christ to describe the future birth of the Church. [8] He is the One who is to come, who is going to enter

[7] Ps. 83:11.
[8] Luke 1:35; 24:49; Acts 1:4, 8.

into mankind and envelop them with power, for the work of divinization is at hand.

III. Merit

The teaching of the Council of Trent on this subject is as follows.

Once men have been justified, whether they always thereafter preserve the grace received or whether they recover it after it has been lost, they should have set before them the words of the Apostle, who tells them to abound in every good work, "knowing that your labor is not in vain in the Lord" (I Cor. 15:58). "For God is not unjust, that He should forget your work and the love which you have shown in His name" (Heb. 6:10). And "Do not lose your confidence, which hath a great reward" (Heb. 10:35). Therefore eternal life is to be held out to those who strive well up to the end and who hope in God, both as a grace mercifully promised to God's sons through Jesus Christ and as a reward that is to be faithfully rendered for their good works and merits, as promised by God Himself. For this is that crown of justice which the Apostle said was laid up for him and was to be rendered to him by the just Judge after the fight was over and the race run; and not to him only but also to them that love His coming (II Tim. 4:7 f.). For, since Jesus Christ Himself continually infuses virtue into the justified, as the head does into the members (Eph. 4:15) and the vine into the branches (John 15:5), and this virtue always precedes, accompanies, and follows their good works, which otherwise could not be pleasing and meritorious before God, we must believe that nothing is wanting to prevent the justified from being accounted to have fully satisfied, by those works performed in God, the divine law according to the state of this life, and to have truly merited eternal life, which is to be obtained in its own proper time, provided they die in grace (Apoc. 14:13). For Christ our Savior says: "He that shall drink of the water that I will give him, shall not thirst forever, but . . . it shall become in him a fountain of water springing up into life everlasting" (John 4:13 f.). Thus our own justice is not established as our own as coming from ourselves, nor is the justice of God ignored or repudiated (Rom. 10:3). For the justice that is said to be ours for the reason that we are justified through its inherence in us, is also the justice of God, for the reason that it is infused into us by God through the merit of Christ.[9]

[9] Council of Trent, Sess. VI, cap. 16 (Denz., 809).

That is the teaching. The task of theology is to expound it scientifically, and the exposition ought to begin with a definition of merit.

Theologians have supplied the definition. They usually phrase it in function of juridical concepts, thus presenting the nature of merit according to the implications of the legal terms employed. They say that merit is a certain right, specifically a right to a reward. They have closely scrutinized this right and have repeatedly studied all its aspects. They have carefully noted the conditions necessary for its exercise. They have investigated how these conditions, as applied to the case of supernaturally good works, are verified in the relations obtaining between God and man.

But theologians are aware and openly confess that the juridical conditions of merit are imperfectly realized in these relations between God and man. And this is just what might have been expected. Legal right is indeed a very human thing, and God has adapted the supernatural economy to man, so that it too is a human thing; and therefore it can be expressed, up to a certain point, in legalistic phraseology. On the other hand, the supernatural economy is impregnated with charity and union, whereas the system of rights essentially implies conflict between several parties, the vindication of personal interests, external relations, legalism, and grim rigorism. The difference between the two amounts to opposition.

Consequently we should not be surprised that Christian thought does not find the Gospel message exactly mirrored in juridical concepts, and that it seeks to express the same realities in a way that corresponds better to the nature of Christianity and its message. The *id quod* remains the same; the *modus quo* differs.

The notion of merit appropriate to the present book is easily set forth. The definition does not have to be sought far afield, for it is imposed by the principles that have been our unvarying point of departure. We take the liberty of proposing it; thus all can see whether it expresses the same reality and has the same sense as the juridical definition.

Our definition tells what merit is in function of Christ and of the life which the mystical body lives in Christ. Merit, we submit, is the causality that Christ and our life in Him should exercise in the moral order; it is a sort of vital causality which moral activity exercises with respect to its end in the supernatural, Christian economy.

Even on the natural plane a special kind of causality comes into play in the sphere of moral life. This is the activity which the moral person exercises in order to obtain his last end; by performing the good actions through which he perfects himself he advances toward the final end, and freely fits himself to attain it. Causality such as this properly belongs to a free act and is natural and intrinsic to it, being its very purpose. Since the end of moral living is essentially some kind of possession of God, the causality in question, even in the natural order which was never more than possible, requires the intervention of God, and hence the intervention of another's free will. This intervention is implied in the very notion of creation and conservation; it is the continuation of the divine concurrence by which the creature is sustained in being and is able to act, and differs from ordinary concurrence only in the intensity by which it leads creatures to their last end.

To acquire an understanding of supernatural merit, we need do no more, in our opinion, than raise all this to the supernatural level, and complete it by the idea of the divinization that in Christ is given to the members of Christ.

Supernatural merit, we should say, is the kind of causality and efficacy proper to the activity of Christ's humanity, considered both in itself and in its mystical prolongation in all Christians, with regard to obtaining or approaching the supernatural end, that is, with regard to divinization as finally achieved or as begun; in other words, with regard to glory or grace. St. Thomas has some instructive texts on this subject. We can judge from them why the causality of merit appears physical and organic to the holy doctor, and how vital is the continuity between grace and its effects.[10]

Apparently we may speak of a connatural causality in connection with merit, in which the cause, adequately considered, has all it needs to produce its effect. Yet this is a moral causality, in the sense that it belongs to the moral order; it is a causality by which a being uses his moral activity, elevated by grace, to actualize, form, and perfect himself in respect to his moral end.

This causality supposes the intervention of a causality distinct from the Christian and from the sacred humanity of Jesus. It supposes the intervention of God Himself, and one that is much greater than the simple concurrence sufficient for natural merit. The end to

[10] St. Thomas, *Summa*, Ia IIae, q.114, a.1; a.3 et ad 3; *In IV Sent.*, d.45, q.3, a.3 ad 4.

be attained is God Himself, *Deus prout est in se*. Such an end cannot be attained unless it is given, and the efficacy of human action on this level is null, unless it is elevated and divinized by an act of God who communicates Himself to the soul.

But this communication of God is precisely what is inaugurated in grace, and it even defines grace. Is not grace an "entity of union," intrinsically adapted to reach its perfection in this supreme union? Is not actual grace a divinization of the energy of our acts, designed to issue in sanctifying grace, and is not sanctifying grace the divinization of the present life of us wayfarers, destined to burst into full flowering when we reach our definitive life? Is it not true that glory is simply the consummation of grace, that vision is the unveiling of what faith believed, and that beatitude is the perfection of charity? The same intervention of God is at work in grace and glory, in the manner befitting each; God acts in the former to enable it truly to cause the latter, in which meritorious activity culminates.

We suggest, therefore, that merit is a "causality through union" truly exercised by man, and that it is a reinforcement of the union which is grace. The elevation it gives to the efficacy of human action crowns the elevation which grace gives to the life and powers of the human soul. It enables human action to do its part in attaining the gift of God which God Himself confers as first cause. It equips human action for this function, so that man may give to himself by his good actions what God gives to man out of His goodness, and thus empowers man to perfect himself. The man who lives by God's gift of divinization merits God with an inherent causality.

In this inherent power is found the explanation of the *ius ad praemium*, the right to a reward, that occurs in the juridical definition mentioned at the beginning of the present section. Some theologians who are excessively fond of juridical clarity and who are wary of a theology they consider too realistic, like to conceive this right as depending completely on a sort of divine engagement. They represent God as obliging Himself by His irrevocable word to give Himself in heaven to those who, aided by grace, faithfully observe His law on earth, Thus all Christian merit is based on God's promises, and not on any intrinsic value possessed by the works of justified men.

St. Thomas is more realistic. When he speaks of the divine ordinance that is necessary for a work to be meritorious in God's sight, he does not mean a merely positive decree that would leave things unchanged, but has in mind a real proportion with eternal life that God bestows on our free acts. With his magnificent simplicity he says: "The law of divine Providence has ordained that nothing should act beyond its powers." [11]

If merit is thus the supernatural causality that is proper to the activity of grace, it must be proportionate to the activity of grace. It is perfect when grace is perfect. Grace has such perfection in the Incarnation. Therefore, since the Incarnation is the source of all merit here on earth, it is not the product of any merit. The Incarnation is the absolutely free gift; it is as gratuitous as it is measureless, and makes everything that flows from it likewise gratuitous.

This merit, understood as a vital causality, is found radically in the transcendent divinization of the assumed humanity. It is found actually in all of Christ's acts. In a special way that recapitulates Christ's whole life, it is found in the act which perfectly manifests and crowns the sacred humanity, that is, in Christ's act of dying, the act by which He acted fully as the God-man in a human way. Through this act of unreserved human donation, He definitively passed over to God, and thereby also to men.

Merit flows from the head to those men who are members of Christ. This is personal with them, and is characterized by all the intensity that is imparted to their personality by their incorporation into Christ. As found in their persons, therefore, it is a derived and secondary merit, such as is proper for members. It is full merit, in all the rigor of justice, as the Scholastics were wont to say, when the member is regarded in his exact position as member, that is, in his actual and living union with the head who is the God-man. It is incomplete and essentially insufficient merit, deriving its value from extraneous circumstances, when the member is regarded as outside of Christ to whom he belongs, that is, when his quality of member is left out of account.

We need not point out that in the case of men having no ties with Christ, merit is null. But are there such men? We considered above how we may behold grace at work in every good deed, and how Christ is present, at least according to the divine vocation and in a rudimentary way, in every man. If that is so, no human action is really good unless it has some connection with Christ and to that

[11] *Summa*, Ia IIae, q.114, a.2; cf. a.1.

extent is efficacious and salutary. But an act of this sort possesses such power only in an imperfect, inchoative, rudimentary way, and so the merit is essentially imperfect. This is what theology has called merit *de congruo* since the thirteenth century, and is not merit *de condigno*.

As we said above, union with Christ is what endows our virtue with meritorious efficacy. This union does not exist fully in the man we are speaking of, nor, consequently, in his action, which therefore lacks the full causative power coming from the union. Whatever comes to him from the goodness of God and the holiness of Christ, comes from outside, and does not arise from the life that only true members can live. It comes from a sort of grace which is not formally the grace that makes a meritorious act possible, even though it is closely allied to such a grace, for it is given in view of eventual union with Christ.

All this enables us to see what distinctions have to be introduced if we undertake to comment, from the point of view of these pages, on the theological proposition: "To him who does what he can, God does not refuse His grace."

Merit, as we have said, is essentially personal. This does not prevent it from being catholic, universal, and social. Is not the Christian's personality supernaturally united to all Christianity by that which makes him intrinsically supernatural? Each Christian's personality is distinct from that of all others, but is not separated. Union requires that everything affecting a Christian's personality should have a repercussion on the whole from which he derives his life. As grace is a union with the whole Christ and hence with all supernaturalized mankind, the merit proceeding from this grace is in union with the supernatural life of all mankind. Merit is no more exclusively individualistic than Christianity or the supernatural is exclusively individualistic.

But we also perceive that this sharing of all the members in the merits of each depends on the unity that makes them all members of a single body of a single Christ. In Christ alone, therefore, merit is fully universal and communicable. He alone can strictly merit *de condigno* for others; indeed, as the head of a body, He can truly merit only in relation to others; as for Himself, He already has everything essential. The merit of all the others derives from Him. Each member is primarily himself, and not the others; that is, if we may say so, he is not interior to them except in his own way and measure. Moreover, his union with others here on earth is still being forged, whereas that of Christ was complete, on His side, from the very first. This is why each member can merit *de condigno* for himself alone; his merit for others is partial and imperfect, and is only *de congruo*. And in our opinion this merit is different from another kind of merit, also called *de congruo*, which the sinner can exercise for himself; for it is an act of the interior life of the mystical body, and hence is more real, more intrinsic, and more powerful.

The congruous merit of Christ's members is exercised spontaneously. This is not true of its accidental efficacy, its application to this or that person, in view of this or that grace; such application remains uncertain, and the bonds of the supernatural organism taken in general do not require it. But what we have said is true of its efficacy on the whole, of its value for the life of the entire Church and of particular souls that have special needs in the collective economy of that life. And this application does not depend necessarily on the express intentions that are made, but pertains to Christian life itself. For charity is what makes merit, and charity is precisely the principle that unites, *virtus unitiva*.

Thus the whole Christ merits in each member, and this merit is the growth He gives to Himself, in His members and through His members, for the fullness of His body, "unto the increase of God." [12]

[12] Col. 2:19.

INDEX

Act: of dying, 262, 264 f., 268; of the human form, 116; of sin, 252

Activity: of charity, 440 ff.; of Christ's members, 438, 440-46; divinization of, 387, 627

Actual grace, 622-39
 caused by sacraments, 556
 in Christ's human nature, 624, 631
 conferred by extreme unction, 572
 conferred by matrimony, 576
 consent to, 631
 definition of, 622
 described at the Vatican Council, 622
 described by Christ, 623
 dialectic of, 624-32
 distinct from sanctifying grace, 595, 623
 effects of, 627
 efficient causality of, 628
 as "entity of union," 628-32, 636
 flowing from Christ to men, 626, 632
 formal causality in, 627
 genesis of, 627, 632
 God as first cause of, 627, 632
 gratuity of, 624
 instrumental causality of, 630
 nature of, 628-32
 power of, 629, 632
 principle in theology of, 623
 purpose of, 623, 627
 as "reinforcement of union," 629, 631
 related to sanctifying grace, 623
 subordinate to sanctifying grace, 624
 theories about, 628
 unique in Christ, 625
 untenable conception of, 629

Actuation of Christ's human nature, 209

Adam: created in grace, 142; figure of Christ, 135, 162; solidarity of mankind in, 150; supernatural union of mankind in, 164

Adoption, divine; see Sonship of Christians

Affirmation of existence, 111

Albert the Great on theology, 64 f. and notes

Alexander of Hales on the object of theology, 63

Amelioration of Christ's human nature, 206-10, 214

Angels, the
 consciousness in, 77
 peccability of, 139
 reparation of, 138
 sin of, 138, 165
 supernatural state of, 138
 unity of, 138

Anselm, St.: redemption theory of, 249

Anti-intellectualism, 13 ff.

Antiquity of scientific endeavor, 28

Apologetic value of theology, 93 ff.

Apologetics: intrinsic to theology, 94; science of, 492

Apostles, the: formation of, 56; as theologians, 43

Apostolicity (note of the Church): emphasized since origin of Christianity, 517; notion of, 517; rooted in Christ, 518

Appropriation of divine adoption to the Father, 354

Aquinas, Thomas; see Thomas Aquinas, St.

Aristotelian current in theology, 61

Aristotle on unity in knowledge, 35

Asceticism, unity sought in, 37

Assimilation, power of, 97

Athanasius, St.: on Christ and the Holy Spirit, 426; on Christian sonship, 343 ff.

Augustine, St.
 on Christ the teacher, 532
 on Christian love, 352
 on Christian sonship, 350 ff.
 on the divine Word, 72 note
 on grace in Christ, 601
 on the grace of Christians, 350 and note
 on the Mass, 585, 587

CARMELITE MONASTERY